ADVANCE PRAISE FOR *GENDER AND DOMESTIC VIOLENCE*

Finally! Perhaps the most comprehensive approach to understanding IPV in terms of policy and practice, this book gathers the work of committed scholars who ignored convention in the face of great opposition and steadfastly pushed for a greater understanding of women's use of violence. Russell and Hamels's book shines light in the dark corners where change and progress are desperately needed and represents more than a decade of effort to transform our thinking—and thus our policies, practices, and treatment approaches—resulting in a paradigmatic shift in the conversations around gender and IPV.
—**Michelle Mohr Carney**, PhD, MSSA, Dean & Professor, School of Social Welfare, University of Kansas, Lawrence, KS

As a former domestic violence prosecutor, I struggled with the one-size-fits-all approach to IPV. As a current defense attorney, I see the havoc this homogenous mindset causes for the wrongfully accused. With a scientific and fact-driven approach, this volume recognizes and reports the nuances of IPV, and asks questions of our current criminal legal system based on research, not stereotypes or politics. Prosecutors, defense attorneys and judges must wrestle with the evidence presented in this volume or risk being well-intentioned agents of injustice.
—**Peter Chambers**, Esq., Law Office of Peter James Chambers, San Rafael, CA

I applaud and admire Brenda Russell and John Hamel for putting together this book. The book is well-researched with chapters written by highly regarded experts in the field. Although destined to be controversial, it's long overdue, and provides solid research and recommendations for both criminal justice and family courts for how to best handle domestic violence cases. It takes on the political controversy and provides evidence-based information on how gender is not the determining predictor for who commits domestic violence. It is a must read for all who work in the field of domestic violence and who encounter domestic violence in the criminal courts, family courts, and service professions.
—**Denise A. Hines**, Associate Professor, George Mason University College of Health and Human Services

As a certified family law specialist in California who has presided for many years as a Judge Pro Tem on the Domestic Violence Calendar in the San Francisco Unified Family Court, I appreciate the significant contribution made by Russell and Hamel in addressing the evolving gender roles in intimate partner violence. Their research offers an enlightened critique of the gender paradigm, and valuable insights into what appears to be equal rates aggression—particularly psychological aggression—between the sexes. As a staunch advocate of Alternative Dispute Resolution, and wary of the current punitive, win-lose mindset, I appreciate the creative solutions presented in the book. Such interventions are sorely needed, to reduce the trauma of court proceedings and its impact on the parties, and provide a safe harbor with long-term benefits to the family.

—**Steve Ruben**, Esq., Ruben Law Firm, San Francisco, CA

Documenting the complex number of factors that contribute to the proliferation of intimate partner violence, this collection provides the evidence to—finally—acknowledge that a narrow conception of the problem has had a devastating impact on those people who are harmed and ignored by the system that claims to be comprehensive and compassionate. None of this negates the important inroads the battered women's movement has made, but rather provides proof that this blinkered approach has prevented us from actually combating it. A must read.

—**Linda G. Mills**, Lisa Ellen Goldberg Professor, New York University

Russell and Hamel have brought together the most thoughtful and talented researchers, clinicians and legal scholars for their edited volume, Domestic violence legal practice and intervention policy: Beyond the gender paradigm. The chapters cover the latest research findings in the field and translates that data into practical guidelines for understanding and addressing the complex dynamics of domestic violence in various settings. Having conducted extensive research in the area of family violence, and having worked as a clinician with domestic violence perpetrators and victims and as an expert witness in numerous criminal and family law cases, I find this book to be a must-read for anyone who is formulating public policy, designing research studies, involved in criminal or civil legal settings, or designing and implementing clinical interventions.

—**Daniel Sonkin**, Author, *Learning to Live Without Violence* and *Domestic Violence on Trial*, San Rafael, CA

This book will serve as an important contribution to the challenging area of responding to interpersonal and domestic violence. Infusing this emotionally laden field with data-driven and evidence-based responses and analysis will guide our justice systems and communities to find more effective responses than our predominant punitive approach.

—**Robert Sand**, Founding Director, Center for Justice Reform, Vermont Law School

This is a refreshing book on the current status of approaches to assessment and intervention in domestic violence and intimate partner violence. It emphasizes data based as opposed to political conceptualizations of DV/IPV. This book provides important information for legislators, criminal justice personnel and treatment providers to assist in the determination of optimal interventions for both victims and perpetrators which take into account the heterogeneity of IPV as opposed to one-size-fits-all approaches.

—**Arthur L. Cantos**, Professor & Director of Clinical Training, Department of Psychological Science, University of Texas Rio Grande Valley

Gender and Domestic Violence

Contemporary Legal Practice and Intervention Reforms

EDITED BY BRENDA RUSSELL

AND

JOHN HAMEL

OXFORD
UNIVERSITY PRESS

Oxford University Press is a department of the University of Oxford. It furthers
the University's objective of excellence in research, scholarship, and education
by publishing worldwide. Oxford is a registered trade mark of Oxford University
Press in the UK and certain other countries.

Published in the United States of America by Oxford University Press
198 Madison Avenue, New York, NY 10016, United States of America.

© Oxford University Press 2022

All rights reserved. No part of this publication may be reproduced, stored in
a retrieval system, or transmitted, in any form or by any means, without the
prior permission in writing of Oxford University Press, or as expressly permitted
by law, by license, or under terms agreed with the appropriate reproduction
rights organization. Inquiries concerning reproduction outside the scope of the
above should be sent to the Rights Department, Oxford University Press, at the
address above.

You must not circulate this work in any other form
and you must impose this same condition on any acquirer.

CIP data is on file at the Library of Congress

ISBN 978-0-19-756402-8

DOI: 10.1093/med-psych/9780197564028.001.0001

Printed by Integrated Books International, United States of America

CONTENTS

Acknowledgments vii
About the Editors ix
Contributors xi

PART I Overview of Research on Domestic Violence

1. Introduction: The Problem with the Gender Paradigm 3
   John Hamel and Brenda Russell

2. What We Currently Know about the Prevalence, Causes, and Dynamics of Intimate Partner Violence 21
   Elizabeth A. Bates and Alexandra Papamichail

3. The Law Enforcement Response to Intimate Partner Violence: Toward a Gender-Neutral Approach 57
   Brenda Russell and Emily Seisler

PART II Litigation

4. Gender, Sex, and the Prosecution of Intimate Partner Violence 85
   Jennifer Cox, Elizabeth MacNeil, and Hannah Lind

5. Challenges and Strategies in Mounting a Legal Defense in Intimate Partner Violence Criminal Cases 110
   Charles Dresow

6. Intimate Partner Homicide and the Battered Person Syndrome 129
   John Hamel, Don Dutton, and Alexandra Lysova

7. Jury Decision-Making: Understanding and Overcoming Bias in the Courtroom 165
   Brenda Russell and Blake McKimmie

PART III Family Law

8. Guidelines for Domestic Violence and Child Custody Litigation 207
   David Pisarra

9. Custody and Intervention Recommendations in Family Law Cases: A Gender-Inclusive Framework 229
   John Hamel and Kelley Baker

10. The Same Coin: Intimate Partner Violence, Child Abuse, and Parental Alienation 276
    Jennifer Harman and Edward Kruk

PART IV Evidence-Based Interventions

11. Holding Perpetrators Accountable: Evidence-Based Interview and Assessment Procedures 307
    John Hamel and Liam Ennis

12. Risk-Needs-Responsivity-Informed Approaches to Batterer Intervention Treatment 337
    Amie Roberts

13. Couples and Family Interventions for Intimate Partner Violence 351
    Victoria E. Bennett, Janella Chu, Deanna Pollard, and Julia Babcock

14. Restorative Justice Alternatives 376
    Briana Barocas and Rei Shimizu

Afterword: Recommendations and Resources 399
    John Hamel, Brenda Russell, Don Dutton, and Jennifer Cox

Index 411

ACKNOWLEDGMENTS

We would like to thank all of the contributors of this book and thank Emily Seisler for her assistance with references. We are also thankful to our friends and family, who inspire and continue to support us through the process.

ABOUT THE EDITORS

Brenda Russell, PhD, is a professor of psychology at The Pennsylvania State University, Berks. Her scholarly and teaching interests include psychology and law, perceptions of victims and perpetrators of domestic violence, homicide defendants, and the social psychological and cognitive aspects of jury decision-making. Dr. Russell is particularly interested in how gender and sexual orientation play a role in evaluating defendants in cases of domestic violence, rape, sexual coercion, and sexual harassment. She has published dozens of scholarly research articles and authored four books to date. Dr. Russell also serves as an expert in criminal homicide cases involving domestic violence and works as a consultant and program evaluator for various federal and state educational, law enforcement, justice, and treatment programs.

John Hamel, PhD, LCSW, has a master's degree in social welfare from UCLA and is currently a research fellow at the University of Central Lancashire, United Kingdom, in the Psychology Department, where he obtained his PhD. He has worked with family violence perpetrators and victims since 1992 and is a court-approved provider of batterer intervention and parent programs in five Greater San Francisco Bay Area counties. Dr. Hamel is the author/editor of three books and has published dozens of articles in peer-reviewed scholarly journals; he is editor-in-chief of *Partner Abuse*, a journal published quarterly by Springer. Dr. Hamel regularly speaks at conferences on domestic violence, has provided case consultation and expert witness testimony, and has trained mental health professionals, victim advocates social service organizations, law enforcement, attorneys, and family court mediators.

CONTRIBUTORS

Julia Babcock, PhD, is a professor in the Department of Psychology at the University of Houston and a licensed clinical psychologist. Her research focuses on laboratory studies of violent and nonviolent couples and community-based evaluations of battering interventions. She is interested in identifying mechanisms of change that translate research into practice and developing and evaluating new techniques that stop intimate partner violence.

Kelley Baker, PhD, received her PhD in developmental, social, and personality psychology from the University of Texas at Austin in 2002. She received a master's degree in program evaluation in 2000 and a master's degree in counseling and guidance in 1994. She is a licensed professional counselor with over 25 years of clinical experience serving families going through separation and divorce. As a therapist she has provided individual, group, couples, marital, family, reunification, and co-parenting therapy. As a forensic consultant in the Austin area of central Texas, she serves as a court-appointed guardian ad litem, a court-appointed custody evaluator, a trial consultant, and subject matter expert on topics related to high-conflict divorce.

Briana Barocas, PhD, is the director of research of New York University's Center on Violence and Recovery and a research associate professor at New York University's Silver School of Social Work. Her interests in trauma, resiliency, and recovery have led to research on first responders, individuals and families affected by domestic violence, and survivors of 9/11. Her research has been supported by the National Institute of Justice, the National Science Foundation, the Department of Homeland Security, and the Department of Defense. She is committed to developing and researching programs and services that better the lives of individuals, families, and communities and has over 15 years of research experience in the specific field of restorative justice applications to domestic violence practice. She holds a PhD in social policy and policy analysis from Columbia University, an MS in gender studies from the London School of Economics and Political Science, and a BS in human development and family studies from Cornell University.

Elizabeth A. Bates, PhD, is a principal lecturer in psychology and psychological therapies at the University of Cumbria. Key areas of interest include intimate partner violence. Her doctoral work highlighted the prevalence of women's aggression and men's victimization, and her more recent postdoctoral work has specialized in exploring men's experiences of domestic violence and abuse. Specifically, her most recent papers have explored their experiences of coercive control, barriers to help seeking, recovery from their experience, and their postseparation abuse. She is also a trustee of the ManKind Initiative, a male victim's charity in England.

Victoria E. Bennett, MA, is a fifth-year doctoral student in the clinical psychology program and a graduate student in the Emotions in Marriage Lab at the University of Houston. She received her BS in psychology from the University of Mary Washington in 2013 and an MA in general psychology in 2016 from the University of North Carolina Wilmington. While at UNCW, she worked with Dr. Caroline Clements and coordinated multiple research studies examining predictors of intimate partner violence (IPV) perpetration and the impact of IPV on victims and child witnesses. At the University of Houston, she has authored and coauthored a number of peer-reviewed publications and book chapters on IPV and couples therapy. She will begin her predoctoral clinical internship in July 2021 at the Michael E. DeBakey VA Medical Center in Houston, Texas.

Janella Chu, BS, is a second-year clinical psychology master's student at the University of Houston-Clear Lake and a research assistant in the Emotions in Marriage Lab. She received a BS in psychology with a minor in health from the University of Houston-Main in 2020. Her current research interests broadly include personality disorders, specifically borderline personality disorder, predictors of intimate partner violence, and the LGBTQ+ population.

Jennifer Cox, PhD, is an associate professor of psychology specializing in clinical psychology law at The University of Alabama, where she directs the Psychology and Legal Decision Making Lab and codirects the Alabama Forensic Assessment and Research Evaluation (FARE) project. Her research interests include the impact of biases on legal decision-making, forensic mental health assessment, psychopathy, and the interaction of psychology and public policy. She is licensed to practice psychology and regularly serves as a forensic mental health expert.

Charles Dresow, Esq., has maintained a criminal defense practice based in Marin County since 2008. Charlie handles a wide range of criminal cases, from simple misdemeanors to complex felony trials and appeals. Charlie understands that even the smallest cases are critical to the life and future of his clients. He primarily handles cases in Northern California, although he serves his clients across the state if necessary. Mr. Dresow has won success for his clients at both the trial court and appellate level. Charlie has represented numerous clients whose cases have faced local, regional, and national media scrutiny. He effectively develops a multifaceted approach to defending these cases, which includes comprehensive crisis management as well as media and public relations strategies. Charlie currently serves as the president of the board of directors for Alternate Defenders Incorporated, which is the governing body for the local conflict indigent defense panel. He was formerly the president of the Marin County Bar Association and remains on the board of directors of multiple regional nonprofits.

Don Dutton, PhD, is a professor emeritus of psychology at the University of British Columbia. He cofounded a court-mandated treatment program for men convicted of wife assault in 1979 and used the men as research subjects for studies on domestic violence. He has published over 100 papers and five books, including *Domestic Assault of Women* (1995), *The Batterer: A Psychological Profile* (1995), *The Abusive Personality* (2006), *Rethinking Domestic Violence* (2006), *The Psychology of Genocide* (2007), and *Religion On Trial* (2019). He has given talks to the World Bank, the U.S. Army and Department of Defense, the University of Washington Law School, the British Forensic Psychological Association, and the Senate of Canada. He serves as an expert witness in civil trials involving intimate abuse and in criminal trials involving family violence.

Liam Ennis, PhD, is a registered psychologist and internationally recognized as an expert in the field of violence risk assessment and management. He previously served as the resident forensic psychologist for Alberta Law Enforcement Response Teams (ALERT), assigned to the Integrated Threat and Risk Assessment Center (ITRAC), where he provided training and consultation to law enforcement and child protective services for the prevention of intimate partner violence, stalking, workplace violence, and other forms of targeted violence. He has been qualified as an expert witness in Provincial Court and Court of Queen's Bench and has published and presented internationally in the areas of threat assessment, violence prevention, and high-risk offender management.

Jennifer Harman, PhD, is an associate professor of psychology at Colorado State University. Her primary research focus is on the study of family violence and the power dynamics that exist in family systems. She has received faculty excellence awards for her teaching and research on parental alienation and has published over a dozen peer-reviewed scientific papers and several books and book chapters on the topic to date. She also serves on the board of the Parental Alienation Study Group, which is an international, nonprofit corporation dedicated to educating the general public, mental health clinicians, forensic practitioners, attorneys, and judges regarding parental alienation.

Edward Kruk, MSW, PhD, is an associate professor of social work at the University of British Columbia. Specializing in child and family policy and practice, he has written extensively on the topics of shared parenting, family violence, and parental alienation. As the inaugural president of the International Council on Shared Parenting, he co-organized and hosted the five international conferences of the Council, the most recent focused on the theme of the intersection of shared parenting and family violence. His most recent books are *The International Handbook on Shared Parenting and the Best Interests of the Child*, published by Routledge, and *The Equal Parent Presumption*, published by McGill-Queen's University Press.

Hannah Lind, BA, is a graduate student in the clinical psychology program at The University of Alabama, specializing in psychology and law. She received her BA in psychology from Vassar College. Her research and clinical interests include legal decision-making, forensic assessment, and issues related to child custody and parental rights.

Alexandra Lysova, PhD, is an associate professor in the School of Criminology at Simon Fraser University in British Columbia, Canada. She has studied intimate partner violence, including violence against women and children, for over 15 years in Russia and currently in Canada. Recently, she has focused on men's experiences of intimate partner violence, including victimization, help-seeking behavior, and issues involving children. In her research, she draws on the results of the international focus groups among male victims in four English-speaking countries, Canadian General Social Survey on Victimization, and Homicide Survey.

Elizabeth MacNeil, BA, is in the clinical psychology doctoral program at The University of Alabama, concentrating in psychology and law. Her research interests include prosecutor and defendant decision-making, psychopathy, and gender biases in the legal processing of prostitution and intimate partner violence cases.

Blake McKimmie, PhD, is a professor and social psychologist in the School of Psychology at the University of Queensland. He does research on jury decision-making and has published over 80 outputs in areas of social cognition and group processes. In the area of psychology and law, he published a book on expert testimony, has made submissions to law reform commissions, and provided training to police officers. His research has been supported by the Australian Research Council, and he is now working with the Queensland Police Service Special Investigations Training team on a multiyear project to redevelop training in response to the Royal Commission into Institutional Responses to Child Sexual Abuse.

Alexandra Papamichail, PhD, completed her doctoral work in developmental psychology and psychopathology investigating the issue of child-to-parent violence from developmental lens. She is a postdoctoral researcher in modern slavery and mental health at King's College London. Prior to this, she worked as a clinical research coordinator in mental health in the NHS. Her primary research interests focus on mental health and violence and early rearing adversities and their impact on children's mental health.

David Pisarra, Esq., is a practicing attorney for over 20 years in the world of family law, appearing in front of judges on domestic violence cases as counsel for both the protected party (victim) and the perpetrator (aggressor). He has primarily represented men (80% of his client base) for the past 15 years. He is the author of three books for men, *A Man's Guide to Divorce Strategy*, *A Man's Guide to Domestic Violence*, and *A Man's Guide to Child Custody*.

Deanna Pollard, MA, is a first-year clinical psychology doctoral student at The University of Houston and a graduate student in the Emotions in Marriage Lab. She graduated with a bachelor's degree in psychology at The University of Texas Rio Grande Valley in 2018 and will graduate with a master's degree in experimental psychology there this summer. Her research interests broadly encompass the study of intimate relationships and addressing gaps in the literature relating to culturally underrepresented groups by examining predictors of intimate partner violence in predominantly young, Hispanic couples.

Amie Roberts, MA, is a licensed mental health counselor and certified public manager of domestic violence intervention treatment. She is the domestic violence intervention treatment (DVIT) program manager for the State of Washington. Prior to her current role, she was a mental health program administrator at the Division of Behavioral Health and Recovery in Washington. She has worked in the mental health field in direct services or administration for over 15 years. She has experience in domestic violence and sexual assault victim services, substance use treatment, domestic violence perpetrator treatment, mental health, and couples counseling. She has been in her current role since December 2015. Amie has served on the Washington State's Gender and Justice Commission's committees regarding domestic violence risk assessments and treatment from HB 1163 and HB 1517.

Emily Seisler, BA, is a graduate of the Pennsylvania State University, with dual degrees in criminal justice and psychology. Emily has a passion to work with children in the criminal justice system. Her research interests include domestic violence and addiction. She hopes to help those in the juvenile probation system while continuing her education to obtain a PhD and further her research interests.

Rei Shimizu, PhD, is currently an assistant professor at the University of Alaska Anchorage and a former research assistant at New York University's Center on Violence and Recovery. She holds a PhD in social work from New York University, an MSW from Columbia University, and an LMSW in New York State. She is a social worker with a clinical background in trauma-focused therapy for survivors of intimate partner violence in the United States and Japan. Her goal as an early career investigator is to design a psychosocial nutrition intervention incorporating restorative justice techniques to improve dietary quality among marginalized young adults by addressing food behaviors in the social/community context.

PART I

Overview of Research on Domestic Violence

1

Introduction

The Problem with the Gender Paradigm

JOHN HAMEL AND BRENDA RUSSELL ■

Physical, psychological, and sexual abuse among intimate partners, commonly known as *domestic violence*, but more recently as *intimate partner violence* (IPV), is a significant social and public health problem in the United States and worldwide. IPV had long been considered private by law enforcement, rarely investigated by social science researchers, and poorly understood by mental health professionals. In the 1980s, a series of well-publicized court cases, such as *Thurman v. City of Torrington* (1985), brought to light the grossly inadequate law enforcement response at the time, which allowed repeat offenders to avoid prosecution while their partners continued to be victimized, often fatally. In response, a grassroots victim advocacy movement established shelter and other *services* for victims while lobbying state legislatures across the United States, and subsequently to Canada, the United Kingdom, and other nations, to enact new laws that would hold offenders accountable (Buzawa & Buzawa, 2002; Russell, 2010).

GENDER PARADIGM ORIGINS, DEFINITIONS, AND PERVASIVENESS

About the same time, researchers at the University of New Hampshire had begun to report on the results of two national representative sample surveys showing IPV victimization rates to be comparable across the sexes, with approximately 6 million men and 6 million women incurring some form of physical assault by their partner each year (Straus, Gelles, & Asplund, 1990). These findings were met with skepticism or dismissed by victim advocates, who had dedicated their efforts exclusively to helping battered women. In retrospect, this resistance was understandable at the time, given that research on IPV was still in its infancy and news accounts focused on severely abused women. It was also known then, as it is known now, that men perpetrate the majority of overall violent crimes (79.5%; Federal Bureau of Investigation, 2017). Around the world, women remain exploited and abused by men in various ways, including dowry murders (Rudd, 2001), sex trafficking (Kotrla, 2010), and rape. Males perpetrate 97.2% of all reported rapes (Federal Bureau of Investigation, 2017), primarily (but not exclusively) upon females.

For these reasons, and because the IPV victim advocacy movement soon merged with the broader feminist political movement—a far more influential force than the social science researchers working in relative obscurity—IPV arrest and intervention policies came to reflect, and continue to reflect, what University of British Columbia professor Donald Dutton and others have called the *gender paradigm*. The gender paradigm frames domestic violence as a problem of men assaulting women, with corollary assumptions regarding risk factors, dynamics, and motives (Dutton & Nicholls, 2005). Research scholars in the United Kingdom and elsewhere have referred to it as the *feminist perspective* (Dixon et al., 2012). In Scotland it is known simply as the *common story* (Dempsey, 2013), alluding to the pervasiveness of this paradigm within society and the judicial system. Whatever the terminology, IPV is assumed to be a "gendered" phenomenon—that is, the use, or threat, of physical abuse and other forms of control by men against intimate female partners to enforce male privilege in a patriarchal society (Dobash & Dobash, 1979, 1988; Kang et al., 2017; Pence & Paymar, 1993; Wood, 2013). Consequently, IPV policies have mainly focused on the arrest and rehabilitation of male suspects and protection of female victims via a range of legal and support services (e.g., restraining orders, shelters).

For several decades now, this view has thoroughly dominated IPV arrest, prosecution, and treatment policies in the United States and has informed child custody decisions in the family court system, largely because it has been so widely and unquestioningly accepted. News rarely reports, if ever, feature stories about men or sexual minorities as the abused party. Suppose one wishes to search beyond the headlines. In that case, accurate IPV statistics can be found within peer-reviewed journals, but these sources are available only to academic scholars. In contrast, there is an endless stream of misinformation about IPV rates, dynamics, and outcomes on Internet sites, accessible to everyone. For example, Hines (2014) examined information pages of prominent victim advocacy organizations, such as the National Coalition Against Domestic Violence and its various local and state chapters, and found that almost a third of agencies presented false facts about IPV. The paradigm informs the way police are trained to conduct IPV investigations (Hamel & Russell, 2013), dominates state statutes that regulate court-mandated intervention programs for offenders (Babcock et al., 2016), and is evident among shelter workers and mental health professionals (see Follingstad et al., 2004; Hamel et al., 2007, 2009; and Russell & Torres, 2020, for a review.)

Despite the serious shortcomings of current arrest and prosecution polices, as amply documented throughout this volume, publications from the American Bar

Association (ABA) focus exclusively on the rights of female victims, frame domestic violence within a long-discredited ideological framework as a "gender" crime, and promulgate false and misleading views regarding the causes, dynamics, and consequences of domestic violence (American Bar Association, 2001; American Bar Association Commission on Domestic & Sexual Violence, 2021; Dutton et al., 2009). Not surprisingly, anecdotal and empirical evidence suggests that practicing attorneys are profoundly misinformed on this subject (Hamel, 2016; Hamel et al., 2009).

Among a growing share of stakeholders involved in IPV intervention policies, there has been some acknowledgment that IPV assault rates are more symmetrical across the sexes than was previously thought. Further, scholars have found the problem to be associated with other risk factors besides patriarchal structures—among them, childhood trauma, mental illness, and substance abuse (Hamel, 2009). When considering motives, however, a core distinction continues to be drawn, falsely, between male and female violence, wherein the former is assumed to be driven by a need to exercise power and control over the victim, and the latter is assumed to be perpetrated primarily in self-defense (Dragiewicz, 2008; Kimmel, 2002), or as a way to express emotions rather than for instrumental purposes (Hamberger et al., 1997; Swan et al., 2008.)

The Research Evidence

Nonetheless, *the contemporary research evidence provides scant support for the gender paradigm, in any of its manifestations, certainly not in the United States and other developed countries.* Among the most notable and relevant findings for criminal justice and mental health responses, discussed in greater detail elsewhere in this book, are as follows:

1. Overall rates of intimate partner abuse, defined as any physical, sexual, and psychological aggression, are comparable across the sexes, and they are also comparable across sexual orientation. However, men perpetrate sexual assaults at significantly higher rates than women.
2. While some men are motivated to assault their partners to maintain male privilege, most do so for personality and relationship reasons—to get what they want, to punish, out of jealousy, in retaliation, when they are under the influence of substances, in self-defense, or to express anger or other emotions. Motives are the same for LGBTQ+ perpetrators as they are for heterosexual perpetrators.
3. Women perpetrate IPV for the same reasons as men, with self-defense one of the least-endorsed motives.
4. In most relationships where there has been physical aggression, both partners are violent, and assaults are instigated on average as often by the female partner as the male partner. When psychological aggression is considered, the percentage of bidirectional aggression is much higher.

5. Women unquestioningly incur the most serious injuries and account for approximately 80% of intimate partner homicide victims. However, most IPV-related injuries are relatively minor and incurred by men and women in comparable numbers. This is a crucial consideration for arrest and prosecution policies, given that injuries are not a requirement in most states for an arrest to be made.
6. Individuals arrested for an IPV-related crime are ubiquitously referred to as *batterers*, commonly defined as a chronic pattern of physical assaults together with dominating and controlling behavior that only becomes worse over time. A small percentage of offenders are responsible for most incidents of repeat violence, and most defendants engage primarily in infrequent, lower-level violence that results in no or minimal injuries. The violence is not part of an overall pattern of dominance and control but instead arises from escalated conflicts and poor impulse control and does not necessarily worsen over time. These patterns also exist among LGBTQ+ populations.
7. The short-term impact of observing IPV by the father, as opposed to the mother, is somewhat greater on children in terms of their emotional states (e.g., anxiety, depression). This is perhaps due to the more frightening nature of father-perpetrated violence. However, children are at risk for displaying conduct and academic problems regardless of the parent's sex. Additionally, because observational learning is not dependent on the actor's size and strength, children who observe IPV by either parent are in the long run at risk for perpetrating IPV in adolescence and adulthood and exhibiting various mental health and substance abuse disorders. These findings are particularly relevant to child custody evaluators, judges, and attorneys.
8. Children who witness one parent physically assault the other are not necessarily more impacted psychologically than children who witness verbal abuse or merely intense arguments unless the physical assaults lead to serious injury.
9. The two most ubiquitous tools used in IPV training, the so-called Duluth "Power and Control Wheel," and Lenore Walker's three-phase "Cycle of Violence," can be helpful in some contexts but are simplistic and can also be misleading. The former purports to be an inclusive category of psychological abuse tactics used by perpetrators to dominate their partners but is incomplete and was originally intended to apply only to heterosexual male offenders; evidence-based measures of psychological abuse currently in use are based on populations of both male and female perpetrators. Furthermore, so-called power and control behaviors, or psychological abuse, are not always accurately defined, and their impact on victims depends on many factors, including the extent to which they constitute a pattern of abuse and whether they are accompanied by physical violence, or the threat of such violence. In disputed child

custody cases, "power and control" charges may sometimes refer merely to intense and hostile but otherwise normal relationship conflict.
10. The latter accurately describes only one type of IPV dynamic—specifically, a heterosexual male perpetrator with features of borderline personality disorder, the sole or dominant aggressor in a relationship, with a heterosexual female who is the sole or primary victim. The Walker model fails to account for the far more common varieties of mutually escalating couple dynamics, the behavior of antisocial or psychopathic offenders, violence by borderline women, or same-sex IPV.

The body of research evidence makes it abundantly clear that the "common story" is just that—a story. For true believers, this narrative either confirms their personal experiences or resonates with their political sensibilities. For most, it seems plausible enough, given some suspension of disbelief, and provides a simple explanation for matters they are not inclined to investigate.[1] But for the unfortunate victims and family members whom IPV policies have adversely impacted on an individual level, the common story is nothing more than a pernicious lie.

PARADIGM CONSEQUENCES

The extent to which current arrest, prosecution, and treatment policies have been effective in reducing rates of IPV, holding perpetrators accountable, and keeping victims safe is an ongoing topic of debate (Buzawa et al., 2017; Eckhardt et al., 2013). Problems with measurement are considerable, including the varying nature of the epidemiological survey and the specific questions used, differentiating the effectiveness of IPV-specific policies with an overall decrease in violent crimes, and determining how to measure desistance (e.g., whether to rely on criminal justice data, victim reports, mental health functioning, relationship satisfaction). Nonetheless, it is universally agreed that more can be done (Buzawa et al., 2017; Hamel, 2009).

There are several possible reasons for the limited effectiveness of current IPV policies. This can include a resistance by many in our society to consider IPV severe enough to report as a crime, victim noncooperation, organizational and bureaucratic limitations, budget restrictions, and traditional religious beliefs. There is also the tension between an overreaching law-and-order response to such a complex problem, presuming all IPV cases to be serious criminal matters akin to the failing war on drugs, and the difficulties of getting convictions in a system where one is presumed innocent until proven guilty. Another reason

---

1. Explanations for symmetry in IPV, compared to much more asymmetrical rates of general violence across the sexes, derive from both cultural and evolutionary/sexual selection theories, and center around the importance of the home and family in women's lives, as well as prevailing norms allowing women more latitude to aggress within this sphere (see Hamel, in press, for a more detailed account).

is the persistence of the gender paradigm that encourages the stereotyping of perpetrators (Boushey, 2016; Douglas & Hines, 2011; Hine et al., 2020; Lysova et al., 2020; Tsu et al., 2010). Ostensibly a liberal, "feminist" ethos, the paradigm depends on, and champions, a law enforcement response that is at best clumsy but well-intended and, at worse, entirely unconcerned with progressive civil rights values (Corvo & Johnson, 2012).

Let us be clear: A great deal of good and long-lasting value has been achieved due to the Battered Women's Movement. Violence between married, cohabitating, and dating partners is now taken seriously, both among the public and the institutions responsible for protecting us. Laws are now in effect that makes IPV a punishable crime, including statutes for offenses (e.g., marital rape) that had not existed before, and no longer do police regard partner violence as merely a family squabble. Nonetheless, these laws have been limited. Clearly, many women remain in danger from severe, potentially lethal violence from male partners who manage to avoid prosecution for their crimes. This is a serious problem.

However, male victims and sexual minorities are even less likely to get justice, as arrest and intervention policies too often continue to frame IPV primarily in terms of male perpetrators and female victims. Research over the past 30 years indicates that IPV stretches far beyond this historical paradigm and is in dire need of criminal justice reform. Aside from stymying our collective efforts to reduce rates of IPV in our communities effectively, the gender paradigm, vigorously defended by individuals who see themselves as champions for women's rights, continues to rely upon anachronistic principles and dismisses empirically based research which can lead to *benevolent sexist ideologies*[2] that only serve to reinforce tired stereotypes about women as helpless, child-like creatures who lack agency (Hamel, 2020b). Instead, this book provides evidence-based data that can hopefully lead to necessary reform toward greater inclusion to accommodate all victims.

Purpose of the Book

To address these misconceptions, this volume will describe the strengths and shortcomings of current IPV arrest and prosecution policies as they are carried out across the United States, considering methodologically sound contemporary research. It will demonstrate that the Battered Women's Movement was long overdue and responsible for several necessary reforms in our criminal justice system that remain as relevant today as ever before, given the lack of protection

---

2. In contrast to *hostile sexism*, the term *benevolent sexism* refers to attitudes and behaviors that regard women as virtuous and to be admired, but also fragile, lacking in agency or competitive drive, often helpless, and in need of protection—what some call the "women are wonderful" effect.

for many of the most vulnerable victims, usually women. While ending violence against women is an admirable aim, this vision continues to neglect other victims of IPV. Therefore, this text focuses on how a more empirically based criminal justice response and practice would be more effective in providing for the safety of all victims. This includes holding offenders accountable and stopping the intergenerational cycle of violence in families while ensuring the civil rights of criminal defendants.

This book is written by scholars, practitioners, and attorneys to provide research and expertise that should be of interest to legal professionals responding to and adjudicating criminal, family court, and tort cases involving accusations of IPV, as well as mental health professionals, policymakers, and others interested in IPV as a societal and criminal issue. We hope that it will be helpful to district attorneys in making more informed decisions about who and how to prosecute so that IPV offenders are forced to take responsibility for their violence. We seek to assist defense attorneys in preventing defendants from being wrongfully convicted or mandated to a course of treatment that fails to address their needs and potentially leaves victims in danger. We also hope that the information presented will help victim advocates and treatment providers by providing a common empirical ground on which to engage and cooperate for the benefit of all involved constructively.

Our concerns regarding the deleterious consequences of current IPV arrest, prosecution, and treatment policies are summarized herein and then elaborated upon elsewhere in the book, and a variety of promising reform recommendations will be advanced. If you are a defense attorney or civil libertarian, you may already share these concerns. If not, we hope you will learn to take them seriously and to give voice to them, whatever your role may be, in the collective effort to combat relationship violence.

Undermining Defendant Rights

In most states, including California, police officers are encouraged to conduct investigations into IPV allegations according to guidelines set forth by mandatory arrest and proarrest statutes. These statutes make sense insofar as they allow police to intervene in situations where a victim may be at significant risk, but evidence of harm (e.g., injuries) is often lacking. Some of the most dangerous perpetrators know how to hurt their victims without leaving marks and can project a calm demeanor, giving the appearance that "there's nothing to see here" (DeLeon-Granados et al., 2006; Miller, 2001). It is also true that when police are encouraged to arrest with minimal evidence that a crime has been committed, many innocent people are likely to find themselves behind bars. This also comes neatly wrapped with the attendant legal, financial, and emotional costs to defendants and their families. Defendants criminally convicted of an IPV offense, even in misdemeanor cases, or arrested but never charged can be denied employment opportunities and, following relationship dissolution, find their parental rights denied or severely curtailed. Among them, low-income individuals, often people of color, cannot meet bail requirements or afford skilled legal counsel to exonerate them. For these reasons, and lack of confidence an attorney may have about going to trial, defendants often take a plea deal to go back to work and provide for their families. Even when the incident is minor, the toll on families is not inconsiderable, as when children are needlessly removed from their mother by Child Protective Services for "failure to protect" (Stark, 2002).

Ideally, a balance should be found between the rights of citizens not to be falsely arrested and keeping people safe. Sadly, among some victim advocates, there appears to be very little concern for defendant constitutional rights—particularly the rights of male suspects or members of sexual minority groups. This lack of concern has been amply demonstrated over the past two decades, following the enactment of mandatory arrest laws and the resulting spike in arrests, including those involving female defendants. Only after this increase of female arrests did victim advocates question mandatory arrest laws, arguing that these laws sometimes led to police officers unknowingly arresting the wrong person. As a legal remedy, advocates helped to enact so-called *predominant aggressor* guidelines. The exact definition varies from state to state. However, they align well with the definition proposed by the International Association of Chiefs of Police (IACP), which defines the term as "the individual who poses the most serious, ongoing threat, which may not necessarily be the initial aggressor in a specific incident" (International Association of Chiefs of Police, 2017).

In theory, these guidelines might indeed serve to protect actual victims who, in some circumstances, may have initiated an act of preemptive aggression against someone who had previously engaged in a pattern of chronic violence and who now threatens further harm (Hamel, 2011; Hamel & Russell, 2013). However, when citing such cases, advocates inevitably refer only to female victimization, despite the gender-neutral language used in predominant aggressor statutes (Chesney-Lind, 2002; McMahon & Pence, 2003). Ideology and political bias aside, these statutes are difficult to properly administer, given the lack of empirically derived criteria upon which to determine precisely how to identify the predominant aggressor. Suppose IPV scholars cannot agree on this term. What can be reasonably expected from poorly informed police officers presented with two plausible but conflicting stories and a lack of reliable eyewitnesses? History of previous IPV, a common criterion, can only be reliably ascertained from criminal justice records, which may or may not say anything meaningful about the aggressor in a particular incident (Hamel, 2011).

Moreover, most IPV is bidirectional in the general population, yet most states discourage mutual arrests, forcing arbitrary distinctions to be made between perpetrator and victim. In arrests involving heterosexual relationships, men's relatively greater size and strength make them convenient targets for arrest. However, female victims may also be arrested for the same reason, or when they are intoxicated or otherwise frustrate the police who arrive at the scene. The opposite problem exists with same-sex couples, where police are even less informed about IPV dynamics (Letellier, 1994; Russell & Torres, 2020). Officers may assume mutuality in violence due to the lesser difference in size and strength between the parties, when, in fact, one partner is the predominant aggressor.

Police officers cannot be blamed for ideologically tinted policies. However, they are nonetheless responsible for enforcing existing laws, and how they do so reflects in part the inherent difficulties in any type of police work. A solid body of forensic psychology research has revealed the extent to which police officers cannot accurately detect deception when interviewing general criminal suspects. Instead, they rely on the same misleading cues as laypeople (e.g., Bond & DePaulo, 2006; Hartwig & Granhag, 2015). Figuring out who is lying and who is telling the truth in IPV cases presents additional difficulties. Given the personal nature of intimate relationships and the possibility of ulterior motives, the person who initially reports an IPV incident may or may not be the actual victim. Other reasons for calling the police include getting someone to mediate a nonviolent but escalating conflict, retribution for actual or imagined infidelity, or as a means to forcibly kick out a partner for purposes of gaining an advantage in a child custody case (e.g., Cook, 2009). False allegations of IPV, a form of coercive control known as legal and administrative abuse, are made by both sexes, including by manipulative men, as previously mentioned, and confirmed by abused women and their allies (DeLeon-Granados et al., 2006; Miller, 2001). Nonetheless, false allegations can also greatly benefit female batterers, who are more likely to be taken seriously because they are female and presumed to be the victimized party (Douglas, 2018; Hines et al., 2015).

Once an arrest is made and charges are filed by the local prosecutor, current "no-drop prosecution" policies in some jurisdictions make it difficult for the complainant to see the charges dismissed, a practice discouraged by the National District Attorneys Association (2017). Battered women advocates correctly argue that victim retraction is often done under duress, either due to threats made by the perpetrator, for economic reasons, or because the perpetrator wore the victim down with a variety of self-serving, manipulative, and guilt-inducing tactics (Bonomi et al., 2011; Hamel, 2020a). This is a serious problem long recognized by district attorneys and advocates alike (Leisenring, 2008). Rarely, if ever acknowledged is the possibility that the presumed "victim" had initiated the violence but lied about it, for whatever reasons, or perhaps called the police during a bilaterally escalated incident in which the parties were equally culpable but later felt genuinely guilty for lying or exaggerating their partner's degree of involvement. Due to the legal consequences of perjury and concern that charges might be brought against them should they want the investigation to continue, complainants are reluctant to fully disclose their culpability in any incident (they make perfunctory statements or provide no information in their retraction statements; Sleath & Smith, 2016). Still, it does not take much imagination to understand that when law enforcement officers arrive at the scene of a domestic disturbance, especially in mandatory arrest states, and primed to make an arrest, it makes sense for all parties to shade the truth. Nobody wants to be arrested.

For all of these reasons, we should all be mindful of limitations and biases inherent in the current criminal justice response to IPV, and the very real threat to defendant rights and procedural justice, as evidenced by the scholarly research literature. In their review, Shernock and Russell (2012) conclude:

> Simulation studies of police officer and mock juror decision making have found that males are viewed as more culpable in IPV situations but have found no significant racial differences. The results of these simulated studies are for the most part borne out in reality regarding the criminal justice response to IPV. In general, it appears that the less favorable treatment of males regarding the issuance of POs, arrest, and prosecution is most salient.... The less favorable treatment of males becomes somewhat more pronounced at each of the subsequent stages of the criminal justice process. (p. 523)

Considering the greater physical danger posed by male perpetrated IPV, it is essential to understand that among the research papers referenced by the authors were many local and nationwide studies on arrest and issuance of restraining orders that controlled for the extent of injuries. These studies confirm a significant pattern of gender bias within the judicial system.

Limited Effectiveness of Arrest, Prosecution, and Intervention Policies

Within proarrest and mandatory arrest states, IPV arrest rates are higher than where police have greater discretion. This is a positive outcome if it helps bring more batterers to justice. Unfortunately, additional arrests lead to fewer successful prosecutions because district attorneys lack the resources to process weak cases (Davis, 2008; Hirschel & Buzawa, 2002). Undoubtedly many of these weaker cases involve situations of high conflict that need not be addressed through the criminal justice system. However, in other cases, victims might be in danger. There are few alternatives to arrest in most jurisdictions other than allowing a potentially violent individual to go free. Save for the issuance of a restraining order, which provides no legal mechanism by which the perpetrator, or perpetrators, might be helped to resolve their issues (e.g., such as deferred prosecution or a mandated assessment protocol with which to determine alternate intervention options) (Young et al., 2007). Particularly troublesome, a lack of alternatives may put victims in danger when they are denied the choice of having the prosecution dropped. This has been demonstrated in studies showing that in proarrest states, they are less likely to call hotlines or report reoffenses to law enforcement, making them feel revictimized by the criminal justice system (Hotaling & Buzawa, 2003; Mills, 2003).

Once a defendant pleads guilty to an IPV charge, he or she may have to serve a jail sentence, but in misdemeanor cases they are typically required instead to complete a course of treatment. Except for Colorado and Washington State, state standards governing such treatment are not based on the particulars of a case, such as a defendant's personality, ability to change, abuse pattern, or risk of reoffending. Treatment recommendations from battered women advocates tend to lean toward one-size-fits-all remedies. These treatments include intervention programs rooted in a same-sex psychoeducational group format, otherwise known as batterer intervention programs (BIPs). Such programs typically emphasize gender role factors and offender use of "power and control" behaviors and discourage or prohibit evidence-based approaches such as couples counseling or anger management. However, such approaches may not be adequate or flexible enough to fully meet the needs of a highly heterogeneous population (Babcock et al., 2016; Maiuro & Eberle, 2008). Therefore, it is not surprising that they affect a mere 5% reduction in recidivistic violence above arrest and court monitoring (Babcock et al., 2004).

The point needs to be stated, however apparent, that when batterers are not arrested or held accountable for their violence, whether they be male or female, gay or straight, they remain a threat to their victims and contribute further to the intergenerational cycle of violence. They are also denied an opportunity to rehabilitate themselves. Of course, IPV does not happen in a vacuum. In most partner-violent relationships, the abuse is bidirectional, and both partners need to be held accountable. However, even when one party dominates or is solely responsible for the violence, treatment is more likely to be effective when it is understood from a systemic perspective (Hamel & Nicholls, 2007). Unfortunately, current policies presume rigid perpetrator/victim distinctions that limit alternative treatment options. This is a problem in dire need of redress.

Throughout this book, an argument is made that arrest, prosecution, and treatment should be based on the research evidence and the facts of each case. There is no reason (other than politics) why this cherished maxim should not apply to violence between intimate partners. To the extent that women are more impacted than men from physical assaults, the system should respond accordingly. Prison cells will no doubt continue to accommodate primarily male homicide perpetrators. On average bigger and stronger, men can more readily protect themselves and are at lesser risk of life-threatening violence. Therefore, they are unlikely to require the same level of shelter services as female victims. Nevertheless, the current reflexive law enforcement response, based on traditional gender stereotypes, makes a mockery of the judicial system, fosters confusion and cynicism, and erodes support from potential allies needed in the fight against IPV. Sadly, it also reaffirms the very stereotypes that feminists have sought to overcome by denying women and sexual minorities—whether victim or perpetrator—a sense of agency.

ORGANIZATION OF CHAPTERS

The information provided in this volume provides a contemporary view associated with all aspects of the adjudicative process and evidence-based interventions surrounding IPV. The book is organized into four parts, including history and research, litigation, issues of family law, and evidence-based interventions. Part I includes an overview of the current research on IPV. Bates and Papamichail (see Chapter 2) examine the evolution of IPV awareness, gender similarities and differences of IPV, prevalence, causes, and dynamics of IPV. The authors also address various typologies of abuse, risk factors, antecedents, and consequences of IPV for victims and families. Part I also explores the history and advances of law enforcement and criminal justice response to IPV. For instance, Russell and Seisler (see Chapter 3) summarize arrest rates for cis-gender and sexual minority victims and perpetrators of IPV. They examine critical legal cases leading to current arrest policies, including mandatory arrest, proarrest, and discretionary arrest, and explore the effectiveness of these policies. The authors also explore how social stereotypes can influence IPV response and the extent to which training and experience can shape how they interpret and handle IPV incidents. Police officers are not immune to IPV within their own ranks; therefore, officer-involved domestic violence (OIDV) is addressed along with considerations of discretion and recommendations for greater inclusiveness in policy and practice.

Part II (Litigation) includes four chapters on the litigation process from prosecution, strategies for mounting a legal defense in IPV criminal cases, intimate partner homicide and the battered person syndrome, and jury decision-making. Cox and colleagues (see Chapter 4) explore how gender and sex influence the prosecution of IPV and address gender-inverted (female-to-male IPV) in addition to IPV in same-sex relationships. They examine legal and extralegal factors associated with prosecutorial decision-making and offer implications for practice and directions for future research. In Chapter 5, Dresow, a San Francisco Bay Area attorney, reflects on the challenges and strategies to mount a legal defense in IPV criminal cases. He provides general guidelines from receiving the first phone call from someone in need of a defense, initial steps upon accepting a case, information gathering, collateral consequences, and the necessity of understanding the universe of the case to build an effective defense. The author stresses the importance of guiding clients through the process while acknowledging the idiosyncrasies of IPV compared to other crime classifications. In this context, he refers to sex and gender, mandatory arrest and dominant aggressor laws, and the consequences of arrest and prosecution on defendants, trial considerations, the use of expert testimony, and sentencing alternatives.

Chapter 6 focuses on intimate partner homicide (IPH). Hamel, Dutton, and Lysova provide an in-depth view of IPH, including prevalence, context, risk factors, and motivation for IPV perpetration. The authors note differences in types of IPV and how situational couple violence differs from intimate terrorism and address male-perpetrated and female-perpetrated IPH in the context of intimate terrorism, violent resistance, and self-defense. The authors also explore risk factors and personality as predictors of IPH, along with a review of the battered woman's syndrome within an IPH context. Similarities and differences across the sexes are provided in conjunction with implications for prosecutors and defense attorneys charged with adjudicating these cases. The last chapter in this section pertains to jury decision-making in IPV and overcoming bias in the courtroom (see Russell and McKimmie, Chapter 7). This chapter covers critical issues for the jury in cases of IPV. Issues address self-defense in confrontational and nonconfrontational issues, why victims do not leave their abuser, motivations for IPH, the gendered nature of IPV, and the role of stereotypes and scripts in jury decision-making. A summary of the literature on jury decision-making in IPV cases is reviewed emphasizing nontypical victims and perpetrators. The authors review the various ways in which jurors make decisions individually and within groups. They explain how juror gender and expert testimony of the battered person syndrome influence decisions in IPV cases and offer suggestions for jury selection, reform, and future research.

Part III (Family Law) covers challenges and strategies in litigating IPV in family law cases, custody and intervention recommendations, and child abuse and parental alienation. Chapter 8 was written by an experienced practicing family law attorney in Southern California. Pissara provides a unique look into the family court system by offering guidelines for domestic violence. The author helps attorneys navigate the family court system and provides an in-depth perspective on how domestic violence affects individuals and families. The author provides recommendations of how custody determinations can be improved so that children's best interests are served. Chapter 9, written by Hamel and Baker, provides a gender-inclusive framework surrounding custody and intervention recommendations in family law. The authors approach IPV from perspectives of the child's best interest and elaborate on the complexities of family abuse. Child custody evaluation procedures, custody protocol, and child custody recommendations are addressed for legal actors, child custody mediators, and evaluators, as the authors provide an in-depth review of the complete process of the evaluation, interviews, observation, to synthesizing data to ensure objectivity reduce potential bias. Lastly, in this part, Chapter 10 authors Harmon and Kruk examine parental alienation, gender bias, and child abuse. They summarize the empirical research on these topics, draw parallels on how IPV and parental alienation behaviors affect the victims of these behaviors, and examine similarities in patterns and motives of abuse and their effect on children.

Finally, Part IV (Evidence-Based Interventions) focuses on cutting-edge gender-inclusive intervention strategies for legal actors, mediators, counselors, and restorative justice practitioners. Hamel and Ennis (Chapter 11) provide ideas for evidence-based interviewing protocols and risk assessment instruments to hold perpetrators accountable. Within this chapter, Hamel and Ennis explore ways to gauge better the actual risk posed by IPV perpetrators through evidence-based interview protocols and assessment techniques utilizing validated, reliable instruments such as the Spousal Assault Risk Assessment (SARA and SARA v3), Brief Spousal Assault Form for the Evaluation of Risk (B-SAFER), Ontario Domestic Assault Risk Assessment (ODARA), Domestic Violence Risk Appraisal Guide (DVRAG), Domestic Violence Screening Instrument (DVSI), and Danger Assessment (DA). Similarly, Roberts (Chapter 12) reviews risk-needs-responsivity (RNR)–informed approaches to batterer intervention programs. Roberts addresses the inconsistencies in most batterer intervention strategies and draws from her work in Washington State that provides an alternative evidence-based approach to IPV treatment. She addresses the risk, needs, responsivity assessment and treatment framework, behavioral assessment standards, differentiated treatment model, core competencies, and a cognitive-behavioral treatment model approach to standardize a core curriculum. Authors in Chapter 13 (Bennett, Chu, Pollard, and Babcock) examine the efficacy of couples and family interventions for IPV as safe and effective interventions for couples experiencing situational couple violence. Their chapter addresses perpetrator typologies, intervention programs such as restorative justice, family interventions for witnessing IPV, and IPV prevention programs. The last chapter in this volume (Chapter 14), by Barocas and Shimizu, provides an overview of restorative justice theory and practice and addresses the research on restorative justice in IPV cases. The authors review the history, definitions in practice, the use of restorative justice to address IPV crimes, including crime severity, various methods used, the timing of restorative justice, and the evidence base for restorative justice interventions.

This volume has two distinct purposes. First, it provides a novel approach by addressing the gendered aspects of IPV and its effects within the legal system, practice, and intervention. Second, this book provides a unique view of contemporary evidence-based research surrounding the adjudication process of IPV. It offers ways to address the problems associated with adjudicating IPV cases in practice and intervention to serve all IPV victims better and hold batterers accountable. The book intends to demonstrate how the gender paradigm has affected (and continues to affect) legal decision-making and practice, and the many ways in which differential treatment exists within the context of IPV. We hope this text demonstrates that the time to move beyond the gender paradigm is now. Armed with the current state of the research, readers of this text have the knowledge and ability to do so. This book provides the expertise and tools necessary to help us to become more cognizant of our own biases and ultimately more inclusive in the adjudicative process and IPV intervention/prevention practice. The information provided in this book provides a foundation from which we can learn and apply by developing tools to improve research, policy, and practice allowing us to move forward toward eradicating IPV and closer to equality. We recognize there are limitations and issues that may not have been addressed. However, we hope this text demonstrates the need for a paradigm shift and revitalizes the debate between traditional gendered perceptions of IPV and those who recognize that IPV is no longer a gender-based crime, but rather a crime that exists beyond gender or sexual orientation/identity. Ideally, this text can serve as a catalyst to spark discourse, empirical research, and improve practice in the adjudicative processes of IPV that can lead to wide-ranging political and ideological changes over time.

REFERENCES

American Bar Association. (2001). Know your basic rights: Domestic violence. https://www.americanbar.org/content/dam/aba/administrative/public_education/resources/domviol.pdf

American Bar Association Commission on Domestic & Sexual Violence. (2021). Recommended legal reforms for inclusion in the U.S. national action plan on gender-based violence, pp. 1–78. https://www.americanbar.org/content/dam/aba/publications/domestic-violence/aba_nap-gbv_report.pdf

Babcock, J., Green, C., & Robie, C. (2004). Does batterers' treatment work: A meta-analytic review of domestic violence treatment. *Clinical Psychology Review, 23*, 1023–1053. https://doi.org/10.1016/j.cpr.2002.07.001

Babcock, J., Armenti, N., Cannon, C., Lauve-Moon, K., Buttell, F., Ferreira, R., Cantos, A., Hamel, J., Kelly, D., Jordan, C., Lehmann, P., Leisring, P. A., Murphy, C., O'Leary, D. K., Bannon, S., Salis, K., & Solano, I. (2016). Domestic violence perpetrator programs: A proposal for evidence-based standards in the United States. *Partner Abuse, 7*(4), 1–107. doi:10.1891/1946-6560.7.4.355

Bond, C., & DePaulo, B. (2006). Accuracy of deception judgments. *Personality and Social Psychology Review, 10*(3), 214–234. doi:https://doi.org/10.1207/s15327957pspr1003_2

Bonomi, A. E., Gangamma, R., Locke C., Katafizsz, H., & Martin, D. (2011). "Meet me at the hill where we used to park": Interpersonal processes associated with victim recantation. *Social Science & Medicine, 73*, 1054–1061.

Boushey, G. (2016). Targeted for diffusion? How the use and acceptance of stereotypes shape the diffusion of criminal justice policy innovations in the American states. *American Political Science Review, 110*(1), 198–214. doi:10.1017/S0003055415000532

Buzawa, E., & Buzawa, C. (2002). *Domestic violence: The criminal justice response* (2nd ed.). Sage.

Buzawa, E. S., Buzawa, C., & Stark, E. (2017). *Responding to domestic violence: The integration of criminal justice response & human services* (5th ed.). Sage.

Chesney-Lind, M. (2002). Criminalizing victimization: The unintended consequences of pro-arrest policies for girls and women. *Criminology and Public Policy, 2*(1), 81–90. https://doi.org/10.1111/j.1745-9133.2002.tb00108.x

Cook, P. (2009). *Abused men: The hidden side of domestic violence* (2nd ed.). Praeger.

Corvo, K., & Johnson, P. (2012). An eye for an eye: Gender revanchisme and the negation of attachment in domestic violence policy. *Partner Abuse, 3*(1), 89–106. doi:10.1891/1946-6560.3.1.89

Davis, R. L. (2008). *Domestic violence: Intervention, prevention, policies, and solutions*. CRC Press.

DeLeon-Granados, W., Wells, W., & Binsbacher, R. (2006). Arresting developments: Trends in female arrests for domestic violence and proposed explanations. *Violence Against Women, 12*(4), 355–371. https://doi.org/10.1177/1077801206287315

Dempsey, B. (2013). Men's experiences of domestic abuse in Scotland. *Edinburgh: Abused Men in Scotland (AMIS)*. https://www.academia.edu/7317930/Mens_experience_of_domestic_abuse_in_Scotland_Full_Report

Dixon, L, Archer, J., & Graham-Kevan, N. (2012). Perpetrator programmes for partner violence: Are they based on ideology or evidence? *Legal and Criminological Psychology, 17*, 196–215. https://doi.org/10.1111/j.2044-8333.2011.02029.x

Dobash, R. E., & Dobash, R. (1979). *Violence against wives: A case against the patriarchy* (pp. 179–206). New York: Free Press.

Dobash, R. E., & Dobash, R. (1988). Research as social action: The struggle for battered women. In K. Yllo & M. Bograd (Eds.), *Feminist perspectives on wife abuse* (pp. 51–74). Sage.

Douglas, E., & Hines, D. (2011). The help-seeking experiences of men who sustain intimate partner violence: An overlooked population and implications for practice. *Journal of Family Violence, 26*, 473–485. https://doi.org/10.1007/s10896-011-9382-4

Douglas, H. (2018). Legal systems abuse and coercive control. *Criminology & Criminal Justice, 18*(1), 84–99. https://doi.org/10.1177/1748895817728380

Dragiewicz, M. (2008). Patriarchy reasserted: Fathers' rights and anti-VAWA activism. *Feminist Criminology, 3*(2), 121–144.

Dutton, D., Corvo, K., & Hamel, J. (2009). The gender paradigm in domestic violence research and practice, part II: The information website of the American Bar Association. *Aggression and Violent Behavior, 14*, 30–38. doi:10.1016/j.avb.2008.08.002

Dutton, D., & Nicholls, T. (2005). The gender paradigm in domestic violence research and theory: The conflict of theory and data. *Aggression and Violent Behavior, 10*, 680–714. doi:10.1016/j.avb.2005.02.001

Eckhardt, C. I., Murphy, C. M., Whitaker, D. J., Sprunger, J., Dykstra, R., & Woodard, K. (2013). The effectiveness of intervention programs for perpetrators and victims of intimate partner violence. *Partner Abuse, 4*(2), 196–231. doi:10.1891/1946-6560.4.2.175

Federal Bureau of Investigation. Crime in the United States Uniform Crime Report Summary Reporting System National Incident-Based Reporting System (NIBRS) (2017). Table 42: Arrests by sex, 2017. https://ucr.fbi.gov/crime-in-the-u.s/2017/crime-in-the-u.s.-2017/topic-pages/tables/table-42

Follingstad, D., DeHart, D., & Green, E. (2004). Psychologists' judgements of psychologically aggressive actions when perpetrated by a husband versus a wife. *Violence and Victims, 19*(4), 435–452. doi:10.1891/vivi.19.4.435.64165

Hamberger, K., Lohr, J., Bonge, D., & Tolin, D. (1997). An empirical classification of motivations for domestic violence. *Violence Against Women, 3*, 401–423. doi:https://doi.org/10.1177/1077801297003004005

Hamel, J. (2009). Toward a gender-inclusive conception of intimate partner violence research and theory: Part II—New directions. *International Journal of Men's Health, 8*(1), 41–59. doi:10.3149/jmh.0801.41

Hamel, J. (2011). In dubious battle: The politics of mandatory arrest and dominant aggressor laws. *Partner Abuse, 2*(2), 224–245. doi:10.1891/1946-6560.2.2.224

Hamel, J. (2016). In the best interests of children: What family law attorneys should know about domestic violence. *Journal of the American Academy of Matrimonial Lawyers, 28*, 201–228.

Hamel, J. (2020a). Perpetrator or victim? A review of the complexities of domestic violence cases. *Journal of Aggression, Conflict and Peace Research, 12*(2), 55–62. https://doi.org/10.1108/JACPR-12-2019-0464

Hamel, J. (2020b). Explaining symmetry across sex in intimate partner violence: Evolution, gender roles, and the will to harm. *Partner Abuse, 11*(3), 228–267. doi:10.1891/PA-2020-0014

Hamel, J., Desmarais, S. L., & Nicholls, T. L. (2007). Perceptions of motives in intimate partner violence: Expressive versus coercive violence. *Violence and Victims, 22*(5), 563–576. doi:10.1891/088667007782312113

Hamel, J., Desmarais, S. L., Nicholls, T. L., Malley-Morrison, K., & Aaronson, J. (2009, July). Domestic violence and child custody: Are family court professionals' decisions based on erroneous beliefs? *Journal of Aggression, Conflict and Peace Research, 1*(2), 37–52. https://doi.org/10.1108/17596599200900011

Hamel, J., & Russell, B. (2013). The Partner Abuse State of Knowledge Project: Implications for law enforcement responses to domestic violence. In B. Russell (Ed.), *Perceptions of female offenders: How stereotypes and social norms affect criminal justice responses* (pp. 151–180). Springer. doi:10.1007/978-1-4614-5871-5

Hartwig, M., & Granhag, P. (2015). Exploring the nature and origin of beliefs about deception: Implicit and explicit knowledge among lay people and presumed experts. In P. Granhag, A. Vrij, & B. Verschuere (Eds.), *Detecting deception: Current challenges and cognitive approaches* (pp. 125–154). John Wiley & Sons.

Hine, B., Noku, L., Bates, E.A., & Jayes, K. (2020). But, who is the victim here? Exploring judgements toward hypothetical bidirectional domestic violence scenarios. *Journal of Interpersonal Violence, 37*(7-8), 1–22. NP5495–NP5516. https://doi.org/10.1177/0886260520917508

Hines, D. (2014). Extent and implications of the presentation of false facts by domestic violence agencies in the United States. *Partner Abuse, 5*(1), 69–82. https://doi.org/10.1891/1946-6560.5.1.69

Hines, D., Douglas, E., & Berger, J. (2015). A self-report measure of legal and administrative aggression within intimate relationships. *Aggressive Behavior, 41*(4), 295–309. https://doi.org/10.1002/ab.21540

Hirschel, D., & Buzawa, E. (2002). Understanding the context of dual arrest with directions for future research. *Violence Against Women, 8*, 1449–1473. https://doi.org/10.1177/107780102237965

Hotaling, G., & Buzawa, E. (2003). *Foregoing criminal justice assistance: The non-reporting of new incidents of abuse in a court sample of domestic violence victims* (NIJ Publication No. 195667). National Institute of Justice.

International Association of Chiefs of Police. (2017). Intimate partner violence response policy and training content guidelines 6. https://www.theiacp.org/sites/default/files/all/i-j/IACPIntimatePartnerViolenceResponse PolicyandTrainingGuidelines2017.pdf

Kang, M., Lessard, D., Heston, L., & Nordmaken, S. (2017). Introduction to women, gender, sexuality studies. University of Massachusetts Amherst. https://scholarworks.umass.edu/cgi/viewcontent.cgi?article=1000&context=wost_ed_materials.

Kimmel, M. (2002). "Gender symmetry" in domestic violence: A substantive and methodological research review. *Violence Against Women, 8*, 1332–1363. https://doi.org/10.1177/107780102237407

Kotrla, K. (2010). Domestic minor sex trafficking in the United Sates. *Social Work, 55*, 181–187. https://doi.org/10.1093/sw/55.2.181

Leisenring, A. (2008). Controversies surrounding mandatory arrest policies and the police response to intimate partner violence. *Sociology Compass, 2*(2), 451–466. https://doi.org/10.1111/j.1751-9020.2008.00095.x

Letellier, P. (1994). Gay and bisexual male domestic violence victimization: Challenges to feminist theory and responses to violence. *Violence and Victims, 9*(2), 95–106.

Lysova, A., Hanson, K., Hines, D., Dixon, L., Douglas, E., & Celi, E. (2020). A qualitative study of the male victims' experiences with the criminal justice response to intimate partner abuse in four English-speaking countries. *Criminal Justice and Behavior, 20*(10), 1–8. https://doi.org/10.1177/0093854820927442

Maiuro, R. D, & Eberle, J. A. (2008). State standards for domestic violence perpetrator treatment: Current status, trends, and recommendations. *Violence and Victims, 23*(2), 133–155. doi:10.1891/0886-6708.23.2.133

McMahon, M., & Pence, E. (2003). Making social change: Reflections on individual and institutional advocacy with women arrested for domestic violence. *Violence Against Women, 9*(1), 47–72. https://doi.org/10.1177/1077801202238430

Miller, S. L. (2001). The paradox of women arrested for domestic violence. *Violence Against Women, 7*(12), 1339–1376. https://doi.org/10.1177/10778010122183900

Mills, L. G. (2003). *Insult to injury: Rethinking our responses to intimate abuse*. Princeton University Press.

National District Attorneys Association (2017). National domestic violence prosecution best practices guidelines. NDAA_National-DV-Prosecution-Best-Practices-Guide_3-16-2017.pdf (ncdsv.org)

Pence, E., & Paymar, M. (1993). *Education groups for men who batter: The Duluth model*. Springer.

Rudd, J. (2001). Dowry-Murder: An example of violence against women. *Women's Studies International Forum, 24*(5), 513–522. https://doi.org/10.1016/S0277-5395(01)00196-0

Russell, B. (2010). *Battered woman syndrome as a legal defense: History, effectiveness and implications*. McFarland & Company.

Russell, B., & Torres, C. (2020). Identifying and responding to LGBT+ intimate partner violence from a criminal justice perspective. In B. Russell (Ed.), *Intimate partner violence and the LGBT+ community* (pp. 257–280). Springer. https://doi.org/10.1007/978-3-030-44762-5_14

Shernock, S., & Russell, B. (2012). Gender and racial/ethnic differences in criminal justice decision making in intimate partner violence cases. *Partner Abuse, 3*(4), 501–530. doi:10.1891/1946-6560.3.4.501

Sleath, E., & Smith, L. (2016, January). Understanding the factors that predict victim retraction in police reported allegations of intimate partner violence. *Psychology of Violence, 7*(1), 140–149. https://doi.org/10.1037/vio0000035

Stark, E. (2002). The battered mother in the child protective service caseload: Developing an appropriate response. *Women's Rights Law Reporter, 23*(2), 107–131.

Straus, M., Gelles, R., & Asplund, L. M. (1990). Physical violence in American families: Risk factors and adaptations to violence in 8,145 families. *Victims and Violence, 5*(4), 297–298. doi:10.1891/0886-6708.5.4.297

Swan, S., Gambone, L., Caldwell, J., Sullivan, T., & Snow, D. (2008). A review of research on women's use of violence with male intimate partners. *Violence and Victims, 23*(3), 302–314. doi:10.1891/0886-6708.23.3.301

Tsui, V., Cheung, M., & Leung, P. (2010). Help-seeking among male victims of partner abuse: Men's hard times. *Journal of Community Psychology, 38*(6), 769–780. https://doi.org/10.1002/jcop.20394

Wood, J. (2013). *Gendered lives: Communication, gender, and culture*. Wadsworth.

Young, C., Cook, P., Smith, S., Turteltaub, J., & Hazelwood, L. R. (2007). Domestic violence: New visions, new solutions. In J. Hamel & T. Nicholls (Eds.), *Family interventions in domestic violence: A handbook of gender-inclusive theory and treatment* (pp. 601–620). Springer.

2

What We Currently Know about the Prevalence, Causes, and Dynamics of Intimate Partner Violence

ELIZABETH A. BATES AND ALEXANDRA PAPAMICHAIL ■

Over the past 50 years, a wealth of literature exploring intimate partner violence (IPV) has developed. Despite a historical focus on men's violence toward women in marriage with causes thought to be around male privilege and gender inequality, an array of work now explores the causes and consequences of IPV for many victims and perpetrator groups. This chapter will present what we currently know about the prevalence, causes, and dynamics of IPV. This will involve exploring the prevalence of different forms of IPV, the dynamics of IPV, including bidirectional or mutual abuse, and the development of typologies thought to help us understand the issue (e.g., Johnson, 1995). It will further explore risk factors and antecedents of IPV perpetration, the links with other forms of family violence, and the consequences of IPV for victims and families. There will also be an exploration of where these issues involve similarity and difference across gender. The chapter will draw on a wide range of academic research, including specifically from the Partner Abuse State of Knowledge (PASK) research as well as national population data such as the National Intimate Partner and Sexual Violence Survey (USA) and the Office for National Statistics data on domestic abuse in England and Wales.

HISTORICAL FOCUS

The historical context of how we have understood IPV within research and practice is critical in understanding IPV within research and practice today (Bates, 2019). Prior to the 1970s, there was a lack of research and social narrative around IPV, something which Dutton (2006) labeled the "age of denial" (p. 16); here the sanctity and privacy of the home were valued above and beyond the safety of those who resided within. This is something that changed during the 1970s; one of the focuses of the feminist movement included fighting against both violence against women and rape within marriage (Dobash & Dobash, 1979, 2004). This movement was significant in raising awareness of the issue. It can be credited with raising the profile of terms such as "domestic violence" and "domestic abuse" within the public narrative. Indeed, during this time, Erin Pizzey opened the first women's shelter in 1971 for women who were escaping abusive relationships, and a research movement began to explore men's violence against women.

During this period, the movement created research and practice that highlighted the magnitude of the issues of domestic violence and its significance as a social issue. For example, the research highlighted the prevalence of men's violence toward women (Rath et al., 1989), the impact of women's victimization (Mullen et al., 1988), and the impact of engaging in services and the positive impacts of working with practitioners (Berk et al., 1986). The origins of this movement started over 50 years ago, but scholars more recently have echoed these original sentiments. For example, DeKeseredy (2021) believes it is problematic that there has been a decline in the feminist sociological analyses of IPV over the last decade. DeKeseredy believes that other explorations of IPV (e.g., nursing, psychology) do not then consider the broader social, cultural, and political factors that influence violence against women. Those who support this model often draw on evidence that finds women experience higher levels of fear and injury (e.g., Caldwell et al., 2012).

This model continues to be influential within practice through the Duluth model (Pence & Paymar, 1993), a psychoeducational model that was developed to re-educate men about male privilege and gender inequality to reduce their violence toward women. The central curriculum of this model is the Power and Control Wheel, which focuses on issues such as men's economic control over women, use of children, male privilege, and use of threats and intimidation. More recent approaches have retained this curriculum and created a hybrid model grounded in cognitive-behavioral therapy (CBT; Gondolf, 2007). There is a significant body of evidence that suggests this approach is not effective in reducing recidivism (e.g., see Babcock et al., 2004). However, despite this, there is evidence from a recent series of reviews (see Hamel, 2016) that this approach is still influential. This is also in contrast to further evidence (to be discussed in more detail later) that highlights women's use of violence, men's victimization, the prevalence of bidirectional abuse, and the myriad of risk factors that predict men's violence other than male privilege and gendered attitudes.

PREVALENCE OF INTIMATE PARTNER VIOLENCE

The prevalence of IPV within the population and gender differences within this context differ depending on the data source. For example, within the United States, according to the CDC's National Intimate Partner and Sexual Violence Survey (NISVS; Smith et al., 2017), 1 in 4 women and 1 in 7 men have experienced severe physical violence by an intimate partner during their lifetime. Black et al.'s (2011) analysis of the 2010 version of the survey revealed that 35.6% of women and 28.5% of men reported lifetime rates of rape, physical violence, and stalking behavior; this was 5.9% and 5%, respectively, for the last 12 months. There were also similarities in reported rates for physical violence; for "slapped, pushed or shoved," the figures were 30.3% for women and 25.7% for men (3.6% and 4.5% for the last 12 months). These figures were 24.3% for women and 13.8% for men (2.7% and 2%, respectively, for the last 12 months) for any severe physical violence. Figures were not presented to be compared for rape due to the low number for men, but when looking at other sexual violence, there was 16.9% for women and 8% as lifetime rates for men; for the last 12 months, these were remarkably similar for men and women with 2.3% and 2.5%, respectively. When exploring figures over the last 12 months, there are few fundamental gender differences seen. It should be noted that there is a tendency to utilize the rates for the previous 12 months instead of lifetime rates due to the perception that these are more accurate.

Within England and Wales, domestic abuse-related prosecutions data suggest that men are the vast majority of perpetrators (92%) and women the majority of victims (77%; ONS, 2020), with a total of 61,169 domestic abuse-related prosecutions. Where crime surveys are utilized, and the focus is around the range of crimes experienced through a random digit dialing survey (e.g., ONS, 2020), we see around 2 million victims annually in England and Wales, and a gender ratio is much closer with statistics suggesting that for every three victims, one is male and two are female. We look toward academic studies and those utilizing self-report measures such as the Conflict Tactics Scale (CTS; Straus, 1979; see more detailed discussion later). We see evidence suggesting gender symmetry in perpetration and victimization (e.g., Archer, 2000; Bates et al., 2014). There have been heated discussions around the use of these figures. For instance, some scholars (e.g., Brown, 2004; Henning & Renauer, 2005) suggest that self-report fails to capture context. Criminal justice figures likely do not depict much of women's aggression due to existing biases in charging and prosecution. Dutton (2010) claimed, "once the criminal justice selective filer is removed, the outcome results homogenize for both genders" (p. 14). The variation in these figures has been the subject of significant debate, but there is some agreement that figures from the justice system are likely to be an underestimate, not only due to barriers women face in disclosing but also the significant additional barriers men are thought to face in reporting abuse.

The disparity in these figures can largely be seen in the origins and methods of the data collection. For example, those collecting data within the criminal justice system through the clinical levels shelter/refuge samples, including those who work with perpetrators, will see the more serious examples of IPV. For example, men who have been arrested and mandated to IPV programs or women who are residing within shelters or refuges typically suggest more serious incidents of IPV. While these samples provide a wealth of information about the experiences of male perpetrators and female victims, the lack of equivalent samples from female perpetrators and male victims means any generalization made from these samples is inappropriate. Women are less likely to be prosecuted and are less likely to receive custodial sentences (e.g., Henning & Renauer, 2005) and less likely to be mandated to a perpetrator program.

Similarly, there are fewer resources to support safe accommodation and refuge for men escaping an abusive relationship, so there is limited access to the same clinical samples for both female perpetrators and male victims. Some proponents of the gendered model would suggest this is because there are fewer female perpetrators and male victims in need of this clinical level response; however, the broader evidence-based research does not support this. It is likely that the biases and inadequate resources within the wider criminal justice system prevent there being equivalent samples to access.

When we focus on more gender-inclusive approaches, including using less loaded language around conflict, we see very different findings in terms of gender when we seek more comprehensive community samples. The CTS (Straus, 1979) was one of the first measures designed to capture the frequency of violence within intimate relationships. Straus designed it to measure IPV by investigating a list of acts they had used in conflict resolution within a set period of time. It is usually used with community and undergraduate samples of married or dating couples and involves respondents completing their own and their partner's behavior (Archer, 1999). Some of the early studies utilizing this demonstrated the prevalence of IPV within the family and the prevalence of women's violence and men's victimization. For example, Szinovacz (1983) used the CTS with a sample of couples and found that women reported higher physical aggression rates than men. Similarly, Arias et al. (1987) used the CTS and found that 30% of men and 32% of women reported using aggression to a partner, with more women reporting using severe acts of aggression.

These findings started developing a body of work that evidenced the nature of family violence; indeed, Archer's (2000) meta-analysis published over 20 years ago was the culmination of 82 studies with over 64,000 participants. This paper concluded that women reported perpetrating significantly more acts of physical aggression within relationships than men (effect size $d = -.05$). This key study in this burgeoning body of literature has (at last check on Google Scholar, May 2021) been cited 3,414 times. Research continued post 2000, with similar findings being seen. For example, in 2012, Desmarais et al. (2012a, 2012b) published two systematic reviews exploring the prevalence of men's and women's perpetration and victimization as part of the PASK project. The PASK project is the world's most extensive domestic violence research database with summaries of 1,700 peer review studies across 17 papers (Hamel et al., 2012). The papers, including the extensive data tables, are available online, to scholars and the general public, at www.domesticviolenceresearch.org. Both the Desmarais et al. papers cover research over the previous 10 years, and so naturally follow on from Archer's work. Their first paper explored the prevalence of victimization through 249 articles (47.4% of which used the CTS); the pooled prevalence figures revealed that 1 in 4 women (23.1%) and 1 in 5 men (19.3%) had experienced IPV with an overall prevalence of 22.4%. Their second study in the project explored the prevalence of perpetration rates across 111 articles (73% used the CTS) with an overall pooled prevalence of 1 in 4 or 24.8%. For women, perpetration rates were 1 in 4 (28.3%) and 1 in 5 for men (21.6%). Women reported higher perpetration rates in clinical samples, with a pooled prevalence of 31.5% and 18.4% for men. Interestingly, the authors note the criticisms of the CTS as overestimating the prevalence of perpetration rates for women. However, the pooled prevalence figures of CTS versus other measures only revealed a 2% difference.

In the years that have followed, many studies have supported the notion that women can be as violent as men within relationships (e.g., Bates et al., 2014). For example, Bates et al. (2014) found no empirical support for this male control (of gendered) theory of IPV and little support for some of the hypotheses derived from Johnson's typology. Women reported using significantly more acts of physical aggression than men and engaged in more coercive controlling behavior than men. Bates and Graham-Kevan (2016) utilized the 1999 General Social Survey data from Canada and found no gender differences in minor, severe, or overall aggression rates. Similarly, men and women reported being the victim of high- and low-controlling aggression at similar rates. They were equally as likely to be classified within the intimate terrorism and situational couple violence categories.

These studies stand in stark contrast to the original gendered models of IPV and indeed point to the complexity of IPV in affecting people in a relationship regardless of gender or sexual orientation. They are not without their critics, however. Indeed, those proponents of the gendered models have criticized both the family violence approach and the CTS specifically. For example, those that suggest they are more susceptible to false positives (e.g., Hamby, 2016), that it is of limited utility without contextual information (e.g., Jones et al., 2017), that it relies on retrospective reports (e.g., Kimmel, 2002), that men overreport it (e.g., Ackerman, 2018), and that the violence is later endorsed as accidental or that neither took it seriously (e.g., Ackerman, 2016). This debate's political and emotive nature can be seen in that those supporting the gender symmetry and family violence argument have been labeled as extremists and men's rights activists (Kimmel, 2002).

Kimmel (2002) believes there are two statistical anomalies to the gender symmetry theory: (1) more women are in shelters and hospitals, thus evidencing injuries and impact; and (2) women are not violent outside the home. To address the first point, the lack of similar funded resources for men (e.g., refugees, safe accommodation) means there are no opportunities for men to utilize these, thus making this a skewed population. Similarly, men who present at the hospital are not always supported or questioned about possible domestic abuse (e.g., Hope et al., in press), so these figures could be skewed again. The fact that women do not engage in violence as much outside the home has presented a paradox that many researchers have explored. Cross et al. (2011) specifically tested this contrasting pattern of gender differences using hypothetical conflict scenarios. Men were found to show less physical aggression to a partner than to a same-sex nonpartner. Women show more physical aggression to a partner than to a same-sex nonpartner. Cross and Campbell (2012) extended this exploration using self-reported aggression and found similar results.

Straus (2012) acknowledged the shortcomings of such a measure as the CTS, including that it is only for current partners and only within the last 12 months. It does not link injury questions directly with the described perpetrated behaviors. However, he argues against criticisms such as it lacks context and consequence, only measures conflict-related violence, and does not capture self-defense or who initiates. He specifically argues against the notion of it suffering from underreporting (as many critics have suggested) by evidencing that it demonstrates several times more violence than other instruments, including the National Crime victimization Survey in the United States, suggesting that the latter has inadequate sensitivity to being able to evidence significant amounts of partner violence. Interestingly, Straus claims that when the CTS demonstrates violence against women, there is much greater acceptability to it as a measure than when it is used to evidence women's violence.

JOHNSON'S TYPOLOGY

Scholars have attempted to address the debate and disagreement about these contrasting figures through various means. One of the most well-known is Michael Johnson, who proposed that the different figures seen within these debates were due to sampling. Johnson (1995) proposed that the two approaches (namely the feminist/gendered approach and that of the family violence approach) were seeing different "types" of IPV within their data sets. Johnson's original typology was an attempt to "bridge the gap" between these two contrasting bodies of work. Earlier, many authors have proposed that the differing methodology would have led to these contrasting findings, but Johnson proposed it was potentially more due to the sample being used. Family violence researchers tend to utilize community samples and self-report methods, and feminist researchers tend to use more "clinical"-level samples from women in refuge/shelters and men who were in either the criminal justice system (e.g., prison, court-mandated treatment) or community treatment programs. For example, Hamberger and Larsen (2015) found in their clinical sample that men and women used abuse, but that women seemed to be using it in response to the violence they had experienced. Indeed, women were more highly victimized and injured. However, their inclusion criteria for their review were studies where participants had been recruited from a clinical or service setting, but there are few equivalent clinical victim settings where male victims could be recruited due to underfunded or a general lack of available services.

Johnson created a typology that initially labeled two types of violence within relationships. He first labeled "patriarchal terrorism" (later renamed intimate terrorism), which he asserted represented the most severe and injurious form of IPV, whereby violence is just one strategy used in a broader pattern of control and domination of women. This pattern of abuse was the most serious, the most likely to have adverse outcomes, and the most likely to escalate. This was the type of violence most likely to be found within the accounts of women in refuges and men in criminal justice samples—with men the overwhelming perpetrators and women the overwhelming victims. The second type of IPV he labeled "common couple violence" (later renamed situational couple violence) was the type of noncontrolling violence that occurs when a conflict or argument gets out of control. Johnson posited this was not particularly serious in its consequences and was unlikely to escalate. This type of violence was captured in the community and self-reported survey samples of the family violence researchers, where we see gender parity.

Support for the typology has been seen in Johnson's own tests of his data with some existing interview data (see Johnson, 2006) and survey data from the National Violence Against Women Survey (see Johnson & Leone, 2005). Some scholars are more critical of the selective or purposeful sample choices for Johnson's tests (e.g., see Archer, 2009). They are selected for higher proportions of male-to-female aggression with no alternative/comparable sample of female to male aggression. Other scholars have found evidence of distinct groups as posited by Johnson (e.g., see Graham-Kevan & Archer 2003a, 2003b), but no support for the gendered hypothesis he derives. For example, Bates et al. (2014) categorized their sample using K-Means cluster analysis of those who displayed aggression into high- and low-control perpetration and victimization, classified as either intimate terrorists or situational couple violence; there was no significant difference—meaning men and women were equally as likely to be classified as "intimate terrorists" or "situational couple violence." Notably, Johnson's typology predicts two distinct clusters of controlling behavior (the use of coercive control and psychologically abusive tactics)—that of no/low control and high control. This pattern was not found within the Bates et al. (2014) study, where the authors found a linear (as opposed to a categorical) relationship between aggression and control.

BIDIRECTIONAL VIOLENCE

In terms of the feminist or gendered theory of IPV, one of the most contentious findings to emerge from the family violence literature has been the prevalence of bidirectional or mutual violence. Indeed, self-report surveys such as the CTS demonstrated the prevalence of IPV generally and women's perpetration/men's victimization. They further highlighted the prevalence of bidirectional and mutual violence, where men and women were fulfilling the roles of both perpetrators and victims within the same relationship. Research has suggested that this type of abuse is seen to be the most common (e.g., Melander et al., 2010; Palmetto et al., 2013; Straus, 2008). When examining the prevalence of abuse and gender within relationships, research has suggested that around 50% of violent relationships involve bidirectional abuse. A further 25% involving male perpetrated only and the final 25% involving female perpetrated unilateral abuse (e.g., Stets & Straus, 1989). However, other research has suggested that women are more commonly the unilateral perpetrators (e.g., Blanco Carranza, 2013; Gray & Foshee, 1997; Renner & Whitney, 2012).

Langhinrichsen-Rohling et al. (2012a) performed a systematic review of the existing literature as part of the earlier described PASK project. They explored 48 studies that reported both unidirectional and bidirectional IPV rates, with the latter being specifically measured instead of simply measuring the relationship between report perpetration and victimization rates. They calculated a weighted rate of violence across the collated studies of 2,991 sampling units (1,615 women and 1,376 men), and the weighted rates showed the prevalence of IPV across these samples was 47.0%. Of this, 59.6% was bidirectional violence. The remaining 40.4% was unidirectional, further categorized into 17.5% male to female and 22.9% female to male.

Research has further applied typologies to this type of IPV. Langhinrichinsen (2010) presented a typology of bidirectional violence, suggesting three subtypes:

1. motivated by control and coercion,
2. related to emotional regulation and behavior control related to partner interdependency, and
3. the least severe IPV with violence restricted to partners with little evidence of any personality disorders or psychopathology.

Indeed, Johnson's (1995) typology was later adapted to include patterns of bidirectional violence. Johnson's (2006) work involved the addition of "violent resistance," which represented a type of noncontrolling violence in response to controlling violence from a partner. Namely, this was meant to capture where women were violent in self-defense. He also added "mutual violent control," representing a particularly destructive relationship where both partners were using controlling aggression. Bates et al.'s (2014) study found, in contrast to Johnson's predictions about gender, that men and women were equally as likely to be found in all categories.

Psychological IPV often occurs independently of other forms of IPV (Hamby & Sugarman, 1999), may precede physical IPV (Salis et al., 2014), and almost always overlaps with physical and sexual IPV. Additionally, individuals who experience psychological IPV without physical IPV may not recognize violence as such, leading to prolonged exposure and, thus, worse outcomes (Follingstad & DeHart, 2000). Although it is the most common form of IPV in Europe and the United States with high prevalence rates (e.g., Black et al., 2011), it has received less attention by the research than physical violence (Lagdon et al., 2014). Black et al. (2011) report on the 2010 NIPSV data demonstrating that there were lifetime rates of psychological abuse of 48.4% and 48.8% for women and men, respectively. These figures were 1.9% and 18.1% for the previous 12 months. Moreover, when split into expressive and coercive types, they reported women experiencing more expressive types (40.3% lifetime and 10.4% last 12 months vs. 31.9% and 9.3% for men) and men experiencing more coercive types (42.5% lifetime and 15.2% last 12 months vs. 41.1% and 10.7% for women). This is like the figures from Carney and Barner's (2012) systematic review as part of the PASK project. They found that 40% of women and 32% of men reporting expressive aggression, 41% of women and 42% of men reporting some form of coercive control.

Johnson's (1995, 2006) typology references the possible reciprocity of psychological abuse/coercive control, but not in physical violence. The extent to which psychological abuse can be reciprocal in nature has been discussed at length but lacks evidence to support it fully (Follingstad, 2007). What little research has explored this has supported that not only is psychological abuse seen to be reciprocal but that this reciprocity is also seen at the most severe end of the continuum of this behavior. For example, Follingstad and Edmundson (2010) suggested that psychological abuse is likely to be more common than physical abuse within relationships due to the lack of social sanctions associated with physical violence. They supported that psychological abuse was reciprocal and that this was seen at both ends of the continuum of severity. Furthermore, Follingstad and Rogers (2012) presented findings that suggested women experiencing no or low psychological abuse were significantly different from those in the "higher "group; they suggested this group was qualitatively and quantitatively different and not just experiencing a higher frequency of these behaviors.

Bidirectional or mutual patterns of abuse remain an overlooked area of IPV within some areas of research and practice. Indeed Bates (2016) highlights that despite the evidence (e.g., the PASK review earlier) of this type of IPV, interventions in practice continue to treat perpetrators and victims unilaterally and often from a gendered position. This type of IPV is an important pattern to recognize as research has suggested that mutually violent relationships are associated with more significant violence and abuse (e.g., Renner & Whitney, 2012) and more severe physical and mental health outcomes (e.g., Rhodes et al., 2009; Temple et al., 2005; Whitaker et al., 2007). For example, Ulloa and Hammett (2016) found through a National Longitudinal Study of Adolescent Health data set that the severity and prevalence of the violence, as well as the outcomes, was highest among people in the bidirectional group (compared to perpetration only, victimization only, and no violence), including negative mental health outcomes.

However, this evidence is not always consistent. For example, when comparing male victims of intimate terrorism and those in the mutual violent control group, Hines and Douglas (2018) found those in the latter group did experience more significant violence. However, the intimate terrorism group experienced more detrimental physical and mental health outcomes. This points to the fact that the aforementioned findings that demonstrate more adverse outcomes may not be solely based on the level of violence experienced.

MOTIVATIONS

One of the tenets from the gendered and feminist theory of IPV is related to the motivations of men's and women's violence. Specifically, gendered theorists (e.g., DeKeseredy, 2011; Dobash & Dobash, 1979) hold that men's violence is driven by male privilege, gender inequality, and patriarchal control and values. Consequently, with men's domination of women, women's violence is recognized or seen as being in self-defense either in the immediate threat of danger or as a reaction to years of being abused. For example, Walker (1992) discusses the use of "battered woman self-defense" (p. 321) as one that can be used as a defense for women who have killed or attempted to kill their partners after experiencing domestic abuse. DeKeseredy et al. (1997) found in their exploration of women's violence that many women were reporting self-defense as a motive, and the majority of women did not initiate the violence. They even suggested that some of the women who did initiate the violence may have "sensed impending violence from their partners and thus initiated assault" (p. 216).

Self-defense as a motivation for women's aggression will undoubtedly be the case in some IPV situations. However, there are several sources of evidence that provide contradictory evidence to this always being the case. The earlier discussion around bidirectional violence is indeed one; the fact that men and women can both be identified as perpetrators and victims within the same relationship does not point to defense or retaliation consistently being a motivation for women. Similarly, the research suggests that women are more often the unidirectional perpetrators (e.g., Gray & Foshee, 1997), and indeed where both partners are violent, more women than men are engaged in "severe" violence (Straus, 2008) is further evidence against this.

There is a wealth of other research that points to a range of different motivations and that there are more similarities than differences between men and women in this context. For example, Bates et al. (2014) found that coercive controlling behavior was a predictor of both men's and women's IPV, indicating the motivation for control is not driven by patriarchal values. Indeed, coupled with the fact that this same coercive control was also predictive of men's aggression in a same-sex nonintimate relationship points instead (as indeed the authors do) to a more generally aggressive and coercive interpersonal style than a type of coercion rooted in gender inequality (e.g., see Corvo & deLara, 2009). Furthermore, the fact that coercive control was a predictor of women's aggression is a further indication that self-defense cannot be seen as the sole motivation for women's violent behavior.

Langhinrichsen-Rohling et al. (2012b) performed a systematic review as part of the PASK project and synthesized all available empirical data around IPV motivations for men and women. Power and control and self-defense are the most commonly measured: 76% and 61%, respectively. Only 18 of 75 samples allowed for a direct gender comparison, but very few gender differences were found. The authors observed that motivations to perpetrate IPV are entirely internal and personal experiences and that it is possible some motivations (e.g., anger) might indeed be underpinned by other things that the perpetrator struggles to identify (e.g., jealously or an inability to communicate). Langhinrichsen et al. (2012b) found in their review that "anger" was often collapsed with a range of other motivations such as retaliation, jealousy, and other emotional regulation issues. An important point noted by the authors also included that many have historically assumed that men's motives are obvious or at least self-evident and so have not been worthy of in-depth exploration. In contrast, some authors (e.g., Bates et al., 2019) have noted that women's violence has received more in-depth attention because of a need to explain or understand why a woman would go against her gender role and be violent.

RISK FACTORS

In contrast to the feminist and gendered models of IPV, a well-developed body of literature details the multitude of risk factors that have predictive power over IPV perpetration for men and women; this includes a range of demographic factors. For example, Cunradi et al. (2002) found that after controlling for other known risk factors of IPV (e.g., age, childhood experiences of IPV between parents, alcohol use and abuse, impulsivity, and relationship factors), annual household income was the most important predictor of IPV perpetration. In a systematic review of 228 studies (170 studies with adult samples and 58 with adolescent samples) investigating the risk factors for physical, psychological, and sexual IPV perpetration, Capaldi et al. (2012) concluded that socioeconomic deprivation, unemployment, and low income are predictive of IPV. Similarly, Abramsky et al. (2011) utilized data from the WHO Multi-country Study on Women's Health and Domestic Violence and found that achieving secondary education and high socioeconomic status was associated with less physical and sexual IPV against women, while according to the authors, the most consistent protective factor was when both women and their partners had completed achieved secondary education. A recent systematic and meta-analytic review of all risk and protective factors for IPV against women by Yakubovich et al. (2018) also concluded that married status was a protective factor for IPV. Low relationship satisfaction and high discord appear to be proximal predictors of IPV, with high discord being a robust predictor (Birkley & Eckhardt, 2015).

ADVERSE CHILDHOOD EXPERIENCES

Moving beyond demographic factors, we see a developing body of work that has indicated the influence of childhood trauma on IPV perpetration and victimization and a range of other adverse life outcomes. Adverse childhood experiences (ACEs) include experiences of intense stress during childhood such as child maltreatment; exposure to IPV; growing up in a household where the parent/carer is mentally distressed; alcohol and/or substance abuse; incarcerated parent; peer, community, and neighborhood violence; losing a parent to death, divorce, or separation; and poverty (e.g., Bellis et al., 2014). Prolonged exposure to stress associated with such experiences can disrupt early brain development and affect the nervous and immune system functioning. ACEs have been linked not only with continued involvement in violence and aggressive behavior (WHO, 2010) but with poor health outcomes, psychological distress and psychopathology across the lifespan, substance abuse and illicit drug use, and unemployment (Baglivio et al., 2014; Bellis et al., 2014; Dube et al., 2003; McLaughlin & Hatzenbuehler, 2009). Longitudinal studies have demonstrated that children with ACEs, in the absence of secure attachments, exhibit disruptions in emotional processing, emotional awareness, and emotional regulation (McLaughlin & Hatzenbuehler, 2009). Those difficulties underlie the association of adverse childhood experiences with psychopathology (McLaughlin et al., 2010; Van der Kolk et al., 1991).

A particular type of ACE that is experiencing IPV between parents/carers during childhood has been linked with later involvement in IPV during adulthood. In a meta-analysis, Stith et al. (2000) found a "weak-to-moderate relationship between growing up in an abusive family and becoming involved in a violent martial relationship" (p. 640). In line with these findings, Ibabe et al. (2020) recently found that among 847 college students aged 18–25 years in Spain, the relationship between experiences of IPV between parents during the previous year and current intimate dating violence was intervened and facilitated by child-to-parent violence and ambivalent sexism.

In their systematic review, Capaldi et al. (2012) found that experiencing IPV between parents/carers during childhood and child maltreatment are significant low to moderate risk factors for future IPV perpetration, especially when mediated by substance abuse and conduct problems in adolescence. It is important to note that no significant gender differences were seen. In yet another systematic review of 25 longitudinal studies investigating childhood and/or adolescent predictors of IPV perpetration and/or victimization, researchers found abuse during childhood and family-of-origin risks (i.e., poor relationships with parents in childhood and adolescence, being raised by a single parent, and experiencing IPV between parents) were consistent predictors of IPV perpetration and victimization (Costa et al., 2015). However, for female perpetrators of IPV involved in the criminal justice system, Mackay et al. (2018) found that although child abuse was associated with IPV perpetration, the experience of IPV during childhood was not. According to the authors, the results of their systematic review of 31 studies show that neither child abuse nor IPV experience can be established as a causal risk factor of female IPV perpetration. However, the authors caution that interpretration of these results may be limited, as they were hampered with methodological limitations of the original studies.

It should be noted that while there is a robust and consistent relationship between ACEs and IPV, associations differ among types of ACEs and types of IPV (Mair et al., 2012). Additionally, these associations are mediated by a range of factors such as severity and frequency of violence, the number of different types of ACEs experienced, gender, attachment history, alcohol and substance abuse, and mental health, as well as resilient factors (e.g., Whitfield et al., 2003). These findings highlight the need to assess IPV experiences and child maltreatment during childhood; they also underscore the importance of early intervention and prevention of intergenerational cycles of violence.

GENERAL OFFENDING AND LINKS WITH OTHER CRIME

Evidence suggests that both men and women who are violent within their relationships are also violent against others outside of the intimate relationship (Bates et al., 2014; Thornton et al., 2010). This finding is in line with other types of family violence, such as child-to-parent violence, where children who are violent against their parents are often violent against their siblings and or against their peers and in school (e.g., Papamichail & Bates, 2020). Research that has explored the relationship between general criminal behavior with IPV evidences a significant relationship between the two; Costa et al. (2015) found that delinquent behavior during adolescence constitutes a significant risk factor for involvement in IPV in young adulthood. Additional research has shown that those involved in serious and persistent criminal behavior are at an increased risk of perpetrating IPV (Moffitt et al., 2002). In addition, research investigating official records rather than self-report data also shows that a significant number of adult IPV offenders have a history of general offending, both nonviolent and violent. For example, Hilton and Eke (2016) found that almost two thirds of IPV offenders had criminal charges before the IPV assault. However, a recent systematic review that investigated the risk indicators for women's IPV perpetration in criminal justice populations found although women perpetrators of IPV were like men in using violence outside of the family home, general criminality cannot be established as a risk factor of IPV among women by the available evidence (Mackay et al., 2018).

It is also important to note that general offending and IPV perpetration share some common risk factors, such as experiences of child maltreatment during childhood (Costa et al., 2015). Although they are distinct types of offending and violence, the findings discussed earlier underscore the relevance of general theories of crime for understanding IPV at least for a considerable proportion of IPV perpetrators and the need for a holistic, integrated theoretical approach to understanding this issue. It is important to note that both Capaldi et al. (2012) and Mackay et al. (2018) in their reviews reported more similarities than differences between genders in the risk factors of IPV perpetration.

IMPACT ON PARTNERS

There has been significant research that has also explored the impact of IPV within the family. IPV has significant adverse mental and physical health outcomes and is a traumatic event for many who experience it. Understanding the broad-ranging impact of IPV, the nested ecological framework is adopted (e.g.,

Bronfenbrenner, 1979; Dutton, 2006). The impact of IPV does not only involve the direct, first-order effects on partners (e.g., the impact on physical and mental health). Rather, it extends on the microsystem environment (e.g., ability to work, impact on relationships with friends and children), on the exosystem (e.g., extended family members taking responsibility of looking after the children), and on the macrosystem (e.g., impact on the economy, unemployment). These levels are not independent of each other; instead, they are nested, each linked to the other. Research evidence demonstrates that IPV constitutes a highly complex and multifaceted experience of violence; perceiving it as a single category is simplistic and impedes researchers and practitioners from capturing the dynamics and the impact on individuals and families holistically.

Several studies have established the first-order effects, for instance, according to a review of 132 studies published from 1989 to 2012 on the impact of physical and psychological IPV on partners, victims of physical IPV (which more often than not involves psychological violence) experience more physical injuries, poorer health outcomes (e.g., chronic pain, abdominal pain, cardiovascular problems, gastrointestinal problems, and childbirth complications, among others), poorer cognitive functioning (e.g., memory problems, traumatic brain injury), maladaptive coping mechanisms (e.g., smoking, substance abuse), and higher rates of mental health problems (e.g., anxiety, depression, posttraumatic stress disorder [PTSD], suicidal ideation and suicide attempts; Lawrence et al., 2012). A meta-analysis of 19 studies inclusive of 13,797 participants on the impact of IPV on men who have sex with men (MSM) found IPV victimization was linked with increased likelihood of substance abuse, depressive symptoms, risky sexual behaviors, and being HIV positive (Buller et al., 2014). Also, IPV links with unintended pregnancy, abortion, miscarriage, and decreased contraceptive use (Garcia-Moreno et al., 2006; Miller et al., 2010).

In comparison with men, the impact of physical IPV is greater on women victims, with women being more likely to be injured, requiring medical hospitalization, fearing for their lives, and dying due to violence (Archer, 2000). Also, because of physical violence, women report higher rates of anxiety, PTSD, and depression than male victims of IPV, are more likely to miss work or be unemployed as a result of IPV, to have lower relationship satisfaction, and to experience isolation (Lawrence et al., 2012).

Although psychological IPV has received less attention than physical violence (Lagdon et al., 2014), we know the outcomes are similar regarding physical and psychological health, maladaptive coping mechanisms, cognitive functioning, and relationship satisfaction. Research evidence suggests that psychological IPV is linked with insomnia and sleep disturbance. It is as strongly related to depression, PTSD, and alcohol abuse as physical IPV (Lawrence et al., 2012, for a review). A more recent systematic review supports that psychological violence alone may cause PTSD, depression, and anxiety (Lagdon et al., 2014). Pico-Alfonso et al. (2006) in Spain also showed that psychological IPV alone is as detrimental to women's mental health as physical IPV and independently contributes to PTSD and depression. According to Taft et al. (2005), psychological IPV links with anxiety, distress, and physical health symptoms for both women and men. In the same study, psychological IPV was linked with higher levels of depression in women but not in men. Those findings highlight the fact that psychological violence is not to be underestimated. Indicatively, the high prevalence and the detrimental impact of this subtype of IPV led some countries such as England and Wales to criminalize nonphysical forms of IPV, including coercive and controlling behavior (Crown Prosecution Service, 2017).

Most research investigating the impact of psychological IPV has focused on women. The consequences of physical and psychological IPV toward men have not received enough attention, and there is a dearth of research exploring men's experiences. However, the interest in this area is growing, especially in Western countries (e.g., Bates, 2020). Indicatively, a recent systematic review of 106 studies published between 2006 and 2016 found that most studies were conducted with heterosexual women victims of IPV ($n = 70$), seven studies were conducted with men victims of IPV, and 11 studies were conducted with LGBTQ+ participants (Laskey et al., 2019). Dixon and Graham-Kevan (2011) explain this dearth of studies as due to the belief that men are victimized only in the context of women's self-defense; another factor might be that the abuse men experience is believed not to be severe. Although the impact of physical IPV is greater on women in comparison with men, recent evidence shows that men can also experience significant and adverse outcomes. Men victimized by their female partners are more likely to engage with substance abuse, and they are more likely to have a diagnosis of more than one psychiatric disorder and suffer from depression and PTSD compared to nonvictimized men (Laskey et al., 2019; Lawrence et al., 2012).

Regarding psychological violence, there is evidence suggesting that victimized men display depressive symptoms and psychological distress (Hines & Douglas, 2010). However, the evidence is mixed; some studies support that those men are more likely to suffer from depression as a result of psychological IPV (e.g., Sabina & Straus, 2008). Other research suggests psychological IPV is linked with higher levels of depression in women but not in men (e.g., Taft et al., 2005). The dearth of studies investigating the impact of psychological IPV on men, the limited samples recruited, and the cross-sectional methodology adopted by the vast majority of studies do not allow for confident conclusions about the impact of psychological IPV on men and how this might differ from the impact on women.

IMPACTS ON THE WIDER FAMILY

A further important aspect of this to consider is how IPV impacts children living in abusive homes. There is little disagreement that a child's family environment is fundamental in development while the interparental relationship influences child psychopathology (Bernet et al., 2016; Sturge-Apple et al., 2012). Although initially, research investigating IPV focused on the prevalence and impact of IPV on female victims (Rivett et al., 2006), during the last 30 years, there has been a growing recognition that children can also be profoundly affected by IPV. They are not just passive or indirect witnesses of IPV. During the last 10 years, research evidence has led to the recognition that children's experiences of IPV constitute a form of maltreatment (e.g., Macmillan et al., 2009). When conceptualizing children's experiences of IPV, it is essential to acknowledge that children not only suffer from the direct impact of violence. Instead, they also experience the impact of living with fear, tension, coercive control, unpredictability, and anxiety within their family homes. Nevertheless, despite these developments and the evidence of the impact of IPV on children, they are still conceptualized mainly as "witnesses," or "secondary victims," rather than direct victims by the criminal justice system and the family courts (Callaghan et al., 2018).

Although not all children will be affected by IPV in the same way, research has established that IPV can adversely affect children's healthy development, relationships, behavior, physical health, cognition, and emotional well-being. A comprehensive literature search of 73 articles that reviewed the state of knowledge about both short- and long-term impact of witnessing mutual IPV and the impact of experiencing both IPV and child maltreatment concluded that mutual IPV is linked with internalizing and externalizing problems, with negative health and cognitive outcomes, and with interpersonal difficulties and relational problems (MacDonell, 2012). Notably, the negative impacts of experiencing mutual IPV in childhood seem to persist into adulthood. However, the author calls for more longitudinal studies, especially regarding the long-term impact on health and intellectual outcomes. It should be noted that acrimonious parental conflict and emotional abuse/control negatively impact children in similar ways with IPV (see Sturge-Apple et al., 2012, for a review). Indicatively, children as young as 6 months show signs of distress, such as elevated heart rate, in response to hostile and overt interparental conflict compared with conflict between nonparental adults (Cummings & Davies, 2002).

Regarding internalizing problems, research has established links with anxiety, depression, mood swings, and lower levels of self-esteem (McGee, 2000). It also shows links with self-worth, shame and self-blame, suicidality, and PTSD (e.g., intrusive re-experiencing of the events in dreams or flashbacks, hyperarousal, and emotional withdrawal; Evans et al., 2008). Of note, there is a high comorbidity between internalizing and externalizing problems in children. Therefore, a clinical diagnosis of conduct disorder does not exclude depressive symptomatology (Kessler et al., 2005). Experiencing IPV is an established risk factor for a range of externalizing difficulties such as aggression, running away from home, hostility, disruptive and oppositional behaviors, bullying victimization and perpetration, violence, delinquency, academic failure, and conduct disorder (e.g., Erath & Bierman, 2006; McTavish et al., 2016; Nagin & Tremblay, 1999; Sternberg et al., 2006). It is important to highlight that conduct disorder in childhood is a risk factor for IPV perpetration in adulthood and a mediator of the intergenerational transmission of IPV. These findings are further supported by the fact that experiencing IPV has been linked with other types of family violence later in childhood and adolescence, namely, child-to-parent violence (Papamichail & Bates, 2020). These patterns and trends highlight the increased risk of continuing the intergenerational cycle of family violence. It is important to note that most children do not imitate violent behavior (Dutton, 1999). Furthermore, experiencing parental or intercouple IPV during childhood has also been associated with additional forms of children's victimization outside of the family, such as sexual misconduct, dating violence, Internet harassment, and property crime (Hamby et al., 2010). Although causality cannot be established, it seems that a stressful familial environment, a lack of parental oversight, low socioeconomic status, and or compromised parenting (due to parental traumatic stress) might contribute to victimization suffered by children exposed to IPV.

While both girls and boys are negatively affected, the literature suggests that boys and girls may react differently to experiences of IPV. However, the evidence is mixed. For instance, several studies suggest that boys who experience IPV are more likely to develop externalizing problems while girls are more likely to develop internalizing problems (e.g., Moylan et al., 2010). Other studies found that girls from violent homes are more likely to exhibit externalizing problems (Sigfusdottir et al., 2004). However, a meta-analysis of 118 studies investigating the psychosocial outcomes of IPV found no evidence of interaction between sex/gender and outcomes (Kitzmann et al., 2003). Wolfe et al. (2003), in another meta-analysis of 41 studies, found no sex/gender differences.

Those mixed findings are due to methodological limitations that probably weaken findings' validity and thus lead to mixed results. A way forward that, nevertheless, has not been sufficiently investigated would have been the investigation of the interaction between the gender of the parent perpetrator and the gender of the child (MacDonell, 2012). According to MacDonell (2012), male-perpetrated IPV has been associated with more trauma symptoms in children, depression and distress, greater aggression toward their fathers in girls, and greater use of aggression toward their peers in boys. Female-perpetrated IPV has been linked with girls' internalizing problems more than boys, more externalized problems toward romantic partners and peers in girls, and more dating aggression in boys. The role of parent gender remains inconclusive at this stage for both physical and emotional IPV due to the lack of studies disentangling men and women-perpetrated IPV; similarly, we cannot draw conclusions about the type of reactions from boys and girls to experiencing IPV, although there are indications of sex-specific modeling effects. The differences noted suggest that outcomes may indeed differ depending on the gender of the perpetrator as well as the gender of the child. However, more research is needed to elaborate on these interactions (MacDonell, 2012).

Having briefly reviewed the evidence on children's outcomes associated with experiencing IPV, it is essential to note that not all children necessarily suffer negative outcomes. For example, in their meta-analysis, Kitzmann et al. (2003) found that 37% of children showed no significant developmental problems. Evidence shows that many children facing this adversity show resilience (Rutter, 2012, for a review). Several examples of widely cited factors contributing to a child's resiliency at the individual level are the child's easy temperament (e.g., Martinez-Torteya et al., 2009), internal locus of control, and academic achievement (e.g.,

Suzuki et al., 2008) and at the interpersonal level, a secure attachment with an adult (Graham-Bermann et al., 2009). Positive parenting skills, parental warmth, and parental mental health have also been acknowledged as contributing to children's positive adaptive functioning (Bowen, 2017; Kolbo, 1996; Levendosky et al., 2006). Maternal good education is also a protective factor (Bowen, 2017), which suggests that socioeconomic advantage may buffer the impact of risk on development. Additionally, the frequency of IPV "exposures" influences resilience processes; greater frequency means a greater negative impact on children's adjustment (Fortin et al., 2011).

The protective factors mentioned earlier suggest that IPV, rather than acting as a single influence on specific outcomes for children (e.g., IPV experiences—child depression), works in concert with other factors. The impact of IPV on children is a process in which a range of individual and contextual characteristics interplaying with each other differentiate how each child responds to the same adversity. There is now a need for a contemporary approach that focuses on processes and mechanisms underlying differences in children's "response" or adaptation to risk factors such as IPV (Sturge-Apple et al., 2012). Simply stated, the focus is shifted toward the factors (mediating and moderating) that explain *why*, *when*, and *how* children are affected by IPV (Cummings & Davies, 2002). Potential mechanisms identified predominantly include the impact of parental conflict but *not violence* on children. Furthermore, emerging studies on IPV that explain the link between IPV and child adverse outcomes and psychopathology include disruptions in the parent–child relationship (e.g., hostile parenting, harsh discipline, lack of parental warmth, insecure attachment, maternal mental health; e.g., Zarling et al., 2013). For instance, abused mothers may experience depressive symptomatology. Depression may reduce their ability to be emotionally available and attentive to children's needs and provide consistent parenting (Letourneau et al., 2007). Such unavailability may be linked to a perceived lack of parental warmth by children and insecure attachment, demonstrating the complexity of the various interconnected dynamics involved. A second pathway involves children's cognitive attributions of the violence and emotional processing (e.g., interpretation of IPV, self-blame, emotion dysregulation; Minze et al., 2010). The third pathway focuses on children's psychophysiological and neurobiological processing (e.g., cortisol levels, vagal regulation, among others; Harold & Sellers 2018, for a review).

INTIMATE PARTNER VIOLENCE AND ITS LINKS WITH OTHER TYPES OF FAMILY VIOLENCE

In general, there are five types of family violence: intimate partner violence (IPV), child maltreatment (CM), child-to-parent violence (CPV), sibling violence, and elder abuse (Browne & Herbert, 1997; Papamichail & Bates, 2019). Research has established that these types of family violence often co-occur; thus, if one type exists, there is an increased risk of other types occurring (Browne & Herbert,

1997). Traditionally the different types of family violence have been researched in isolation providing a fragmented picture of family violence and blurring the context and the continuum of family violence (Williams, 2003). Also, prevention or intervention programs and funding often target specific populations within the family (e.g., women victims of IPV) rather than adopting a holistic, integrated approach that addresses the common risk factors and acknowledges the impact of family violence on the family.

Nevertheless, there is increasing recognition of the associations between the different forms of family violence (Browne & Herbert, 1997), the need to research different forms of the family dynamics (Heise, 2011), and the associated need for interagency collaboration and treatment for the families affected (Williams, 2003). The process of studying different types of family violence in isolation has provided valuable and essential insights and was perhaps necessary, especially when taking into consideration the complexities of the topic studied and the fact that this field of study is relatively young. However, we argue that we now need to move forward to holistic, integrated, and nuanced understandings of family violence. Integration of knowledge is a prerequisite to identify common issues, risk, and protective factors in different types of family violence (Heise, 2011). There is a need to focus on the connections between different forms of violence, links with larger structural inequalities, connections between violence at different life course stages and its impact, and the mechanisms that sustain such violence across generations.

Child maltreatment is a global public health issue that affects more than 1 in 3 children globally (WHO, 2017). In 2018, approximately 678,000 children were victims of child maltreatment in the United States, with neglect being the most prevalent type of maltreatment (60.8%) (United States Department for Health and Human Services, 2018). The victimization rate for girls (9.6 per 1000 in the population) was higher than boys (8.7 per 1000). Most perpetrators were parents (77.5%).

Similarly, with other types of family violence (e.g., child-to-parent violence), child maltreatment is challenging to define primarily due to different cultural understandings about the acceptability of various parenting practices. Furthermore, it is difficult to research due to the shame and stigma associated with such experiences. According to the World Health Organization (WHO, 1999, p. 15), child maltreatment "constitutes all forms of physical and/or emotional ill-treatment, sexual abuse, neglect, or negligent treatment or commercial or other exploitation, resulting in actual or potential harm to the child's health, survival, development, or dignity in the context of a relationship of responsibility, trust or power." The main types of child maltreatment are physical abuse, psychological abuse, sexual abuse, and neglect. Before proceeding, it is important to highlight that in line with other researchers (e.g., Macmillan et al., 2009), we view children experiences of IPV as an additional type of maltreatment and children who experience IPV as direct victims of IPV and not just passive witnesses (Callaghan et al., 2018). Therefore, when we refer to child maltreatment in this section, we refer to victimization *in addition to* IPV experiences.

The elevated risk of child maltreatment in the context of IPV is an area of growing attention among researchers (e.g., Carlson et al., 2020). Although not every child who experiences IPV is a victim of maltreatment, it does constitute an established significant risk factor for types of child maltreatment such as physical abuse, neglect, psychological abuse, and sexual abuse (e.g., Appel & Holden, 1998; Hamby et al., 2010; Kerker et al., 2001). According to Hamby et al. (2010), in a study using a nationally representative sample of children up to 17 years in the United States, of the children with IPV experiences during the last year, 33.9% had experienced maltreatment. A longitudinal study conducted with a sample of 2,544 at-risk mothers showed that an assessment of IPV during the first 6 months of a child's life more than tripled the likelihood of physical abuse and doubled the likelihood of psychological abuse and neglect during the child's first 5 years (McGuigan & Pratt, 2001). Serious case file reviews of fatal child maltreatment in the United Kingdom covering 4 years (4/2005 to 3/2009) also underscore the overlap of IPV with child maltreatment; in 20% of cases in which children were killed, there was IPV noted, although this is likely to be an underestimate (Sidebotham et al., 2011).

Prevalence rates of co-occurrence vary considerably among different studies that use different definitions of maltreatment, short referent periods that usually decrease co-occurrence, and different methodologies and samples that result in discrepancies. For instance, Appel and Holden (1998) found that in a clinical sample of women victims of IPV, the median prevalence of child abuse was 41% while the rate of co-occurrence dropped at 6% for a nationally representative community sample. Finkelhor et al. (2009), in the United States, demonstrated that 40% of all child abuse victims report violence in the home between their parents. Despite the differences in the prevalence of occurrence and the methodological limitations across studies, there is a consensus in the literature about a considerable overlap between IPV and child maltreatment estimated at 30%–60% (e.g., Edleson, 1999).

Research shows that both men and women perpetrators of IPV and or victims of IPV have the potential to maltreat their children (Smith-Slep & O'Leary, 2005). Gender differences identified include mothers having a higher prevalence of mental health problems, isolation, and a history of violent relationships. In contrast, fathers were seen as being more likely to have convictions for physical and or sexual violence, aggression during childhood, and more stress, depression, and adverse life events (Dixon et al., 2007; Smith-Slep & O'Leary, 2005). Co-occurrence can take multiple forms. For example, it can occur as *within an individual pattern* where one person abuses his or her partner *and* his or her children. Dixon et al. (2007) found that male perpetrators of IPV were more likely to abuse their children. Another type of co-occurrence is the *sequential perpetrator model*, the one that occurs *across individuals*. For instance, a man is abusive to his female partner, and she, in turn, maltreats the children. Indeed, Straus and Gelles (1990) found that female victims of IPV were twice as likely to abuse their children physically compared to nonabused women. Similarly, Kerker et al. (2000)

showed that mothers who reported IPV victimization were significantly 1.6 times more likely to report "hitting their child hard enough to leave a mark" than those not reporting IPV victimization.

The majority of studies investigating IPV and child maltreatment have been conducted separately, which has lessened our understanding of how dual exposure impacts children; even fewer studies have investigated the long-term impact of dual exposure in adulthood. The literature on child maltreatment documents that child maltreatment is associated with a range of physical (e.g., risk markers for inflammatory disease) and mental health problems across the life course. It negatively affects children's psychosocial development (e.g., cognition), academic and career attainment, and interpersonal relationships, and it increases the likelihood of IPV in adulthood (e.g., Moylan et al., 2010, for a review). Child maltreatment correlates with a range of factors, including anxiety, depression, attention deficit-hyperactivity disorder (ADHD), PTSD, eating disorders, bipolar disorder, personality disorders, self-harm, suicidality, loneliness, and substance abuse (e.g., Boyda & McFeeters, 2015; Read & Bentall, 2012). Evidence suggests that there are gender differences in the impact of maltreatment (e.g., Fisher et al., 2009), with girls being more likely to internalize difficulties, while boys are more likely to exhibit externalizing behavior problems.

Despite the shortcomings of the literature on the overlap of child maltreatment with IPV, it becomes apparent that child maltreatment and family violence, more broadly, are embedded in a web of family relationships; they are not single acts that break a supposed continuum of nonviolence. Instead, they should be approached as a process in the context of a cycle of violence and counterviolence. The next session discusses another type of family violence linked with IPV and child maltreatment, namely, child-to-parent violence, and further highlights the cyclical character, the complexity, and the continuum of family violence.

Child-to-parent violence (CPV) refers to systematic *patterns* of violence directed toward parents/carers by children and adolescents legally recognized as children. It includes physical, psychological, financial, and sexual violence (e.g., Papamichail, 2018). According to Paterson et al. (2002, p. 92), "behaviour (is) considered to be violent if others in the family feel threatened, intimidated or controlled by it and if they believe that they must adjust their own behaviour to accommodate threats or anticipation of violence." It should be highlighted here that more often than not, CPV coexists with violence against siblings and children's conduct behavior problems at school (Papamichail & Bates, 2020).

In contrast with other types of family violence, such as IPV, CPV is an understudied and undertheorized type of family violence, although the interest in the field is growing (Ibabe, 2019). Indicatively, the topic lacks a widely accepted definition and terminology (Papamichail & Bates, 2019, for a review). The prevalence of violence against parents is difficult to establish due to the shame and stigma surrounding such experiences and partly due to the lack of widely accepted definition and the lack of consistency in the measurements used. However, a recent review estimates CPV ranges between 5% and 21% (Simmons et al., 2018).

Regarding the child's and the parent's gender in CPV, similarly with IPV, the existing literature documents that boys represent the majority of the initiators of violence and mothers are the main targets of violence among studies that recruit samples from the criminal justice system (e.g., Condry & Miles, 2013). In contrast, studies with community samples and clinical samples (e.g., Biehal, 2012) show no statistically significant difference between boys and girls. Calvete et al. (2013), in Spain, found no gender difference in physical violence against parents, but for verbal and psychological violence, girls had significantly higher scores than boys. A more recent study in Germany also found no gender differences in physical violence between boys and girls; however, girls were more verbally violent against parents than boys (Beckmann et al., 2019).

Regarding parents' gender in CPV, mothers are found to be the main targets of violence (e.g., Ibabe & Jaureguizar, 2010). Other studies found that the rates of physical violence against fathers and mothers are similar (Ibabe et al., 2013). Additional research is needed to clarify those aspects; there is a gap in the literature on whether mothers are more likely to report CPV than fathers and whether boys' violence against mothers is taken more seriously by the police in comparison with girls' violence (Papamichail & Bates, 2019; Selwyn & Meakings, 2016).

Similarly, with IPV, child maltreatment, and other forms of violence, CPV is a highly complex, multifaceted, and multifactorial issue, and no single factor alone can account for the totality of this issue. As discussed previously in this chapter, the experience of IPV during childhood and adolescence is a risk factor for a range of difficulties such as aggression, conduct disorder, violence, academic failure, and mental health difficulties, among others (McTavish et al., 2016). A review of the existing literature indicates that the most commonly reported adversity associated with CPV is children's experiences of IPV between parents/adults (e.g., Simmons et al., 2018). IPV is an established risk factor of CPV (e.g., Boxer et al., 2009). Verbal IPV between parents has also been linked with CPV. A retrospective study of 1,681 Spanish university students found that experiencing verbal violence (e.g., threats) between parents was associated with physical CPV (Gámez-Guadix & Calvete, 2012).

In addition to IPV, recent studies have demonstrated that parent-to-child violence constitutes an additional risk factor of CPV (Ibabe, 2019). In Germany, Beckmann et al. (2019) recruited a large community sample ($N = 6,444$) of adolescents aged 13 to 19 years. They found that parent-to-child violence (both physical and verbal) during childhood was the strongest predictor of CPV for both girls and boys. Similarly, a recent meta-analytic review of 19 primary studies found that the probability of CPV for children victimized by parents increased 71% compared with nonvictimized children (Gallego et al., 2019).

In the United Kingdom, Biehal (2012) showed that 32% of the 112 participants who exhibited CPV had experienced physical and sexual violence and neglect. In the same study, professionals reported that they were concerned that half of those with experience of maltreatment might still be subject to emotional abuse, whereas 47% of those who had experienced maltreatment also had experiences of

IPV, showing that children and adolescents were embedded in broader contexts of violence. This finding is supported by the evidence discussed in the previous section and the literature that demonstrates that IPV and child maltreatment often co-occur (e.g., Hamby et al., 2010).

Although the majority of children who experience IPV or child maltreatment do not exhibit violent behavior or aggression later in life, the link between those adverse childhood experiences with CPV highlights the intergenerational cycles of violence. It further highlights the failure of the various systems around families to intervene early and prevent those cycles. Researchers investigating CPV in Australia concluded that in the case of CPV, we are working "10 years too late" (Campbell et al., 2020, p. 15). In addition to the intergenerational cycle of violence, such as normalization of violence as a means to resolve conflict, we argue that researchers and practitioners in the field should incorporate complex or developmental trauma in their conceptualizations of the impact of such adversities on development (McTavish et al., 2016; Nowakowski-Sims & Rowe, 2017).

A small qualitative study with adolescents who exhibited CPV, Papamichail and Bates (2020) found both experiences of IPV and parent-to-child violence. Adolescents perceived their parents as rejecting and perceived their relationships with their parents as unsatisfactory due to persistent conflicts. According to adolescents, feelings of rejection and parental favoritism toward their siblings were some of the reasons they were violent against their siblings. According to the authors, these relational qualities and emotional dysregulation, poor psychosocial competence, difficulties sustaining healthy interpersonal relationships, and defiant and oppositional behaviors indicate that participants were susceptible to the traumatic effects of childhood adversities and disrupted attachments with parents. However, due to this study's exploratory and qualitative character, the findings cannot be generalized, and there is a need for more research investigating those aspects further.

CONCLUSION

This chapter aimed to present a review of what we currently know about the prevalence, causes, and dynamics of IPV. The evidence presented points to the fact that IPV is an issue that affects people of all genders and sexual orientations. It directly contrasts the gendered models that have dominated the sector for decades but have yielded little effect in terms of reducing the prevalence or impacts of this abuse. The research presents evidence that contradicts this through (1) evidence of women's perpetration of violence and men's perpetration; (2) evidence of abuse within the LGBTQ+ community; (3) evidence of bidirectional violence; (4) evidence of a variety of risk factors that predict IPV perpetration above and beyond gender, including the similarities that exist between men and women; and (5) evidence of the overlap between IPV and other forms of offending, including other forms of family violence.

It is vital that services and support organizations both within and outside the criminal justice system recognize the complexity of the nature of IPV. It is an issue that affects anyone regardless of gender or sexual orientation. The importance of an effective service response has been seen within the previous literature; for example, our research has indicated that effective service responses can be vital in helping women leave an abusive relationship (Waldrop & Resick, 2004).

Furthermore, removing barriers to help seeking is key for several reasons, not least because research indicates that those who seek help may indeed have better outcomes (e.g., health outcomes) than those who do not (Cho et al., 2020). Indeed, missed opportunities or inappropriate service responses have also been seen to be involved within domestic homicide in England and Wales (see Hope et al., in press). Better service engagement and protective action for all victim groups could prevent escalation and missed opportunities to address serious risk.

There needs to be a consistent approach to ensuring victims are given appropriate help and support. Saxton et al. (2021) indicate that there is a narrative around being "lucky" in finding the "right" (p. 2048) person to speak to, having a significant impact in terms of an effective and helpful response. We must work toward ensuring that all criminal justice, service, and other practitioner responses ensure inclusivity.

REFERENCES

Abramsky, T., Watts, C. H., Garcia-Moreno, C. Devries, K., Ellsberg, K. M., Jansen, H., & Heise, L.(2011). What factors are associated with recent intimate partner violence? Findings from the WHO multi-country study on women's health and domestic violence. *BMC Public Health*, *11*, 1–17. https://doi.org/10.1186/1471-2458-11-109

Ackerman, J. (2018). Assessing conflict tactics scale validity by examining intimate partner violence overreporting. *Psychology of Violence*, *8*(2), 207–217. https://doi.org/10.1037/vio0000112

Ackerman, J. M. (2016). Over-reporting intimate partner violence in Australian survey research. *British Journal of Criminology*, *56*(4), 646–667. https://doi.org/10.1093/bjc/azv066

Appel, A. E., & Holden, G. W. (1998). The co-occurrence of spouse and physical child abuse: A review and appraisal. *Journal of Family Psychology*, *12*(4), 578–599. https://doi.org/10.1037/0893-3200.12.4.578

Archer, J. (1999). Assessment of the reliability of the conflict tactics scales: A meta-analytic review. *Journal of Interpersonal Violence*, *14*(12), 1263–1289. https://doi.org/10.1177/088626099014012003

Archer, J. (2000). Sex differences in aggression between heterosexual partners: A meta-analytic review. *Psychological Bulletin*, *126*, 651–680. https://doi.org/10.1037/0033-2909.126.5.651

Archer, J. (2009). Refining the sexual selection explanation within an ethological framework. *Behavioral and Brain Sciences*, *32*(3–4), 292–311. https://doi.org/10.1017/S0140525X09990963

Arias, I., Samios, M., & O'Leary, K. D. (1987). Prevalence and correlates of physical aggression during courtship. *Journal of Interpersonal Violence, 2*(1), 82–90. https://doi.org/10.1177/088626087002001005

Babcock, J. C., Green, C. E., & Robie, C. (2004). Does batterers' treatment work? A meta-analytic review of domestic violence treatment. *Clinical Psychology Review, 23*, 1023–1053. https://doi.org/10.1016/j.cpr.2002.07.001

Baglivio, M. T., Epps, N., Swartz, K., Huq, M. S., & Hardt, N. S. (2014). The prevalence of adverse childhood experiences (ACE) in the lives of juvenile offenders. *Journal of Juvenile Justice, 3*, 1–23.

Bates, E. A. (2016). Current controversies within intimate partner violence: Overlooking bidirectional violence. *Journal of Family Violence, 31*(8), 937–940. https://doi.org/10.1007/s10896-016-9862-7

Bates, E. A. (2019). Challenging the gendered approach to men's violence towards women. In E. A. Bates & J. C. Taylor (Eds.), *Intimate partner violence: New perspectives in research and practice* (pp. 11–19). Taylor and Francis.

Bates, E. A. (2020). "No one would ever believe me": An exploration of the impact of intimate partner violence victimization on men. *Psychology of Men & Masculinities, 21*(4), 497–507. https://doi.org/10.1037/men0000206

Bates, E. A., & Graham-Kevan, N. (2016). Is the presence of control related to help-seeking behavior? A test of Johnson's assumptions regarding sex-differences and the role of control in intimate partner violence. *Partner Abuse, 7*(1), 3–25. https://doi.org/10.1891/1946-6560.7.1.3

Bates, E. A., Graham-Kevan, N., & Archer, J. (2014). Testing predictions from the male control theory of men's partner violence. *Aggressive Behavior, 40*(1), 42–55. https://doi.org/10.1002/ab.21499

Bates, E. A., Klement, K. R., Kaye, L. K., & Pennington, C. R. (2019). The impact of gendered stereotypes on perceptions of violence: A commentary. *Sex Roles, 81*(1), 34–43. https://doi.org/10.1007/s11199-019-01029-9

Beckmann, L., Bergmann, M. C., Fischer, F., & Mößle, T. (2019). Risk and protective factors of child-to-parent violence: A comparison between physical and verbal aggression. *Journal of Interpersonal Violence, 36*(3-4), NP1309–1334NP. https://doi.org/10.1177/0886260517746129

Bellis, M. A., Lowey, H., Leckenby, N., Hughes, K., & Harrison, D. (2014). Adverse childhood experiences: Retrospective study to determine their impact on adult health behaviours and health outcomes in a UK population. *Journal of Public Health, 36*, 81–91. https://doi.org/10.1093/pubmed/fdt038

Berk, R. A., Newton, P. J., & Berk, S. F. (1986). What a difference a day makes: An empirical study of the impact of shelters for battered women. *Journal of Marriage and the Family, 48*(3), 481–490. https://doi.org/10.2307/352034

Bernet, W., Wamboldt, M. Z., & Narrow, W. E. (2016). Child affected by parental relationship distress. *Journal of the American Academy of Child and Adolescent Psychiatry, 55*, 571–579. https://doi.org/10.1016/j.jaac.2016.04.018

Biehal, N. (2012). Parent abuse by young people on the edge of care: A child welfare perspective. *Social Policy and Society, 11*(2), 251–263. https://doi.org/10.1017/S1474746411000595

Birkley, E. L., & Eckhardt, C. I. (2015). Anger, hostility, internalizing negative emotions, and intimate partner violence perpetration: A meta-analytic review. *Clinical Psychology Review, 37*, 40–56. https://doi.org/10.1016/j.cpr.2015.01.002

Black, M., Basile, K., Breiding, M., Smith, S., Walters, M., Merrick, M., & Stevens, M. (2011). *National Intimate Partner and Sexual Violence Survey (NISVS): 2010 summary report*. National Center for Injury Prevention and Control, Centers for Disease Control and Prevention.

Blanco Carranza, A. (2013). *Non-suicidal self-injury in unidirectional and bidirectional intimate partner violence* [Doctoral dissertation, University of British Columbia].

Bowen, E. (2017). Conduct disorder symptoms in pre-school children exposed to intimate partner violence: Gender differences in risk and resilience. *Journal of Child & Adolescent Trauma, 10*(2), 97–107. https://doi.org/10.1007/s40653-017-0148-x

Boxer, P., Gullan, R. L., & Mahoney, A. (2009). Adolescents' physical aggression toward parents in a clinic-referred sample. *Journal of Clinical Child & Adolescent Psychology, 38*(1), 106–116. https://doi.org/10.1080/15374410802575396

Boyda, D., & McFeeters, D. (2015). Childhood maltreatment and social functioning in adults with sub-clinical psychosis. *Psychiatry Research, 226*(1), 376–382. https://doi.org/10.1016/j.psychres.2015.01.023

Bronfenbrenner, U. (1979). *The ecology of human development*. Harvard University Press.

Brown, G. A. (2004). Gender as a factor in the response of the law-enforcement system to violence against partners. *Sexuality and Culture, 8*(3/4), 3–139. https://doi.org/10.1007/s12119-004-1000-7

Browne, K. D., & Herbert, M. (1997). *Preventing family violence*. Wiley.

Buller, A. M., Devries, K. M., Howard, L. M., & Bacchus, L. J. (2014). Associations between intimate partner violence and health among men who have sex with men: A systematic review and meta-analysis. *PLoS Medicine, 11*(3), 1–12. https://doi.org/10.1371/journal.pmed.1001609

Caldwell, J. E., Swan, S. C., & Woodbrown, V. D. (2012). Gender differences in intimate partner violence outcomes. *Psychology of Violence, 2*(1), 42–57. https://doi.org/10.1037/a0026296

Callaghan, J., Alexander, J., Sixsmith, J., & Fellin, L. C. (2018). Beyond "witnessing": Children's experiences of coercive control in domestic violence and abuse. *Journal of Interpersonal Violence, 33*(10), 1551–1581. https://doi.org/10.1177/0886260515618946

Calvete, E., Orue, I., & Gámez-Guadix, M. (2013). Child-to-parent violence: Emotional and behavioral predictors. *Journal of Interpersonal Violence, 28*, 755–772. https://doi.org/10.1177/0886260512455869

Campbell, E., Richter, J., Howard, J., & Cockburn, H. (2020). *The PIPA project: Positive Interventions for Perpetrators of Adolescent Violence in the Home (AVITH)*. ANROWS. https://apo.org.au/sites/default/files/resource-files/2020-03/apo-nid277191_1.pdf

Capaldi, D. M., Knoble, N. B., Shortt, J. W., & Kim, H. K. (2012). A systematic review of risk factors for intimate partner violence. *Partner Abuse, 3*, 231–280. https://doi.org/10.1891/1946-6560.3.2.231

Carlson, C., Namy, S., Norcini, P. A., Wainberg, M. L., Michau, L., Nakuti, J., Knight, L., Allen, E., Ikenberg, C., Naker, D., & Devries, K. (2020). Violence against children and intimate partner violence against women: Overlap and common contributing factors among caregiver-adolescent dyads. *BMC Public Health, 20*(124), 1–13. https://doi.org/10.1186/s12889-019-8115-0

Carney, M. M., & Barner, J. R. (2012). Prevalence of partner abuse: Rates of emotional abuse and control. *Partner Abuse*, *3*(3), 286–335. https://doi.org/10.1891/1946-6560.3.3.286

Cho, H., Seon, J., Han, J. B., Shamrova, D., & Kwon, I. (2020). Gender differences in the relationship between the nature of intimate partner violence and the survivor's help-seeking. Violence Against. *Women*, *26*(6–7), 712–729. https://doi.org/10.1177/1077801219841440

Condry, R., & Miles, C. (2013). Adolescent to parent violence: Framing and mapping a hidden problem. *Criminology and Criminal Justice*, *14*(3), 1–19. https://doi.org/10.1177/1748895813500155

Corvo, K., & deLara, E. (2009). Towards an integrated theory of relational violence: Is bullying a risk factor for domestic violence? *Aggression and Violent Behavior*, *15*, 181–190. https://doi.org/10.1016/j.avb.2009.12.001

Costa, B. M., Kaestle, C. E., Walker, A., Curtis, A., Day, A., Toumbourou, J. W., & Miller, P. (2015). Longitudinal predictors of domestic violence perpetration and victimization: A systematic review. *Aggression and Violent Behavior*, *24*, 261–272. https://doi.org/10.1016/j.avb.2015.06.001

Cross, C. P., & Campbell, A. (2012). The effects of intimacy and target sex on direct aggression: Further evidence. *Aggressive Behavior*, *38*(4), 272–280. https://doi.org/10.1002/ab.21430

Cross, C. P., Tee, W., & Campbell, A. (2011). Gender symmetry in intimate aggression: An effect of intimacy or target sex? *Aggressive Behavior*, *37*(3), 268–277. https://doi.org/10.1002/ab.20388

Crown Prosecution Service. (2017). Controlling or coercive behaviour in an intimate or family relationship. https://www.cps.gov.uk/legal-guidance/controlling-or-coercive-behaviour-intimate-or-family-relationship

Cummings, E., & Davies, P. (2002). Effects of marital conflict on children: Recent advances and emerging themes in process-oriented research. *Journal of Child Psychology and Psychiatry and Allied Disciplines*, *43*, 31–63. https://doi.org/10.1111/1469-7610.00003

Cunradi, C. B., Caetano, R., & Schafer, J. (2002). Predictors of intimate partner violence among White, Black, and Hispanic couples in the United States. *Journal of Family Violence*, *17*(4), 377–389. https://doi.org/10.1023/A:1020374617328

DeKeseredy, W. S. (2011). Feminist contributions to understanding woman abuse: Myths, controversies, and realities. *Aggression and Violent Behavior*, *16*(4), 297–302. https://doi.org/10.1016/j.avb.2011.04.002

DeKeseredy, W. S. (2021). Bringing feminist sociological analyses of patriarchy back to the forefront of the study of woman abuse. *Violence Against Women*, *27*(5), 621–638. https://doi.org/10.1177/1077801220958485

DeKeseredy, W. S., Saunders, D. G., Schwartz, M. D., & Alvi, S. (1997). The meanings and motives for women's use of violence in Canadian college dating relationships: Results from a national survey. *Sociological Spectrum*, *17*(2), 199–222. https://doi.org/10.1080/02732173.1997.9982160

Desmarais, S. L., Reeves, K. A., Nicholls, T. L., Telford, R. P., & Fiebert, M. S. (2012a). Prevalence of physical violence in intimate relationships, Part 1: Rates of male and female victimization. *Partner Abuse*, *3*(2), 140–169. https://doi.org/10.1891/1946-6560.3.2.140

Desmarais, S. L., Reeves, K. A., Nicholls, T. L., Telford, R. P., & Fiebert, M. S. (2012b). Prevalence of physical violence in intimate relationships, Part 2: Rates of male and female perpetration. *Partner Abuse, 3*(2), 170–198. https://doi.org/10.1891/1946-6560.3.2.170

Dixon, L., & Graham-Kevan, N. (2011). Understanding the nature and etiology of intimate partner violence and implications for practice and policy. *Clinical Psychology Review, 7*, 1145–1155 https://doi.org/10.1016/j.cpr.2011.07.001

Dixon, L., Hamilton-Giachritsis, C., Browne, K. D., & Ostapuik, E. (2007). The co-occurrence of child and intimate partner maltreatment in the family: Characteristics of the violent perpetrators. *Journal of Family Violence, 22*, 675–689. https://doi.org/10.1007/s10896-007-9115-x

Dobash, R. P., & Dobash, R. E. (2004). Women's violence to men in intimate relationships: Working on a puzzle. *British Journal of Criminology, 44*, 324–349. https://doi.org/10.1093/bjc/azh026

Dobash, R. E., & Dobash, R. P. (1979). *Violence against wives: A case against the patriarchy*. Open Books.

Dube, S. R., Felitti, V. J., Dong, M., Chapman, D. P., Giles, W. H., & Anda, R. F. (2003). Childhood abuse, neglect, and household dysfunction and the risk of illicit drug use: The Adverse Childhood Experiences Study. *Pediatrics, 111*(3), 564–573. https://doi.org/10.1542/peds.111.3.564

Dutton, D. G. (1999). *Limitations of social learning models in explaining intimate aggression*. In X. B. Arriaga & S. Oskamp (Eds.), *Violence in intimate relationships* (pp. 73–87). Sage. https://doi.org/10.4135/9781452204659.n4

Dutton, D. G. (2006). *Rethinking domestic violence*. Ubc Press.

Dutton, D. G. (2010). The gender paradigm and the architecture of antiscience. *Partner Abuse, 1*(1), 5–25. https://doi.org/10.1891/1946-6560.1.1.5

Edleson, J. (1999). The overlap between child maltreatment and woman battering. *Violence Against Women, 5*, 134–154.

Erath, S. A., & Bierman, K. L. (2006). Aggressive marital conflict, maternal harsh punishment, and child aggressive-disrupted behavior: Evidence for direct and mediated relations. *Journal of Family Psychology, 20*(2), 217–226. https://doi.org/10.1037/0893-3200.20.2.217

Evans, S. E., Davies, C., DiLillo, D. (2008). Exposure to domestic violence: A meta-analysis of child and adolescent outcomes. *Aggression and Violent Behavior, 13*, 131–140. https://doi.org/10.1016/j.avb.2008.02.005

Finkelhor, D., Turner, H., Ormrod, R., Hamby, S. L. (2009). Violence, abuse, and crime exposure in a national sample of children and youth. *Pediatrics, 124*(5), 1411–1423. http://doi.org/10.1542/peds.2009-0467

Fisher, H., Morgan, C., Dazzan, P., Craig, T. K., Morgan, K., Hutchinson, G., Jones, P. B., Doody, G. A., Pariante, C., McGuffin, P., Murray, R. M., Leff, J., & Fearon, P. (2009). Gender differences in the association between childhood abuse and psychosis. *The British Journal of Psychiatry, 194*(4), 319–325. http://doi.org/10.1192/bjp.bp.107.047985

Follingstad, D. R. (2007). Rethinking current approaches to psychological abuse: Conceptual and methodological issues. *Aggression and Violent Behavior, 12*(4), 439–458. https://doi.org/10.1016/j.avb.2006.07.004

Follingstad, D. R., & DeHart, D. D. (2000). Defining psychological abuse of husbands toward wives: Contexts, behaviors, and typologies. *Journal of Interpersonal Violence*, 15(9), 891–920. https://doi.org/10.1177/088626000015009001

Follingstad, D. R., & Edmundson, M. (2010). Is psychological abuse reciprocal in intimate relationships? Data from a national sample of American adults. *Journal of Family Violence*, 25(5), 495–508. https://doi.org/10.1007/s10896-010-9311-y

Follingstad, D. R., & Rogers, M. J. (2012). Women experiencing psychological abuse: Are they a homogenous group? *Journal of Aggression, Maltreatment & Trauma*, 21(8), 891–916. https://doi.org/10.1080/10926771.2012.708012

Fortin, A., Doucet, M., & Damant, D. (2011). Children's appraisals as mediators of the relationship between domestic violence and child adjustment. *Violence and Victims*, 26(3), 377–392. http://doi.org/10.1891/0886-6708.26.3.377

Gallego, R., Novo, M., Fariña, F., & Arce, R. (2019). Child-to-parent violence and parent-to-child violence: A meta-analytic review. *European Journal of Psychology Applied to Legal Context*, 11(2), 51–59. https://doi.org/10.5093/ejpalc2019a4

Gámez-Guadix, M., & Calvete, E. (2012). Violencia filioparental y su asociación con la exposicón a la violencia marital y la agresón de padres a hijos. [Child-to-parent violence and its association with exposure to marital violence and parent-to-child violence]. *Psicothema*, 24, 277–283.

Garcia-Moreno, C., Jansen, H. A., Ellsberg, M., Heise, L., & Watts, C. H. (2006). Prevalence of intimate partner violence: findings from the WHO multi-country study on women's health and domestic violence. *Lancet*, 368, 1260–1269. http://doi.org/10.1016/S0140-6736(06)69523-8

Gondolf, E. W. (2007). Theoretical and research support for the Duluth Model: A reply to Dutton and Corvo. *Aggression and Violent Behavior*, 12(6), 644–657. https://doi.org/10.1016/j.avb.2007.03.001

Graham-Bermann, S. A., Gruber, G., Howell, K. H., & Girz, L. (2009). Factors discriminating among profiles of resilience and psychopathology in children exposed to intimate partner violence (IPV). *Child Abuse & Neglect*, 33(9), 648–660. http://doi.org/10.1016/j.chiabu.2009.01.002

Graham-Kevan, N., & Archer, J. (2003a). Intimate terrorism and common couple violence: A test of Johnson's predictions in four British samples. *Journal of Interpersonal Violence*, 18(11), 1247–1270. https://doi.org/10.1177/0886260503256656

Graham-Kevan, N., & Archer, J. (2003b). Physical aggression and control in heterosexual relationships: The effect of sampling. *Violence and Victims*, 18(2), 181–196. https://doi.org/10.1891/vivi.2003.18.2.181

Gray, H. M., & Foshee, V. (1997). Adolescent dating violence: Differences between one-sided and mutually violent profiles. *Journal of Interpersonal Violence*, 12, 126–141, https://doi.org/10.1177/088626097012001008

Hamberger, L. K., & Larsen, S. E. (2015). Men's and women's experience of intimate partner violence: A review of ten years of comparative studies in clinical samples; Part I. *Journal of Family Violence*, 30(6), 699–717. https://doi.org/10.1007/s10896-015-9732-8

Hamby, S. (2016). Self-report measures that do not produce gender parity in intimate partner violence: A multi-study investigation. *Psychology of Violence*, 6(2), 323–335. https://doi.org/10.1037/a0038207

Hamby, S., Finkelhor, D., Turner, H., & Ormrod, R. (2010). The overlap of witnessing partner violence with child maltreatment and other victimizations in a nationally representative survey of youth. *Child Abuse & Neglect, 34*(10), 734–741. https://doi.org/10.1016/j.chiabu.2010.03.001

Hamby, S. L., & Sugarman, D. B. (1999). Acts of psychological aggression against a partner and their relation to physical assault and gender. *Journal of Marriage and the Family, 61*(4), 959–970. https://doi.org/doi:10.2307/354016

Hamel, J. (2016). Domestic violence and perpetrator programs around the world. *Partner Abuse, 7*(3), 223–225. https://doi.org/10.1891/1946-6560.7.3.223

Hamel, J., Langhinrichsen-Rohling, J., & Hines, D. (2012). More than a literature review: The partner abuse state of knowledge manuscripts and online data base. *Partner Abuse, 3*(2), 131–139. https://doi.org/ 10.1891/1946-6560.3.2.131

Harold, G. T., & Sellers, R. (2018). Annual research review: Interparental conflict and youth psychopathology: An evidence review and practice focused update. *Journal of Child Psychology and Psychiatry, 59*(4), 374–402. https://doi.org/10.1111/jcpp.12893

Heise, L. (2011). *What works to prevent partner violence? An evidence overview.* STRIVE, London School of Hygiene and Tropical Medicine.

Henning, K., & Renauer, B. (2005). Prosecution of women arrested for intimate partner abuse. *Violence and Victims, 20*(3), 361–376. https://doi.org/10.1891/vivi.20.3.361

Hilton, N. Z., & Eke, A. W. (2016). Non-specialization of criminal careers among intimate partner violence offenders. *Criminal Justice and Behavior, 43*(10), 1347–1363. https://doi.org/10.1177/0093854816637886

Hines, D. A., & Douglas, E. M. (2010). A closer look at men who sustain intimate terrorism by women. *Partner Abuse, 1*(3), 286–313. https://doi.org/10.1891/1946-6560.1.3.286

Hines, D. A., & Douglas, E. M. (2018). Influence of intimate terrorism, situational couple violence, and mutual violent control on male victims. *Psychology of Men & Masculinity, 19*(4), 612–623. https://doi.org/10.1037/men0000142

Hope, K. A., Bates, E. A., Brooks, M., & Taylor, J. C. (2021). What can we learn from domestic homicide reviews with male victims? *Partner Abuse, 12*(4), 384–408.

Ibabe, I. (2019). Adolescent-to-parent violence and family environment: The perceptions of same reality? *International Journal of Environmental Research and Public Health, 16*(12), 2215. https://doi.org/10.3390/ijerph16122215

Ibabe, I., Arnoso, A., & Elgorriaga, E. (2020). Child-to-parent violence as an intervening variable in the relationship between inter-parental violence exposure and dating violence. *International Journal of Environmental Research and Public Health, 17*(5), 1–19. https://doi.org/10.3390/ijerph17051514

Ibabe, I., & Jaureguizar, J. (2010). Child-to-parent violence: Profile of abusive adolescents and their families. *Journal of Criminal Justice, 38*(4), 616–624. https://doi.org/10.1016/j.jcrimjus.2010.04.034

Ibabe, I., Jaureguizar, J., & Bentler, P. M. (2013). Risk factors for child-to-parent violence. *Journal of Family Violence, 28*(5), 523–534. https://doi.org/10.1007/s10896-013-9512-2

Johnson, M. P. (1995). Patriarchal terrorism and common couple violence: Two forms of violence against women. *Journal of Marriage and the Family, 57*, 282–294. https://doi.org/10.2307/353683

Johnson, M. P. (2006). Conflict and control: Gender symmetry and asymmetry in domestic violence. *Violence Against Women, 12*, 1003–1018. https://doi.org/10.1177/1077801206293328

Johnson, M. P., & Leone, J. M. (2005). The differential effects of intimate terrorism and situational couple violence: Findings from the National Violence Against Women Survey. *Journal of Family Issues, 26*(3), 322–349. https://doi.org/10.1177/0192513X04270345

Jones, R. T., Browne, K., & Chou, S. (2017). A critique of the revised Conflict Tactics Scales-2 (CTS-2). *Aggression and Violent Behavior, 37*, 83–90. https://doi.org/10.1016/j.avb.2017.08.005

Kerker, B. D., Horwitz, S. M., Leventhal, J. M., Plichta, S., & Leaf, P. J. (2000). Identification of violence in the home: Pediatric and parental reports. *Archives of Pediatrics and Adolescent Medicine, 154*(5), 457–462 https://doi.org/10.1001/archpedi.154.5.457

Kessler, R. C., Chiu, W. T., Demler, O., & Walters, E. E. (2005). Prevalence, severity, and comorbidity of 12-month DSM-IV disorders in the National Comorbidity Survey replication. *Archives of General Psychiatry, 62*(6), 617–627. https://doi.org/10.1001/archpsyc.62.6.617

Kimmel, M. S. (2002). "Gender symmetry" in domestic violence: A substantive and methodological research review. *Violence Against Women, 8*(11), 1332–1363. https://doi.org/10.1177/107780102237407

Kitzmann, K. M., Gaylord, N. K., Holt, A. R., & Kenny, E. D. (2003). Child witnesses to domestic violence: A meta-analytic review. *Journal of Consulting and Clinical Psychology, 71*, 339–352. https://doi.org/10.1037/0022-006X.71.2.339

Kolbo, J. R. (1996). Risk and resilience among children exposed to family violence. *Violence and Victims, 11*(2), 113–128. https://doi.org10.1891/0886-6708.11.2.113

Lagdon, S., Armour, C., & Stringer, M. (2014). Adult experience of mental health outcomes as a result of intimate partner violence victimisation: A systematic review. *European Journal of Psychotraumatology, 5*(1), 24794. https://doi.org/10.3402/ejpt.v5.24794

Langhinrichsen-Rohling, J. (2010). Controversies involving gender and intimate partner violence in the United States. *Sex Roles, 62*, 179–193. https://doi.org/10.1007/s11199-009- 9628-2

Langhinrichsen-Rohling, J., Misra, T. A., Selwyn, C., & Rohling, M. L. (2012a). Rates of bidirectional versus unidirectional intimate partner violence across sample, sexual orientations, and race/ethnicities: A comprehensive review. *Partner Abuse, 3*(2), 199–230. https://doi.org/10.1891/1946-6560.3.2.199

Langhinrichsen-Rohling, J., McCullars, A., & Misra, T. A. (2012b). Motivations for men and women's intimate partner violence perpetration: A comprehensive review. *Partner Abuse, 3*(4), 429–468. https://doi.org/10.1891/1946-6560.3.4.429

Laskey, P., Bates, E. A., & Taylor, J. C. (2019). A systematic literature review of intimate partner violence victimisation: An inclusive review across gender and sexuality. *Aggression and Violent Behavior, 47*, 1–11. https://doi.org/10.1016/j.avb.2019.02.014

Lawrence, E., Orengo-Aguayo, R., Langer, A., & Brock, R. L. (2012). The impact and consequences of partner abuse on partners. *Partner Abuse, 3*(4), 406–428. https://doi.org/10.1891/1946-6560.3.4.406

Letourneau, N. L., Fedick, C. B., & Willms, J. D. (2007). Mothering and domestic violence: A longitudinal analysis. *Journal of Family Violence, 22*(8), 649–659. https://doi.org/10.1007/s10896-007-9099-6

Levendosky, A. A., Leahy, K. L., Bogat, G. A., Davidson, W. S., & von Eye, A. (2006). Domestic violence, maternal parenting, maternal mental health, and infant externalizing behavior. *Journal of Family Psychology, 20,* 544–552. https://doi.org/10.1037/0893-3200.20.4.544

MacDonell, K. W. (2012). The combined and independent impact of witnessed intimate partner violence and child maltreatment. *Partner Abuse, 3*(3), 358–378. https://doi.org/10.1891/1946-6560.3.3.358

Mackay, J., Bowen, E., Walker, K., & O'Doherty, L. (2018). Risk factors for female perpetrators of intimate partner violence within criminal justice settings: A systematic review. *Aggression and Violent Behavior, 41,* 128–146. https://doi.org/10.1016/j.avb.2018.06.004

Macmillan, H. L, Wathen, C. N, Barlow, J, Fergusson, D. M., Leventhal, J. M., & Taussig, H. N. (2009). Interventions to prevent child maltreatment and associated impairment. *Lancet, 373,* 250–266. http://doi.org/10.1016/S0140-6736(08)61708-0

Mair, C., Cunradi, C. B., & Todd, M. (2012). Adverse childhood experiences and intimate partner violence: testing psychosocial mediational pathways among couples. *Annals of Epidemiology, 22*(12), 832–839. https://doi.org/10.1016/j.annepidem.2012.09.008

Martinez-Torteya, C., Anne Bogat, G., Von Eye, A., & Levendosky, A. A. (2009). Resilience among children exposed to domestic violence: The role of risk and protective factors. *Child Development, 80*(2), 562–577. https://doi.org/10.1111/j.1467-8624.2009.01279.x

McGee, C. (2000). *Childhood experiences of domestic violence.* Jessica Kingsley.

McGuigan, W. M., & Pratt, C. C. (2001). The predictive impact of domestic violence on three types of child maltreatment. *Child Abuse & Neglect, 25*(7), 869–883. https://doi.org/10.1016/S0145-2134(01)00244-7

McLaughlin, K. A., & Hatzenbuehler, M. L. (2009). Mechanisms linking stressful life events and mental health problems in a prospective, community-based sample of adolescents. *Journal of Adolescent Health, 44,* 153–160. https://doi.org/10.1016/j.jadohealth.2008.06.019

McLaughlin, K. A., Kubzansky, L. D., Dunn, E. C., Waldinger, R. J., Vaillant, G. E., & Koenen, K. C. (2010). Childhood social environment, emotional reactivity to stress, and mood and anxiety disorders across the life course. *Depression and Anxiety, 27,* 1087–1094. https://doi.org/10.1002/da.20762

McTavish, J. R., MacGregor, J. C., Wathen, C. N., & MacMillan, H. L. (2016). Children's exposure to intimate partner violence: An overview. *International Review of Psychiatry, 28*(5), 504–518. https://doi.org/10.1080/09540261.2016.1205001

Melander, L. A., Noel, H., & Tyler, K. A. (2010). Bidirectional, unidirectional, and nonviolence: A comparison of the predictors among partnered young adults. *Violence and Victims, 25*(5), 617–630. https://doi.org/10.1891/0886-6708.25.5.617

Miller, E., Jordan, B., Levenson, R., & Silverman, J. G. (2010). Reproductive coercion: connecting the dots between partner violence and unintended pregnancy. *Contraception, 81*(6), 457–459. https://doi.org/10.1016/j.contraception.2010.02.023

Minze, L. C., McDonald, R., Rosentraub, E. L., & Jouriles, E. N. (2010). Making sense of family conflict: intimate partner violence and preschoolers' externalizing problems. *Journal of Family Psychology, 24*(1), 5–11. https://doi.org/10.1037/a0018071

Moffitt, T. E., Caspi, A., Harrington, H., & Milne, B. J. (2002). Males on the lifecourse—persistent and adolescence-limited antisocial pathways: Follow-up at age 26 years. *Development and Psychopathology, 14*(1), 179–207. https://doi.org/10.1017/S0954579402001104

Moylan, C. A., Herrenkohl, T. I., Sousa, C., Tajima, E. A., Herrenkohl, R. C., & Russo, M. J. (2010). The effects of child abuse and exposure to domestic violence on adolescent internalizing and externalizing behavior problems. *Journal of Family Violence, 25*, 53–63. https://doi.org/10.1007/s10896-009-9269-9

Mullen, P., Walton, V., Romans-Clarkson, S., & Herbison, G. P. (1988). Impact of sexual and physical abuse on women's mental health. *The Lancet, 331*(8590), 841–845. https://doi.org/10.1016/S0140-6736(88)91600-5

Nagin, D., & Tremblay, R. E. (1999). Trajectories of boys' physical aggression, opposition, and hyperactivity on the path to physically violent and nonviolent juvenile delinquency. *Child Development, 70*(5), 1181–1196. https://doi.org/10.1111/1467-8624.00086

Nowakowski-Sims, E., & Rowe, A. (2017). The relationship between childhood adversity, attachment, and internalizing behaviors in a diversion program for child-to-mother violence. *Child Abuse & Neglect, 72*, 266–275. https://doi.org/10.1016/j.chiabu.2017.08.015

Office for National Statistics (ONS). (2020). Domestic abuse in England and Wales overview: November 2020. https://www.ons.gov.uk/peoplepopulationandcommunity/crimeandjustice/bulletins/domesticabuseinenglandandwalesoverview/november2020#:~:text=The%20CSEW%20is%20a%20face,months%20prior%20to%20the%20interview.

Palmetto, N., Davidson, L. L., & Rickert, V. I. (2013). Predictors of physical intimate partner violence in the lives of young women: Victimization, perpetration, and bi-directional violence. *Violence and Victims, 28*(1), 103–121. https://doi.org/10.1891/0886-6708.28.1.103

Papamichail, A. (2018). *Young people who are violent towards their parents in the UK* [Unpublished doctoral dissertation, University of Brighton, Brighton, UK].

Papamichail, A., & Bates, E. A. (2019). The appropriateness of the Duluth model for intimate partner violence and child-to-parent violence: A conceptual review. *Partner Abuse, 10*(4), 517–532. http://dx.doi.org/10.1891/1946-6560.10.4.517

Papamichail, A., & Bates, E. A. (2020). "I want my mum to know that I am a good guy...": A thematic analysis of the accounts of adolescents who exhibit child-to-parent violence in the United Kingdom. *Journal of Interpersonal Violence*, 1–24. https://doi.org/10.1177/0886260520926317

Paterson, R., Luntz, H., Perlesz, A., & Cotton, S. (2002). Adolescent violence towards parents: Maintaining family connections when the going gets tough. *Australian and New Zealand Journal of Family Therapy, 23*(2), 90–100. https://doi.org/10.1002/j.1467-8438.2002.tb00493.x

Pence, E., & Paymar, M. (1993). *Education groups for men who batter: The Duluth model.* Springer.

Pico-Alfonso, M. A., Garcia-Linares, M. I., Celda-Navarro, N., Blasco-Ros, C., Echeburúa, E., & Martinez, M. (2006). The impact of physical, psychological, and sexual intimate male partner violence on women's mental health: Depressive symptoms, posttraumatic stress disorder, state anxiety, and suicide. *Journal of Women's Health, 15*(5), 599–611. https://doi.org/10.1089/jwh.2006.15.599

Rath, G. D., Jarratt, L. G., & Leonardson, G. (1989). Rates of domestic violence against adult women by men partners. *The Journal of the American Board of Family Practice*, *2*(4), 227–233. https://doi.org/10.3122/jabfm.2.4.227

Read, J., & Bentall, R. P. (2012). "Negative childhood experiences and mental health: Theoretical, clinical and primary prevention implications": Correction. *The British Journal of Psychiatry*, *201*(4), 328. https://doi.org/10.1192/bjp.201.4.328

Renner, L. M., & Whitney, S. D. (2012). Risk factors for unidirectional and bidirectional intimate partner violence among young adults. *Child Abuse & Neglect*, *36*(1), 40–52. https://doi.org/10.1016/j.chiabu.2011.07.007

Rhodes, K. V., Houry, D., Cerulli, C., Straus, H., Kaslow, N. J., & McNutt, L. A. (2009). Intimate partner violence and comorbid mental health conditions among urban male patients. *The Annals of Family Medicine*, *7*(1), 47–55. https://doi.org/10.1370/afm.936

Rivett, M., Howarth, E., & Harold, G. (2006). "Watching from the stairs": Towards an evidence-based practice in work with child witnesses of domestic violence. *Clinical Child Psychology and Psychiatry*, *11*(1), 103–125. https://doi.org/10.1177/1359104506059131

Rutter, M. (2012). Resilience as a dynamic concept. *Development and Psychopathology*, *24*(2), 335–344. https://doi.org/10.1017/S0954579412000028

Sabina, C., & Straus, M. A. (2008). Polyvictimization by dating partners and mental health among U.S. college students. *Violence and Victims*, *23*(6), 667–682. https://doi.org/10.1891/0886-6708.23.6.667

Salis, K. L., Salwen, J., & OLeary, K. D. (2014). The predictive utility of psychological aggression for intimate partner violence. *Partner Abuse*, *5*, 83–97. https://doi.org/10.1891/1946-6560.5.1.83

Saxton, M. D., Olszowy, L., MacGregor, J. C., MacQuarrie, B. J., &Wathen, C. N. (2021). Experiences of intimate partner violence victims with police and the justice system in Canada. *Journal of Interpersonal Violence*, *36*(3–4), NP2029–NP2055. https://doi.org/10.1177%2F0886260518758330

Selwyn, J., & Meakings, S. (2016). Adolescent-to-parent violence in adoptive families. *British Journal of Social Work*, *46*(5), 1224–1240. https://doi.org/10.1093/bjsw/bcv072

Sidebotham, P., Bailey, S., Belderson, P., & Brandon, M. (2011). Fatal child maltreatment in England, 2005–2009. *Child Abuse & Neglect*, *35*(4), 299–306. https://doi.org/10.1016/j.chiabu.2011.01.005

Sigfusdottir, I.-D., Farkas, G., & Silver, E. (2004). The role of depressed mood and anger in the relationship between family conflict and delinquent behavior. *Journal of Youth and Adolescence*, *33*, 509–522. https://doi.org/10.1023/B:JOYO.0000048065.17118.63

Simmons, M., McEwan, T., Purcell, R., & Oglo, J. (2018). Sixty years of child-to-parent abuse research: What do we know and where do we go? *Aggression and Violent Behavior*, *38*, 31–52. https://doi.org/10.1093/bjsw/bcv072

Smith, S. G., Chen, J., Basile, K. C., Gilbert, L. K., Merrick, M. T., Patel, N., Walling, M., & Jain, A. (2017). *The National Intimate Partner and Sexual Violence Survey (NISVS): 2010–2012 State Report*. National Center for Injury Prevention and Control, Centers for Disease Control and Prevention.

Smith-Slep, A. M. S., & O'Leary, S. G. (2005). Parent and partner violence in families with young children: Rates, patterns, and connections. *Journal of Consulting and Clinical Psychology*, *73*(3), 435–444. https://doi.org/10.1037/0022-006X.73.3.435

Sternberg, K. J., Baradaran, L. P., Abbott, C. B., Lamb, M. E., & Guterman, E. (2006). Type of violence, age, and gender differences in the effects of family violence on children's behavior problems: A mega-analysis. *Developmental Review*, 26, 89–112. https://doi.org/10.1016/j.dr.2005.12.001

Stets, J. E., & Straus, M. A. (1989). The marriage license as a hitting license: A comparison of assaults in dating, cohabiting, and married couples. *Journal of Family Violence*, 4(2), 161–180. https://doi.org/10.1007/BF01006627

Stith, S. M., Rosen, K. H., Middleton, K. A., Busch, A. L., Lundeberg, K., & Carlton, R. P. (2000). The intergenerational transmission of spouse abuse: A meta-analysis. *Journal of Marriage and Family*, 62, 640–654. https://doi.org/10.1111/j.1741-3737.2000.00640.x

Straus, M. A. (1979). Measuring intrafamily conflict and violence: The Conflicts Tactics (CT) scales. *Journal of Marriage and the Family*, 41, 75–88

Straus, M. A. (2008). Dominance and symmetry in partner violence by male and female university students in 32 nations. *Children and Youth Services Review*, 30(3), 252–275. https://doi.org/10.1016/j.childyouth.2007.10.004

Straus, M. A. (2012). Blaming the messenger for the bad news about partner violence by women: The methodological, theoretical, and value basis of the purported invalidity of the Conflict Tactics Scales. *Behavioral Sciences & The Law*, 30(5), 538–556. https://doi.org/10.1002/bsl.2023

Straus, M. A., & Gelles, R. J. (1990). Societal change and change in family violence from 1975 to 1985 as revealed by the two national surveys. In M. A. Straus & R. J. Gelles (Eds.), *Physical violence in American families, risk factors and adaptations to violence in 8145 families* (pp. 113–131). Transaction.

Sturge-Apple, M. L., Davies, P. T., Cicchetti, D., & Manning, L. G. (2012). Interparental violence, maternal emotional unavailability and children's cortisol functioning in family contexts. *Developmental Psychology*, 48(1), 237–249. https://doi.org/10.1037/a0025419

Suzuki, S. L., Geffner, R., & Bucky, S. F. (2008). The experiences of adults exposed to intimate partner violence as children: An exploratory qualitative study of resilience and protective factors. *Journal of Emotional Abuse*, 8(1–2), 103–121. https://doi.org/10.1080/10926790801984523

Szinovacz, M. E. (1983). Using couple data as a methodological tool: The case of marital violence. *Journal of Marriage and the Family*, 45(3), 633–644. https://doi.org/10.2307/351668

Taft, C. T., Murphy, C. M., King, L. A., Dedeyn, J. M., & Musser, P. H. (2005). Posttraumatic stress disorder symptomatology among partners of men in treatment for relationship abuse. *Journal of Abnormal Psychology*, 114(2), 259–268. https://doi.org/10.1037/0021-843X.114.2.259

Temple, J. R., Weston, R., & Marshall, L. L. (2005). Physical and mental health outcomes of women in nonviolent, unilaterally violent, and mutually violent relationships. *Violence and Victims*, 20(3), 335–359. https://doi.org/10.1891/vivi.20.3.335

Thornton, A. J. V., Graham-Kevan, N., & Archer, J. (2010). Adaptive and maladaptive personality traits as predictors of violent and nonviolent offending behavior in men and women. *Aggressive Behavior*, 36, 177–186. https://doi.org/10.1002/ab.20340

Ulloa, E. C., & Hammett, J. F. (2016). The effect of gender and perpetrator–victim role on mental health outcomes and risk behaviors associated with intimate partner violence. *Journal of Interpersonal Violence, 31*(7), 1184–1207. https://doi.org/10.1177/0886260514564163

United States Department for Health and Human Services. (2018). Child maltreatment. https://www.acf.hhs.gov/sites/default/files/documents/cb/cm2018.pdf

Van der Kolk, B., Perry, J. C., & Herman, J. L. (1991). Childhood origins of self destructive behavior. *American Journal of Psychiatry, 148*, 1665–1671.

Waldrop, A. E., & Resick, P. A. (2004). Coping among adult female victims of domestic violence. *Journal of Family Violence, 19*(5), 291–302. https://doi.org/10.1023/B:JOFV.0000042079.91846.68

Walker, L. E. (1992) Battered women syndrome and self-defense. 6 *Notre Dame J.L. Ethics & Public Policy*, 321. http://scholarship.law.nd.edu/ndjlepp/vol6/iss2/3

Whitaker, D. J., Haileyesus, T., Swahn, M., & Saltzman, L. S. (2007). Differences in frequency of violence and reported injury between relationships with reciprocal and nonreciprocal intimate partner violence. *American Journal of Public Health, 97*(5), 941–947. https://doi.org/10.2105/AJPH.2005.079020

Whitfield, C. L., Anda, R. F., Dube, S. R., & Felitti, V. J. (2003). Violent childhood experiences and the risk of intimate partner violence in adults: Assessment in a large health maintenance organization. *Journal of Interpersonal Violence, 18*(2), 166–185. https://doi.org/10.1177/0886260502238733

WHO. (1999). *Report of the consultation on child abuse prevention*, 29–31 March 1999, World Health Organization (document WHO/HSC/PVI/99.1). https://apps.who.int/iris/handle/10665/65900

WHO. (2010). *Violence prevention: The evidence. Series of briefings on violence prevention*. World Health Organization.

WHO. (2017). *Violence info—child maltreatment*. http://apps.who.int/violence-info/child-maltreatment/

Williams, L. M. (2003). Understanding child abuse and violence against women: A life course perspective. *Journal of Interpersonal Violence, 18*(4), 441–451. https://doi.org/10.1177/0886260502250842

Wolfe, D. A., Crooks, C. V., Lee, V., McIntyre-Smith, A., & Jaffe, P. G. (2003). The effects of children's exposure to domestic violence: A meta-analysis and critique. *Clinical Child and Family Psychology Review, 6*, 171–187. https://doi.org/10.1023/A:1024910416164

Yakubovich, A. R., Stöckl, H., Murray, J., Melendez-Torres, G. J., Steinert, J. I., Glavin, C., & Humphreys, D. K. (2018). Risk and protective factors for intimate partner violence against women: Systematic review and meta-analyses of prospective-longitudinal studies. *American Journal of Public Health, 108*(7), 1–11. https://doi.org/10.2105/AJPH.2018.304428

Zarling, A. L., Taber-Thomas, S., Murray, A., Knuston, J. F., Lawrence, E., Valles, N. L., DeGarmo, D. S., & Bank, L. (2013). Internalizing and externalizing symptoms in young children exposed to intimate partner violence: examining intervening processes. *Journal of Family Psychology, 27*(6), 945–955. https://doi.org/10.1037/a0034804

The Law Enforcement Response to Intimate Partner Violence

Toward a Gender-Neutral Approach

BRENDA RUSSELL AND EMILY SEISLER ■

Domestic abuse has historically been perceived as a heterosexual phenomenon, with males as perpetrators and females as victims. As chapters throughout this volume will attest (see Bates & Papamichail, Chapter 2; and Hamel et al., Chapter 6), this is not always the case, as women can be motivated to abuse their partner in many of the same ways as men. Intimate partner violence (IPV) knows no boundaries. It exists beyond the boundaries of age, race, gender, or sexual orientation. However, despite over 30 years of research demonstrating the boundless nature of IPV, our societal beliefs continue to be constrained within the gender binary or gender paradigm, where IPV is considered a crime perpetrated by men against women. This chapter examines how the vestiges of these beliefs can influence law enforcement response and addresses ways to better assist victims while holding perpetrators accountable.

IPV is a human problem, and until we acknowledge this problem, we do a disservice to victims. This is not intended to minimize the victimization among women but rather reflects upon the victimization of all individuals. Women experience a more comprehensive range of violence, including stalking and sexual assault, and suffer more significant injury (Archer, 2000; Chen et al., 2020) and intimate partner homicide than men in IPV incidents (see Hamel et al., Chapter 6, this volume). This chapter will demonstrate how law enforcement training and procedures leading to IPV arrest should be reassessed to meet the needs of all IPV victims. Those supporting patriarchal gendered notions of IPV argue IPV is innately gendered, injury severity is greater for women, and studies supporting gender symmetry are not sensitive to inherent gender differences; hence, this suppresses the reality of IPV as a crime against women (Buttell & Star, 2013;

Dobash et al., 1992). Research over the last 30+ years suggests the actual number of women initiating abusive behavior is about equal to men (Carney et al., 2006; Dutton & Nicholls, 2005; Langhinrichsen-Rohling et al., 2012; Straus & Gelles, 1990; Wexler, 2020). Such findings have led family violence scholars to reject this point of view and believe IPV is not driven by gender patriarchy, but rather motivations and behaviors associated with IPV perpetration are shared by all, far beyond the confines of gender. Despite this belief and its empirical support, we continue to experience greater disdain for male perpetrators of IPV initiating such violence, which often leads to arrest. In contrast, the same IPV initiated by a female perpetrator seems insignificant (Buttell & Star, 2013). Similarly, racial and sexual minorities are negatively impacted by disparities of IPV response within the criminal justice system, and despite years of empirical evidence demonstrating such disparities, not much has changed within criminal justice response to recognize this issue.

This is evident in our scholarly research and crime databases. Many law enforcement agencies, advocates, and proponents of the gender paradigm often turn to statistics of crime databases that demonstrate that women are victims of IPV more often than men. Crime databases estimate that about 9 times as many men as women perpetrate violence. However, these estimates only reflect rates of arrest and or conviction; therefore, they do not reflect the broader picture of IPV victimization. Shernock and Russell's (2012) review of 90 scholarly research articles addressing IPV arrest found male suspects were arrested more than females even when controlling for severity of injury. Additional research examining over 4,000 defendants found female defendants were treated more leniently throughout the adjudicative process, even when legal and extralegal factors were statistically controlled (Henning & Feder, 2005). Renauer and Henning (2005) found these findings were replicated specifically in terms of IPV arrests, especially when a woman assaulted a male, but also extended into other domestic offenses, including other types of relationships (i.e., familial and lesbian relationships). If law enforcement officers are inherently biased toward the heterosexual nature of IPV and female victimization and their training reinforces this bias, then it is no wonder why IPV rates of arrest are highly asymmetrical.

Male victims and sexual minorities continue to be neglected or treated differently in criminal justice response related to IPV. According to the National Intimate Partner and Sexual Violence Survey (NISVS), almost 60% of bisexual women and 40% of lesbians have reported lifetime rates of IPV compared to 32.3% of heterosexual females. Similarly, 25% of gay men and 28.7% of heterosexual men reported IPV in their lifetime (Breiding et al., 2013). Further, as the National Crime Victimization Survey just began to include gender identity in 2019, research on IPV in transgender and nonconforming individuals is scarce. However, a meta-analysis compared cis-gender IPV survivors to transgender victims and found transgender victims were 1.7 times more likely to experience IPV and 2.2 to 2.5 times more likely to experience physical and sexual IPV than cis-gender individuals (Peitzmeier, 2020). Further, a recent study examining IPV among 750 transgender individuals aged 65 years and older found prevalence rates of IPV was 51% (Hillman, in press). Research examining transgender and nonconforming adults found that 72% of their sample experienced at least one form (physical, psychological, sexual) of IPV in their lifetime (Henry et al., 2021).

Sexual minorities are also more likely to be involved in the criminal justice system and incarcerated. Researchers (e.g., Edwards et al., 2020; Majd et al., 2009) have explored national data on sexual minority adults' (those who identify as lesbian, gay, and bisexual) interactions with the criminal justice system and found that sexual minority adults are 3 times more likely than heterosexual adults to be incarcerated. Previous research (Hirschel et al., 2007), utilizing 2005 data from 1,401 arrestees from 19 states, found that while arrests rates for opposite and same-sex couples were similar (ranging between 49.7% and 50.7%), there was a stark contrast for dual arrests. The dual arrest was 0.8% for female victims with male perpetrators and 3.0% for male victims with female perpetrators but 26%–27% for lesbian and gay couples. A more recent analysis of IPV arrests, Hirschel and McCormack (2021) found that this trend continues today. Researchers examined 10 years of data (2000–2009) and over 2,675,198 cases using the National Incident-Based Reporting Systems (NIBRS). They found IPV arrests were more likely to occur in opposite-sex couples (49.9%) compared to lesbian (43.7%) or gay (46.1%) couples. Moreover, when arrests were made, dual arrests were much more likely in same-sex couples (54.8% lesbians and 61.9% gays) than opposite-sex couples (2.9%). This is consistent with research from the National Coalition of Anti-Violence Programs (NCAVP) (2016) that showed that in 2015, 31% of same-sex IPV victims said they had been arrested rather than the abusive partner. These results demonstrate differential treatment and reveal the gravity of the extent of unjust arrests taking place for sexual minorities (Hirschel & McCormack, 2021).

IPV and domestic violence is not a gendered issue; it is a societal issue that can occur despite gender or sexual minority status. The stark contrast from crime studies and empirical research examining the prevalence and incidence of IPV boldly demonstrates the need for acknowledgment and reform in law enforcement and the criminal justice system.

Historically, societal views about domestic violence have largely been the result of political pressure for legal reform from women's rights groups and advocates in legal cases (*Bruno v. Codd*, 1977; *Scott v. Hart*, 1976; *Thurman v. City of Torrington*, 1984) that ultimately paved the way to contemporary law enforcement response.

THE FOUNDATION AND EVOLUTION OF THE LAW ENFORCEMENT RESPONSE

On the front lines of response to IPV are well-intentioned law enforcement officers doing their best to protect and serve victims and apprehend perpetrators. However, the history of police response to IPV has witnessed tremendous changes over the years. The criminalization of IPV is a relatively new phenomenon. The women's rights movements of the late 1800s began to shed light on the issue of domestic violence. Historically, arrests were discouraged as IPV was believed to be a matter dealt with exclusively within the family, with little objection to a man's use of physical force against his wife (Bruns et al., 2005; Martin, 1994). If an officer did respond to an IPV incident, they often acted as mediators between parties, separating the couple and recommending the offender "cool off" or get counseling. At the time, officers could not arrest unless the offense was a felony or committed in the officer's presence.

Public awareness of domestic violence became popular starting in the 1970s when there was an influence from the Battered Women's Movement. Women joined together and recognized three major contributors of domestic violence: economic disparity, traditional gender roles expectations, and a criminal justice system that did not hold men accountable (The Pennsylvania Child Welfare Resource Center, n.d.). In essence, domestic violence had been treated differently than any other form of assault, wherein officers called to the scene often refused to act, make an arrest, offer support, or render services simply because the perpetrator was the husband.

During the 1970s, the police and criminal courts were accused of being too lenient with IPV offenders. Feminists, activists, and advocates for domestic violence victims began to fight for legitimate police response in IPV incidents. Two legal cases calling for protection from their physically abusive partners, obtaining police protection, educating the criminal justice system about IPV, and treating IPV as any other crime or assault were heard in the late 1970s (*Scott v. Hart*, 1979; *Bruno v. Codd*, 1978). These cases led to limited discretion to refuse to arrest, monitoring provisions, or case dismissal. In October 1982, Charles Thurman attacked his wife, Tracey Thurman, and took their son, Charles Thurman Jr. He was sentenced to 6 months in prison, with a 2-year conditional discharge, and was ordered to stay away from Tracey and to commit no further crimes. Once released, Charles violated the conditions of his parole.

After countless attempts at contacting the Torrington Police Department regarding these violations, nothing was done. On June 10, 1983, Charles Thurman went to Tracey Thurman's residence, and Tracey called the police. Twenty-five minutes later, one police officer arrived at the scene to see Charles drop a knife, kick Tracey in the head, and run into the house. Charles had stabbed Tracey in the chest, neck, and throat. Charles proceeded to drop Charles Thurman Jr. on top of his mother and kick Tracey again. Even when more police officers arrived at the scene, they watched Charles kick Tracey and did not arrest him until he approached Tracey again, this time on the stretcher. The court found that Tracey was discriminated against because of a domestic dispute, and her civil rights were violated. Evidence showed that police provided consistently less protection when the victim was a woman or assaulted by a spouse. Tracey was awarded $2.3 million by the court. Because of *Thurman v. Torrington* (1984), the General Assembly passed the Family Violence Act in 1986. The new law defines family or household members to include spouses, former spouses, parents, individuals aged 18 years or older related by blood or marriage, and unrelated individuals aged 16 years or older who are either living together or who have lived together. The Family Violence Act created changes in police behavior to domestic disputes. The law prohibits police from considering the victim's relationship to the suspect and from discouraging requests for police intervention in domestic violence cases (C.G.S. § 46b-38b(a)). New training guidelines were created for police. The training must stress the enforcement of the criminal law in these cases and the use of community resources and include the nature and extent of family violence, the legal rights and remedies available to victims, and techniques for handling these cases by minimizing the likelihood of injury to the officers (C.G.S. § 46b-38b(f)).

Following the Thurman case, police agencies had also been successfully sued for having inadequate or nonexistent domestic violence training materials (*Ricketts v. Columbia*, 1993). In *Ricketts*, evidence was shown that police had been trained that it was permissible to provide a minimal response to domestic violence calls than to non–domestic violence calls. A 5-year review of arrests in that agency showed officers of Columbia, Missouri Police Department arrested 2 to 3 times more often in non–domestic violence assault cases than they did in domestic violence assault cases. This led to a $1.2 million settlement for the plaintiff.

Along with this awareness of domestic violence came continued criticism about how police were responding to calls of domestic violence. In essence, critics and advocates continued to assert that IPV offenders were not being arrested as often, prosecuted as vigorously, or sentenced as severely as other violent criminals (Davis & Smith, 1995). They also charged police officers minimized and even ignored IPV against women. The Violence Against Women Act was passed in 1996 in the United States to protect women from IPV with a more vigorous law enforcement response by fostering awareness of domestic violence and improving services and provisions for victims (Sacco, 2015). The main crimes targeted in the Violence Against Women Act included IPV, dating violence, sexual assault, and stalking. Since the passage of this act, changes have been made. In 2000, Congress added protection for abused foreign nationals and created more programs for elderly and disabled women (Sacco, 2015). In 2005, Congress increased penalties for repeat stalking offenders and added protection for battered and trafficked foreign nationals, as well as created additional programs (Sacco, 2015). In 2013, the Violence Against Women Act was again reauthorized and included sex trafficking; it also gave Indian tribes authority to enforce domestic violence laws. The new reauthorization of the Violence Against Women Act in 2021 will add a nondiscrimination requirement to guarantee protection for all victims regardless of gender. As a response to increased political pressure to take IPV more seriously and hold perpetrators accountable, most states and police departments created and implemented proarrest policies such as mandatory arrest or dominant/primary aggressor laws.

MANDATORY ARREST, PROARREST, AND DISCRETIONARY ARREST

In 1977, Oregon was the first state to enact a mandatory arrest law (Branch et al., 2018). This involved granting police officers the power to arrest for a misdemeanor that did not occur in their presence and often dictate an arrest must be made in an incident of IPV, regardless of whether the incident was minor, mutual, or without evidence of who initiated the offense (Davis, 2008). Further, "no drop" policies were enacted and unique in that they removed discretion from law enforcement officers and the victim. However, removing discretion from the victim can reduce the victim's empowerment, and the possibility of a dual arrest can lead victims to become more hesitant to report. A study examining the effects of this new approach (Sherman & Berk, 1984) demonstrated recidivism rates decreased 50% when arrests were made. Following law enforcement's concerns about liability and the promising effects of Sherman and Berk's (1984) study led to the adoption of mandatory arrest laws in 23 states (Hirschel et al., 2007). The rush to enact such laws came despite Sherman and Berk's (1984) reservations about this policy becoming a widespread practice until further research was conducted. In fact, Sherman's subsequent research (Sherman et al., 1991; Sherman & Harris, 2015) would come to find unintended effects of this practice led to greater abuse in poor and ethnic minority women, and the stress associated with a partner's arrest led women to suffer an early death. While some studies (Eitle, 2005; Hirschel et al., 2007) have found mandatory arrest reduces violence against women, other scholars continue to warn about the consequences and unintended effects of this approach. For example, while the widespread use of mandatory arrest removed discretion and assisted officers in responding more appropriately, it ultimately led to much higher arrest rates. Prior to mandatory arrest laws, arrest rates for IPV ranged between 7% and 15% but increased to 49% after it was enacted (Hirschel et al., 2007). Rates of arrest ultimately led to dramatic increases in female arrests as single perpetrators or in dual arrest (Chesney-Lind, 2002; DeLeon-Granados et al., 2006; Hirschel & Buzaawa, 2002), and they resulted in increased arrest rates for male victims. One study (Jones & Belknap, 1999) found that male victims in Boulder, Colorado, were over 3 times as likely to be a part of a dual-arrest couple than female victims.

Similarly, a Massachusetts study (Buzawa & Hotaling, 2000, 2006) found that when a male was the victim, females were 5 times less likely to be arrested than a male. While there were wide variations of female arrests among different states (typically between 5% and 33%), arrests in California increased an unprecedented 446%. Unintended effects of increased arrests also led to greater difficulty prosecuting these cases, as prosecutors had to sift out cases of "couple conflict" versus more serious cases of battering (Davis, 2008; Hamel, 2011), not to mention families who had been torn apart by losing custody of children in family court (Dutton et al., 2010). It was clear that modifications and corrective actions should be made to reduce victim arrests, so other forms of proarrest policies were considered. This problem ultimately led to backing off mandatory arrest and moving to primary/dominant aggressor or proarrest policies (Hamel, 2011; Stop Abusive and Violent Environments [SAVE], 2010).

Proarrest (or presumptive arrest) policies encourage an arrest is made; however, officers are not required to make arrests, even when probable cause is evident (Goodmark, 2018), providing a small amount of discretion not to make an arrest.

States worked closely with feminists and advocates for battered women to push for primary/dominant aggressor guidelines that sought to decrease the number of victim arrests and consider the relationship behind the assault (DeLeon-Granados et al., 2006). This law would encourage officers to identify the most significant aggressor or the one that poses the most serious threat (not necessarily the first aggressor), which directly contrasts with how police respond to their crimes (Davis, 2008). While each state's definition of primary aggressor may be different, the International Association of Chiefs of Police (IACP, 2018) presented a model policy for domestic violence that included 21 elements of consideration when determining the predominant aggressor. These elements included who uses threats and intimidation in the relationships; whether isolation or emotional abuse is present; use of minimization, blame, or denial; using children to get their way; control of finances; use of coercion/threats; history of committing violent offenses; physical size differences; whether one of the parties has an existing or prior protection order; who appears more capable of assaulting the other; injury severity and whether injuries were offensive or defensive; whether self-defense was used; who has the potential of future violence; the existence of firearms or weapons; who expresses fear; and evidence provided by witnesses.

Unfortunately, not all these criteria correlate with perpetration, and no formula has yet to be described for how they should be weighed (Hamel, 2011). Moreover, officer response depends upon several issues, including legal and extralegal factors (Mele, 2018). Legal factors can include many factors such as immediate or future risk and victim fear (Trujillo & Ross, 2008), victim injury (Feder, 1998), the seriousness of the offense, and criminal history (Buzawa & Hotaling, 2000). However, when we combine legal elements associated with the identification of a primary aggressor with extralegal factors (gender, race, relationship status, socioeconomic status, etc.), it becomes much more difficult to disentangle the legal from the extralegal.

Scholars (Hamel, 2011; Hamel & Russell, 2013) have noted that many of these elements are inherently vague. For example, Hamel (2011) noted it was uncertain whether "dominant aggressor" should refer to who dominates the relationship or who is dominant during the incident. To further complicate matters, our gendered perceptions can implicitly affect officer decision-making. For example, research consistently finds that male-to-female IPV is perceived as more serious, more likely to induce fear of injury, and lead to greater injury (Rhatigan et al., 2011; Russell & Kraus, 2016) compared to female-to-male or same-sex IPV (Felson & Feld, 2009; Hamby & Jackson, 2010; Russell & Kraus, 2016; Seelau & Seelau, 2005). Masculinity is also associated with dominance and has been related to a greater likelihood of arousing fear in an IPV victim and leading to increased blame (Russell & Sturgeon, 2019). While criminal history and IPV are related (Gondolf, 1996), it is unclear whether such history should include arrests, convictions, or phone calls (Hamel, 2011).

Even consideration of past and future harm can be influenced by gender. Research (Russell, 2018) examining police officers' perceptions of past and future harm showed that police officers believed heterosexual male IPV perpetrators were a greater threat of danger than female heterosexual and same-sex couples. Both lesbian and heterosexual male perpetrators were believed to have inflicted harm to their partner in the past while female heterosexual perpetrators were least likely to be perceived as having inflicted physical harm in the past. Officers were also more likely to rate victims of female perpetrators as more likely to inflict harm in the future. The inherent problems with physical size also render men more likely to be suspected as the dominant aggressor simply because they are typically larger and stronger than women and have the potential of causing physical injury. However, it does not necessarily mean they always use this to their advantage (Hamel, 2011). These questions and empirical findings place men at a disadvantage when presumptions are made to identify the primary aggressor.

The issue of physical size certainly can lead to greater difficulties identifying the primary aggressor in cases of IPV in same-sex couples. Despite which proarrest policies or the extent to which discretion is used, our biases and gendered beliefs can lead to difficulty identifying the primary aggressor and increasing dual or no arrests. Stereotypes and assumptions surrounding same-sex couples suggest perpetrators and victims would be of equal strength and size, and IPV among lesbian couples would be considered less serious (Hassouneh & Glass, 2008; Ristock, 2002). Durfee and Goodmark (2020) examined arrest rates of same-sex and opposite-sex couples and race/ethnicity, comparing mandatory and proarrest laws. They found that gay male couples were more likely to be arrested under mandatory arrest laws than proarrest or discretionary arrest laws. Incidents in same-sex couples with Black victims were less likely to lead to arrest compared to White victims. This is evidence of how our biases and social stereotypes associated with perpetrators and victims of IPV undoubtedly influence decisions of arrest. Studies suggest these stereotypes are alive and well in law enforcement response to IPV.

Social Stereotypes and Law Enforcement Response to Intimate Partner Violence

Studies in the general population have found that IPV perpetrated by a heterosexual male is considered more serious and in need of reporting and intervention compared to IPV perpetrated by heterosexual females and those in same-sex relationships (Archer, 2000; Felson & Cares, 2005; Poorman et al., 2003; Sorenson & Thomas, 2009). Others have found that men who assault women are blamed or sentenced more often than female perpetrators (Poorman et al., 2003; Ragatz & Russell, 2010; Rhatigan et al., 2011; Russell et al., 2009, 2010; Sorenson & Taylor, 2005). In fact, violence against women regardless of sexual orientation is considered more serious (Poorman et al., 2003; Seelau & Seelau, 2005; Sorenson & Thomas, 2009). Heterosexual women and those in same-sex relationships are less likely to be perceived as perpetrators of IPV, and their assaultive behaviors are considered less illegal than heterosexual males (Sorenson & Thomas, 2009). Researchers have demonstrated that this consistent bias over time can undoubtedly affect first responders' responses to IPV incidents. However, the research on rates of arrest is mixed. While some earlier studies have found evidence suggesting male perpetrators are arrested more than female perpetrators (Buzawa & Hotaling, 2000; Durfee, 2012; Felson & Pare, 2007; Tjaden & Thoennes, 2000), other studies have found no effect of offender/victim gender on arrest decisions (Eitle, 2005; Ho, 2003; Jones & Belknap, 1999; Pattavina et al., 2007; Simpson et al., 2006). However, studies find greater leniency in the adjudicative process for women following arrest (Henning & Feder, 2005). Nevertheless, an officer's response during an IPV incident can make or break trust within its community and ultimately lead to a victim's willingness to report IPV. Stereotypes and lack of resources for heterosexual male and sexual minority victims leave them much less likely to report IPV.

The relationship between the LGBTQ+ community and the criminal justice system is tenuous at best. Differential treatment by sexual orientation and gender identity persists in delivery systems designed to assist victims of violence, including screening, access to programs, therapeutic interventions, shelters, and prevention programs. Perpetrators of violence also face differential treatment in both the legal and prison system (Brown & McDuffie, 2009). LGBTQ+ individuals continue to experience bias and discrimination regularly because of their sexual minority identity (Herek et al., 2007). Although resources and services for IPV victims, in general, have increased, there remains an extreme shortage of LGBTQ+-affirming resources for sexual and gender minority victims. Homophobic beliefs and reliance on victims' and offenders' stereotypes can lead to discriminatory police practices and subsequent mistrust of police officers (Russell & Torres, 2020). When the police respond to an IPV incident, studies have detailed how responding officers often act inappropriately or insensitively toward the victims by not using preferred gender pronouns, not taking same-sex IPV seriously, and an overall failure to recognize an incident as IPV (Guadalupe-Diaz & Jasinski, 2017; Langenderfer-Magruder et al., 2016). Sexual minority victims are often arrested along with their abusers, and few culturally competent advocates are available to help them navigate the criminal justice system (Los Angeles Gay and Lesbian Community Center, 2010). Similarly, pervasive beliefs/myths about male power and control dictate that men cannot be victims of IPV, and this can easily lead to inequality in criminal justice response.

Such mistrust breeds reluctance to report IPV incidents. Studies examining help seeking (Kay & Jeffries, 2010; Langenderfer-Magruder et al., 2016) in sexual minority populations found participants were reluctant to involve law enforcement for fear of discrimination. Therefore, they only considered doing so in more extreme circumstances. Incidents where police were called revealed detailed responses of how law enforcement acted inappropriately or callously toward victims or generally failed to recognize an incident as IPV (Ciarlante & Fountain, 2010; Guadalupe-Diaz & Jasinski, 2017).

Research on police perceptions of sexual minorities in IPV incidents has demonstrated that officers also adhere to these gender biases and stereotypes. Two studies (Russell, 2018; Russell & Sturgeon, 2019) examined police perceptions of an IPV perpetrator and victim in terms of culpability, risk of harm/injury, credibility, and arrest options (mediation, providing informal advice, threats to arrest, arrest). Results found that officers considered nonarrest options fairer when the perpetrator was gay or a heterosexual female. Officers also rated injury severity higher when the perpetrator was a heterosexual male and the victim was a heterosexual female. These findings were not influenced by the frequency or recency of officer IPV training, suggesting training had minimal, if any, effect as biases continue to seep into the decision-making process. Additional findings showed that heterosexual men were perceived as a greater threat of danger than gay male lesbian or heterosexual female perpetrators, and gay and female heterosexual perpetrators were least likely to be perceived as harming their partner in the past. The study also found that victims of female perpetrators were considered more responsible for the IPV incident while victims of male perpetrators were considered more credible.

Additional research by Franklin et al. (2019) examined 467 officers' perceptions about an IPV incident utilizing vignettes manipulating sexual orientation (heterosexual couple male perpetrator, lesbian couple, and a gay couple) and physical evidence in decisions to arrest. The researchers also examined the extent to which officers endorsed homophobic attitudes and heteronormative myths about IPV. The authors found that arrest was less likely when the couple was same sex. While the authors found some adherence to homophobia, this did not interact with arrest decisions. In contrast, while officers did not firmly adhere to IPV myths, those who did adhere to heteronormative IPV myths were less likely to arrest after controlling for victim cooperation and physical evidence. So how do we train law enforcement officers to recognize the gender paradigm embedded within the social system and work to ensure equal justice in IPV? The following section addresses some movement toward gender-neutral terminology and officer training.

Officer Training and Intimate Partner Violence

Although domestic violence is a complex problem, it becomes even more complicated as states vary in their definition of domestic violence. Many states have resorted to using broad definitions of domestic violence, battery, simple assault, and aggravated assault in family violence contexts. Most states also include broad definitions, including stalking, harassment, and even nonphysical abuse such as intimidation and psychological abuse. To create a judicial system where all victims and perpetrators are acknowledged, definitions must align. Pressure for reform has led states to more gender-neutral definitions of IPV. For example, Texas's definition of the relationship between domestic violence victim and offender is as follows: "by one family member against another . . . family violence also includes abuse against a family or household member and dating violence" (Texas Family Code §§ 71.004; 261.001(1); 71.0021(a)). Other states include definitions that specifically include the sharing of a child (Arizona, California, Florida, Georgia, Kansas, New York, North Carolina, Utah, and Wisconsin). (For more information on each state's definition, see the National Conference of State Legislatures State Laws on Domestic Violence or Abuse [NCSL].)

While there is very little empirical research on officer training in IPV, empirical research suggests that many police departments continue to rely on the gender paradigm for their training materials and generally do not include or rely upon contemporary empirical research (Hamel & Russell, 2013). Training is often provided by academy staff and or domestic violence advocates who may or may not be familiar with empirical research. Often specific modules are provided academy or continuing education training on the topic of IPV. However, scholars (Eigenberg et al., 2012) who have conducted IPV training for officers believe training experiences tend to focus almost exclusively on intimate terrorism. The most common form of IPV is "situational couple violence" (Kelly & Johnson, 2008; also see Hamel et al., Chapter 6, this volume), which comprises the majority (66%-75% of IPV incidents). These types of incidents may include one or both partners and can lead to behaviors such as pushing, shoving, and so on, but rarely result in injury. One study examining the seriousness of IPV incidents found that most IPV arrests were misdemeanors (Buttell & Carney, 2008).

In contrast, the more severe and dangerous type of IPV is "intimate terrorism" (Kelly & Johnson, 2008), which includes patterns of physical abuse, use of coercive control, and emotional abuse. While there are distinct differences in the motivations, patterns, and use of each type of IPV, it is essential to note that many incidents of police response to IPV may not necessarily fall into the latter category. However, police training rarely acknowledges the important nuances and distinctions between the two forms of IPV. As Abraham Maslow stated, "If all you have is a hammer, everything looks like a nail."

However, while police officers realize women can be abusive, they are not offered the contextual framework to distinguish between "intimate terrorism" and "situational couple violence" (for more information, see Hamel et al., Chapter 6, this volume). Officers are often not instructed about the nature of mutual violence and the various forms of IPV and often turn to focus on who is most at risk for serious injury (Eigenberg et al., 2012).

While the IACP provides guidance on evidence collection, officers do not routinely collect evidence in IPV incidents (Belknap et al., 2000; Eigenberg et al., 2012). For instance, some officers do not take photos of injuries (Deutsch et al., 2017), and while some injuries may be apparent when first responders arrive, other injuries may not be apparent until days later. This can also influence the perceived seriousness of the offense. Durfee and Goodmark (2019) found that incidents with Black victims led to fewer arrests, but this can also be attributed to the visibility of injuries as some injuries are more apparent in lighter-skinned individuals (Deutsch et al., 2017). Cases should use an evidence-based process to include witness statements, crime scene evidence, injury pattern evidence, and so on. However, in many cases, such evidence is not collected and presented, which can lead to deadly consequences. For example, the first author of this chapter testified in a trial where the defendant was in a same-sex relationship. The defendant had made previous calls to the police preceding the incident and a request for a protection order (which was denied). In one report by a law enforcement officer, the claimant stated his partner had a handgun and placed it to his head, playing roulette multiple times. The officer phoned the partner, who denied having a gun. Both had been drinking; the officer took no action because the officer believed there was no probable cause a crime had occurred. There were no witness accounts, photos of injuries, or follow-ups. Unfortunately, this case ultimately led to homicide a month later.

Officers' personal characteristics (gender, academy training, and experience) can also shape how they interpret and handle an IPV incident. For instance, Saunders (1980) used scenarios of IPV depicting male-to-female violence to examine officer characteristics associated with decisions to arrest or the use of minimal actions (general referrals, warnings) or informal (mediation, referrals, etc.). Results showed that officers who endorsed a more masculine sex role and had less training in family crisis identity were more likely to make arrests while undifferentiated sex-role identity and family crisis training related to the choice of minimal action. Additional research (Russell & Sturgeon, 2019; Stalans & Finn, 1995) also found that older, more experienced officers chose fewer legal options to resolve the issue, while younger, less experienced officers were more likely to choose arrest. Experienced officers tended to perceive victims who conformed to social norms as more credible and less dangerous. Further, mental illness and the use of alcohol also influence the extent to which officers provide information about domestic violence shelters and mental health treatment (Stalans & Finn, 1995). Lastly, Farris and Holman's (2015) research found that sheriffs who endorse victim-blaming myths about violence against women are less likely to enact mandatory arrest policies or encourage their deputies to complete training on sexual assault and IPV response.

While there have been substantial changes in officer IPV training over the years, there is much more to be done. In 2011, Hamel conducted an in-depth content analysis of the California POST manual (California Commission on Peace Officer Standards and Training, 2010) and the State of Maine's training manuals. As a state with primary/dominant aggressor laws, he noted officers were provided with little to no instructions to determine the relative importance of each criterion. He also examined the use of gender-neutral language within the manuals and found gendered language was primarily used in both training manuals suggesting males were the primary aggressors. For example, the California manual included 34 training examples of male-to-female IPV. However, only one example demonstrated female-to-male IPV, one for a lesbian couple and one for mutual abuse, and 7 out of 8 of Maine's training examples suggested the male perpetrator should be arrested as the primary aggressor.

Hamel and Russell (2013) further investigated how gendered language was used in definitions, criteria, and training examples provided to aid in identifying the primary aggressor. Law enforcement academy training materials for domestic violence were obtained from 16 of the 23 states with primary aggressor laws. Researchers found that 44% of states used the term "battered woman" or "women who are battered" throughout the manuals. While some manuals had disclaimer statements that males were not always abusers and females were not always the victim and that IPV can occur in same-sex relationships, the manuals did not suggest how an officer should handle those situations, nor was this mentioned subsequently within the manuals. All states but one included information on power and control specifically within heterosexual relationships, and only one state included three scholarly references (out of 31 resources). Of the 17 training examples used to assist officers in identifying the dominant aggressor in three unilateral examples, one was a female aggressor, and two were a male aggressor. In 12 bilateral examples, the man was deemed the dominant aggressed and targeted for arrest in 75% of situations, and one example included a same-sex couple.

In yet another study, Tesch et al. (2010) surveyed officers in five towns in Illinois to examine IPV officer knowledge of training, policies, and procedures related to IPV encounters with the LGBTQ+ community. Even though officers had regular encounters with this population, 81% knew of no departmental procedures addressing the specifics of same-sex IPV calls, and over 70% had no official training in LGBTQ+ IPV situations. While a few law enforcement departments have created policies and procedures regarding interaction with sexual minorities, most of these policies offer little information regarding the needs of sexual minorities. Complaints made by sexual minorities about the discrimination and police misconduct against LGBTQ+ individuals led to recommendations in the Williams Institute Report (Mallory et al., 2015). These recommendations suggest that state and local departments adopt internal policies and practices that include outreach and liaisons to the LGBTQ+ community and provide sensitivity and diversity training to police officers. Many of the pitfalls in service provider response within the criminal justice system begin with training. Ford et al. (2013) found low levels of training for outreach staff, failure to document sexual orientation or gender identity, and that they utilized practices that did not consider the unique needs of the LGBTQ+ clients that proved detrimental to victims and survivors in the community. Officers may feel woefully unprepared to assess the needs of LGBTQ+ victims.

Officer-Involved Domestic Violence

Just as discretion can play a role in decisions based on gender, sexual orientation, race, and so on, police often use discretion when policing themselves. If we seek to become more inclusive, then that includes IPV among law enforcement officers. Although the IACP has developed model policies for officer-involved domestic violence (OIDV), little is known about the extent to which agencies have adopted these policies. Early studies of OIDV have found that somewhere between 24% (Neidig et al., 1992) and 40% (Johnson, 1991; Neidig et al., 1992) of officer families experience domestic violence. OIDV statistics can be alarming to the public and propagate mistrust, calling for transparency and accountability of police misconduct. Russell and Tannenbaum (2016) obtained data from 299 officers in 27 states. They found that more than half (51.3%, $n = 156$) reported that they had been called to respond to a domestic violence incident that involved another law enforcement officer. Based on these findings, OIDV is a common occurrence, but it remains challenging to understand OIDV due to a lack of information. Victims of OIDV are in a precarious situation because their abuser knows local shelter locations and training with firearms. Domestic violence victims of law enforcement are a particularly vulnerable population. Victims of IPV perpetrators may also fear their accusations will not be taken seriously by officers or prosecutors, resulting in a lack of reporting.

Research suggests that penalties for OIDV remain lenient and rarely result in unemployment (Domestic Violence Task Force, 1997). Stinson and Liederbach (2012) analyzed 324 cases of OIDV that resulted in arrests between 2005 and 2007. Only 32% of officers had lost their jobs, and in 40% of cases, simple assault was the most severe charge. More often, these officers were charged with much lesser offenses to avoid an assault charge. It is suggested that OIDV is often pled down to avoid assault charges because of the Lautenberg Amendment (Stinson & Liederbach, 2012). The Lautenberg Amendment (1996) refers to a federal gun control act that prohibits individuals (including officers) from owning or using a gun if they have been convicted of the misdemeanor crime of domestic violence. An officer who has a misdemeanor charge of domestic violence could therefore be dismissed from the police department. It is crucial to consider the limitations of OIDV studies before making a broad generalization. Little is known about the outcomes of OIDV cases, and each state has its own statutes, definitions, and charges associated with domestic violence. Furthermore, management information systems, early intervention systems, officer training, intervention, and prevention in OIDV vary among states. The IACP recognized some of these issues while creating a model policy to attempt to encourage a more standardized approach to domestic violence.

In 1999, the IACP National Law Enforcement Policy Center enacted The Model Policy on Police Officer Domestic Violence. This model is currently used throughout the United States and consists of six tenets: prevention, education and training, early warning and intervention, incident response protocols, victim safety and protection, and postincident administrative/criminal case actions. According to this model policy, those training for OIDV should affiliate with domestic violence professionals in their community, complete at least 40 hours of baseline training, communicate effectively with police dispatchers, and receive proper instruction. Some states have adopted their own model policy, but although these guidelines do exist, research demonstrates that many police departments are hesitant to adopt and reinforce these policies (Cheema, 2016). With only a tiny portion of agencies adopting and reinforcing OIDV policies, there is a gap within the justice system, resulting in a wide variation in response tactics. Police may be less likely to report their colleague when they know that an arrest may prohibit them from using a firearm and jeopardize their job (Lonsway, 2006). Unfortunately, there is little information about the extent to which officers are reporting known incidents of suspicions of OIDV to supervisors or internal affairs. When considering candidates for employment, it is important to conduct background checks and psychological examinations to identify violent or abusive tendencies (Russell & Pappas, 2018). While departments have adopted a "zero-tolerance" policy for all law enforcement agency employees, some question the effectiveness of this method of handling OIDV (Wetendorf & Davis, 2003). However, there is hope that training in OIDV can assist officers in identifying behaviors associated with domestic violence.

Traditional academy training and education rarely provide in-depth information on responding to OIDV (Russell & Pappas, 2018). According to Wetendorf and Davis (2003), effective training on OIDV should include specific issues, specifically understanding issues with victim vulnerability and how police subculture can influence willingness to report an abusive colleague. Effective training should also stress ethics, professional decision-making, victim assistance and safety, making referrals, and prioritizing victim safety in response to alleged OIDV (Oehme et al., 2016; Wetendorf & Davis, 2003). Although training and resources to prevent OIDV are becoming more accessible, they are underutilized despite little research that suggests it is beneficial through implementation. Additional research is needed to identify whether OIDV training results in higher reporting rates and leads to a reduction in OIDV. Despite guidelines such as the model policy, agencies lack uniformity in their adoption and implementation of policies, training, and reports of OIDV. A more uniform approach would allow for valuable data and greater transparency by standardization of terminology and conditionality. Currently, there is no government agency or state or national data repository collecting information on OIDV, despite the suspected prevalence of this phenomenon.

Police Officer Discretion and Additional Considerations

It is evident that since proarrest policies have been enacted, despite efforts toward change, further improvement is sorely needed to accommodate all victims of IPV and ensure equal justice. When we think about police response, there is a great deal of discretion leading to decisions of arrest and charging. Officers must first decide whether to take official action when a suspect is identified and then decide which action(s) to take. However, in cases of IPV, sometimes just identifying the suspect can be difficult. Legal actors may be especially vulnerable to bias in incidents that are more ambiguous, less severe, and nonphysical (see Cox et al., Chapter 4, this volume). Of course, injuries will be examined, but sometimes it is difficult to determine self-defense injuries from other forms of injury (Hamel, 2011). Officers work with danger on a regular basis, and IPV incidents are typically perceived as dangerous if there is physical evidence (Barlow & Walklate, 2020). However, many other IPV factors that should be considered can be minimized or simply not recognized as potential risk behaviors for future harm (Medina et al., 2016). For example, Myhill (2017) found that police officers had difficulty identifying coercive controlling, abusive behaviors. Further, if individuals are the same size, strength, and status, how is the primary aggressor determined (Hamel, 2011;

Hamel & Russell, 2013)? This has been, no doubt, difficult for officers as research consistently finds more arrests are made in opposite-sex couples compared to same-sex couples, and when arrests are made in same-sex IPV incidents, they are dual arrests (Hirschel et al., 2007; Hirschel & McCormack, 2021). Moreover, the ways in which a victim interacts with officers can influence their risk of future harm. When victims are ignored or minimized, they are less likely to report future violence and mistrust law enforcement (Ciarlante & Fountain, 2010; Guadalupe-Diaz & Jasinski, 2017; Medina et al., 2016). Simply identifying a primary aggressor upon a set of vague criteria may not be sufficient, particularly when officers are not informed about some of the unique issues related to male and sexual minority victimization.

Officers can take many different paths of official action (Shernock, 2005; Shernock & Russell, 2012). They can choose to charge the offender with IPV and issue a citation rather than arrest or taking a suspect into custody. They can also choose to arrest for other reasons such as disorderly conduct, violation of protection order, or release. Finally, officers must determine whether the incident constitutes simple or aggravated assault. Choosing one direction or another simply because of one's gender and sexual orientation can lead to differential response and treatment at every rung within the criminal justice system. This is evident in research studies that suggest that while IPV arrests among men and women in opposite-sex couples are about equal, women are treated more leniently in subsequent legal proceedings. For example, Henning and Feder (2005) found that female and minority defendants were more likely to be released on their own recognizance (ROR). Females were more likely to be ROR, more likely to have their charges dropped by the prosecutor, less likely to be convicted, and when convicted, received shorter sentences. This demonstrates the need to carefully consider dispositions in each incident as it can affect victim safety.

One could say that that to minimize potential bias, we could tighten the reins of law enforcement decision-making to reduce discretion. However, mandatory arrest laws have demonstrated similar problems to that of states with greater discretion. A policy can also encroach upon discretion (Myhill & Johnson, 2016) and does not always lead to actual changes within the natural landscape, patterns, and culture of policing (Henry & Smith, 2007).

Stark (2012) noted it is not discretion itself but rather police understanding of IPV. Training is essential and can go a long way in helping police better understand IPV. For example, providing greater clarity and instruction in police training and implementation may be helpful (Hamel, 2011), but will this assist in the process of inclusion if we do not get to the root of the problem? To do so would entail reshaping and rethinking our paradigm foundations about IPV and restructuring our academy and law enforcement officer curriculums to become more inclusive. Law enforcement personnel should be instructed on emerging research and encouraged to reflect on their own personal biases (see Cox et al., Chapter 4, this volume). However, the extent to which training alone can solve the underlying gendered based attitudes associated with IPV and inappropriate use of discretion is challenging, given the belief of some officers who minimize IPV or believe it is a waste of police time (Barlow & Walklate, 2020; Buzawa & Buzawa, 1996). Education and training can provide "guidance" for police about legal changes and assist in understanding and implementing procedural issues (Waddington, 2012), but it is doubtful this can translate into attitude change and appreciation for the seriousness of IPV (Barlow & Walklate, 2020). Perhaps attitude change is exactly what should be examined in future research. Some researchers (i.e., Franklin et al., 2019) examined homophobia and heteronormative myths about IPV and found no effects of homophobia. However, their results revealed that officers endorsing heteronormative myths were less likely to arrest.

Additionally, Bruns and colleagues (2005) examined 266 police academy recruits who were provided with pre-posttraining scores on IPV general knowledge, victim blame, and sexist beliefs as measured by the Ambivalent Sexism Inventory (Glick & Fiske, 1996). Their results found that general knowledge increased from pretest to posttest, and officers were less likely to endorse victim blame. However, officer's level of sexism influenced the knowledge they retained. General knowledge increased significantly more for nonsexist recruits compared to recruits that embraced ambivalent sexist attitudes. These results emphasize the need to address how awareness of sexism and their own biases can influence how they respond to victims of crime.

Young et al. (2006) provided possible recommendations to evolve IPV criminal justice response and policy further. The authors suggest finding ways to distinguish between serious and situational couple violence and battering, and they encourage more research on the consequences of mandatory and presumptive arrest policies and consideration of the victim's plea to not prosecute when no serious injury has occurred. Also, initial response could be provided by a specialized team of trained community professionals who could have access to prior calls, as well as reporting agencies that could serve as intermediaries to assess the situation and determine physical danger, the extent to which additional action is necessary, and alternatives to arrest. Further, to control potential misuse of restraining orders in divorce or child custody cases, expedited evidentiary hearings can be held shortly after a restraining order is issued to ensure the legitimacy of the order. In the same regard, in cases of mutual abuse, the court can order temporary shared custody and assessments of both parties. Lastly, while government and advocacy groups have played an integral part in creating IPV policy, advocacy groups should not be the only voices. Policy changes are best informed by involving many individuals, including LGBTQ+ groups, scholars, mental health professionals, and criminologists.

Efforts toward changing the criminal justice response will require the community's involvement and changes in the ways officers think about IPV. This is not just a first-responder discretionary issue, as the path toward recognizing and responding to IPV within the criminal justice system is filled with discretion. Suppose we hope for officers and others within the criminal justice system to be accountable and utilize discretion in ways that ensure justice. In that case, this should include all aspects of societal social services, including resources for all victims and the criminal justice system's accountability in terms of criminal and civil law.

REFERENCES

Archer, J. (2000). Sex differences in aggression between heterosexual partners: A meta-analytic review. *Psychological Bulletin, 126*, 651–680. https://psycnet.apa.org/doi/10.1037/0033-2909.126.5.651

Barlow, C., & Walklate, S. (2020). Policing intimate partner violence: The "Golden Thread" of discretion. *Policing: A Journal of Policy and Practice, 14*(2), 404–413. https://doi.org/10.1093/police/pay001

Belknap, J., Graham, D., Hartman, J., Lippend, V., Allen, G., & Sutherland, J. (2000). *Factors related to domestic violence court dispositions in a large urban area: The role of victim/witness reluctance and other variables.* U.S. Department of Justice, National Institutes of Justice.

Branch, K. A., Khan, S., & Dretsch, E. (2018). Same sex intimate partner violence. In *Contemporary issues in victimology: Identifying patterns and trends* (pp. 115–130).

Breiding, M. J., Chen, J., & Walters, M. L. (2013). The National Intimate Partner and Sexual Violence Survey (NISVS). 2010 findings on victimization by sexual orientation.

Brown, G. R., & McDuffie, E. (2009). Health care policies addressing transgender inmates in prison systems in the United States. *Journal of Correctional Health Care, 15*(4), 280–291. https://doi.org/10.1177/1078345809340423

Bruno v. Codd, 396 N.Y.S. 2d 974, 976–77 (Sup.Ct. 1977). https://1-next-westlaw-com.ezaccess.libraries.psu.edu/Link/Document/FullText?findType=Y&serNum=1977128032&pubNum=602&originatingDoc=I768786e04a6411dba16d88fb847e95e5&refType=RP&originationContext=document&transitionType=DocumentItem&ppcid=989df378252f4741a1d7057054402c37&contextData=(sc.Recommended)

Bruns, D., Russell, B., Bruni, J., & Fuller, J. (2005). Domestic violence training: Are sexism and victim blame mediators in training? *The Canadian Journal of Police & Security Services, 3*(3), 161–174.

Buttell, F., & Carney, M. (2008). A large sample investigation of batterer intervention program attrition: Evaluating the impact of state program standards. *Research on Social Work Practice, 22*, 20–28. doi:10.1177/1049731508314277

Buttell, F., & Star, E. (2013). Lifting the veil: Foundations for a gender-inclusive paradigm of intimate partner violence. In B. Russell (Ed.), *Perceptions of female offenders* (pp. 117–132). Springer. https://doi.org/10.1007/978-1-4614-5871-5_8

Buzawa, E., & Buzawa, C. G. (1996). *Do arrests and restraining orders work?* Sage.

Buzawa, E., & Hotaling, G. (2000). *The police response to domestic violence calls for assistance in three Massachusetts towns: Final report.* National Institute of Justice.

Buzawa, E., & Hotaling, G. (2006). The impact of relationship status, gender, and minor status in the police response to domestic assaults. *Victims & Offenders, 1*(1), 323–360. doi:10.1080/15564880600798681

Carney, M., Buttell, F., & Dutton, D. (2006). Women who perpetrate intimate partner violence: A review of the literature with recommendations for treatment. *Aggression and Violent Behavior, 12*, 108–115. https://doi.org/10.1016/j.avb.2006.05.002

Cheema, R. (2016). Black and blue bloods: Protecting police officer families from domestic violence. *Family Court Review, 54*(3), 487–500. https://doi.org/10.1111/fcre.12226

Chen, J., Walters, M. L., Gilbert, L. K., & Patel, N. (2020). Sexual violence, stalking, and intimate partner violence by sexual orientation, United States. *Psychology of Violence, 10*(1), 110–119. https://doi.org/10.1037/vio0000252

Chesney-Lind, M. (2002). Criminalizing victimization: The unintended consequences of pro-arrest policies for girls and women. *Criminology & Public Policy, 2*, 81–90.

Ciarlante, M., & Fountain, K. (2010). *Why it matters: Rethinking victim assistance for lesbian, gay, bisexual, transgender, and queer victims of hate violence and intimate partner violence.* The National Center for Victims of Crime, the National Coalition of Anti-Violence Programs.

Davis, R. C., O'Sullivan, C. S., Farole, D. J., & Rempel, M. (2008). A comparison of two prosecution policies in cases of intimate partner violence: Mandatory case filing versus following the victim's lead. *Criminology & Public Policy, 7*, 633–662. https://doi.org/10.1111/j.1745-9133.2008.00532.x

Davis, R. C., & Smith, B. (1995). Domestic violence reforms: Empty promises or fulfilled expectations. *Crime & Delinquency, 41*, 541–552. https://doi.org/10.1177%2F0011128795041004010

DeLeon-Granados, W., Wells, W., & Binsbacher, R. (2006). Arresting developments: Trends in female arrests for domestic violence and proposed explanations. *Violence Against Women, 12*, 355–371. https://doi.org/10.1177/1077801206287315

Deutsch, L. S., Resch, K., Barber, T., Zuckerman, Y., Stone, J. T., & Cerulli, C. (2017). Bruise documentation, race and barriers to seeking legal relief for intimate partner violence survivors: A retrospective qualitative study. *Journal of Family Violence, 32*(8), 767–773. https://doi.org/10.1007/s10896-017-9917-4

Dobash, R. E., Dobash, E., Wilson, M., & Daley, M. (1992). The myth of sexual symmetry in marital violence. *Social Problems, 39*, 71–91. https://doi.org/10.2307/3096914

Domestic Violence Task Force. (1997). *Domestic violence in Los Angeles Police Department: How well does the Los Angeles Police Department police its own?* Office of the Inspector General.

Durfee, A. (2012). Situational ambiguity and gendered patterns of arrest for intimate partner violence. *Violence Against Women, 18*(1), 64–84. https://doi.org/10.1177%2F1077801212437017

Durfee, A., & Goodmark, L. (2020). Gender, protection orders, and intimate partner violence in later life: A study of protective order filings in Arizona. *Journal of Interpersonal Violence, 36*(21–22), 10479–10498. doi:10.1177/0886260519884688

Dutton, D. G., Hamel, J., & Aaronson, J. (2010). The gender paradigm in family court processes: Re-balancing the scales of justice from biased social science. *Journal of Child Custody, 7*(1), 1–31. https://doi.org/10.1080/15379410903554816

Dutton, D. G., & Nicholls, T. L. (2005). The gender paradigm in domestic violence research and theory: The conflict of theory and data. *Aggression and Violent Behavior, 10*(6), 680–714. https://doi.org/10.1016/j.avb.2005.02.001

Edwards, K. M., Shorey, R. C., & Glozier, K. (2020). Primary prevention of intimate partner violence among sexual and gender minorities. In B. Russell (Ed.), *Intimate partner violence and the LGBT+ community* (pp. 161–176). Springer. https://doi.org/10.1007/978-3-030-44762-5_9

Eigenberg, H. M., Kappeler, V. E., & McGuffee, K. (2012). Confronting the complexities of domestic violence: Social prescription for rethinking police training. *Journal of Police Crisis Negotiations, 12*(2), 122–145. https://doi.org/10.1080/15332586.2012.717045

Eitle, D. (2005). The influence of mandatory arrest policies, police organizational characteristics, and situational variables on the probability of arrest in domestic violence cases. *Crime & Delinquency, 51*, 573–597. https://doi.org/10.1177%2F0011128705277784

Farris, E. M., & Holman, M. R. (2015). Public officials and a "private" matter: Evaluations and policies in the county sheriff office regarding violence against women. *Social Science Quarterly, 96*(4), 1117–1135. https://doi.org/10.1111/ssqu.12182

Feder, L. (1998). Police handling of domestic and non-domestic assault calls: Is there a case for discrimination? *Crime & Delinquency, 44*(2), 335–349. https://doi.org/10.1177%2F0011128798044002009

Felson, R. B., & Cares, A. C. (2005). Gender and the seriousness of assaults on intimate partners and other victims. *Journal of Marriage and Family, 67*(5), 1182–1195. https://doi.org/10.1111/j.1741-3737.2005.00209.x

Felson, R. B., & Feld, S. L. (2009). When a man hits a woman: Moral evaluations and reporting violence to the police. *Aggressive Behavior, 35*(6), 477–488. https://doi.org/10.1002/ab.20323

Felson, R. B., & Pare, P. (2007). Does the criminal justice system treat domestic violence and sexual assault offenders leniently? *Justice Quarterly, 24*, 435–459. https://doi.org/10.1080/07418820701485601

Ford, C. L., Slavin, T., Hilton, K. L., & Holt, S. L. (2013). Intimate partner violence prevention services and resources in Los Angeles: Issues, needs and challenges for assisting lesbian, gay, bisexual and transgender clients. *Health Promotion Practice, 14*(6), 841–849. https://doi.org/10.1177/1524839912467645

Franklin, C. A., Goodson, A., & Garza, A. D. (2019). Intimate partner violence among sexual minorities: Predicting police officer arrest decisions. *Criminal Justice and Behavior, 46*(8), 1181–1199. https://doi.org/10.1177/0093854819834722

Glick, P., & Fiske, S. T. (1996). The ambivalent sexism inventory: Differentiating hostile and benevolent sexism. *Journal of Personality and Social Psychology, 70*, 491–512. https://psycnet.apa.org/doi/10.1037/0022-3514.70.3.491

Gondolf, E. (1996). Characteristics of batterers in a multi-site evaluation of batterer intervention systems. *Mincava.* http://www.mincava.umn.edu/documents/gondolf/batchar.html

Goodmark, L. (2018). *Decriminalizing domestic violence.* University of California Press.

Guadalupe-Diaz, X. L., & Jasinski, J. (2017). "I wasn't a priority, I wasn't a victim": Challenges in help seeking for transgender survivors of intimate partner violence. *Violence Against Women, 23*, 772–792. https://doi.org/10.1177/1077801216650288.

Hamby, S., & Jackson, A. (2010). Size does matter: The effects of gender on perceptions of dating violence. *Sex Roles, 63*, 324–331. https://doi.org/10.1007/s11199-010-9816-0

Hamel, J. (2011). In dubious battle: The politics of mandatory arrest and dominant aggressor laws. *Partner Abuse, 2*(2), 224–245. https://doi.org/10.1177%2F1077801212437017

Hamel, J., & Russell, B. L. (2013). The Partner Abuse State of Knowledge Project: Implications for law enforcement responses to domestic violence. In B. L. Russell (Ed.), *Perceptions of female offenders: How stereotypes and social norms affect criminal justice responses* (pp. 151–179). Springer Science + Business Media. https://doi.org/10.1007/978-1-4614-5871-5_10

Hassouneh, D., & Glass, N. (2008). The influence of gender role stereotyping on women's experiences of female same-sex intimate partner violence. *Violence Against Women, 14*, 310–325. https://doi.org/10.1177/1077801207313734.

Henning, K., & Feder, L. (2005). Criminal prosecution of domestic violence offenses: An investigation of factors predictive of court outcomes. *Criminal Justice and Behavior, 32*(6), 612–642. https://doi.org/10.1177/0093854805279945

Henry, A., & Smith, D. J. (2007). *Transformations of policing.* Ashgate.

Henry, R. S., Perrin, P. B., Coston, B. M., & Calton, J. M. (2021). Intimate partner violence and mental health among transgender/gender nonconforming adults. *Journal of Interpersonal Violence, 36*(7–8), 3374–3399. https://doi.org/10.1177%2F0886260518775148

Herek G. M., Chopp R., & Strohl, D. (2007) Sexual stigma: Putting sexual minority health issues in context. In I. H. Meyer & M. E. Northridge (Eds.), *The health of sexual minorities* (p. 171). Springer.https://doi.org/10.1007/978-0-387-31334-4_8

Hirschel, D., Buzawa, E., Pattivina, A., & Faggiani, D. (2007). Domestic violence and mandatory arrest laws: To what extent do they influence police arrest decisions. *Journal of Criminal Law and Criminology, 98*(1), 255–298.

Hirschel, D., & McCormack, P. D. (2021) Same-sex couples and the police: A 10-year study of arrest and dual arrest rates in responding to incidents of intimate partner violence. *Violence Against Women, 27*(9), 119–149. doi:10.1177/1077801220920378

Hirschel, D., & Buzawa, E. (2002). Understanding the Context of Dual Arrest With Directions for Future Research. *Violence Against Women, 8*(12), 1449–1473. https://doi.org/10.1177/107780102237965

Ho, T. (2003). The influence of suspect gender in domestic violence arrests. *American Journal of Criminal Justice, 27*, 183–195.

International Association of Chiefs of Police. (2018). *Intimate partner violence response policy and training content guidelines 6.* https://www.theiacp.org/sites/default/files/2018-08/DomesticViolenceBinder2018.pdf

Johnson, L. (1991). *On the front lines: Police stress and family well-being.* Hearing Before the Select Committee on Children, Youth, and Families, House of Representatives, 102 Congress, First Session, May 20. U.S. Government Printing Office.

Jones, D. A., & Belknap, J. (1999). Police responses to battering in a progressive pro-arrest jurisdiction. *Justice Quarterly, 16*, 249–273. https://doi.org/10.1080/07418829900094131

Kay, M., & Jeffries, S. (2010). Homophobia, heteronormativism and hegemonic masculinity: Male same-sex intimate partner violence from the perspective of Brisbane Service Providers. *Psychiatry, Psychology and Law, 17*(3), 412–423. https://doi.org/10.1080/13218710903566953

Kelly, J. B., & Johnson, M. P. (2008). Differentiation among types of intimate partner violence: Research update and implications for interventions. *Family Court Review, 46*(2), 476–499. https://doi.org/10.1111/j.1744-1617.2008.00215.x

Langenderfer-Magruder, L., Whitfield, D. L., Walls, N. E., Kattari, S. K., & Ramos, D. (2016). Experiences of intimate partner violence and subsequent police reporting among lesbian, gay, bisexual, transgender, and queer adults in Colorado: Comparing rates of cisgender and transgender victimization. *Journal of Interpersonal Violence, 31*, 855–871. https://doi.org/10.1177/0886260514556767

Langhinrichsen-Rohling, J., Misra, T. A., Selwyn, C., & Rohling, M. (2012). Rates of bi-directional versus unidirectional intimate partner violence across samples, sexual orientations, and race/ethnicities: A comprehensive review. *Partner Abuse, 3*(2), 199–230. doi:10.1891/1946-6560.3.2.199

Lonsway, K. A. (2006). Policies on police officer domestic violence: Prevalence and specific provisions within large police agencies. *Police Quarterly, 9*(4), 397–422. https://doi.org/10.1177/ 1098611104268884423

Majd, K., Marksamer, J., & Reyes, C. (2009). *Hidden injustice: Lesbian, gay, bisexual, and transgender youth in juvenile courts.* Legal Services for Children, National Juvenile Defender Center, National Center for Lesbian Rights.

Mallory, C., Hasenbush, A., & Sears, B. (2015). *Discrimination and harassment by law enforcement officers in the LGBT community.* The Williams Institute.

Martin, M. E. (1994). Mandatory arrest for domestic violence: The courts' response. *Criminal Justice Review, 19*, 212–227. https://doi.org/10.1177%2F073401689401900203

Medina, A. J., Robinson, A., & Myhill, A. (2016). Cheaper, faster, better: Expectations and achievements in police risk assessment of domestic abuse. *Policing, 10*, 341–350. https://doi.org/10.1093/police/paw023

Mele, M. (2018). Police response to domestic violence: The influence of extra-legal factors on arrest decisions. *Partner Abuse, 9*(3), 215–229. https://doi.org/10.1891/1946-6560.9.3.215

Myhill, A. (2017). Renegotiating domestic violence: Police attitudes and decisions concerning arrest, *Policing and Society, 29*(1), 52–68. https://doi.org/10.1080/10439463.2017.1356299

Myhill, A., & Johnson, K. (2016). Police use of discretion in response to domestic violence. *Criminology & Criminal Justice, 16*(1), 3–20. https://doi.org/10.1177%2F1748895815590202

National Conference of State Legislatures State Laws on Domestic Violence or Abuse (2019). https://www.ncsl.org/research/human-services/domestic-violence-domestic-abuse-definitions-and-relationships.aspx

Neidig, P., Russell, H., & Seng, A. (1992). Interspousal aggression in law enforcement families: A preliminary investigation. *Police Studies, 15*(1), 30–38. https://policing.umhistorylabs.lsa.umich.edu/files/original/5528df2d5b5c33cfeaa930146cfe20ccb5cad0cd.pdf

Oehme, K., Prost, S. G., & Saunders, D. G. (2016). Police responses to cases of officer-involved domestic violence: The effects of a brief web-based training. *Policing, 10*(4), 391–407. https://doi.org/10.1093/police/paw039

Pattavina, A., Buzawa, E., Hirschel, D., & Faggiani, D. (2007). Policy, place, and perpetrators: Using NIBRS to explain arrest practices in intimate partner violence. *Justice Research and Policy, 9*, 31–51. https://doi.org/10.3818%2FJRP.9.2.2007.31

Peitzmeier, S. M., Hughto, J. M. W., Potter, J., Deutsch, M. B., & Reisner, S. L. (2020). Development of a novel tool to assess intimate partner violence against transgender individuals. *Journal of Interpersonal Violence, 34*, 2376–2397. https://doi.org/10.1177/0886260519827660

The Pennsylvania Child Welfare Resource Center. (n.d.). *Domestic violence timeline.* http://www.pacwrc.pitt.edu/Curriculum/310DomesticViolenceIssuesAnIntroductionforChildWelfareProfessionals/Handouts/HO3DomesticViolenceTimeline.pdf

Poorman, P. B., Seelau, E. P., & Seelau, S. M. (2003). Perceptions of domestic abuse in same-sex relationships and implications for criminal justice and mental health responses. *Violence and Victims, 18*(6), 659–669. http://dx.doi.org/10.1891/vivi.2003.18.6.659

Renauer, B., & Henning, K. (2005). Investigating intersections between gender and intimate partner violence recidivism. *Journal of Offender Rehabilitation, 41*(4), 99–124. https://doi.org/10.1300/J076v41n04_05

Rhatigan, D. L., Stewart, C., & Moore, T. M. (2011). Effects of gender and confrontation on attributions of female perpetrated intimate partner violence. *Sex Roles, 64,* 875–887. https://doi.org/10.1007/s11199-011-9951-2

Ricketts v. Columbia, N. 90-4099-CV-C66BA (U.S. Dist. Ct. W. D. Mo.). National Criminal Justice Reference Service.

Ristock, J. L. (2002). *No more secrets: Violence in lesbian relationships.* Psychology Press.

Russell, B. (2018). Police perceptions in intimate partner violence cases: The influence of gender and sexual orientation. *Journal of Crime and Justice, 41*(2), 193–205. https://doi.org/10.1080/0735648X.2017.1282378

Russell, B., & Kraus, S. (2016). Perceptions of partner violence: How aggressor gender, masculinity/femininity, and victim gender influence criminal justice decisions. *Deviant Behavior, 37*(6), 679–691. doi:10.1080/01639625.2015.1060815

Russell, B., & Pappas, N. (2018). Officer involved domestic violence: A future of uniform response and transparency. *International Journal of Police Science & Management, 20*(2), 134–142. https://doi.org/10.1177%2F1461355718774579

Russell, B., Ragatz, L., & Kraus, S. (2010). Self-defense and legal decision making: The role of defendant and victim gender and gender-neutral expert testimony of the battered partner's syndrome. *Partner Abuse, 1*(4), 399–419. doi:10.1891/1946-6560.1.4.399

Russell, B., Ragatz, L. L., & Kraus, S. W. (2009). Does ambivalent sexism influence verdicts for heterosexual and homosexual defendants in a self-defense case? *Journal of Family Violence, 24*(3), 145–157. doi:10.1007/s10896-008-9210-7

Russell, B., & Sturgeon, J. A. (2019). Police evaluations of intimate partner violence in heterosexual and same-sex relationships: Do experience and training play a role? *Journal of Police and Criminal Psychology, 34,* 34–44. https://doi.org/10.1007/s11896-018-9279-8

Russell, B., & Tannenbaum, R. (2016). Strengthening police psychological and law enforcement response to domestic and intimate partner violence: Applying empirical findings. Presentation at the International Association of Chief of Police, San Diego, CA.

Russell, B., & Torres, C. (2020). Identifying and responding to LGBT+ intimate partner violence from a criminal justice perspective. In B. Russell (Ed.), *Intimate partner violence and the LGBT+ community* (pp. 257–280). Springer. https://doi.org/10.1007/978-3-030-44762-5_14

Sacco, L. N. (2015). The Violence Against Women Act: Overview, legislation, and federal funding. *Congressional Research Service.* https://fas.org/sgp/crs/misc/R42499.pdf

Saunders, D. G. (1980). *The police response to battered women: Predictors of officers' use of arrest, counseling, and minimal action* [Doctoral dissertation, University of Wisconsin-Madison, 1979]. Dissertation Abstracts International, *40,* 6446-A.

Scott v. Hart (1976). C76-2395 (N.D. Cal.).

Seelau, S. M., & Seelau, E. P. (2005). Gender-role stereotypes and perceptions of heterosexual, gay, and lesbian domestic violence. *Journal of Family Violence, 20,* 363–371. https://doi.org/10.1007/s10896-005-7798-4

Sherman, L., & Berk, R. (1984). The specific deterrent effect of arrest for domestic assault. *American Sociological Review, 49*(2), 261–276.

Sherman, L., & Harris, H. M. (2015). Increased death rates of domestic violence victims from arresting vs. warning suspects in the Milwaukee Domestic Violence Experiment (MilDVE). *Journal of Experimental Criminology, 11*(1), 1–20. https://doi.org/10.1007/s11292-014-9203-x

Sherman, L. W., Schmidt, J. D., Rogan, D. P., Gartin, P. R., Cohn, E. G., Collins D. J., & Bachich, A. R. (1991). From initial deterrence to long-term escalation: Short custody arrest for ghetto poverty violence. *Criminology, 29*(4), 821–849. https://doi.org/10.1111/j.1745-9125.1991.tb01089.x

Shernock, S. (2005). Police categorization and disposition of non-lethal partner violence incidents involving women offenders in a statewide rural jurisdiction with presumptive arrest policy. *Family Violence & Sexual Assault Bulletin, 21*(2–3), 11–17.

Shernock, S., & Russell, B. (2012). Gender and racial/ethnic difference in criminal justice decision making in intimate partner violence cases. *Partner Abuse, 3*(4), 501–530. https://doi.org/10.1891/1946-6560.3.4.501

Simpson, S. S., Bouffard, L. A., Garner, J., & Hickman, L. (2006). The influence of legal reform on the probability of arrest in domestic violence cases. *Justice Quarterly, 23*, 297–316. https://doi.org/10.1080/07418820600869087

Sorenson, B., & Taylor, C. A. (2005). Female aggression toward male intimate partners: An examination of social norms in a community-based sample. *Psychology of Women Quarterly, 29*(1), 78–96. https://doi.org/10.1111/j.1471-6402.2005.00170.x

Sorenson, S. B., & Thomas, K. A. (2009). Views of intimate partner violence in same— and opposite sex relationships. *Journal of Marriage and Family, 71*(2), 337–352. https://doi.org/10.1111/j.1741-3737.2009.00602.x.

Stalans, L. J., & Finn, M. A. (1995). How novice and experienced officers interpret wife assaults: Normative and efficiency frames. *Law & Society Review, 29*, 287–321. https://doi.org/10.2307/3054013

Stark, E. (2012). Looking beyond domestic violence: Policing coercive control. *Journal of Police Crisis Negotiations, 12*(2), 199–217. https://doi.org/10.1080/15332586.2012.725016

Stinson, P. M., & Liederbach, J. (2012). Fox in the henhouse: A study of police officers arrested for crimes associated with domestic and/or family violence. *Criminal Justice Policy Review, 24*(5), 601–625. https://doi.org/10.1177%2F0887403412453837

Stop Abusive and Violent Environments (SAVE). (2010). Predominant aggressor policies: Leaving the abuser unaccountable. http://www.saveservices.org/pdf/SAVE-Predominant_Aggressor.pdf

Straus, M. A., & Gelles, R. J. (1990). *Physical violence in American families*. Transaction.

Tesch, B. P., Bekerian, D. A., English, P., & Harrington, E. (2010). Same-sex domestic violence on police officers' assessment of intimate partner violence risk. *Journal of Family Violence, 32*(1), 125–134. https://doi.org/10.1350%2Fijps.2010.12.4.204

Thurman v. City of Torrington, DC, 595 F.Supp.1521 (D. Conn. 1984).

Tjaden, P., & Thoennes, N. (2000). *Extent, nature, and consequences of intimate partner violence*. National Institute of Justice and Centers for Disease Control and Prevention.

Trujillo, M. P., & Ross, S. (2008). Police response to domestic violence: Making decisions about risk and risk management. *Journal of Interpersonal Violence, 23*(4), 44–473. https://doi.org/10.1177%2F0886260507312943

Waddington, T. (2012). Cop culture. In T. Newburn & J. Peay (Eds.), *Policing: Politics, culture and control* (pp. 89–109). Hart.

Wetendorf, D., & Davis, D. (2003). *The misuse of police powers in officer-involved domestic violence*. Advocate and Officer Dialogues: Police perpetrated domestic violence. Davis Corporate Training.

Wexler, D. (2020). When women abuse men: What we now know about female intimate partner violence. *Partner Abuse, 11*, 415–436. http://dx.doi.org/10.1891/PA-2020-0026

Young, C., Cook, P., Smith, S., Turltletaub, J., & Hazelwood, L. (2006). Domestic violence: New visions, new solutions. In J. Hamel & T. Nicholls (Eds.), *Family interventions in domestic violence: A handbook of gender-inclusive theory and treatment* (pp. 601–619). Springer.

PART II

Litigation

4

Gender, Sex, and the Prosecution of Intimate Partner Violence

JENNIFER COX, ELIZABETH MACNEIL, AND HANNAH LIND ∎

In the United States, approximately 90% of criminal charges do not proceed to trial ("Criminal Cases," n.d.), with the vast majority of cases resulting in guilty verdicts subsequent to plea bargaining or outright charge dismissals. Typically, federal, state, and local jurisdictions afford US prosecutors with a substantial amount of discretion to determine if and how to move arrests forward to formal charges, whether to engage in plea negotiations, and what their trial strategy will be; in some instances, they may provide sentencing recommendations (Albonetti, 1987). Some level of discretion is necessary, considering the impossible amount of resources needed to progress every criminal arrest through the investigative and trial process (O'Neill, 2004). Although not supported by empirical evidence, concerns about unchecked prosecutorial power have entered popular discourse (Balko, 2013; Reynolds, 2016), and social science and legal scholars are increasingly considering the decision-making processes in this population (Baker & Hassan, 2021; Spohn & Tellis, 2019).

Intimate partner violence (IPV) is one type of criminal offense for which prosecutors are tasked with applying the law. Historically, law enforcement entities largely ignored or underplayed IPV, notably when the violence did not include serious physical injury (see Erez, 2002). The notion of intimate relationship physical abuse as a crime emerged in the United States in the 1970s, propelled by victims' advocacy groups and cultural changes related to the women's movement (Goodman & Epstein, 2008). Due mainly to proarrest laws and policies, the last three decades have witnessed increased IPV-related arrests. However, documented IPV prosecution and conviction rates vary significantly across empirical studies and are likely jurisdictionally specific (Garner & Maxwell, 2009).

This chapter will review theory and research regarding prosecutorial decision-making broadly defined. We will then examine perceptions and attitudes about

IPV and consider how these perceptions shape prosecutorial discretion through criminal case processing. Traditionally IPV is conceptualized as a "gendered" crime (Kubicek et al., 2015); however, we will specifically consider "gender-inverted" (woman aggressor/man victim), same-sex IPV, and trans and gender-diverse (TDG) IPV, as there are high rates of IPV within these dyads, yet relatively less scholarship (Archer, 2000; Peterman & Dixon, 2003; Straus & Ramirez, 2007). Finally, we summarize research implications and provide recommendations for practice and future research.

PROSECUTORIAL DECISION-MAKING

Social science literature has examined a multiplicity of concerns that prosecutors hold as relevant to decision-making. Employing a mixed-methods research design, Frederick and Stemen (2012) sought to better understand prosecutorial decision-making through the trajectory of criminal case processing. Researchers conducted multiple focus groups, administered surveys, and analyzed administrative data to examine four specific questions: What are prosecutorial conceptions of justice? What factors are associated with prosecutorial decisions at each stage of the adjudicative process? What contextual factors guide prosecutorial decisions? Moreover, how do prosecutors interpret case-specific factors?

According to Frederick and Stemen (2012), when determining whether and how to proceed with criminal charges, prosecutors consider two basic questions: *Can* I prove this case? And *should* I prove this case? The question of whether one *can* prove a case was important early in the case trajectory and driven primarily by the strength of the evidence. However, when considering whether one *should* prove a case, factors such as characteristics of the defendant/victim, the seriousness of the offense, and the defendant's criminal history emerged as important considerations. This indicates that prosecutors consider both legal (e.g., strength of evidence, victim injuries) and extralegal (e.g., perceptions of victim credibility, the status of the victim/perpetrator relationship) factors when determining case processing. A handful of other studies have supported these data, suggesting prosecutors consider resource availability, victim credibility, political factors, and, perhaps not surprisingly, their own perceptions of the likelihood of a conviction (O'Neill, 2004; Spohn et al., 2001).

In fact, prosecutor overall estimation of securing a conviction is a robust predictor of case processing decisions. This concept is typically discussed in terms of the "shadow of a trial" model (herein known as the "shadow model"). Originating from Landes's (1971) model of plea bargaining, this theory posits that the interested parties negotiate plea outcomes with some anticipation of the expected trial outcome. Perhaps the popularity of this model partially stems from its simplicity and appeal to intuition; as Bushway et al. (2014) note, a defendant will plead guilty if the "offered sentence is less than or equal to his or her expected value of the trial. For example, if the expected sentence for a conviction at trial is 20 years and the defendant believes his or her probability of conviction at trial is 0.8, then a plea to a sentence of no more than 16 years (80% of 20) represents a rational choice for a risk-neutral defendant" (p. 724).

As an illustrative example of the shadow model, Bushway and colleagues (2014) tested the model with a large sample of judges, prosecutors, and defense attorneys across the United States. Researchers presented participants with a brief scenario describing a hypothetical robbery followed by 31 fact files which each described a different piece of information pertaining to the case. Participants then estimated the probability of conviction at trial, the least severe sentence that would be acceptable for a plea deal, and their likely course of action. Researchers subsequently estimated a structural model and considered participant decision-making within the context of the model. Defense attorney and prosecutor participants rendered decisions in a manner consistent with the shadow model, although the plea discounts from prosecutor participants were smaller than defense attorney participant expectations, particularly when the trial sentence is low. This suggests prosecutors may be more willing to "reward" defendants (i.e., offer a lighter sentence) when they are willing to avoid the high fixed costs of a trial.

It stands to reason that prosecutors with significant experience prosecuting IPV cases would formulate certain appraisals of the likelihood of success at trial and exercise their discretion regarding charges, plea bargaining, and case dismissals accordingly. Yet the model has been criticized for its simplicity and assumption of rationality. For example, Redlich and Summers (2012) contest that a lack of complete information, cognitive biases, and data processing heuristics can serve as psychological impediments to rational decision-making. Further, Bibas (2004) argues the shadow model is particularly flawed within the context of plea bargaining in the US system because of the number of potentially influential variables unaccounted for, such as attorney effectiveness across cases, judicial discretion, or jury composition. Stuntz (2004) asserts that the shadow model may not be appropriate given the reality of the US criminal justice system. Specifically, US prosecutors do not necessarily try to maximize prison time, and, in some jurisdictions, prosecutors have resources and alternative prosecutorial methods (e.g., mental health court, veterans court). Thus, a determination of "convictability" may be practically impossible for some prosecutors, while for others, the shadow of a trial may register as little more than a peripheral concern based on jurisdictional, political, or personal priorities.

THEORIES OF INTIMATE PARTNER VIOLENCE

Prior to examining the justice system's approach to prosecuting IPV specifically, it is important to understand general perceptions of the crime, as these attitudes subsequently influence the lawmakers crafting criminal codes and the prosecutors enforcing the law. The Violence Against Women Act (VAWA) was perhaps the most comprehensive federal legislation aimed at the investigation and prosecution of violent crimes against women. Initially passed in 1994, in 2019, the US

Congress failed to reauthorize the now-defunct law, and, as of February 2021, funding for this program has dried up. Despite the name, the Violence Against *Women* Act applied to victims, regardless of gender or sex.

The language inherent in the VAWA is not surprising when considering traditional characterizations of IPV as a phenomenon between abusive men and victimized women (Kubicek et al., 2015). Historically, empirical research has closely aligned with these perceptions, with researchers typically relying on "gender-based" violence, positing that IPV may stem from patriarchal power dynamics and toxic masculinity (Russell et al., 2009). Indeed, although prevalence rates of IPV arrest wax and wane, women only make up a small minority of all arrests (National Coalition Against Domestic Violence, 2020).

Researchers have applied innumerable theories and typologies to understand and explain IPV, such as family system theory, cognitive-behavioral theory, feminist theory, learned helplessness, and Johnson's (2005) controlled-based typology. The extent to which these theories focus on the gender of the individuals involved varies significantly. For example, the feminist theory posits that IPV is the result of systematic male oppression of women, making gender a central factor in understanding the phenomenon (Dobash & Dobash, 1979). In contrast, general strain theory proposes that negative emotions such as stress, anger, and frustration cause all criminal behavior (Agnew, 1992), and it has been applied as a framework for IPV (Zavala & Kurtz, 2016).

Instead of relying on a single theory or typology to understand this complex phenomenon, it is likely that empirical frameworks must be as varied, nuanced, and dynamic as the individuals involved. This flexibility will prove beneficial to legal decision-makers as they apply the law and identify appropriate interventions. We now move to review research regarding perceptions of IPV in same-sex and gender-inverted dyads and consider how these perceptions are associated with prosecutorial interpretation and application of the law.

PERCEPTIONS OF "GENDER-INVERTED" INTIMATE PARTNER VIOLENCE

Prior to reviewing this scholarship, it is important to note that researchers and policymakers have traditionally failed to differentiate between sex and gender. Sex is biologically determined and refers to an individual's reproductive system and secondary sex characteristics. In contrast, gender refers to social and culturally derived behaviors, traits, and interpersonal patterns based on sex. In conflating these two constructs, researchers have ignored large communities of individuals who identify as transgender, gender diverse, or gender nonbinary, highlighting the extent to which erasure and discrimination are systemic. We echo the call from previous scholars for more research with this important population (Vincent, 2018). Although imperfect, when reviewing the following research, we intentionally adhere to terms and definitions used by the original researchers or justify deviations.

Female-to-male abuse is often referred to as "gender-inverted" IPV because female aggression (and male victimization) is inconsistent with lay perceptions of the crime (Seelau et al., 2003). However, female-to-male violence occurs more than commonly believed (Archer, 2000; Straus & Ramirez, 2007). The Center for Disease Control's (CDC; Smith et al., 2018) *National Intimate Partner and Sexual Violence Survey* (NISVS) indicates that approximately 1 in 3 men experience IPV as a victim at some point in their lifetime, and it is likely this is an underestimation of the true rates.

Much of the research examining perceptions and attitudes of "gender-inverted" IPV had specifically focused on the gender of the aggressor, regardless of the gender of the victim. Thus, many studies include both "gender-inverted" IPV and same-sex IPV with women aggressors. We appreciate that a comprehensive understanding of IPV requires researchers to consider all types of relationship dyads. However, members of the lesbian, gay, bisexual, transgender, queer plus community (LGBTQ+) have unique experiences with law enforcement and the criminal justice system (Nadal et al., 2015), and we believe it is important to honor these experiences by examining the nuances specifically within same-sex and TGD IPV dyads. Thus, in the following section, we first review research findings pertaining to "gender-inverted" IPV, followed by data regarding same-sex IPV.

Regardless of perpetrator gender, IPV involving female victims is considered more severe, serious, and in need of intervention than incidences with male victims (Hamby & Jackson, 2010; Poorman et al., 2003; Stanziani et al., 2018). For example, when presented with a case of IPV in which researchers manipulated offender and victim sex, undergraduates rated the violence as more reasonable and milder forms of intervention as more appropriate when the victim was male (Seelau et al., 2003). Male IPV victims are also seen as more responsible for inciting their own abuse, and that such abuse is less serious (Erickson et al., 2017; Poorman et al., 2003).

Hamby and Jackson (2010) argue that gender asymmetry may be one explanation for these disparate perceptions. Specifically, the perceived physical strength of men and the accompanied ability to cause injury and invoke fear may be a primary factor in subsequent perceptions of violence severity. Indeed, the researchers determined that participants viewed physical differences as more impactful for male-to-female perpetration than any other dyad (i.e., male to male, female to male, female to female). Similarly, police officers believed victim injury to be significantly more severe when presented with male-to-female IPV scenarios compared to female-to-male IPV (Russell & Sturgeon, 2019).

Criminal justice professionals and service providers alike perceive men to possess a different kind of power than women (e.g., physical and controlling power), resulting in more justified and expressed fear by women (Miller, 2001). Notably, men perpetrators may inflict greater injury on women victims (Kingsnorth & MacIntosh, 2007). However, research indicates that a notable percentage of women offenders appear to be the primary aggressors. This percentage may be highly underestimated due to gender biases held by law enforcers (Renauer &

Henning, 2005). For example, many criminal justice professionals and service providers handling IPV cases endorsed the idea that "if men wanted to defend themselves, they could easily do so" (Miller, 2001, p. 1353).

The validity of such perceptions is one much debated in the research. Many sociopolitical researchers advocate that most women perpetrators are acting in self-defense and that new arrest laws have led to wrongfully arresting women as primary aggressors or alongside men (i.e., "dual arrests"; Miller, 2001). Compared to men, women are more likely to be dually arrested, and those dually arrested are more likely to have their case dismissed (84%) compared to those arrested as the sole aggressor (29% dismissal rate: Henning & Renauer, 2005). Understanding whether police officers dually arrest due to socialized incongruence of a woman aggressor or if it accurately reflects the situation remains an important research question.

In one sample of both men and women convicted of assault against an opposite-gender intimate partner, researchers found that women (65.4%) were much more likely than men (50.0%) to cite self-defense as a reason for the assault (Henning et al., 2005). Interestingly, men and women were equally likely to respond in a socially desirable way that minimized, denied, and placed blame on the other partner. However, in a different sample of men and women arrested for domestic violence and court-referred for intervention, there were minimal differences between groups regarding self-defense as a motive (Elmquist et al., 2014). A slightly greater percentage of women, compared to men, endorsed the power and control motive (67.0% versus 61.1%), as well as that of self-defense (65.0% versus 57.4%), and women endorsed communication difficulties and expression of negative emotions as motives more frequently than men. Because offenders, regardless of gender, appear to respond in a socially desirable way, Henning and colleagues (2005) note the difficulty in disentangling whether gender differences represent real-life differences or not.

When looking at females convicted for assaulting their male intimate partners, patterns continue in which the females identify the male as the primary aggressor (Henning et al., 2006). Specifically, female offenders reported that males were more likely to use coercion and physical aggression within the relationship. Coercive behaviors include jealousy-driven surveillance of the partner's whereabouts and activities, controlling the finances, and threats (e.g., harming or taking the children). Further, in prior arrest records for the same sample, the female offenders were identified as the primary aggressor only 18% of the time, compared to 60% for their male partners. These findings remained after controlling for social desirability, adding support to the validity of the self-report data. In contrast, when assessing for power and control motivations using a gender-inclusive measure (the Controlling and Abusive Tactics Questionnaire [CAT]), the survey of batterer intervention clients by Hamel et al., (2015) found comparable rates across sex, and both males and females to have reported higher victimization than perpetration. In the general population, according to the NISVS survey cited earlier (Black et al., 2011), the number of men who report having been victims of coercive control in a given year exceeds the number of women—17.2 million compared to 12.6 million.

An additional consideration is "coabuse," or the extent to which both partners are involved in the aggression. Victim surveys indicate bidirectional violence accounts for about 40%–70% of all reported IPV (Straus, 2008; Whitaker et al., 2007), which can complicate identification of the "victim" and the "perpetrator." In a study of undergraduates' judgments of bidirectional IPV, Hine and colleagues (2020) found that, while many participants could recognize the bidirectional nature of the abuse, in scenarios featuring an opposite-sex couple, it was the woman who was almost always labeled as "victim" and the man who assumed the role of "perpetrator." Participants infrequently labeled the woman as "perpetrator" and man as "victim," even when the violence was predominantly female perpetrated, regardless of who initiated the violence. Thus, the pervasive gendered stereotypes painting men as "powerful" and "aggressive" and women as "powerless" and "meek" may be more influential in decision-making than the facts of the incident.

PERCEPTIONS OF SAME-SEX AND INTIMATE PARTNER VIOLENCE

In addition to "gender-inverted" IPV, over the last three decades, scholars have increased research into same-sex IPV. Similar to gender-inverted IPV, same-sex IPV is generally perceived to be less serious and believable than opposite-sex IPV (Poorman et al., 2003; Russell et al., 2015, Stanziani et al., 2020). For example, Brown and Groscup (2009) recruited staff members at a suburban crisis center and provided them with a vignette outlining a case of alleged IPV. Researchers manipulated the sex and sexual orientation of the people involved, creating same-sex and opposite-sex conditions. Participants perceived the victim to have more difficulty leaving the relationship in the opposite-sex conditions. Further, participants rated the violence as more intense and more likely to escalate in the opposite-sex condition. In a separate study, Wasarhaley and colleagues (2017) manipulated victim and offender features to represent "femininity" or "masculinity" in a scenario of same-sex IPV between two women. Male undergraduate students endorsed higher levels of anger toward the masculine defendant when the victim was feminine. Meanwhile, female participants assigned more responsibility to a masculine offender when the victim was masculine.

However, some perceptions of IPV appear to be independent of dyad sex (e.g., Hamby & Jackson, 2010; Sorenson & Thomas, 2009). For example, IPV crisis center staff rated victim capacity to defend, the severity of victim injury, perpetrator's intent to injure, and perpetrator responsibility similarly, regardless of scenarios describing same-sex or opposite-sex IPV (Brown & Groscup, 2009). Similarly, Stanziani and colleagues (2018) reported dyad sex was not associated with perceptions of victim blameworthiness, defendant treatment amenability, or defendant recidivism risk, further highlighting the nuance of these attitudes.

One consistent finding across studies is that IPV is perceived as most serious when the perpetrator is male (regardless of victim sex) and the victim is female (regardless of perpetrator sex; Ahmed et al., 2013; Poorman et al., 2003; Russell et al., 2015). Further, variability in the perception of IPV severity between same-sex versus opposite-sex dyads may dissipate among more explicitly violent cases (Ahmed et al., 2013; Basow & Thompson, 2012), suggesting that less severe cases leave more room for biases. For example, Basow and Thompson (2012) reported opposite-sex female victims (i.e., male perpetrators) compared to same-sex female victims (i.e., female perpetrators) were more likely to be identified as a victim by service providers. However, this trend was only observed in vignettes describing psychological and emotional abuse rather than physical abuse, suggesting stereotypes and "perceptual shorthand" may drive attitudes when processing less severe offenses or when evidence is vague (Steffensmeier et al., 1998).

Although discrepancies are apparent in perceptions of same-sex IPV, the extent to which these attitudes lead to differential treatment is unknown. For example, service providers and IPV crisis staff are no more likely to recommend counseling to opposite-sex IPV female victims compared to same-sex IPV female victims (Basow & Thompson, 2012; Brown & Groscup, 2009). Further, Russell and Sturgeon (2019) reported that police officer participants evaluated potential arrest options similarly for same-sex and opposite-sex alleged IPV incidences. In contrast, US police officers believed that mediating an argument and providing informal advice was more appropriate for same-sex male couples than for opposite-sex (male aggressor) couples (Russell & Sturgeon, 2019). Similarly, law enforcers were more likely to rate the belief that allowing the alleged aggressor to leave the premises to "cool off" was fairer for same-sex male couples and gender-inverted couples. In sum, these data also highlight the nuance in perceptions and actions, suggesting factors such as participant role (e.g., law enforcement, layperson) and strength of intervention action (e.g., mediation, arrest) are important factors to consider when examining IPV attitudes.

Perceptions of Trans and Gender-Diverse Intimate Partner Violence

Relative to the other IPV dyads discussed thus far, very little scholarship has considered perceptions of TGD IPV. Despite this, TGD IPV is a pervasive and problematic phenomenon; Peitzmeier and colleagues (2020) conducted a systematic review and meta-analysis of quantitative research concerning TGD IPV. Compared to cis-gender individuals, TGD individuals were 1.7 times more likely to experience physical IPV and 2.5 times more likely to experience sexual IPV. Official statistics indicate TGD individuals experience IPV at disproportionate rates (National Coalition Against Domestic Violence, 2020) and established rates of these crimes are likely underestimations considering the general distrust of law enforcement within this community (Lambda Legal, 2015).

One qualitative study highlights the pervasiveness of gender role expectations in identifying IPV and help-seeking behaviors for this community. Guadalupe-Diaz and Jasinski (2016) found TGD IPV survivors experienced conflict due to gendered notions of victimization and navigating resources built exclusively for victims who are assigned the female sex. Kurdyla and colleagues (2019) found TGD IPV survivors were more likely to seek help from friends, family, and mental health care providers than formal community resources such as police, medical doctors, or survivor hotlines. Further, when seeking help, Seelman (2015) found that TGD people of color, those with disabilities, and those more frequently perceived as TGD are more likely to experience unequal treatment at community-based IPV programs. Thus, although research specifically assessing *perceptions* of IPV in this population is relatively scarce, there is convincing evidence to suggest that TGD IPV survivors experience disparate treatment when attempting to engage with community resources (Kattari et al., 2017; Klein et al., 2018).

DIFFERENCES IN THE EYE OF THE BEHOLDER

Research has consistently shown that women are much more likely to perceive IPV as serious and in need of intervention than men (Ahmed et al., 2013; Erickson et al., 2017; Russell et al., 2015). Further, women are less likely to blame the victim and justify the perpetrator's actions and are more likely to assign guilt to perpetrators and believe the victim to be distressed and fearful (Hamby & Jackson, 2010). Further, Poorman and colleagues (2003) found that male participants were more likely to respond that they believed a couple was unlikely to encounter future "domestic problems" when the index IPV offense was perpetrated by a man against a woman; female participants did not perceive a difference in the likelihood of future "domestic problems" based on perpetrator sex. Additionally, men were much less likely to believe criminal justice system intervention was appropriate in gender-inverted or same-sex IPV.

In a study sampling individuals identifying with the LGBTQ+ community, Guadalupe-Diaz and Yglesias (2013) found that women rated domestic violence law more favorably as it applied to same-gender dyads. Notably, a large portion of these differences was due in part to lesbian and bisexual women having a more positive perception of law enforcement than gay or bisexual men. However, these differences may also be somewhat related to gender role stereotyping and stalking myth acceptance, which is consistently endorsed at higher rates by men (Erickson et al., 2017; Herzog, 2007; Wasarhaley et al., 2017). For example, Stanziani and colleagues (2020) found hegemonic masculinity is related to perceptions of IPV seriousness and defendant treatment amenability. Given the predominately male demographic of US prosecutors (Women Donors Network, 2019), this research highlights how prosecutor individual differences and held beliefs may be associated with blunted perception of the seriousness of IPV and likelihood of defendant recidivism, ultimately leading to discrepant case outcomes when compared to female prosecutors.

PROSECUTION OF INTIMATE PARTNER VIOLENCE

Legal terming and operationalizing of IPV have continually changed over the past four decades. Modern definitions have expanded to encompass psychological and sexual abuse as well as stalking in addition to physical violence (Sorenson & Thomas, 2009). Although the movement away from the term "domestic violence" to "intimate partner violence" allows for the inclusion of gender minorities, dating adolescents, and noncohabiting couples, the use of the word "violence" continues the historical conceptualization of abuse as purely physical, potentially explaining the difficulties of some agencies with labeling psychological abuse and coercion as IPV.

During the late 1980s, many US jurisdictions enacted "mandatory arrest" statutes, requiring that an arrest occur when law enforcement responds to a report of IPV and probable cause exists. In tandem, some jurisdictions employed "no-drop" policies that generally prohibited prosecutorial discretion to drop criminal IPV charges solely because a victim is uncooperative (Buzawa & Buzawa, 2003). Although originally heralded by victim advocates as important strides toward combating IPV (see Goolkasian, 1986), these policies have come under considerable debate among researchers and practitioners. Regarding mandatory arrest policies, data summarizing the effectiveness of these policies in reducing IPV recidivism are inconsistent. For example, in reviewing data from six experiments associated with the National Institute of Justice's Spouse Assault Replication Program, Maxwell and colleagues (2001) found that arresting male aggressors was associated with a reduction in subsequent aggression against female intimate partners, although this association was modest when compared to the relationship between aggressor previous criminal history and future IPV recidivism. However, Iyengar (2009) examined the FBI Supplementary Homicide Reports and found that mandatory arrest laws increase intimate partner homicide. Further, Maxwell and colleagues (2001) reported the majority of IPV aggressors discontinued aggressive behaviors, regardless of arrest status, while others argue that, under these policies, victims are at risk of arrest due to self-defensive battering, retaliatory battering, or escalating the violence. Thus, some argue mandatory arrests may siphon community resources away from identifying the most violent offenders and most vulnerable victims, as well as increase the most violent IPV, such as intimate partner homicide.

No-drop policies are similarly controversial, with some arguing legally mandated prosecution is detrimental to victims and the interests of justice (Goodman & Epstein, 2005). Generally, no-drop policies require that, once criminal charges have been filed, prosecutors will move forward with the case regardless of victim cooperation. Mills (1999) states no-drop policies take the decision-making power from the victim, hindering the survivor's efforts to regain control of their life and move past abusive experiences. Mills suggests female victims may be less likely to report future violence if the original arrest led to prosecution of their male partner and if the victim felt she had no rights or input during the criminal adjudicative process. Although there are few rigorous empirical studies of no-drop policy outcomes, it is likely these policies have led to an increase in convictions and a decrease in dismissal rates (Davis et al., 2001). However, Davis and colleagues (2008) examined differences in rearrest rates between two boroughs of New York City (Brooklyn and the Bronx), and data suggest the Brooklyn policy, which required IPV charges filed regardless of victim cooperation, was more costly and more likely to result in dismissed cases but did not differ significantly in IPV rearrest rates after 6 months. Although no-drop policies are widespread, increasingly jurisdictions provide flexibility, outlining specific circumstances under which charges can be dropped (Buzawa & Buzawa, 2003).

An additional prosecutorial route in many jurisdictions includes a deferred prosecution agreement, which is a contract between the defendant and prosecutor's office outlining specific requirements the defendant must meet (e.g., mental health treatment, community service, restitution) within a specific period of time. Typically, if the defendant successfully completes the requirements, the prosecutor will drop the charges. However, if the defendant fails to meet the requirements within the specified timeframe, the prosecutor will reopen the case and move forward with adjudication. Instances of deferred prosecution are increasing, although exact rates are unknown (Barkow & Barkow, 2011), and research on the effectiveness of this prosecutorial mechanism is scarce. In one empirical study, Ford and Regoli (1993) randomly assigned IPV defendants to three different prosecutorial strategies: deferred prosecution with counseling, prosecution with counseling recommended as a stipulation of probation, or no-drop prosecution with conviction and sentencing. Researchers concluded there were no differences in violence between groups at 6-month follow-up. The authors concluded empowering victims to determine whether to drop charges is associated with more control in other areas of the relationship.

Evidence-based prosecution refers to reliance on evidentiary strategies that are independent of victim testimony (Gewirtz et al., 2006). Instead of building a case around the victim's testimony, evidence-based prosecution requires prosecutors to focus on evidentiary factors such as medical records, photographs, witness testimony, and previous arrest records. Evidence-based prosecution is relatively less common, and there is a lack of data regarding the efficacy of this approach in reducing violence. Despite the relative lack of data, evidence-based prosecution may become more normative considering US Supreme Court decisions that prohibit the admission of testimonial statements by witnesses who have since become unavailable (e.g., victims who evoke spousal privilege), rendering it as hearsay (*Crawford v. Washington*, 2004; *Crawford v. Washington*, 2006).

Finally, the National District Attorneys Association (2017) suggests vertical case processing is particularly important in IPV cases. Vertical prosecution, or the presence of a single, specially trained prosecutor handling the case from filing to disposition, may allow prosecutors to build relationships and establish trust with victims. A single prosecutor will reduce the extent to which the victim must recount their experiences and increase the consistency and continuity in communication between victim and prosecutor. Despite the potential benefits of this prosecutorial approach, there is no research examining victim experiences and perceptions of vertical prosecution.

A plethora of factors may influence prosecutorial decision-making in IPV charging decisions. O'Neal and colleagues (2015) examined California prosecutorial charging decisions in approximately 50 IPV arrests. They determined prosecutors moved forward with charges for approximately 30% of referred cases and most frequently cited insufficient evidence as the catalyst for rejecting cases. Further, analysis of qualitative data from attorney charge evaluation forms maintained by the Los Angeles (California) District Attorney's Office indicated factors relevant to prosecutor charging decisions included suspect weapon use and victim cooperation (O'Neal & Spohn, 2017). This is consistent with a report by Henning and Feder (2005), which determined prosecutors were more likely to move forward with criminal charges if the IPV incident involved a weapon or the victim sustained serious injury.

Messing (2014) examined prosecutorial decision-making in urban California IPV cases from 2005 and found that police decisions to take the perpetrator into custody at the scene of the crime had the greatest effect on prosecutors' decision to proceed, increasing the likelihood over sixfold. Yet victim's willingness to assist with prosecution was also found to be a significant factor, increasing the likelihood of prosecution nearly fivefold. In addition to underscoring the importance of victim cooperation, the results from this study seem to indicate a reliance on police decision-making to inform later prosecutorial decision-making. In the United States, prosecutorial offices and policing agencies act independently in their respective roles yet rely significantly on each other to carry out their tasks (Harris, 2011; Orton & Weick, 1990). Petersen (2017) conceptualizes this relationship as a loosely coupled system in that the two entities are responsive to each other but maintain distinct identities. Holleran and colleagues (2010) found congruence between charges filed by police at arrest and final charges filed by the prosecutor, with differences largely reflecting jurisdictional variance. This suggests the very first decision prosecutors face when a case lands on their desk may already be contingent on earlier handling of the case by the police.

The vast majority of IPV prosecution research has focused on women victims in opposite-sex couples. Cultural expectations of gender roles, gender norms, and violence likely perpetuated this hyperfocus, further exacerbated by some US jurisdictional prohibitions on same-sex marriages prior to the US Supreme Court's *Obergefell v. Hodges* (2015) ruling solidifying marriage as a fundamental right. Although we acknowledge the importance of understanding and eradicating opposite-sex/women-victim IPV, we also aim to highlight that IPV is not gender exclusive and occurs in all types of intimate relationships. Thus, IPV prosecution must similarly reflect the diversity of the aggressor–victim dyad.

PROSECUTING GENDER-INVERTED INTIMATE PARTNER VIOLENCE

Considering IPV is traditionally conceptualized as a gendered crime, with men as the abusers and women as the abused, it is thus unsurprising that males make up the vast majority of those arrested for IPV (National Coalition Against Domestic Violence, 2020). As such, it also follows that ample research indicates that women receive more leniency in prosecution (Henning & Reneauer, 2005; Lantz, 2020). For example, when presenting prosecutors with mock opposite-sex IPV cases in which researchers manipulated defendant sex, MacNeil and colleagues (2020) found that prosecutors recommended less punitive charges and a more lenient plea deal to the female defendant compared to the male defendant.

However, this leniency may collapse given the severity of the crime and the extent to which the female defendant's behavior is inconsistent with traditional gender roles. For example, Henning and Feder (2004) found that women are more likely to be charged with a felony than men in IPV cases, which they attribute to the fact that, although women are less likely to be arrested, when arrested, the incident is more likely to include a weapon or result in serious victim injury (Lantz, 2020). Further, Romain and Freiburger (2013) determined that females were less likely to have their cases dismissed compared to males and suggested that this may be due to perceiving violent women as incongruent with gender role norms and as more of a danger to their families.

Adhering to the traditional conceptualization of IPV or IPV myths and gender role norms appears to be a pertinent extralegal factor that influences decision-making. A 2009 study found that family law attorneys and judges correctly answered only 3.17 items from a 10-item quiz of IPV myths, performing just slightly better than undergraduate students with no IPV training (Hamel et al., 2009). Notably, these attorneys and judges were particularly misinformed about the high rates of serious physical gender-inverted IPV. Given these findings, scholars, activists, and practitioners have pushed for a more nuanced understanding of the IPV phenomenon and a more holistic approach to combating this public health crisis (Coston, 2019; Kozuch, 2020; Parry & O'Neal, 2015).

PROSECUTING SAME-SEX AND TRANS AND GENDER-DIVERSE INTIMATE PARTNER VIOLENCE

Considering the extent to which police work in tandem with prosecutorial offices (Harris, 2011; Orton & Weick, 1990), police officers serve as an important gateway to transitioning incidences of IPV from allegation to prosecution. However, this system can be problematic, considering members of the LGBTQ+ community frequently report experiencing harassment and discrimination from law enforcement officers (Mallory et al., 2015), and perceptions of police legitimacy may be particularly low among this population (Dario et al., 2020; Owen et al., 2018).

These negative experiences with law enforcement may continue into later stages of case processing. Specifically, a survey of LGBTQ+ experiences with police, courts, and jails suggests victims experience significant homophobia and do not perceive that the justice system applies equally to them (Lambda Legal, 2015). Unsurprisingly, male, non-White LGBTQ+ individuals are less likely to report same-sex IPV (Guadalupe-Diaz, 2016), and many victims of same-sex or TGD

IPV report formal help services are unequipped to assist sexual and gender minority populations (Alhusen et al., 2010; Edwards et al., 2015; Guadalupe-Diaz & Jasinski, 2016). Indeed, Lantz (2020) found victims of same-sex IPV were significantly less likely to cooperate with police compared to victims of opposite-sex IPV. The ruptured trust between LGBTQ+ victims and law enforcement translates into very palpable concerns over equal justice in light of research findings that victim cooperation is a factor often heavily considered by prosecutors when proceeding with IPV cases (e.g., Belknap & Graham, 2000; Cerulli et al., 2014).

Lantz (2020) examined the criminal justice system's response to same-sex and opposite-sex IPV using data from the National Incident-Based Reporting System. They found male-perpetrated IPV, regardless of victim sex, was more likely to be prosecuted. In contrast, Henning and Renauer (2005) found females arrested for same-sex IPV were more likely to have their cases dismissed than females arrested for gender-inverted IPV, again suggesting that *gender* (and beliefs about power differentials) may be more influential than sexual minority status.

In one of the first published empirical studies of prosecutorial discretion in same-sex IPV, Cox and colleagues (2019) presented over 100 US prosecutors with a vignette summarizing the arrest of an alleged IPV incident. The researchers manipulated the gender and sexual orientation of the couple involved via gender stereotypic names and pronouns, creating four conditions (opposite-sex couple/female victim, opposite-sex couple/male victim, same-sex couple/female victim, same-sex couple/male victim). There were no differences between conditions regarding prosecutor decision to proceed with charges, the severity of charges imposed, or the harshness of the initial plea bargain. However, prosecutors were more likely to proceed without the victim's cooperation when the victim was female, regardless of her partner's gender. Further, prosecutors rated the male aggressor in the opposite-sex couple/female victim condition as more aggressive than the female aggressors. As such, it is possible that gender and sex do not impact substantial case processing decisions such as whether to file charges or enter into plea negotiations. Instead, these extralegal factors may be associated with decision-making in more nuanced ways.

PRACTICE IMPLICATIONS

Considering women, compared to men, are more likely to be victims of severe, injury-inducing IPV, some scholars have raised concerns regarding the complete erasure of a gender-based framework when combating this phenomenon (Reed et al., 2010). It is impossible to extricate gender, sex, and intersectionality from individual lived experiences and effective prosecution, and subsequent interventions must consider the entire person. Although a significant proportion of intervention efforts focus on aspects of power, control, and the patriarchal dynamics of heteronormative relationships thought central to IPV, the reality is usually more complex. We echo Lantz's (2020) assertion that the criminal justice response to IPV must reflect the diversity of the phenomenon. Undoubtedly, commonalities exist between heterosexual, gender-inverted, and same-sex IPV; however, important differences also exist, indicating a single theoretical framework or generic legal response is insufficient for tackling this crisis. The following recommendations may be more applicable to gender-inverted, same-sex, and TGD IPV; however, prosecutors may also find this information useful when considering any IPV case.

Although there has been an increase in research regarding gender-inverted, same-sex, and TGD IPV over the last two decades, the general lack of data on this phenomenon is troubling. Already dated, Hamel's and colleague's (2009) survey of attorneys and judges suggests this group is misinformed about the complexities and diverse presentations of IPV. Attorneys who rely on gender stereotypes and archaic notions of relational power differentials are ill-equipped to prosecute a case. As such, it is imperative that legal decision-makers receive the necessary education and relevant information to effectively seek justice. While this education should come in the form of formal training and continuing education programs, mental health experts who work with the legal system are also well poised to inform attorneys about the most recent research and to dispel IPV myths.

Prosecutors faced with determining how to move forward with a criminal arrest may wrestle with deciding the most appropriate and applicable charges given the strength of the evidence and the victim's wishes. First, we encourage prosecutors to take the time to reflect on their personal beliefs regarding gender roles and identify gender stereotypes they may hold. Unconscious attitudes are implicit associations between a social concept (e.g., man) and an evaluation (e.g., powerful; Greenwald & Banaji, 1995). Although unconscious attitudes are, by definition, unconscious, one may become aware of these associations through active self-reflection, while deliberative decision-making may reduce their impact on tangible actions.

Further, prosecutors tasked with pursuing these cases should carefully consider the National District Attorney Association's (NDAA) 2017 National Domestic Violence Prosecution Best Practices Guidelines. NDAA outlines specific areas of consideration for effective IPV case processing, including victim autonomy, cultural competency, and the prosecutor's role. For example, the report details effective victim interviewing and advocacy, trauma-informed prosecution, and risk assessment and safety planning. Undoubtedly, every jurisdiction is different, and every case requires a nuanced, educated, and compassionate approach to prosecution. This best practices guide allows prosecutors to consider and apply relevant recommendations.

Hamel (2018) encourages attorneys to seek continuing education regarding IPV research. However, he also highlights the importance of ensuring any educator/trainer is an expert in their field and thus able to accurately communicate the latest research. Hamel further emphasizes the flaws inherent in many IPV laws, such as mandatory arrest laws and no-drop policies. While tasked with prosecuting criminal acts as defined by legal statutes, the prosecutor's primary duty is to seek justice (American Bar Association, 2017). As such, prosecutors should use discretion when applying laws with little empirical support.

Further, Hamel (2018) outlines 22 questions prosecutors should consider when a defendant is claiming to also be an IPV victim ("battered person syndrome"). These include questions regarding the event (e.g., "Did the defendant use only a reasonable amount of force to counter the perceived danger?"), defendant presentation (e.g., "Does the defendant evidence signs of trauma, and how are these symptoms relevant to the defendant's actions against the victim"), and relationship history (e.g., "When previously assaulted, or threatened with assault by the victim, did the defendant make efforts to seek help?"). Prosecutors may consult these items when determining how to apply criminal law.

DIRECTIONS FOR RESEARCH

Led by prolific scholars such as Cassia Spohn and Eryn O'Neal, scientific investigations of IPV prosecution have increased rapidly over the last 30 years. However, this remains a relatively understudied area, particularly when considering the vast research base on law enforcement and jury decision-making. Next, we outline specific topics we believe will advance our understanding of prosecutorial decision-making and inform lawmakers and clinical practitioners in addressing IPV. Nevertheless, this discussion is not exhaustive; instead, we hope this will serve as a springboard for researchers to consider future lines of impactful research.

Perhaps the most profound and obvious contribution social science researchers can make to the prosecutorial decision-making literature is the application of experimental research. The dearth of experimental literature examining this topic is puzzling, and social science researchers have the necessary training and tools to address this gap. Experimental methodology would allow researchers to isolate the specific impact of variables and measure this impact more precisely. Importantly, as noted earlier, the experimental methodology also allows researchers to draw causal inferences, significantly contributing to our basic understanding of the factors that influence prosecutor decision-making.

Another area ripe for additional research concerns the role of prosecutors as officers of the court and the interrelatedness of this role with law enforcement (e.g., police entities). Although independent agencies, both prosecutors and police officers depend on each other in the administration of justice (Harris, 2011; Orton & Weick, 1990); thus, they may be conceptualized as distinct yet connected systems (Petersen, 2017). Prosecutors rely on the police to investigate crimes, interview witnesses, and collect the best evidence possible. Police, however, depend on prosecutors to move a case through the criminal court system and bring arrested suspects to justice. Thus, although potentially valuable, research that fails to consider the entire system is not comprehensive.

Prosecutors have many "tools" in their toolbox when determining an appropriate case outcome, including plea bargaining and deferred prosecution. Relative to the plea-bargaining research base, there is substantially less scientific data concerning deferred prosecution. Thus, we have no general sense of the circumstances under which prosecutors negotiate deferred prosecution and the factors that influence these decisions.

Much of the existing research that has examined the impact of extralegal factors on prosecutorial discretion has produced mixed results. Most of this research has focused on victim and defendant characteristics (e.g., Cox et al., 2021; Petersen, 2017). We believe the exploration of prosecutor individual differences (e.g., demographic variables), sociopolitical factors (e.g., elected vs. appointed position), and prosecutor personality characteristics and value structures (e.g., right-wing authoritarianism, need for cognition) are all avenues psycholegal scholars may pursue to better understand the prosecutorial decision-making process. For example, Bandyopadhyay and McCannon (2014) suggest prosecutors may be more likely to bring a case forward to trial during political election years, while St. George and Spohn (2018) report that prosecutor beliefs about rape myths may impact charging decisions in sexual assault cases. Given the research regarding individual differences and perceptions of IPV among laypeople (Stanziani et al., 2020), it is conceivable that constructs such as gender role attitudes or attitudes toward the LGBTQ+ community may play a role in IPV case processing.

Similarly, there is a relative lack of data examining gender-inverted IPV and prosecutorial discretion with female aggressors. Considering the increase in female IPV arrests subsequent to mandatory arrest policies, an increased understanding of the dynamics inherent to these cases is imperative. To that end, research that concerns prosecutors' decision-making processes in cases of "coabuse" would also be crucial, given the high prevalence of bidirectional violence among intimate partners reporting IPV. Further, considering the disproportionate number of incarcerated people of color involved in the criminal justice system throughout the United States (Hartney & Vyong, 2009), when examining the differential treatment of men and women in the criminal justice system, research should consider the intersectionality of race and gender. Anderson (1976) theorized women of color do not benefit equally from the court's paternalistic approach to decision-making. Bishop and Frazier (1984) hypothesized legal decision-makers (e.g., judges, attorneys) are typically White men and may be less likely to consider women of color as wives, mothers, daughters, and sisters. There is some support for this theory (e.g., Farnworth & Teske, 1995; Leiber & Mack, 2003; cf. Franklin & Fearn, 2008); however, future research is needed to understand if and how an intersectional approach may elucidate prosecutorial decision-making.

CONCLUSION

Understanding how prosecutors perceive and prosecute cases of IPV is riddled with nuances produced by differences in policies, case characteristics, study methodology, and an ever-evolving understanding of the IPV public crisis. The confluence of these factors has resulted in an unclear picture as to whether and how extralegal factors, such as gender and sex, influence criminal case processing.

This lack of clarity is strong evidence of unequal treatment, but more nuanced and methodologically rigorous research is needed.

We resonate with Lantz's (2020) call for adaptive prosecutorial response to IPV cases, yet simultaneously caution against unbridled prosecutorial discretion, as legal actors may be more subject to bias with less severe, nonphysical, or more ambivalent IPV cases (e.g., Sorenson & Thomas, 2009; Steffensmeier et al., 1998). As such, we urge prosecutorial offices to educate and train personnel on IPV myths and emerging research and to encourage active self-reflection on biases. We also call for research to expound on this phenomenon through experimental methods focusing on the legal system in its entirety, alternative case outcomes (e.g., deferred prosecution), the influence of personal and sociopolitical factors on prosecutor decision-making, and diversity within the IPV crisis, specifically the intersectionality of race and gender.

REFERENCES

Agnew, R. (1992). Foundation for a general strain theory of crime and delinquency. *Criminology, 30*(1), 47–88. https://doi.org/10.1111/j.1745-9125.1992.tb01093.x

Ahmed, A., Aldén, L., & Hammarstedt, M. (2013). Perceptions of gay, lesbian, and heterosexual domestic violence among undergraduates in Sweden. *International Journal of Conflict and Violence, 7*(2), 249–260. https://doi.org/10.4119/ijcv-3022

Albonetti, C. A. (1987). The effects of uncertainty. *Law & Society Review, 21*(2), 291–314. https://doi.org/10.2307/3053523

Alhusen, J. L., Lucea, M. B., & Glass, N. (2010). Perceptions of and experience with system responses to female same-sex intimate partner violence. *Partner Abuse, 1*(4), 443–462. https://doi.org/10.1891/1946-6560.1.4.443

American Bar Association. (2017). https://www.americanbar.org/groups/criminal_justice/standards/ProsecutionFunctionFourthEdition/

Anderson, E. A. (1976). The "chivalrous" treatment of the female offender in the arms of the criminal justice system: A review of the literature. *Social Problems, 3*, 49–57.

Archer, J. (2000). Sex differences in aggression between heterosexual partners: A meta-analytic review. *Psychological Bulletin, 126*, 651–680. https://doi.org/10.1037/0033-2909.126.5.651

Baker, D. B., & Hassan, S. (2021). Gender and prosecutorial discretion: An empirical assessment. *Journal of Public Administration Research and Theory, 31*(1), 73–90. https://doi.org/10.1093/jopart/muaa017

Balko, R. (2013). *Rise of the warrior cop: The militarization of America's police forces.* Radley Balko.

Bandyopadhyay, S., & McCannon, B. C. (2014). The effect of the election of prosecutors on criminal trials. *Public Choice, 161*(1–2), 141–156. https://doi.org/10.1007/s11127-013-0144-0

Barkow, A. S., & Barkow, R. E. (Eds.). (2011). *Prosecutors in the boardroom: Using criminal law to regulate corporate conduct.* NYU Press.

Basow, S. A., & Thompson, J. (2012). Service providers' reactions to intimate partner violence as a function of victim sexual orientation and type of abuse. *Journal of Interpersonal Violence*, *27*(7), 1225–1241. https://doi.org/10.1177/0886260511425241

Belknap, J., & Graham, D. L. R. (2000). Factors related to domestic violence court dispositions in a large urban area: The role of victim/witness reluctance and other variables. Final Report. U.S. Department of Justice. https://www.ojp.gov/pdffiles1/nij/grants/184232.pdf

Bibas, S. (2004). Plea bargaining outside the shadow of trial. *Harvard Law Review*, *117*(8), 2463–2547. https://www.jstor.org/stable/4093404

Bishop, D. M., & Frazier, C. R. (1984). The effects of gender on charge reduction. *Sociological Quarterly*, *25*, 358–396.

Black, M. C., Basile, K. C., Breiding, M. J., Smith, S. G., Walters, M. L., Merrick, M. T., Chen, J., & Stevens, M. R. (2011). The National Intimate Partner and Sexual Violence Survey (NISVS): 2010 summary report. National Center for Injury Prevention and Control, Centers for Disease Control and Prevention. http://www.cdc.gov/ViolencePrevention/pdf/NISVS_Executive_Summary-a.pd

Brown, M. J., & Groscup, J. (2009). Perceptions of same-sex domestic violence among crisis center staff. *Journal of Family Violence*, *24*(2), 87–93. https://doi.org/10.1007/s10896-008-9212-5

Bushway, S. D., Redlich, A. D., & Norris, R. J. (2014). An explicit test of plea bargaining in the "shadow of the trial." *Criminology*, *52*(4), 723–754. https://doi.org/10.1111/1745-9125.12054

Buzawa, E. S., & Buzawa, C. G. (2003). *Domestic violence: The criminal justice response*. Sage.

Cerulli, C., Kothari, C. L., Dichter, M., Marcus, S., Wiley, J., & Rhodes, K. V. (2014). Victim participation in intimate partner violence prosecution: Implications for safety. *Violence Against Women*, *20*(5), 539–560. https://doi.org/10.1177/1077801214535105

Coston, B. M. (2019). Disability, sexual orientation, and the mental health outcomes of intimate partner violence: A comparative study of women in the U.S. (2019). *Disability and Health Journal*, *12*(2), 164–170. https://doi.org/10.1016/j.dhjo.2018.11.002

Cox, J., Meaux, L. T., Stanziani, M., Coffey, C. A., & Daquin, J. (2021). Partiality in prosecution? Discretionary prosecutorial decision making and intimate partner violence. *Journal of Interpersonal Violence*, *36*(17-18), 8471–8493. https://doi.org/10.1177/0886260519849689

Crawford v. Washington, 541 U.S. 36 (2004).

Criminal Cases. (n.d.). http://www.uscourts.gov/about-federal-courts/types-cases/criminal-cases

Dario, L. M., Fradella, H. F., Verhagen, M., & Parry, M. M. (2020). Assessing LGBT people's perceptions of police legitimacy. *Journal of Homosexuality*, *67*(7), 885–915. https://doi.org/10.1080/00918369.2018.1560127

Davis, R. C., O'Sullivan, C. S., Farole, D. J., & Rempel, M. (2008). A comparison of two prosecution policies in cases of intimate partner violence: Mandatory case filing versus following the victim's lead. *Criminology & Public Policy*, *7*(4), 633–662. https://doi.org/10.1111/j.1745-9133.2008.00532.x

Davis, R. C., Smith, B. E., & Davis, H. J. (2001). Effects of no-drop prosecution of domestic violence upon conviction rates. *Justice Research and Policy*, 3(2), 1–13. https://journals.sagepub.com/doi/pdf/10.3818/JRP.3.2.2001.1

Dobash, R. E., & Dobash, R. (1979). *Violence against wives: A case against the patriarchy* (pp. 179–206). Free Press.

Edwards, K. M., Sylaska, K. M., & Neal, A. M. (2015). Intimate partner violence among sexual minority populations: A critical review of the literature and agenda for future research. *Psychology of Violence*, 5(2), 112–121.

Elmquist, J., Hamel, J., Shorey, R. C., Labrecque, L., Ninnemann, A., & Stuart, G. L. (2014). Motivations for intimate partner violence in men and women arrested for domestic violence and court referred to batterer intervention programs. *Partner Abuse*, 5(4), 359–374. https://www.ncbi.nlm.nih.gov/pmc/articles/PMC4201052/

Erez, E. (2002). Domestic violence and the criminal justice system: An overview. *The Online Journal of Issues in Nursing*, 7(1), 1–18. www.nursingworld.org/ojin/MainMenuCategories/ANAMarketplace/ANAPeriodicals/OJIN/TableofContents/Volume72002/No1Jan2002/DomesticViolenceandCriminalJustice.aspx

Erickson, K. A., Jonnson, M., Langille, J. I., & Walsh, Z. (2017). Victim gender, rater attitudes, and rater violence history influence on perceptions of intimate partner violence. *Violence and Victims*, 32(3), 533–544. http://dx.doi.org/10.1891/0886-6708.VV-D-15-00086

Farnworth, M., & Teske, Jr., R. H. (1995). Gender differences in felony court processing: Three hypotheses of disparity. *Women & Criminal Justice*, 6(2), 23–44. https://doi.org/10.1300/J012v06n02_02

Ford, D. A., & Regoli, M. J. (1993). *The Indianapolis domestic violence prosecution experiment: Final report*. U.S. Department of Justice, National Institute of Justice United States.

Franklin, C. A., & Fearn, N. E. (2008). Gender, race, and formal court decision-making outcomes: Chivalry/paternalism, conflict theory or gender conflict? *Journal of Criminal Justice*, 36(3), 279–290. https://doi.org/10.1016/j.jcrimjus.2008.04.009

Frederick, B., & Stemen, D. (2012). *The anatomy of discretion: An analysis of prosecutorial decision making technical report* (Report for Award No. 2009-IJ-CX-0040). Vera Institute of Justice. https://www.ncjrs.gov/pdffiles1/nij/grants/240334.pdf

Garner, J. H., & Maxwell, C. D. (2009). Prosecution and conviction rates for intimate partner violence. *Criminal Justice Review*, 34(1), 44–79. https://doi.org/10.1177/0734016808324231

Gewirtz, A., Weidner, R. R., Miller, H., & Zehm, K. (2006). Domestic violence cases involving children: Effects of an evidence-based prosecution approach. *Violence and Victims*, 21(2), 213–229.

Goodman, L., & Epstein, D. (2005). Refocusing on women: A new direction for policy and research on intimate partner violence. *Journal of Interpersonal Violence*, 20(4), 479–487. https://doi.org/10.1177/0886260504267838

Goodman, L. A., & Epstein D. (2008). *Psychology of women: Listening to battered women: A survivor-centered approach to advocacy, mental health, and justice*. American Psychological Association.

Goolkasian, G. A. (1986). *Confronting domestic violence: A guide for criminal justice agencies*. National Institute of Justice. https://www.ojp.gov/library/abstracts/confronting-domestic-violence-guide-criminal-justice-agencies

Greenwald, A. G., & Banaji, M. R. (1995). Implicit social cognition: Attitudes, self-esteem, and stereotypes. *Psychological Review, 102*(1), 4–27.

Guadalupe-Diaz, X. (2016). Disclosure of same-sex intimate partner violence to police among lesbians, gays, and bisexuals. *Social Currents, 3*(2), 160–171. https://doi.org/10.1177/2329496515604635

Guadalupe-Diaz, X. L., & Jasinski, J. (2016). "I wasn't a priority, I wasn't a victim": Challenges in help seeking for transgender survivors of intimate partner violence. *Violence Against Women, 23*(6), 772–792. https://doi.org/10.1177/1077801216650288

Guadalupe-Diaz, X. L., & Yglesias, J. (2013) "Who's protected?" Exploring perceptions of domestic violence law by lesbians, gays, and bisexuals. *Journal of Gay & Lesbian Social Services, 25*(4), 465–485. https://doi.org/10.1080/10538720.2013.806881

Hamby, S., & Jackson, A. (2010). Size does matter: The effects of gender on perceptions of dating violence. *Sex Roles, 63*(5–6), 324–331.

Hamel, J. (2018). Intimate partner violence: Gender issues and the adjudication of homicide and other cases. *Journal of Criminological Research, Policy, and Practice, 4*(4), 226–237. https://doi.org/10.1108/JCRPP-01-2018-0008

Hamel, J., Desmarais, S. L., Nicholls, T. L., Malley-Morrison, K., & Aaronson, J. (2009). Domestic violence and child custody: Are family court professionals decisions based on erroneous beliefs? *Journal of Aggression, Conflict, and Peace Research, 1*(2), 37–52.

Hamel, J., Jones, D. N., Dutton, D. G., & Graham-Kevan, N. (2015). The CAT: A gender-inclusive measure of controlling and abusive tactics. *Violence and Victims, 30*(4), 547–580. https://doi.org/10.1891/0886-6708.W-D-13-00027

Harris, D. A. (2011). *The interaction and relationship between prosecutors and police officers in the U.S., and how this affects police reform efforts*. University of Pittsburgh Legal Studies Research Paper Series (Working Paper No. 2011-19).

Hartney, C., & Vuong, L. (2009, March). *Created equal: Racial and ethnic disparities in the U.S. criminal justice system*. National Council on Crime and Delinquency. Retrieved from https://www.nccdglobal.org/sites/default/files/publication_pdf/created-equal.pdf

Henning, K., & Feder, L. (2005). Criminal prosecution of domestic violence offenses: An investigation of factors predictive of court outcomes. *Criminal Justice and Behavior, 32*, 612–642. https://doi.org/10.1177/0093854805279945

Henning, K., Jones, A. R., & Holdford, R. (2005). "I didn't do it, but if I did I had a good reason": Minimization, denial, and attributions of blame among male and female domestic violence offenders. *Journal of Family Violence, 20*(3), 131–139. https://doi.org/10.1007/s10896-005-3647-8

Henning, K., & Renauer, B. (2005). Prosecution of women arrested for intimate partner abuse. *Violence and Victims, 20*(3), 361–376. https://doi.org/10.1891/vivi.20.3.361

Henning, K., Renauer, B., & Holdford, R. (2006). Victim or offender? Heterogeneity among women arrested for intimate partner violence. *Journal of Family Violence, 21*(6), 351–368. https://doi.org/10.1007/s10896-006-9032-4

Herzog, S. (2007). An empirical test of feminist theory and research. *Feminist Criminology, 2*(3), 223–244. http://doi.org/10.1177/1557085107301836

Hine, B., Noku, L., Bates, E. A., & Jayes, K. (2020). But, who is the victim here? Exploring judgments toward hypothetical bidirectional domestic violence scenarios. *Journal of Interpersonal Violence*. https://doi.org/10.1177/0886260520917508

Holleran, D., Beichner, D., & Spohn, C. (2010). Examining charging agreement between police and prosecutors in rape cases. *Crime & Delinquency Volume*, *56*(3), 385–413. https://doi.org/10.1177/0011128707308977

Iyengar, R. (2009). Does the certainty of arrest reduce domestic violence? Evidence from mandatory and recommended arrest laws. *Journal of Public Economics*, *93*(1–2), 85–98. https://doi.org/10.1016/j.jpubeco.2008.09.006

Johnson, M. P. (2005). Domestic violence: It's not about gender: Or is it? *Journal of Marriage and Family*, *67*(5), 1126–1130. https://www.jstor.org/stable/3600300

Kingsnorth, R. F., & MacIntosh, R. C. (2007) Intimate partner violence: The role of suspect gender in prosecutorial decision-making. *Justice Quarterly*, *24*(3), 460–495. https://doi.org/10.1080/07418820701485395

Kittari, S. K., Walls, N. E., & Speer, S. R. R. (2017). Differences in experiences of discrimination in accessing social services among transgender/gender nonconforming individuals by (dis)ability. *Journal of Social Work in Disability & Rehabilitation*, *16*(2), 116–140. https://doi.org/10.1080/1536710X.2017.1299661

Klein, A., Mountz, S., & Bartle, E. (2018). Factors associated with discrimination in social-service settings among a sample of transgender and gender-nonconforming adults. *Journal of the Society for Social Work and Research*, *9*(3), 431–448. https://doi.org/10.1086/699538

Kozuch, E. (2020, June 25). HRC report shows that LGBTQ people are more likely to be victims of interpersonal violence. Human Rights Campaign. https://www.hrc.org/news/hrc-report-shows-lgbtq-people-are-more-likely-to-be-victims-of-interpe

Kubicek, K., McNeeley, M., & Collins, S. (2015). "Same-sex relationship in a straight world": Individual and societal influences on power and control in young men's relationships. *Journal of Interpersonal Violence*, *30*, 83–109. https://doi.org/10.1111/j.1471-6402.1990.tb00013.x

Kurdyla, V., Messinger, A. M., & Ramirez, M. (2019). Transgender intimate partner violence and help-seeking patterns. *Journal of Interpersonal Violence*, *36*(19-20), NP11046–NP11069. https://doi.org/10.1177/0886260519880171

Lambda Legal. (2015). Protected and served? Survey of LGBT/HIV contact with police, courts, prisons, and security. https://www.lambdalegal.org/protected-and-served

Landes, W. M. (1971). An economic analysis of the courts. *The Journal of Law and Economics*, *14*(1), 61–107. https://doir.org/10.1086/466704

Lantz, B. (2020). Victim, police, and prosecutorial responses to same-sex intimate partner violence: A comparative approach. *Journal of contemporary criminal justice*, *36*(2), 206–227. https://doi.org/10.1177/1043986219894429

Leiber, M. J., & Mack, K. Y. (2003). The individual and joint effects of race, gender, and family status on juvenile justice decision-making. *Journal of Research in Crime and Delinquency*, *40*(1), 34–70. https://doi.org/10.1177/0022427802239253

MacNeil, E., Cox, J., & Daquin, J. (2020, August 5–7). Gender role attitudes and prosecutorial decision-making [Poster presentation]. American Psychological Association.

Mallory, C., Hasenbush, A., & Sears, B. (2015). *Discrimination and harassment by law enforcement officers in the LGBT community*. The Williams Institute. https://escholarship.org/content/qt5663q0w1/qt5663q0w1.pdf

Maxwell, C., Garner, J., & Fagan, J. (2001). *The effects of arrest on intimate partner violence: New evidence from the spouse assault replication program*. National Institute of Justice.

Messing, J. T. (2010). Evidence-based prosecution of intimate partner violence in the post-Crawford era: A single-city study of the factors leading to prosecution. *Crime & Delinquency, 60*(2), 238–260. https://doi.org/10.1177/0011128710362056

Miller, S. L. (2001). The paradox of women arrested for domestic violence: Criminal justice professionals and service providers respond. *Violence Against Women, 7*(12), 1339–1376.

Mills, L. G. (1999). Killing her softly: Intimate abuse and the violence of state intervention. *Harvard Law Review, 113*(2), 550–613. https://doi.org/10.2307/1342332

Nadal, K. L., Quintanilla, A., Goswick, A., & Sriken, J. (2015) Lesbian, gay, bisexual, and queer people's perceptions of the criminal justice system: Implications for social services. *Journal of Gay & Lesbian Social Services, 27*(4), 457–481. https://doi.org/10.1080/10538720.2015.1085116

National Coalition Against Domestic Violence. (2020). Domestic violence. https://assets.speakcdn.com/assets/2497/domestic_violence-2020080709350855.pdf?1596811079991

National District Attorneys Association. (2017). *National domestic violence prosecution best practices guidelines.* NDAA_National-DV-Prosecution-Best-Practices-Guide_3-16-2017.pdf (ncdsv.org)

Obergefell v. Hodges, 135 S. Ct. 2071–2017.

O'Neal, E. N., & Spohn, C. (2017). When the perpetrator is a partner: Arrest and charging decisions in intimate partner sexual assault cases—A focal concerns analysis. *Violence Against Women, 23*(6), 707–729. https://doi.org/10.1177/1077801215591630

O'Neal, E. N., Tellis, K., & Spohn, C. (2015). Prosecuting intimate partner sexual assault: Legal and extra-legal factors that influence charging decisions. *Violence Against Women, 21,* 1237–1258. https://doi.org/10.1177/1077801215591630

O'Neill, M. E. (2004). Understanding federal prosecutorial declinations: An empirical analysis of predictive factors. *American Criminal Law Review, 41,* 1439–1498.

Orton, J. D., & Weick, K. E. (1990). Loosely coupled systems: A reconceptualization. *Academy of Management Review, 15*(2), 203–223. https://doi.org/10.5465/amr.1990.4308154

Owen, S. S., Burke, T. W., Few-Demo, A. L., & Natwick, J. (2018). Perceptions of the police by LGBT communities. *American Journal of Criminal Justice, 43,* 668–693. https://doi.org/10.1007/s12103-017-9420-8

Parry, M. M., & O'Neal, E. N. (2015). Help-seeking behavior among same-sex intimate partner violence victims: An intersectional argument. *Criminology, Criminal Justice Law & Society, 16*(51), 51–67.

Peitzmeier, S. M., Malik, M., Kattari, S. K., Marrow, E., Stephenson, R., Agenor, M., & Reisner, S. L. (2020). Intimate partner violence in transgender populations: Systematic review and meta-analysis of prevalence and correlates. *American Journal of Public Health, 110*(9), e1–e14.

Peterman, L. M., & Dixon, C. G. (2003). Domestic violence between same-sex partners: Implications for counseling. *Journal of Counseling and Development, 81,* 40–53. https://doi.org/10.1002/j.1556-6678.2003.tb00223.x

Petersen, N. (2017). Examining the sources of racial bias in potentially capital cases: A case study of police and prosecutorial discretion. *Race and Justice, 7*(1), 7–34. https://doi.org/10.1177/2153368716645842

Poorman, P. B., Seelau, E. P., & Seelau, S. M. (2003). Perceptions of domestic abuse in same-sex relationships and implications for criminal justice and mental health responses. *Violence and Victims, 18*, 659–669. https://doi.org/10.1891/vivi.2003.18.6.659

Redlich, A. D., & Summers, A. (2012). Voluntary, knowing, and intelligent pleas: Understanding the plea inquiry. *Psychology, Public Policy, and Law, 18*(4), 626–643. https://doi.org/10.1037/a0026066

Reed, E., Raj, A., Miller, E., & Silverman, J. G. (2010). Losing the "gender" in gender-based violence: The missteps of research on dating and intimate partner violence. *Violence Against Women, 16*(3), 348–354. https://doi.org/10.1177/1077801209361127

Renauer, B., & Henning, K. (2005). Investigating intersections between gender and intimate partner violence recidivism. *Journal of Offender Rehabilitation, 41*(4), 99–124. https://doi.org/10.1300/J076v41n04_05

Reynolds, G. H. (2016, April 6). Prosecutors have too much power. Juries should rein them in. https://www.washingtonpost.com/news/in-theory/wp/2016/04/06/prosecutors-have-too-much-power-juries-should-rein-them-in/

Romain, D. M., & Freiburger, T. L. (2013). Prosecutorial discretion for domestic violence cases: An examination of the effects of offender race, ethnicity, gender, and age. *Criminal Justice Studies, 26*(3), 289–307. http://dx.doi.org/10.1080/1478601X.2012.745399

Russell, B., Chapleau, K. M., & Kraus, S. W. (2015). When is it abuse? How assailant gender, sexual orientation, and protection orders influence perceptions of intimate partner abuse. *Partner Abuse, 6*(1), 47–64. http://dx.doi.org/10.1891/1946-6560.6.1.47

Russell, B., Ragatz, L. L., & Kraus, S. W. (2009). Does ambivalent sexism influence verdicts for heterosexual and homosexual defendants in a self-defense case? *Journal of Family Violence, 24*(3), 145–157.

Russell, B., & Sturgeon, J. A. D. (2019). Police evaluations of intimate partner violence in heterosexual and same-sex relationships: Do experience and training play a role? *Journal of Police and Criminal Psychology, 34*(1), 34–44. https://doi.org/10.1007/s11896-018-9279-8

Seelau, E. P., Seelau, S. M., & Poorman, P. B. (2003). Gender and role-based perceptions of domestic abuse: Does sexual orientation matter? *Behavioral Sciences and the Law, 21*, 199–214. https://doi.org/10.1002/bsl.524

Seelman, K. L. (2015). Unequal treatment of transgender individuals in domestic violence and rape crisis programs. *Journal of Social Service Research, 41*(3), 307–325. https://doi.org/10.1080/01488376.2014.987943

Smith, S. G., Zhang, X., Basile, K. C., Merrick, M. T., Wang, J., Kresnow, M., & Chen, J. (2018). *The National Intimate Partner and Sexual Violence Survey (NISVS): 2015 data brief updated release.* National Center for Injury Prevention and Control, Centers for Disease Control and Prevention. https://www.cdc.gov/violenceprevention/pdf/2015data-brief508.pdf

Sorenson, S. B., & Thomas, K. A. (2009). Views of intimate partner violence in same-and opposite-sex relationships. *Journal of Marriage and Family, 71*(2), 337–352. https://doi.org/10.1111/j.1741-3737.2009.00602.x

Spohn, C., Beichner, D., & Davis-Frenzel, E. (2001). Prosecutorial justifications for sexual assault case rejection: Guarding the "gateway to justice." *Social Problems, 48*(2), 206–235. https://doi.org/10.1525/sp.2001.48.2.206

Spohn, C., & Tellis, K. (2019). Sexual assault case outcomes: Disentangling the overlapping decisions of police and prosecutors. *Justice Quarterly*, *36*(3), 383–411. https://doi.org/10.1080/07418825.2018.1429645

St. George, S., & Spohn, C. (2018) Liberating discretion: The effect of rape myth factors on prosecutors' decisions to charge suspects in penetrative and non-penetrative sex offenses. *Justice Quarterly*, *35*(7), 1280–1308. https://doi.org/10.1080/07418825.2018.1529251

Stanziani, M., Cox, J., & Coffey, C. A. (2018). Adding insult to injury: Sex, sexual orientation, and juror decision-making in a case of intimate partner violence. *Journal of Homosexuality*, *65*, 1325–1350. https://doi.org/10.1080/00918369.2017.1374066

Stanziani, M., Newman, A. K., Cox, J., & Coffey, C. A. (2020). Role call: Sex, gender roles, and intimate partner violence. *Psychology, Crime, and Law*, *26*, 208–225. https://doi.org/10.1080/1068316X.2019.1652746

Steffensmeier, D., Ulmer, J., & Kramer, J. (1998). The interaction of race, gender, and age in criminal sentencing: The punishment cost of being young, black, and male. *Criminology*, *36*(4), 763–798. http://doi.org/10.1111/j.1745-9125.1998.tb01265.x

Straus, M. A. (2008). Dominance and symmetry in partner violence by male and female university students in 32 nations. *Children and Youth Services Review*, *30*(3), 252–275. https://doi.org/10.1016/j.childyouth.2007.10.004

Straus, M. A., & Ramirez, I. L. (2007). Gender symmetry in prevalence, severity, and chronicity of physical aggression against dating partner partners by university students in Mexico and USA. *Aggressive Behavior*, *33*, 281–290. https://doi.org/10.1002/ab.20199

Stuntz, W. J. (2004). Plea bargaining and criminal law's disappearing shadow. *Harvard Law Review*, *117*(8), 2548–2569. http://doi.org/10.2307/4093405

Vincent, B. W. (2018). Studying trans: Recommendations for ethical recruitment and collaboration with transgender participants in academic research. *Psychology & Sexuality*, *9*(2), 102–116. https://doi.org/10.1080/19419899.2018.1434558

Wasarhaley, N. E., Lynch, K. R., Golding, J. M., & Renzetti, C. M. (2017). The impact of gender stereotypes on legal perceptions of lesbian intimate partner violence. *Journal of Interpersonal Violence*, *32*(5), 635–658. https://doi.org/10.1177/0886260515586370

Whitaker, D. J., Haileyesus, T., Swahn, M., & Saltzman, L. S. (2007). Differences in frequency of violence and reported injury between relationships with reciprocal and nonreciprocal intimate partner violence. *American Journal of Public Health*, *97*(5), 941–947. https://doi.org/10.2105/AJPH.2005.079020

Women's Donor Network. (2019, October). Tipping the scales: Challengers take on the old boys' club of elected prosecutors. https://wholeads.us/wp-content/uploads/2019/10/Tipping-the-Scales-Prosecutor-Report-10-22.pdf

Zavala, E., & Kurtz, D. L. (2016). Applying differential coercion and social support theory to police officers' misconduct. *Deviant Behavior*, *37*(8), 877–892. https://doi.org/10.1080/01639625.2016.1153365

Challenges and Strategies in Mounting a Legal Defense in Intimate Partner Violence Criminal Cases

CHARLES DRESOW ■

This chapter is intended for attorneys representing those arrested or charged with domestic violence offenses, sometimes known as intimate partner violence (IPV). The author is a criminal defense attorney who has represented those accused of domestic violence for over a decade. His practice is based in the San Francisco Bay Area. He has represented individuals at all stages of the proceeding, in his practice, from postarrest/prefiling to jury trials and appeals. The views and opinions expressed herein are primarily based on the author's experience and that of his family. The author's father was a criminal defense attorney for over 40 years, and his paternal grandfather was a career public defender. All were trial attorneys who represented individuals accused of domestic violence at jury trial. The lessons learned by my grandfather were passed to my father, who then passed them to this author. These lessons have assisted the author in understanding the unique dynamics of a domestic violence case successfully.

FIRST STEPS

The phone rings in your office. You pick it up. A voice on the other line says they need a lawyer because they were arrested for domestic violence. Your evaluation of the case and client must begin immediately. An arrest or accusation of domestic violence is a traumatic experience for both the arrestee and the complaining witness. In the immediate aftermath of a domestic violence–related arrest, both individuals face a potentially life-changing odyssey through the criminal justice system. As a lawyer, you must immediately begin building trust and rapport with your potential client. I will not discuss the business-related process of retainer agreements and setting fees in this chapter other than to say the best practice ethically is to receive your payment from your client. Do not take payment of your fee from the alleged victim. This can cause a conflict of interest or lead to ethical concerns down the road.

From the moment the phone rings, you must start evaluating the case, the individuals involved, and the context in which the alleged domestic violence incident occurred. Generally, on a first phone call or meeting with a new client, they will be somewhat scattered and want to dump tons of relevant and irrelevant information in the meeting. Do not worry about formally interviewing them or asking a checklist of questions at this point. For the first meeting, just listen. In subsequent meetings just listen, and take notes. You can return to the information you need or questions you have later. In the first meeting or call, it is essential to understand the relationship between parties, how the incident was initiated, and the history of the parties—the universe of the case. At some point in the first call, you will need to find out what the client does for a living and whether they have a professional license or job that requires a background check. Here is some information that is useful to gather during the first meeting with a client who was arrested for or charged with a crime of domestic violence:

- Relationship type (married, dating, living together, broken up, family member)
- Job and any professional licenses or certifications
- Possession of any firearms which may have to be turned in pursuant to the issuance of a protective order (a conviction for a crime of violence or domestic violence may preclude your client from possessing firearms for the rest of their life)
- Prior arrests, cases, or allegations along with probationary or parole status
- Prior military service
- Physical and mental health issues
- Substance abuse or use-related issues
- Whether either party consumed any intoxicating substances before the incident
- Presence of children or witnesses
- Any pending litigation between the parties, such as a divorce or civil restraining orders
- Your client's goals in the representation—do they need a full acquittal, dismissal, or nonfile, or are they most concerned with avoiding jail?
- Citizenship status

This is not a comprehensive list. You need to start understanding the universe of the case from the moment the client first contacts you. This can include noting the client's tone and demeanor toward you. Are they aggressive and confrontational with you or passive? Do they appear to be forthcoming or have any noticeable cognitive lapses? Was a substance abuse or mental health–related issue involved in the incident? To understand the universe of the case, you must understand your client. You need to build a relationship of trust with the client from the first contact. Do not be offended if the client does not tell you the whole story or even lies to you during the first contact. At the first meeting, you should focus on listening and gathering information. If you are meeting in person, you may want to avoid taking notes at the first meeting. This can be impersonal and break your personal connection with the client. Eye contact and open ears are most important at the first meeting. You can leave a 20- or 30-minute period in your schedule after the first meeting to write down notes and list any follow-up questions.

COLLATERAL CONSEQUENCES

It is critical to be aware of a pending domestic violence prosecution's impact on your client's life and livelihood. A conviction for a crime of domestic violence can have severe negative consequences, including deportation or denial of citizenship for a noncitizen client. A conviction for domestic violence likely precludes an individual from owning or possessing a firearm for the rest of their life. Professional licensing boards can deny certification or seek to discipline the individuals professionally. A client convicted of a crime may face termination from their employment. It is always wise to ask your client to review their employee handbook to look for any language or policies regarding arrests and or convictions.

The goal of every representation needs to be full acquittal or dismissal. You do need to identify potential safe harbors for resolution along the way. For instance, a noncitizen may face deportation if they are convicted of charged offenses, a crime of moral turpitude, and domestic violence. This client will not face immigration consequences if they plead to a non–domestic violence/non–moral turpitude crime such as disturbing the peace. This client may not wish to gamble for a full acquittal at jury trial if an immigration safe plea is available.

You must understand that you are required to give accurate immigration advice to a noncitizen before they accept a plea: "[t]o satisfy this responsibility, we now hold that counsel must inform her client whether his plea carries a risk of deportation. Our longstanding Sixth Amendment precedents, the seriousness of deportation because of a criminal plea, and the concomitant impact of deportation on families living lawfully in this country demand no less" (*Padilla v. Kentucky* (2010) 559 U.S. 356, 374). You must have an immigration specialist review any proposed plea bargains for noncitizens. Given the complexity and ever-changing nature of immigration-related law, an expert in that area is necessary.

THE UNIVERSE OF THE CASE

You can begin to build your defense theme and identify areas for further investigation as you start to understand the universe of the case. To build your defense theme, it is vital to understand the relationship that exists between the accused and the alleged victim. A critical first step in this process is evaluating the power dynamic between the two. Who is the dominant party in the relationship? This is not as easy to identify as it seems. There may be both a private power dynamic and a public power dynamic. For instance, one individual may have a meaningful, highly paid, powerful, public-facing job with significant responsibilities. At the same time, the other is a stay-at-home parent or has a job that provides little income or responsibility. The individual with the high income and big job would appear to hold the power in the relationship to an outside observer. This is not always true behind closed doors. The individual who stays at home may be verbally and psychologically abusive to the other individual. You need to understand and evaluate the power dynamic between your client and the alleged victim.

Power Dynamics

In some cases, generally involving short-term dating relationships, no power dynamic has developed between the parties. Tinder and other casual social media contacts have changed the nature of how individuals view dating and relationships. On some occasions, the relationship between two individuals who have met on a casual dating app might not fall within the coverage of the domestic violence laws. In these instances, you need to check your jurisdiction's definition of domestic relationships to determine if the parties even fall within the domestic violence laws.

Consider this example. Your client met and had a singular consensual sexual encounter with the alleged victim through a dating app. Six months elapse with no contact. Then they reconnect through a dating app and have another consensual encounter. After another few months with no contact, the two see each other in a bar. They argue that your client has allegedly pushed the victim out of anger while in the bar. In this type of case, the relationship between the parties and the dynamics of the incident may not qualify as domestic battery because their relationship fails to qualify. Given the enhanced penalties and eligibility restrictions for diversions and sentencing alternatives, it is essential to evaluate whether the relationship falls within your jurisdiction's definition of a domestic relationship. Alternatively, individuals who met through casual dating apps may fall within the relationship definition of domestic violence without knowing so or considering themselves to be in a relationship.

Your understanding of the universe of the case will evolve as your investigation of your client and their relationship with the alleged victim grows. Equally important as your understanding of your client is your understanding of the alleged victim. You conduct a thorough investigation of the alleged victim and their personal circumstances. Do not meet with the alleged victim alone or have them attend office meetings with your client during this process. If you need a statement from them, get it through a private investigator. Communicating with a victim, especially without a private investigator present, is a recipe for disaster. You do not want to become a witness and be forced to conflict off the case if the alleged victim makes a statement to you and then later denies or changes that statement. Meeting with an alleged victim without a private investigator can also leave you vulnerable to claims that you manipulated or intimidated them. The best rule is to use a private investigator instead of personally interacting with the alleged victim.

The process of understanding the parties and the power dynamic between them continues throughout the case. Once you have a good initial handle on the parties as individuals and understand the power dynamic, you are well on the way to the point where you can continue developing your defense theme. As you gather more information, you will start to see the universe of the case form. You must be agile and understand that a newly discovered fact may upend your understanding of the case and the parties involved.

Guiding Clients through the Process

During this time of gaining competency over the facts of the case, you must continue to communicate with your client and keep them updated. "Client control" is a term used by many attorneys to describe their interaction with the person they represent. You should not think of client relations in this way. You were hired to guide them through a potentially life-altering experience, not control them. Your client may be facing the loss of their marriage or relationship while they are considering the impact of a potential conviction on their job or professional license. They may be facing the reality of going to jail or potentially losing custody of a child. At times they may call you while on a spiral of emotion caused by fear of the unknown. The unknown is terrifying. To many individuals, the criminal justice system is one big unknown. While remembering you are a lawyer, not a therapist, you may be able to address your client's fears by listening to them and changing the unknown to the known. This will reduce their stress significantly. For instance, your client may be terrified about the first court date and wondering how they will prepare for their "trial" with so little time. By explaining to a client that the first court date is simply an arraignment where the formal criminal court process starts and there is no "trial" on that day, this client's stress and terror will be reduced accordingly. Consider that many clients' perceptions of the court system stem from getting a traffic ticket and going to court to fight it or pay the fine. This is a very different process than the criminal process, and it is worth explaining the differences between the two types of procedures if it appears your client is confusing the two.

As you get to know your client, their fears, and their personality, you must constantly evaluate whether you think they can testify in their own defense at trial. This is a separate evaluation from the question of whether they *should* testify at trial. Although this is an ongoing evaluation and can change, you must conceptualize whether the client can testify in their own defense as you develop your theme. Evaluating whether your client *can* testify will rest on their personality, credibility, ability to stand up to pressure, and other case-specific facts. The determination of whether your client *should* testify includes any prior convictions or evidence that will come into evidence only if they testify. In a case that proceeds to trial, deciding whether your client testifies may rest on what evidence was admitted during the people's case. To develop your defense theme and understanding the universe of the case, the consideration of whether your client *can* testify will evolve as the case proceeds.

Most criminal cases are resolved short of jury trial through either plea bargaining, diversion, or dismissal. Only a small number of criminally charged cases proceed to trial. Domestic violence cases tend to go to trial more often than other types of crimes. The moment you are retained by a client charged with a domestic violence–related offense, you must consider that the universe of the case may include a jury trial. You must explain to your client that their case may have to go to a jury trial if it is not settled or dismissed. Even if the alleged victim does not wish to prosecute, the District Attorney may take the case to the jury. It is worth explaining to your client that a criminal case is prosecuted in the name of the state. The prosecutor does not represent the alleged victim. The prosecutor will consider the alleged victim's desires but is not mandated to dismiss the case if the alleged victim wants the case dismissed. Explaining this early in the representation will help your client better understand the process and likelihood of dismissal pretrial. Explaining early avoids the inevitable confused client later.

Throughout the criminal process, recall that while you handle cases in the criminal court's system every day, your client's knowledge of the court process may come solely from TV shows or pop culture media coverage of notorious cases. You frequently will have to spend some time explaining the actual court procedure and how it differs from TV or pop culture procedure. Explaining the reality of the criminal process early and often during a representation will assist your client in navigating through an incredibly confusing and stressful period of their life.

CONSIDERATIONS IN DOMESTIC VIOLENCE CASES

As discussed elsewhere in this volume, domestic violence cases that travel through the criminal justice system differ from other crimes classifications. Understanding of your jurisdiction's arrest policies and prosecutorial filing process can help you effectively communicate expectations to your client and soothe some of their concerns. In most jurisdictions a police officer is mandated to arrest when there is any allegation or evidence of physical abuse. An officer responding to a domestic violence report will generally identify a dominant aggressor and then make an arrest. These mandatory arrest laws were developed to prevent the scenario where an officer responds to the scene of a domestic violence incident, makes no arrest, and then is dispatched out later to a homicide or serious bodily injury incident. A reality that permeates domestic violence cases is that at each level, there is a fear that if the arresting officer, prosecutor, judge, and so on do nothing, subsequently something like a homicide can occur, leaving the person who had a chance to act but did not to be blamed.

How domestic violence cases are handled is as much related to the political climate, risk avoidance, and societal views on domestic violence as the facts of any specific case. Your client needs to understand this. Just because an arrest was made does not mean that there will be charges filed. In some jurisdictions, domestic violence offenses can be filed as either felonies or misdemeanors. If a felony arrest was made, it does not mean that the charges will not be filed at a reduced level by the prosecutor. As discussed earlier, your phone generally will ring after an arrest when the client is looking to hire a lawyer to assist them. Once you receive that call and take the case, you must be prepared for the case to run its course in unexpected ways. You have to tailor your defense strategy to the specific facts of the case and the characters that develop in the universe of the case.

Consider the following examples of domestic violence cases that went to trial and notice how a defense theme was developed early and that theme built into a successful defense at trial. (Names and some facts have been altered to protect the identity of the parties involved.)

Example 1. Judy was a young African American female who had met and casually dated a slightly older Caucasian male police detective. The police detective was frequently verbally abusive and demeaning toward her. She responded verbally in kind. On the night of Judy's arrest, both individuals videoed and audiotaped each other as they hurled terrible insults at each other. They had been drinking at a bar together in a jurisdiction next to where the detective worked. He was off duty at the time. Neither party looked or sounded sympathetic on these videos, and one video was made while the intoxicated off-duty detective threatened to kick Judy out of his car in a random parking lot. She refused to get out of his car, and they returned to his apartment, where he claimed she hit and kicked him. He videotaped himself trying to remove her from his couch physically. He then called the police and identified himself as an off-duty officer. Massive police response ensued, and Judy was arrested for felony domestic violence causing injury. She was allowed to write her statement in a jail cell while the alleged victim was left at home to type his statement and turn it in the next day.

Misdemeanor charges were filed against Judy. Early on, the power differential between the alleged victim and client was developed as a theme. He was White, and she was African American. She was a female who was employed as a school aide, while he was an established police detective. Judy would lose her ability to work if she was convicted of a domestic violence–related offense. The case proceeded

Challenges and Strategies

to trial. Through investigation, it was discovered that the alleged victim had made a prior police report claiming an ex-girlfriend victimized him. The report was disclosed to the defense and revealed an incredibly similar set of facts to Judy's case. The detective, while off duty, had engaged in a mutually abusive verbal fight with a girl he was dating. He then called the police and claimed physical abuse. She was arrested but not charged due to a lack of evidence. A secondary theme was developed that the alleged victim was using his law enforcement employment to gain favoritism from the investigating officers.

The cross-examinations of the alleged victim and investigating officers were calibrated to develop the themes discussed earlier. The investigating officers were questioned about their knowledge of the alleged victim's law enforcement background and how they had treated him differently than Judy. Ultimately Judy was acquitted of all charges.

Example 2. Tania was a female who was not married but was in a relationship and shared a child with the alleged victim. The alleged victim told Tania that he was working late and would not be home. Tania located the alleged victim in a cheap motel with another female. The alleged victim then claimed Tania attacked him. Tania claimed he attacked her, and she defended herself. Responding officers identified Tania as the dominant aggressor because she had traveled to the motel and arrested her for felony domestic violence. The other woman in the motel was not identified by the investigating officers and was not available as a trial witness. The case essentially became a credibility contest. Cross-examination and argument were used to develop the theme that if the alleged victim would lie to the mother of his child, then he would easily lie to the police and jury about being attacked first. The jury acquitted the client.

Each defense theme was developed independently of the defendant being a female and the victim being a male in these examples. The jury will consider that aspect of the case, and you do not need to waste time pointing it out. The best themes use the facts of the case to tell a story that concludes with a not-guilty verdict. Jurors want to do the right thing. Your job is to present your case in a fashion that persuades them that the only right thing to do is vote not guilty.

Another example of this involving a female defendant was when the male alleged victim filed divorce papers but did not serve them or notify the client. She had been the sole breadwinner of the family while he failed at various jobs. Her salary had primarily paid for their house. The alleged victim was incredibly verbally abusive and taunted the client about her postpregnancy weight gain. She eventually was alleged to have pushed him after a series of verbal insults. He called the police, and she was arrested and charged with misdemeanor domestic battery. He then served her with the divorce papers and sought a move-out order in a family law court because he had been "abused." His actions were used to develop a theme that he had planned to divorce her and fabricated the domestic violence allegation to gain an advantage over her in the family law proceeding. The jury acquitted her quickly. Although the theme did not attempt to paint the client as a hero, it certainly was persuasive in showing that the accuser was no victim.

Sex and Gender

Each of the examples presented so far was related to female defendants. Juries tend to be biased against men who treat women poorly or abusively and then call the police when they get hit. Although the battered woman defense has been limited in several jurisdictions, you still can develop a theme that incorporates the alleged victim's conduct into your defense. Jurors are people, and people are persuaded by themes that connect with their beliefs and personal experiences. They do not like to feel like they are siding with or protecting the villain.

Structuring your trial theme for a case where a male is accused of domestic violence against a female involves different considerations from when you represent a female accused of domestic violence against a male. This is because the jurors are not sympathetic to a male accused of violence against a female when the roles are reversed. In many cases involving a female accused of domestic violence against a male, the jurors will give the female a pass for some conduct that violates the domestic violence statutes. A famous Texas lawyer, Racehorse Haynes, understood that jurors had sympathy toward a female accused of domestic violence against an abusive male victim:

> He made something of a specialty of "Smith & Wesson divorces," as he called them: cases in which wives solved their marital problems by killing their husbands. "I won all but two of those cases," he told ABA Journal in 2009. "And I would have won them if my clients hadn't kept reloading their gun and firing." (Curriden, 2009)

In these defenses, Mr. Haynes essentially presented a case that portrayed the alleged male victim as abusive, someone whose actions required the female defendant to use self-defense. As the earlier quote illustrates, the only cases he lost were when the immediate need for self-defense was resolved.

Male clients rarely are perceived by jurors as the weaker or more vulnerable party in a relationship and therefore look at claims of self-defense by a male defendant with more significant doubt (see Russell & McKimmie, Chapter 7, this volume). When you represent a male client, you must evaluate whether relationship stereotypes must be countered with the true dynamics of the relationship. These stereotypes include but are not limited to identifying the male as the dominant partner in a relationship, the male as the aggressive party in a relationship, and the controlling party of a relationship. The universe of the case may include facts that contradict these stereotypes. Investigate for these facts. For instance, consider the case of Richard. Richard was in his mid-twenties and married to a very successful and well-paid partner at a CPA firm named Donna. She worked while he stayed at home and took care of the kids. Before their relationship, Richard made a healthy living managing a chain of bars. The couple had met when her firm was hired to perform an audit of the books. Once they had children, it was agreed by the couple that he would give up his career and she would be the breadwinner. Donna began to work longer hours and treat Richard as more of a housekeeper than a partner. She verbally emasculated him multiple times a week. After an argument, Donna called the police and claimed that Richard had punched her in the leg while she was lying in bed. In her statement to police, Donna claimed that Richard was controlling, verbally abusive, and had instigated the argument that led to the police report.

Donna received an emergency protective order, and Richard was forced to move out of their house. She rapidly decided she did not wish the case to proceed, but the District Attorney filed charges against her wishes. The District Attorney had body-worn camera video of her allegations from when the police responded to the scene. Donna refused to cooperate with the prosecution other than to notify them she did not want the case prosecuted. The District Attorney chose to proceed, using the body-worn camera video as their evidence. They presented an expert to explain why an abused woman would stay with her abuser and refuse to cooperate with the prosecution. This expert claimed that women would stay with their abusers and protect them because the abuser controls the alleged victim's finances, children, and livelihood. The abuser has the power over the alleged victim. The alleged victim is then afraid to leave the abuser because they feel they will lose everything and have no financial support. This expert was cross-examined vigorously to show how the "power and control" was held by that alleged victim rather than Richard. The jury acquitted.

Expert Witnesses

The earlier examples involved the representation of both males and females accused of domestic violence. Although there are different considerations in representing each type of client, your understanding of the universe of the case and the development of a defense theme are equally important. When planning your cross-examinations for trial, you must make sure that the questions support your theme. In Richard's example, the cross-examination of the expert supported the theme that Donna was the power persona in the relationship and that the government's case was based on the flawed premise that Richard was the power party.

The government will sometimes present an expert as part of their case to explain why someone they perceive as a victim has not left the accused or is not cooperating in the prosecution. You must carefully evaluate the credentials of the expert and any personal biases they may have. It is well worth ordering copies of any reports or training they have attended to gain their expertise. Commonly government-side domestic violence experts will be either retired law enforcement officers or domestic violence advocates who have worked in the field. A careful review of their credentials and training may reveal that they have only attended law enforcement side seminars and training. Ask yourself why is this person's testimony relevant or, stated another way, what does it prove? Do they simply bolster the government's case, or do they present something new or different?

Mandatory Arrest and Dominant Aggressor Laws

Richard's case is an excellent example of how the outside politics of domestic violence and the societal context of this type of crime can lead to cases going to trial which should have been dismissed or not filed. Mandatory arrest laws lead to situations where police respond to a mutual argument or mutual fight and then are forced to identify and arrest the dominant aggressor. This then turns what may have been a private argument into a public court proceeding. California's arrest statute authorizes a warrantless arrest in domestic violence incidents (California Legislative Information, 2021a):

> (d) Notwithstanding paragraph (1) of subdivision (a), if a suspect commits an assault or battery upon a current or former spouse, fiancé, fiancée, a current or former cohabitant as defined in Section 6209 of the Family Code, a person with whom the suspect currently is having or has previously had an engagement or dating relationship, as defined in paragraph (10) of subdivision (f) of Section 243, a person with whom the suspect has parented a child, or is presumed to have parented a child pursuant to the Uniform Parentage Act (Part 3 (commencing with Section 7600) of Division 12 of the Family Code), a child of the suspect, a child whose parentage by the suspect is the subject of an action under the Uniform Parentage Act, a child of a person in one of the above categories, any other person related to the suspect by consanguinity or affinity within the second degree, or any person who is 65 years of age or older and who is related to the suspect by blood or legal guardianship, a peace officer may arrest the suspect without a warrant where both of the following circumstances apply:
> (1) The peace officer has probable cause to believe that the person to be arrested has committed the assault or battery, whether or not it has in fact been committed.
> (2) The peace officer makes the arrest as soon as probable cause arises to believe that the person to be arrested has committed the assault or battery, whether or not it has in fact been committed. (Pen. Code, § 836)

The California Penal Code encourages peace officers to arrest the dominant aggressor in a domestic violence incident (California Legislative Information, 2021b):

> (a) Every law enforcement agency in this state shall develop, adopt, and implement written policies and standards for officers' responses to domestic violence calls by January 1, 1986. These policies shall reflect that domestic violence is alleged criminal conduct. Further, they shall reflect existing policy that a request for assistance in a situation involving domestic violence is the same as any other request for assistance where violence has occurred.

(b) *The written policies shall encourage the arrest of domestic violence offenders if there is probable cause that an offense has been committed.* These policies also shall require the arrest of an offender, absent exigent circumstances, if there is probable cause that a protective order issued under Chapter 4 (commencing with Section 2040) of Part 1 of Division 6, Division 10 (commencing with Section 6200), or Chapter 6 (commencing with Section 7700) of Part 3 of Division 12, of the Family Code, or Section 136.2 of this code, or by a court of any other state, a commonwealth, territory, or insular possession subject to the jurisdiction of the United States, a military tribunal, or a tribe has been violated. These policies shall discourage, when appropriate, but not prohibit, dual arrests. Peace officers shall make reasonable efforts to identify the dominant aggressor in any incident. The dominant aggressor is the person determined to be the most significant, rather than the first aggressor. In identifying the dominant aggressor, an officer shall consider the intent of the law to protect victims of domestic violence from continuing abuse, the threats creating fear of physical injury, the history of domestic violence between the persons involved, and whether either person acted in self-defense. These arrest policies shall be developed, adopted, and implemented by July 1, 1996. Notwithstanding subdivision (d), law enforcement agencies shall develop these policies with the input of local domestic violence agencies. (Pen. Code, § 13701)

The dominant aggressor is not defined in California as the person who started the incident or even struck the first physical blow (California Legislative Information, 2021a):

The dominant aggressor is the person determined to be the most significant, rather than the first, aggressor. In identifying the dominant aggressor, an officer shall consider the intent of the law to protect victims of domestic violence from continuing abuse, the threats creating fear of physical injury, the history of domestic violence between the persons involved, and whether either person acted in self-defense. (Pen. Code, § 13701(b))

This statute forces the investigating officer to decide whom to arrest based on limited or unreliable information at the scene. The officer is essentially directed to arrest based on initial investigation and first impression (see Hamel & Russell, Chapter 1; and Russell & Seisler, Chapter 3, this volume). This does not mean the District Attorney will file a case made based on that determination.

When your client is in your office shortly after their arrest, they will likely be confused about how the officer could have arrested them or why they arrested them when the alleged victim asked the officers not to arrest while at the incident scene. Penal Code 13701 is why. It is helpful to explain to your client that although California law encourages actual arrest in domestic violence incidents, the same standard of proof exists for conviction—that of proof beyond a reasonable doubt. Just because an arrest was made does not mean there will be a conviction. The District Attorney's office has the same discretion to file a domestic violence-related offense as they do in any other type of case. A thorough investigation of the incident may reveal facts unknown to the arresting officer that cause the filing Deputy District Attorney to reject the case. The arresting officer's on-scene conclusion about who was the dominant aggressor can cause an innocent person to face the indignity of an arrest, booking, and eventual prosecution.

The mandatory and encouraged arrest laws are designed to protect victims from abuse starting all over again once the police leave. This is a noble goal. In practice, police officers who are statutorily encouraged to make an arrest are unlikely to respond to a domestic violence call and leave without one of the parties handcuffed in the back of their squad car. If the officer fails to make an arrest, and then one of the parties is seriously injured or killed after the officer leaves, the officer likely will face professional consequences along with personal guilt. This fear of a tragedy occurring because of lack of intervention permeates how the criminal justice system handles domestic violence cases. A filing Deputy District Attorney will review a case and worry if they reject it. Subsequently, the alleged victim is killed or seriously injured by the same suspect; they will face severe scrutiny for their decision. A Deputy District Attorney assigned to handle the case once it is filed will have the same concern, and so will a Judge if the decision to dismiss falls to them. This is a reality of handling domestic violence cases. In order to effectively persuade the decision-maker not to file or dismiss a domestic violence case, you must deal with their fear of a reoccurrence. This fear of reoccurrence is separate and distinct from the merits of a given case or accusation, and this factor is present in the universe of any domestic violence case.

The fear of the reoccurrence factor exists independently of the merits or provability of the accusation. Occasionally an individual will out and out fabricate a domestic violence accusation and lie to the police to have someone arrested. False allegations are made for various reasons and considered a subset of legal and administrative aggression, a form of "power and control" behavior and psychological abuse that is often used in disputed child custody cases (see the chapters by Pisarra, Chapter 8; and Hamel & Baker, Chapter 9, this volume.) These cases have a very distinct universe, and your focus needs to be on proving the claim's falsity. This is done through the investigation with a focus on locating independent evidence which contradicts the accusation. Your evidence then is presented to the filing deputy to show the claim is false. In a different scenario, your client was arrested by police, dispatched to the scene, and identified your client as the dominant aggressor. In this type of case, a neighbor, the alleged victim, or another individual called the police for help. The California Penal Code prioritizes police response to reports of domestic violence (California Legislative Information, 2021b):

> Every law enforcement agency in this state shall develop, adopt, and implement written policies and standards for dispatchers' response to domestic

violence calls by July 1, 1991. These policies shall reflect that calls reporting threatened, imminent, or ongoing domestic violence and the violation of any protection order, including orders issued pursuant to Section 136.2, and restraining orders, shall be ranked among the highest priority calls. Dispatchers are not required to verify the validity of the protective order before responding to the request for assistance. (Pen. Code, § 13702)

The Penal Code directive that domestic violence calls be ranked among the highest priority results in a police response to nearly every report of domestic violence received by dispatch. The statutory encouragement for the arrest of the individual identified as the dominant aggressor increases the probability of the dispatch call ending in an arrest. In other classifications of cases, the investigating officer might choose not to make an arrest and instead send the reports to the District Attorney for a decision. In most domestic violence cases, the arrest is made either at the incident scene or shortly after the incident. In these cases, the filing deputy district attorney may understand that their evidence is weak but are concerned about another incident. This is especially true when the evidence reflects mutual combat or self-defense-gone-too-far situations. To persuade the filing deputy to reject cases like this for prosecution, it is helpful to understand that the universe of the case reflects that something happened. However, it may be unprovable precisely what happened. These cases are challenging to prove in front of a jury, so the filing deputy might be persuaded to reject the case if you can show him or her that steps have been taken to ensure a similar situation will not happen again. Depending on the specific universe of a case and its parties, these steps can include some form of deferred prosecution as well as couples counseling, anger management, alcohol or substance abuse treatment, mediation, or some action that addresses the root cause of the incident, which triggered a police response. For more information on sentencing alternatives, see Chapter 4 by Cox et al. in this volume and those included in the last section.

Your client, who was arrested, taken to jail, and possibly forced to pay significant bail, may balk at taking affirmative steps to address the behavior which led to their arrest. Perhaps because they may feel that they were the true victim, or the other person lied, and so on. They might make a point of "why should I do any of this—I'm innocent." Persuading a filing deputy to reject a marginal case because steps have been taken to address behavior that led to a police intervention helps ease their fear of reoccurrence. If effective, this will end a case much more quickly than having to defend a jury trial. Identifying factors or behaviors which contributed to the situation which led to police intervention can also pay dividends if the case is filed. If the trial deputy district attorney feels their case is slipping away from them for whatever reason, they still may be afraid to dismiss out of fear they will be blamed for letting the defendant off the hook if it happens again. At this stage in the case, it is important to speak frankly to the deputy and explaining that although your client is not guilty of the charged offense, they have taken steps to address the root causes of the incident.

Take, for example, the case of Tony. Tony was 26 years old and was working toward his real estate license. He had a college degree and had never really left his fraternity lifestyle behind when he graduated. Tony had a dating relationship with Becca, who was a heavy drinker. Both would fall into the category of high-functioning alcoholics. They occasionally would do cocaine together. Neither drank heavily nor did drugs during the workweek, but both would party and drink to blackout almost every weekend. After a night at the bars that included cocaine together, Tony was seen speaking to an ex. Becca unleashed a verbal tirade on him in front of the bar as other patrons were leaving. She threw a glass at the ground by his feet and then pushed him. Witnesses then observed him push her back, knocking her to the ground. He then left, and another patron called the police. The police arrived and interviewed Becca. She was heavily intoxicated and combative with the officers. She said Tony had pushed her but denied pushing him first or throwing a glass at his feet. The police located Tony at his apartment and arrested him for domestic battery. The officer reasoned that he was the dominant aggressor because witnesses had seen him push her with enough force to knock her to the ground while her push had only caused him to step back.

The District Attorney filed the case. Becca sent emails and left messages with the assigned deputy that she did not want Tony prosecuted, nor would she cooperate with the prosecution. Becca hired her own attorney, who then advised the prosecutor that his client would be asserting her Fifth Amendment privilege against self-incrimination if called to testify at a trial. The assigned prosecutor felt she could prove the case because of the independent witnesses. Becca was on the fence because she had not been hurt, and she wanted to consider the alleged victim's desires for no prosecution. Post arrest Tony started attending Alcholics Anonymous (AA)/Narcotics Anonymous (NA) and then enrolled in a 6-month intensive outpatient program for substance abuse. He completed the program successfully and continued to attend aftercare and AA/NA meetings. This information was provided to the filing deputy. The information was used to argue that the incident between Tony and Becca was more a substance abuse–related incident than a classic domestic abuse case. Since Tony was sober and continuing treatment, there was little chance he would reoffend because the root cause of his conduct was his substance abuse. The case was then dismissed.

This example illustrates how identifying the factors leading to specific behavior and having your client address them early can lead to a dismissal in marginal cases. A 52-week batterers' treatment program is required as a term of probation after a domestic violence conviction in California. This treatment program is relatively one size fits all and can seem either punitive or rehabilitative to a client. Your client might have gotten into a fight with their partner while heavily intoxicated. The incident may have had more to do with overconsumption of alcohol than anger management. A client whose issues do not fall within those addressed by the 52-week program will feel punished rather than rehabilitated. Identifying client-specific treatment before a conviction can undoubtedly help persuade a prosecutor that your client, the alleged victim, and society, in general, are better served and protected through the course of treatment you developed than that of the standard batterer's treatment program. Penal Court 1203.097 allows the court to approve a more individual treatment program to satisfy the 52-week requirement (California Legislative Information, 2021c):

> (6) Successful completion of a batterer's program, as defined in subdivision (c), or if none is available, another appropriate counseling program designated by the court, for a period not less than one year with periodic progress reports by the program to the court every three months or less and weekly sessions of a minimum of two hours class time duration. The defendant shall attend consecutive weekly sessions, unless granted an excused absence for good cause by the program for no more than three individual sessions during the entire program and shall complete the program within 18 months, unless, after a hearing, the court finds good cause to modify the requirements of consecutive attendance or completion within 18 months. (Pen. Code, § 1203.097)

This section allows a defense attorney to present an individual treatment plan to the court for approval. It is wise to have a mental health, substance abuse, or other treatment expert draft the plan. The treatment provider must provide updates to the court and probation.

THE TRIAL

To handle domestic violence cases effectively, you must understand the societal, political, and community climate that exists around this segment of cases. This climate is where your jurors come from, and they walk into the courtroom with their preconceived notions of domestic violence. A vigorous and thorough jury selection strategy is necessary to eliminate the potential jurors who cannot be fair to your client. To do this, you must once again have a thorough understanding of the universe of your client's case and all the worlds that exist within it. You must identify both the weak points in the prosecution's case and your best evidence. Focus your jury selection on the evidentiary issues and other turning points of the case. Eliminate potential jurors who have opinions and views that are unsympathetic to your position. Most trials have one or two moments that turn the tide of the case and lead to a verdict one way or another.

The most well-known example of this is when the glove did not fit in the O.J. Simpson trial. There was a moment of truth that focused the jury's attention on a singular piece of evidence. That moment broke in the defense's favor and led directly to Johnny Cochran's closing argument theme, "If the glove doesn't fit, you must acquit." And acquit the jury did. Identify the moments of truth in your case and focus your jury selection on eliminating jurors that will likely fall against you when the moment occurs. The most straightforward example of this is in a case where you will develop that the investigating officer exaggerated the alleged victim's statements. Some jurors will be willing to discount police exaggerations.

In contrast, others will find the idea of an officer putting something other than the exact truth in a report offensive to the idea of justice. If this distinction is going to be the critical turning point of the case, eliminate potential jurors who will give the officer a pass for the exaggerations. Your case theme should be introduced to the potential jurors during the jury selection process.

Your defense theme must remain consistent throughout the entire case. Everything you do in a trial should support the theme or originate from it. Your defense theme becomes the narrative arc of the story you are trying to tell at trial. You want to develop the facts of the case to tell a story to the jury, which ends with them writing the conclusion: an acquittal. Jurors are humans, and humans have a long history of storytelling. Themes that build into the narrative arc of a story are compelling because they are comfortable to jurors. Legendary trial lawyer Gerry Spence (2005) explains:

> We view most of our lives in terms of story. We are fascinated by movies because of their stories in which we inhabit the life of those on the screen. Most advertisements we suffer on television are in story form. Even the nightly news is conveyed as story. *The Wall Street Journal* and *The New York Times* most often begin a feature with the story of an individual caught up in it. Elizabeth Ellis said, "Storytelling is the grandmother of all our knowledge." (pp. 85–86)

A good story is more persuasive to the jury than a disjointed attack on the facts or credibility of the witnesses. A good story fits your attacks on the facts and credibility of the witnesses into your theme, leading to your desired result. Stated another way, your story must answer the "Why does it matter?" question. If a witness lied or an officer exaggerated in their report, the jury might overlook it unless your story illustrates why the lie or exaggeration creates reasonable doubt. When preparing for trial, you need to identify the facts upon which the case will turn and focus on building those facts into your theme or finding an excellent way to rebut or discredit them. Your opening statement, cross-examinations, and any evidence you present must be consistent these aims and your theme. A disjointed presentation is not credible to the juror.

When the trial begins, the jury will know nothing of the case other than the charges read by the court. You will fully understand the universe of the case as you stand to give your opening statement. In preparing for this moment, you can't disregard that you are part of the universe of the case to the jury. You can think of yourself as the jury's narrator as you tell them the story of the case. Your questions during cross-examination and direct examination are the guideposts. The narrator is part of the story to the juror. Be aware of how you carry yourself, dress, and support your theme with your physical presence. Be yourself and understand how the tone of your questioning and arguments can impact your ability to persuade the jury.

Make sure that your client understands that he or she will be scrutinized by the jurors exhaustively. Ensure your client can avoid any outbursts or combative body language. It is not a stretch for the jury to believe your client was the aggressor in a domestic violence incident if they have aggressive or hostile body language during the trial. Make sure that your client is aware that when on trial, they must behave like they are being watched from the moment they leave their house in the morning to the moment they close the door at the end of the day. If your client cuts someone off and flicks them off or yells at them on the way to the court, odds are it will be a juror or a juror will see it. A good illustration of this is when the author was handling a reckless driving and hit-and-run jury trial. After a long day of trial, the client raced out of the courtroom because he was late for an appointment. The jurors were exiting the courthouse when they observed the client driving his truck at a high rate of speed and rolling through a red light as he made a right turn. The client was ultimately acquitted, but several jurors noted how his behavior outside of the courthouse gave them pause. Fortunately for the client, the evidence was so weak in the case that the jury overlooked what they had observed. In a closer case, his out-of-court conduct might have stolen a conviction out of the jaws of reasonable doubt.

This risk is somewhat mitigated if the bailiffs manage your client's commute to the courthouse. Even when your client is in custody, they need to understand that the jury will evaluate their every movement. Make sure that your client stands when the jury leaves and does not look back at the bailiffs to take him or her away until every juror has left the room. The jurors are not supposed to know that an individual is in custody during the trial. It would be best to avoid tip-offs that your client is housed courtesy of the government during the trial.

Each jury trial is different. A thorough understanding of the dynamics of your case, the client, and the alleged victim is necessary to succeed at trial. Your jury selection strategy, opening statement, witness examinations, and closing should follow a consistent theme. The theme should correlate with the specific universe of your case.

CONCLUSION

The author hopes that you have found these observations helpful. Every domestic violence case is different. Each demands a careful understanding of the universe of the case and all its inhabitants. You must be prepared to walk into court representing someone charged with a crime that offends society. It takes skill, dedication, and a healthy heap of intestinal fortitude to handle this type of case successfully. Good luck.

REFERENCES

California Legislative Information. (2021a). Penal code, Part 2 of criminal procedure, Title 3, additional provisions regarding criminal procedure, Chapter 5. https://leginfo.legislature.ca.gov/faces/codes_displaySection.xhtml?sectionNum=836.&lawCode=PEN

California Legislative Information. (2021b). Penal code, Part 4, prevention of crimes and apprehension of criminals, Title 5, law enforcement response to domestic violence. https://leginfo.legislature.ca.gov/faces/codes_displaySection.xhtml?lawCode=PEN&sectionNum=13701

California Legislative Information. (2021c). Part 2 of criminal procedure, Title 8, of judgement and execution, Chapter 1. https://leginfo.legislature.ca.gov/faces/codes_displaySection.xhtml?sectionNum=1203.097.&lawCode=PEN

Curriden, M. (2009). Richard 'Racehorse" Haynes. ABA Journal, (2009, March 2nd). https://www.abajournal.com/magazine/article/richard_racehorse_haynes

Grimes, W. (2017, April). Richard Haynes, flashy and successful Houston lawyer, dies at 90. https://www.nytimes.com/2017/04/28/us/richard-racehorse-haynes-dead-texas-defense-lawyer.html

Spence, G. (2005). *Win your case: How to present, persuade, and prevail—every place, every time*. St. Martin's Press.

6

Intimate Partner Homicide and the Battered Person Syndrome

JOHN HAMEL, DON DUTTON, AND ALEXANDRA LYSOVA ■

Intimate partner homicide (IPH) became a topic of social science research in the late 1970s, raising awareness about domestic violence, also known as intimate partner violence (IPV). This chapter presents a comprehensive overview of research on the prevalence, context, risk factors, and motivation for IPH perpetration, including similarities and differences across the sexes, with implications for the judicial system, in particular prosecutors and defense attorneys tasked with adjudicating such cases. We argue that IPH is not a unitary phenomenon and requires consideration of different types of homicides. Such disaggregation of IPH into subtypes could help improve our understanding and assessment of, as well as responses to, IPH.

The literature on the classification of different IPH cases is limited (Caman et al., 2017; Ioannou & Hammond, 2015). The focus is on the sex of a perpetrator/victim and risk factors (Belknap et al., 2012; Spencer & Stith, 2020). Given close interpersonal relationships between any two parties involved in IPH, we discuss such cases along with major categories of couple-based IPV (Johnson, 2008). These types of IPH cases are not meant to fit neatly with certain IPV types but rather provide a framework for researchers and practitioners to consider a variety of IPHs. We also add the discussion of individual risk factors for IPH that can interact with couple-related risk factors. Different theoretical perspectives apply to different types of IPH. In this chapter, we focus on the feminist gender paradigm, evolutionary psychology, and social learning to explain cases of male-perpetrated IPH. The critical examination of these perspectives allows for the explanation of other types of IPH, including the female-perpetrated intimate terrorism type of IPH and the male-perpetrated violent resistance type of homicide. In discussing personality-related risk factors, we focus on attachment theory to explain how the lack of secure attachment can lead to abandonment IPH.

We begin by reviewing research data on IPV, commonly known as *domestic violence*, which describes three prevalent types of aggression between intimate partners in dating, cohabitating, and marital relationships, that is, *situational couple violence, intimate terrorism*, and *violent resistance*. Then we examine IPH as a subset of various IPV types. Finally, we move on to discuss the implications of these findings for the judicial system with the focus on the *battered woman syndrome* that is sometimes used for self-defense pleas in homicide cases.

IPV has historically comprised a type of social problem that governments have found challenging because traditional norms of family protection and family privacy from the state clashed with each other (Pleck, 1987). Early in the 20th century, Theodore Roosevelt advocated corporal punishment for "wife beaters" (Pleck, 1987), leading to new laws in three US states. Throughout the rest of the century, there was a waxing and waning of criminal justice, and social work approaches enacted. Since the 1990s, there has been a vigorous criminal justice response to IPV, and the problem is no longer regarded as a private matter (Buzawa & Buzawa, 2003). An evolution in the legal system's views of perpetrators and victims of IPV/IPH was reflected in the defense seeking to introduce expert testimony at trial on the psychological effects of IPV in 1979 (Paradis et al., 2020). In past decades, US and Canadian courts became more accepting of expert testimony on the behaviors known as *battered woman syndrome* (BWS) and *battered person syndrome* (BPS) (Paradis et al., 2020).

IPH, as a subset of IPV, is recognized as significant health problem in the world (Stöckl et al., 2013). Domestic homicide reviews suggest that many IPH cases appear predictable and preventable with hindsight, whereas only a minority are highly unexpected (Jaffe et al., 2020). Many gaps in professional training and service delivery, and a lack of interagency cooperation are likely to hinder the prevention of IPH in similar circumstances in the future. This chapter highlights a variety of IPH situations and motives and critically reviews various explanations that expand our understanding of IPH.

TYPES OF INTIMATE PARTNER VIOLENCE

As discussed at greater length elsewhere in this volume (e.g., Bates & Papamichail, Chapter 2), rates of both physical and psychological IPV are comparable across the sexes. Based on a meta-analysis of 249 studies published from 2000 to 2010, Desmarais et al. (2012) found that in large population surveys, males reported more IPV victimization in the past year than did females. Past-year victimization is generally considered the more reliable measure than lifetime victimization because of memory issues (Straus, 1999). According to the National Intimate Partner and Sexual Violence Survey (NISVS), the largest, most recent IPV survey conducted in the United States, the total overall number of past-year combined physical and nonphysical victims of IPV, including sexual abuse, were 23,560,000 women and 26,239,000 men (Black et al., 2011). The majority of incidents involved psychological abuse and controlling behaviors. In his meta-analytic study of sex differences in IPV, Archer (2000) found women to be slightly more likely to be injured than men (d = .16).[1]

However, large surveys and meta-analyses such as these provide scant information about the complexities and dynamics of IPV. For this, we turn to a brief discussion of typology research.

Situational Couple Violence

One of the most popular approaches to classifying different types of IPV is a couple-based approach developed by Johnson (2008, 2011). According to this classification, most IPV (66%–75%) consists of noninjurious physical assaults such as grabbing and pushing that are not likely to lead to serious injuries (Archer, 2002; Black et al., 2011; Hines et al., 2013). Although one or both partners can be violent, neither of the partners is particularly controlling of the other. It has been called *situational couple violence* because it typically occurs during escalating conflicts among couples and is characterized by high levels of anger, poor communication skills, and a lack of impulse control (Johnson, 2008, 2011). Based on perpetrator typologies widely used in the field, men and women who engage in this type of behavior would fit best in a category called *family or partner only*, consisting of individuals with no criminal histories and little, if any, mental health issues (Babcock et al., 2003; Holtzworth-Munroe & Stuart, 1994).

Intimate Terrorism

The most consequential type of IPV features a pattern of physical abuse, often severe, together with emotional abuse and various controlling behaviors, and is known as *intimate terrorism* (Johnson, 2008, 2011), *controlling-coercive violence*, or more commonly, *battering*. In these couples, it is often the case that one individual is violent and controlling and the partner is not, although other cases involve two intimate terrorists, known as *mutual violent control*. In the Holtzworth-Munroe typology, batterers are categorized as *dysphoric-borderline* (low criminal history, highly possessive, insecure, and reactive) and *generally violent/antisocial* type (high criminal history and substance abuse, violence used instrumentally, distancing emotional style). Female perpetrators in such couples are categorized as *generally violent* women (Babcock et al., 2003).

Based on these definitions, national surveys in the United States and Canada have found comparable prevalence rates of both *situational couple violence* and *intimate terrorism* across sex (Jasinski et al., 2014; Laroche, 2005; Lysova et al., 2019). In cases of *intimate terrorism*, more commonly known as *battering*, sex

---

1. *d* is a measure of the difference between two distributions—of the size of an effect, a d of .06 is 1/16 of a standard deviation difference between male and female distributions.

differences in IPV impact are more pronounced. Although men and women incur minor injuries at comparable rates and women can also terrorize their partners emotionally, women sustain a larger share of serious injuries and express much greater fear of victimization due to their relatively lesser size and strength and difficulty defending themselves (Jasinski et al., 2014; Lawrence et al., 2012; Lysova et al., 2019). This is an important factor in understanding domestic violence dynamics, especially at extreme levels, for example, in cases of repeated rape, kidnapping, forced prostitution, and homicide (Hamel & Russell, 2013; Stark, 2007). That being said, the rates of extreme IPV ("severe violence" on the Conflict Tactics Scale, the most common measure of victim reports) are quite low and are in the 4%–5% range for reports of male violence by women (Stets & Straus, 1992). Aside from physical injuries, victims of intimate terrorism report high levels of anxiety and depression, low self-esteem, posttraumatic stress disorder (PTSD), and other evidence of trauma (Coker et al., 2002; Hines & Douglas, 2013, 2019; Williams & Frieze, 2005).

Violent Resistance

An additional type of IPV identified in Johnson's typology is *violent resistance*. This is the type of couple violence where a noncontrolling partner can become violent to protect themselves and resist a violent and controlling partner (Johnson, 2008). It is often a response to *intimate terrorism*. Although some consider it an entirely woman's type of violence (Johnson, 2008), male victims of intimate terrorism use violent resistance against their violent and controlling female partners much more often than previously thought (Hines & Douglas, 2019).

GENDER SYMMETRY IN INTIMATE PARTNER VIOLENCE PERPETRATION

Despite the findings mentioned earlier about the similar rates of perpetration of various types of IPV by men and women, many still find it difficult to explain female involvement in IPV other than violent resistance to IPV initiated by their male partners. One of the theories that shed light on the sex/gender symmetry in IPV perpetration by examining women's involvement in violence outside and inside the home is an evolutionary approach (Campbell, 2013; Wilson & Daly, 1993). Having evolved to compete for partners against same-sex rivals and amass resources, men are naturally more prone to take risks, display aggression, and overcome their fears of danger. In contrast, women are wired to experience higher levels of fear to avoid situations that would threaten successful child-rearing (and the survival of the human species) (Campbell, 2013; Cross & Campbell, 2011). Not surprisingly, women are far less outwardly aggressive in general than men, who perpetrate the great majority of violent crimes and engage in the majority of public displays of aggression, including verbal aggression (Archer, 2004).

However, women have been shown to use comparable or higher rates of indirect aggression (Archer, 2004), such as using malicious gossip and ostracizing others from their social groups. In laboratory studies, women will engage in direct aggression (e.g., administering a series of electric shocks) when they feel justified or when they can do so anonymously (Frodi et al.,1977; Richardson, 2005). Furthermore, anger and hostile intentions are experienced at comparable levels between the sexes (Brody & Hall, 2008). When women use physical violence outside the home, it is generally against female rivals.

What then, from an evolutionary perspective, explains the symmetry among men and women in violence within the home and intimate relationships? It has been suggested that women's normal fear instincts are disinhibited in the home, where they are motivated to defend their natural maternal and resource-seeking interests (Cross et al., 2011; Saini et al., 2017; Straus, 1999). Emerging research indicates that the hormone oxytocin, involved in pair-bonding and childbirth, may also be involved through its stress and fear-reducing properties (Cross & Campbell, 2011). Cultural norms reinforce these tendencies. Greater societal tolerance for female-perpetrated IPV, combined with norms of chivalry and the greater disapproval of violence by husbands, may help motivate women to overcome their natural fears and defend their interests. Even in the most patriarchal societies, women regard the home as their domain.

There are, however, alternative explanations for the high rates of female-perpetrated IPV. Among them are those from social learning theory. Boys and girls who witness IPV by either parent are at risk of acting out against peers; and later to perpetrate IPV against dating partners in adolescence and, later, in their adult intimate relationships (Ehrensaft et al., 2003; Kimber et al., 2018). Observational learning does not depend on the size and strength of the parties. In another line of research, Eriksen and Jensen (2006, 2009) found that boys in their teens were more likely to be punished for sibling violence than were girls. The boys' aggression was deemed more serious by their parents and was more severely punished. Consequently, the frequency of male sibling violence diminishes during the teen years while female sibling violence does not. This means females have higher rates of intimate aggression at an age where they first enter intimate relationships.

In addition, the research literature finds little support for the theory that men are motivated to batter their female partners to enforce traditional gender roles, at least in the United States (Sugarman & Frankel, 1996). Individuals arrested for domestic violence give a variety of reasons for assaulting their partners, among them self-defense, retaliation, failures in communication and anger regulation, jealousy, and to exercise control, but common to all battering is a need to dominate one's partner, coupled with poor impulse control and beliefs that violence is acceptable (Capaldi et al., 2012; Dutton, 2006). Straus and colleagues' famous National Family Violence surveys in the 1980s (Straus & Gelles, 1990) found a positive correlation between IPV and household dominance by either the husband or wife. Also, in Straus's (2008) international survey of 13,601 university students in 32 countries, male and female respondents who endorsed such items as "my partner needs to remember that I am in charge" were equally likely to use severe violence against their partner. In fact, men and women attempt to control their partners for many reasons, having more to do with personality and circumstances than gender roles.

BIDIRECTIONAL INTIMATE PARTNER VIOLENCE

Victims of IPV may elicit sympathy from others, but often it is difficult to distinguish between victim and perpetrator, given that approximately 58% of physical IPV is bidirectional and initiated at similar rates across the sexes (Langhinrichsen-Rohling et al., 2012). Five independent large-sample US surveys, totaling a combined sample size of 23,106, found that 50% of all IPV reported in victim surveys was bilateral, matched for level of severity (Dutton et al., 2017). The breakdown of perpetrator sex and bilaterality in these surveys was remarkably consistent, with age being the only demographic factor that had a large effect on IPV incidence.[2] When emotional abuse and controlling behaviors are considered, the percentage of abusive relationships in which both partners engage in any type of abuse is even greater. Furthermore, and of major significance for the adjudication of both IPV and IPH, male and female perpetrators report a similar array of motives and at comparable rates. These include a wish to control or punish the partner, in retaliation, as a means of expressing anger or to communicate, and sometimes in self-defense (Langhinrichsen-Rohling & McCullars, 2012).

Bidirectionality is often the case, even with victims who have entered a shelter. Approximately half of the women living in the first shelters established in the United Kingdom were co-batterers of violence toward husbands and or their children (Pizzey, 1982). Similarly, in the United States a shelter survey found that 67.1% of female victims had perpetrated severe violence at least once toward their male partners in the previous year (McDonald et al., 2009). In a large majority of abusive relationships, it is more accurate to view the parties neither as perpetrators nor victims but rather as co-perpetrators, particularly when nonphysical forms of abuse are considered. When asked in another shelter survey about their relationship abuse, victimized women said their own violence was perpetrated in self-defense less than 50% of the time (Saunders, 1996). Research also found that the female partners of men arrested for domestic violence initiate physical assaults in 40% of the cases (Gondolf, 1996; Stacey et al., 1994). Abused men who seek help through domestic violence hotlines sometimes report having engaged in IPV of their own, mostly in self-defense (Cook, 2009; Douglas & Hines, 2011; Hines & Douglas, 2019).

Bidirectional IPV is not necessarily perpetrated at equal levels of severity or chronicity; often, one person is the dominant aggressor who drives the

---

2. Racial differences diminish when correlated factors such as network embeddedness are controlled (Cazaneave & Straus, 1992).

relationship abuse. Among couples who are bidirectionally violent but who call the police only when violence levels increase, it is the male member of the couple who is typically arrested, even in dual-arrest states, and even when it is the man who experienced the most serious victimization (Capaldi et al., 2009). Therefore, a history of abuse victimization must be considered in the context of the entire relationship and the personalities of the parties involved. Attorneys litigating IPV cases should become familiar with the latest, most accurate information on the subject, including its prevalence, causes, characteristics, and consequences. They are advised to become familiar with findings from the National Intimate Partner and Sexual Violence Survey (Black et al., 2011; Smith et al., 2018), and the more comprehensive 2,687-page *Partner Abuse State of Knowledge Project*, a compendium of IPV research available for free online (www.domesticviolenceresearch.org). Helpful information and suggestions can also be found in Hamel (2016), especially for those practicing family law.

PREVALENCE RATES OF INTIMATE PARTNER HOMICIDE

A major distinction between lethal and nonlethal IPV is the much lower prevalence rates for the former in comparison with the latter. Wilson and Daly (1993) reported three larger datasets of IPH with baseline rates as follows: Chicago, male perpetrator 3.6/100,000 (per hundred thousand [PHT]), female perpetrator 3.5 PHT; New South Wales, Australia, male perpetrator 7 PHT, female perpetrator 3 PHT; Canada, male perpetrator 8 PHT, female perpetrator 3 PHT. Since then, IPH rates have steadily abated, until recently, when the number of victims rose from 1,875 per year in 2014 to 2,237 in 2017 (Fridel & Fox, 2019)—a noticeable increase, yet nonetheless, IPH is a rare event.

Another important distinction between lethal and nonlethal IPV is that women are much more likely to be victims of male-perpetrated IPH. One literature review, reporting data from 66 countries worldwide, found that IPH accounted for 38.5% of all female homicide victims, compared to 6.3% for male victims (Stöckl et al., 2013). In contrast to men, women are proportionately more likely to be killed by an intimate partner than a stranger and account for the large majority of IPH victims (Bourget & Gagne, 2012; Catalano, 2012; Crawford & Gartner 1992; Garcia et al., 2007; Spencer & Stith, 2020; Velopulos et al., 2019). In part, this is because homicide victimization rates outside of marriage are higher for men (Browne et al., 1999). Crawford and Gartner (1992) reviewed 551 femicides in Ontario, Canada, from 1974 to 1990 and found that 61% to 78% of women were killed by intimate partners, depending on the specific definition of intimate femicide used. They identified one motive as dominant; that is, rage over impending separation or suspected infidelity was present in 43% of the cases. Female perpetrators are far less likely than male perpetrators to overpower their victims physically and beat them to death, and to use knives, guns, and other weapons instead (Cooper & Smith, 2011; Jurik & Winn, 1990; Mann, 1988; Mize et al., 2009; Mize & Shackelford, 2008; Smith et al., 2014; Swatt & He, 2006,

Velopulos et al., 2019). They are also less likely to have a previous criminal record of violent crime (Block & Christakos, 1995; Jordan et al., 2012).

INTIMATE PARTNER HOMICIDE TYPES

Male-Perpetrated Intimate Partner Homicide in the Context of Intimate Terrorism

A prevailing set of assumptions, with roots in Marxist sociology (MacKinnon, 1989) and collectively known as the *gender paradigm* (Dutton et al., 2009; Dutton & Nicholls, 2005; Felson & Lane, 2010), views IPH as primarily male perpetrated, in order to enforce dominance over their female partners, assumed to be their right in a patriarchal society (Dobash & Dobash, 2011; Saunders & Browne, 2000; Serran & Firestone, 2004). Feminist analysis also views wife killing as an endpoint in escalating male domestic violence (Campbell et al., 2003). Interviews with perpetrators, and collateral interviews with relatives and others, indicate that possessiveness and jealousy, along with fears of abandonment, are significant motivators for male-perpetrated IPH (Dobash & Dobash, 2011; Harden et al., 2019; Liem & Roberts, 2009). Dutton (2006) has argued that fear of abandonment has psychological origins in the process of attachment, not the sociological origins implied by the gender paradigm.

Furthermore, the higher rates of suicide by male homicide perpetrators are thought to be an indication of guilt, although Dutton has argued that it is indicative of a more severe emotional reaction by males to feelings of relationship dissolution, overwhelming loss, or abandonment (Dutton, 2006). For every hundred thousand divorcing men in the United States, four will kill their wives and 207 will kill themselves, an eightfold increase (Kposowa, 2000). Comparable suicide statistics for females do not increase with separation. This seems to indicate that the more frequent target for abandonment aggression by males is the self, not the spouse. Feminist analysis does not consider male suicide statistics.

Another prevailing explanation for the male-perpetrated IPH in the context resembling intimate terrorism is provided by a *proprietariness theory*, a subset of the gender paradigm. These views were developed in evolutionary psychology within a broader theory known as the *sexual selection theory* (Daly et al., 1982; Wilson & Daly, 1992). This theory holds that natural selection processes over the past 200,000 years have resulted in a differentiation between men and women in their reproductive strategies for ensuring descendants (Geary, 2010). Due to the prolonged period of gestation, a woman's reproductive interests are best served to seek a mate, or mates, who will provide resources to enhance the survival of her offspring. Although men can mate with numerous partners, monogamous relationships are advantageous to men because an investment of resources in one partner increases the odds of the children surviving, with greater certainty of paternity (Harris, 2003; Miller & Fishkin, 1997). In selecting partners that will further their respective reproductive ends, men seek young and physically attractive women because these features correlate with fertility, which is why women often complain of being treated as "sex objects."

According to the *proprietariness theory*, men will jealously guard their mates against other men and exercise control over partners whom they suspect of wanting to stray. When they suspect their partner might cheat on them or leave the relationship, men will employ various strategies in response to avoid losing the partner or being cuckolded (unwittingly having to raise another man's child). Such "mate retention" strategies include working harder to earn more money, showering the partner with attention and gifts, and letting her have her way—as well as what is known as "mate guarding," which involves a variety of possessive behaviors (Albert & Arnocky, 2016; Schmitt, 2004). In some circumstances, this control will escalate to physical violence, sometimes with lethal results (Daly et al., 1982; Wilson & Daly, 1992).

Killing one's mate is clearly not a sound reproductive strategy because, at the very least, a dead partner can no longer reproduce. However, neither is suicide or any other number of human self-destructive behaviors. Evolution and sexual selection account for reproductive failures as well as success. In homicide cases, when a man is overwhelmed with jealousy, rage, and deep feelings of insecurity and hopelessness, such interests are negated, along with the customary norms of chivalry. Whatever self-restraint mechanisms he may once have had are overridden, perhaps due to a particularly disordered personality, mental illness, or substance abuse.

Female-Perpetrated Intimate Partner Homicide in the Context of Violent Resistance

Within the *gender paradigm*, women who kill their intimate partners are presumed to do so in self-defense or after years of psychological and physical abuse. Based on the work of Lenore Walker, the term *battered woman syndrome* (BWS) was formulated to explain the effects of such abuse, wherein victims become conditioned through a process of "learned helplessness" to stay in the most abusive relationships until the violence reaches a certain level of dangerousness. At that point, some of these victims will kill their abusers, believing that this is the only way they have to prevent further assaults (Walker, 1983).

Several arguments have been put forth in support of the gender paradigm and BWS. Women who kill their intimate partners are statistically more likely than men who kill their intimate partners to report having been previously assaulted (Browne, 1987; Garcia et al., 2007; O'Keefe 1997; Saunders & Browne, 2000). Compared to men, women are more likely to kill their partners at some point during the relationship, possibly due to ongoing abuse, rather than after a breakup, thought to be due to pathological jealousy (Jordan et al., 2012, Wilson & Daly, 1993). Feminist analysis also argues that the decreasing rates of female-perpetrated IPH relative to those by men of the past several decades provide evidence for the self-defense motive, as the increased level of services for battered women has lessened their need to take matters into their own hands (Caman et al., 2017; Cooper & Smith, 2011; Dugan et al., 1999; Titterington & Harper, 2005). Women would not harm themselves if they had killed their partner in self-defense and sought safety from further abuse (Browne, 1987; Carmichael et al., 2018; Morton et al., 1998; Salari & Sillito, 2016). Females may tolerate relationship dissolution better than males (Kposowa, 2000).

Female-Perpetrated Intimate Partner Homicide in the Context of Intimate Terrorism

Left out of this gendered account are the evolutionary forces that drive female behavior. Women, attracted to men who are physically fit and who can successfully compete with other men (socially, economically, politically, or physically) to secure needed resources, are predisposed to view men as "success objects." Women will seek to improve their looks or grant more sexual favors to hold on to their mates and the resources they provide and sometimes engage in the same mate guarding behaviors used by men. Mate retention tactics have been studied with a questionnaire known as the Mate Retention Inventory (MRI; Shackelford et al., 2005). The MRI category known as Direct Mate Guarding includes the subcategories of Vigilance (e.g., "called at unexpected times to see who my partner was with"), Concealment of Mate (e.g., "refused to introduce my partner to my same-sex friends"), and Monopolization of Time (e.g., "insisted that my partner stay at home rather than go out"). Results from mate retention studies conducted with married couples in the United States (Buss & Shackleford, 1997), Spain (De Miguel & Buss, 2011), and Croatia (Kardum et al., 2006) indicate that women use these tactics at rates at least equal to men, and in some studies at higher rates, that correlate with IPV.

The mate guarding tactics found in these studies among jealous, insecure men and women are roughly the same as those identified in the general population, among dating partners, and in clinical samples, including IPV offenders court-mandated to treatment (Black et al., 2011; Carney & Barner, 2012; Graham-Kevan & Archer, 2009; Hamel et al., 2015; Jasinski et al., 2014). Some IPH studies find similar rates of male- and female-perpetrated IPH motived by sexual jealousy. For example, a review of 2,556 IPH cases in Chicago over several decades (1965–1993) confirmed the oft-cited finding that male-perpetrated IPH is more likely than female-perpetrated IPH to be due to a partner's attempt to leave the relationship (13% versus 4%), but found sexual jealousy, whether imagined or involving an actual love triangle, to be the motive for about the same percentage of male and female perpetrators (Block & Christakos, 1995). One difference between the sexes is that women tend to use coercive mate retention tactics throughout the relationship. In contrast, men are more likely to use them when suspecting their partner of cheating, which explains why women are so often killed when they try to leave. Another difference is that men score significantly in the Submission and Debasement category (e.g., "became a slave to my partner," "gave in to my partner's every wish").

Male-Perpetrated Intimate Partner Homicide in the Context of Violent Resistance

There has been limited research on this type of IPH, but given women's involvement in intimate terrorism, some homicides perpetrated by men are motivated by violent resistance. In the large study based on interviews with a national sample of 2,124 male and female prison inmates, questions about victimization and perpetration experiences in childhood and adulthood at the hands of intimate partners and other adults were asked (Felson & Lane, 2010). Although not without methodological limitations (e.g., the results come from self-reports and do not include individuals outside the prison system or murder-suicides that skew in the male direction), this study yields findings that are in sharp contrast to other IPH studies that typically depend on criminal justice data (arrests, restraining orders) and therefore underestimate the frequency of female-perpetrated assaults:

> Men and women who killed or assaulted their partners tended to be like other violent male and female offenders. The women who attacked their partners were not particularly likely to have been abused by their partners. Rather, we found that men who attacked their partners were particularly likely to have suffered partner abuse. This result challenges the idea that these women were responding to a history of abuse. Violence against partners and victimization by partners were strongly correlated for both men and women, which indicates that a considerable amount of mutual violence was present in the relationship. (Felson & Lane, 2010, pp. 329–330)

A review of 45 IPH cases in another study in Sweden concluded:

> We found that more than half of the female perpetrators had been threatened and physically abused by their male victims, as opposed to a minority of the male perpetrators. However, we also found that the majority of the male victims had been threatened, and half of them physically abused by the female perpetrators. (Caman et al., 2016, p. 31)

FEMALE- AND MALE-PERPETRATED INTIMATE PARTNER HOMICIDE: COUPLE CONFLICT AND SELF-DEFENSE

While disentangling the various motives and circumstances around IPH is a difficult task, a clearer picture emerges from a broader reading of the empirical research literature, which does not support the gender paradigm and male proprietariness theory in cases of IPH and finds self-defense to be a much less common motive for female-perpetrated IPH than commonly thought. Although "the literature does not provide a detailed contextual picture of female offenders" (Jordan et al., 2012, p. 429), it does indicate, as one research team has observed, that "intimate partner homicide is not simply a dual phenomenon, with aggressive men and defenseless women driven under the worst of interpersonal circumstances to kill one another. To adequately address the issue in both sociological and psychological terms, it must be understood more fully" (Titterington & Harper, 2005, p. 86).

Research studies have questioned the gender paradigm and have found a broad range of motives for female-perpetrated IPH. The review by Mann (1988) of 145 randomly selected cases of female-perpetrated IPH in several US cities indicated that 58.3% were premeditated, and 30% of the defendants had previously been charged with a prior felony assault. The review of female-perpetrated IPH cases between 1985 and 1995 in the province of Victoria, Australia, found that 59% of the offenders had "killed partners in response to their violence" (Kirkwood, 2003, p. 158); however, some of the women killed their partners in response to "nonphysical forms of abuse, such as lack of support in parenting and in pregnancy" (p. 158). According to an analysis of court records and presentence reports of 158 IPH cases in Arizona, in 56% of cases involving female perpetrators, there was no reported history of physical abuse against the defendant (Jurik & Winn, 1990) undermining claims of self-defense. Moreover, a previous study found that 60% of women who murdered their partners had previous criminal records and that only 21% of the homicides were preceded by a history of previous abuse or threats of abuse by the partner (Jurik & Gregware,1989).

An analysis of 276 IPH cases from 1991 to 2010 in Quebec, Canada (Bourget & Gagne, 2012), found evidence of previous assaults by the male victim in only 26.2% of the female-perpetrated homicides, no evidence for assaults in 21.4% of the cases, and previous assaults could not be determined in another 40.5%. The presence of intent to kill was found for 45% of the female perpetrators and 62% for the male perpetrators among cases in which information about intent was available. A history of previous assaults as a precipitant for IPH could not be found in about half of the 207 London cases reported by Sebire (2017), neither for the male nor the female perpetrators. In a Colorado study of 117 IPH cases (Belknap et al., 2012), approximately half of the female-perpetrated homicides were found to not have been committed in self-defense; the others involved proxy killings where women, previously abused by ex-partners, took out their rage against a current mate or were driven by purely instrumental motives (e.g., financial gain) or by jealousy. "Future research and policy," the authors suggested, "needs to acknowledge the issue-problem that prior victims of IPH may be at risk of killing future partners, especially if these partners are at all abusive, and that sexual proprietary killings of mates are not restricted to men" (Belknap et al., 2012, p. 373).

In Finland, an investigation of police records and psychiatric interviews of 145 IPH cases adjudicated during the period 1994–2005 revealed that about 78% of the male perpetrators and 89% of the female perpetrators killed their partner in the context of a quarrel (Weizmann-Henelius et al., 2012). A higher rate of female-perpetrated IPH than male-perpetrated IPH was committed in self-defense (36.0% versus 1.1%), but again, as other studies have shown, the majority of IPH, by either sex, is perpetrated for other reasons.

The analysis by Felson and Messner (1998) of 2,058 partner homicide cases in 33 of the most populated US counties found that 54% of female spousal murderers had not been physically assaulted by their partner before the incident, and less than 10% were judged to have acted strictly in self-defense. By comparison, 10% of male murder victims had suffered previous assaults, and in very few cases (0.5%) were the homicides deemed to be in self-defense. Unfortunately, the authors were unable to distinguish between the violence perpetrated immediately before the homicide from violence perpetrated in the past, thus leaving unclear which cases might be explained by some version of battered person syndrome and which cases involved simple retribution in a cycle of mutual abuse.

The survey by Velopulos et al. (2019) was somewhat more illuminating. As with other major surveys, reported percentages of female IPH victims were much larger than male victims (79% versus 21%). Escalating violence was rare: Only 5.0% of the male victims and 0.8% of the female victims had assaulted their partner in the month preceding the homicide, and very few cases were categorized as justifiable self-defense—certainly for male perpetrators (0.1%) but also for female perpetrators (6.4%). Jealousy was a motive in a small number of cases (10.5% of the male perpetrators, 6.4% for female perpetrators). In only 22.8% of cases was there evidence of prior IPV against female victims, and only 10% for male victims. Hence, most cases involved no prior domestic violence, nor was it escalating.

Some have proposed that nonlethal and lethal IPV are similar enough phenomena to be conceptualized as being on a continuum:

> Fatal and non-fatal IPV may not necessarily differ meaningfully, and perhaps to better understand violence involving intimate partners we must stop being distracted by the search for risk factors that differentiate or predict fatality. There has been tremendous attention on lethality and femicide. Instead, we should focus on severity, frequency, and imminence of IPV. When evaluating risk, the concern should be for determining risk for the presence and severity of future violence, by using broad-based IPV risk assessments . . . Fatality may be merely as result of where the knife struck or where the gun was directed. There is no doubt that the intention of the perpetrator was to harm, perhaps even to kill the victim, but the dividing line between an act that is fatal vs. not-fatal may also be arbitrary. (Jung & Stewart, 2019, p. 165)

Nonetheless, much of the prior research on IPH finds that a history of IPV does not always precede the IPH (Bourget & Gagne, 2012; Felson & Messner, 1998; Jurik & Winn, 1990; Sebire, 2017; Velopulos et al., 2019). This suggests that IPH may have more than one profile with different factors involved in homicides preceded by IPV than those with no IPV. Clearly, the guilt or innocence of a defendant facing IPH charges cannot be assumed on a lack of previous IPV alone.

RISK FACTORS AND PERSONALITY AS PREDICTORS OF INTIMATE PARTNER HOMICIDE

In addition to IPH types based on couple violence dynamics, various risk factors and personality characteristics of IPH perpetrators and victims can interact with couple aggression dynamics. With the notable exception of offender sex, risk factors for nonfatal and fatal IPV overlap considerably. Younger age is one prominent risk factor for IPH victimization, with male and female victims alike at greatest risk between ages 20 and 29 years (Garcia et al., 2007). One literature review found evidence of previous battering behavior in 22% of male-perpetrated cases (Kivisto, 2015). Other significant risk factors include abuse of alcohol and drugs; unemployment; a history of violence outside the home; and having previously stalked the victim, forced her to have sex, or threatened to kill her (Aldridge & Browne, 2003; Harden et al., 2019; Saunders & Browne, 2000; Spencer & Stith, 2020). According to a survey of men who contacted a national domestic violence hotline, abused men appeared to be at greater risk of life-threatening violence when in a relationship with a partner who is low-income and has been psychologically and physically abusive, and when the man has sought help in the past (Hines & Douglas, 2013). Block and Christakos (1995), in their large-scale study of homicide in Chicago, found that African American males were the most likely victims of spousal homicide (annual rate 5.8/100,000 PHT), followed by African American females (3.9 PHT), Latinos, and Whites. The rate for White female victims was (.9 PHT) and for White males (0.1 PHT). These findings, which can largely be explained according to lower socioeconomic status among marginalized ethnic minority groups, were later confirmed in a more extensive review of the national violent death reporting system (Velopulos et al., 2019).

The defendant's personality, which may provide clues to motive, is a crucial element in the adjudication of any criminal case and cannot be dismissed, particularly when it comes to sentencing. Longitudinal studies trace adult IPV in both male and female perpetrators to a history of antisocial behavior arising from a combination of genetic predisposition and family dysfunction in childhood (Dutton, 2006; Ehrensaft et al., 2004). Men and women who engage in battering behavior have been found to evidence personality traits or a personality constellation often associated with interpersonal aggression, including borderline, antisocial, narcissistic, histrionic, and sadistic traits that are stable and consistent across relationships (Henning et al., 2003; Johnston & Campbell, 1993; Simmons et al., 2005).

A major prison study (Jordan et al., 2012) found that male and female perpetrators of lethal as well as serious nonlethal IPV were equally likely to have mental health issues, although the women were less likely to have had problems with alcohol and drugs. The recent and comprehensive survey of 6,131 IPH cases reported through the National Violent Death Reporting System (Velopulos et al., 2019) found mental illness an equally contributing factor (about 7%) among both male and female perpetrators. The Quebec study mentioned earlier (Bourget & Gagne, 2012) determined that 42% of the women and 53% of the men had what the researchers termed a "psychiatric/pathological motive" for the killings (not fully explained). Sebire's (2017) study of 207 IPH cases in London, based on police reports covering the years 1998–2009, reported a higher percentage of mental illness among female perpetrators (29.4%) than male perpetrators (19.7%). It is not clear whether mental illness assessments in these studies included personality disorders.

Few studies have reported on the specific personality characteristics of IPH offenders, as measured by validated assessment instruments. One of the few studies to investigate the personalities of both male and female intimate IPH perpetrators, drawing on a very small sample (Kalichman, 1988), reported higher ratings for females compared to males on the Minnesota Multi-Phasic Personality Inventory (MMPI) on scales for paranoid, antisocial, and dependency traits. A classification scheme for male offenders, based on a file review of 90 male prison inmates in the United Kingdom who were incarcerated for killing their partners between 1975 and 2003, was proposed by Dixon and colleagues (Dixon et al., 2008), akin to the one developed by Holtzworth-Munroe and Stuart (1994) for male IPV perpetrators. About 15% of the men were placed in the *Low Criminality/Low Psychopathology* category, roughly the same as the *Family Only* type. Among the rest, 48.6% best fit the category of *High Criminality/Low-Moderate Psychopathology* (similar to Generally Violent/Antisocial), and 36.1% best fit the category of *Moderate–High Criminality/High Psychopathology*, akin to the Dysphoric-Borderline classification, but reflecting the higher number of criminal histories in the IPH sample.

Dutton and Kerry (1999) interviewed 90 men incarcerated for spousal homicide in Canadian prisons and 50 nonlethal spouse abusers in a court-mandated treatment group and reviewed their prison and criminal records. Spousal killers had a higher incidence of personality disorders, although not of the type typically expected. So-called overcontrolled personalities (Passive-Aggressive, Dependent, and Borderline on the MCMI) were more frequent in the spousal killer group, while antisocial personality disorder was more frequent in the nonlethal batterer group. When those with antisocial personality disorder did kill, it was typically to gain a monetary advantage, such as life insurance. When those with overcontrolled personality disorders killed, it was typically a type of abandonment killing (more about this later) and frequently accompanied by a suicide attempt. These individuals tend to be emotionally dependent on partners and react poorly to perceived or actual abandonment. After reviewing the IPH literature, Kivisto (2015) proposed a typology of male IPH offenders that included, aside from the overcontrolled types, an *undercontrolled/dysregulated* category consisting of men with mostly borderline personality disorder; *chronic batterers*, with antisocial and narcissistic personalities; and a *mentally ill* group of offenders with no discernable Axis II diagnoses (i.e., personality disorders).

Attachment Theory

One of the theories that fare well at explaining rare events, such as IPH, and focuses on the internal events (cognitions, emotions, learned behaviors patterns, etc.) that generate violence has been attachment theory. Attachment theory has been demonstrated as having some specificity and predictive ability with aggression and intimate aggression (Dutton et al., 1994; Dutton & White, 2013). Unlike broad-based theories, it assesses individual differences in attachment security and has empirically related these to aggression.

Attachment theory, as originally developed by Bowlby (1969, 1973, 1977, 1980), held that attachment to a stronger other was the primary human motive necessary for survival in a being that had a prolonged period of dependency on another. Based in sociobiology and psychoanalysis and tested through lengthy observation of children separated from their parents during the Battle of Britain, attachment theory held that an "attachment behavioral system" developed, based on aversive arousal when an "attachment object" (typically a mother) was not visually present. The aversive arousal could only be ameliorated by locomotion toward and physical reunification with the attachment object. Failure to reattach led to what Bowlby called "an anger born of fear" and may be the prototype for later abandonment rage (Dutton, 2006, 2008; Dutton et al., 1994, 1996). Since attachment is so essential in infancy, it was initially thought to only apply to infants.

However, a landmark study in 1987 (Hazan & Shaver, 1987) found that adult attachment styles (personality traits that manifest in intimate relations) were distributed similarly to infant styles. Eventually, empirical studies connected insecure attachment styles to adult behaviors (Mikulincer & Shaver, 2007), adolescent aggression (Fearon et al., 2010; van IJzendoorn et al., 1999), and the frequency and severity of IPV (Dutton et al., 1994; Mauricio et al., 2007). Dutton (2006) showed that certain DSM personality disorders (e.g., borderline personality disorder and dependent personality disorder) were attachment-based and related to expression of aggression. Borderline personality is highly emotionally unstable, undergoes cyclical swings in mood and perspective, and is highly reactive to potential abandonment by an intimate other (Lieb et al., 2004). Borderline personality is, in fact, the psychological basis for the "cycle of violence" reported by Lenore Walker's respondents in describing their perpetrators (Walker, 1979) and is now considered to be a general "g" factor in psychopathology (Sharp et al., 2015). In short, borderline personality is a broad-based psychological deficit with special problems in emotional management, ego stability, and intimate relationships. Assessments of court-mandated batterers have found a high incidence of borderline personality in these groups (Dutton & Starzomski, 1993; Mauricio et al., 2007). Given its reactivity to abandonment, borderline personality is also a risk factor for the perpetration of IPH (Dutton & Kerry 1999). Insecure attachment and borderline personality generate extreme affective reactions to abandonment, due, in part, to inherited neural deficits in borderlines (Lieb et al., 2004; Lis et al., 2007; Schmahl et al., 2004). These reactions can be so extreme as to generate transitory, abandonment-precipitated psychotic states (Lieb et al., 2004). The case against using borderline personality disorder as a defense is the lack of familiarity the general public has with the diagnosis and the term "borderline," which refers to the border between neuroticism and psychoticism.

Attachment is based on a complex neurological set of connections involving emotion governing neural structures (Dutton, 2002; Schore, 1994, 2003), many of which exhibit rapid growth during the first 2 years of life. Severe disruptions of secure attachment during that time can lead to affective dysfunction throughout life (Pynoos & Eth, 1985; Schore, 2003). Dutton (2002) argued that attachment dysfunction interferes with the development of the orbitofrontal cortex, a center for emotional control. These disruptions can be caused by childhood exposure to family violence (Cicchetti et al., 1990; Godbout et al., 2009; Sroufe et al., 2005) or major family conflicts. Lyons-Ruth and her colleagues (Lyons-Ruth, 1996, 2008; Lyons-Ruth & Jacobwitz, 2008), as part of the Harvard Family Pathways Study, found that with lifetime trauma exposure and genetic factors controlled, the quality of mother–child interaction did contribute to the variance of later aggression. Serbin and colleagues (2004) found that aggression in girls measured as early as grade 1 predicted the likelihood of their later perpetration of IPV and physical child abuse. A lifelong profile termed "negative emotionality," which shares many standard features with borderline personality, is a predictor of life-course antisociality (Magdol et al., 1997; Moffitt et al., 2001). Dutton (2006) argued that exposure to abuse in the family of origin led to a propensity for abusiveness not so much through behavioral modeling as through the development of dysfunctional emotionality, especially in intimate relationships.

One notable subset of IPH related to the lack of secure attachment is *abandonment homicide*. A significant trigger for male-perpetrated IPH is abandonment by his spouse (Wilson & Daly, 1993) or what Wilson and Daly called "estrangement," based on an examination of police records for three large samples. It is abandonment (being left behind); however, that is the trigger—not estrangement. Abandonment homicides are described as highly emotional and involving overkill, violence beyond that would be necessary to kill the victim (Crawford & Gartner, 1992), and appear to generate high levels of physiological arousal in the perpetrator (Dutton, 2002). This view is consistent with Schore's developmental emphasis on failures in the "automodulation of rage" (Schore, 2003) as having early origins. These psychological factors, not "proprietariness" (men's presumed desire to control their wives to maintain male privilege), generate abandonment IPH.

RISK ASSESSMENT AND DOMESTIC VIOLENCE FATALITY REVIEWS

Classification schemes may be helpful, but determining risk with any particular victim is not an exact science. The most popular instrument for predicting lethality in IPV cases, the Danger Assessment (DA) Scale, at best predicts an attempted or completed murder in less than 50% of cases (Campbell et al., 2009).

The DA Scale was developed from a risk study by Campbell and her associates (Campbell et al., 2003) that examined 220 female homicide victims and nonlethal battered woman controls. The victims were represented by a best friend to collect police and medical research data. The battered women controls were drawn from the same metropolitan area as the homicide victims. Unfortunately, the levels of abuse reported by the control were fairly low (e.g., only 25% reported controlling behaviors by their partner, 15% reported threats to kill); consequently, virtually every "risk factor" examined in the study was found to be significant, but what they were confusing was lethality with severe abuse. As a rare event, IPH may be better explained using clinical or psychopathological factors than the more common forms of IPV. IPH may reveal a perpetrator profile consistent only with severe (and rarer) IPV. Consideration of various types of IPH based on a couple's violent dynamics can also prove helpful.

Beginning in the early 1990s, various domestic violence stakeholders have formed domestic violence fatality review teams (DVFRTs) in the United Kingdom and more than 20 US states, at both the local and state levels, to learn more about the nature, and causes and consequences of IPH. The purpose of these domestic homicide reviews, as articulated by Hope et al. (in press) in their assessment of 22 male homicide victim cases in the United Kingdom, is to "establish the involvement of multiple agencies (where there was knowledge of the abuse) in terms of understanding any missed opportunities and to establish what lessons can be learned from this." Their review found systemic failures across institutions in preventing female-perpetrated homicides due to prevailing beliefs about men as perpetrators. In the United States, only about half of fatality reviews in the United States have provided specific details about the cases examined (aside from basic demographic information). One report found that only 43% of cases reviews included information about abuse perpetrated before the homicide. Those reports that included case details provided information only about legal outcomes (Marsh-Pow et al., 2015). Specific information about defendant motives, the most pertinent in adjudicating these cases, was not reported. Echoing Hope et al. (in press), Marsh-Pow et al. (2015) stressed the "inherent value of conducting fatality reviews in that the comprehensive review process can highlight places where victims "slipped through the cracks" and where opportunities for potentially valuable intervention may have been missed (p. 215).

THE BATTERED WOMAN SYNDROME

Having discussed the research on the prevalence, context, and risk factors of various types of IPH, we proceed to review the literature on the battered woman syndrome (BWS). As discussed in an earlier section on theories of male entitlement, the term was coined by Lenore Walker to describe a constellation of reactions to chronic battering culminating in self-defensive homicide of the abuser, commonly used as a legal strategy to explain why an abused woman may resort to deadly force in situations in which she is not at imminent risk of a physical assault, in the legal definition (Follingstad, 2003; Walker, 1979, 1984, 2009). The syndrome consists of lowered self-esteem, lack of initiative to leave the relationship, abnormal attachment, and trauma symptoms (Dutton & Painter, 1981, 1993a, 1993b). The paradoxical emotional attachment was an added reason for the woman's inability to leave the relationship (Griffing et al., 2002), what Walker termed "learned helplessness," a term borrowed from previous laboratory research (Walker, 1984).

As Follingstad (2003) pointed out, however BWS was introduced in courts before it had been empirically validated. By 2003, about 20 years after its first use in court, the syndrome still had not been conceptually clarified. The one empirical study conducted (Dutton & Painter, 1993a) showed merely a concurrence of symptoms (lowered self-esteem, heightened attachment, and trauma symptoms). BWS does not present a coherent model whereby aggression, even self-defensive aggression, would be used, given the high prevalence of bidirectional violence among abusive couples. It does attempt to explain certain cognitions (e.g., the likelihood of receiving severe violence, the impossibility of escape, etc.). However, even given these cognitions, other responses are available and are often used, including psychic freezing and other "passive" reactions (Turan & Dutton, 2010). According to legal scholars (Faigman et al., 2020):

> In most legal cases, the relevant question is, of those people who have been battered, which ones manifest a "state of mind" that is relevant to the fact in issue. Certainly, not all battering victims respond identically to the violence. Since the research provides no diagnostic criteria, it is impossible for any expert, judge, or jury to determine which victims of battering have developed the legally relevant state of mind and which have not. In short, because the research is definitional and not diagnostic, once a woman is defined as battered, she, ipso facto, is diagnosed as suffering from the battered woman syndrome. Courts have confused definition with diagnosis, concepts that should be kept entirely separate and which are ordinarily distinct in the scientific lexicon. (p. 373)

While the term *battered person syndrome* has gained favor as a gender-neutral version of BWS (Russell et al., 2012), there is weak evidence for an actual syndrome or its ability to meet Daubert testimony standards (Dahir et al., 2005; Russell, 2010) for relevance and reliability. The term is vague, never operationally defined, or confirmed by replication studies (Dutton, 1996). For example, a definition of "battering" includes not only threats to harm or constant monitoring of the partner but also lesser slights such as coming home late (Downs & Fisher, 2005). Walker's theory was, in fact, based on a self-selected sample of subjects who were asked leading questions and whose responses were subjectively interpreted, and none of the women's partners were interviewed. Walker failed to provide comparison groups to gauge levels of BWS symptoms between abused and nonabused women or differences between abused women who have BWS and those who do not (Dixon & Dixon, 2003); specific criteria are lacking for measuring symptoms such as "low self-esteem"; and the theory fails to account for symptom variance due to mediators of psychological effects of battering (e.g., vulnerability factors, resources, support, other stressors, the severity of the abuse; Follingstad, 2003). There is, in fact, inconsistent support for an actual cycle—for example, less than 50% of subjects experienced all three phases, no time frame was proposed for the duration of a cycle, and no data provided on how often the tension stage does not lead to a battering incident, or why some men (e.g., psychopaths) can strike without a tension build-up and never offer a third-phase apology (Faigman, 1986).

These and other flaws in BWS have been amply documented elsewhere (Coughlin, 1994; Downs & Fisher, 2005; Faigman et al., 2020; Russell, 2010; Schopp et al., 1994). Notably, it has been criticized for providing an unconvincing "abuse excuse" for the defendant and lack of justice for the victim:

> In self-defense law, the devil properly lies in the details. For example, while intentional homicides are committed for a variety of motives, BWS tends to reduce the abuse victim's motivation to kill to simplistic terms. Though fear of an attack and a sense of futility about escaping are predominant, other motives may also enter the picture. . . . Other motives include anger over finding out about the abuse of their children, jealousy and simple greed. Anyone who has studied cases in this area has encountered all of these motives for homicide. Battered women are human beings like the rest of us, and the use of BWS should not obscure the fact that battered women, despite the sympathy they deserve for their plights, sometimes kill for reasons that the criminal law cannot excuse or justify. (Downs & Fisher, 2005, p. 247)

Additionally, a defense strategy based on BWS can backfire, because some features of the syndrome—particularly, learned helplessness—conflict with the legal standards of "reasonableness." This is especially true in cases involving nonconfrontational situations (e.g., the woman shoots her batterer while he is sleeping), even though these are far less prevalent than the confrontational ones (Osthoff & Maguigan, 2005). In this regard, juries may be sympathetic to female IPH defendants, even when they do not conform to the stereotype of a passive, helpless woman, when their defense is mounted within the framework of what psychologists call *social agency* theory, a better fit for imperfect self-defense cases not involving an immediate threat (Buchhandler-Raphael, 2017; Ramsey, 2010; Russell, 2010; Terrance et al., 2012). The focus of this theory, within the legal system, is on "social framework evidence," a clearer and more credible way to explain the actions of someone with a history of IPV victimization:

> Courts have recognized that past violence by an aggressor toward the defendant influences the defendant's assessment of the current danger posed by the aggressor's actions. The evidence is routinely received in murder trials because most homicides involve people who were either acquainted with each other or in family relationships. A defendant in such a circumstance uses his or her experience with the decedent as a basis for evaluating

whether the decedent posed an imminent threat of serious injury. (Osthoff & Maguigan, 2005, pp. 231–232)

In contrast to BWS, PTSD is an accepted diagnosis, supported by a wealth of compelling social science data finding high rates of trauma-related disorders among victims of IPV, and providing a much more solid empirical basis for mitigating factors in cases involving both male and female victims who fight back against an abuser. It has been estimated that 31%–84% of battered women experience PTSD (M. Dutton & Goodman, 1994), depending on whether the diagnosis is based on formal DSM-V criterion or the more expansive definitions inherent in the increasingly popular diagnosis of complex PTSD (Courtois, 2008). Surveys have found abused men to experience PTSD at a rate more than 15 times that of men in the general population, as evidenced by a clinically significant cut-off score for PTSD on the PTSD Checklist for DSM-5 (PDL-5). As with female victims (Johnson & Leone, 2005), the highest scores are reported by victims of battering rather than situational violence (Hines & Douglas, 2015). Focusing on trauma symptoms has many advantages, both diagnostically and legally. PTSD and complex PTSD are well-defined terms, referring to actual behaviors, known etiologies, and the predictable existence of relevant symptoms, with a correlation between levels of violence suffered and PTSD symptoms (Terrance & Matheson, 2003).

Trauma-related categories better account for research findings on the consequences of battering on male and female victims, including the relatively gender-neutral impact of emotional abuse. When included in a social framework evidence defense, they more accurately explain the various types of battering phenomena, including memory lapses, aggressive episodes, and other contradictions that might otherwise compromise a BWS defense (e.g., the victim is thought to be helpless but can accurately predict future acts of violence and seek support). Thus, the constellation of mitigating factors included in the term "battered woman syndrome," and presented in expert testimony, can be better described as "testimony on battering and its effects" (Osthoff & Maguigan, 2005, p. 230), and may make the difference between manslaughter, rather than, murder, conviction. Excellent discussions on the complexities of BWS can be found among the publications listed in the reference section, from the point of view of forensic psychologists (e.g., Russell, 2010) and legal scholars (e.g., Faigman et al., 2020), including how research and existing legal codes may be applied in classic self-defense, diminished capacity, duress, and other legal defenses and strategies. The reader is also directed to the chapter by Russell and McKimmie (Chapter 7) in this volume, on jury decision-making. Basic research-informed guidelines, from Hamel (2018), can be found in the Appendix.

CONCLUSIONS

There is now a convincing body of research to indicate that both women and men can experience severe and sometimes lethal IPV at the hands of their intimate partners. The findings discussed herein are especially compelling, given growing concerns around the concept of BWS and the proliferation of research on the role of trauma. Even if the Felson and Lane (2010) prison study previously cited is dismissed as an outlier, the body of evidence indicates that rates of previous violence by IPH victims may not differ across sex as much as commonly assumed. It is not always clear, in any particular case, exactly what effects previous abuse may have on IPH perpetration, and there is no agreed-upon calculus available to dependably determine that role, especially given the multiplicity of possible motives and situations. The research makes it quite clear that female victims of IPV are, overall, more physically and emotionally impacted than male victims, providing perhaps more robust support for the consideration of mitigating circumstances in those cases. However, sex differences are relative, not absolute. While a person's sex "plays a role in determination of incidents as IPV, arrest, trial, conviction, and dispensations from the court, ultimately these considerations fail to address the relational context of these incidents" (Carney & Barner, 2012, p. 161).

Life-threatening and lethal IPV is perpetrated for various reasons other than self-defense, including jealousy, financial gain, revenge, and the desire to maintain control over one's partner and relationship, with roots deep in cultural practices and evolutionary principles. Some individuals who kill their partners (more often, but not always, women) have experienced previous abuse at the hands of the victim. However, even when such a history has been established, its relevance will vary depending on the nature of that history, the particular dynamics of the abuse, the motives and mindset of the parties involved, and the circumstances surrounding the incident.

ACKNOWLEDGMENTS

The authors would like to thank Aaron Kivisto, PhD, and Victoria Titterington for taking the time to review earlier drafts of this chapter and providing helpful comments.

REFERENCES

Albert, G., & Arnocky, S. (2016). Use of mate retention strategies. In T. K. Shackelford & V. A. Weekes-Shackleford (Eds.), *Encyclopedia of evolutionary psychological science* (pp. 1–11). Springer.

Aldridge, M. L., & Browne, K. D. (2003). Perpetrators of spousal homicide: A review. *Trauma, Violence, & Abuse, 4*(3), 265–276. https://doi.org/10.1177/1524838003004003005

Archer, J. (2000). Sex differences in physical aggression to partners: A reply to Frieze (2000), O'Leary (2000), and White, Smith, Koss, and Figueredo (2000). *Psychological Bulletin, 126*(5), 697–702. https://doi.org/10.1037/0033-2909.126.5.697

Archer, J. (2002). Sex differences in physically aggressive acts between heterosexual partners: A meta-analytic review. *Aggression and Violent Behavior, 7*, 313–351. https://doi.org/10.1016/S1359-1789(01)00061-1

Archer, J. (2004). Sex differences in aggression in real-world settings: A meta-analytic review. *Review of General Psychology, 8*(4), 291–322. https://doi.org/10.1037/1089-2680.8.4.291

Babcock, J. C., Miller, S. A., & Siard, C. (2003). Toward a typology of abusive women: Differences between partner-only and generally violent women in the use of violence. *Psychology of Women Quarterly, 27*(2), 153–161. https://doi.org/10.1111/1471-6402.00095

Belknap, J., Larson, D., Abrams, M., Garcia, C., & Anderson-Block, K. (2012). Types of intimate partner homicides committed by women—Self-defense, proxy-retaliation, and sexual proprietariness. *Homicide Studies, 16*(4), 359–379. https://doi.org/10.1177/1088767912461444

Black, M. C., Basile, K. C., Breiding, M. J., Smith, S. G., Walters, M. L., Merrick, M. T., Chen, J., & Stevens, M. R. (2011). *The National Intimate Partner and Sexual Violence Survey (NISVS): 2010 summary report*. National Center for Injury Prevention and Control, Centers for Disease Control and Prevention. http://www.cdc.gov/ViolencePrevention/pdf/NISVS_Executive_Summary-a.pd

Block, C. R., & Christakos, A. (1995). Intimate partner homicide in Chicago over 29 years. *Crime & Delinquency, 41*(4), 496–526. https://doi.org/10.1177/0011128795041004008

Bourget, D., & Gagne, P. (2012). Women who kill their mates. *Behavioral Sciences and the Law, 30*(5), 598–614. https://doi.org/10.1002/bsl.2033

Bowlby, J. (1969). *Attachment and loss: Attachment*. Basic Books.

Bowlby, J. (1973). *Attachment and loss: Separation* (Vol. 2). Basic Books.

Bowlby, J. (1977). The making and breaking of affectional bonds. *British Journal of Psychiatry, 130*(3), 201–210. https://doi.org/10.1192/bjp.130.3.201

Bowlby, J. (1980). *Attachment and loss* (Vol. 3). Basic Books.

Brody, L., & Hall, J. (2008). Gender and emotion in context. In M. Lewis, J. Haviland-Jones, & L. Feldman Barnett (Eds.), *Handbook of emotions* (pp. 395–408). Guilford.

Browne, A. (1987). *When battered women kill*. Free Press.

Browne, A., Dutton, D. G., & Williams, K. W. (1999). Homicide between intimate partners. In M. D. Smith & M. A. Zahn (Eds.), *Homicide studies: A sourcebook of social research* (pp. 149–164). Sage.

Buchhandler-Raphael, M. (2017). Fear-based provocation. *American University Law Review, 67*, 1719–1796. https://heinonline.org/HOL/LandingPage?handle=hein.journals/aulr67&div=47&id=&page=

Buss, D., & Shackelford, T. K. (1997). From vigilance to violence: Mate retention tactics in married couples. *Journal of Personality and Social Psychology, 72*(2), 346–361. https://doi.org/10.1037/0022-3514.72.2.346

Buzawa, E. S., & Buzawa, C. G. (2003). *Domestic violence: The criminal justice response*. Sage.

Caman, S., Howner, K., Kristiansson, M., & Sturup, J. (2016). Differentiating male and female intimate partner homicide perpetrators: A study of social, criminological and clinical factors. *The International Journal of Forensic Mental Health, 15*(1), 26–34. https://doi.org/10.1080/14999013.2015.1134723

Caman, S., Kristiansson, M., Granath, S., & Sturup, J. (2017). Trends in rates and characteristics of intimate partner homicides between 1990 and 2013. *Journal of Criminal Justice, 49*, 14–21. https://doi.org/10.1016/j.jcrimjus.2017.01.002

Campbell, A. (2013, October). The evolutionary psychology of women's aggression. Philosophical Transactions of the Royal Society of Biological Sciences.

Campbell, J., Glass, N., Sharp, P., Laughon, K., & Bloom, T. (2007). Intimate partner homicide: Review and implications of research and policy. *Trauma, Violence & Abuse, 8*(3), 246–269. https://doi.org/10.1177/1524838007303505

Campbell, J., Webster, D., & Glass, N. (2009). The danger assessment: Validation of a lethality risk assessment instrument for intimate partner femicide. *Journal of Interpersonal Violence, 24*(4), 653–674. https://doi.org/10.1177/0886260508317180

Campbell, J., Webster, D., Koziol-McLain, J., Block, C., Campbell, D., Curry, M., Gary, F. A., McFarlane, J. M., Sachs, C. J., Sharps, P., Ulrich, Y., & Wilt, S. A. (2003). Assessing risk factors for intimate partner homicide. *National Institute of Justice Journal, 250*, 14–19.

Campbell, J. C., Webster, D., Koziol-McLain, J., Block, C., Campbell, D., Curry, M. A., & Laughon, K. (2003). Risk factors for femicide in abusive relationships: Results from a multisite case control study. *American Journal of Public Health, 93*(7), 1089–1097. https://doi.org/10.2105/AJPH.93.7.1089

Capaldi, D. M., Knoble, N. B., Shortt, J. W., & Kim, H. K. (2012). A systematic review of risk factors for intimate partner violence. *Partner Abuse, 3*(2), 231–280. doi:10.1891/1946-6560.3.2.231

Capaldi, D. M., Wu Shortt, J., Kim, H. K., Wilson, J., Crosby, L., & Tucci, S. (2009). Official incidents of domestic violence: Types, injury and associations with non-official couple aggression. *Violence and Victims, 24*(4), 502–519. doi:10.1891/0886-6708.24.4.502

Carmichael, H., Jamison, E., Bol, K., McIntyre, R., & Velopulos, C. (2018). Premeditated versus "passionate": Patterns of homicide related to intimate partner violence. *Journal of Surgical Research, 230*, 87–93. https://doi.org/10.1016/j.jss.2018.04.050

Carney, M., & Barner, J. (2012). Prevalence of partner abuse: Rates of emotional abuse and control. *Partner Abuse, 3*(3), 286–335. doi:10.1891/1946-6560.3.3.286

Catalano, S. (2012, November). Intimate partner violence, 1993–2010. http://bjs.ojp.usdoj.gov/content/pub/pdf/ipv9310.pdf

Cazaneave, N. A., & Straus, M. A. (1992). Race, class, network embeddedness and family violence. In M. Straus & R. Gelles (Eds.), *Physical violence in American families* (pp. 321–340). Transaction.

Cicchetti, D., Cummings, M., Greenburg, M., & Marvin, R. (1990). An organizational perspective on attachment beyond infancy: Implications for the theory, measurement, and research. In M. Greenberg, D. Cicchetti, & E. M. Cummings (Eds.), *Attachment during the preschool years: Theory, research, and intervention* (pp. 3–51). University of Chicago Press.

Coker, A., Davis, K., Arias, I., Desai, S., Sanderson, M., Brandt, H., & Smith, P. (2002). Physical and mental health effects of intimate partner violence for men and women. *American Journal of Preventive Medicine, 23*(4), 260–268. https://doi.org/10.1016/S0749-3797(02)00514-7

Cook, P. (2009). *Abused men: The hidden side of domestic violence* (2nd ed.). Praeger.

Cooper, A., & Smith, E. (2011). *Homicide trends in the United States, 1980–2008*. NCJ 236018, U.S. Department of Justice.

Coughlin, A. (1994). Excusing women. *California Law Review, 82,* 1–93. https://heinonline.org/HOL/LandingPage?handle=hein.journals/calr82&div=10&id=&page=

Courtois, C. A. (2008). Complex trauma, complex reactions: Assessment and treatment. *Psychological Trauma: Theory, Research, Practice and Policy, 1,* 86–100. http://dx.doi.org.proxy.lib.sfu.ca/10.1037/1942-9681.S.1.86

Crawford, M., & Gartner, R. (1992). *Woman killing: Intimate femicide in Ontario 1974–1990.* Woman's Directorate: Ministry of Community and Social Services.

Cross, C., & Campbell, A. (2011). Women's aggression. *Aggression and Violent Behavior, 16*(5), 390–398. https://doi.org/10.1016/j.avb.2011.02.012

Cross, C., Tee, W., & Campbell, A. (2011). Gender symmetry in intimate aggression: An effect of intimacy or target sex? *Aggressive Behavior, 37*(3), 268–277. https://doi.org/10.1002/ab.20388

Dahir, V. B., Richardson, J. T., Ginsburg, G. P., Gatowski, S. I., Dobbin, S. A., & Merlino, M. L. (2005). Judicial application of Daubert to psychological syndrome and profile evidence: A research note. *Psychology, Public Policy, and Law, 11*(1), 62–82. https://doi.org/10.1037/1076-8971.11.1.62

Daly, M., Wilson, M., & Weghorst, S. (1982). Male sexual jealousy. *Ethnology and Sociobiology, 3*(1), 11–27. https://doi.org/10.1016/0162-3095(82)90027-9

De Miguel, A., & Buss, D. (2011). Mate retention tactics in Spain: Personality, sex differences, and relationship status. *Journal of Personality, 79*(3), 563–585. https://doi.org/10.1111/j.1467-6494.2011.00698.x

Desmarais, S. L., Reeves, K. A., Nicholls, T. L., Telford, R. P., & Fiebert, M. S. (2012). Prevalence of physical violence in intimate relationships, Part 1: Rates of male and female victimization. *Partner Abuse, 3*(2), 140–169. doi:10.1891/1946-6560.3.2.140

Dixon, J., & Dixon, K. (2003). Gender-specific clinical syndromes and their admissibility under the federal rules of evidence. *American Journal of Trial Advocacy, 27*(1), 25–66. https://heinonline.org/HOL/LandingPage?handle=hein.journals/amjtrad27&div=8&id=&page=

Dixon, L., Hamilton-Giachritsis, C., & Browne, K. D. (2008). Classifying partner femicide. *Journal of Interpersonal Violence, 23*(1), 74–93. https://doi.org/10.1177/0886260507307652

Dobash, R. E., & Dobash, R. P. (2011). What were they thinking? Men who murder an intimate partner. *Violence Against Women, 17*(1), 111–134. https://doi.org/10.1177/1077801210391219

Douglas, E., & Hines, D. (2011). The help seeking experiences of men who sustain intimate partner violence: An overlooked population and implications for practice. *Journal of Family Violence, 26*(6), 473–485. https://doi.org/10.1007/s10896-011-9382-4

Downs, D., & Fisher, J. (2005). Battered woman syndrome: Tool of justice or false hope in self-defense cases? Explaining without pathologizing: Testimony on battering and its effects. In D. Loseke, R. Gelles, & M. Cavanaugh (Eds.), *Current controversies on family violence* (2nd ed., pp. 241–256). Sage.

Dugan, L., Nagin, D., & Rosenfeld, R. (1999). Explaining the decline in intimate partner homicide: The effects of changing domesticity, women's status, and domestic violence resources. *Homicide Studies, 3*(3), 187–214. https://doi.org/10.1177/1088767999003003001

Dutton, D. G. (2002). The neurobiology of abandonment homicide. *Aggression and Violent Behavior, 7*(4), 407–421. https://doi.org/10.1016/S1359-1789(01)00066-0

Dutton, D. G. (2006). *Rethinking domestic violence.* UBC Press.

Dutton, D. G. (2008). Anger in intimate relationships. In M. Potegal, G. Stemmler, & C. D. Spielberger (Eds.), *Handbook of anger* (pp. 535–544). Springer.

Dutton, D. G., Corvo, K., & Hamel, J. (2009). The gender paradigm in domestic violence research and practice: Part 11: The website of the American Bar Association. *Aggression and Violent Behavior, 14*(1), 30–38. https://doi.org/10.1016/j.avb.2008.08.002

Dutton, D. G., & Kerry, G. (1999). Modus operandi and personality disorder in incarcerated killers. *International Journal of Law and Psychiatry, 22*(3–4), 287–299. https://doi.org/10.1016/S0160-2527(99)00010-2

Dutton, D. G., & Nicholls, T. (2005). The gender paradigm in domestic violence research and theory: Part 1—The conflict of theory and data. *Aggression and Violent Behavior, 10*(6), 680–714. https://doi.org/10.1016/j.avb.2005.02.001

Dutton, D. G., & Painter, S. L. (1981). Traumatic bonding: The development of emotional bonds in relationships of intermittent abuse. *Victimology: An International Journal, 6*(1–4), 139–155.

Dutton, D. G., & Painter, S. L. (1993a). The Battered Woman Syndrome: Effects of severity and intermittency of abuse. *American Journal of Orthopsychiatry, 63*(4), 614–622. https://doi.org/10.1037/h0079474

Dutton, D. G., & Painter, S. L. (1993b). Emotional attachments in abusive relationship: A test of traumatic bonding theory. *Violence and Victims, 8*(2), 105–120. doi:10.1891/0886-6708.8.2.105

Dutton, D. G., & Starzomski, A. (1993). Borderline personality in perpetrators of psychological and physical abuse. *Violence and Victims, 8*(4), 327–337. doi:10.1891/0886-6708.8.4.327

Dutton, D. G., Starzomski, A., & Ryan, L. (1996). Antecedents of borderline personality organization in wife assaulters. *Journal of Family Violence, 11*(2), 113–132. 10.1007/BF02336665

Dutton, D. G., Starzomski, A., Saunders, K., & Bartholomew, K. (1994). Intimacy-anger and insecure attachment as precursors of abuse in intimate relationships. *Journal of Applied Social Psychology, 24*(15), 1367–1386. https://doi.org/10.1111/j.1559-1816.1994.tb01554.x

Dutton, D. G., Tetreault, C., & White, K. (2017). Violence in the family. In P. Sturmey (Ed.), *The Wiley handbook on violence and aggression.* Wiley.

Dutton, D. G., & White, K. (2013). Attachment insecurity and intimate partner violence. *Aggression and Violent Behavior, 17*(5), 475–481. https://doi.org/10.1016/j.avb.2012.07.003

Dutton, M. A. (1996). Critique of the battered woman syndrome model. https://www.vawnet.org/DomesticViolence/Research/VAWnetDocs/AR_bws.php

Dutton, M. A., & Goodman, L. (1994). Posttraumatic stress disorder among battered women: Analysis of legal implications. *Behavioral Sciences and the Law, 12*(3), 215–234. https://doi.org/10.1002/bsl.2370120303

Ehrensaft, M., Moffit, T., & Caspi, A. (2004). Clinically abusive relationships in an unselected birth cohort: Men's and women's participation and developmental antecedents. *Journal of Abnormal Psychology, 113*(2), 258–270. https://doi.org/10.1037/0021-843X.113.2.258

Ehrenshaft, M. K., Cohen, P., Brown, J., Smailes, E., Chen, H. N., & Johnson, J. G. (2003). Intergenerational transmission of partner violence: A 20-year prospective study. *Journal of Consulting and Clinical Psychology, 71*(4), 741–753. https://doi.org/10.1037/0022-006X.71.4.741

Eriksen, S., & Jensen, V. (2006). All in the family? Family environment factors in sibling abuse. *Journal of Family Violence, 21*(8), 497–507. doi:10.1007/s10896-006-9048-9

Eriksen, S., & Jensen, V. (2009). A push or a punch: Distinguishing the severity of sibling violence. *Journal of Interpersonal Violence, 24*(1), 183–208. https://doi.org/10.1177/0886260508316298

Faigman, D. L. (1986). The battered woman syndrome and self-defense. *Virginia Law Review, 72*, 619–647. https://doi.org/10.2307/1072974

Faigman, D. L., Cheng, E. K., Mnookin, J. L., Murphy, E. E., Sanders, J., & Slobogin, C. (2020). *Modern scientific evidence: The law and science of expert testimony* (Vol. 1). Thomson Reuters.

Fearon, R. P., Bakermans-Kranenburg, M. J., van Izendoorn, M. H., Lapsley, A., & Roisman, G. I. (2010). The significance of insecure attachment and disorganization in the development of children's externalizing behavior: A meta-analytic study. *Child Development, 81*(2), 435–456. https://doi.org/10.1111/j.1467-8624.2009.01405.x

Felson, R., & Lane, K. (2010). Does violence involving women and intimate partners have a special etiology? *Criminology, 48*(1), 321–338. https://doi.org/10.1111/j.1745-9125.2010.00186.x

Felson, R., & Messner, S. (1998). Disentangling the effects of gender and intimacy on victim precipitation in homicide. *Criminology, 36*(2), 405–424. https://doi.org/10.1111/j.1745-9125.1998.tb01253.x

Follingstad, D. R. (2003). Battered woman syndrome in the courts. In A. M. Goldstein (Ed.), *Handbook of psychology: Forensic psychology* (Vol. 11, pp. 485–507). John Wiley and Sons.

Fridel, E. E., & Fox, J. A. (2019). Gender differences in patterns and trends in U.S. homicide, 1976–2017. *Violence and Gender, 6*(1), 27–36. https://doi.org/10.1089/vio.2019.0005

Frodi, A., Macaulay, J., & Thome, P. R. (1977). Are women always less aggressive than men? A review of the experimental literature. *Psychological Bulletin, 84*(4), 634–660. https://doi.org/10.1037/0033-2909.84.4.634

Garcia, L., Soria, C., & Hurwitz, E. (2007). Homicides and intimate partner violence: A review. *Trauma, Violence & Abuse, 8*(4), 370–383. https://doi.org/10.1177/1524838007307294

Geary, D. (2010). *Male, female: The evolution of human sex differences* (2nd ed.). APA.

Godbout, N., Dutton, D. G., Lussier, Y., & Sabourin, S. (2009). Early exposure to violence, domestic violence, attachment representations and martial adjustment. *Personal Relationships, 16*(3), 365–384. https://doi.org/10.1111/j.1475-6811.2009.01228.x

Gondolf, E. (1996). Characteristics of batterers in a multi-site evaluation of batterer intervention systems. Mincava. http://www.mincava.umn.edu/documents/gondolf/batchar.html

Graham-Kevan, N., & Archer, J. (2009). Control tactics and partner violence in heterosexual relationships. *Evolution and Human Behavior, 30*(6), 445–452. https://doi.org/10.1016/j.evolhumbehav.2009.06.007

Griffing, S., Ragin, D. F., Sage, R. E., Madry, L., Bingham, L. E., & Primm, B. J. (2002). Domestic survivors' self-identified reasons for returning to abusive relationships. *Journal of Interpersoanl Violence, 13*(3), 306–319. https://doi.org/10.1177/0886260502017003005

Hamel, J. (2016). In the best interests of children: What family law attorneys should know about domestic violence. *Journal of the American Academy of Matrimonial Lawyers, 28,* 201–228. https://heinonline.org/HOL/LandingPage?handle=hein.journals/jaaml28&div=21&id=&page=

Hamel, J. (2018). Intimate partner violence: Gender issues and the adjudication of homicide and other cases. *Criminological Research Policy and Practice, 4*(4), 226–237. https://doi.org/10.1108/JCRPP-01-2018-0008

Hamel, J., Jones, D. N., Dutton, D. G., & Graham-Kevan, N. (2015). The CAT: A gender-inclusive measure of controlling and abusive tactics. *Violence and Victims, 30*(4), 547–580. DOI:10.1891/0886-6708.VV-D-13-00027

Hamel, J., & Russell, B. (2013). The Partner Abuse State of Knowledge Project: Implications for law enforcement responses to domestic violence. In B. Russell (Ed.), *Perceptions of female offenders: How stereotypes and social norms affect criminal justice responses* (pp. 151–180). Springer.

Harden, J., Du, J., Spencer, C., & Stith, S. (2019). Examining attempted and completed intimate partner homicides: A qualitative synthesis. *Violence & Victims, 34*(6), 869–888. doi:10.1891/0886-6708.VV-D-18-00128

Harris, C. (2003). A review of sex differences in sexual jealousy, including self-report data, psychophysiological responses, interpersonal violence, and morbid jealousy. *Personality and Social Psychology Review, 7*(2), 102–128. https://doi.org/10.1207/S15327957PSPR0702_102-128

Hazan, C., & Shaver, P. (1987). Romantic love conceptualized as an attachment process. *Journal of Personality and Social Psychology, 52*(3), 511–524. https://doi.org/10.1037/0022-3514.52.3.511

Henning, K., Jones, A., & Holdford, R. (2003). Treatment needs of women arrested for domestic violence: A comparison with male offenders. *Journal of Interpersonal Violence, 18*(8), 839–856. https://doi.org/10.1177/0886260503253876

Hines, D., & Douglas, E. (2013). Predicting potentially life-threatening partner violence by women toward men: A preliminary analysis. *Violence and Victims, 28*(5), 751–771. doi:10.1891/0886-6708.VV-D-12-00104

Hines, D., & Douglas, E. (2015). Health problems of partner violence victims: Comparing help-seeking men to a population-based sample. *American Journal of Preventive Medicine, 48*(2), 136–144. https://doi.org/10.1016/j.amepre.2014.08.022

Hines, D., Malley-Morrison, K., & Dutton, L. (2013). *Family violence in the United States: Defining, understanding, and combating abuse* (2nd ed.). Sage.

Hines, D. A., & Douglas, E. M. (2019). An empirical test of Johnson's typology of intimate partner violence in two samples of men. *Partner Abuse, 10*(2), 180–198. doi:10.1891/1946-6560.10.2.180

Holtzworth-Munroe, A., & Stuart, G. (1994). Typologies of male batterers: Three subtypes and the differences among them. *Psychological Bulletin, 116*(3), 476–497. https://doi.org/10.1037/0033-2909.116.3.476

Hope, K., Bates, E. A., Brooks, M., & Taylor, J. C. (in press). What can we learn from Domestic Violence Homicide Reviews with male victims? *Partner Abuse, 12*(4), 384–408.

Ioannou, M., & Hammond, L. (2015). The changing face of homicide research: The shift in empirical focus and emerging research trends. *Journal of Criminal Psychology*, 5(3), 157–162. https://doi.org/10.1108/JCP-06-2015-0019

Jaffe, P., Scott, K., & Straatman, A-L. (2020). Future directions on promoting domestic homicide prevention in diverse populations. In Peter Jaffe, Katreena Scott, & Anna-Lee Straatman (Eds.), *Preventing domestic homicides: Lessons learned from tragedies* (pp. 281–297). Academic Press. https://doi.org/10.1016/B978-0-12-819463-8.00013-7

Jasinski, J., Blumenstein, L, & Morgan, R. (2014). Testing Johnson's typology: Is there gender symmetry in intimate terrorism? *Violence and Victims*, 29(1), 73–88. doi:10.1891/0886-6708.VV-D-12-00146

Johnson, M. (2008). *A typology of domestic violence: Intimate terrorism, violence resistance, and situational couple violence*. Northeastern University Press.

Johnson, M. (2011). Gender and types of intimate partner violence: A response to antifeminist literature review. *Aggression and Violent Behavior*, 16(4), 290–296. https://doi.org/10.1016/j.avb.2011.04.006

Johnson, M. P., & Leone, J. M. (2005). The differential effects of intimate terrorism and situational couple violence: Findings from the National Violence Against Women Survey. *Journal of Family Issues*, 26(3), 322–349. https://doi.org/10.1177/0192513X04270345

Johnston, J., & Campbell, L. (1993). A clinical typology of interpersonal violence in disputed-custody cases. *American Journal of Orthopsychiatry*, 63(2), 190–199. https://doi.org/10.1037/h0079425

Jonason, P. K., Li, N. P., & Buss, D. M. (2010). The costs and benefits of the dark triad: Implications for mate poaching and mate retention tactics. *Personality and Individual Differences*, 48(4), 373–378. https://doi.org/10.1016/j.paid.2009.11.003

Jordan, C., Clark, J., Pritchard, A., & Charnigo, R. (2012). Lethal and other serious assaults: Disentangling gender and context. *Crime & Delinquency*, 58(3), 425–455. https://doi.org/10.1177/0011128712436412

Jung, S., & Stewart, J. (2019). Exploratory comparison between fatal and non-fatal cases of intimate partner violence. *Journal of Aggression, Conflict and Peace Research*, 11(3), 158–168. https://doi.org/10.1108/JACPR-11-2018-0394

Jurik, N., & Gregware, P. (1989). *A method for murder: An interactionist analysis of homicides by women*. Arizona State University, School of Justice Studies.

Jurik, N., & Winn, R. (1990). Gender and homicide: A comparison of men and women who kill. *Violence and Victims*, 5(4), 227–242. doi:10.1891/0886-6708.5.4.227

Kalichman, S. C. (1988). MMPI profiles of women and men convicted of domestic homicide. *Journal of Clinical Psychology*, 44(6), 847–853. https://doi.org/10.1002/1097-4679(198811)44:6<847

Kardum, I., Hudek-Knezevic, J., & Gracanin, A. (2006). Sociosexuality and mate retention in romantic couples. *Psychological Topics*, 15(2), 277–296.

Kimber, M., Adhama, S., Gillb, S., McTavisha, J., & MacMillana, H. L. (2018). The association between child exposure to intimate partner violence (IPV) and perpetration of IPV in adulthood—A systematic review. *Child Abuse & Neglect*, 76, 273–286. https://doi.org/10.1016/j.chiabu.2017.11.007

Kirkwood, D. (2003). Female perpetrated homicide in Victoria between 1985 and 1995. *The Australian and New Zealand Journal of Criminology*, 36, 152–172. https://doi.org/10.1375/acri.36.2.152

Kivisto, A. (2015). Male perpetrators of intimate partner homicide: A review and proposed typology. *Journal of the American Academy of Psychiatry and the Law, 43,* 300–312.

Kposowa, A. (2000). Marital status and suicide in the National Longitudinal Mortality Study. *Journal of Epidemiological Community Health, 54,* 254–261. http://dx.doi.org/10.1136/jech.54.4.254

Langhinrichsen-Rohling, J., & McCullars, A. (2012). Motivations for men and women's intimate partner violence perpetration: A comprehensive review. *Partner Abuse, 3*(4), 429–468.

Langhinrichsen-Rohling, J., Misra, T. A., Selwyn, C., & Rohling, M. L. (2012). Rates of bi-directional versus unidirectional intimate partner violence across samples, sexual orientations, and race/ethnicities: A comprehensive review. *Partner Abuse, 3*(2), 199–230. doi:10.1891/1946-6560.3.2.199

Laroche, D. (2005). *Aspects of the context and consequences of domestic violence: Situational couple violence and intimate terrorism in Canada in 1999.* Institut de la statistique du Quebec. https://www.stat.gouv.qc.ca

Lawrence, E., Oringo, A., & Brock, R. (2012). The impact of partner abuse on partners. *Partner Abuse, 3*(4), 406–428. doi:10.1891/1946-6560.3.4.406

Lieb, K., Zanarini, M. K., Schmahl, C., Linehan, M., & Bohus, M. (2004). Borderline personality disorder. *The Lancet, 364*(23), 453–461. https://doi.org/10.1016/S0140-6736(04)16770-6

Liem, M., & Roberts, D. (2009). Intimate partner homicide by presence or absence of a self-destructive act. *Homicide Studies, 13,* 339–354. https://doi.org/10.1177/1088767909347988

Lis, E., Greenfield, B., Henry, M., Guilé, J. M., & Dougherty, G. (2007). Neuroimaging and genetics of borderline personality disorder: A review. *Journal of Psychiatry & Neuroscience, 32*(3), 162–173.

Lyons-Ruth, K. (1996). Attachment relationships among children with aggressive behavior problems: The role of disorganized early attachment patterns. *Journal of Consulting and Clinical Psychology, 64*(1), 64–73. https://doi.org/10.1037/0022-006X.64.1.64

Lyons-Ruth, K. (2008). Contributions of the mother-infant relationship to dissociative, borderline and conduct symptoms in young adulthood. *Infant Mental Health Journal, 23*(3), 203–218. https://doi.org/10.1002/imhj.20173

Lyons-Ruth, K., & Jacobwitz, D. (2008). Attachment disorganization: Unresolved loss, relational violence, and lapses of behavioral and attentional strategies. In J. Cassidy & P. R. Shaver (Eds.), *Handbook of attachment: Theory, research, and clinical applications.* (pp. 520–554). Guilford.

Lysova, A., Dim, E. E., & Dutton, D. (2019). Prevalence and consequences of intimate partner violence in Canada as measured by the national victimization survey. *Partner Abuse, 10*(2), 199–221. doi:10.1891/1946-6560.10.2.199

MacKinnon, C. (1989). *Toward a feminist theory of state.* Harvard University Press.

Magdol, L., Moffitt, T. E., Caspi, A., Newman, D. L., Fagan, J., & Silva, P. A. (1997). Gender differences in partner violence in a birth cohort of 21-year-olds: Bridging the gap between clinical and epidemiological approaches. *Journal of Consulting and Clinical Psychology, 65*(1), 68–78. https://doi.org/10.1037/0022-006X.65.1.68

Mann, C. R. (1988), Getting even? Women who kill in domestic encounters. *Justice Quarterly, 5*(1), 33–51. https://doi.org/10.1080/07418828800089601

Marsh-Pow, A., Murray, C. E., Flasch, P. S., Bodenheimer-Brown, B., Doom, E., & Snyder, M. (2015). Learning from experience: A content analysis of domestic violence fatality review team reports. *Partner Abuse*, *6*(2), 197–216. doi:10.1891/1946-6560.6.2.197

Mauricio, A. M., Tein, J. Y., & Lopez, F. G. (2007). Borderline and antisocial personality scores as mediators between attachment and intimate partner violence. *Violence and Victims*, *22*(2), 139–157. doi:10.1891/088667007780477339

McDonald, R., Jouriles, E., Tart, C., & Minze, L. (2009). Children's adjustment problems in families characterized by men's severe violence toward women: Does other family violence matter? *Child Abuse & Neglect*, *33*(2), 94–101. https://doi.org/10.1016/j.chiabu.2008.03.005

Mikulincer, M., & Shaver, P. R. (2007). *Attachment in adulthood: Structure, dynamics, and change*. Guilford Press.

Miller, L. C., & Fishkin, S. A. (1997). On the dynamics of human bonding and reproductive success: Seeking windows on the adapted-for-human environmental interface. In J. A. Simpson & D. T. Kenrick (Eds.), *Evolutionary social psychology* (pp. 197–236). Erlbaum.

Mize, K., & Shackelford, T. (2008). Intimate partner homicide methods in heterosexual, gay, and lesbian relationships. *Violence & Victims*, *23*(1), 98–114. doi:10.1891/0886-6708.23.1.98

Mize, K., Shackelford, T., & Shackelford, V. (2009). Hands-on killing of intimate partners as a function of sex and relationship status/state. *Journal of Family Violence*, *24*, 463–470. https://doi.org/10.1007/s10896-009-9244-5

Moffitt, T. E., Caspi, A., Rutter, M., & Silva, P. A. (2001). *Sex differences in antisocial behavior*. Cambridge University Press.

Morton, E., Runyan, C., Moracco, K., & Butts, J. (1998). Partner homicide victims: A population based study in North Carolina, 1988–1992. *Violence and Victims*, *13*(2), 91–106. doi:10.1891/0886-6708.13.2.91

O'Keefe, M. (1997). Incarcerated battered women: A comparison of battered women who killed their abusers and those incarcerated for other offenses. *Journal of Family Violence*, *12*(1), 1–18. https://doi.org/10.1023/A:1021989732032

Osthoff, S., & Maguigan, H. (2005). Explaining without pathologizing: Testimony on battering and its effects. In D. Loseke, R. Gelles, & M. Cavanaugh (Eds.), *Current controversies on family violence* (2nd ed., pp. 225–240). Sage.

Paradis, C., Bowen, M., & McCullough, G. (2020). Intimate partner violence: Psychological effects and legal defenses. In R. Javier, E. Owen & J. Maddux (Eds.), *Assessing Trauma in Forensic Contexts* (pp. 351–378). New York: Springer Nature.

Pizzey, E. (1982). *Prone to violence*. Hamlyn Press.

Pleck, E. (1987). *Domestic tyranny: The making of American social policy against family violence from colonial times to the present*. Oxford University Press.

Pynoos, R. S., & Eth, S. (1985). Children traumatized by witnessing acts of personal violence: Homicide, rape, or suicide behavior. In S. Eth & R. S. Pynoos (Eds.), *Posttraumatic stress disorder in children* (pp. 17–44). American Psychiatric Press.

Ramsey, C. (2010). Provoking change: Comparative insights on feminist homicide law reform. *The Journal of Criminal Law & Criminology*, *100*(1), 33–106.

Richardson, D. (2005). The myth of female passivity: Thirty years of revelations about female aggression. *Psychology of Women Quarterly*, *29*, 238–247. https://doi.org/10.1111/j.1471-6402.2005.00218.x

Russell, B. (2010). *Battered woman syndrome as a legal defense: History, effectiveness and Implications*. McFarland & Company.

Russell, B., Ragatz, L., & Kraus, S. W. (2012). Expert testimony of the battered person syndrome, defendant gender, and sexual orientation in a case of duress: Evaluating legal decisions. *Journal of Family Violence, 27*(7), 659–670. https://doi.org/10.1007/s10896-012-9459-8

Saini, M. A., Drozd, L. M., & Olesen, N. W. (2017). Adaptive and maladaptive gatekeeping behaviors and attitudes: Implications for child outcomes after separation and divorce. *Family Court Review, 55*(2), 260–272. https://doi.org/10.1111/fcre.12276

Salari, S., & Sillito, C. (2016). Intimate partner homicide-suicide: Perpetrator primary intent across young, middle and elder adult age categories. *Aggression and Violence Behavior, 26*, 26–34. https://doi.org/10.1016/j.avb.2015.11.004

Saunders, D. (1996). When battered women use violence. *Violence and Victims, 1*(1), 47–60. doi:10.1891/0886-6708.1.1.47

Saunders, D., & Browne, A. (2000). Intimate partner homicide. In R. Ammerman & M. Hersen (Eds.), *Case studies in family violence* (2nd ed., pp. 415–449). Plenum.

Schmahl, C. G., Vermetten, E., Elzinga, B. M., & Bremner, J. D. (2004). A positron emission tomography study of memories of childhood abuse in borderline personality disorder. *Biological Psychiatry, 55*(7), 759–765. https://doi.org/10.1016/j.biopsych.2003.11.007

Schmitt, D. (2004). Patterns and universals of mate poaching across 53 nations: The effects of sex, culture, and personality on romantically attracting another person's partner. *Journal of Personality and Social Psychology, 86*(4), 560–584. https://doi.org/10.1037/0022-3514.86.4.560

Schopp, R., Sturgis, B., & Sullivan, M. (1994). Battered woman syndrome, expert testimony, and the distinction between justification and excuse. *University of Illinois Law Review, 1*, 45–113.

Schore, A. N. (1994). *Affect regulation and the origin of the self: the neurobiology of emotional development*. Erlbaum.

Schore, A. N. (2003). *Affect dysregulation and the disorders of the self*. Norton.

Sebire, J. (2017). The value of incorporating measures of relationship concordance when constructing profiles of intimate partner homicides: A descriptive study of IPH committed within London, 1998–2009. *Journal of Interpersonal Violence, 32*(10), 1476–1500. https://doi.org/10.1177/0886260515589565

Serbin, L., Stack, D., De Genna, N., Grunzeweig, N., Temcheff, C. E., Schwartzmann, A. E., & Ledingham, J. (2004). When aggressive girls become mothers. In M. Putallaz & K. L. Bierman (Eds.), *Aggression, antisocial behavior, and violence among girls* (pp. 262–285). Guilford Press.

Serran, G., & Firestone, P. (2004). Intimate partner homicide: A review of the male proprietariness and the self-defense theories. *Aggression and Violent Behavior, 9*, 1–15. https://doi.org/10.1016/S1359-1789(02)00107-6

Shackelford, T. K., Goetz, A. T., & Buss, D. M. (2005). Mate retention in marriage: Further evidence of the reliability of the Mate Retention Inventory. *Personality and Individual Differences, 39*(2), 415–425. https://doi.org/10.1016/j.paid.2005.01.018

Sharp, C., Wright, A., Fowler, C. J., Frueh, B. C., Allen, J. G., Oldham, J., & Clark, L. A. (2015). The stucture of personality pathology: Both general ("g") and specific ("s") factors? *Journal of Abnormal Psychology, 124*(2), 387–398.

Simmons, C., Lehmann, P., Cobb, N., & Fowler, C. (2005). Personality profiles of women and men arrested for domestic violence: An analysis of similarities and differences. *Journal of Offender Rehabilitation, 41*(4), 63–81. doi:10.1300/J076v41n04_03

Smith, S., Fowler, K., & Nioolon, P. (2014). Intimate partner homicide and corollary victims in16 states: National violent death reporting system, 2003–2009. *American Journal of Public Health, 104*(3), 461–467. https://doi.org/10.2105/AJPH.2013.301582

Smith, S. G., Zhang, X., Basile, K. C., Merrick, M. T., Wang, J., Kresnow, M., & Chen, J. (2018). *The National Intimate Partner and Sexual Violence Survey (NISVS): 2015 data brief—Updated release*. National Center for Injury Prevention and Control, Centers for Disease Control and Prevention.

Spencer, C., & Stith, S. (2020). Risk factors for male perpetration and female victimization of intimate partner homicide: A meta-analysis. *Trauma, Violence & Abuse, 21*(3), 527–540. https://doi.org/10.1177/1524838018781101

Sroufe, L. A., Egeland, B., Carlson, E. A., & Collins, W. A. (2005). *The development of the person: The Minnesota study of risk and adaptation from birth to adulthood*. Guilford Press.

Stacey, W., Hazelwood, L., & Shupe, A. (1994). *The violent couple*. Praeger.

Stark, E. (2007). *Coercive control: The entrapment of women in personal life*. Oxford University Press.

Stöckl, H., Devries, K., Rotstein, A., Abrahams, N., Campbell, J., Watts, C., & Moreno, C. (2013). The global prevalence of intimate partner homicide: A systematic review. *Lancet, 382*, 859–865. https://doi.org/10.1016/S0140-6736(13)61030-2

Straus, M. (1999). The controversy over domestic violence by women: A methodological, theoretical, and sociology of science analysis. In X. Arriaga & S. Oskamp (Eds.), *Violence in intimate relationships* (pp. 17–44). Sage.

Straus, M. (2008). Dominance and symmetry in partner violence by male and female university students in 32 nations. *Children and Youth Services Review, 30*(3), 252–275. https://doi.org/10.1016/j.childyouth.2007.10.004

Straus, M., & Gelles, R. (1990). *Physical violence in American families*. Transaction.

Sugarman, D., & Frankel, S. (1996). Patriarchal ideology and wife-assault: A meta-analytic review. *Journal of Family Violence, 11*(1), 13–39. https://doi.org/10.1007/BF02333338

Swatt, M., & He, N. (2006). Exploring the difference between male and female intimate partner homicides. *Homicide Studies, 10*(4), 279–292. https://doi.org/10.1177/1088767906290965

Terrance, C., & Matheson, K. (2003). Undermining reasonableness: Expert testimony in a case involving a battered woman who kills. *Psychology of Women Quarterly, 27*, 37–45. https://doi.org/10.1111/1471-6402.t01-2-00005

Terrance, C., Plumm, K., & Rhyner, K. (2012). Expert testimony in cases involving battered women who kill: Going beyond the battered woman syndrome. *North Dakota Law Review, 88*(92), 922–955.

Titterington, V., & Harper, L. (2005). Women as the aggressors in intimate partner homicide in Houston, 1980s to 1990s. In F. Buttell & M. Carney (Eds.), *Women who perpetrate relationship violence* (pp. 83–98). Routledge. doi:10.1300/J076v41n04_04

Turan, S., & Dutton, D. G. (2010). Psychic freezing to lethal malevolent authority. *Journal of Aggression, Conflict and Peace Studies, 2*(3), 4–15. https://doi.org/10.5042/jacpr.2010.0332

van IJzendoorn, M. H., Schlengel, C., & Bakermans-Kranenburg, M. J. (1999). Disorganized attachment in early childhood: Meta analysis of precursors, concomitants and sequelae *Development and Psychopathology, 11*, 225–249.

Velopulos, C., Carmichael, H., Zakrison, T., & Crandall, M. (2019). Comparison of male and female victims of intimate partner homicide and bidirectionality—An analysis of the national violent death reporting system. *Journal of Acute Care Surgery, 87*(2), 331–336. doi:10.1097/TA.0000000000002276

Walker, L. (1979). *The battered woman*. Harper and Row.

Walker, L. (1983). The battered woman syndrome study. In D. Finklehor (Ed.), *The dark side of families* (pp. 31–48). Springer.

Walker, L. (1984). *The battered woman syndrome*. Springer.

Walker, L. (2009). *The battered woman syndrome* (3rd ed.). Springer.

Weizmann-Henelius, G., Grönroos, M., Putkonen, H., Eronen, M., Lindberg, N., & Häkkänen-Nyholm, H. (2012). Gender-specific risk factors for intimate partner homicide: A nationwide register-based study. *Journal of Interpersonal Violence, 27*, 1519–1539. https://doi.org/10.1177/0886260511425793

Williams, S., & Frieze, I. (2005). Patterns of violent relationships, psychological distress, and marital satisfaction in a national sample of men and women. *Sex Roles, 52*(11/12), 771–785. https://doi.org/10.1007/s11199-005-4198-4

Wilson, M., & Daly, M. (1992). Who kills whom in spouse killings? On the exceptional sex ratio of spousal homicides in the United States. *Criminology, 30*, 189–215. https://doi.org/10.1111/j.1745-9125.1992.tb01102.x

Wilson, M., & Daly, M. (1993). Spousal homicide risk and estrangement. *Violence and Victims, 8*(1), 3–16.

APPENDIX: QUESTIONS RELEVANT TO THE ADJUDICATION OF INTIMATE PARTNER HOMICIDE

QUESTIONS REGARDING THE EVENT

1. Did the defendant plan to assault the victim?
2. Did the assault occur during a confrontational situation, and if so, what was the defendant's role in the confrontation—e.g., did he or she initiate violence or contribute to the escalation process?
3. Was there intent to injure or kill?
4. If there was such an intent, did the defendant believe he or she was in imminent danger of unlawful bodily harm?
5. To what extent was this belief based on objective evidence of imminent danger, and not simply subjective? For example, did the defendant have a naturally anxious or paranoid personality? Was the fear of harm based

on memories of past abuse by others? In other words, did the victim's behavior (e.g., arguing, yelling), not previously associated with serious, life-threatening abuse, trigger an exaggerated fear response in the defendant?

6. Did he or she use only a reasonable amount of force to counter the perceived danger?
7. Was either party under the influence of drugs or alcohol?
8. What unusual circumstances did the defendant and victim face at the time of the assault?
9. What other motives, aside from fear, may have driven the defendant's actions—such as revenge for something the victim did (e.g., having an affair) or might do (leave the relationship, report them to law enforcement for past or current abuse), to avoid spousal or child support payments, collect on a life insurance policy, or for other monetary gain?

Questions Regarding Defendant and Victim Histories

1. Was the defendant previously subjected to a pattern of battering, consisting of physical assaults leading to serious bodily harm, threats to seriously injure or kill his or her family, and/or emotionally abusive and controlling behaviors?
2. To what extent was the defendant under the influence of the victim throughout the course of their relationship? To what extent was this influence due directly to the victim's physical and psychological abuse, threats, and controlling behaviors, as opposed to situational or personality differences (e.g., lack of assertiveness, emotionally dependent)?
3. Is there confirmation of such a pattern of battering and influence aside from the defendant's self-report—e.g., prior calls to police, arrest reports, eyewitnesses, medical reports, or trauma symptoms?
4. Does the defendant evidence signs of trauma, and how are these symptoms relevant to the defendant's actions against the victim?
5. How have these symptoms impacted how the defendant has been able to present himself or herself in court, and perhaps undermined his or her credibility?
6. Does the defendant have a history of prior trauma (in childhood or previous relationships) that might account for these symptoms (rather than abuse at the hands of the victim)?
7. Was the defendant able to predict, based on the victim's pattern of violence against him or her, when he or she would be violent again?
8. How often when he or she recognized signs of impending violence did violence actually occur?
9. When previously assaulted, or threatened with assault by the victim, did the defendant make efforts to seek help? If not, is there evidence of previous life-threatening threats by the victim?

10. If he or she did seek help, was help available? For example, was the local shelter full, police slow to respond, a restraining order issued but ignored, etc.?
11. If there is evidence of prior bidirectional abuse between the defendant and victim, was there a dominant aggressor? Bidirectionality, by itself, does not necessarily imply mutual culpability.
12. Is there a record of the defendant, or the victim, perpetrating any previous battering behavior upon other partners?
13. What are the characteristics of the defendant's personality? Does he or she present with characteristics typical of perpetrators rather than victims—e.g., angry temperament, need to dominate and control, jealous, impulsive, with borderline, narcissistic, paranoid, or antisocial traits?
14. What are the characteristics of the victim's personality? Does he or she present with characteristics typical of perpetrators rather than victims?
15. Did the defendant subject the victim to a pattern of battering, consisting of physical assaults leading to serious bodily harm, threats to seriously injure or kill him or her or family, and/or emotionally abusive and controlling behaviors?
16. Is there confirmation of such a pattern of battering aside from the victim's self-report—e.g., prior calls to police, arrest reports, eyewitnesses, or medical reports?

7

Jury Decision-Making

Understanding and Overcoming Bias in the Courtroom

BRENDA RUSSELL AND BLAKE MCKIMMIE ■

Our inherent gender roles inform stereotypes surrounding intimate partner violence (IPV) and stereotypes throughout the legal system (Bates et al., 2019). IPV originated as a "crime against women" and continues to be perceived as such despite the research that suggests anyone can be a victim of IPV. While heterosexual women certainly do experience IPV, our beliefs, assumptions, and stereotypes (often unconsciously) can lead to differential treatment of others who may not fit the stereotype of a victim of IPV. Although members of the criminal justice system remain committed to the service of others, they, too, are susceptible to these stereotypes. Society is less likely to recognize partner violence as a serious social problem affecting all individuals, regardless of demographic characteristics and intersectionality. Such lack of awareness and neglect creates an environment where IPV continues, and victims do not receive the same protection from the law compared to other crimes.

A juror brings to the courtroom their previous knowledge about the legal system and their stereotypes about the different people involved in the legal system. For example, many believe that defendants with a criminal record or a history of violence or dishonesty are all part of a "guilty" stereotype; in other words "good cases have good victims and bad offenders" (Rauma, 1984, p. 384). While not all defendants have these characteristics, being consistent with a negative stereotype can lead to the defendant being more likely to be seen as guilty. Offences are also viewed through the lens of stereotypes. IPV has historically been considered a gender-based crime where (heterosexual) women are perceived as the primary victims, and (heterosexual) men are the stereotypical perpetrators. In this regard, women may be perceived as acting in self-defense or under duress when or if they do commit a crime. While women do endure more significant injury (Archer, 2000) and victimization in intimate partner homicide cases (see Hamel, Dutton,

& Lysova, Chapter 6, this volume), as this volume demonstrates there are certainly cases involving heterosexual male and female and sexual minority perpetrators and victims.

This chapter will review empirical research that examines how underlying heteronormative beliefs about gender and partner violence can influence jury decision-making and what some of the critical aspects of jury decision-making are that create a reliance on those beliefs. We will begin by addressing some critical issues in jury cases about IPV. As the primary cases that come in front of a jury often revolve around homicide, crimes of passion, and duress, we will focus on the common elements and essential factors involved in these cases.

CRITICAL ISSUES FOR THE JURY IN CASES OF INTIMATE PARTNER VIOLENCE

IPV can be deadly, and juries are primarily used in cases of IPV involving homicide due to the seriousness of this offense. Intimate partner homicide (IPH) is the most dangerous consequence and outcome. IPH can be defined as involving a victim killed by an intimate partner such as a husband, wife, boyfriend, same-sex partner, or ex-partner. Various defenses are used in such cases, and historically insanity was used as a defense for homicide against a partner. However, since the 1980s, self-defense has become the more common defense used in IPH cases to obtain an acquittal (Brewer, 1988; Maguigan, 1991). There are vital issues to consider surrounding IPH and self-defense, which are reviewed next.

Self-Defense

Self-defense is the most common defense used to justify intentional homicide committed to fending off an attacker. It rests on the notion that a defendant may take reasonable steps to defend themselves from physical harm (LaFave & Scott, 1972). The primary objective of the defendant who claims self-defense is to convince the judge and jury that the homicide was justified, proper, proportionate, or appropriate given the circumstances surrounding the incident (Schneider, 1980). When deciding whether a response is justified, the difficulty in self-defense is to reach a mutual understanding of a reasonable person and the defendant's subjective perception of what they believe as imminent danger. In other words, one's behavior is "justified" or "excused" based on the victim's behavior and circumstances.

While each state's statutes vary slightly in wording, most self-defense is justified when "the use of force upon or toward another person is justifiable when the actor believes that such force is immediately necessary for protecting himself against the use of unlawful force by another person on the present occasion" (§ 505 Section (a) Title 18 Pa.C.S.A. Crimes and Offenses). In the same regard, there are additional elements the defendant must demonstrate. For example, "the actor believes such force is necessary to protect himself against death or serious bodily injury" (§ 505 Section (C) Title 18 Pa.C.S.A. Crimes and Offenses), and "presumed to have a reasonable belief that deadly force is immediately necessary to protect himself against death, serious bodily injury, kidnapping or sexual intercourse compelled by force or threat" (§ 505 Section (2.1) Title 18 Pa.C.S.A. Crimes and Offenses). Other relevant elements for the chapter include provoking the use of force and the inability for retreat (§ 505 Sections (2. i; 2.2ii;2.3) Title 18 Pa.C.S.A. Crimes and Offenses).

As state statutes and jury instructions relating to self-defense may vary, most have three essential elements: deadly force may be used when the threat of death or serious bodily injury is imminent, the force used is proportional to the threat, and the defendant believes such force is necessary.

Previously, scholars have argued that the original self-defense law was designed for men of equal size and stature. It did not consider the plight of a battered woman who is typically unequal in size and stature and often economic power (Crocker, 1985). Consequently, women might use a knife or gun during a direct confrontation or respond in a nonconfrontational way, such as killing a sleeping abuser, killing when the abuser has their back turned (e.g., *State v. Allery*, 1984; *LaVallee v. Regina*, 1990; *R. v. Lavallee*, 1990; *State v. Norman*, 1989), or killing after an abuser completes their attack (*Ibn-Tamas v. U.S.*, 1979; *State v. Kelly*, 1984). Other situations can include when an attacker threatens further abuse (*State v. Allery*, 1984) or murder for hire (*People v. Yaklich*, 1988). While most women who kill their abusers do so in direct confrontation (Browne, 1987; Maguigan, 1991), it is not unusual that victims of battering would respond in a nonconfrontational way. The element of imminence is particularly relevant in nonconfrontational cases.

Imminent Danger

The imminence requirement typically focuses on what occurred before or during the incident and neglects the cumulative impact of abuse. The ongoing nature of domestic violence places victims in precarious situations, and while killing someone in direct confrontation can be extremely difficult to impart to jurors, doing the same in a nonconfrontational situation can seem overwhelming. Using deadly force toward an individual to protect oneself against an unarmed attacker casts doubt on the reasonableness and necessity for their actions (Schuller et al., 1994).

The main objective of the defendant who claims self-defense is to convey to the court that the homicide was justified, that it was the correct response, or that it was suitable given the circumstances (Schneider, 1980). The difficulty comes in finding the middle ground between the objective understanding of a reasonable person and the defendant's subjective understanding of imminent danger (Russell, 2010). This often leads to considering the defendant's moral and mental status at the time of the crime, wherein the defendant must convey and convince a jury of their perceptions at the time of the crime. Often this is a difficult task, dependent upon a myriad of issues, such as the interpretation of the law and evidence to be allowed at trial. A defense lawyer must then consider the best way to impart their client's perceptions at the time of the crime. Typically, this if often provided by an expert, but what type of expert? Considerations include psychiatric testimony and or social framework testimony which can provide a broad overview about the effects of battering to a jury and whether the defendant will waive their Fifth Amendment right and testify.

Individuals who apply the law (police, attorneys, judges, and juries) tend to turn to common law perceptions of two men engaged in combat of equal size, strength, and force, provocation, and imminence required for reasonable self-defense. These perceptions are also based on the belief that an individual has autonomy or is free to leave/exit the situation. The issues of time (immediate, imminent, cyclical), a distinctive truth of which defendants are compared (Angel, 2007), does not always capture the plight of a victim of abuse. Victims of IPV may not be free to exit the situation. The killing may or may not have occurred based on provocation or events taken place immediately before the killing. Further, even when faced with the immediate danger of death or bodily injury, the consideration of deadly and nondeadly force will be considered. Many courts have held that the use of deadly force against nondeadly force was unreasonable. In cases of female perpetrators and male victims of homicide, size and strength differences between the victim and defendant are taken into consideration (*State v. Wanrow*, 1977). However, power and control of an individual do not always correspond with size and strength, leaving many gender minorities and heterosexual male victims at a disadvantage in the courtroom.

Imminence in Confrontational versus Nonconfrontational Situations

Another aspect to consider regarding imminence is whether the homicide occurred within a confrontational or nonconfrontational situation. While most cases are directly confrontational (actively engaged in direct conflict) (Browne, 1987; Maguigan, 1991), there are times when a defendant kills in a nonconfrontational situation. These incidents may include killing a sleeping abuser, killing when the abuser has their back turned (e.g., *State v. Allery*, 1984; *LaVallee v. Regina*, 1990; *State v. Norman*, 1989), or killing after an abuser completes their attack (*Ibn-Tamas v. U.S.*, 1979; *State v. Kelly*, 1984). Other situations can include when an attacker threatens further abuse (*State v. Allery*, 1984) or murder for hire (*People v. Yaklich*, 1988). Using deadly force toward an individual to protect oneself against an unarmed attacker casts doubt on the reasonableness and necessity for their actions (Schuller, 1994). Nonconfrontational cases present a particular challenge for defense attorneys in terms of elements of imminence and reasonableness. Courts often question the amount of time and space needed for a defendant to believe they were in imminent danger leading to the decision to use deadly force (*People v. Sandoval-Ceron*, 2010; *People v. Yaklich*, 1991).

Deadly Force

In self-defense cases, the courts will examine the amount of force a defendant used, and the force used must be determined as reasonable for self-defense to be a viable option (Russell, 2010). In *People v. Bush* (1978), the defendant had been abused throughout her relationship and attempted to leave her home and call the police. The defendant's efforts to leave were thwarted when the victim stopped her, severely beat her, and threatened to kill her. The defendant grabbed a kitchen knife from the counter and tried to fend off the victim, fatally stabbing him. While the jury had been informed of the victim's past violence, they found Bush guilty of involuntary manslaughter because resorting to a weapon to defend herself did not justify her use of deadly force. This case reflects that even in the defendant's eyes, self-defense can go wrong when strict adherence to the doctrine is used and the jury is unable to consider the cumulative effects of battering.

One's actions must be reasonable, and one's honest belief in the need to use deadly force is relevant in objective and subjective tests in self-defense (*State v. Frei*, 2013). This requires that the defendant must believe that they are in danger and that belief must be reasonable. Most courts will require juries to focus on the objective reasonableness of the defendant's belief they were in imminent danger. In other words, they believed self-defense was necessary, and the belief must be reasonable by the standards of an ordinary person. The subjective test used in some jurisdictions will require only that the defendant have honestly believed that self-defense action was necessary; the extent to which the act was reasonable does not play a role (Faigman et al., 2020; Lafave & Scott, 1972). While some courts will address the cumulative effects of abuse, to the extent that it relates to the reasonable belief in the need to use deadly force (*State v. Kelly*, 1984), other courts might use a more subjective standard by comparing a "reasonable battered person" to a typical reasonable person (*State v. Hundley*, 1985).

Why Didn't They Just Leave the Relationship?

In most jurors' minds, the predominant question is, "Why didn't they just leave the abuser?" Many victims of IPV do attempt to leave their partner but are unsuccessful (Campbell et al., 1994). It is estimated that women attempt to leave their partner five times before successfully ending the relationship (Okun, 1986). The question is also based on the premise that "leaving will end the violence" (Browne, 1987, p. 109). It is unclear how many abused victims stay with their abusers, as studies have varied from 38% to 63% (Campbell et al., 1994), but separating from an abuser can be the most dangerous time for a female victim. Rates of more frequent, serious violence leading to injury occur more often upon separation of the abuser than when victims remain with their abuser (Rennison & Welchans, 2000). Abuse, threats, assaults, stalking, and even murder do not end with separation. In fact, leaving an abusive partner is often a trigger leading to more violent responses (Walker et al., 2004; Wilson & Daly, 1993). Studies on male victims' separation from their abusers are sparse. However, one large-scale study including 2.8 million Canadians (Trainor & Mihorean, 2001) found that 28% of women and 22% of men reported violence perpetrated by an ex-partner (living together or after separation). For most respondents (63%), the violence ended at separation, while approximately one third reported continued violence, with more women (39%) experiencing assault after separation than men (32%). Both women and men reported experiencing more severe forms of violence after separation than those assaulted in their current relationships. To date, studies examining the LGBTQ+ community and reasons for separation and or examination of probability of violence and or homicide are minimal (Edwards et al., 2015).

While reasons for leaving differ based on gender, sexual minority status, socioeconomic status, culture, religion, age, length of the relationship, and many more factors beyond the scope of this chapter, the act of leaving entails many stressors. These can include moving, economic instability, child custody issues, leaving supportive social networks, and leaving an abuser to whom they are emotionally attached. One way of leaving an abusive relationship is to obtain a protection (or restraining) order (PO). However, it may not be as easy for a heterosexual man or sexual minority individual to obtain one. Studies have found judges are more likely to grant POs to females than male plaintiffs (Basile, 2005; Muller et al., 2009; Shernock & Russell, 2012), be charged with a PO offense (Jordan et al., 2010), or convicted of a PO offense (Frantzen et al., 2011). In one study examining men pursuing POs (Mele et al., 2011), more than 80% of men claimed they obtained the PO because of physical abuse and or psychological/emotional abuse. There is little research available on obtaining POs or the effectiveness of POs for sexual minorities. While some states provide mutual restraining orders, this is rare in heterosexual couples. Dual arrests in domestic violence incidents and mutual restraining orders that follow occur in about 1% of cases (Masri, 2018).

Nevertheless, for same-sex couples, this increases to 30% of cases (Hirschel, 2008). This is associated with greater difficulty identifying the primary aggressor or lack of police training with LGBTQ+ IPV (see Russell & Seisler, Chapter 3, this volume). A great deal of empirical research on this topic for women and not for other populations implies a lack of scientific investigation into this critical topic.

It should be noted that there are obstacles for all those who seek to leave an abusive relationship. There are some similarities among men with women's reasons for staying or leaving (Eckstein, 2011). While there is a great deal of research on this topic for women, studies on why heterosexual men leave are recent. Research on men's help-seeking behavior in IPV is growing but remains in its infancy. The context and motives for abuse tend to be similar for men and women. However, the internal and external barriers to help-seeking or leaving an abuser differs among heterosexuals and sexual minorities (availability of services, biases, etc.) (Dixon et al., 2022; Hines & Douglas, 2011; Lysova et al., 2020). Researchers (Eckstein, 2011; Lysova et al., 2020) surveyed men and women about their experiences with IPV victimization to explore how they communicated messages about why they stay in abusive relationships. Eckstein (2011) found that men's and women's internal justifications (how they justified the IPV to themselves) were similar. Shared reasons about decisions to stay related to the promise of a better future, excuses for partner's behavior, parenting, religious reasons, lacking resources, fear, and shame. Men were significantly more likely to believe they had to be the strong one in the relationship, to stay in the relationship to protect their partner, and to believe that children need both parents. Lysova et al. (2020) also explored internal and external barriers to help-seeking in a sample of male victims of female-perpetrated IPV. They found that many men did not recognize their experience as abuse, sought to preserve their relationships, refused to seek help to maintain their masculine identity, and made excuses for their partner's behavior. External barriers consisted of fear of seeking help and having nowhere to go. Similarly, Bates (2020) examined a sample of 161 non-help-seeking male victims of IPV to determine reasons why they chose not to seek help. Her results found that societal perceptions of gender norms and male roles made them uncomfortable seeking help as society is less likely to believe male victims and related concerns of being "weak" and uncomfortable with the term "victim."

It is necessary to stress that IPV in heterosexual and sexual minority and immigrant populations is similar in terms of the cycle of violence and its effects (Amanor-Boadu et al., 2012; Duthu, 1996). However, further considerations for sexual minorities and or illegal immigrants should include forms of coercive controls associated with societal prejudice and discrimination due to their sexual orientation and or immigration status. For example, identity abuse is a common threat used in sexual minority populations; it includes threats to disclose one's partner's sexual identity status to family and employers that can compromise a person's job, family, livelihood, and safety. Sexual minorities and illegal immigrants often seek help using informal sources such as friends, family, and coworkers (Hymen et al., 2006; Scheer et al., 2020). Inadequate criminal justice or social resources (e.g., nonenforcement of protection orders, shelters) also inhibit help-seeking and leaving abusive partners. When subject to further marginalization because of race, class, and immigration status, LGBTQ+ victims face additional obstacles to escape from these dominating relationships.

A victim's undocumented status no doubt contributes to their reticence to report abuse. A recent survey of 715 advocates and attorneys from 46 states and the District of Columbia (Tahirih Justice Center, 2017 Advocate and Legal Service Survey Regarding Immigrant Survivors,; Domestic Violence, 2017) found that 78% of immigrant sexual and domestic violence victims expressed concerns about contacting police. Nearly half of the advocates reported they worked with immigrants who dropped their civil and criminal cases because they feared going forward with the case.

UNDERSTANDING DIFFERENT FORMS OF INTIMATE PARTNER VIOLENCE

While this topic continues to be a scholarly and political hotbed of debate, studies have found that women initiate mild-to-moderate physical assaults at about the same rates as men (Stets & Straus, 1990), though women do experience more sexual coercion and experience more significant injury in IPV incidents (Archer, 2000). Women also use mental and criminal justice services more often than men (Tjaden & Thoennes, 2000). What is now coined as "gender symmetry" has been found in hundreds of studies (Straus, 2012) (readers can also refer to Bates & Papmichail, Chapter 2, this volume). Further, as noted in previous chapters (Hamel et al., Chapter 6), bidirectional violence is one of the most common subcategories of IPV (Johnson, 2008). IPV can take many forms, including physical, sexual, and psychological abuse (Smith et al., 2015). Physical behaviors include pushing, shoving, kicking, and the use of a weapon. Sexual abuse includes participating in sexual activity without consent or consent obtained under duress. While most criminal juries are involved in cases where physical violence is used, it is stressed that IPV cannot be understood simply within the context of physical violence.

Controlling and Coercive Behaviors

IPV characterizes abuse as a pattern of coercive/controlling behaviors that could include physical, psychological, and verbal threats, sexual assault, and bodily injury (for a more in-depth review, see Hamel et al., Chapter 6, in this volume). The patterns, models, and effects of partner violence among sexual minorities are virtually identical to heterosexual abuse. Researchers believe that virtually all forms of abuse are about power and control.

Domestic violence's power and control model has historically been used to explain IPV more contextually. Within this model, there is an event of physical, emotional/verbal, or sexual violence. Once violence occurs, the threat of future abuse is enough to make the victim live in fear of the abuser. The goal of an abuser's behavior is to exert power and control over their partner by depriving the victim of independence and resources. Shechter (1982) and Stark (2007) have introduced the concept of coercive control to describe a wide range of behaviors used by abusers to maintain power.

Overall, it is believed that heterosexual men and sexual minorities are just as likely and, in some ways, more likely to experience IPV than their heterosexual counterparts (Black et al., 2011). Studies on heterosexual male victims have demonstrated that men experience coercive control at the same rate as female victims (Black et al., 2010). For instance, male victims experience verbal, physical, and sexual aggression, threats, intimidation, manipulations of the legal system, blackmail, and financial damage (Bates, 2020; Hines et al., 2007). Some scholars (Hines et al., 2016; Tilbrook et al., 2010) have found that male victims report experiencing manipulation of the legal system by their female partner more than they perpetrate this behavior. Others (Tilbrook et al., 2010) suggest this tactic may be used more often by women than men because of the gendered notions associated with who can and cannot be victims of abuse.

Coercive control and physical IPV are also found in equal or higher rates in LGBTQ+ relationships (Messinger, 2011; Walters et al., 2013). Rates of IPV victimization in LGBTQ+ adults can range from 17% to 74%. However, according to a CDC report of the NISVS report (Walters et al., 2013), 36% of lesbians, 55% of bisexual women, and 30% of heterosexual women were slapped, pushed, or shoved by an intimate partner in their lifetime, and rates of coercive control ranged from 48% to 68%. Similarly, 25% of gay, heterosexual, and bisexual males have been pushed, slapped, or shoved. Lifetime psychological aggression rates among women were 63% for lesbians and 76% for bisexual women compared to 47.5% for heterosexual women. These statistics can be compared to rates of psychological aggression for men, wherein approximately 60% of gays, 53% of bisexual men, and 49.3% of heterosexual men experienced psychological aggression with levels of coercive control ranging from 43% to 48%; moreover, in a study (National Coalition of Violence Programs [NCAVP]) of over 2,000 LGBTQ+ IPV victims, 48% suffered injuries. While rates of IPV are rare for transgender individuals, a recent meta-analysis (Peitzmeier et al., 2020) found that compared to cisgender IPV victims, transgender victims were 1.7 times more likely to experience IPV and 2.2 to 2.5 times more likely to experience physical and sexual IPV. A large national study on transgender individuals found that 54% of transgender individuals experienced IPV, of which 24% suffered severe physical violence. A more recent study examined 732 transgender older adults (65+ years) and found that 30% reported IPV uniquely associated with their transgender identity (Hillman, in press).

While we are learning more about IPV in sexual minority populations, even the CDC states that there is still much to be learned about the national prevalence of IPV in LGBTQ+ relationships. Researchers suspect prevalence rates are severely underrepresented because of fear of reporting to the police among the LGBTQ+ community or law enforcement not taking such reports seriously (Alexander, 2002). Further, even if reports to criminal justice officers are made, victims' sexual and gender identity is often not recognized or reported in police reports. Transgender victims are frequently misgendered and or reported in the media using a birth name. Intimate partner relationships of same-sex couples can be misidentified as friendships or "other relationships" (e.g., "roommates"), making accurate prevalence rates of LGBTQ+ identities of IPV and IPH victims' obscure. Bisexual, gender-nonconforming, and other nonbinary identities are rarely considered and may not be reported accurately. Until LGBTQ+ identities are calculated and confirmed, it will be challenging to understand the true prevalence of IPV in the LGBTQ+ community.

One unique aspect of abuse in the LGBTQ+ community includes threats to "out" one's sexual orientation or anything (children, welfare, immigration status) an abuser can hold against them as a tool in violent relationships. While each member of the LGBTQ+ community endures unique forms of coercive control, they are further marginalized because of sexual minority status, race, class, or immigration status, leaving LGBTQ+ victims to face additional obstacles to seeking help and escaping from abusive relationships.

Motivations for Intimate Partner Violence and Intimate Partner Homicide

Early studies examining motivations for committing IPV and IPH have suggested that IPV and IPH are committed in self-defense due to fear based on previous, imminent, or future assault leading to bodily injury or death (Campbell et al., 2003, 2007; Dobash et al., 2004; Jurik & Winn, 1990). Other studies suggest that motivations for IPV are similar among men and women (also see Hamel et al., Chapter 6, this volume). For example, studies have investigated additional motives such as jealousy. For example, researchers (Belknap et al., 2012; Block & Christakos, 1995) found no differences in male/female perpetrators of IPH over sexual jealousy. Previous studies on self-defense tended to rely upon one or two items that assessed whether a victim's actions were in self-defense. Bates developed a more valid structured survey to better assess the frequency of IPV perpetrated in self-defense. In her survey of 180 couples, 70% reported the use of bidirectional IPV. This finding is consistent with research on male and female offenders incarcerated for IPV, which has found a strong relationship between IPV and mutual violence and retaliation among partners (Felson & Lane, 2010).

STEREOTYPES AND SCRIPTS

One of the challenges victims of IPV face is the stereotypes and scripts associated with IPV and gender more generally. Stereotypes and scripts are examples of a more general construct, schemas. These are our cognitive representations of our knowledge about a concept or a thing. They are based on experience and represent our theories for how the social world works (Alba & Hasher, 1983). They are functional in that they help us efficiently encode and store information about events, people, and the social world more generally (Macrae et al., 1994). They also facilitate the retrieval of information and help us form impressions and make inferences based on that information (Alba & Hasher, 1983; Fiske & Taylor, 1991; Kunda & Thagard, 1996).

Stereotypes are a type of person schema that represents information about social groups such as ethnicity and gender. There are also stereotypes about victims and perpetrators of IPV. Scripts, also referred to as event schemas, are representations of activities and events associated with a particular situation. Thus, just as we might have a script about regular day-to-day activities such as going to a movie, we also have scripts to represent our understanding of events such as IPV. Role schemas are related in a way to both stereotypes and event schemas and are sometimes called scripts. These are the roles or parts that we expect people to play in a particular social position, and as such, role schemas can be thought of as being nested within the context of an event schema (Fiske & Taylor, 1991, p. 119). They are also related to stereotypes when associated with social groups. They represent the prescriptive behaviors that people from that social group are expected to enact if they are behaving in stereotypical ways.

While schemas generally serve a functional purpose, due to their effect on memory storage, memory retrieval, and inference, a problem can arise when schemas are inaccurate. While some argue that stereotypes' accuracy is often neglected or undervalued (Ottati & Lee, 1995, p. 29; Ryan, 2003), it seems that accuracy does vary substantially between individuals, especially for stereotypes around gender (Hall & Carter, 1999). In cases of IPV, schemas often do not accurately represent the different forms of violence. The nature of the relationship between the perpetrator and the victim is also a poor match for more general stereotypes related to sexual violence, which is sometimes a feature of IPV. For example, Monson and his colleagues (1996) found that participants thought that a scenario describing the rape of a woman by her husband was less serious than when the perpetrator was a stranger.

Stereotypes and the Gendered Nature of Intimate Partner Violence

Our beliefs, assumptions, and stereotypes (often unconsciously) can lead to differential treatment. Even though members of the criminal justice system remain committed to the service of others, they, too, are susceptible to these stereotypes. Findings show that underlying heteronormative beliefs about gender and partner violence influence societal and criminal justice response. Society is less likely to recognize partner violence as a serious social problem that affects heterosexual men and LGBTQ+ individuals.

Research shows the impact of gendered notions surrounding IPV lead men to be much less likely to report IPV for fear of ridicule, embarrassment, loss of child custody, and lack of domestic violence resources available; furthermore, they are less likely to call the police for fear they will be identified as the primary aggressor. Some believe that the burden of proof for male victims is higher for men than women (Cook, 2009). A study by Hines and Douglas (2011) examined the help-seeking experiences of male victims of IPV. Men were more likely to seek help from informal sources such as friends/family, online support, or male attorneys. Those seeking help from medical or mental health professionals were rated as most helpful to male victims. Men rated domestic violence victim services and police as least helpful.

Much like heterosexual men, perceptions of IPV victimization are affected by the gendered perspective of IPV violence. Stereotypes of IPV victims and offenders can lead to discriminatory policies and practices. Homophobic beliefs coupled with heterosexist beliefs about IPV leave LGBTQ+ victims at a disadvantage. Many victims receive little to no relief or resources for abuse. Social services, health care, and domestic violence programs are often not trained or equipped to assist LGBTQ+ victims (Russell & Torres, 2020). For instance, pervasive myths about LGBTQ+ (same size and status, less severe victimization) and elder LGBTQ+ (too frail or sweet to inflict violence) can undermine victim support. These services also demonstrate a culture of heteronormative and anti-LGBTQ+

bias. Reports of IPV among the LGBTQ+ community are suspected to be even higher than those found by the CDC. Some of the reasons for this can be explained by victim reporting systems and police reports. Transgender, bisexual, gender, and gender-nonconforming individuals and those in same-sex relationships are often misreported as they may be considered "friends" or "other relationships," making true prevalence rates of IPV victimization in LGBTQ+ communities elusive (Tillery et al., 2018).

Victims of IPV have reported fears of being dismissed due to their sex and have experienced homophobia, discrimination, and discouraging responses that prevented them from seeking help (Alhusen et al., 2010; Guadalupe-Diaz & Jasinski, 2017). IPV victims in LGBTQ+ relationships often do not report abuse to police in fear that they will not be taken seriously and or experience discrimination. In one study (NCAVP, 2016), of 1,976 IPV LBGTQ victims, 57% did not contact police. Of those who contacted police, only 33% filed a report. Like heterosexual male victims (Alhusen et al., 2010; Guadelupe-Diaz & Jasinski, 2017; Russell & Torres, 2020), police mistrust is a huge problem. Studies have found that abuse is most likely to be recognized in the context of our gendered assumptions of a male perpetrator and female victim. Victimization of heterosexual males and gays is less likely to be considered abuse compared to female victims in heterosexual or lesbian relationships (Russell et al., 2015).

Further, research on laypersons and police officers found that injuries among heterosexual males and same-sex couples are considered less serious than injuries incurred by female victims (Russell & Sturgeon, 2019; Seelau & Seelau, 2005). Police officers tend to minimize abuse in gay relationships. They are more likely to perceive nonarrest options (such as mediating) as a more fair and appropriate response in abusive relationships among two men (Russell, 2018). Officers are less likely to arrest sexual minorities in IPV incidents (Franklin et al., 2019). Finneran and Stephenson (2013) found that 40% of gay and bisexual respondents believed contacting the police in response to a violent incident from an intimate partner would be unhelpful or very unhelpful. Fifty-nine percent of respondents also believed that the police would be less helpful to a gay or bisexual man than a heterosexual woman in the same situation. These results illustrate the power of stereotypical constructs associated with victims of IPV. For instance, victims who feel less likely to be believed, helped, or supported by police tend to be non-White, male, or LGBTQ+ (Guadelupe-Diaz & Jasinski, 2017). Structural and institutional stereotypes leave many victims with little to no relief or resources for abuse. Also, legal definitions can exclude same-sex couples. Many abuse shelters prohibit men from entering their facilities, and finding appropriately trained staff to help them can be challenging. Most support groups and shelters are designed for female victims of male partners.

Political leanings that lead to greater silence about IPV in LGBTQ+ relationships can include a fear that IPV might further stigmatize the LGBTQ+ community and lead to additional oppression (Ristock, 2001). Further, acknowledging LGBTQ+ victimization runs contrary to the feminist patriarchal explanation for IPV, particularly when explaining lesbian IPV (Ristock & Timbang, 2005; Rolle et al., 2018). Therefore, our stereotypes and resulting biases, such as homophobia, continue to minimize the seriousness of IPV in the LGBTQ+ population (McClennen, 2005; Russell et al., 2015). Moreover, finding appropriately trained staff to help them can be tough, as most support groups and shelters are primarily designed for female victims of male partners.

Syndrome Stereotypes and Jury Decision-Making

Scholars have noted instances when the testimony on the BWS/BPS has not been admitted because the defendant did not fit the stereotype of a "typical" battered woman. In *State v. Anaya* (1983) testimony of the BWS was not admitted as the defendant had, on a previous occasion, stabbed her boyfriend, was employed, and had not exhibited characteristics such as reacting passively or being dependent on their abuser. Researchers (Russell & Melillo, 2006; Schuller & Hastings, 1996; Terrance & Matheson, 2003) find that the further the defendant's characteristics deviate from the norm, the more likely their motives are scrutinized.

Another stereotype associated with the battered woman syndrome (BWS)/battered person syndrome (BPS) or "typical" IPV victim is their active or passive response history. The overarching belief is that IPV victims (mainly women) are meek and passive. Researchers (Schuller & Hastings, 1996) presented scenarios to mock jurors in which the defendant's response history was manipulated. Half of the mock jurors received information that the defendant provoked or fought back against their abuser (active), and the other half received information that the defendant reacted passively. This study found no effects for defendant response history of active/passive response. However, it concluded this was since there are usually multiple attributes that define a person's stereotype of a victim of abuse. A subsequent study by Russell and Melillo (2006) expanded on the previous study to include an active/passive history and defendant typicality/atypical attributes regarding the defendant's physical, social, and psychological characteristics to determine effects on judgments of self-defense guilt and verdict. Results showed that respondents in atypical scenarios (deviating from the stereotype of a victim of abuse) rendered more verdicts of second-degree murder or manslaughter. In comparison, participants rendered significantly more self-defense verdicts when the defendant was portrayed as typical/passive. Findings also showed that defendants in the typical conditions were more likely to meet the legal requirements of self-defense and consider the situation less in the defendant's control. In contrast, atypical defendants were perceived as having more control over the situation, more options available to them than killing, and less likely to meet the requirements than typical defendants.

Jury Decision-Making and Nontypical Victims and Perpetrators

Problematically, the stereotype of IPV describes a violent act performed by a man against a woman (Boonzaier, 2008; Bosson & Vandello, 2011; Little, 2020).

One of the implications of the nature of schemas about IPV and the stereotypes about perpetrators and victims is that those victims who do not match these representations face additional barriers due to their minority or nontypical status. This includes issues such as gender, sexual minority status, race, and socioeconomic status.

Gender

The basic assumption held by many that women are the primary victims and men are the perpetrators is widely held. With that assumption come heterosexist beliefs inherent in jury decision-making. However, stereotypes associated with BWS/BPS often relate to our understanding of who can and cannot be a victim. Typical attributes of female abuse victims include women who are emotional, submissive, meek, passive, and gentle (Gillespie, 1989), all of which reflect societal norms associated with women (Allard, 1991). There are also stereotypes associated with perpetrators of IPV (e.g., male, dominant, strong, controlling, aggressive, etc.) that also align with the general stereotype of a male.

Such beliefs are inherent in our society and play a significant role in all legal decision-making processes. This is evident in our criminal justice system, as men are more likely to be arrested and prosecuted for IPV (see Shernock & Russell, 2012, for review). While an earlier review of 24 studies on the prosecution of males and females, results overwhelmingly found males were consistently treated more severely at every stage of the adjudicative process, particularly in decisions to prosecute, even when evidential variables were controlled (Shernock & Russell, 2012). However, in a recent experimental study (Cox et al., 2019), 107 prosecutors completed an experimental study of an ambiguously initiated IPV case. The defendant and victim sex were manipulated and asked whether to prosecute the case. Their results found that defendant and victim sex (and sexual orientation) did not affect their decisions to prosecute. While these results are encouraging, it will be interesting to see whether these results can be replicated in the courtroom.

Heterosexual Males and LGBTQ+ Victimization

IPV involving male victimization and same-sex couples can also be considered outside of the realm of the IPV victim stereotype or atypical. Many research studies have examined how defendant/victim sex and sexual orientation affect legal decision-making. This is particularly salient when women are the victim as female victims tend to lead to more negative case outcomes for the defendant in IPV (Cox & Kopkin, 2016; Poorman et al., 2003; Russell et al., 2015; Seelau & Seelau, 2005; Stanziani et al., 2018). Studies (Henning & Feder, 2005; Rhatigan et al., 2011; Russell et al., 2015, 2016; Poorman et al., 2003; Stanziani et al., 2020; Strub & McKimmie, 2015) consistently find IPV perpetrated by a male victim/defendant is more likely to lead to more severe penalties, as their behaviors are considered more abusive, blameworthy, responsible, more likely to initiate the violence, more serious, fear-inducing, and injurious, compared to the same crime committed by a female. These results occur regardless of sexual orientation.

Studies have also found that abuse among heterosexual couples is considered more serious than IPV in same-sex couples. Gender stereotypes might explain phenomena. Male victims may be more likely to be perceived as feminine in terms of meekness and vulnerability to attack, which challenges the stereotype that men are aggressive. This can lead to inferences that male victims were remiss in failing to protect themselves and consequently deviating from their prescribed gender role (Stanziani et al., 2018). This stereotype can extend to same-sex IPV. Sexual minorities and heterosexual male victims violate social norms as they do not fall under the umbrella of heteronormative binary views associated with IPV.

Stereotypes associated with gays and lesbians are often inversely related to their sexual orientation. For example, while heterosexual females are stereotyped as feminine, lesbians are perceived as masculine. Similarly, gay men are often stereotyped as feminine. While a defendant's appearance as masculine or feminine should not be related to victimization or perpetration of IPV (Balsam & Szymanski, 2005), our gender role and IPV victim stereotypes can negatively affect defendants and victims, particularly when they violate prescribed gender roles. In *People of New York v. Arlene Mohammed* (1987), the defendant was accused of assaulting her partner. The prosecution called attention to the defendant's "masculine" appearance, contrasting her partner's feminine appearance. While this should be unrelated to the case, the prosecution knowingly or unknowingly cued juror gender-role and lesbian relationship stereotypes (Renzetti, 1994). One study involving mock jurors' evaluations of a lesbian defendant physically assaulting their partner (Wasarhaley et al., 2017) showed mock jurors believed the victim had a more legitimate claim and the defendant was more responsible for the victim's injuries when they were portrayed as masculine versus feminine (Wasarhaley et al., 2017).

Most research on IPV finds that same-sex defendants tend to fall in the middle, with heterosexual male defendants as most culpable, typically followed by lesbian, gay, and heterosexual females as least culpable (Russell et al., 2009, 2010; Stanziani et al., 2018). One study (Stanziani et al., 2018) found mock jurors' opinions of the crime of IPV in same-sex relationships when parties are assumed to be similar in size/strength to be considered mutually initiated, less severe, and less serious (Brown, 2008). This may be due to the belief that same-sex relationships are more egalitarian than heterosexual relationships (e.g., Hassouneh & Glass, 2008). Therefore, the violence is mutual. This belief persists despite the research that shows IPV among LGBTQ+ relationships shares the same motivations of power and control as heterosexual couples.

Additional studies examining police officer perceptions of gender and sexual orientation (Russell, 2018) found that officers rated heterosexual males as a greater threat of danger than gay males, lesbians, or heterosexual perpetrators. Gay and heterosexual females were least likely to be perceived as harming their partner compared to lesbian and heterosexual males. Female victims were perceived as exhibiting more behaviors indicative of mental illness. Additional research examining mock jurors' decisions in a case of duress (Russell et al., 2012) found that heterosexual females and lesbian defendants were more likely to be coerced and their actions committed in duress compared to gay and heterosexual men. Similarly, in research examining a crime of passion, heterosexual defendants were perceived as more likely to have mitigating circumstances, experience sudden passion, be more provoked, and have less self-control compared to same-sex defendants. Same-sex defendants were less likely to meet the legal requirements of voluntary manslaughter, which may be explained by mock jurors' belief that infidelity in same-sex relationships is less serious and less likely to justify legal elements associated with crimes of passion.

Race, Ethnicity, and Socioeconomic Differences in Jury Decision-Making

Stereotypes associated with Black women tend to be related to strength, assertiveness, and promiscuity (Mossière et al., 2018), all of which tend to go against the stereotype of a meek, passive battered woman. The intersectionality of variables such as race, socioeconomic status, and gender can all play a significant role in evaluations of defendants in the context of IPV. With a few exceptions, research tends to find little differential treatment in jury decision-making in IPV cases, while other scholars have demonstrated mixed results. For example, one experimental study in an IPV homicide case (Braden-Maguire et al., 2005) found no significant differences regarding African American or White female defendants who killed their abusers. However, Willis et al. (1996) found that study subjects rated the defendant less responsible when the victim was Black. In a more recent study (Mossière et al., 2018), the Black defendant was more likely to be found not guilty by reason of self-defense than a White defendant, and mock jurors attributed more options available to the White defendant, suggesting a more remarkable intersection of race, socioeconomic status, and gender.

However, some studies (Esqueda & Harrison, 2005; Maeder et al., 2013) have found that Black women were perceived as more responsible for their own abuse than White women. Further, while some research on interracial-interethnic dyads found no significant differences in interracial-interethnic dyads concerning convictions of felony or misdemeanor charges and sentences imposed (Kingsnorth et al., 2001), Maeder et al.'s (2013) examination of mock jurors in a case of Asian/White couples in an IPV case attributed more guilt to interracial couples compared to same-race couples.

Socioeconomic Differences

Anyone can be a victim of IPV, yet even the demographics of the defendant can influence a jury. For instance, it can be more surprising or atypical when it occurs in an older affluent individual. Researchers (Green et al., 1989) conducted a study that compared IPV experts and juror responses when researchers manipulated an IPV victim's age and socioeconomic status. While the victim's age had no effect, juror responses corresponded more with experts of abuse when the victim was portrayed as low socioeconomic status. Given that one of the stereotypes surrounding IPV is low socioeconomic status, this suggests higher socioeconomic status falls out of the realm of the "typical victim."

There are also stereotypes associated with gender and race that can play a role in IPV legal decision-making. Henning and Feder's (2005) examination of legal and extralegal factors in IPV case outcomes found extralegal factors such as race and SES played a more prominent role in sentencing than legal factors. In cases of IPV, the authors found that, overall, females were treated more leniently in the legal system. Caucasian defendants from higher economic status were more likely to have their cases dropped by the prosecution, and minorities were less likely to be released on their own recognizance than Caucasian defendants.

Overall, we have seen how extralegal factors can play a role in jury decision-making. However, the fact is that it depends upon the content in which a defendant's actions are congruent with the gender and crime stereotype and building a narrative that best describes the crime. Jurors often make decisions using such narratives.

HOW DO JURORS MAKE DECISIONS?

Story Model

One of the most commonly applied models used to understand how jurors make decisions is the cognitive story model (Pennington & Hastie, 1986). According to this model, jurors seek to create a narrative around the evidence to help them organize the evidence and interpret the meaning of the evidence. These narratives are used to help give meaning to subsequent evidence as it is presented. Jurors may construct multiple possible narratives aligned with the different verdict options and then adopt the story that best fits the evidence as presented. Importantly, jurors' schemas and stereotypes may play an influential role in shaping these narratives. Such pre-existing beliefs represent expectations about how particular events unfold and the sorts of behaviors expected of people in particular roles. Thus, the expectation that IPV is a violent act by a man against a woman could influence the nature of the story that jurors create and how that maps on to the verdict options.

Such an expectation can help jurors create a story describing events in cases where the evidence matches the stereotype and, therefore, is subsequently likely to be consistent with a guilty verdict. Conversely, the stereotype is more difficult to fit into a story aligned with a guilty verdict when the events do not match. This means that a conviction is less likely for other common forms of IPV, for example, those involving non–physically violent acts of control or emotional violence, or those where the perpetrator is not male, or the relationship involves two people of the same gender.

Dual-Process Models

Stereotypes may also have an increased effect on jurors when cases involve ambiguous, missing, or complex information. Such cases make it more difficult for jurors to create stories based on the evidence itself, as the evidence may be contradictory or difficult to understand. Not only that, but under these conditions, it is more difficult for jurors to reason through the evidence even if they are highly motivated to do so. Dual-process models of persuasion, such as the elaboration likelihood model (Petty & Cacioppo, 1986) and the heuristic systematic model (Chaiken, 1980), describe how information ambiguity and complexity can influence attitudes and decisions and how peripheral cues such as stereotypes come to have an increased influence.

These models describe two distinct ways in which information is processed and were initially proposed to understand persuasion and attitude change. Both models have been widely applied to the decision-making context, which is not surprising as a jury trial can be conceptualized as a series of persuasive messages directed at the jury by the prosecution, defense, witnesses, and even the judge. The models disagree on some crucial points, but both describe two distinct modes of information processing. The first is a central route or high-elaboration mode that requires effortful thinking, and evaluations are influenced by the overall balance of positive and negative reactions to the considered information. The second is a peripheral route or low-elaboration mode that requires less effortful thinking and relies more on associations with positive cues or heuristics to help arrive at an evaluation.

While the central route/high-elaboration mode of thinking seems to be the most desirable, perceivers obviously do not, or cannot, always use this way of thinking about the evidence to arrive at a verdict. Using effortful thinking to evaluate information requires that perceivers are both motivated to do so and have the ability to engage in that thinking. A lack of either motivation or ability will mean that perceivers tend to rely more on lower-effort peripheral cues such as schemas and stereotypes. An early assumption by researchers was that perceivers were "cognitive misers" (Fiske & Taylor, 1984). Perceivers are reluctant to engage in effortful thinking when they could suffice by relying on a peripheral cue to make an evaluation. However, motivation is increased when an issue is self-relevant or seen as important (Fiske & Taylor, 1984). However, jurors' ability to think effortfully is likely to be impaired by a lack of time to think about information, high information load, distraction, and the ambiguity of the information. The duration of a typical trial and a reliance on the oral transmission of evidence are also likely to undermine jurors' ability to effortfully evaluate information due to the demands placed on their memory (Pritchard & Keenan, 1999). So, while research suggests that jurors report a strong motivation to carry out their duties well (McCabe &

Purves, 1974) and some argue that evidence is the biggest predictor of verdicts (Vidmar & Diamond, 2001), research suggests that they are often influenced by stereotypes in arriving at their verdicts, at least to a degree (Bornstein et al., 2017; Mazzella & Feingold, 1994; Nitschke et al., 2019).

However, one point worth making before proceeding is that such findings are often construed as an argument against using juries and instead relying on judges or other specialist decision-makers, especially in particular matters that might require specialist training, such as cases involving IPV. Such a conclusion would misconstrue the implications of the research findings. These findings demonstrate that jurors are like other humans and use the same sorts of cognitive strategies to make sense of the world when asked to be jurors as they do in their regular lives. If we accept this conclusion, then it is also not surprising that research has shown that judges are largely influenced by the same cognitive biases that affect jurors (Guthrie et al., 2002; Rachlinksi et al., 2008; Wistrich et al., 2005; see also Landsman & Rakos, 1994). Years of legal training did not protect against being influenced by legally prejudicial inadmissible information and racial stereotypes. Vidmar (2011) notes the presence of a racial disparity in sentences given by judges as being consistent with this conclusion.

Perhaps a more constructive way of thinking about the role of stereotypes and how they might be leveraged is that they can help perceivers encode more information than they might otherwise be able to—enabling perceivers to act as "cognitive optimizers." By enabling more efficient encoding of stereotype-consistent information, perceivers can expend more resources on encoding other information about the case that does not align with a stereotype (McKimmie et al., 2013). This is consistent with research on how people form impressions, which shows that perceivers try to engage in as much thinking about unexpected, or stereotype-inconsistent, information as possible (Stern et al., 1984). They found that participants spent more time reading and thinking about stereotype-inconsistent behaviors and consequently recalled a greater number of these behaviors than stereotype-consistent behaviors. Research by Macrae and colleagues also suggests that perceivers who used stereotypes could redirect their cognitive resources to other tasks they had been given (Macrae et al., 1994). In sum, stereotypes enable more strategic information processing that allows effortful thinking concerning stereotype-incongruent targets (e.g., Sherman et al., 1998, 2004).

Group Decision-Making

Although groups are sometimes seen as a remedy for biasing factors, such as stereotypes, that affect individual decision-making due to bringing together different perspectives, there is mixed evidence about the effect of group decision-making. Despite Kalvin and Zeisel's (1966) early conclusion that jury deliberation has a limited effect on decisions, many juries do not start with unanimous agreement about the verdict. Hastie and colleagues (1983) showed that minority jurors prevail in a significant number of deliberations, managing to change the mind of the majority in up to one quarter of cases. Sandys and Dillehay (1995) suggest that to some extent. Both conclusions might be correct if we distinguish between different types of jury deliberation. Lieberman and Krauss (2009) argued that deliberations could be characterized as either verdict driven or evidence driven. The former is based around seeking agreement on the verdict and involves repeated voting to identify individuals who disagree with the majority and subsequently increased pressure for conformity. The latter is characterized by discussion involving effortful evaluation of the evidence before voting on the appropriate verdict.

Group size and the decision rule also influence the quality of the jury's decision. Nemeth's (1981) research found that majority decision rules, compared to unanimous decision rules, were associated with less participation by minority jurors because the majority paid less attention to them, there were fewer hung decisions, and deliberations were taking a shorter time. Of most concern, this decision rule was also associated with a greater likelihood of conviction and more errors in recalling the evidence presented at trial—suggesting that majority decision rules resulted in a lower-quality group decision.

Jury size has a similar effect, with smaller juries producing lower-quality decisions compared to larger juries. Juries vary in size across jurisdictions and case types from twelve to as low as four. Although some have argued based on probability theory that juries of six and twelve are equivalent in terms of how they arrive at their decisions (Thomas & Pollack, 1992), research on what jurors do suggests this conclusion is not warranted. Juries comprised of six people communicate less, are less accurate and thorough in their recall of the evidence, and are more likely to reach an agreement (Saks, 1977). Smaller juries are also less representative of the community, and like those operating under a majority rule, are more likely to convict (Hans & Vidmar, 1986).

The effect of jury size is likely due to much the same processes as the effect of decision rule—the pressure for conformity. Asch's (1956) work on conformity demonstrated unambiguously that smaller groups produce greater pressure on group members to conform with the group position, even when individuals know it is incorrect. Increased pressure for conformity is likely to inhibit sharing different perspectives, which is necessary for higher-quality group decision-making, as demonstrated by the research on hidden profiles (Stasser, 1988). As such, the presence of dissenting viewpoints within the jury is essential for encouraging discussion and increasing the pool of information that the decision is made on (Greitemeyer et al., 2006) and for ensuring a more accurate decision that is less influenced by stereotypes (Rijnbout & McKimmie, 2012, 2014)

Despite these factors, which can impair the quality of a jury's decision, group deliberation does appear to reduce the effect of factors such as stereotypes relative to the decisions made by individuals (Kaplan & Miller, 1978). Thus, to some extent, when there is a unanimous decision rule and a larger jury to undermine the effect of the pressure for conformity during deliberations, the jury as a collective decision-maker may provide some protection against the influence of stereotypes about IPV. Rose and Ogloff (2001) found that deliberating as a group does not improve comprehension of judicial instruction, which is essential for how the jury makes its decision.

Judicial Instructions

A judge's instructions are often thought to be an essential influence on how jurors make their decisions. These instructions are given to protect the jury's verdict against a possible appeal, to ensure that jurors make their decisions in a way that is consistent with the relevant law, and to ensure that the jury relies on the evidence as presented at trial rather than any biasing factor (McKimmie et al., 2014). One way to assist jurors in their decisions in cases involving IPV would be to give them instructions about how they should make their decisions, particularly relating to suppressing their negative stereotypes about IPV or correcting misperceptions about IPV through education. Whether instructions are effective at doing this has been a subject of substantial research.

Research suggests that instructions designed to have jurors put biases and preconceptions out of their minds when arriving at a decision are not so effective. Some studies show that instructions to ignore legally prejudicial information were ineffective at countering the influence of inadmissible evidence on decision-makers (Landsman & Rakos, 1994). Likewise, such instructions are not adequate when negative pretrial publicity exists in cases (Devine et al., 2001). Such findings are not surprising. Research on stereotyping more generally suggests that telling people to ignore or not think about stereotypes and biasing information is unlikely to be successful. The act of trying to suppress negative stereotypical information requires that the perceiver actively monitor their thoughts for the presence of the stereotype, thus making it more accessible in one's mind. Consequently, active instructions to suppress the influence of negative stereotypes have the perverse effect of increasing their influence on judgments, with those judgments becoming more negative than perceivers who are not asked to actively suppress those negative stereotypes (Macrae et al., 1994).

Instructions that are designed to educate jurors about their stereotypic misperceptions seem to be somewhat more effective. For in the case of intoxicated victims of sexual assault, educative instructions about the effect of intoxication on the ability to consent to sexual intercourse were effective at countering the typically negative effect of victim intoxication on decisions in such cases (Nitschke et al., 2018). Educative instructions have also been effective at correcting misperceptions about the reliability of children's memory, resulting in more accurate decisions (Sumner-Armstrong & Newcombe, 2007) and countering misperceptions about child sexual abuse (Cossins et al., 2009; Goodman-Delahunty et al., 2010).

This difference in the effectiveness appears to be due to the different goals of instructions—correcting misperceptions versus instructing jurors on how to use or not use the information according to legal rules. The latter may be more difficult for jurors to comprehend due to the reliance on legal rules and terminology. Thus, while jurors indeed report that they are conscientious and try to do their job well (McCabe & Purves, 1974), they may struggle to understand what they are asked to do. Often jurors will report that they think they know what they are meant to be doing when arriving at a decision (Jackson, 1992) and that instructions are clear and understandable (Cutler & Hughes, 2001), it is clear these self-reports are not necessarily providing the complete picture about jurors' level of comprehension.

For example, Reifman and colleagues (1992) found that less than half of jurors understood the law they were meant to apply when tested objectively. They also found that those given instructions did just as well as those who did not get instructions. McKimmie and colleagues (2014) found that only one third of jurors in criminal trials understood the two fundamental instructions about burden and standard of proof—that the prosecution must prove that the defendant is guilty beyond a reasonable doubt. Severance et al. (1992) found that jurors do not understand the differences between legal concepts. A consequential example of this was demonstrated in research by Sarat (1994)—jurors could not understand or remember the legal rules that were relevant to the decision about whether the death penalty should be imposed. Further, jurors fail to separate the decisions about guilt and punishment in capital cases, despite judicial instructions specifying that these are separate decisions (Sandys, 1995).

Assessing comprehension is somewhat controversial and not straightforward (see Baguley et al., 2019). Severance and Loftus (1982) argue that the use of paraphrasing to test comprehension just assesses jurors' ability to remember the instructions rather than their comprehension of those instructions. Other methods of assessing comprehension suggest a different conclusion. For example, Bornstein and Greene (2011) estimate that across studies, about half of people understand the judicial instructions. Heuer and Penrod's (1994) research suggests that jurors seem to be aware of this, as jurors reported that as cases became more complex, they felt less confident that their verdict reflected a proper understanding of instructions. Law reform entities and other professional bodies such as the American Bar Association have recommended rewriting instructions to be simpler to help overcome such difficulties with comprehension (Bornstein & Greene, 2011).

Rewriting instructions using more straightforward language does appear to improve comprehension (Brewer et al., 2004; Elwork et al., 1977; Rose & Ogloff, 2001). Simplification of instructions can have a negative adverse effect (Baguley et al., 2017)—although comprehension increases as conceptual complexity decreases, mock jurors become more punitive the more they report understanding the instructions. This perhaps reflects an increase in task-related confidence and so a greater willingness to convict.

Thus, although instructions to ignore biases related to IPV are unlikely to change how jurors make decisions due to comprehension issues and with failure of suppression, educative instructions that correct stereotypical misperceptions are more likely to be successful. It is important not to provide a false sense of decision-related simplicity in providing such instructions to ensure that jurors do not become overconfident.

Juror Gender Differences in Intimate Partner Violence Decision-Making

Research using experimental designs has found that participant mock jurors' gender and other demographic characteristics can influence IPV jury decision-making. Many studies have found that women render more severe verdicts and sentences in IPV and sexual assault cases (Kern et al., 2007; Poorman et al., 2003; Stanziani et al., 2020), mainly when the victim is female and the defendant is male. Women also have greater sympathy for battered women defendants (Mossière et al., 2018: Pozzulo et al., 2010; Terrance & Matheson, 2003) than male jurors.

Mock juror gender also differs as a function of typical and atypical defendants. Researchers (Russell & Mellilo, 2006) found that female mock jurors who evaluated atypical defendants were less likely to render a guilty verdict than men who evaluated atypical defendants (there were no gender differences in typical conditions). However, results found that women were more likely than men to believe the female defendants across all conditions met the requirements of self-defense more often than men. Men were more likely to believe the defendant had more options available than women, particularly when the defendant had an active (aggressive) history.

A juror's gender role beliefs can also permeate legal decision-making. For example, Stanziani et al. (2020) found that men who held higher levels of hegemonic masculinity perceived the IPV crime as less serious. Women were more likely to believe the defendant was less likely to benefit from treatment. Men and women both believed the crime was more serious when the victim was female and found the female victim less blameworthy than a male victim. Female jurors held more unfavorable attitudes about an IPV crime and defendant when the defendant was male and the victim was female, which could be due to a woman's increased probability of experiencing physical and or sexual assault (Catalano, 2013). Female mock jurors were more likely to identify with the victim. Individual experiences with IPV can affect attributions of blame.

Researchers (Rhatigan et al., 2011) found that male and female participants attributed blame and responsibility differently, particularly when the perpetrator was provoked. Male and female mock jurors endorsed less responsibility and blame to perpetrators of bidirectional violence. Mock jurors who themselves have been victims of dating abuse leading to injury attributed greater blame and responsibility to violent perpetrators. Mock jurors who were perpetrators of injuries and or dating abuse attributed less blame and responsibility to the perpetrator, suggesting a juror's personal experience with childhood, dating violence, and or IPV victimization can also affect their perceptions of the defendant and victim.

Why Does Juror Gender Matter?

One explanation for the effect of juror gender in cases such as IPV is defensive attributions styles based on a perceiver's similarity to the perpetrator or victim. As one perceives themselves as more like the perpetrator, this often leads to less perpetrator blame (Shaver, 1970). As similarity to a victim increases, victim blame decreases (Grubb & Harrower, 2008). Thus, in the most common cases where a perpetrator is a man and the victim is a woman, male jurors are less likely to blame the perpetrator and less likely to convict the perpetrator than female jurors. This style of attributing blame reassures observers that they would not be responsible for such events (Key & Ridge, 2011; Shaver, 1970). Such similarity effects are seen across multiple social categories, suggesting that defensive attributions are a more general defense mechanism. For example, similarity in terms of gender, race, culture, and social status all produce similar patterns of decreased blame for targets who are more similar (Bongiorno et al., 2016; Grubb & Harrower, 2008; Van Der Bruggen & Grubb, 2014).

Another explanation for the effect of juror gender is like the similarity hypothesis but based instead on shared group membership. According to social identity theory (Tajfel & Turner, 1979), group identities are important for how we see ourselves, and so we evaluate our own ingroups more positively than other groups. Consequently, we also favor ingroup members compared to those who do not share a group membership with ourselves. For example, observers in one study were less likely to blame victims of rape who were from the same university compared to victims from another university (Harrison et al., 2008). Gender is a very salient social cue to shared or nonshared group membership, particularly for some types of crime (see Wayne et al., 2001). This is especially relevant in cases where the victim and perpetrator roles are highly gendered (Mazzella & Feingold, 1994). Such findings can account for gender differences in how jurors view cases involving IPV.

Does Expert Testimony Help Jurors Make Better Decisions?

Cases involving IPV typically involve testimony about the BWS/BPS or the effects of battering. Expert testimony offered on this topic has garnered more attention and acceptance into the courts than most other areas in the field of psychology (Faigman et al., 2020). Testimony of the syndrome is typically presented by a clinical psychologist, psychiatrist, or another expert knowledgeable on the topic of abuse, with its content often relying on the work of Lenore Walker (1979) and her theory of the cycle of battering. Testimony has typically been used in criminal cases and offers the defense a vehicle to explain the conduct of a victim of abuse who fights back and kills their abuser in self-defense. It has been successfully admitted in various crimes of duress (*Dunn v. Roberts*, 1992; *United States v. Dixon*, 2005; *United States v. Homick*, 1992; *United States v. Marenghi*, 1995), child neglect/murder (*Labastida v. State*, 1999; *People v. Hernandez*, 2000; *State v. Long*, 1995), conspiracy and accomplice to murder (*People v. Yachlich*, 1988; *State v. Frazier*, 2002), issues surrounding protection orders (*Castle Rock v. Gonzales*, 2005), and prosecutorial use of testimony regarding pretrial statements often to explain the behavior of a witness (*Clenny v. State*, 1986), to support the prosecution of abusers (*People v. Birse*, 2014), or when victims recant their testimony (*Arcoren v. U.S.*, 1991).

BWS/BPS is a descriptive term and not intended to be a diagnostic tool (Faigman et al., 2020) though some courts have suggested it was diagnostic of the victim's frame of mind (*State v. Haines*, 2006). In fact, many courts' interpretations of its use in the courts differ. Courts can offer case-specific or general testimony. Case-specific testimony typically includes an IPV evaluation of type and severity of abuse, whether the defendant exhibits BPS or symptomology associated with the syndrome for a psychiatric illness, the defendant's mental state at the time of the crime. These findings must be communicated to the attorney. General social framework testimony about battering and its effects can also be admitted that explains relevant research about abuse to help explain a defendant's state of mind, instead of offering a case-specific opinion on the day of the crime (*Chandler v. Cate*, 2012). Experts can address violence, coercion, and prior abuse to provide a rich context of the situation for jurors to evaluate whether the defendant's perceptions and actions were reasonable at the time of the crime. Such testimony can be used to explain the unique psychological distress victims of abuse endure, why they perceive themselves to be in imminent danger, and their inability to perceive alternatives to homicide. It can also address common myths or misconceptions about victims of abuse. There are four main objectives of admitting syndrome testimony: (1) to evoke sympathy, (2) to assist judges and jurors in understanding the psychological effects associated with abuse and how these can distort perceptions of the situation, (3) to show how this affects abilities such as leaving an abuser, and (4) to convince judges and jurors that their reactions were reasonable given the circumstances (Follingstad, 2003). In this respect, testimony has been helpful in providing a framework in which to view the defendant's actions, and this may explain why it has been more helpful in reducing the severity of an offense rather than winning acquittals (Ewing, 1987; Faigman et al., 2020).

Initially, scholars feared introducing the syndrome into evidence would connote an emotionally/psychologically damaged defendant (Schneider, 1986). Scholars in the 1980s and 1990s worried that the syndrome would lead to inferences of mental illness and pathology rather than demonstrate the reasonableness of a defendant's actions in self-defense. Originally, the testimony of the BWS often focused on actions associated with learned helplessness and posttraumatic stress disorder (PTSD) to explain why a victim would not leave their abuser or interpret their actions within the context of pathology. Early studies comparing BWS testimony with no expert testimony cases (Finkel et al., 1991) found that when testimony was provided that provided a diagnosis of the BWS, jurors perceived the defendant as more distorted in their thinking, less capable of making reasonable choices, and less culpable for their actions. These results suggest jurors might shift their beliefs closer to diminished capacity or insanity. Similarly, Schuller (1992, Study 2) utilized mock jurors who deliberated in either no expert testimony or expert testimony scenarios and concluded that when the defendant fit the characteristics of the syndrome, there was a small to moderate effect toward manslaughter, a verdict of diminished capacity in the expert testimony conditions.

The use of testimony often comes as a double-edged sword when the defendant does not fit the stereotype of a victim of abuse. In the previously noted case, *State v. Anaya* (1993), the female defendant accused of killing her partner did not display the typical characteristics associated with the syndrome. Schuller and Hastings (1996) were the first to examine student and nonstudent mock jurors in an IPV case modeled after *Lavelle v. Regina* (1990), depicting the female defendant in terms of fitting in with the syndrome by either having a history of fighting back physically or threatening their abuser (active history) or a history of passivity toward the aggressor and the type of expert testimony (i.e., presence/absence of BWS testimony or social agency testimony (e.g., with less emphasis on PTSD and learned helplessness) or no expert conditions. Their results found there more lenient verdicts in both expert testimony conditions than no-expert conditions, and there were no differences in active or passive response histories.

Researchers (Russell & Melillo, 2006; Terrance & Matheson, 2003) found that the further a defendant moves away from jurors' beliefs of what a victim of abuse should be, the harsher the verdict. Most mock juror studies using the BWS historically examined female defendants and male victims in self-defense cases. Studies have also investigated the use of (presence/absence) expert testimony of the BPS in a case of self-defense depicting heterosexual and same-sex couples (Russell et al., 2009). They found that female mock jurors provided the lowest guilt ratings to heterosexual female and gay defendants who received expert testimony. However, when heterosexual male defendants received expert testimony, their ratings of guilt significantly increased. Jurors' own sexist attitudes and legal elements, such as the defendant's actions were justifiable given the circumstances and belief that a reasonable person would have reacted the same way, were critical predictors of defendant culpability.

Researchers also examined mock juror responses in a case of duress (Russell et al., 2012). They examined whether expert testimony would be more effective for heterosexual female defendants than heterosexual male and same-sex defendants. Their results found that heterosexual male and lesbian defendants received longer sentences than heterosexual female and gay defendants. Furthermore, heterosexual females were more likely to meet the legal requirements for duress, while lesbians were less likely to be believed to have experienced coercion. However, the presence of expert testimony of the BPS decreased guilt and sentence outcomes, ratings of legal elements, and attributes for all defendants.

While there has been some recognition by the courts for the need to expand elements of the BWS/BPS into cases for atypical cases and/or same-sex victims (*People v. Colberg*, 1999), experts still have further to go toward incorporating testimony that truly incorporates the plight of all victims. Such would be more effective instead of modifying that which was originally designed for female victims. Otherwise, it is more like trying to fit a circle into a square peg.

Social psychological factors involved in jury decision-making suggest that jurors evaluate typical and atypical cases differently, although both are evaluated against the backdrop of prevailing stereotypes (Terrance & Matheson, 2003). For example, even the gender of the expert and timing of the expert testimony can affect jury decision-making. Previous studies have evaluated an expert's gender in relation to a child custody dispute (Swenson et al., 1984) and found that the female expert was considered to have more expertise than male experts. The authors suggested that gender congruency associated with the stereotype of traditional female roles may have led to the belief that women were better judges of the needs of children. Additional research by Schuller and Cripps (1998) examined expert gender and timing of testimony in a case of self-defense involving a female killing her abusive husband. They found that mock jurors returned more lenient verdicts when the expert was a woman and testimony was presented prior to the defendant's testimony. While this study demonstrated success with a female expert, it may be associated with gender congruence related to the crime and defendant (female defendant in self-defense). Unfortunately, there have been no studies to our knowledge that have examined the extent to which an expert's gender can be effective when the defendant is a gay or heterosexual male.

While research examining the efficacy of expert testimony is limited, it is difficult to determine the effectiveness of testimony in all cases. Cases with LGBTQ+ defendants should be able to address the unique stressors and emotional abuse strategies used. In some cases, defense teams have resorted to defendant testimonies about their IPV experiences (*People v. Sheehan*, 2013); however, the use of testimony can dictate the direction of the case at any time (plea negotiations, verdicts, sentencing). Compelling testimony can result in acquittals but more often results in lesser charges such as manslaughter (Paradis et al., 2020). Some cases that include expert testimony and evidence of physical abuse can still result in a conviction (*State v. Norman*, 1989).

WHERE TO NEXT?

Understanding how jurors make decisions in the context of our heteronormative biases can leave subsets of the population neglected, misunderstood, and lacking equal justice. Even though sexual minority and heterosexual males suffer from similar or higher rates of IPV, there remains a shortage of resources in terms of services, policies, and training in the criminal justice system that can have severe implications in all aspects of legal decision-making. Changes in terms of increased resources, policies, and training can increase help seeking and reduce the stigma and or revictimization of victims.

As legal actors come to acknowledge the larger context of IPV as a human problem, not just a crime committed against women, it is easier to address some of the implicit and explicit biases in jury decision-making. For instance, the more knowledgable judges and attorneys are about the inherent stereotypes and biases that jurors bring into the courtroom, the more we can promote equality in the courtroom. In such cases, this can involve developing educational instructions to assist jurors and challenge their misperceptions and stereotypes about IPV, atypical behavioral responses to IPV, and how IPV can affect a victim or perpetrator. Such instructions are likely to be more effective than admonishments to ignore any preconceived ideas or biases that one may have. Further research is needed to identify what content and form will ensure that such educational instructions are most effective at helping jurors make evidence-based decisions.

Further, it is important to ask relevant questions during the jury selection process and to simplify instructions in cases of IPV so that jurors can focus on applying the evidence to factual questions. Providing jurors with searchable transcripts of evidence is also likely to enhance the accuracy of the information that they rely on when making decisions. Moreover, the use of unanimous decision rules with larger juries can support the sharing of more diverse views during deliberation and ultimately more accurate decisions. While existing research suggests that such strategies are likely to be effective, further research is necessary in the context of IPV to examine how such information can affect case outcomes. Lastly, we must understand how the intersectionality of gender, race, sexual minority status, and other biases such as socioeconomic statuts and age is typically associated with IPV in legal decision-making.

REFERENCES

Alba, J. W., & Hasher, L. (1983). Is memory schematic? *Psychological Bulletin*, *93*(2), 203–231. https://doi.org/10.1037/0033-2909.93.2.203

Allard, S. A. (1991). Rethinking battered women's syndrome: A Black feminist perspective. *UCLA Women's Law Journal*, *1*, 191–207.

Alexander, C. J. (2002). Violence in gay and lesbian relationships. *Journal of Gay and Lesbian Social Services*, *14*(1), 95–98. https://doi.org/10.1300/J041v14n01_06

Alhusen, J. L., Lucea, M. B., & Glass, N. (2010). Perceptions of and experience with system responses to female same-sex intimate partner violence. *Partner Abuse*, *1*(4), 443–462. doi:10.1891/1946-6560.1.4.443

Amanor-Boadu, Y., Messing, J. T., Stith, S. M., Anderson, J. R., O'Sullivan, C. S., & Campbell, J. C. (2012). Immigrant and nonimmigrant women: Factors that predict leaving an abusive relationship. *Violence Against Women*, *18*(5), 611–633. doi:10.1177/1077801212453139

Angel, M. (2007). Why Judy Norman acted in a reasonable self-defense: An abused woman and a sleeping man. *Buffalo Women's Law Journal, Article 8*, 65–88. https://digitalcommons.law.buffalo.edu/bwlj/vol16/iss1/8

Archer, J. (2000). Sex differences in aggression between heterosexual partners: A meta—analytic review. *Psychological Bulletin*, *126*, 651–680. https://doi.org/10.1037/1089-2680.8.4.291

Arcoren v. U.S., 929 F.2d 1235, 32 Fed. R. Evid. Serv 769, 116 A.L.R. Fed. 839 (Sth Cir. 1991).

Asch, S. E. (1956). Studies of independence and conformity: I. A minority of one against a unanimous majority. *Psychological Monographs: General and Applied, 70*(9), 1–70. doi:10.1037/h0093718

Baguley, C. M., McKimmie, B. M., & Masser, B. M. (2017). Deconstructing the simplification of jury instructions: How simplifying the features of complexity affects jurors' application of instructions. *Law Human Behavior, 41*(3), 284–304. https://doi.org/10.1037/lhb0000234

Baguley, C. M., McKimmie, B. M., & Masser, B. M. (2019). Re-evaluating how to measure jurors' comprehension and application of jury instructions. *Psychology, Crime & Law, 26*(1), 1–14. https://doi.org/10/gf4bxn

Balsam, K. F., & Szymanski, D. M. (2005). Relationship quality and domestic violence in women's same-sex relationships: The role of minority stress. *Psychology of Women Quarterly, 29*(3), 258–269. doi:10.1111/j.1471-6402.2005.00220.x

Basile, S. (2005). A measure of court response to requests for protection. *Journal of Family Violence, 20*(3), 171–179. https://doi.org/10.1007/s10896-005-3653-x

Bates, E., Klement, K. R., Kaye, L. K., & Pennington, C. R. (2019). The impact of gendered stereotypes on perceptions of violence: A commentary. *Sex Roles, 81*, 34–43. https://doi.org/10.1007/s11199-019-01029-9

Bates, E. A. (2020). "No one would ever believe me": An exploration of the impact of intimate partner violence victimization on men. *Psychology of Men & Masculinities, 21*(4), 497–507. https://doi.org/10.1037/men0000206

Belknap, J., Larson, D.-L., Abrams M. L., Garcia, C., & Anderson-Block, K. (2012). Types of intimate partner homicides committed by women: Self-defense, proxy/retaliation, and sexual proprietariness. *Homicide Studies, 16*(4), 359–379. doi:10.1177/1088767912461444

Black, M., Basile, K., Breiding, M., Smith, S., Walters, M., Merrick, M., . . . Stevens, M. (2011). National intimate partner and sexual violence survey: 2010 summary report. Atlanta, GA: National Center for Injury Prevention and Control, Centers for Disease Control and Prevention; 2011.

Block, C. R., & Christakos, A. (1995). Intimate partner homicide in Chicago over 29 years. *Crime & Delinquency, 41*(4), 496–526. doi:10.1177/0011128795041004008

Bongiorno, R., McKimmie, B. M., & Masser, B. M. (2016). The selective use of rape-victim stereotypes to protect culturally similar perpetrators. *Psychology of Women Quarterly, 40*(3), 398–413. https://doi.org/10.1177/0361684316631932

Boonzaier, F. (2008). "If the man says you must sit, then you must sit": The relational construction of woman abuse: Gender, subjectivity, and violence. *Feminism & Psychology, 18*(2), 183–206. https://doi.org/10/cmdcjc

Bornstein, B. H., Golding, J. M., Neuschatz, J., Kimbrough, C., Reed, K., Magyarics, C., & Luecht, K. (2017). Mock juror sampling issues in jury simulation research: A meta-analysis. *Law Human Behavior, 41*(1), 13–28. https://doi.org/10.1037/lhb0000223

Bornstein, B. H., & Greene, E. (2011). Jury decision making: Implications for and from psychology. *Current Directions in Psychological Science, 20*(1), 63–67. doi:10.1177/0963721410397282

Bosson, J. K., & Vandello, J. A. (2011). Precarious manhood and its links to action and aggression. *Current Directions in Psychological Science, 20*(2), 82–86. https://doi.org/10/fg4g7n

Braden-Maguire, J., Sigal, J., & Perrino, C.S. (2005). Battered women who kill: Variables affecting simulated jurors' verdicts. *Journal of Family Violence, 20*, 403–408.

Brewer, K. R. (1988). Missouri's new law on "battered spouse syndrome": A moral victory, a partial solution. *Saint Louis University Law Journal, 33*(1), 227–255.

Brewer, N., Harvey, S., & Semmler, C. (2004). Improving comprehension of jury instructions with audio-visual presentation. *Applied Cognitive Psychology, 18*(6), 765–776. doi:10.1002/acp.1036

Brown, C. (2008). Gender-role implications on same-sex intimate partner abuse. *Journal of Family Violence, 23*, 457–462. http://dx.doi.org/10.1007/s10896-008-9172-9

Browne, A. (1987). *When battered women kill*. Free Press.

Campbell, J., Webster, D., Koziol-McLain, J., Block, C., Campbell, D., Curry, M., Gary, F., Glass, N., McFarlane, J., Sachs, C., Sharps, P., Ulrich, Y., Wilt, S. A., Manganello, J., Xu, X., Schollengurger, J., Frye, V., & Laughon, K. (2003). Risk factors for femicide in abusive relationships: Results from a multi-site case control study. *American Journal of Public Health, 93*(7), 1089–1097. doi:10.2105/ajph.93.7.1089

Campbell, J. C., Glass, N., Sharps, P. W., Laughon, K., & Bloom, T. (2007). Intimate partner homicide: Review and implications of research and policy. *Trauma, Violence, and Abuse, 8*(3), 246–269. https://doi.org/10.1177/1524838007303505

Campbell, J. C., Miller, P., Cardwell, M. M., & Belknap, R. A. (1994). Relationship status of battered women over time. *Journal of Family Violence, 9*, 99–111. https://doi.org/10.1007/BF01531957

Catalano, S. M. (2013). *Intimate Partner Violence--attributes of Victimization, 1993--2011*. Washington, DC: US Department of Justice, Office of Justice Programs, Bureau of Justice Statistics.

Chaiken, S. (1980). Heuristic versus systematic information processing and the use of source versus message cues in persuasion. *Journal of Personality and Social Psychology, 39*(5), 752–766. https://doi.org/10.1037/0022-3514.39.5.752

Chandler v. Cate, WL 4120385 *7 (N.D. Cal. 2012).

Cook, P. W. (2009). *Abused men: The hidden side of domestic violence* (2nd ed.). Praeger.

Cossins, A., Goodman-Delahunty, J., & O'Brien, K. (2009). Uncertainty and misconceptions about child sexual abuse: Implications for the criminal justice system. *Psychiatry, Psychology and Law, 16*(3), 435–452. https://doi.org/10/fhk329

Cox, J., & Kopkin, M. R. (2016). Defendant and victim sex, sexism, and decision making in an ambiguous assault case. *Women & Criminal Justice, 26*(5), 381–393. 10.1080/08974454.2016.1167153

Cox, J., Meaux, L. T, Stanziani, M., Coffey, C. A., & Daquin, J. (2021). Partiality in prosecution? Discretionary prosecutorial decision making and intimate partner violence. *Journal of Interpersonal Violence, 36*(17-18), 8471–8493. doi:10.1177/0886260519849689

Crocker, L. (1985). The meaning of equality for battered women who kill men in self-defense. *Harvard Women's Law Journal, 8*, 121–139.

Cutler, B. L., & Hughes, D. M. (2001). Judging jury service: Results of the North Carolina administrative office of the courts juror survey. *Behavioral Sciences & the Law, 19*(2), 305–320. doi:10.1002/bsl.439

Devine, D. J., Clayton, L. D., Dunford, B. B., Seying, R., & Pryce, J. (2001). Jury decision making: 45 years of empirical research on deliberating groups. *Psychology, Public Policy, and Law, 7*(3), 622–727. doi:10.1037//1076-8971.7.3.622

Dixon, L., Treharne, G. J., Celi, E. M., Hines, D. A., Lysova, A. V., & Douglas, E. M. (2022). Examining men's experiences of abuse from a female intimate partner in four English-speaking countries. *Journal of Interpersonal Violence, 37*(3-4), 1311–1337. doi:10.1177/0886260520922342

Dobash, R. E., Dobash, R. P., Cavanagh, K., & Lewis, R. (2004). Not an ordinary killer; just an ordinary guy: When men murder an intimate woman partner. *Violence Against Women, 10*(6), 577–605. doi:10.1177/1077801204265015

Domestic Violence. Volume XXI, (2) (Annual Review 2020). In X. He, E. Johnson, L. Katz, B. Pecatore, A. Rogers, & E. Schlitz (Eds.), *Georgetown Journal of Gender and the Law*. https://www.law.georgetown.edu/gender-journal/wp-content/uploads/sites/20/2021/01/GT-GJGL200002.pdf

Dunn v. Roberts, 963 F.2d 308, 309, 310 (10th Cir. 1992).

Duthu, K. F. (1996). Why doesn't' anyone talk about gay and lesbian domestic violence? *Thomas Jefferson Law Review, 18*(1), 23–40.

Eckstein, J. J. (2011). Reasons for staying in intimately violent relationships: Comparisons of men and women and messages communicated to self and others. *Journal of Family Violence, 26*, 21–30. https://doi.org/10/cgdjmr

Edwards, K. M., Sylaska, K. M., & Neal, A. M. (2015). Intimate partner violence among sexual minority populations: A critical review of the literature and agenda for future research. *Psychology of Violence, 5*(2), 112–121. https://doi.org/10.1037/a0038656

Elwork, A., Sales, B. D., & Alfini, J. J. (1977). Juridic decisions: In ignorance of the law or in light of it? *Law and Human Behavior, 1*(2), 163–189. doi:10.1007/bf01053437

Esqueda, C. W., & Harrison, L. A. (2005). The influence of gender role stereotypes, the woman's race, and level of provocation and resistance on domestic violence culpability attributions. *Sex Roles, 53*(11), 821–834.

Ewing, W. A. (1987). Domestic violence and community health care ethics: Reflections on systemic intervention. *Family and Community Health, 10*(1), 54–62.

Faigman, D. L., Cheng, E. K., Mnookin, J., Murphy, E. E., Sanders, J., & Slobogin, C. (2020). The battered woman syndrome and other psychological effects of domestic violence against women. In Thomas Reuters (Ed.), *Modern scientific evidence: The law and science of expert testimony*, 2020-2021 (pp. 365–490). Thompson West.

Felson, R. B., & Lane, K. J. (2010). Does violence involving women and intimate partners have a special etiology? *Criminology, 48*(1), 321–338. https://doi.org/10.1111/j.1745-9125.2010.00186.x

Finkel, N. J., Meister, K. H., & Lightfoot, D. M. (1991). The self-defense and community sentiment. *Law and Human Behavior, 15*(6), 585–602. https://doi.org/10.1007/BF01065854

Finneran, C., & Stephenson, R. (2013). Intimate partner violence among men who have sex with men: A systematic review. *Trauma Violence Abuse, 14*, 168–185. doi:10.1177/1524838012470034

Fiske, S. T., & Taylor, S. E. (1984). *Social cognition: Topics in social psychology*. Random House.

Fiske, S. T., & Taylor, S. E. (1991). *Social cognition* (2nd ed.). McGraw-Hill.

Follingstad, D. R. (2003). Battered woman syndrome in the courts. In A. M. Goldstein (Ed.), *Handbook of psychology*, vol. 11, *Forensic psychology* (pp. 485–507). John Wiley & Sons. https://doi.org/10.1002/0471264385.wei1124

Franklin, C. A., Goodson, A., & Garza, A. D. (2019). Intimate partner violence among sexual minorities: Predicting police officer arrest decisions. *Criminal Justice and Behavior, 46*(8), 1181–1199. doi:10.1177/0093854819834722

Frantzen, D., San Miguel, C., & Kwak, D. H. (2011). Predicting cases conviction and domestic violence recidivism: Measuring the deterrent effects of conviction and protection order violations. *Violence and Victims, 26*(4), 395–409. doi:10.1891/0886-6708.26.4.395

Gillespie, C. K. (1989). *Justifiable homicide*. Columbus, OH: Ohio State University Press.

Goodman-Delahunty, J., Cossins, A., & O'Brien, K. (2010). Enhancing the credibility of complainants in child sexual assault trials: The effect of expert evidence and judicial directions. *Behavioral Sciences & the Law, 28*(6), 769–783. https://doi.org/10/b8n4zt

Greene, E., Raitz, A., & Linblad, H. (1989). Jurors' knowledge of battered women. *Journal of Family Violence, 4*(2), 105–125. https://doi.org/10.1007/BF01006624

Greitemeyer, T., Schulz-Hardt, S., Brodbeck, F. C., & Frey, D. (2006). Information sampling and group decision making: The effects of an advocacy decision procedure and task experience. *Journal of Experimental Psychology: Applied, 12*(1), 31–42. doi:10.1037/1076-898X.12.1.31

Grubb, A., & Harrower, J. (2008). Attribution of blame in cases of rape: An analysis of participant gender, type of rape and perceived similarity to the victim. *Aggression and Violent Behavior, 13*(5), 396–405. https://doi.org/10.1016/j.avb.2008.06.006

Guadalupe-Diaz, X. L., & Jasinski, J. (2017). "I wasn't a priority, I wasn't a victim": Challenges in help seeking for transgender survivors of intimate partner violence. *Violence Against Women, 23*(6), 772–792. doi:10.1177/1077801216650288

Guthrie, C., Rachlinski, J. J., & Wistrich, A. J. (2002). Judging by heuristic-cognitive illusions in judicial decision making. *Judicature, 86*, 44.

Hall, J. A., & Carter, J. D. (1999). Gender-stereotype accuracy as an individual difference. *Journal of Personality and Social Psychology, 77*(2), 350–359. https://doi.org/10.1037/0022-3514.77.2.350

Hans, V. P., & Vidmar, N. (1986). The evolution of the American jury. In *Judging the jury* (pp. 31–44). Springer.

Harrison, L. A., Howerton, D. M., Secarea, A. M., & Nguyen, C. Q. (2008). Effects of ingroup bias and gender role violations on acquaintance rape attributions. *Sex Roles, 59*(9), 713–725. https://doi.org/10/fczwn8

Hassouneh, D., & Glass, N. (2008). The influence of gender role stereotyping on women's experiences of female same-sex intimate partner violence. *Violence Against Women, 14*(3), 310–325. doi:10.1177/1077801207313734

Hastie, R., Penrod, S. D., & Pennington, N. (1983). What goes on in a jury deliberation. *American Bar Association Journal, 69*, 1848–1853.

Henning, K., & Feder, L. (2005). Criminal prosecution of domestic violence offenses: An investigation of factors predictive of court outcomes. *Criminal Justice and Behavior, 32*(6), 612–642. doi:10.1177/0093854805279945

Heuer, L., & Penrod, S. (1994). Trial complexity: A field investigation of its meaning and its effects. *Law and Human Behavior, 18*(1), 29–51. doi:10.1007/bf01499142

Hillman, J. (in press). Lifetime prevalence of intimate partner violence and health-related outcomes among transgender adults age 50+. *The Gerontologist*.

Hines, D. A., Brown, J., & Dunning, E. (2007). Characteristics of callers to the domestic violence abuse helpline for men. *Journal of Family Violence*, *22*(8), 63–72. https://doi.org/10.1007/s10896-006-9052-0

Hines, D. A., & Douglas, E. M. (2011). Symptoms of posttraumatic stress disorder in men who sustain intimate partner violence: A study of helpseeking and community samples. *Psychology of Men & Masculinity*, *12*(2), 112–127. https://doi.org/10.1037/a0022983

Hines, D. A., Douglas, E. M., & Straus, M. A. (2016). Controversies in partner violence. In C. A. Cuevas, & C. M. Rennison (Eds.), *The Wiley handbook on the psychology of violence* (pp. 411–438). John Wiley and Sons. doi:10.1002/9781118303092

Hirschel, D. (2008). Domestic violence cases: What research shows about arrest and dual arrest rates. Office of Justice Programs, National Institute of Justice. https://law.tulane.edu/sites/law.tulane.edu/files/Files/pubs/05-l27covtoc.pdf

Hymen, I., Forte, DuMont, J. Romans, S., & Cohen, M. M. (2006). Help-seeking rates of intimate partner violence (IPV) among Canadian immigrant women. *Health Care for Women International*, *27*(8), 682–694, doi:10.1080/07399330600817618

Ibn-Tamas v. United States, 455 A.2d 893, D.C. Cir. (1983).

Jackson, J. D. (1992). Law's truth, lay truth and lawyers' truth: The representation of evidence in adversary trials. *Law and Critique*, *3*(1), 29–49. doi:10.1007/BF01128242

Johnson, M. (2008). Intimate Terrorism. *Violent Resistance, and Situational Couple Violence*. Hanover, NH: Northeastern University Press.

Jordan, C. E., Pritchard, A. J., Duckett, D., & Charnigo, R. (2010). Criminal offending among respondents to protective orders: Crime types and patterns that predict victim risk. *Violence Against Women*, *16*(12), 1396–1411. doi:10.1177/1077801210389680

Jurik, N. C., & Winn, R. (1990). Sex and Homicide: A Comparison of Men and Women Who Kill. *Violence and Victims*, *5*, 227–242.

Kalvin, H., & Zeisel, H. (1966). *The American jury*. Little Brown.

Kaplan, M. F., & Miller, L. E. (1978). Reducing the effects of juror bias. *Journal of Personality and Social Psychology*, *36*(12), 1443–1455. doi:10.1037/0022-3514.36.12.1443

Kern, R., Libkuman, T. M., & Temple, S. L. (2007). Perceptions of domestic violence and mock jurors' sentencing decisions. *Journal of Interpersonal Violence*, *22*(12), 1515–1535. doi:10.1177/0886260507306476

Key, C. W., & Ridge, R. D. (2011). Guys like us: The link between sexual harassment proclivity and blame. *Journal of Social and Personal Relationship*, *28*(8), 1093–1103. doi:10.1177/0265407511402420

Kingsnorth, R. F., Macintosh, R. C., Berdahl, T., Blades, C., & Rossi, S. (2001). Domestic violence: The role of interracial/ethnic dyads in criminal court processing. *Journal of Contemporary Criminal Justice*, *17*(2), 123–141. doi:10.1177/1043986201017002004

Kunda, Z., & Thagard, P. (1996). Forming impressions from stereotypes, traits, and behaviors: A parallel-constraint-satisfaction theory. *Psychological Review*, *103*, 284–308. https://doi.org/10.1037/0033-295X.103.2.284

Labastida v. State, 986 P.2d 443 (1999).

LaFave, W., & Scott, A. (1972). *Handbook of criminal law*. West Publishing Co.

Landsman, S., & Rakos, R. F. (1994). A preliminary inquiry into the effect of potentially biasing information on judges and jurors in civil litigation. *Behavioral Sciences & the Law*, *12*(2), 113–126. doi:10.1002/bsl.2370120203

Lavallee v. Regina, 55 C.C.C. 3d 97 (1990).

Lieberman, J. D., & Krauss, D. A. (2009). *Jury psychology: Social aspects of trial processes*: Ashgate.

Little, B. (2020). Who's the victim here? The role of gender, social norms, and heteronormativity in the IPV gender symmetry debate. In B. Russell (Ed.), *Intimate partner violence and the LGBT+ community* (pp. 69–88). Springer. https://doi.org/10.1007/978-3-030-44762-5_5

Lysova, A., Hanson, K., Dixon, L., Douglas, E. M., Hines, D. A., & Celi, E. M. (2020). Internal and external barriers to help seeking: Voices of men who experienced abuse in the intimate relationships. *The International Journal of Offender Therapy and Comparative Criminology*, 1–22. doi:110.1177/0306624X20919710

Macrae, C. N., Bodenhausen, G. V., Milne, A. B., & Jetten, J. (1994). Out of mind but back in sight: Stereotypes on the rebound. *Journal of Personality and Social Psychology*, 67(5), 808–817. https://doi.org/10.1037/0022-3514.67.5.808

Macrae, C. N., Milne, A. B., & Bodenhausen, G. V. (1994). Stereotypes as energy-saving devices: A peek inside the cognitive toolbox. *Journal of Personality and Social Psychology*, 66(1), 37–47. https://doi.org/10.1037/0022-3514.66.1.37

Maeder, E. M., Mossière, A., & Cheung, L. (2013). Canadian mock juror attitudes and decisions in domestic violence cases involving Asian and White interracial and intraracial couples. *Journal of Interpersonal Violence*, 28(4), 667–684. 10.1177/0886260512455871

Maguigan, H. (1991). Battered women and self-defense: Myths and misconceptions in current reform proposals. *University of Pennsylvania Law Review*, 140(2), 379–460. https://scholarship.law.upenn.edu/penn_law_review/vol140/iss2/1

Masri, A. (2018). Equal rights, unequal protection: Institutional failures in protecting and advocating for victims of same-sex domestic violence in post-marriage equality era. *Tulane Journal of Law & Sexuality*, 27, 75–91.

Mazzella, R., & Feingold, A. (1994). The effects of physical attractiveness, race, socioeconomic status, and gender of defendants and victims on judgments of mock jurors: A meta-analysis. *Journal of Applied Social Psychology*, 24(15), 1315–1344.

McCabe, S., & Purves, R. (1974). *The shadow jury at work: An account of a series of deliberations and verdicts where "shadow" juries were present during actual trials*. Blackwell for the Oxford University Penal Research Unit.

McClennen, J. C. (2005). Domestic violence between same-gender partners: Recent findings and future research. *Journal of Interpersonal Violence*, 20(2), 149–154. doi:10.1177/0886260504268762

McKimmie, B. M., Antrobus, E., & Baguley, C. (2014). Objective and subjective comprehension of jury instructions in criminal trials. *New Criminal Law Review: An International and Interdisciplinary Journal*, 17(2), 163–183. doi:10.1525/nclr.2014.17.2.163

McKimmie, B. M., Masters, J. M., Masser, B. M., Schuller, R. A., & Terry, D. J. (2013). Stereotypical and counterstereotypical defendants: Who is he and what was the case against her? *Psychology Public Policy and Law*, 19(3), 343–354. doi:10.1037/A0030505

Mele, M., Roberts, J. C., & Wolfer, L. (2011). Men who seek protection orders against female intimate partners, *Partner Abuse*, 2(1), 61–75. doi:10.1891/1946-6560.2.1.61

Messinger, A. M. (2011). Invisible victims: Same-sex IPV in the National Violence Against Women survey. *Journal of Interpersonal Violence*, 26(11), 2228–2243. https://doi.org/10/bwct7h

Monson, C. M., Byrd, G. R., & Langhinrichsen-Rohling, J. (1996). To have and to hold: Perceptions of marital rape. *Journal of Interpersonal Violence*, *11*(3), 410–424. https://doi.org/10/bfnrwp

Mossière, A., Maeder, E. M., & Pica, E. (2018). Racial composition of couples in battered spouse syndrome cases: A look at juror perceptions and decisions. *Journal of Interpersonal Violence*, *33*(18), 2867–2890. doi:10.1177/0886260516632355

Muller, H. J., Desmarais, S. L., & Hamel, J. M. (2009). Do judicial responses to restraining order requests discriminate against male victims of domestic violence? *Journal of Family Violence*, *24*, 625–637. https://doi.org/10.1007/s10896-009-9261-4

National Coalition of Anti-Violence Programs. (2016). Lesbian, gay, bisexual, transgender, queer, and HIV-affected intimate partner violence in 2015. http://avp.org/wp-content/uploads/2017/04/2015_ncavp_lgbtqipvreport.pdf

National Coalition of Anti-Violence Programs. (2017). Lesbian, gay, bisexual, transgender, queer and HIV-affected intimate partner violence in 2016. http://4cv6673q3rq92smo7p3grp2z-wpengine.netdna-ssl.com/wp-content/uploads/2017/11/NCAVP-IPV-Report-2016.pdf

Nemeth, C. J. (1981). Jury trials: Psychology and law. In B. Leonard (Ed.), *Advances in experimental social psychology* (Vol. 14, pp. 309–367). Academic Press.

Nitschke, F. T., Masser, B. M., McKimmie, B. M., & Riachi, M. (2018). Intoxicated but not incapacitated: Are there effective methods to assist juries in interpreting evidence of voluntary complainant intoxication in cases of rape? *Journal of Interpersonal Violence*, *36*(9-10), 4335–4359. https://doi.org/10.1177/0886260518790601

Nitschke, F. T., McKimmie, B. M., & Vanman, E. J. (2019). A meta-analysis of the emotional victim effect for female adult rape complainants: Does complainant distress influence credibility? *Psychological Bulletin*, *145*(10), 953. https://doi.org/10/ggc7rg

Okun, L. E. (1986). *Woman abuse: Facts replacing myths*. State University of New York Press.

Ottati, V., & Lee, Y.-T. (1995). Accuracy: A neglected component of stereotype research. In C. R. McCauley, L. J. Jussim, & Y. T. Lee (Eds.), *Stereotype accuracy: Toward appreciating group differences* American Psychological Association (pp. 29–59).

Paradis, C., Bowen, M., & McCullough, G. (2020). Intimate Partner Violence: Psychological Effects and Legal Defenses. *Assessing Trauma in Forensic Contexts*, 351-378.

Peitzmeier, S. M., Malik, M., Kattari, S. K., Marrow, E., Stephenson, R., Agénor, M., & Reisner, S. L. (2020). Intimate partner violence in transgender populations: Systematic review and meta-analysis of prevalence and correlates. *American Journal of Public Health*, *110*(9), e1–e14., https://doi.org/10.2105/AJPH.2020.305774

Pennington, N., & Hastie, R. (1986). Evidence evaluation in complex decision making. *Journal of Personality and Social Psychology*, *51*, 242–258. doi:10.1037/0022-3514.51.2.242

People v. Barbara Sheehan, 1124/08, NYLJ 1202602218280, at *1 (App. Div., 2nd, Decided May 19, 2013).

People v. Birse, 2014 WL5148191, *2 (Cal. App. 3d Dist. 2014).

People v. Bush, 84 3d 294 148 Cal App. (1978).

People v. Carl Colberg, 182 Misc. 2d 798, 701 N.Y.S.2d 608 (1999).

People v. Hernandez, 2d Crim. B120703 (Cal. 2000).

People v. Sandoval-Ceron, 2010 WL 3021861, at *4 n.1 (Mich. Ct.App. 2010).

People of the State of New York v. Arlene Mohammed. (1987). Supreme Court, Appellate Division, Second Department, New York.

People v. Yaklich, 744 P.2d 504 (Colo. 1988).

People v. Yaklich, 833 P.2d 758 (Colo. Ct. App. 1991).

Petty, R. E., & Cacioppo, J. T. (1986). The elaboration likelihood model of persuasion. *Advances in Experimental Social Psychology, 19*, 123–205. doi:10.1016/s0065-2601(08)60214-2

Poorman, P. B., Seelau, E. P., & Seelau, S. M. (2003). Perceptions of domestic abuse in same-sex relationships and implications for criminal justice and mental health responses. *Violence and Victims, 18*(6), 659–669. http://dx.doi.org/10.1891/vivi.2003.18.6.659

Pozzulo, J. D., Dempsey, J., Maeder, E., & Allen, L. (2010). The effects of victim gender, defendant gender, and defendant age on juror decision making. *Criminal Justice and Behavior, 37*(1), 47–63.

Pritchard, M. E., & Keenan, J. M. (1999). Memory monitoring in mock jurors. *Journal of Experimental Psychology: Applied, 5*(2), 152. https://doi.org/10/d7sdgz

R. v. Lavallee, CanLII 95 (SCC), [1990] 1 SCR 852 (1990).

Rachlinski, J. J., Johnson, S. L., Wistrich, A. J., & Guthrie, C. (2008). Does unconscious racial bias affect trial judges? *Notre Dame Law Review, 84*, 1195–1246. http://scholarship.law.cornell.edu/facpub/786

Rauma, D. (1984). Going for gold: Prosecutorial decision making in cases of wife assault. *Social Science Research, 13*, 321–351. https://doi.org/10.1016/0049-089X(84)90008-5

Reifman, A., Gusick, S. M., & Ellsworth, P. C. (1992). Real jurors' understanding of the law in real cases. *Law and Human Behavior, 16*, 539–554. https://doi.org/10.1007/BF01044622

Rennison, C. M., & Welchans, S. (2000). *Intimate partner violence* (Special report). U.S. Bureau of Justice Statistics, National Institute of Justice (NCJ 178247).

Renzetti, C. M. (1994). On dancing with a bear: Reflections on some of the current debates among domestic violence theorists. *Violence and Victims, 9*(2), 195–200.

Rhatigan, D. L., Stewart, C., & Moore, T. M. (2011). Effects of gender and confrontation on attributions of female-perpetrated intimate partner violence. *Sex Roles, 64*, 875–887. http://dx.doi.org/10.1007/s11199-011-9951-2

Rijnbout, J. S., & McKimmie, B. M. (2012). Deviance in organizational group decision-making: The role of information processing, confidence, and elaboration. *Group Processes & Intergroup Relations, 15*(6), 813–828. doi:10.1177/1368430212447136

Rijnbout, J. S., & McKimmie, B. M. (2014). Deviance in organizational decision making: Using unanimous decision rules to promote the positive effects and alleviate the negative effects of deviance. *Journal of Applied Social Psychology, 44*(7), 455–463. doi:10.1111/jasp.12238

Ristock, J. L. (2001). Decentering heterosexuality. *Women & Therapy, 23*(3), 59–72. https://doi.org/10.1300/J015v23n03_05

Ristock, J. L., & Timbang, N. (2005). *Relationship violence in lesbian/gay/bisexual/transgender/queer (LGBTQ) communities.* Violence Against Women Online Resources. https://pdfs.semanticscholar.org/23b6/1c0642d6b09fe881fc4c3e465e59905dccc6.pdf

Rolle, L., Giardina, G., Caldarera, A. M., Gerino, E., & Brustia, P. (2018). When intimate partner violence meets same sex couples: A review of same sex intimate partner violence. *Frontiers in Psychology, Psychology, Medicine,* (9), 1506. doi:10.3389/fpsyg.2018.01506

Rose, V. G., & Ogloff, J. R. P. (2001). Evaluating the comprehensibility of jury instructions: A method and an example. *Law and Human Behavior, 25*(4), 409–431.

Russell, B. (2010). *Battered woman syndrome as a legal defense*. McFarland & Co.

Russell, B. (2018). Police perceptions in intimate partner violence cases: The influence of gender and sexual orientation. *Journal of Crime and Justice, 41*(2), 193–205. https://doi.org/10.1080/0735648X.2017.1282378

Russell, B., Chapleau, K., & Kraus, S. W. (2015). When is it abuse? How assailant gender, sexual orientation, and protection orders influence perceptions of intimate partner abuse. *Partner Violence, 6*(1), 47–64. doi:10.1891/1946-6560.6.1.47

Russell, B., & Kraus, S. (2016). Perceptions of partner violence: How aggressor gender, masculinity/femininity, and victim gender influence criminal justice decisions. *Deviant Behavior, 37*(6), 679–691. doi:10.1080/01639625.2015.1060815

Russell, B., Ragatz, L., & Kraus, S. (2010). Self-defense and legal decision making: The role of defendant and victim gender and gender-neutral expert testimony of the battered partner's syndrome. *Partner Abuse, 1*(4), 399–419. doi:10.1891/1946-6560.1.4.399

Russell, B., Ragatz, L., & Kraus, S. W. (2012). Expert testimony of the battered person syndrome, defendant gender, and sexual orientation in a case of duress: Evaluating legal decisions. *Journal of Family Violence, 27*, 659–670. https://doi.org/10.1007/s10896-012-9459-8

Russell, B., Ragatz, L. L., & Kraus, S. W. (2009). Does ambivalent sexism influence verdicts for heterosexual and homosexual defendants in a self-defense case? *Journal of Family Violence, 24*(3), 145–157. doi:10.1007/s10896-008-9210-7

Russell, B., & Sturgeon, J. A. (2019). Police evaluations of intimate partner violence in heterosexual and same-sex relationships: Do experience and training play a role? *Journal of Police and Criminal Psychology, 34*, 34–44. https://doi.org/10.1007/s11896-018-9279-8

Russell, B., & Torres, C. (2020). Identifying and responding to LGBT+ intimate partner violence from a criminal justice perspective. In B. Russell (Ed.), *Intimate partner violence and the LGBT+ community* (pp. 257–280). Springer. https://doi.org/10.1007/978-3-030-44762-5_14

Russell, B. L., & Melillo, L. S. (2006). Attitudes toward battered women who kill: Defendant typicality and judgments of culpability. *Criminal Justice and Behavior, 33*(2), 219–241. https://doi.org/10/c9h87j

Ryan, C. (2003). Stereotype accuracy. *European Review of Social Psychology, 13*(1), 75–109. https://doi.org/10.1080/10463280240000037

Saks, M. J. (1977). *Jury verdicts: The role of group size and social decision rule*. Lexington Books.

Sandys, M. (1995). Kentucky Capital Jury Project in progress: Guided discretion or negotiated peace of mind? (Part II). *Advocate, 17*(1), 14–19.

Sandys, M., & Dillehay, R. C. (1995). First-ballot votes, predeliberation dispositions, and final verdicts in jury trials. *Law and Human Behavior, 19*(2), 175–195. https://doi.org/10.1007/BF01499324

Sarat, A. (1994). Violence, representation, and the responsibility in capital trials: The view from the jury. *Indiana Law Journal, 70*, 1103–1136. https://www.repository.law.indiana.edu/ilj/vol70/iss4/3

Scheer, J. R., Martin-Storey, A., & Baams, L. (2020). Help-seeking barriers among sexual and gender minority individuals who experience intimate partner violence victimization. In B. Russell (Ed.), *Intimate partner violence and the LGBT+ community* (pp. 139–158). Springer. https://doi.org/10.1007/978-3-030-44762-5_8

Schneider, E. M. (1980). Equal rights to trial for women: Sex bias in the law of self defense. *Harvard Civil Rights and Civil Liberties Law Review, 115*, 623–641.

Schneider, E. M. (1986). Describing the changing women's self-defense work and the problem of expert testimony on battering. *Women's Rights Law Reporter, 9*, 195–222.

Schuller, R. A. (1992). The impact of battered woman syndrome evidence on jury decision processes. *Law & Human Behavior, 16*, 597–620. https://doi.org/10.1007/BF01884018

Schuller, R. A., Smith, V. L., & Olson, J. M. (1994). Juror's decisions in trials of battered women who kill: The role of prior beliefs and expert testimony. *Journal of Applied Social Psychology, 24*(4), 316–337. https://doi.org/10.1111/j.1559-1816.1994.tb00585.x

Schuller, R. A., & Cripps, J. (1998). Expert evidence pertaining to battered women: The impact of gender of expert and timing of testimony. *Law and Human Behavior, 22*(1), 17–31. https://doi.org/10.1023/A:1025772604721

Schuller, R. A., & Hastings, P. A. (1996). Trials of battered women who kill: The impact of alternative forms of expert evidence. *Law and Human Behavior, 20*(2), 131–146. https://doi.org/10.1007/BF01499353

Seelau, S. M., & Seelau, E. P. (2005). Gender-role stereotypes and perceptions of heterosexual, gay and lesbian domestic violence. *Journal of Family Violence, 20*, 363–370. https://doi.org/10.1007/s10896-005-7798-4

Severance, L. J., Goodman, J., & Loftus, E. F. (1992). Inferring the criminal mind: Toward a bridge between legal doctrine and psychological understanding. *Journal of Criminal Justice, 20*(2), 107–120. doi:http://dx.doi.org/10.1016/0047-2352(92)90002-Q

Severance, L. J., & Loftus, E. F. (1982). Improving the ability of jurors to comprehend and apply criminal jury instructions. *Law & Society Review, 17*(1), 153–197. doi:10.2307/3053535

Shaver, K. (1970). Defensive attribution: Effects of severity and relevance on the responsibility assigned for an accident. *Journal of Personality and Social Psychology, 14*(2), 101–113. doi:10.1037/h0028777

Sherman, J. W., Conrey, F. R., & Groom, C. J. (2004). Encoding flexibility revisited Evidence for enhanced encoding of stereotype-inconsistent information under cognitive load. *Social Cognition, 22*(2), 214–232. doi:10.1521/soco.22.2.214.35464

Sherman, J. W., Lee, A. Y., Bessenoff, G. R., & Frost, L. A. (1998). Stereotype efficiency reconsidered: Encoding flexibility under cognitive load. *Journal of Personality and Social Psychology, 75*(3), 589–606. https://doi.org/10.1037/0022-3514.75.3.589

Shernock, S., & Russell, B. (2012). Gender and racial/ethnic differences in criminal justice decision making in intimate partner violence cases. *Partner Abuse, 3*(4), 501–530. doi:10.1891/1946-6560.3.4.501

Smith, S. G., Zhang, X., Basile, K. C., Merrick, M., Wang, J., Kresnow, M., & Chen, J. (2015). National Intimate Partner and Sexual Violence Survey: 2015 data brief. Center for Disease Control and Prevention. https://www.cdc.gov/violenceprevention/datasources/nisvs/2015NISVSdatabrief.html

Stanziani, M., Cox, J., & Coffey, C. A. (2018). Adding insult to injury: Sex, sexual orientation, and juror decision-making in a case of intimate partner violence. *Journal of Homosexuality, 6*(10), 1325–1350. https://doi.org/10.1080/00918369.2017.1374066

Stanziani, M., Newman, A. K., Cox, J., & Coffey, C. A. (2020). Role call: Sex, gender roles, and intimate partner violence. *Psychology, Crime & Law, 26*(3), 208–225. doi:10.1080/1068316X.2019.1652746

Stark, E. (2007). *Coercive control: How men entrap women in personal life*. Oxford University Press.

Stasser, G. (1988). Computer simulation as a research tool: The DISCUSS model of group decision making. *Journal of Experimental Social Psychology, 24*(5), 393–422. doi:10.1016/0022-1031(88)90028-5

State v. Allery, 682 P.2d 312; 101 Wash.2d 591 (1984).

State v. Anaya, 456 A.2d 1255 (Me. 1983).

State v. Dunn, 5ct. 85-CR-59T (Kans. 1992).

State v. Frazier, SD 66, 646 N.W.2d 744 (2002).

State v. Frei, 831 N.W.2d 70 (Iowa 2013).

State v. Haines, 112 Ohio St. 3d 393, 2006-Ohio-6711, 860N.E.2d 91 (2006).

State v. Hundley, 236 Kan. 461, 693 P.2d 475, 479 (1985).

State v. Long, 192 Wis. Ct. App. 2d 762, 532 N.W.29 468 (1995).

State v. Norman, 1989, 378 S.E.2d 8 (N.C. 1989).

State v. Wanrow, 88 Wash. 2d 221, 559 P.2d 548 (1977).

Stern, L. D., Marrs, S., Millar, M. G., & Cole, E. (1984). Processing time and the recall of inconsistent and consistent behaviors of individuals and groups. *Journal of Personality and Social Psychology, 47*(2), 253–262. https://doi.org/10.1037/0022-3514.47.2.253

Stets, J. E., & Straus, M. A. (1990). Gender differences in reporting of marital violence and its medical and psychological consequences. In M. A. Straus & R. J. Gelles (Eds.), *Physical violence in American families: Risk factors and adaptations to violence in 8,145 famiiles* (pp. 151–165). Transaction.

Straus, M. A. (2012). Blaming the messenger for the bad news about partner violence by women: The methodological, theoretical, and value basis of the purported invalidity of the conflict tactics scales. *Behavioral Science and the Law, 30*, 538–556. doi:10.1002/bsl.2023

Strub, T., & McKimmie, B. M. (2015). Sugar and spice and all things nice: The role of gender stereotypes in jurors' perceptions of criminal defendants. *Psychiatry, Psychology and Law, 23*(4), 487–498. https://doi.org/10.1080/13218719.2015.1080151

Sumner-Armstrong, C., & Newcombe, P. A. (2007). The education of jury members: Influences on the determinations of child witnesses. *Psychology, Crime & Law, 13*(3), 229–244. https://doi.org/10/b7jbwc

Swenson, R. A., Nash, D. L., & Roos, D. C. (1984). Source credibility and perceived expertness of testimony in a simulated child-custody case. *Professional Psychology: Research and Practice, 15*, 891–898. https://doi.org/10.1037/0735-7028.15.6.891

Tahirih Justice Center. (2017). Advocate and Legal Service Survey Regarding Immigrant Survivors. Falls Church, VA. Retrieved December 1, 2017 (http://www.tahirih.org/wpcontent/uploads/2017/05/2017-Advocate-and-Legal-Service-Survey-Key-Findings.pdf).

Tajfel, H., & Turner, J. C. (1979). An integrative theory of intergroup conflict. In W. G. Austin & S. Worchel (Eds.), *The social psychology of intergroup relations* (pp. 33–47). Brooks-Cole.

Terrance, C., & Matheson, K. (2003). Undermining reasonableness: Expert testimony in a case involving a battered woman who kills. *Psychology of Women Quarterly, 27*(1), 37–45. doi:10.1111/1471-6402.t01-2-00005

Thomas, G. C., & Pollack, B. S. (1992). Rethinking guilt, juries, and jeopardy. *Michigan Law Review, 91*(1), 1–33. doi:10.2307/1289787

Tilbrook, E., Allan, A., & Dear, G. (2010). *Intimate partner abuse of men report*. Edith Cowan University.

Tillery, B., Ray, A., Cruz, E., & Waters, E. (2018). Lesbian, gay, bisexual, transgender, queer and HIV-affected hate and intimate partner violence in 2017. A report from the National Coalition of Anti-Violence Programs. http://avp.org/wp-content/uploads/2019/01/NCAVP-HV-IPV-2017-report.pdf

Tjaden, P., & Thoennes, N. (2000). Extent, nature, and consequences of intimate partner violence: Findings from the National Violence Against Women Survey. Bureau of Justice Statistics.

Town of Castle Rock, CO v. Jessica Gonzales, 125 S. Ct. 2796, 162 L. Ed. 2d 658 (2005).

Trainor, C., & Mihorean, K. (2001). *Family violence in Canada: A statistical profile 2001*. Minister of Industry.

U.S. v. Homick, 964 F.2d 899,906 (9th Cir. 1992).

U.S. v. Marenghi, 893 F. Supp.85 (D. Me. 1995).

United States v. Dixon, 04-10250 5 Ct. (2005).

Van Der Bruggen, M., & Grubb, A. (2014). A review of the literature relating to rape victim blaming: An analysis of the impact of observer and victim characteristics on attribution of blame in rape cases. *Aggression and Violent Behaviour, 19*(5), 523–531. doi:10.1016/j.avb.2014.07.008

Vidmar, N. (2011). The psychology of trial judging. *Current Directions in Psychological Science, 20*(1), 58–62. doi:10.1177/0963721410397283

Vidmar, N., & Diamond, S. S. (2001). Juries and expert evidence. *Brooklyn Law Review, 66*(4), 1121–1180. https://brooklynworks.brooklaw.edu/blr/vol66/iss4/5

Walker, L. (1979). *The battered woman*. Harper and Row.

Walker, R., Logan, T., Jordan, C. E., & Campbell, J. C. (2004). An integrative review of separation in the context of victimization: Consequences and implications for women. *Trauma, Violence, & Abuse, 5*(2), 143–193. doi:10.1177/1524838003262333

Walters, M. L., Chen, J., & Breiding, M. J. (2013). *The national intimate partner and sexual violence survey (NISVS): 2010 findings on victimization by sexual orientation*. National Center for Injury Prevention and Control, Centers for Disease Control and Prevention. http://www.cdc.gov/violenceprevention/pdf/nisvs_sofindings.pdf.

Wasarhaley, N. E., Lynch, K. R., Golding, J. M., & Renzetti, C. M. (2017). The impact of gender stereotypes on legal perceptions of lesbian intimate partner violence. *Journal of Interpersonal Violence, 32*(5), 635–658. doi:10.1177/0886260515586370

Wayne, J. H., Riordan, C. M., & Thomas, K. M. (2001). Is all sexual harassment viewed the same? Mock juror decisions in same- and cross-gender cases. *Journal of Applied Psychology, 86*(2), 179–187. https://doi.org/10.1037/0021-9010.86.2.179

Willis, C. E., Hallinan, M. N., & Melby, J. (1996). Effects of sex role stereotyping among European American students on domestic violence culpability attributions. *Sex Roles, 34*, 475–491. doi:10.1007/BF01545027

Wilson, M., & Daly, M. (1993). An evolutionary psychological perspective on male sexual proprietariness and violence against wives. *Violence and Victims, 8*, 271–294. doi:10.1111/1467-8721.EP10772668

Wistrich, A. J., Guthrie, C., & Rachlinski, J. J. (2005). Can judges ignore inadmissible information? The difficulty of deliberately disregarding. *University of Pennsylvania Law Review, 153*, 1251–1345. https://doi.org/10.2307/4150614

PART III

Family Law

8

Guidelines for Domestic Violence and Child Custody Litigation

DAVID PISARRA ■

As Mark Twain's adage goes, there are "liars, damned liars, and statistics." In probably no other area of sociological research (including sex) is this old trope more appropriate, truer, and more abused (pardon the reference) than in the area of *intimate partner violence*, commonly known as *domestic violence*. According to the United Nations (2012):

> Domestic abuse, also called "domestic violence" or "intimate partner violence," can be defined as a pattern of behavior in any relationship used to gain or maintain power and control over an intimate partner. Abuse is physical, sexual, emotional, economic, or psychological actions or threats of actions that influence another person. This includes any behaviors that frighten, intimidate, terrorize, manipulate, hurt, humiliate, blame, injure, or wound someone. Domestic abuse can happen to anyone of any race, age, sexual orientation, religion, or gender. It can occur within a range of relationships, including couples who are married, living together, or dating. Domestic violence affects people of all socioeconomic backgrounds and education levels.

In the United States, domestic violence is a national problem that impacts 10 million adults annually, as cited by National Intimate Partner and Sexual Violence Survey (NISVS; Black et al., 2011). There are over 19,000 daily calls to domestic violence hotlines nationally, which is over 6.9 million calls for help each year (Morgan & Ouderkerk, 2019). In California, 31.1% of men and 34.9 % of women experience intimate partner physical violence, sexual abuse, or stalking at some point in their lifetime (Black et al., 2011). The actual numbers of those affected by domestic abuse are certainly unknown, and the underreporting of domestic abuse is one the most chronic problems in the domestic violence community (Buzawa et al., 2015; Tjaden & Thoennes, 2003).

Only in the past few decades has domestic violence become recognized as a pervasive public health and social problem. For all intents and purposes (in court at least), domestic violence crimes were infrequently prosecuted, except in cases of extreme physical damage to one partner, usually the female. The murder of Nicole Simpson and her friend Ronald Goldman was a watershed moment in our society. It was so shocking to the senses, so appalling in its brutality, that the domestic violence community was mobilized to create the change needed to reduce the impact, if not the incidence of, domestic violence in our society. These changes were greatly accelerated at the federal level with the passing in the 1990s of the Violence Against Women Act (which also applies to male victims of domestic violence), implemented at the state level by local legislation such as the California Domestic Violence Prevention Act.

THE RANGE OF THE PROBLEM

The definitions of the terms *domestic violence* and *abuse* have expanded dramatically in the past 25 years from the extreme and primarily limited view of physical abuse and or murder, à la Ms. Simpson, to today's expansive understanding of domestic violence as *coercive control* and or "disturbing the peace of the other party." Such terms are slippery and facile and open to personal interpretation by judges, lawyers, domestic violence professionals, and victims and perpetrators, who often bring their mental health issues, along with ulterior motives, in their determination of what is, or is not, domestic violence and abuse.

The definition of coercive control is fluid, but as a working definition, I will use this from MedicalNewsToday.com: "Coercive control refers to a pattern of controlling behaviors that create an unequal power dynamic in a relationship. These behaviors give the perpetrator power over their partner, making it difficult for them to leave" (Morales-Brown, 2020). As a functional definition, this is wide enough to drive a pair of A380s through, side by side.

For a fuller understanding of "disturbing the peace," we must look to California Family Code §6320a and c (CFC 6320). We begin with CFC 6320(a) (California Legislative Information, 2021a):

(a) The court may issue an ex parte order enjoining a party from molesting, attacking, striking, stalking, threatening, sexually assaulting, battering, credibly impersonating as described in Section 528.5 of the Penal Code, falsely personating as described in Section 529 of the Penal Code, harassing, telephoning, including, but not limited to, making annoying telephone calls as described in Section 653m of the Penal Code, destroying personal property, contacting, either directly or indirectly, by mail or otherwise, coming within a specified distance of, or disturbing the peace of the other party, [emphasis added] and, in the discretion of the court, on a showing of good cause, of other named family or household members.

The Legislature (California Legislative Information, 2021b) has codified the meaning of "disturbing the peace of the other party" as:

> (c) As used in this subdivision (a), "disturbing the peace of the other party" refers to conduct that, based on the totality of the circumstances, destroys the mental or emotional calm of the other party. This conduct may be committed directly or indirectly, including using a third party, and by any method or through any means including, but not limited to, telephone, online accounts, text messages, internet-connected devices, or other electronic technologies. This conduct includes but is not limited to coercive control, which is a pattern of behavior that, in purpose or effect, unreasonably interferes with a person's free will and personal liberty. Examples of coercive control include, but are not limited to, unreasonably engaging in any of the following:
> (1) Isolating the other party from friends, relatives, or other sources of support.
> (2) Depriving the other party of basic necessities.
> (3) Controlling, regulating, or monitoring the other party's movements, communications, daily behavior, finances, economic resources, or access to services.
> (4) Compelling the other party by force, threat of force, or intimidation, including threats based on actual or suspected immigration status, to engage in conduct from which the other party has a right to abstain or to abstain from conduct in which the other party has a right to engage.

When it comes to a working definition of "disturbing the peace of the other party," which can be extended to members of one's household on a showing of "good cause," again this definition suggests a fluidity and expansiveness that any first-year attorney should be able to draft a declaration meeting the minimum standards for at least a temporary restraining order. On the one hand, this is meant to allow a victim to demonstrate need in the easiest and most expansive manner so that his or her legitimate safety concerns are considered. As these cases are emotionally fraught, actual victims are often in a state of shock. They have difficulty conveying information succinctly and logically, often due to the existence of symptoms of posttraumatic stress disorder (PTSD). On the other hand, through the zealous advocacy of an aggressive lawyer, expansive definitions of domestic violence may not always be in the children's best interests, who are unnecessarily denied access to a loving parent. Misinterpretations and manipulations of existing statutes on domestic violence invite continued conflict between the parents, adding stress on the family and perpetuating a cynical view of the legal process in which victims of "real abuse" are significantly disadvantaged. I recognize that making a statement like that is potentially explosive. However, after 20-plus years of fighting in the family courts, I have had cases where one party filed for a temporary restraining order (TRO), alleging years of domestic abuse, was awarded the home and had the other party forcefully removed from the home with nothing more than their personal belongings, only to drop the TRO once it became apparent the charges were exaggerated or falsified. Once the new living conditions are established, and often control the children's living situation (usually in the complaining party's favor), there is no further need for the restraining order, and the matter is dropped.

This is commonly referred to as the "silver bullet strategy," for it will take out the other party with great dispatch. Once a person has had their home, children, and often their bank accounts taken from them, there is little left for them to fight for, let alone with. The impact of this expansion is that in Family Court, the power of a Domestic Violence Prevention Temporary Restraining Order (Order of Protection in some jurisdictions) has been to rewrite how litigants and their attorneys approach divorce and paternity cases. Happily, at least in California, recent court decisions have provided limitations, or "guardrails," on how broadly current statutes are interpreted, so as to conform to the original intent of the legislature (State of California, 2021).

THE INTERSECTION OF DOMESTIC VIOLENCE AND CHILD CUSTODY

One of the largest judicial systems in the nation, Los Angeles County, covering some 4,753 square miles and with over 10 million people, has over 90,000 family law cases a year, on both the "civil" and "criminal" side of the courts. In its 2016/2017 Annual Report, the Superior Court of that county documented 92,544 "Family Law" filings involving Dissolutions (divorce) Nullity, Legal Separation, Adoption, and Domestic Violence cases (Los Angeles Superior Court, 2017).

The intersection of domestic violence and child custody cases arises in statutes such as California Family Code 3044 (California Legislative Information, 2021a), which states that:

> (a) Upon a finding by the court that a party seeking custody of a child has perpetrated domestic violence within the previous five years against the other party seeking custody of the child, or against the child or the child's siblings, or against any person in subparagraph (C) of paragraph (1) of subdivision (b) of Section 3011 with whom the party has a relationship, *there is a rebuttable presumption that an award of sole or joint physical or legal custody of a child to a person who has perpetrated domestic violence is detrimental to the best interest of the child,* [emphasis added] pursuant to Sections 3011 and 3020. A preponderance of the evidence may only rebut this presumption. This presumption may only be rebutted by a preponderance of the evidence.

Here is the wedge that drives many litigants to seek a bogus or fraudulent, or to be charitable, "stretched basis" for a domestic violence restraining order (DVRO). The "rebuttable presumption" is somewhat tricky for most abusers to overcome, particularly those who are in pro per (without legal representation or lawyer) and trying to fight for their custodial rights. This means the "victim" parent, and presumably, a child who is the subject of a custody battle, has the upper hand in any custody case. They are presumed to be the better parent. They, therefore, are awarded sole legal and sole physical custody of the subject child. This advantage brings with it many significant benefits in any paternity or divorce case, from the psychological empowerment that happens by having the strength of the court system recognize the abuse and a distinct disadvantage for the abuser. One should also consider the significant financial motivations that occur under the court-ordered determination of child support based on a 100% custodial timeshare versus a 0% visitation rate. The abuser will now be paying the maximum amount of child support payable based on their income, which in some cases can be a significant motivating factor. Further, for the parent seeking to relocate out of state, or even out of the country, a determination by a court that they are the presumed better parent with sole legal custody and sole physical custody means the relocation process is then made into an expedited process versus a full-court hearing. This process requires a determination of the child's best interests, which can take up to 6 months and costs tens of thousands of dollars, versus a no-fee filing and a hearing in 21 days for a permanent award of protection and custody.

HOW DOMESTIC VIOLENCE AFFECTS INDIVIDUALS AND FAMILIES

Domestic violence/abuse has both short- and long-term impacts on the victims. The short-term consequences on adult victims are obviously any physical effects such as bruising or broken limbs, but they also include the loss of work and productivity, which is estimated to be 8 million days of paid work annually (World Health Organization, 2004).

Witnessing domestic violence, now considered among the various adverse childhood experiences (ACEs), has a broad, lasting impact on the psychosocial and physical development of the individual. In the short run, child witnesses can experience anxiety and depression and are at risk for exhibiting poor school performance and acting-out behavior with peers (MacDonnel, 2012). In the long run, experiencing ACEs such as domestic violence as a child correlates with higher depression and suicidal ideation rates, along with lifetime increases in heart disease, lung cancer, diabetes, and many autoimmune diseases, as well as depression, violence, being a victim of violence, and suicide (AcesTooHigh.com, 2021). The intergenerational effects include an increased risk to perpetrate domestic violence in adolescent and adult intimate relationships (Straus et al., 1990) and for victims to become entangled in abusive relationships themselves (Stith et al., 2000).

Estimating the financial impact of domestic violence is a herculean task that, in many ways, has no outer limit. How can one ever fully quantify the loss of productivity in those lives that have been negatively impacted by PTSD, diminished self-esteem, dreams destroyed, and lives ended by homicide and suicide? One can only loosely grasp aspects of the many sides of this tragedy. For example, the National

Coalition of Domestic Violence (NCADV) reports that $5.8 billion a year is the cost of domestic violence, of which $4.1 billion is in direct medical and mental health services (Tjaden & Thoennes, 2003).

THE COSTS OF LITIGATION

The costs to the court system, both on the civil side for DVROs and the criminal side for prosecutions of assault, battery, and homicide, are astronomical. If we consider how much time is taken up with police investigations, district attorneys prosecuting, judges and juries ruling on guilt or innocence, and the high cost of incarceration, along with lost productivity of the guilty, one can see that the calculus spins out of control quickly.

For those individuals who are seeking representation, there are two primary sources of assistance: (1) the nonprofit model of legal aid that is generally open to low-income parties, and they generally only represent one side of the litigation—whoever gets to them first, which is frequently the victim, thus leaving the alleged perpetrator with no access to free legal aid; and (2) the private attorney model, which commands high hourly rates of compensation and large upfront retainers.

The court system provides self-help centers like the Restraining Order Center (ROC) in Los Angeles County Superior Court in downtown Los Angeles for victims. Those seeking a DVRO can obtain assistance in preparing and filing the papers required to get a TRO. This same type of service is available with private pay attorneys, and the fees range from nominal amounts to tens of thousands of dollars.

Alleged perpetrators have resources available to them through the ROC for assistance with the filing of a response. They can seek out the aid of nonprofits such as Bet Tzedek, Legal Aid Foundation, and so on; however, they run into the problem that, for the most part, nonprofits are victim focused.

IMPACT ON CUSTODY AND PARENTAL RIGHTS

The determination by a court that a party is an abuser will have a detrimental impact on that party's custody and parenting rights. The court's primary concern in domestic violence cases is to protect the children from abuse in the first place and any further abuse if there is a history. Therefore, code sections such as California Family Code $3044 were created. In recognizing the long-term negative impact that domestic violence/abuse has on children, the legislature and the courts say that it is less damaging to have an absent parent than an abusive one. However, the courts have the inherent ability to fashion solutions that will allow an abusive party to maintain a parent–child relationship. A court can order supervised visitation, both familial and professional, to continue the parenting relationship and ensure safeguards to protect the child from any abusive behavior. However, this requirement is often an obstacle due to the high costs of professional monitors who range from $35 an hour to hundreds of dollars per hour. Thus, this solution becomes unrealistic for the parent who is paying the maximum amount of child support, perhaps is unemployed due to the judicial determination of their status as an abuser, and loss of economic resources in a divorce or break-up.

CONSTITUTIONAL RIGHTS IMPLICATED

The power of the Domestic Violence Prevention Act reaches to the suspension of certain constitutional rights: gun ownership and free speech being the two most visibly impacted rights. This chapter cannot cover those in depth; however, the short course on them is this. The court has the power and obligation to prevent violence and further harassment and abuse by suspending a perpetrator's rights because of their prior bad acts of abuse. This is analogous to the termination of the right to own a gun by a formerly incarcerated person.

While the suspension is "temporary" for the duration of the restraining order, usually issued from 6 months to 5 years with a default amount of 3 years from the date of issuance, the victim can request a renewal of the restraining order before the expiration of the current restraining order, and this is almost always granted. As stipulated in California Code §6345 (California Legislative Information, 2021b), "These orders *may be renewed*, [emphasis added] upon the request of a party, either for five years or permanently, without a showing of further abuse since the issuance of the original order." This suggests there is no need for a further showing of violation or abuse if the applicant/protected party still feels the need for the protection of the court. In which case, they can extend the restraining order for either 5 years or permanently, and if it chooses to make a permanent order, effectively then the perpetrator's constitutional rights have been permanently terminated concerning both gun ownership and or free speech.

Complexities in Family Law

Justice is supposed to be blind so that all are treated equally, friend and stranger, rich and poor, female and male. The hope is that an impartial, objective trier of fact would be able to discover the truth easily and then apply hard and fast rules, so that litigants going into court would know what to expect, attorneys would be able to make clear recommendations, and truth and justice would carry the day.

But This Is Family Law

Family law is messy and complex, filled with competing interests, meanings, interpretations, personal biases, histories, and agendas of the parties, the judges, the social workers, the police, the evaluators, and the lawyers. All the litigation happens in a world where the party that is to be most protected, the child, is rarely, if ever, in a particular case, heard from directly. The statements of the child provided to the court are filtered through the lens of a parent's perceptions, feelings about the other parent, goals in the litigation, and social constructs. They are then often contradicted by the other parent, who filters the statements through their perceptions, and so on. The attorneys themselves then take a whack at reframing, slanting, emphasizing, de-emphasizing, minimizing, or evading the statements in favor of their client's objectives. Finally, a judicial officer is charged with divining the "truth" of all this through their lens of perceptions, biases, training, lived experiences, and beliefs.

Judges interpret this area of law with great flexibility for two main reasons. One, the nature of the beast is highly complex, fluid, and hard to define. Human interactions are inherently subjective; what one person views as abusive, another may view as "my communication style" and not abusive. Absent clear indicators of abuse, the courts and society have, for the most part, set as a default position that abuse is in the eye of the victim, which opens the definition to anything that someone does not like. The second main reason is that the appellate courts have a predisposition to confirm a trial court's rulings since the trier of fact is the one who had the opportunity to make a determination about the witnesses and the parties to determine credibility. The judge saw the victim on the stand and could conclude from the multitude of factors like body language, demeanor, and emotional state the true import of what was being testified to, versus an appellate judge looking at the bare words on paper and trying to discern their meaning.

WHAT ARE THE "BEST INTERESTS OF THE CHILD"?

As Justice Potter Stewart wrote when dealing with a definition of "hardcore pornography" and finally capitulating to an "I know it when I see it" standard, the "best interests of the child (BIC)" is similarly slippery to define. The California Legislature has attempted to codify some standard factors a judicial officer may resort to in any case, with Family Code 3011, 3020, and 3040 et seq. The starting point for all BIC is with Family Code 3011 (California Legislative Information, 2021a):

(a) In making a determination of the best interests of the child in a proceeding described in Section 3021, the court shall, among any other factors it finds relevant and consistent with Section 3020, consider all of the following:
   (1) The health, safety, and welfare of the child.
   (2) (A) A history of abuse by one parent or any other person seeking custody against any of the following:
      (i) A child to whom the parent or person seeking custody is related by blood or affinity or with whom the parent or

person seeking custody has had a caretaking relationship, no matter how temporary.
(ii) The other parent.
(iii) A parent, current spouse, or cohabitant, of the parent or person seeking custody, or a person with whom the parent or person seeking custody has a dating or engagement relationship.

(B) As a prerequisite to considering allegations of abuse, the court may require independent corroboration, including, but not limited to, written reports by law enforcement agencies, child protective services or other social welfare agencies, courts, medical facilities, or other public agencies or private non-profit organizations providing services to victims of sexual assault or domestic violence. As used in this paragraph, "abuse against a child" means "child abuse and neglect" as defined in Section 11165.6 of the Penal Code and abuse against any of the other persons described in clause (ii) or (iii) of subparagraph (A) means "abuse" as defined in Section 6203.

(3) The nature and amount of contact with both parents, except as provided in Section 3046.

The primacy of the "health, safety and welfare" of the child is where domestic violence starts. In any case, where domestic violence is alleged, and the child was present in the home and could hear the abusive behavior, from yelling, threatening, or angry exchanges to the witnessing of physical violence, we know the child's ACE score is increasing. That, in and of itself, is grounds for the court to make custody determinations to protect the child. This becomes a murky blend of conflicting interpretations where one person's yelling is normative human behavior. Another says it is an abusive attack on the peace and serenity and, therefore, should be prevented under the Domestic Violence Prevention Act (DVPA).

Not all child custody cases have prior DVROs issued. The fact is that under §3011(a)(2)(B), the court is empowered to perform an investigation and to demand independent corroboration. This indicates that there need not be a DVRO, but just a history of abuse in the relationship that impacts the child to justify a determination of sole legal and sole physical custody to the nonoffending parent. According to California Family Code 3020 (California Legislative Information, 2021a):

(a) The Legislature finds and declares that it is the public policy of this state to ensure that the health, safety, and welfare of children shall be the court's primary concern in determining the best interests of children when making any orders regarding the physical or legal custody or visitation of children. The Legislature further finds and declares that children have the right to be safe and free from abuse. The perpetration of child abuse or domestic violence in a household where a child

resides is detrimental to the health, safety, and welfare of the child. [emphasis added]
(b) The Legislature finds and declares that it is the public policy of this state to ensure that children have frequent and continuing contact with both parents after the parents have separated or dissolved their marriage or ended their relationship, and to encourage parents to share the rights and responsibilities of child-rearing in order to effect this policy, except when the contact would not be in the best interests of the child, as provided in subdivisions (a) and (c) of this section and Section 3011.

The emphasis in Family Code §3020 that the *primary* [emphasis added] concern in child custody is the health, safety, and welfare of the child living in a home free from abuse and violence points to how seriously the Legislature and the Courts are taking the issue of domestic violence. Freedom from abuse is now a "right" the child has, and it is a right that can trump a parent's right to be a parent. As a society, we are stating that it is more important to be free of abuse and violence than have one's biological parents be a part of one's life. The state is exerting its police powers in the protection of children. Even when the other parent has not sought and been granted a DVRO, they can still come into court, make allegations of a history of abuse, and if the court determines them to be credible, can regulate to the point of practical termination, a parent's rights to their child.

When a perpetrator has committed domestic violence or abuse within the previous 5 years, Family Code §3044 (California Legislative Information, 2021) is triggered, which states that there is a rebuttable presumption that an award of joint or sole legal and physical custody to the perpetrator is "detrimental to the best interest of the child."

> Family Code §3044: (a) Upon a finding by the court that a party seeking custody of a child has perpetrated domestic violence within the previous five years against the other party seeking custody of the child or against the child or the child's siblings, or against any person in subparagraph (C) of paragraph (1) of subdivision (b) of Section 3011 with whom the party has a relationship, there is a rebuttable presumption that an award of sole or joint physical or legal custody of a child to a person who has perpetrated domestic violence *is detrimental to the best interest of the child*, [emphasis added] pursuant to Sections 3011 and 3020. This presumption may only be rebutted by a preponderance of the evidence.

The perpetrator has the right to contest such a "detrimental" determination by reviewing the factors listed and complying with them, along with making an argument to the court that such prior domestic abuse/violence was not witnessed or experienced by the child. However, the expansive meaning of CFC 3020 indicates that the mere fact that the child was resident in a home where domestic violence occurred is determinative in and of itself that an award of custody to the perpetrator is detrimental.

In this author's experience, litigating this type of case is extremely difficult. In one case, where a prior determination of domestic violence was made, and the perpetrator had completed all court-ordered classes and programs and was seeking to reunify with the child, the court found that evidence presented by the victim of current social media posts violated the existing DVRO and denied the perpetrator's request.

KEY QUESTIONS

How do we know that what is alleged is actually domestic violence and has adversely affected the child? When does an allegation become a determination?

In Family Court, the allegation of an abusive relationship is widely upheld based on the victim's statements. The judicial review standard is "reasonable proof of a past act or acts of abuse." Therefore, when an applicant for a restraining order believes they have been abused, so long as the court has some measure of reasonable proof (i.e., testimony in a declaration, email and or text messages, photos, video summations, witness statements, police incident reports, medical reports), the standard for an initial finding of abuse is met.

In child custody litigation, the determination that a child is living in an abusive household is conclusive proof that they had been adversely affected. There is no extrinsic requirement to prove that a child is experiencing any symptoms of PTSD, anxiety, neuroses, or adverse impacts. It is presumptive under the Family Code. Therefore, this is the basis for the determination that placement with the perpetrator, unless under supervised visitation conditions and or proof to the court's satisfaction that the perpetrator has remediated their behavior, is detrimental to the child's best interest.

How Do We Know Who Is Telling the Truth?

This is a difficult question that presumes there *is* truth. I use the example of two people on the opposite side of a numeral painted on the sidewalk. One sees a 6, the other a 9. Who is right? Who is wrong? What is the truth?

In Family Court, the dynamics of a relationship play out in scenes for a judge to review and then extrapolate an entire movie from. For example, I had a case where my client, a 6'2" heavy-set Hispanic project foreman for a construction company, was allegedly abusing the mother of his three children. She was 5'9" and a bit heavy-set herself. We had a video of her threatening to tear up my client's blueprints for his projects. These were work-related, and he was terrified that she would destroy them, and he would have to explain it to his employer. In another video, she was swinging a Dyson vacuum at his head and screaming that he was a terrible lover and a horrible father and provider.

Her DVRO application alleged that he was abusive and terrorized her and the children. She claimed that he yelled at her, and she was scared he was going to hit her. That was the level of specificity in her declaration. Her testimony was that he tried to "choke me during sex," and she was afraid he would kill her. This is a "red flag" for judicial officers who are trained in lethality factors, and as soon as it is mentioned, it pretty much guarantees that a court will issue the restraining order.

The court reviewed the videos of her actions, listened to her tearful testimony, found that she was abused, and gave her sole legal and physical custody of the children. Supervised visitation was ordered for my client.

When I asked him about the "choking," he admitted it, telling me she asked for it, she liked it during sex, and it was part of their sex play. They had been doing it for years.

What is the truth? Was he abusive? Was she? Did he choke her? Was he a threat to her?

I do not know.

When I talked with her in the hallway, she was a strong, independent woman that I would not describe as a victim. She was clear on what she wanted from him; her demeanor in dealing with me was neither fearful nor overly demanding. I would describe her frankly as a strong negotiator. I pay attention to the affect and the demeanor of the other side. In her, I did not detect any of the indicia that I would usually find in what I would call a "true victim." I have worked with many a person who has been a domestic violence survivor, and there are certain moments where they leak the trauma, and it is evident that, yes, there was abusive behavior happening. Nevertheless, I did not see that with this person. This does not mean it was not there, just that I did not see it.

I walked out of the court, questioning all of it. The judge saw a woman defending herself with the blueprints and the vacuum from an oppressive and violent man who choked her. What was the truth? I have no idea.

Is It Parental Alienation or Legitimate Concern for the Victims?

For parents who have been separated from their children due to a DVRO and do not recognize their part in the cycle of violence, it is an oft-heard refrain that they are the "wronged party" who is being alienated from their children. Parental alienation (PA) accusations fly in family court freely by those who are not familiar with the true definition of PA and with little or no understanding of the actual dynamics and underlying causes, conditions, and factors to be evaluated.

PA experts generally designate PA into three main categories. There is mild PA, which is usually experienced by couples who are separating. In my experience, this is the generic "your mother/father is being a jerk" level of accusations. They tend to dissipate after a few months as the family finds a new normal. The moderate level of PA is when the accusations and involvement of the child in the proceedings are more substantial and accusatory. This is the "your mother/father will not agree that you should go to your favorite activity, aren't they terrible? How could they want to deny you that?" Again, this hopefully tends to wind down over the course of the litigation as the parties reach a conclusion and routines are established.

The most extreme form of PA, and which in my opinion is actual abuse, is when the alienating parent is attempting to sever the relationship between the child and the parent to serve their own psychological needs. This is exemplified by the parentification of the child, maternal/paternal enmeshment, and the rejection of the other parent by the child without valid justification or cause, such as actual emotional, physical, or sexual abuse by that parent. This last element makes the difference between PA and a valid response to an abusive situation. If the courts separate a parent after a determination of actual domestic violence, it is "by definition" *not* PA.

Where the intersection of PA and domestic violence cases get confusing is in the case of the "victim" parent who is manipulating the process, through either false or exaggerated abuse claims to effectuate an extended plan of revenge, and or to satisfy their own emotional needs to "own" the child and eliminate the other parent. Given the court's sympathetic position to view all claims by a victim that are "reasonable," this becomes an easily manipulatable vehicle for affecting a malicious severance of the parent–child relationship.

In my experience, this type of case is tough to prove, painful to defend, and heartbreaking for the targeted parent who has, in reality, done nothing to justify the rejection of their child. This is an area ripe for abuse by unethical litigants who find attorneys that wish to be standard-bearers for the victims in our system but are taken advantage of and turned into complicit child abusers, albeit unknowingly.

WORKING WITH CHILD CUSTODY EVALUATORS AND OTHER EXPERTS

In high-conflict child custody cases, the use of child custody evaluators is a common occurrence. These are specially trained individuals with a background in psychology appointed by the court under Evidence Code §730 or more appropriately under Family Code §3111 et seq, which outlines the requirements and expectations of the evaluator.

A child custody evaluation will generally involve psychological testing of both parents, interviews of the child with each parent, and interviews with collateral witnesses such as teachers, family members, caretakers, and so on, who have direct knowledge of the parenting skills and abilities of the parties. After a significant expenditure of time and money, the evaluator may make recommendations to the court on the custody plan in the child's best interest.

In cases involving domestic violence where one party has been determined to be a victim, and one party a perpetrator, use of a child custody evaluation may be employed by the perpetrator in their efforts to re-establish their parenting rights under Family Code §3644. Frequently this is in conjunction with the perpetrator's belief that they are the "true victim" and that the protected party is, in fact, the abuser who is perpetrating abuse not only on the other parent but also on the child in the form of fomenting the rejection of the parent.

In general, courts are averse to accepting the theory that one parent alienates the children out of malice. The preference is to believe all victims out of an abundance of caution. Given how hard it is for so many victims to come forward, this is understandable. Additionally, on some level, judicial officers want to protect themselves (their ego and or their professional reputation) as it is safer to believe that the alleged perpetrator is abusive or violent and to protect the child than run the risk of letting an abusive or violent parent have access to a child whom they then harm.

This level of protection and hesitancy carries over into the highly contested cases. It makes the use of child custody evaluators valuable in those cases where there is, in fact, an "abusive victim." However, it is extremely difficult to prove this. In many cases, the evaluation is just stalling the inevitable rejection by the court in favor of keeping the perpetrator away from the child under Family Code §3644.

USE AND MISUSE OF TEMPORARY RESTRAINING ORDER AND RESTRAINING ORDERS

The power of a TRO in California under the Domestic Violence Prevention Act is nearly unchecked. Consequently (intended or unintended), they are helpful for divorce attorneys who wish to abuse them to effectuate what is commonly referred to as the "Divorce by Ambush." A well-drafted Request for a DVRO will kick someone out of their home; take custody of the home, children, and pets; and order the ongoing payment of expenses such as rent/mortgage, car payments, bills, and so on. Further, the request can also establish the basis for spousal support, order attorney's fees to be paid, transfer wireless phone accounts, request any other orders so desired, and emotionally gut the other side, all without an actual appearance in front of a judge.

Many litigants use the powerful tool of a DVRO to get the upper hand in the divorce proceedings to speed the process. As noted earlier, this can make relocation easier if contemplated. For the alleged perpetrator who has had their home taken from them, is living in their car, who has had their tools of the trade and or their business taken from them, and children withheld, this is a psychological blow that renders many of them incapable of finding resources to pay an attorney and defend themselves.

To add to the distress, there is the shortened time frame the Family Code requires for a hearing to be held within 21 days of the temporary orders being issued. The 21 days are frequently extended out so that the alleged perpetrator can gather funds, seek counsel, and get their bearings under them again. These extensions are granted as a matter of right to the perpetrator, and the TROs are extended to provide protection to the victim.

RELEVANCE AND IMPACT OF DOMESTIC VIOLENCE GIVEN OTHER PROBLEMS

It is not uncommon in family law cases for a cluster of issues that have led to the dysfunction in the family unit. One parent's substance abuse, whether legal such as alcohol, marijuana, and/or prescribed, or illegal, such as methamphetamine, heroin, and cocaine, will lead to a breakdown in the parents' relationship, which can quickly morph into an abusive situation. The question of who started the abuse, or what was the primary cause, is much like a chicken-and-egg conundrum that frankly has little value beyond laying blame. In many of the cases that I have litigated over the years involving substance abuse, there is more than enough blame and miscommunication to go around and completely obscure the failed relationship's origins. The more significant question is how to get the family back on some level ground so that the child suffers the least amount of long-term damage.

Substance abuse brings with it a cadre of emotional frustrations and ills for the family. The abusers themselves often have anger outbursts while using their drug of choice, especially alcoholics, when their usage is challenged. Spouses of active substance abusers tend to exhibit similar mental health issues and reactions to the substance abuse, which can lead to their outbursts of anger and frustration that can lead to fights, scuffles, and arguments that the children then witness. Now there is domestic abuse happening in the home (Potter-Efron, 2007), and we know that the Family Code deems that to be not in the child's best interest and damaging to them.

There are cases of direct abuse of a child caused by a parent's anger management problems, or poor parenting skills, along with emotional and mental health issues that result in harm to a child. Those cases tend to end up in the Dependency Court or Child Protective Services jurisdiction and not often in the Civil/Family Court. Parents in Family Court who are involved in high-conflict custody cases often claim that there is child abuse happening and that this should be the basis for a DVRO. The Code allows any parent with legal custody to file a Request for a Temporary DVRO on behalf of the child. However, most claims of what constitutes "abuse" in the other parent's household are looked at with a jaundiced eye as merely "a custody battle" and are not given the same level of deference that a DVRO gets when made by an adult claiming that they were abused and that the child was a secondary victim.

In my experience, I have handled cases where there were allegations that the new stepfather was abusive, and the claims were substantiated in the Partial Parenting Plan Assessment by the social worker when the mother wanted to move away. The child had been hit repeatedly by the stepfather with a belt on his buttocks in a manner reminiscent of a 1950s "wait until your father gets home" style of parenting. The judge's response was to order the stepfather not to do that again. My client, a 210 pound, 6'0" tall man, became a crying mess when we left the courtroom at the thought that his son was being abused, the mother was tolerating it, and the stepfather had no consequences for his behavior.

When significant mental health issues are involved, unless the mentally ill party is hospitalized, the diagnosis will generally have little impact on the proceedings, either as a straight custody case or a hybrid domestic violence case. In a straight custody matter, the question for the court becomes, "Is this parent an adequate parent?" "Adequate" means are the basics of providing for the health, safety, and welfare of the child being met? If so, the parent's mental illness is not dispositive of their right to parent. In a hybrid case where the mental illness may have led to domestic violence or abuse, the question proceeds along the lines laid down in Family Code 3020 and focused more on the domestic violence issues than the mental illness issues.

CHALLENGES IN LITIGATING FAMILY LAW CASES INVOLVING DOMESTIC VIOLENCE ACCUSATIONS

Complainants

The most significant challenge of litigating on behalf of complainants is their hesitancy to proceed and risk the wrath of the perpetrator. The ongoing fear and anxiety of the victim is a significant obstacle that I must confront and overcome for my clients who are seeking a DVRO. This is true whether my client is male or female—although I will add in that when I represent a male seeking a DVRO, it is much harder to get them to act and seek the court's intervention. My observation has been that they struggle with their internalized ideals of what being a man means. They are confronted with a hard societal view that, as a man, they should be able to protect themselves, on the one hand. On the other hand, if they do so physically, they are berated for "attacking a woman"—so they are caught in a Catch-22 situation.

However, female complainants have a genuine fear that the supposed protections of a piece of paper will not actually protect them from a former spouse who is dedicated to causing harm. Given estimate from 66 countries across the world, intimate partner homicide constitutes 38.5% of all female homicide victims, compared to 6.3% for male victims (Stöckl et al., 2013). Given the number of actual deaths each year of women whom their former male mates have killed, this fear is not unreasonable or poorly taken.

Respondents

Primarily respondents are blindsided by the paperwork. They are often removed from their homes and have lost access to their computers, cameras, on-site security systems, and documents that would support their version of the story that they were not the aggressor. This leads to a major problem in representing respondents in that they have so little evidence to back up what their claims are, and this is usually in response to an avalanche of claims and supporting documentation from the complainant who has spent weeks, if not months, preparing their case. The respondent has 21 days to file a response unless they seek a continuance to allow for the proper preparation of their case.

As previously noted, the respondent is often at a significant disadvantage because of a lack of money, which is often a source of conflict, and or the joint account is liquidated the same day as the DVRO is issued. Finally, the perpetrator is experiencing a huge emotional blow; even if they are an abuser, the challenge to their identity will set them back as they prepare a defense.

The respondent's self-image frequently will not allow them to see their behavior as fitting within the current definition of abuse. In my experience, the public is still unaware of the actual impact that anger, yelling, and creating an anxious environment have on a person, and especially on the child. In my 20-plus years of experience in representing dozens of male individuals in domestic violence cases, the respondents almost all say, "I never hit her," as if that were the only definition of domestic abuse.

Educating individuals about what constitutes abuse is a profound need in our community. Everyone needs to be taught that abuse is so much more than physical conduct, and this is where the intersection of the perpetrator's belief and the victim's belief collide. A victim can be abusive in their language, tone, and content of what they say. Therefore, it is so difficult to tease out the truth of who is the "true" first aggressor. I say this based not only on my years as a family law attorney but also as someone who was raised in a household that had extensive domestic abuse. If today's standards were applied to my childhood experience, certainly the physical behavior that was experienced and perpetrated by both my parents would constitute abuse. Additionally, the way that they talked to each other would be considered verbal abuse in today's world, and honestly, my mother was the more cutting and vicious of the two.

Times change, and awareness increases. As we continue to evolve and understand the long-term impacts of abuse, we are expanding the situations that qualify for a DVRO. Yet there is a lag in the common understanding and, until it meets with wider acknowledgment, there will be an imbalance in who gets to court first and the reasons why.

Mothers

When I represent mothers, they are frequently afraid of being killed, and this fear keeps them in the relationship dynamic. There is a thought process that if the relationship maintains, as bad as it is, at least he won't kill me or the child. Navigating this very real fear in some cases is the most difficult challenge as it leads to repeated attempts and pullbacks before finally severing the relationship.

Domestic violence experts (e.g., Walker, 2009) estimate that it takes several attempts before a woman is ready to leave an abusive and violent relationship, assumed to be about seven by victim advocacy organizations (e.g., Women Against Abuse, 2021). In my experience, that is a fairly accurate estimate. I had a case where the mother came to me, wanting to leave her abusive husband, and we prepared the documents five times before she was ready to let me file them. We spent literally 2 years planning strategy and positioning her for a safe exit. In the end, we were awarded the permanent restraining order, and she was able to move on with her life, but we spent many hours discussing her fears and how to prepare for his reaction to the divorce.

Often the mother has put the consistency of the child's life ahead of her safety concerns. This imbalance needs to be unpacked and the situation clarified to see a way forward for her and the child. In situations where leaving home for a domestic violence shelter is the appropriate course of action, there are additional concerns such as whether she will have to give up her job, how she will provide for her child if the abuser withholds money, and how the child attends school and other activities that the sudden removal of the father will impact. Of course, there are safety concerns for the child.

A stark division happens when a restraining order is issued, which can be a relief and a traumatic event for the mother and the child. These concerns need to be addressed, for they can engender a sense of loss and confusion about what to do next. When the household has revolved around the abuser and avoiding violence, the sudden removal of that focus can bring anxiety. Finding appropriate mental health professionals to assist the mother and child is one more obstacle to be addressed. While there is an immediate need for therapy, there may not be the resources available, and or there may be resistance on the part of the mother and the child to seek help when they are in the early stages of shock and denial of just how bad things were in the home.

Fathers

Fathers present unique challenges in litigating when they are the complainant. They are faced with overcoming the social stigma of being a man who is abused, which many equate with being "less than a man." Society tells men they should be able to defend themselves and protect their families. However, society also says a man should never hit a woman, even if she is hitting him. The concept of a male engaging in self-defense against a female aggressor runs counter to our social mores. Thus, the horns of a dilemma are born: On one side is the "never hit a woman," and the other side is if you were beaten up by a woman, you're not "a real man." Navigating these choppy waters when a man is being abused is difficult because much of what is needed to secure the DVRO requires the man to confront his self-image and be willing to face the inevitable arrows of insults sure to come from his abuser: "What kind of man are you?" "Such a coward—you hit a woman!" "You're no real man, I can beat you up!" (All of these, by the way, are what my mother would say to my father.) And let alone what he thinks other men will say to him. Oddly though, in my work with men, I have found that most of my clients (admittedly a self-selecting group that is not representative of all men) not only have been abused but exhibit compassion for other men who have also been in similar situations.

This, of course, occurs when there is an education campaign that tells men that only they can teach other men not to be abusers and to stand up when they see a man being abusive. There is no similar campaign to teach women that only they can teach women not to be abusers.

Conflicting messages, evolving gender roles, and the evolution of the domestic violence community have all combined to make representing men as victims a problematic practice. As more men become "stay at home" parents, they confront spousal support issues when they divorce. This, of course, raises the specter of what constitutes "a real man" for if he has sacrificed a career to raise a child, he is often demeaned for being a "loser" who can't provide for himself, which is, of course, a form of abuse in and of itself, thus driving him to avoid requesting spousal support. Simultaneously that creates a motive for the mother to seek a DVRO to have him declared an abuser so that she will not have to pay him spousal support. In this topsy-turvy world of domestic violence, where courts are more likely to see a man as abusive than a woman, this presents an opportunity to misuse the DVPA to avoid a legal obligation.

SUGGESTIONS ON IMPROVING THE CURRENT FAMILY LAW SYSTEM

The Adversarial Process

To paraphrase Winston Churchill, "Many forms of domestic violence prevention have been tried and will be tried in this world of sin and woe. No one pretends that the current system is perfect or all-wise. It has been said that what we have now is the worst form of protection, except for all those other forms that have been tried from time to time." Family law is widely considered the most challenging area of law to practice, for it is the intersection of all other areas. The family law arena must handle financial, emotional, psychological, criminal, and sexual issues while trying to be as hands-off as possible. The courts and the judicial officers do their level best to fashion solutions that will accomplish the opposing goals of staying out of people's lives while simultaneously being asked to make orders that will have an impact for this family's lifetime. They do all this with tight budgets, crowded dockets, not nearly enough training in the psychodynamics of families and cross-cultural studies, let alone the ever-changing landscape of what are appropriate gender roles and evolving family structures.

On the one hand, the adversarial system allows individuals to plead their case to hopefully a sympathetic and understanding judge who can see through the fog of a relationship breakup to discern some ill-defined "truth" of what is happening. On the other hand, there is such a zealous advocacy of attorneys and litigants who are slinging mud and blowing smoke to confuse and confound the courts so that their side can "win" that the "truth" may be lost in the mix.

A less adversarial system might be better. If there were behavioral analyses done prior to filing a request for a DVRO, perhaps that would redirect some of the heavily litigated cases into an alternative resolution process. Something akin to a court-facilitated break-up plan that was less painful for the family would be beneficial. The work required to develop such a program could be a pilot program in large counties such as Los Angeles, which has so many cases that statistical significance could be determined relatively quickly.

CLETS versus Non-CLETS Orders

As the law now stands, when a DVRO is made on the Judicial Council forms in California, it *must* be entered into the California Law Enforcement Telecommunications System (CLETS) that allows law enforcement to see that an order was made and who the parties are. This automatic registration will show up in a person's background check, and it stigmatizes everyone the same way, even if the abuse or violence is not the same.

Suppose the courts engaged in a more mediated process that allowed for some level of protection for the victim without stigmatizing the perpetrator. In that case, this may reduce the acrimony and result in a more effective resolution to the break-up and the long-term family dynamics often implicated in child custody cases.

Currently, the courts can issue orders on non–Judicial Council forms that are non-CLETS and yet still can be enforced. This type of creative resolution, advocated by Judge Hank Goldberg in his article "Settling Domestic Matters in Family Court," is a possibility that deserves greater training of both judicial officers and the family law bench.

Sanctions Imposed for False Accusations

What is true and what is false are the ever-present questions in family law. However, there are times when the demonstrably false is offered in court by a litigant to sway the court to their side. This behavior is rarely ever punished; at best, it usually results in the court determining that the credibility of the proponent is weak or nil and then finds for the other side. However, this ignores the emotional, psychological, and financial toll that has been put upon the falsely accused. The oft-cited reasoning is that we want to encourage people to come forward, and if we were to punish the liars in court, it would have a chilling effect, and those who needed help would be too scared to come forward. To this, I call bunk. The true victims will always be heard, but the false accusers need to have some real-world consequences for their lies, which would also cut down on the caseloads if more of the false accusers thought twice about filing bogus claims.

There is a way to have a tiered program of falsity evaluated. For example, the "lie" that "he did not use 10 of his 12 visits" when in fact he did not use 6 of them is a lie, but one of degree, not character. The "lie" that he hit me when the video clearly shows he did not is one of character that goes to the actual final determination of abuse or not. Those are two very different types of lies and should be treated differently. As it stands now, neither is likely to be punished beyond the mere decision of credibility by the court.

Cultural Awareness

There is an issue with the imposition of our cultural values on all situations equally. It must be asked if the broader cultural view of abuse should be applied in all cases to all families equally. As has been said, everyone comes to court with their own set of prejudices, biases, and agendas. How we see them and recognize their applicability is the question. Should the couple who have a history and pattern of mutual aggressive behaviors be seen through the same lens as the couple who never fought, but suddenly one partner becomes physically abusive? The variety of human experiences, relationships, motivations, and sensitivities are implicated and dealt with in family court.

As the saying goes, if all you have is a hammer, you will view all problems as nails. The courts need to recognize that they have more than just a hammer at their disposal. As a society, we need to develop additional tools to better fix the multitude of problems that human relations create.

REFERENCES

ACES Too High. (2021). What ACES/PCES do you have? *ACES Too High News*. https://acestoohigh.com/got-your-ace-score/

Black, M. C., Basile, K. C., Breiding, M. J., Smith, S. G., Walters, M. L., Merrick, M. T., Chen, J., & Stevens, M. R. (2011). The National Intimate Partner and Sexual Violence Survey (NISVS): 2010 summary report. National Center for Injury Prevention and Control, Centers for Disease Control and Prevention. http://www.cdc.gov/ViolencePrevention/pdf/NISVS_Executive_Summary-a.pd

Buzawa, E., Buzawa, C., & Stark, E. (2015). *Responding to domestic violence: The integration of criminal justice and human services* (5th ed.). Sage.

California Legislative Information. (2021a). Division 8: Custody of children. https://leginfo.legislature.ca.gov/faces/codes_displayexpandedbranch.xhtml?tocCode=FAM&division=8.&title=&part=&chapter=&article=&nodetreepath=10

California Legislative Information. (2021b). Division 10: Prevention of family violence. https://leginfo.legislature.ca.gov/faces/codes_displayexpandedbranch.xhtml?tocCode=FAM&division=10.&title=&part=&chapter=&article=

Los Angeles Superior Court. (2017). 2016/2017 annual report. http://www.lacourt.org/newsmedia/uploads/142017105142756AnnualReport2017-compressedfile.pdf#:~:text=ANNUAL%20REPORT%202016%2F2017%20EDITION%20

The%20Los%20Angeles%20Superior,and%20more%20than%2090%20law%20 enforcement%20agencies.%20It

MacDonnel, K. W. (2012). The combined and independent impact of witnessed interparental violence and child maltreatment. *Partner Abuse, 3*(3), 358–378. doi:10.1891/1946-6560.3.3.358

Morales-Brown, L. (2020). What are the signs of coercive control? https://www.medicalnewstoday.com/articles/coercive-control

Morgan, R. E., & Ouderkerk, B. A. (2019). Criminal victimization, 2018. Bureau of Justice Statistics. https://www.bjs.gov/content/pub/pdf/cv18.pdf

Potter-Efron, R. (2007). Anger, aggression, domestic violence and substance abuse. In J. Hamel (Ed.), *Intimate partner and family abuse: A casebook of gender inclusive therapy* (pp. 437–456). Springer.

State of California Court of Appeal. (2021, July). In Re the Marriage of L.R. and K.A. https://www.courts.ca.gov/opinions/documents/D077533.PDF

Stith, S. M., Rosen, K. H., Middleton, K. A., Busch, A. L., Lundeberg, K., & Carlton, R. P. (2000). The intergenerational transmission of spouse abuse: A meta-analysis. *Journal of Marriage and Family, 62*(3), 640–654. https://doi.org/10.1111/j.1741-3737.2000.00640.x

Straus, M., Gelles, R., & Smith, C. (1990). *Physical violence in American families: Risk factors and adaptations to violence in 8,145 families*. Transaction.

Stöckl, H., Devries, K., Rotstein, A., Abrahams, N., Campbell, J., Watts, C., & Moreno, C. (2013). The global prevalence of intimate partner homicide: A systematic review. *Lancet, 382*, 859–865. https://doi.org/10.1016/S0140-6736(13)61030-2

Tjaden, P., & Thoennes, N. (2003). *Costs of intimate partner violence against women in the United States*. Centers for Disease Control and Prevention. National Centers for Injury Prevention and Control.

United Nations. (2012). COVID-19 response. https://www.un.org/en/coronavirus/what-is-domestic-abuse

Walker, L. (2009). *The battered woman syndrome* (3rd ed.). Springer.

Women Against Abuse. (2021). Why it's so difficult to leave. https://www.womenagainstabuse.org/education-resources/learn-about-abuse/why-its-so-difficult-to-leave

World Health Organization. (2004). The economic dimensions of interpersonal violence. http://apps.who.int/iris/bitstream/10665/42944/1/9241591609.pdf

Custody and Intervention Recommendations in Family Law Cases

A Gender-Inclusive Framework

JOHN HAMEL AND KELLEY BAKER ■

Consider the following case summaries:

Case 1
The father secures primary physical custody of his 8-year-old son, Dylan, despite having been previously arrested twice on domestic violence charges, once against the mother, and once against a previous partner that led to a misdemeanor conviction and completion of an anger management course. He is an investment banker, with an outgoing personality and a large circle of friends, and presents a calm, confident demeanor in court. The expensive attorney he has hired to represent him cites parental alienation on the part of the mother for his client's strained relationship with their son. Testimony is given on the mother's history of emotional instability and alcohol abuse, including having picked up Dylan late from school on multiple occasions, and frequently allowing him to watch cartoons for hours as he binges on junk food.

Case 2
During a protracted custody dispute, the mother seeks a restraining order against the father for threatening to kill her. In the application she alleges several incidents of physical assault, as well as a pattern of coercive

psychological abuse against her, which she says were witnessed by their 4-year-old twins. This is the first time she has alleged such abuse, and she cannot find independent corroboration. The father agrees that they have had strong disagreements in the past, particularly in the period following their separation a year earlier but denies perpetrating any form of abuse. In his rebuttal, the father further claims the mother had previously threatened to have him arrested on a domestic violence charge if he disputed her custody demands, that she is manipulative and prone to outbursts of anger, and that she spanks the children and constantly puts him down in front of them. The judge nevertheless grants the temporary restraining order, mandates the father to a batterer intervention program, and allows him only minimal visitation, supervised.

These examples illustrate some of intimate partner abuse (IPA) allegations made in approximately half of disputed child custody cases litigated throughout the United States (Kelly & Johnson, 2008). Was the correct decision made in each? Individuals who are primarily concerned with protecting battered women and their children are likely to agree with the custody decision made in the second case, but to question the conclusions reached in the first; whereas those concerned mostly with the rights of fathers to have shared custody are likely to hold the opposite point of view, approving of the conclusions made in the first case, but reluctant to accept those in the second without further inquiry. For example, a victim advocate would cite research indicating that the psychological symptoms exhibited by abused women, such as those evidenced in the first case, can impair one's judgement and coping skills. This, they would say, better accounts for the mother's drinking and compromised supervision of Dylan than a lack of concern for his welfare. In response, a fathers' rights activist might point out that men are disproportionately arrested on domestic violence charges compared to women, even for the same level of offense, and that the husband's plea bargain was an understandable legal strategy to avoid incarceration rather than evidence of wrongdoing. A similar bias claim might be made on behalf of the father in the second case, namely that a woman merely needs to make accusations of abuse against one's partner, no matter how frivolous, and will be taken seriously, even though she may be abusing the children. Such accusations, in turn, would inevitably be viewed by the mother and her representatives as the usual victim blaming characteristic of controlling male abusers.

Child custody mediators and evaluators regularly hear some version of these arguments, which they are expected to evaluate fairly and objectively. Numerous questions remain unanswered about each. Given what is known about the effects of family conflict and violence on children, all points of view must be considered, and all allegations taken seriously and evaluated on what is in the best interests of the children (Gould & Martindale, 2013). This is a daunting task because, as discussed in the chapter by Pisarra (Chapter 8) and others in this volume: (1) Disputed child custody litigants are motivated to lie, omit, exaggerate, and otherwise shade the truth in ways that make fact-finding difficult; and

(2) intimate partner violence (IPV), more so than other mental health and behavioral problems (e.g., substance abuse), has been highly politicized over the years, with implications for how family court professionals understand this problem (e.g., Brinig et al., 2014; Drozd et al., 2004; Dutton, 2006a; Dutton et al., 2010; Hardesty et al., 2012; Johnson, 2005; Kelly & Johnson, 2008; Saunders, 2015).

Incorrect assumptions based on the prevailing gender paradigm, discussed elsewhere in this volume, certainly play a part, as reflected by two of the most widely known researchers in the field of family violence, in one of their earlier works:

> Although the terms family violence and domestic violence are commonly used, the most accurate term is the maltreatment of women and children because women and children represent the vast majority of victims. Men are also abused, but in most instances, men's violence against women creates greater injury, pain, and suffering, and a large proportion of women's violence toward men is in self-defense. (Jaffe & Geffner, 1998, p. 374)

Fortunately, an increasingly growing number of child custody experts have since come to recognize some of these fallacies and to challenge them:

> Advocates believe research supporting the overwhelming prevalence of males as perpetrators in classic battering should be considered probative in the individual case and that women must routinely be given the benefit of the doubt when conflicting allegations exist. Because a classic batterer minimizes, denies, and blames the victim when violence is alleged, it follows that any male doing so is exhibiting behaviors that confirm his guilt. This catch-22, however, does not allow for the possibility of a false accusation. (Salem & Dunford-Jackson, 2008, p. 446)

The most rigorously gender-neutral evaluator will also be confronted with perhaps a more fundamental challenge: how to sort out the complexities of IPA, not only among the parents but within the context of family relations. All the different types of partner aggressive behaviors—physical, sexual, psychological—must be considered, along with their frequency, chronicity, impact, and degree of bidirectionality; and the relative impact of witnessed IPA on children must be weighed against the impact of direct child abuse or neglect, child alienation, and other types of family dysfunction—as well as the possible psychological harm done to children when they are denied access to one of their parents.

INTIMATE PARTNER ABUSE AND THE BEST INTERESTS OF CHILDREN STANDARDS

Thanks to the efforts of mental health professionals and concerned citizens, laws protecting children from abuse and neglect strengthened in the 1960s, and IPV has been recognized as a significant social problem, with criminal statutes enacted in the 1980s making domestic violence a crime. However, it was not until the 1990s that the impact of IPA on children was acknowledged and given consideration in disputed child custody cases as reflected in new family law code sections throughout the United States (Advisory Committee, 1994; Jaffe & Geffner, 1998). For example, in California, Division 8 of the Family Code, Custody of Children, section 3044 (California Legislative Information, 2021a) stipulates that:

(a) Upon a finding by the court that a party seeking custody of a child has perpetrated domestic violence within the previous five years against the other party seeking custody of the child, or against the child or the child's siblings, or against any person in subparagraph (C) of paragraph (1) of subdivision (b) of Section 3011 with whom the party has a relationship, there is a rebuttable presumption that an award of sole or joint physical or legal custody of a child to a person who has perpetrated domestic violence is detrimental to the best interest of the child, pursuant to Sections 3011 and 3020. This presumption may only be rebutted by a preponderance of the evidence.

Statutes have been enacted in nearly every state, containing either the rebuttable position provision or similar language stipulating that the effects of domestic violence on children should be considered a factor in custody decisions (American Bar Association, 2014). How such terms as "abuse" and "domestic violence" are defined varies from state to state. In California, Division 10 of the Family Code on Prevention of Domestic Violence defines "abuse" in section 6203 (California Legislative Information, 2021b) as "intentionally or recklessly cause or attempt to cause bodily injury; sexual assault; placing a person in reasonable apprehension of imminent serious bodily injury to that person or to another"; or engaging in "any behavior that has been or could be enjoined pursuant to Section 6320." Section 6203 further indicates that abuse is not to be limited to "the actual infliction of physical injury or assault," and section 6320(a) stipulates that family courts can issue ex-parte orders enjoining a party from engaging in a number of behaviors, including "molesting, attacking, striking, threatening, sexually assaulting" and "battering." An ex-parte order can also be issued to prevent a party from stalking or "disturbing the peace" of the other party. In 2020, this section was amended so that "disturbing the peace" was defined as follows:

(c) As used in this subdivision (a), "disturbing the peace of the other party" refers to conduct that, based on the totality of the circumstances, destroys the mental or emotional calm of the other party. This conduct includes, but is not limited to coercive control, which is a pattern of behavior that in purpose or effect unreasonably interferes with a person's free will and personal liberty. Examples of coercive control include, but are not limited to, unreasonably engaging in any of the following:
(1) Isolating the other party from friends, relatives, or other sources of support.
(2) Depriving the other party of basic necessities.

(3) Controlling, regulating, or monitoring the other party's movements, communications, daily behavior, finances, economic resources, or access to services.

(4) Compelling the other party by force, threat of force, or intimidation, including threats based on actual or suspected immigration status, to engage in conduct from which the other party has a right to abstain or to abstain from conduct in which the other party has a right to engage.

RESEARCH ON INTIMATE PARTNER ABUSE AND FAMILY VIOLENCE

How exactly the use of coercive control and physical assaults by one parent against the other impacts children's best interests is not discussed within these family code sections. Explanations are left to the forensic professionals who provide expert consultation and testimony, as well as the evaluators tasked with making recommendations on child custody and visitation. As demonstrated by the fictitious case studies cited earlier, these explanations are subject to the distorting influences inherent in an adversarial system. Differences among child custody researchers on best practices for evaluating cases involving IPA allegations may also reflect personal bias due to personality or life experience or due to the vague and sometimes contradictory legal statutes that guide them, exacerbated by a lack of knowledge about IPA.

Lack of Accurate Intimate Partner Abuse Knowledge

Without accurate knowledge about IPA, the custody evaluator is at higher risk of relying on specific mental shortcuts, such as representativeness and availability heuristics, which in turn can produce confirmatory bias (Nicholls et al., 2013). A survey of 465 child custody evaluators found that the amount of custody and visitation given to fathers who were alleged to have perpetrated IPA was greater if the evaluator was male, scored high on the Modern Sexism Scale, or believed that mothers sometimes engage in parental alienation and make false allegations (Saunders et al. 2013). These results should be understood in the context of the authors' focus on fathers as perpetrators. Clearly, the pro-father bias among evaluators who hold sexist attitudes toward women should be of concern. However, meanings attributed to correlations found between custody/visitation time and beliefs that women are capable of manipulating the court system are open to interpretation—as a failure by some evaluators to properly assess the significance of IPA or, alternatively, reflecting an accurate understanding of the problem and a willingness to take it seriously. The authors assume the first, leaving the reader with the not-so-subtle suggestion that false allegations and alienating behaviors are not relevant. Additional findings by Saunders et al. (2013) that greater workshop attendance predicted custody decisions favoring the mother are also open to interpretation. The assumption is that training on IPA for family court professionals are reliable; however, there is evidence that many of the mental health professionals, victim advocates, and child custody researchers who might provide such training remain very much under the spell of the gender paradigm and fail to draw from the full body of accurate, reliable, and up-to-date scholarly research (Hamel, 2014; Hines, 2014).

After many years working with male and female domestic violence perpetrators and victims at his clinical practice in the San Francisco Bay Area, it became apparent to the first author that treatment recommendations for custody litigants often failed to meet best practice standards and that the referring parties were alarmingly uninformed about the prevalence, dynamics, consequences, and proper assessment of IPV (Hamel, 2019). For example, fathers who were found to have perpetrated any IPA, regardless of its level of severity or chronicity, were nearly always required to complete a full, 52-week batterer intervention program. In contrast, partner-abusive mothers were referred either to individual counseling, a shorter course in anger manger management, or no treatment at all, even if they had demonstrated a clear pattern of serious physical and/or psychological assaults upon their partners.

Accordingly, the first author created a 10-item quiz to measure basic IPA knowledge among family court professionals (Hamel et al., 2009). Online and paper-and-pencil versions were administered to members of the Association of Family and Conciliation Courts (mediators, evaluators, and family law attorneys), family court judges, shelter workers, and victim advocates drawn from a directory published by the National Coalition Against Domestic Violence and state chapters of the National Coalition Against Domestic Violence, and to undergraduate psychology students in partial fulfillment of their introductory psychology research requirement. The results of the study were troubling. The average respondent answered only 2.8 questions correctly. For example, 43% of respondents believe the percentage of IPA perpetrated by men in the general population to be between 85% and 95% (it is in fact about half). Further, 48% assume it is almost always the man, but sometimes the woman, who perpetrates verbal and emotional abuse and controlling behaviors (it is roughly symmetrical across gender); and more than a third (37%) incorrectly believe that in abusive households the violent father is more likely than the mother to also hit the children. Despite extensive training, the family court professionals did not score significantly better than the undergraduates, and females scored below males. The lowest scores were found among the battered women's advocates, a major source of information and training on IPA (Hines, 2014). Furthermore, the authors found it very telling that:

> For those items in which a clear choice was given between opposite but equally incorrect options, one of them consistent with the patriarchal paradigm (i.e., abuse is primarily male-perpetrated), the other in the opposite direction (i.e., abuse is primarily female-perpetrated), that respondents invariably selected the former. Thus, we would suggest that the incorrect

responding was not by chance alone, nor due to a general lack of knowledge about IPA. (Hamel et al., 2009, p. 45)

Typologies

Since the incorporation of the Model Code into family court proceedings, an evolving body of research has generated a more complete and accurate account of IPA dynamics, risk factors, and impact on adult victims and children than earlier formulations (e.g., Jaffe & Geffner, 1998). As summarized in Hamel (2016) and the introduction to this volume, and explored at length by Bates and Papamichail in Chapter 2 of this volume, IPA is neither completely symmetrical nor asymmetrical across sex. Rather, there is considerable symmetry with respect to rates of physical and psychological abuse and controlling behaviors, and their combination, and the risk factors associated with perpetration and victimization—primarily low income, poor impulse control, domineering personality, trauma, and family of origin issues, substance abuse, and relationship conflict. Moreover, men and women report similar motives for perpetration, including self-defense, revenge, jealousy, and control, and in the general population, most IPA cases involve bidirectional abuse (Hamel, 2020a; Langhinrichsen-Rohling et al. 2012). However, women are sexually assaulted at much higher rates than men, incur a much larger share of serious injuries leading to hospitalization, and account for approximately 80% of homicide victims. The emotional impact of physical assaults also disproportionately affects women, although male and female victims appear to be similarly impacted by psychological abuse and coercive control. Except for severe, life-threatening assaults, male and female victims alike report that the worse kind of abuse is ongoing emotional abuse (Arias & Pape, 2001; Hines & Douglas, 2015, 2018; Simonelli & Ingram, 1998), resulting in mental health problems as serious, or more so, than those produced by physical assaults (Harned, 2001; Lawrence et al., 2012).

Although scholars may differ somewhat on how to define and categorize such terms as "abuse" or "domestic violence," there is a consensus that they comprise a highly heterogeneous set of behaviors and dispositions, with varying etiologies, characteristics, and consequences for victims and children (Austin & Drozd, 2012; Ver Steegh, 2005). It is difficult to "conduct a valid parenting evaluation for a family without knowing and understanding the specific domestic violence context" (Ganley, 2009, p. 5). In a pioneering study of disputed child custody cases involving IPA allegations, using various sound, validated questionnaires, Johnston and Campbell (1993) found an equal number of cases where the father or the mother was the primary relationship aggressor (13.6% and 13.5%, respectively). A pattern of bidirectional IPA was found in 19.3% of the cases, and 5.7% of the violence was due to severe psychopathology. Most significantly, in almost half (46.7%) of the relationships, there had been no history of violence until the period of separation and divorce. "In general," the authors noted, "physical violence was perpetrated by the partner who felt abandoned, and this could be either the man or the woman" (p. 197). Violence was limited to a few incidents, some episodes more severe than others, during the separation and divorce, and the perpetrators later expressed contrition and embarrassment about their behavior.

As indicated in the Association of Family and Conciliation Courts publication *Guidelines for Examining Intimate Partner Violence* (AFCC, 2016), evaluations should distinguish between, on the one hand, aggression that arises due to poor impulse control and conflict management or is "a reaction to the stress of separation or divorce without any history of violence or propensity for future violence" versus, on the other hand, aggression where "one partner exercises power to intimidate, isolate, denigrate, control and subordinate the other partner" (p. 3). Various forms of IPV perpetration have been linked to an insecure attachment style, especially one characterized by *anxiety over abandonment* (Dutton, 2006; Sonkin & Hamel, 2019). Parents whose motive is primarily to dominate their partner, whether male or female, are also likely to exhibit signs of personality disorder, mostly borderline personality disorder (BPD) or antisocial personality disorder (APD), and their abuse is often chronic and severe, featuring both physical and psychological abuse (Babcock et al., 2000; Dutton, 2006; Holtzworth-Munroe & Stewart, 1994; Mauricio et al., 2007; Munro & Sellbom, 2020). Simmons et al. (2005) found evidence of BPD and APD between one third to one half of perpetrators mandated to batterer treatment, but high scores for narcissistic and histrionic traits were found as well, particularly among the women, and dependent personality traits among the men. Of relevance to child custody, parents who engage in this type of IPA are more likely to harass, stalk, or assault the other parent after separation, and or perpetrate physical, sexual, or psychological abuse in subsequent relationships, with deleterious consequences for child witnesses. For more information about personality and other risk factors for consequential IPV, including intimate partner homicide (IPH), the reader is referred to Chapter 6 by Hamel, Dutton, and Lysova in this volume.

As helpful as the AFCC guidelines may be, the various types of relationship aggression that they delineate are based on research that is often misunderstood and overly politicized (Dutton, 2006; Dutton et al., 2010). In the typology proposed by Michael Johnson, IPA related to poor impulse control and escalated conflict is known as *situational couple violence* (SCV), where physical assaults are infrequent, lead to minor or no injuries, and are perpetrated at comparable rates across sex. Abuse perpetrated with the intention to dominate and control, featuring severe physical assaults and chronic psychological aggression, has been variously called *coercive-controlling violence* (CCV), *intimate terrorism*, or simply *battering*, and regarded as overwhelmingly male perpetrated. Johnson also identified two other types: *mutual violence control*, involving two batterers, and *violent resistance*, where a victim, presumed to be the woman, fights back physically against her batterer (Johnson, 2008, 2011). While these categories recognize the heterogeneity of IPA, they have been tainted by the gender paradigm, insofar as the extant scholarly research finds few differences across sex concerning rates of physical assaults, psychological abuse, the control motive, or rates of self-defense (see Bates and Papamichail, Chapter 2, this volume).

Unfortunately, Johnson's erroneous proposition that CCV is primarily or exclusively male perpetrated has remained unquestioned by many child custody experts (e.g., Ganley, 2009; Hardesty et al., 2012; Jaffe et al., 2008; Kelley & Johnson, 2008). In fact, large-scale population surveys indicate that rates of CCV are comparable across the sexes, both in the United States (Jasinski et al. 2014) and Canada (Laroche, 2005). Hardesty et al. (2012) correctly cite statistics from Canada, finding rates of postseparation violence to be around 39% for female victims. However, we must not neglect to mention that the same survey reported that 32% of men who had previously been victimized were revictimized after separation (Statistics Canada, 2001).

Still, while rates of CCV are comparable across sex as defined by Johnson (high levels of physical and psychological abuse), it would be misleading to suggest that men and women are equally impacted or *terrorized*. There are, in fact, several forms of "battering" (Hamel, 2014):

(1) *Common battering*. It resembles SCV but includes a control motive and moderate levels of physical and psychological abuse and often stalking. This is roughly gender symmetrical.
(2) *Physical terrorism*. Far less frequent in the general population, it is characterized by extreme violence and control. The control is maintained through physical force, or the threat of physical force, much like the way a pimp might maintain control over his prostitutes (Stark, 2007). It is mostly male-perpetrated.
(3) *Emotional terrorism*. It may involve physical aggression, but dominance is established primarily with psychological abuse and emotional control. The victim is not necessarily in danger of being killed and not entirely helpless to protect him/herself. Perpetrated by men and women. Here is an example of emotional terrorism:

Throughout his 8-month relationship with Laura, Bill's life has been hell. Laura is highly critical of Bill and will force him to stay up until 3 a.m., browbeating him with complaints. As a result of not sleeping and Laura's harassing calls to his workplace, Bill was fired from his job. Now she refers to him as a "loser" and "a worthless piece of shit." When he shows disinterest in sexual relations, she ridicules him, questioning the size of his penis, and calls him a "faggot." During her rages, she bites, kicks, punches, slaps, and throws objects at Bill. . . . When Bill attempted to call the police, Laura threatened to fabricate spousal abuse charges, claim self-defense, and have Bill arrested, boasting that "they'll believe me because I'm a woman." (Hamel, 2014, p. 23)

An additional limitation of the Johnson typology is the considerable overlap across categories. One clinical study of 273 couples (Simpson et al., 2007) identified two categories resembling Johnson's categories of CCV and SCV, consisting of one low-violence and one moderate-to-severe violence group. However, a number of the low-violence couples perpetrated higher levels of psychological abuse than those in the moderate-to-severe physical violence group. Similar profiles have been found among same-sex partners (Stanley et al., 2006), suggesting that IPA dynamics can best be understood when placed on a continuum. Findings such as these should caution child custody evaluators from developing offender profiles based on limited information. For instance, the inability by victim advocates to distinguish between SCV and battering has unnecessarily caused concern that SCV dads often obtain custody time when they pose minimal danger to the children (Morrill et al., 2005; Rosen & O'Sullivan, 2005). However, "there does not seem to be any research," according to Austin and Drozd (2012), "to support a conclusion ... that coercive controlling fathers are often successful in gaining primary custody" (p. 293). It should be stressed that *the majority of partner violence consists of lower-level assaults that do not lead to significant injury or trauma.*

Psychological Abuse and Coercive Control

The code sections previously discussed provide a general guide for determining whether a parent has perpetrated "domestic violence." Specific examples are given for conducts that would "disturb the peace of the other party," including isolating one's partner, monitoring their movements, and other "coercive control" behaviors. PC 6320 correctly defines coercive control not as a discrete incident but rather as a "pattern of behavior that in purpose or effect unreasonably interferes with a person's free will and personal liberty." Still, there are limitations to these codes and how they should be applied (Follingstad, 2007). There are many other ways by which perpetrators engage in coercive control aside from the examples given, such as legal and administrative abuse, which includes making false reports of domestic violence or child abuse, threats to leave and take the children, and ruining a partner's reputation in the community (Hines et al., 2015). Parental alienation, a form of child abuse, can also be considered a form of IPA (see Harman & Kruk, Chapter 10, this volume). Existing measures on psychological abuse/coercive control are not entirely in accord with what items should be included, and the examples given are open to interpretation. How do we determine if someone is forcibly isolated from friends? What was the baseline prior to a reduction in visits, and what percentage would constitute "isolation"? A 10% reduction? A 90% reduction?

Furthermore, what is defined as coercive control may be a simple disagreement—for example, when a woman asks that her boyfriend not associate with drug users. If a husband cancels his wife's credit card after she makes extravagant purchases they cannot afford, is that coercive control or responsible limit setting? How do we measure the extent to which any act of coercive control actually "interferes with a person's free will and personal liberty"? Many forms of psychological abuse are only coercive if the victim is actually controlled, for example, by threats of violence (Saunders, 2015). Some individuals are more resilient than others, whereas those who are psychologically fragile, having experienced prior trauma, may feel constrained regardless of the partner due to internal processes of shame and low self-esteem. Finally, whether an act is "intended" to be coercive is difficult to ascertain. One party, with a more extroverted and dominant personality, may remind, suggest, and initiate activities at higher rates than the other party. Are constant admonitions to avoid junk food examples of coercive control or irritating but well-intended attempts to help?

Ample research can be found supporting the victim advocacy point of view illustrated by the first case study in the introduction to this chapter, that certain male batterers manipulate the family court system by effectively projecting a nonabusive image (Bow & Boxer, 2003; Jacobsen & Gottman, 1998); while their victims, as a result of the physical and psychological consequences of the abuse, may appear as overly hostile and to be a less "fit" parent (Hardesty et al., 2012; Kernic et al., 2005). Research has well-documented the effects of IPV victimization on mothers' caregiving capabilities, what is known as the *spillover effect* (Chiesa et al., 2018). When mothers attempt to leave the abuser, they sometimes will find resistance among their children, who miss their friends and neighbors, and who will even blame the mother for the abuse (Jaffe & Geffner, 1998). Some women, of course, also manipulate the court system and project a "nonabusive" image, and their efforts to gain custody have more to do with a sense of entitlement or punishing the partner than what is best for the children.

We recognize that no matter how politicized, both battered women's advocates and fathers' rights organizations have voiced valid concerns regarding the way IPA and parental alienation complaints are assessed and litigated within the family court system. We agree with Johnston and Sullivan (2020) that parental alienation is multidetermined and not sex-specific, just as we acknowledge the same regarding other forms of abuse between partners. We further agree with Harman and Kruk (Chapter 10, this volume) that IPA and parental alienation are not merely two sides of the same coin, but the same coin of coercive control that includes legal and administrative abuse and child abuse and neglect. All threaten the best interests of children, and neither men nor women have a monopoly on these behaviors.

THE COMPLEXITIES OF FAMILY ABUSE

A significant fact, rarely if ever acknowledged in the family court system, is that conclusions about the impact of IPA on children—which informed the Model Code for child custody evaluations—were based on research conducted almost exclusively with battered women and their children in the 1980s and 1990s. Despite the obvious limitations in generalizing from convenience samples such as these, the path by which family violence was presumed to affect children was assumed to originate with the father, who physically assaults the mother and the children, increasing the levels of stress and pathology within the family, sometimes leading the victimized mother to act out against the children with harsh or abusive parenting. Subsequent research has identified the limitations of this model. In one methodologically sound study, based on a large community sample of 453 couples and their children (Slep & O'Leary, 2005), a higher percentage of mothers, compared to fathers, were found to have perpetrated both IPA and child abuse (44.4% vs. 37.3%, and 78.1% vs. 68.2%, respectively). Only 2% of the families with severe violence featured a so-called battering dad pattern of combined severe physical assaults on the mother and abuse of the children.

Recent comprehensive literature reviews have identified other paths where IPA impacts the family. According to MacDonnel (2012), children who have witnessed physical aggression by *either* parent against the other are at significantly greater risk of experiencing internalizing symptoms (e.g., anxiety, depression) as well as externalizing symptoms (e.g., school problems, aggression) than other children. In the short term, internalizing symptoms are experienced to a somewhat greater degree when the child is exposed to IPA by the father or the father figure because men's violence is relatively more consequential (and more frightening) than violence by women. However, children and teens who are exposed to physical assaults by either parent are significantly more likely to aggress against peers, family members, and dating partners, and to evidence trauma symptoms and depression later in adulthood (also see Ehrensaft et al., 2003; Fergusson et al., 2006; Kimber et al., 2018; Straus, 1992).

Children are as much at risk living in a household with an abusive mother as one with an abusive father. In fact, except for sexual abuse, their perpetrator is more likely to be the mother (McDonald et al., 2006), not because mothers are inherently more abusive but because they are the primary caregivers and spend more time with their children than fathers. There is some correlation between physical partner abuse and child abuse, for female and male perpetrators, as high as 67% based on studies using shelter samples, but lower in representative community samples (see Dutton et al., 2010; Jouriles et al., 2008). Although the combined impact of the two types of abuse has not yet been clearly determined (MacDonell, 2012), children are affected by both. Some studies find the impact of direct child abuse on children to be comparable to witnessed physical IPA, based on research with battered women (Kitzmann et al., 2003); but other research, drawn from Child Protective Services samples (Salzinger et al., 2002), finds child abuse to have more deleterious consequences. Such contradictory findings can be explained by other research, showing any chronic form of severe abuse most impacts children—as witnesses to battering serious enough to necessitate refuge in a shelter or as the victim of abuse that has come to the attention of child welfare workers (e.g., Jouriles et al., 2001). Some studies suggest that the highest levels of internalizing and externalizing symptomology in children are more likely due to verbal abuse. For instance, comments by the mother, or the father, intended to shame and denigrate the child (e.g., "You're worthless," "Little bitch") can be just as or more impactful than most forms of corporal punishment or witnessed violence between the parents (Dutton, 2006b; English et al., 2003; Moore & Pepler, 1998).

Family violence is a heterogeneous, multidimensional phenomenon, characterized by a variety of possible pathways of abuse (Appel & Holden, 1998; Davies et al., 2006), with stress as a central mediator (Margolin & Gordis, 2003; Salzinger et al., 2003). According to the old model, it may be driven by a controlling-coercive father or by a controlling-coercive mother, whereby one parent, or both, may assault the other and abuse the children; or the partner-abused parent may respond to the stress of victimization by abusing the children. Marital discord and violence may follow rather than precede other forms of family abuse. Sometimes the abuse is initiated by the children against one another, to which the parents may respond with harsh punishment, in turn causing friction within the parental unit leading to an escalation of interparental conflict. In other cases, the abuse originates from a child and is directed at the parents. Mothers are the more frequent victims (Lynch & Cicchetti, 1998) and are often targeted in response to a history of child abuse (Ulman & Straus, 2003). Lynch and Cicchetti (1998) determined that the existence of child behavior problems prior to having been exposed to marital violence contributes significantly to overall levels of family stress, which in turn may aggravate both marital and parent–child relationships. "Violence anywhere in the family," according to Kitzmann et al. (2003), "may be sufficient to disrupt child development" (p. 346).

However, it is important to note that the less severe types of family violence alleged by family court litigants do not necessarily impact on children to a significantly greater degree than having grown up in a high-conflict, dysfunctional, but nonviolent home or experiencing the inevitable stress of marital conflict and impending divorce (Fantuzzo et al., 1991; Grych & Fincham, 1990; Laumakis et al., 1998):

> Pervasive conflict that takes the form of overt verbal hostility or violence harms children by causing stress, impairing effective parent-child relationships, and training children to be aggressive . . . children from violent homes appear to be at greater risk for showing clinical-level behavioral and emotional problems, but it is likely that some symptoms are caused by the conflict and not necessarily the violence. (Wolak & Finkelhor, 1998, pp. 91–92)

Another review (Sturge-Apple et al., 2006), focused on the impact of parental conflict, found children to be more impacted by exposure to conflict characterized by contempt, hostility, and withdrawal compared to those characterized only by anger; and more impacted when the topic under discussion concerns the child (e.g., disagreements over child-rearing, comments blaming the child). As with physical violence, the impact can be direct or indirect, when chronic, intense conflict leads to a decrease in parental sensitivity, warmth, and consistent discipline and an increase in harsh discipline. Parental conflict is more likely to undermine mother–child relationships throughout the toddler years and father–child relationships in the school-age years. Overall, however, parental conflict (especially when characterized by high levels of hostility) seems to have a more pronounced effect on mothers, perhaps because "men generally face fewer responsibilities and challenges in their caregiving roles than women . . . Therefore, interpersonal conflict may only increase parental difficulties for men under conditions of severe perturbances in the marital subsystem" (Sturge-Apple et al., 2006, p. 1638).

EVALUATION PROCEDURES

Child custody evaluators do not always follow sound, evidence-based evaluation procedures. A national survey of 115 evaluators by Bow and Boxer (2003) found that 37% of child custody referrals involve allegations of partner violence. Asked to cite the signs or characteristics to substantiate the abuse allegations, 60% of the respondents listed shame, guilt, fear, low self-esteem, financial vulnerability, or inability to leave—which may simply be symptoms of being involved in a highly charged child custody dispute. Only 31% of the evaluators secured independent confirmation by eyewitness reports or police records, and only 30% said they used a comprehensive risk assessment model, neither specifically for use in child custody cases nor any general IPA questionnaire (e.g., 20% used the Spousal Abuse Risk Assessment). Other evaluators presume "battering" from restraining orders alone (e.g., Morrill et al., 2005; Rosen & O'Sullivan, 2005). Although the issuance of a restraining order provides some degree of substantiation, they are based on a lower standard of evidence required for a criminal conviction, are more liberally given to mothers than to fathers (Muller et al., 2009), and without other information (e.g., offender's mental health history) do not by themselves indicate the type of abuse and its impact on the family.

Still, evidence-based assessment protocols have been developed for custody evaluations involving IPA that consider the credibility of the allegations within the context of other forms of family abuse and dysfunction and require the inclusion of corroborating evidence (e.g., Austin, 2001; Austin & Drozd, 2012; Drozd et al., 2004; Drozd & Oleson, 2004). They have been found to significantly increase the probability that offenders are mandated to complete counseling programs (e.g., anger management, batterer intervention, substance abuse treatment), and that victims and their children are provided legal protections (Kernic, 2020). In this section, we draw upon these efforts in light of the emerging scholarly findings on the dynamics, causes, and consequences of intimate partner and family abuse. As articulated by Austin and Drozd (2012), we strive to avoid two types of errors: overpredicting the risk of future IPA and the possible risks for victims (false positive), and underpredicting that risk (false negative):

> The aversive effects of concluding that a person has committed violence, or that there is sufficient risk to diminish parenting time, can have profound effects on the parent–child relationship and the quality of life of both. Not heeding risk factors or red flags that follow from a parent's conspicuously alarming behaviors can place the children at risk and can be lethal to children and ex-partners. If evaluators "miss it" for the court on issues of violence risk and the implications for parenting and co-parenting, the consequences can be extreme with the errors going in either direction. The stakes are high. When there has been severe form of IPV, the evaluator needs to assist the court to reduce uncertainty for the child and parent's future. The court wants to raise the odds in favor of safety, or to have a low threshold for protective action when there has been high harm in the past, while also appreciating

that a parent who perpetrated IPV may have important psychosocial resources to offer the child. (p. 267)

To what extent false or exaggerated claims of abuse are used to secure custody and alienate the children from the other parent is still open to debate. Within Johnston and Campbell's earlier family court sample (Johnston and Campbell, 1993), 13% of the parents had filed false or exaggerated domestic violence claims, at a rate 7 times more often by mothers compared to fathers. In a later publication, Johnston et al. (2005) found higher substantiated rates of "adult abuse" by fathers than by mothers; however, whether these pertained more to substance abuse or IPV was not clarified. Also, as with other child custody studies, this was a nonrandom study that may not generalize beyond the particular sample, criteria for substantiation were not standardized, and "the range or degree of severity of the abuse was not rated" (p. 16).

Clearly, the possibility of such false or exaggerated allegations should remind family court mediators, evaluators, and judges to proceed with caution and to refrain from viewing all IPA as the same or perpetrated mostly by men. There are few sex differences in the inclination of custody litigants to behave unethically or otherwise attempt to harm the partner (Clemente et al., 2019). The tendency by some parents to overcontrol the other parent's activities may be indicative of alienating behaviors aimed at interfering in the child's relationship with the other parent, or they may represent a form of "gatekeeping," wherein a concerned parent is legitimately looking out for a child's interests, possibly to prevent abuse or neglect (Saini et al., 2017). Therefore, custody evaluators are encouraged to follow protocols that help them differentiate between accusations aimed at gaining advantage and genuine abuse concerns while also following legal requirements and professional guidelines.

CUSTODY PROTOCOLS

This portion of the chapter describes protocols for conducting child custody evaluations when domestic violence is a factor. The discussion is divided into four sections: (1) preparing to conduct custody evaluations, (2) beginning the evaluation process, (3) gathering data during the evaluation, and (4) evaluating and synthesizing the data.

Preparing to Conduct Evaluations

Professionals interested in conducting child custody evaluations (CCEs) should review minimum requirements set forth by licensing boards and state laws, review professional guidelines, obtain specialized training, and familiarize themselves with the relevant social psychological research on the topic. State laws may vary regarding minimum requirements for professionals. For instance, the second author practices in Texas, where chapter 107, section 107.104 of the Texas Family Code states that a custody evaluator must have "at least a master's degree from an accredited college or university in a human services field of study and a license to practice in this state as a social worker, professional counselor, marriage and family therapist, or psychologist, or have a license to practice medicine in this state and a board certification in psychiatry" (Texas Family Code, 2019, p. 159). Additional requirements include years of experience, specialized training, supervision, licensure, and at least 8 hours of training in domestic violence

The American Psychological Association (APA, 2010) and the Association for Families and Conciliation Courts (AFCC, 2006) have comprehensive guidelines for conducting custody evaluations. Together, these publications offer custody evaluators guidance in many areas such as informed consent, maintaining neutrality, collateral sources of data, communication with attorneys, record keeping, reducing the potential for bias, and the importance of data-informed recommendations.

The AFCC (2016) subsequently issued a supplement to the Model Standards called Guidelines for Examining Intimate Partner Violence, calling for professionals conducting child custody evaluations to acquire specialized training on IPV to assess abuse allegations adequately, understand the effects of abuse on parents and children, and know how to design parenting plans that sufficiently addressed future risks. IPV research has shown an increased likelihood of violence at the time of separation and during divorce (Austin, 2001). Professionals conducting CCEs can benefit from the knowledge that includes not merely the ability to identify IPV but also an understanding of possible risk factors for future violence and how to consider safety needs for children and parents in their recommendations (Saunders, 2015). Therefore, training should include topics such as assessing the credibility of abuse allegations, awareness of one's own biases particularly related to gender and domestic violence, types of IPV, screening for IPV, interview techniques for adults and children, and creating appropriate parenting plans when IPV is a factor. Understanding the current social psychological research should include topics on shared parenting, alienation, suggestibility, gender biases in custody litigation, outcomes for children in divorce, the effect of domestic violence on children and co-parenting, and therapeutic recommendations for families going through separation and divorce.

Professional guidelines differ from licensure standards and legal mandates outlined in state laws with licensing and legal repercussions if not followed. Professionals wanting to ensure their work has gone beyond minimum standards, exceeded judicial requirements, and is based on current evidenced-based practices should strive to meet these guidelines, as can be found in the AFCC Model Standards (2006).

Beginning the Assessment

The initial tasks for conducting a CCE include defining the professional's role, ensuring that the professional does not have a conflict with litigants or their family members (e.g., having served in another capacity such as a therapist), determining the scope of the evaluation, and obtaining informed consent (APA, 2010). Mental health professionals (MHPs) can play many roles in family law litigation. When the role includes or is exclusive to that of a custody evaluator, it is best stated in a court order, making clear to litigants and lawyers that the professional is not providing therapeutic services but is fulfilling a role under the jurisdiction of the court with authority to make custody and parenting time recommendations.

The terminology used to define a MHP's role can vary from state to state; some roles include the possibility of opining on custody and parenting time without explicitly stating that a custody evaluation will be performed. For example, a guardian ad litem may be able to make custody and parenting time recommendations under the umbrella of their duty to assist the court in furthering the children's best interest. It is the second author's recommendation that when the state's legal statutes include specific rules for custody evaluations, the court order should include that statute when the professional's opinions on custody, parenting time (access and possession), and decision-making rights could be expected by the litigants, lawyers, and/or the court. Attorneys wanting to exclude expert opinion about custody that differs from their client's agenda may find support from the court when the role is not defined in the court order to specifically include the right to make custody recommendations pursuant to the duties outlined by the statute.

The scope of the evaluation refers to issues of concern before the court and provides the parameters for the evaluator's investigation (APA, 2010). The AFCC Model Standards (2006) state:

> Evaluators shall establish the scope of the evaluation as determined by the court order or by a signed stipulation by the parties and their attorneys. . . . When circumstances demand that an evaluation be limited in scope, evaluators shall take steps to ensure that the boundaries to the evaluation and the evaluator's role are clearly defined for the litigants, attorneys, and the court. (pp. 13–14)

Referral questions are best defined in the court order but can also be conveyed by attorneys, judges, and the parties during initial consultations (Gould, 1999).

Referral questions can be worded in broad terms such as "What is the best interest of the child?" or specific terms such as "Is the child resisting contact with the mother/father because of harsh parenting?" A recent article by Garber (2020) discussed the potential for extremely narrow referral questions to contribute to confirmation bias by creating an evaluation process that seeks to confirm the stated hypothesis. Garber recommended the following wording in situations where a child is resisting or refusing contact with a parent:

> Parties will enlist a qualified mental health professional to conduct an evaluation intended to summarize the history and quality of the child's relationship with each parent, seeking in particular: (1) to identify the circumstances and precipitant(s) of any change in the quality of those relationships; and (2) to recommend the specific constellation of interventions best suited to

facilitating the child's opportunity to enjoy a healthy relationship with both/all caregivers. (p. 390)

It has been the second author's experience that attorneys seldom ask how to phrase the evaluator's appointment or the referral questions within the court order. However, when evaluators have the opportunity, the wording suggested by Garber could be useful in many family law situations involving custody issues.

Obtaining informed consent respects each person's right to understand the process of an evaluation, the limits to confidentiality, and how the information obtained may be used before agreeing to participate in the process. The APA (2010) recognizes informed consent as a process that "honors the legal rights and personal dignity" of each person (p. 865). While the evaluator's intake forms should include descriptions of services, the process of the evaluation, and the limits of confidentiality, this author recommends that evaluators also discuss these topics in their initial meeting with the client. The dialogue provides an opportunity for the client to ask questions and build trust. It has been this author's experience that most clients have never been through a custody evaluation, and many are extremely nervous. Predictability and knowing what to expect can calm a client who feels overwhelmed and frightened.

Discussion about the evaluation process might include a description of how information is obtained (i.e., interviews, home visits, parent–child observations, collateral information, and documentation submitted by the client and attorney). Limits to confidentiality can be used to build trust with the client and clarify how the evaluation process differs from a therapeutic relationship. Many clients do not understand that a custody evaluation report is public information when included in their file at the courthouse. They also do not know that hearings are public, and information about their family obtained during the evaluation may be shared during testimony. This is extremely pertinent since COVID-19 created the need for video conference hearings. Some jurisdictions have created their own YouTube channels to ensure that hearings are public. Clients appreciate knowing that they can request that their hearing not be televised when testimony includes personal health information and/or private information about their children and that reports including private information can be sealed from public view.

Information Gathering

The primary format for gathering information from parents and children is through interviews, observation, and documentation. Hence, this part of the evaluation process includes individual interviews with each parent, individual interviews with each child, parent–child observations, home visits, testing (either by the evaluator or someone else), collateral contacts, and amassing documentation relevant to the issues. States may vary in the extent to which they outline the duties of the evaluator, but evaluators should confirm that their protocol meets requirements in their state for conducting custody evaluations, realizing that these minimum requirements do not often meet professional expectations. For instance, a custody evaluator in Texas, according to section 107.109 in The Elements of Child Custody Evaluation (Texas Family Code, 2019), is required to conduct a personal interview with the parties, an interview with the child, an observation of the child with each parent, and an interview of each child living in the home. This author has not found one interview with each parent and the child to be sufficient in meeting evidenced-based practices or professional guidelines for conducting child custody evaluations.

Information-gathering activities should minimize the possibility of bias by maintaining neutrality, ensuring that balance and equity are practiced (tasks performed with one parent are also performed with the other), remaining cognizant of diversity issues and issues affecting persons who are victims of abuse (AFCC, 2006, 2016; APA, 2010). Specific to victims of interpersonal violence, evaluators should consider how fear of retaliation or fear of negatively affecting the outcome of the custody litigation may cause the client to minimize their experiences (AFCC, 2016). Evaluators should continue screening for violence between partners, violence directed at children, and assessing risk factors throughout the information gathering process (Austin & Drodz, 2012).

When answers include allegations of violence or indicate high levels of aggression, conflict, and control, follow-up questions should ascertain specific details of the interaction(s) such as dates, who was present, the location, how the incident began, who saw or heard the interaction, whether the client told anyone else about the incident, or if the police were called. This line of questioning helps the evaluator generate a list of collateral contacts and or documents, which can be used to assess the credibility of the allegation (Austin & Drodz, 2012). Additionally, evaluators should identify the form(s) of the violence, the frequency, whether one or both partners initiated the violence, and other situational and contextual variables such as the use of substances, the use of weapons, the involvement of children, and differentiating between an isolated occurrence and a pattern of violence. These variables reflect current frameworks for assessing IPV and child abuse during child custody evaluations (Austin & Drodz, 2012; Jaffe et al. 2008; Kelly & Johnston, 2008).

As mentioned previously in this chapter, legal and administrative aggression is a form of IPV that is particularly relevant to custody litigation, where the parent attempts to use the court, police, and child protective services to gain more custodial time and authority over the children (Harman & Lorandos, 2021). Examples of this type of IPV are filing frequent and unnecessary lawsuits, making false allegations of abuse, making disparaging comments and discrediting public statements that affect employment, and making threats to take or destroy things of value (Berger et al., 2016; Hines et al., 2015). Clients may not identify these behaviors as abusive when answering general questions about conflict. This author has found that this type of controlling and threatening behavior can be easily identified by asking for a history of previous court action, including identification of the person responsible for initiating the action. Each court action can then be explored in more detail during the interview sessions.

Evaluators should not immediately discount abuse allegations when the client does not have corroborating evidence or witnesses. They need to be sensitive to the fact that victims of abuse often do not report the abuse and or hesitate to make it a central focus in divorce litigation (AFCC, 2016). Likewise, they should strive to maintain objectivity and consider that persons involved in divorce litigation may also have motivations to distort negative information to gain an advantage in custody litigation (Austin, 2000). Males have reported a reluctance to leave their marriages because of fear that their wives will make false abuse claims against them, which could limit their time with the children (Hines & Douglas, 2010). Females have reported fears of retaliation if they expose their partner's abusive behaviors during custody litigation (Saccuzzo et al., 2004). Therefore, custody evaluators need to ensure that their relationship-building efforts and interview style allow the client an opportunity to build trust and feel safe enough to disclose these behaviors if they have occurred.

Testing Instruments

Custody evaluators often use testing instruments to help identify incidents and patterns of abuse, personality disorders, and parenting attitudes and to assess the credibility of abuse allegations. The APA Guidelines (2010) and AFCC Model Standards (2006) direct evaluators to articulate specific reasons for the testing instruments selected, document the ways custody litigation could affect testing results, familiarize themselves with the validity and reliability of the instruments chosen, and gain experience and training in administering, scoring, and interpreting the tests they use.

The Controlling and Abusive Tactics Questionnaire (CAT-2-C) is a 37-item questionnaire that specifically looks at the frequency with which the client and their partner engaged in psychologically and emotionally abusive behaviors (Hamel et al., 2015). The CTS and the Conflict Tactic Scales (CTS-2) are the most widely used and accurate measures of relationship abuse and consider roles of victimization and perpetration within the context of conflict. The CTS-2 measures physical, psychological, and sexual abuse as well as rates of injuries (Straus et al., 1996). The reader should refer to Chapter 11 in this volume by Hamel and Ennis for an in-depth discussion of the CTS and other instruments that can help the evaluator assess deception. Other sources for assessing the presence and type(s) of abuse include the Mediator's Assessment of Safety Issues and Concerns (MAISC; Holtzworth-Munroe et al., 2010), the Battered Women's Justice Project (BWJP, 2015) initial screening form (the questions are applicable to female and male victims), or the Domestic Violence in Child Custody (DVCC) questionnaire (Drodz, 2008).

Personality and characterological disorders are often found in perpetrators of abuse. The Minnesota Multiphasic Personality Inventory (MMPI-2), the Millon Clinical Multiaxial Inventory (MCMI-III), and the Personality Assessment Inventory (PAI) are the most widely used objective personality tests for custody evaluations. Projective tests, such as the Rorschach and the Thematic Apperception Test (TAT), are often used to infer personality traits/dynamics from stories told by clients as they view realistic or amorphous pictures. The Rorschach is the most widely used and researched projective test for use in custody evaluations. Parenting inventories such as the Parenting Stress Index (PSI; Abidin, 1990), the Parent-Child Relationship Inventory (PCRI; Gerard, 1994), and the Parent Behavior Checklist (PBC; Fox, 1994) are used by some custody evaluators and are most helpful when combined with other testing data, collateral information, documentation, and interview data (Stahl, 2011).

The MMPI-2, MCMI-III, and the PAI include validity scales that, when combined with other testing results and interview data, can increase the evaluator's level of confidence in the overall validity of the client's reporting. The Miller Forensic Assessment of Symptoms Test (M-FAST; Miller, 2001) is a 25-item questionnaire that assesses the likelihood that a client is exaggerating mental health symptoms related to victimization. The Children's Exposure to Domestic Violence (CEDV) is a 45-item questionnaire that provides a measure, from the child's perspective, of their exposure to domestic violence (Edelson et al., 2008). Custody evaluators who do not conduct psychological testing should consult with the testing psychologist to ensure their understanding of the personality testing results are accurate and discuss additional variables that impacted the client's validity scale scores. Many of the instruments mentioned here do not require the administrator to be a licensed psychologist, but evaluators should ensure they are working within their licensing parameters and seek consultation for testing results when necessary.

When there are allegations of IPV, it is recommended that evaluators strive to fully understand the events and the context in which the behavior occurred, including whether aggressive behaviors between the parents were caused by one or both parties. Violence between one or both parents should also include to what extent the children observed or were involved in the conflict. Research has shown that children of divorce are most affected by parental conflict when they observe it or are caught in the middle of it, which can include being told about the conflict, being cautioned about the danger of the other parent, being used as a messenger between the parents, being asked to keep notes on the parent, and/or being asked to report abusive behavior that they did not witness to other people (Baker & Darnall, 2006; Harman et al., 2018; Nielson, 2017). When parents compartmentalize their conflict so that the children are not involved, current research indicates that children are not negatively affected. Their long-term outcomes improve by having as much time possible with both parents after divorce (Nielson, 2017).

Identification of the type of violence, how often it occurred, the nature of the injuries sustained, who was responsible or instigated the aggression, who was affected by the behavior, future risks to parents and children, the potential impact on parenting, and lethality risks help the evaluator organize the data by type and level of concerns and potential risks, and makes the synthesis of the data more manageable (AFCC 2016; Austin & Drodz, 2012; Johnston et al., 2009).

INTERVIEWS

The importance of an evaluator's interview style while assessing for IPV was acknowledged by Holtzworth et al., (2010) in the development of the Mediators Assessment of Safety Issues and Concerns (MASIC). A semistructured interview format includes aspects of an unstructured and structured interview style. The questions given to both parents are the same, which is typically in a structured format. However, the evaluator may pursue additional information when responses warrant further explanation or description. It is recommended that additional questions be reserved for clients until both parents have completed the same set of initial questions. Current research has not provided reliability and validity measurements for semistructured interviews. However, the literature in forensic science supports a consensus that a semistructured format has greater reliability than unstructured formats, where evaluators may ask a myriad of various questions to each party, some of which may not be the same (Gould & Martindale, 2007).

The second author uses an intake form and a semistructured interview questionnaire composed of many questions suggested by Stahl (2011), which allow parents to respond independently and during individual interviews with the evaluator. Both include questions that provide opportunities for the evaluator to assess, among other things, parental conflict, aggression, discipline, substance abuse, and power and control dynamics. Some examples include the following: How do you think the conflict between you and _____ (the other parent) affects the child(ren)? How do you think your feelings about _____ affect the child(ren)? What do you like about _____? How do you discipline? How do you contribute to the conflict between you and (spouse or ex-spouse)? What can you do to improve the co-parenting relationship? What happens when you try to talk to _____?

The author has found that conducting the semistructured interview in three to six 1-hour increments over a 2- to 6-week period allows multiple opportunities to interact with clients. The variety of questions gives parents the chance to share positive memories and information about their children and consider more difficult issues related to past and present conflict and its effects. This timing allows parents to reflect on the questions and their answers. Often, clients remember an example that describes something they mentioned in the previous session, or they expand on their answer, providing reasons why they acted or responded during the marriage in a certain way, or they may remember that a friend or relative witnessed a concerning event and want to add that person to their collateral list. However, if the essential facts regarding domestic violence incidents are reported differently from one interview session to the next, the evaluator makes a note of the inconsistencies in the client's report, as it reduces credibility and the ultimate weight of the incident on final recommendations.

In general, interviews with parents should elicit information that helps the evaluator identify and assess historical patterns of relationship, family dynamics, the quality of parent–child relationships, how conflict is managed, child development knowledge, parenting skills and characteristics, co-parenting ability and future capacity, concerns the parents have for one another's parenting and/or relationship with the children, major physical and/or emotional health issues, risk factors for future abusive behavior and/or exposure to violence, preferences for custody and parenting time (including justifications for their preferences), work schedules and child care options/plans, and each parent's willingness to support and nurture the child's relationship with the other parent (Austin & Drodz, 2012; Gould & Martindale, 2007; Gould & Stahl, 2000; Stahl, 1994, 2011).

Interviews with children should be age-appropriate and aim to provide the evaluator with information that helps the evaluator understand the quality of the child's relationship with each parent and with each of their siblings, the child's current functioning, the child's educational, emotional, and physical well-being, the child's preferences for parenting time with each parent, and the child's exposure to violence, in order to provide the evaluator some sense of the child's personality, unique interests, and temperament (Stahl, 2011). When the child's answers regarding likes, interests, activities, friends, and school reflect the parents' answers about the child on the same topics, the evaluator has some assurance that the parents know and understand the unique aspects of their child, which in part speaks to the quality of the relationship between them.

A semistructured format can be used with children over the age of 4 years and can be conducted while children are engaged in age-appropriate activities like Legos, arts and crafts, or sand tray. For example, information that speaks to the child's relationship with each parent might be ascertained by asking, "What are your favorite things to do with your mom/with your dad? Tell me something you do not like about your mom/dad? Who do you go to when you need help with something? Who helps you with your homework? How do they help you? How do you get to school in the morning? Who else is awake when you get up?" Assessing after-school routines helps the evaluator understand the differences between the households and differences in the caretaking behaviors of the parents (e.g., How do you get home from school? Who is home when you get there? What do you do when you get home? Who cooks dinner? Where does everyone eat?). Asking questions about favorite activities with each parent can provide the evaluator with information about quality time and caretaker involvement in child-centered activities (Stahl, 2011). Asking the child how it feels when their parents speak negatively about each other provides the evaluator with information regarding potentially alienating behaviors and the extent to which the child may be experiencing loyalty binds. Depending on the answer to this question, the evaluator may need to follow up and ask for specific examples about what is being said to the child. Parental alienation behaviors include badmouthing a parent to the child or where the child can hear, limiting time with a parent, asking the child to spy on the parent, making the child choose between the parents, and telling the child that they are not safe with the other parent or that the other parent has abused or neglected them (Baker & Darnall, 2006; Kelly & Johnston, 2001). Parents in the early stages of divorce often make mistakes and knowingly or unknowingly expose their children to negative comments or adult information. When these behaviors are severe and rise to the level of causing harm to the child's relationship with the other parent, they are recognized as a form of psychological and emotional abuse (Clawar & Rivlin, 2013, Harman et al., 2018; Warshak, 2013). For additional information on alienating behaviors, the reader can refer to Chapter 10 in volume text by Harman and Kruk.

The parent–child relationship can be overlooked in a custody evaluation where the concerns of the parents are more focused on each other and their deficiencies as spouses than they are on the parents' relationship with and their parenting of the children (Gould & Martindale, 2007). When one parent appears to be taking on more responsibility than the other parent, the author finds it useful to ask some additional questions about caretaking when the parents were still living together to assess how the parents divided responsibilities during the marriage. Evaluators may need to consider the amount of time a parent has been functioning as a single parent before concluding that the parent is unwilling or incapable of managing certain tasks and include some follow-up questions about how the parent would like to share in parenting more and why they have not done so yet. The extent to which the parent is child focused, can relate to the child in developmentally appropriate ways, keep the child safe, respond to their emotional and physical needs, and nurture the relationship between the child and the other parent are qualities that the evaluator will want to assess. Protocols that require each parent to bring the child to an interview session address the need for equity in the evaluation process and provide additional opportunities to observe the child in each parent's care.

Parent–Child Observations

Parent–child observations allow evaluators to gain information that informs "goodness of fit" criterion. They can be conducted in an office or home setting and are recommended by the APA and required by some state laws governing custody evaluations (APA, 2010; Texas Family Code, 2019). Home visits provide opportunities to assess parenting skills and the parent–child relationship in the family's natural environment, while in-office observations provide information from a more controlled environment. When the child is under 4 years of age, this author performs an unstructured parent–child observation in her office playroom, where the parent and the child interact in nondirected play, and observes the parent–child interactions in each parent's home. Parent–child observations can be structured or unstructured.

A structured observation involves the parent and the child engaging in a structured activity designated by the evaluator (e.g., build something together with these blocks, or the parent might instruct the child in a clean-up activity). An unstructured observation allows the evaluator to observe the parent and child in free play (Acklin & Cho-Statler, 2006). AFCC (2006) advises that "Evaluators shall be mindful of the fact that their presence in the same physical environment as those being observed creates a risk that they will influence the very behaviors and interactions that they are endeavoring to observe." The value of parent–child observations has been debated by some psychologists who believe that the information gained is most likely tainted by the presence of the evaluator (Bricklin,

1995). Others have noted the value of seeing parents and children interact in neutral as well as natural settings such as their home, despite the lack of scientific evidence to support that the observations yield reliable information (Ackerman, 1995; Hynan, 2003; Stahl, 1994).

The author has found observations of children, both in the office and in their home environment, to be particularly useful. The neutral office setting provides privacy for conducting the semistructured interview questions, some of which may be difficult for a child to answer in the home when an honest answer may include negative comments about the parent. A natural observation in each home yields a different type of information, such as the style and quality of sibling interactions, parent–child interactions, family dynamics, the differences/similarities in the parents' homes, and whether the home environment reflects the child's interests and achievements. Hynan (2003) recommends a minimum of two 45- to 60-minute sessions between each parent and child. This author conducts at least one 60-minute observation at each home and considers the extent to which her presence may have affected the behavior of those observed. She does not hesitate to visit the home more than once, especially if the child and/or parent's behavior during the home visit was notably different than what was observed during other interactions. An additional consideration is given to the amount of time the parent and child have lived in the home. When parents have recently separated, the parent with the new home may not have an equal number of pictures, toys, furniture, or child memorabilia as the parent who remained in the marital residence. This should not be construed as a lack of interest in the child's activities and achievements unless other information supports that hypothesis.

There are formal and informal coding systems available for parent–child observations. The reader can refer to Hynan (2003) for a discussion on the System for Coding Interactions and Family Functioning (SCIFF) and the Family Problem Solving Guide (FAMPROS). Additional options for formal coding systems are discussed in Kerig and Lindhahl (2001). An informal coding system should include notes on reciprocity during interactions, attunement, compliance, overcontrol or undercontrol, intrusiveness, encouraging autonomy, cooperation, limit setting, negative behaviors toward the parent, and avoidance of the parent. Information obtained from parent–child observations that does not converge with other collateral data provided by teachers, therapists, or coaches should have limited diagnostic value regarding its accurate representation of the parent–child relationship (Acklin & Cho-Statler, 2006).

Collateral Information

Collateral information is part of the information-gathering phase and often confirms and disconfirms information about the events and topics discussed by parents and children during individual interview sessions. As with other evaluation tasks, professionals should consult their state family law statutes to determine legal requirements regarding information gained from third parties as part of a custody evaluation. In Texas, the code directs the evaluator to talk to all persons with relevant information about the child (Texas Family Code, 2019). However, the determination of what constitutes relevant information, who possesses that information, and to what extent it affects recommendations is left to the judgment of the evaluator (AFCC, 2016).

Professional guidelines encourage the use of multiple and diverse methods of information gathering to enhance the reliability and validity of the evaluator's findings, opinions, and recommendations (AFCC, 2006; APA, 2010). Possible sources of collateral information are teachers, therapists, school counselors, special education directors, doctors, coaches, friends, family members, camp directors, preschool directors, private childcare providers, ex-spouses/significant others, current significant others, police officers, and housekeepers. Collaterals may provide information through written or oral means and may submit relevant records about the parents and/or the child such as email communications, school records, therapy notes, bank statements, CPS reports, legal reports, school reports, diaries and journals, audio and video recordings, letters and cards, and psychological testing. The evaluator uses their own judgment to determine the weight and credibility of the information obtained (AFCC, 2016). The Model Standards (AFCC, 2006) state, "Valid collateral source information is critical to a thorough evaluation. Sufficiency and reliability of collateral source information is a determination to be made by the child custody evaluator" (p. 12). The Model Standards remind evaluators to gather information from many sources, consider alternative hypotheses, consider whether the collateral has relevant and important information, include oral and written sources of information, and reveal limitations in their reports when collateral information was not available or could not be obtained.

Collateral sources should help in making informed decisions on how to share information about the family. Limits of confidentiality, the scope of the evaluator's work, and the way in which the information may be used (e.g., in a written report as support for recommendations and/or findings) are disclosures that should be included, as they can increase the safety for collaterals. This is particularly important for collaterals which are providing information or have witnessed abuse between the parents and/or between the parent(s) and the child(ren).

A determination of who should provide collateral information occurs throughout all stages of the evaluation. This author has no knowledge of research suggesting that identification of collaterals should be limited to one specific phase. She strives for a complete and thorough investigation such that information gained from new collaterals which can confirm, disconfirm, or otherwise increase her knowledge of an event or family dynamic may serve to strengthen the reliability and validity of her findings and recommendations. Initial paperwork includes a release of a confidential information form used for professionals such as teachers, lawyers, therapists, and doctors, and a form for references who are nonprofessionals with relevant information about the parents and the children. The process of gathering history and answering the semistructured interview questions may reveal several additional people who need to be added to the reference form and the release of information form. Additionally, if events occur during the evaluation process, new collaterals who witnessed the event may be included. For example, if a parent angrily confronts the other parent at the child's basketball game, other parents who witnessed the exchange become relevant collateral sources.

Professional judgment is used in determining the weight of the information provided by collateral sources (AFCC, 2006). Eyewitness accounts are generally more valuable than information that was shared with the collateral by a parent or by someone else and are reflected in the court's value for evidence gained firsthand as opposed to hearsay. However, when assessing all forms of abuse, the evaluator must consider that domestic violence often occurs without anyone ever seeing it, many times going unreported to lawmakers or therapists. Clients may minimize them for fear of retaliation. In these cases, a relative or close friend may have been the only person sought out after a particular incident. These collaterals can provide information that increases the credibility of the partners' accounts regarding the event, even though they did not witness the interaction. They can also provide information about the emotional, psychological, and physical injuries sustained. When collateral information is limited, it should be noted as limited in its reliability, and the reasons for the limitations should be shared in the report (AFCC, 2006; Gould & Martindale, 2007).

Synthesis of the Data

At this point in the process, the evaluator should continually revise hypotheses as collected data confirm or disconfirm them. This back-and-forth process continues as the data are categorized and organized around the significant events, the primary concerns of the clients, and the themes that have been identified (Drodz et al., 2013). Data should be viewed in terms of the potential impact of IPV behaviors on co-parenting capacity; quality of parenting; maintaining a secure relationship with each child; ability to engage in activities that support developmentally appropriate and enriching activities, respect of the child's unique personality, and nurture a positive sense of self; ability to provide physically, emotionally, and financially for the child; encourage age-appropriate responsibility and autonomy; engage in appropriate discipline and monitoring; and allow the child age-appropriate social activity and independence (AFCC, 2016; Austin, 2000; Austin & Drodz, 2012; Gould & Martindale, 2013; Saunders, 2013).

The data supporting partner violence and child abuse should describe how the violence impacted the parent and the child during the marriage and consider the potential of how it could affect the parent and the child after divorce. By organizing collateral information and data provided by the clients, an evaluator can assess future risks of violence, which consider patterns of aggression, level of aggression, type of aggression, the harm sustained, and the persons affected. Recommendations for parenting time, decision-making, and co-parenting should reflect findings and consider the future safety of the parent and the children (AFCC, 2016; Austin, 2000; Austin & Drodz, 2012; Saunders, 2013).

In situations when a child is resisting or rejecting contact with a parent, an evaluator will need to analyze and organize the data so that it informs the court as to the reasons for the child's resistance/rejection. There can be many reasons why a child is refusing contact with a parent during separation and divorce, ranging from justified reasons such as abuse and poor parenting to unjustified reasons such as psychological manipulation and alienation (Drodz & Olesen, 2004; Garber, 2020; Harman et al., 2018). Sorting out the data can be complicated by the fact that extremely alienated children can distort normal parenting flaws during interviews with the evaluator (Baker, 2018; Baker & Darnall, 2006; Clawar & Rivlin, 2013; Warshak, 2013). Evaluators should review Amy Baker's (2018) Four Factor Model for assessment of parental alienation; the Decision-Making Tree for differentiating estrangement from alienation (Drodz & Olesen, 2004; Drodz et al., 2013); and Clawar and Rivlin (2013) for programming and brainwashing strategies used by parents in custody litigation. Bernet et al. (2020) found evidence that the Parental Acceptance Rejection Questionnaire (PARQ) differentiated alienated children from abused children.

There is no one "official" way to write a custody evaluation report. The evaluation needs to have collected the required information as defined by family law statutes and recommended by professional guidelines. However, the organization of the information within the report is left to the discretion of the evaluator. Professionals need to find the format that works best for them. This author suggests asking for feedback from lawyers and clients and reading reports written by other seasoned professionals. In an organized and clear manner, the report should explain the integration of the clinician's judgments, grounded in the data obtained and using the scientific literature to support the recommendations and data interpretation (Gould & Stahl, 2000). The recommendations for custody and treatment (if needed) usually follow the body of the report, such that it is clear to the reader why certain recommendations were made. Citations for research supporting the recommendations and the evaluator's judgments conclude the report.

CHILD CUSTODY RECOMMENDATIONS

Consider these additional brief case summaries:

Case 3
The father admits to having grabbed his wife on a couple of occasions in the past, after their children were born, each time during a period of tension and escalated marital conflict. He has not been physically violent for more than 2 years but sometimes yells at her. She yells back and often initiates the verbal abuse. The father, due to how he was raised, does not spank his kids, and monitors carefully how he speaks to them, whereas the mother often yells at the kids, and recently slapped her 13-year-old daughter in the face for being disrespectful. Who should get custody, and why?

Case 4

The mother is seen on video screaming at her husband, begging him not to leave, while holding a frightened child in her arms, as he pleads for her to calm down. He has been arrested twice on misdemeanor domestic violence charges, has cheated on her, and has left her alone at home for days at a time. By herself, she can barely manage their young children. Her attorney says her screaming is an understandable emotional reaction to his abuse; his attorney claims that he only leaves to get away from her unpredictable physical and emotional outbursts. Who should get custody, and why?

General Considerations

Based on the principle that custody time, visitation, orders of protection, and counseling recommendations should reflect the extent of substantiated partner abuse and child abuse, the recommendations in Table 9.1 are listed from least restrictive to most restrictive, alongside the four major abuse levels, listed from least to most severe: low, low/moderate, moderate/high, and high. The levels reflect, in general terms, the severity, frequency, and time frame of the abuse (e.g., did it emerge long before, or during, the period of separation) and whether it was physical, sexual, or psychological. The latter include parental alienation behaviors and legal and administrative abuse. The highest priority is given to "the safety of the child, the parties, and other involved individuals" (AFCC, 2016, p. 4).

Due to space limitations and for purposes of flexibility, we give a range of custody and intervention options for each level, considering whether the abuse was perpetrated against the children, against a partner, or both. We also factor in whether the partner conflict or abuse was witnessed by the children and whether it was unidirectional or bidirectional. Recommendations for counseling include mediation, co-parent counseling, individual therapy, child therapy, anger management, batterer intervention programs, and child–parent reunification therapy. Not included is substance abuse or other mental health counseling, depending on the needs of the family. For an intervention to work, it must address the risk factors relevant to the client. These are implied within each of the four levels (e.g., high-conflict couples lack adequate impulse control and conflict resolution skills), but the full panoply of risk factors and how a client might respond to the intervention(s) can only be determined on a case-by-case basis.

Custody and Visitation

The suggestions in Table 9.1 are generic, meant as a rough guide with which to navigate the myriad of factors warranting investigation in child custody evaluations, rather than a specific set of recommendations for any particular case. The types of child and partner abuse included at each level do not always match up with one another in real-world settings (e.g., couples who engage in SCV may engage in moderate to severe child abuse). There is some overlap between the levels (in a high-conflict relationship, the parties may have, in some circumstances, behaved like batterers, e.g., highly jealous, making threats). Within the spectrum of recommended treatment for a given level (e.g., up to 26 weeks of anger management and or parenting counseling for SCV/separation and divorce violence), the amount should be lowest when there is only one type of abuse and highest when both are present. The extent of bidirectionality in abuse between the parents does not in itself indicate what form the abuse takes. Are both physically violent, or is one more likely to perpetrate physical aggression and the other psychological aggression? As indicated in an earlier section, victims often find the latter more impactful, but only when chronic and severe. Not factored in Table 9.1 is whether other forms of family abuse, such as abuse between the siblings or by a child toward a parent, contribute to family stress and dysfunction. The extent to which they do will determine whether family-centered modalities of treatment should be recommended.

The presence of child witnesses is an important consideration. In cases of high-conflict or SCV/separation and divorce violence, there is a lesser risk to a child, even if they have witnessed or heard some of the violence, if the offending party or parties are getting help and a restraining order is in place. In cases involving chronic battering or intimate terrorism, however, it must be assumed that the children are at least indirectly affected (the victim's parenting abilities have been compromised) or likely to witness the abuse later, either against the victimized parent or a new partner. A competent evaluation must investigate the extent to which the children were impacted by the abuse they witnessed. Which parent is the greater threat to the child when one parent primarily engages in psychological abuse and the other primarily engages in physical abuse? The seriousness of the threat also depends on severity and chronicity, as does the existence of partner abuse by one parent and child abuse and neglect by another, illustrated in Case 3. Here, careful interviewing and testing can provide some guidance. One child may articulate greater fear of the father's spankings than mother's physical assaults on the dad, whereas it may be the exact opposite for another child, perhaps a sibling in the same house. If the child does not exhibit any symptoms, internalized (e.g., anxiety) or externalized (aggression), how should that affect visitation or counseling recommendations? As with children who did not witness the violence that nonetheless had a severe impact on the adult victim, it must be assumed that the functioning of a child who has experienced high levels of family abuse may eventually deteriorate if the offending parent is not held accountable.

In Table 9.1, we note the importance of child preferences as one way to resolve custody decisions when both parents are abusive, short of severe child abuse or intimate terrorism. However, child preferences must be weighed in the context of their age and development and the favored parent's ability to adequately care for the child, including the use of positive parenting practices. A key consideration is whether the attachment bond between parent and child is a healthy one, not shaped by the effects of parental alienating behaviors nor toxic identification with a highly domineering parent. Given the complexities of family relationships, it would seem to be a herculean task to tease out precisely the extent to which the perpetration of domestic violence by one parent against the other is indeed "detrimental to the best interest of the child." Research indicates that a child need not have witnessed incidents of physical abusive or coercive control to be affected if the abuse has interfered with the victim's ability to parent. If the latter, how does that impact, in turn, affect the child, independent of the victimized parent's own parenting behaviors?

An example would be when a mother is depressed due to the chronic battering she has experienced, and she takes her frustrations out on the children and/or is so psychologically compromised that she is unable to properly care for them. Who is the greater threat—the father or the mother? If both are a threat, should preference be given to the mother, who can be presumed to re-establish a loving relationship with her children once she has escaped the violence, or to the father if he shows rapid progress in a batterer intervention program? Research suggests that abused mothers do overcome the effects of the abuse once they are safe (e.g., Bogat et al., 2004; Levendosky et al., 2007). Is the mother more deserving of our sympathy because she is an IPA victim, or the father, whose behavior may be driven by long-standing family-of-origin trauma? In the example given in Case 4, the picture is even more complicated, given mom's mental health issues. Her emotional outbursts are a threat to the children, yet how dependable a caregiver could the father be, given his philandering? The research does not provide clear-cut answers to these questions. Value judgments seem almost inevitable, so the evaluator must be especially attentive to personal biases. A guiding principle is that a child's best interests are compromised when the benefits gained from avoidance of further abuse exposure and its consequences are less than the psychological impact of separation from an otherwise good parent.

Intervention Options

Custody evaluators should make treatment recommendations based on the risk posed by family abusers to the children and the victimized party. Treating therapists, in turn, are expected to follow the relevant guidelines set forth by their licensing bodies and, where they apply, guidelines for cases involving child custody. According to the California Association of Family and Conciliation Courts, court-involved therapists (CITs) should have competence and knowledge in child development, child interviewing and suggestibility, domestic violence, child abuse, special needs issues such as substance abuse, and high-conflict dynamics, including risks to children from exposure to parental conflict, parental undermining, alienation, and estrangement (AFCC, 2010).

The Risk-Needs-Responsivity Model

The intervention recommendations in Table 9.1 follow long-established principles established by the governing bodies of professional mental health organizations, which are presented in the corrections field, including domestic violence, as the risk-needs-responsivity (RNR) model of treatment (see Roberts, Chapter 12, this volume). In this model, the first R refers to the amount of treatment necessary to proportionately address the level of risk posed to the victims. This translates in child custody cases as the amount of treatment based on future risk to children of being directly abused or having to witness partner abuse, and the risk posed to the victimized parents that such abuse might have on their parenting abilities, as determined by the evaluation procedures described in the previous section. In criminal cases, some of the most widely used and established domestic violence risk assessment instruments include the SARA and the ODARA (see Hamel & Ennis, Chapter 11, this volume). The N refers to the various client needs (problems) that must be addressed for treatment to be effective (e.g., low income, poor impulse control, aggressive personality, relationship conflict). Risk and need are addressed in Table 9.1, with more extended periods of perpetrator treatment suggested for cases involving battering, where behavior is chronic and likely to persist, and rooted more in personality rather than situational factors involving poor communication and conflict resolution skills. Finally, the second R stands for how treatment is delivered. "The responsivity principle," as described by Stewart et al. (2013), "stresses . . . the successful matching of treatment strategies to their learning styles, motivation level, and cultural context" (pp. 512–513).

Perpetrator Treatment

Criminal justice statutes regulating batterer intervention programs (BIPs) for criminally convicted domestic violence offenders vary from state to state, mandating as few as 16 and as many as 52 group sessions. These one-size-fits-all programs, which usually prohibit individual and family treatment, were established at the behest of victim advocates as a very generic response to domestic violence, with little input, if any, from mental health professionals or family violence researchers. They can be effective with family court litigants, but the length and modality of the intervention should be case specific (Babcock et al., 2016). SCV and separation and divorce/violence offenders do not fit a "batterer" profile; unless they have been criminally convicted, referral to a BIP is contraindicated. A standard, skills-building cognitive-behavioral-type anger management program is the more appropriate option for such clients, with a parenting component or additional parenting counseling when child abuse and neglect have been found. When the abuse is primarily directed at the children, one option is a so-called child abuser program. In California, such programs are regulated under PC 271.3; allow for a combination of group, individual, and family therapy; and services must be delivered by a licensed mental health professional (California Legislative Information, 2021c). An in-depth discussion of the San Francisco Bay Area program can be found in Pratt and Chapman (2007).

For the various types of batterers described in Table 9.1, a BIP is an appropriate intervention, where, depending on the treatment model, clients can acquire the impulse control and relationship-building skills available in anger management, along with help overcoming their deeply ingrained aggressive tendencies, childhood-of-origin and trauma issues, and gendered attitudes of entitlement (Hamel, 2014). Examples of the latter include dismissing one's partner as being too "emotional" or expecting sex on demand (male entitlement); or expecting the partner to work an exorbitant number of hours to maintain an extravagant lifestyle, assuming that children "belong" with the mother, or justifying physical assaults on one's partner because he's a man and should just "take it" (female entitlement). In cases involving a chronic history of serious abuse perpetration, especially when testing reveals evidence of serious personality disfunction, a separate course of individual psychotherapy should be recommended in addition to the batterer intervention program.

Child custody evaluators should be aware that professional licensure is not required of BIP group facilitators in many states. Some, such as California, allow peer counselors who lack many of the AFCC competency requirements cited earlier and have a surprisingly poor understanding of domestic violence dynamics (Cannon et al., 2016). It should also be pointed out that many of the programs that identify as "pro-feminist," such as the Duluth model, while appropriate for men who hold misogynistic or highly patriarchal attitudes, is contraindicated for most other men, who have different issues and would feel uncomfortable and unmotivated in such an environment. Research supports the responsivity principle, according to which the relationship between therapist and client, or group facilitator and members, is more important than the particular philosophy of treatment, and client preferences are a key in establishing a working therapeutic relationship. Such a relationship is compromised when there is too much of a mismatch between client needs and intervention model, and thus a lack of responsivity (Babcock et al., 2016; Hamel, 2020b). The responsivity principle also suggests that the treatment modality should be tailored to the client's learning style. Therefore, notwithstanding the unique benefits of the group format, family court litigants should be allowed to work on anger/battering issues in individual therapy if they have such a preference. In one-on-one sessions, clients can learn the same impulse control and conflict skills while exploring the issues causing and maintaining their abusive behavior in greater depth. An in-depth treatment model is available in the excellent volume by Murphy and Eckhardt (2005).

Conjoint and Family Counseling

Most IPA is bidirectional, and both parents, in some way or another, are involved in the complexities of family abuse, given the multiple pathways of abuse and its effects and the central mediating role of stress. Often, then, the treatment recommendations for family abuse perpetrators outlined in Table 9.1 apply to both parents.

Wherever possible, then, the parents should be encouraged to participate in conjoint sessions and or therapy involving other family members. The advantages of these modalities include an opportunity for the clinician to observe couples

Table 9.1 Custody Plans and Family Abuse

Type of Family Abuse	Child Witness to PA	Interventions	Custody Limitations
LOW LEVEL—CA/N: Yelling, anger displays. PA: High conflict	No	None	None
	Yes	Mediation, co-parent counseling if conflict is chronic and intense. Therapy for the children, if necessary. Up to 16 sessions of anger management counseling/parenting class for dominant aggressor.	None
LOW/MODERATE LEVEL—CA/N: Verbal abuse, mild CP, no injuries. PA: SCV/ separation and divorce violence	No	Mediation, co-parent counseling. Up to 26 weeks of anger management counseling for perpetrators.	None
	Yes	Mediation, co-parent counseling. Therapy for the children, victim. Up to 26 weeks of anger management counseling/ parenting for perpetrators.	Limited period of supervised visitation for perpetrator. If both partners are abusive, primary custody should be determined by child preferences, parental strengths.

Level	CA/N	Treatment	Custody/Visitation
MODERATE/HIGH LEVEL—CA/N: Moderate physical and psychological abuse, neglect. PA: Common battering	No	Mediation, co-parent counseling only if safe. Therapy for the children. Up to 52-week batterer intervention/parent group for perpetrators.	Short-term order of protection. Limited period of supervised visitation for perpetrator; regular visitation determined by (1) evidence of stalking/harassment; (2) impact of IPA on victim's ability to parent, (3) extent of direct child abuse, and (4) how quickly offending parent takes responsibility. If both parents are abusive, primary custody should be determined by child preferences, parental strengths.
	Yes	Mediation, co-parent counseling only if safe. Therapy for the children, victim. Up to 52-week batterer intervention/parent group for perpetrator.	Order of protection. Supervised visits/reunification therapy until perpetrator has demonstrated sufficient treatment progress. If both parents are abusive, primary custody should be determined by child preferences, parental strengths, and verified ability of at least one parent to assume responsibility.
HIGH LEVEL—CA/N: Severe physical, psychological abuse and neglect. PA: Intimate terrorism	No/Yes	Therapy for the children. Refer victim to shelter services and individual therapy. 52-week batterer intervention/parenting group, and individual therapy for perpetrator.	Long-term order of protection. No visitations initially for perpetrator. Supervised visits/reunification therapy can commence when perpetrator has demonstrated sufficient treatment progress, and children feel safe. Remove children from home if both parents are abusive.

CA/N, child abuse and neglect; IPA, intimate partner abuse; PA, partner abuse.

and family dynamics, gauge client progress, and provide an environment in which everyone is learning the same information and acquiring the same set of skills more accurately. There is no attempt to reunite the parents, as with intact families, but rather to facilitate cooperation and begin the healing process. Sound guidelines for family interventions in custody cases can be found in Greenberg et al. (2019). The reader is referred to Hamel (2014), Hamel and Nicholls (2007), and Cooper and Vetere (2005) for resources on working with violent families. Suggestions on how to work with families disputing custody can be found in Carolla (2007). They include a description of *therapeutic supervised visitation*, an alternative to standard visitation arrangements that can provide a bridge to later parent–child reconciliation and other family therapy sessions. See Hamel (2008) for an account of the initial resistance to family interventions for IPA and the many safe and effective approaches that have since been developed, many by staunch self-identified feminist therapists. The review by Eckhardt et al. (2013) documents best practices for working with IPA victims.

Johnston et al. (2009) outlines the best therapeutic practices in cases involving parental alienation, with the aligned parent, the rejected parent, and the children. Therapeutic interventions for alienation cases are determined by the severity of the child's resistance to the parent. The reader should refer to Warshak (2020) for the most current discussion on managing and treating parental alienation cases.

Because the parental subsystem is key to the safety and well-being of a family, systemic interventions in child custody cases involving high conflict and abuse must begin with the parents. Sessions should be conducted by competent therapists who have expertise with divorcing couples and domestic violence, are competent in managing highly charged situations, can effectively set limits, and can intervene when there is evidence of power and control behaviors (Gutierrez, 2008). "A lack of appropriate structure, clarity, and definition at the outset of the treatment," writes Smith (2016), "can later undermine the progress of the therapy" (p. 500). Johnston et al. (2009) suggest that co-parenting sessions should be conducted in stages, beginning with an initial agreement. This is followed by an assessment of the issues and how parental conflict and abuse have impacted the children, and then a neutral reformulation of the issues to engage cooperation. Throughout the course of treatment, the clinician copes with client resistance and ongoing conflict and, ideally, can help the clients resolve their issues. Termination comprises the final stage, with follow-up sessions as necessary.

> The therapist should always be on the lookout for any signs of bullying or, alternatively, evidence of fear, but discussions about past events, including incidents of partner violence, are to be avoided. Working with average or high conflict couples the therapist may allow some bickering and conflict in order to assess the couple's level of dysfunction; however, this is a dubious luxury when conducting co-parenting sessions. The therapist must insist that the parties talk to one another with respect and focus on solutions and be prepared to instruct them in how this is to be done. (Hamel, 2014, p. 195)

Except for cases involving chronic battering, claims by custody litigants that they are "not safe" if in the same room with the ex-partner should be given consideration but not automatically believed. Especially in an adversarial setting such as the family court system, reports by litigants that they are in fear should be interpreted with caution, given the highly subjective nature of emotions and the possibility of legal and administrative abuse. Still, conjoint sessions would not be appropriate for couples who are unable to work productively during the sessions or still acting out with aggression outside the therapy office. In such cases, parallel conjoint sessions are a reasonable alternative. These should be conducted by the same therapist, who, ideally, works in close collaboration with other treatment providers—the batterer intervention, anger management, and parenting programs, as well as those working with other family members, including the victims. When interparental conflict is protracted, some states allow for a court-ordered parent coordinator to act as the de facto case manager, but more directly and with more authority (Deutsch et al., 2018; Sullivan & Burns, 2020), and having "a much greater likelihood of succeeding and having a positive impact on children's adjustments" (Sullivan, 2008, p. 11).

Motivational Factors

Studies with court-mandated offenders find they are motivated to change less by fear of incarceration and more by a desire to be a better person and to spare their children from further abuse (Hamel, 2020b). Family court litigants can be induced to actively participate in treatment to share custody of their children. These natural motivators are not always sufficient if clients are not sufficiently engaged. This can occur for many reasons, first and foremost the unwillingness of some perpetrators to take responsibility for their actions. Other factors include a mismatch between the client and the type of recommended intervention, as mentioned earlier, as well as failure by the courts to provide and enforce a reasonable reunification schedule. The first author has seen firsthand how much more involved BIP and anger management clients are in the therapeutic process when they are able to incrementally secure additional visitation with their children, and how discouraged they become when those visits are unnecessarily postponed despite evidence of verifiable progress. Properly rewarded clients become further motivated, which in turn accelerates the change process, leading to long-term changes and, ultimately, greater safety to victims than what a temporary order of protection may provide.

REFERENCES

Abidin, R. (1990). *Parenting Stress Index*. Pediatric Psychology Press.
Ackerman, M. J. (1995). *Clinician's guide to child custody evaluations*. John Wiley & Sons.

Acklin, M. W., & Cho-Statler, L. (2006). The science and art of parent-child observation in child custody evaluation. *The Journal of Forensic Psychology Practice*, 6(1), 51–62. https://doi.org/10.1300/J158v06n01_03.

Advisory Committee of the Conrad N. Hilton Foundation Model Code Project of the Family Violence Project. (1994). *Model code on domestic and family violence*. National Council of Juvenile and Family Court Judges.

AFCC. (2006). Model standards of practice for child custody evaluations. Retrieved 4/19/21 from: https://portal.ct.gov/-/media/OCPD/Child_Protection/Training/Day6/AFCCModelStandardsofPracticeforChildCustodyEvaluationpdf.pdf

AFCC. (2010). Guidelines for court-involved therapy. https://www.afccnet.org/Portals/0/PublicDocuments/CEFCP/Guidelines%20for%20Court%20Involved%20Therapy%20AFCC.pdf

AFCC. (2016). Guidelines for examining intimate partner violence: A supplement to the AFCC model. http://niwaplibrary.wcl.american.edu/wp-content/uploads/AFCC-Guidelines-for-Examining-Intimate-Partner-Violence.pdf

American Bar Association. (2014). Joint custody presumptions and domestic violence exceptions. ABA Commission on Domestic & Sexual Violence. https://www.americanbar.org/groups/domestic_violence/Initiatives/statutory_ summary charts

APA. (2010). Guidelines for child custody evaluations in family law proceedings. Retrieved 4/19/21 from: https://www.apa.org/pubs/journals/features/child-custody.pdf

Appel, A. E., & Holden, G. W. (1998). The co-occurrence of spouse and physical child abuse: A review and appraisal. *Journal of Family Psychology*, 12(4), 578–599. https://doi.org/10.1037/0893-3200.12.4.578

Arias, I., & Pape, K. (2001). Psychological abuse: Implications for adjustment and commitment to leave violent partners. In K. D. O'Leary & R. D. Maiuro (Eds.), *Psychological abuse in violent relations* (pp. 137–151). Springer.

Austin, W. (2000). Assessing credibility in allegations of marital violence in the high-conflict child custody case. *Family and Conciliation Courts Review*, 38(4), 462–477. https://doi.org/10.1111/j.174-1617.2000.tb00585.x

Austin, W. (2001). Partner violence and risk assessment in child custody evaluations. *Family Court Review*, 39(4), 483–496. https://doi.org/10.1111/j.174-1617.2001.tb00627.x

Austin, W., & Drozd, L. (2012). Intimate partner violence and child custody evaluations, Part I: Theoretical framework, forensic model, and assessment issues. *Journal of Child Custody*, 9, 250–309. http://dx.doi.org/10.1080/15379418.2012.749717

Babcock, J., Armenti, N., Cannon, C., Lauve-Moon, K., Buttell, F., Ferreira, R., Cantos, A., Hamel, J., Kelly, D., Jordan, C., Lehmann, P., Leisring, P., Murphy, C., O'Leary, KD., Bannon, S., Salis, K., & Solano, I. (2016). Domestic violence perpetrator programs: A proposal for evidence—based standards in the United States. *Partner Abuse*, 7(4), 1–107. https://doi.org/ 10.1891/1946-6560.7.4.355

Babcock, J. C., Jacobson, N. S., Gottman, J. M., & Yerington, T. P. (2000). Attachment, emotional regulation, and the function of marital violence: Differences between secure, preoccupied, and dismissing violent and nonviolent husbands. *Journal of Family Violence*, 15, 391–409. doi:10.1023/A: 1007558330501

Baker, A. J. (2018). Reliability and validity of the four-factor model of parental alienation. *Journal of Family Therapy*, 42(1), 100–118. https://doi.org/10.1111/1467-6427.12253

Baker, A. J. L., & Darnall, D. (2006). Behaviors and strategies employed in parental alienation: A survey of parental experiences. *Journal of Divorce and Remarriage, 45*(1/2), 97–124. http://dx.doi.org/10.1300/J087v45n01_06

Battered Women's Justice Project. (2015). Practice guides for family court decision-making in domestic abuse-related child custody matters. Office of Violence Against Women, U.S. Department of Justice. practice-guides-for-family-court-decision-making-ind.pdf (bwjp.org)

Berger, J. L., Douglas, E. M., & Hines, D. A. (2016). The mental health of male victims and their children affected by legal and administrative partner aggression. *Aggressive Behavior, 42*, 346–361. https://doi.org/10.1002/ab.21630

Bernet, W., Gregory, N., Rohner, R. P., & Reay, K. M. (2020). Measuring the difference between parental alienation and estrangement: The PARQ-Gap. *Journal of Forensic Sciences, 65*, 1225–1234. doi:10.1111/1556-4029.14300

Bogat, G. A., Levendosky, A. A., DeJonghe, E., Davidson, W. S., & von Eye, A. (2004). Pathways of suffering: The temporal effects of domestic violence on women's mental health. *Maltrattamento e abuso all'infanzia, 6*, 97–112.

Bow, J., & Boxer, P. (2003). Assessing allegations of domestic violence in custody evaluations. *Journal of Interpersonal Violence, 18*(12), 1394–1410. https://doi.org/10.1177/0886260503258031

Bricklin, B. (1995). *The custody evaluation handbook: Research-based solutions and applications*. Brunner/Mazel.

Brinig, M. F., Frederick, L. M., & Drozd, L. M. (2014, April). Perspectives on joint custody presumptions as applied to domestic violence cases. *Family Court Review, 52*(2), 271–281. https://doi.org/10.1111/fcre.12090

California Legislative Information. (2021a). Division 8: Custody of children. https://leginfo.legislature.ca.gov/faces/codes_displayexpandedbranch.xhtml?tocCode=FAM&division=8.&title=&part=&chapter=&article=&nodetreepath=10

California Legislative Information. (2021b). Division 10: Prevention of family violence. https://leginfo.legislature.ca.gov/faces/codes_displayexpandedbranch.xhtml?tocCode=FAM&division=10.&title=&part=&chapter=&article=

California Legislative Information. (2021c). Abandonment and neglect of children. https://leginfo.legislature.ca.gov/faces/codes_displaySection.xhtml?lawCode=PEN&sectionNum=273.1

Cannon, C., Hamel, J., Buttell, F. P., & Ferreira, R. J. (2016). A survey of domestic violence perpetrator programs in the U.S. and Canada: Findings and implications for policy intervention. *Partner Abuse, 7*(3), 226–276. http://dx.doi.org/10.1891/1946-6560.7.3.226

Carolla, M. (2007). Therapy with clients accused of domestic violence in disputed child custody cases. In J. Hamel & T. Nicholls (Eds.), *Family interventions in domestic violence: A handbook of gender-inclusive theory and treatment* (pp. 457–476). New York: Springer.

Chiesa, A. E., Kallechey, L, Harlaar, N., Ford, C. R., Garrido, E. F., Betts, W. R., & Maguire, S. (2018). Intimate partner violence victimization and parenting: A systematic review. *Child Abuse & Neglect, 80*, 285–300. https://doi.org/10.1016/j.chiabu.2018.03.028

Clawar, S., & Rivlin, B. (2013). *Children held hostage: Identifying brainwashed children, presenting a case, and crafting solutions* (2nd ed.). American Bar Association.

Clemente, M., Espinosa, P., & Padilla, D. (2019). Moral disengagement and willingness to behave unethically against ex-partner in a child custody dispute. *PLoS ONE*, *14*(3). e0213662.https://doi. org/10.1371/journal.pone.0213662

Cooper, J., & Vetere, A. (2005). *Domestic violence and family safety: A systemic approach to working with violence in families*. Whurr.

Davies, P., Sturge-Apple, M., Winter, M., Cummings, E., & Farrell, D. (2006). Child adaptational development in contexts of interparental conflict over time. *Child Development*, *77*(1), 218–233. https://doi.org/10.1111/j.1467-8624.2006.00866.x

Deutsch, R., Misca, G., & Ajoku, C. (2018). A critical review of research evidence of parenting coordination's effectiveness. *Family Court Review*, *56*(1), 119–134. https://doi.org/10.1111/fcre.12326

Drozd, L. M. (2008). DVCC protocol. *Journal of Child Custody*, *4*(3–4), 19–31. https://doi.org/10.1300/J190v04n03_02

Drozd, L. M., Kuehnle, K., & Walker, L. E. A. (2004). Safety first: A model for understanding domestic violence in child custody and access disputes. *Journal of Child Custody*, *1*(2), 75–103. https://doi.org/10.1300/J190v01n02_04

Drozd, L. M., & Olesen, N. (2004). Is it abuse, alienation, and/or estrangement? A decision tree. *Journal of Child Custody*, *1*(3), 65–106. https://doi.org/10.1300/J190v01n03_05

Drodz, L. M., Olesen, N., & Saini, M. (2013). *Parenting plan and child custody evaluations: Using decision tress to increase evaluator competence & prevent avoidable error*. Professional Resource Press.

Dutton, D., Hamel, J., & Aaronson, J. (2010). The gender paradigm in family court processes: Re-balancing the scales of justice from biased social science. *Journal of Child Custody*, *7*(1), 1–31. https://doi.org/10.1080/15379410903554816

Dutton, D. G. (2006a). *Rethinking domestic violence*. UBC Press.

Dutton, D. G. (2006b). On comparing apples to apples deemed non-existent: A reply to Johnson. *Journal of Child Custody*, *2*(4), 53–63. https://doi.org/10.1300/J190v02n04_04

Eckhardt, C. I., Murphy, C. M., Whitaker, D. J., Sprunger, J., Dykstra, R., & Woodard, K. (2013). The effectiveness of intervention programs for perpetrators and victims of intimate partner violence. *Partner Abuse*, *4*(2), 196–231. https://doi.org/10.1891/1946-6560.4.2.196

Edelson, J. L., Shin, N., & Armendariz, K. K. (2008). Measuring children's exposure to domestic violence: The development and testing of the Child Exposure to Domestic Violence (CEDV) Scale. *Child and Youth Services Review*, *30*(5), 502–521. https://doi.org/10.1016/j.childyouth2007.11.006

Ehrenshaft, M. K., Cohen, P., Brown, J., Smailes, E., Chen, H. N., & Johnson, J. G. (2003). Intergenerational transmission of partner violence: A 20-year prospective study. *Journal of Consulting and Clinical Psychology*, *71*(4), 741–753. https://doi.org/10.1037/0022-006x.71.4.741

English, D. J., Marshall, D. B., & Stewart, A. J. (2003). Effects of family violence on child behavior and health during early childhood. *Journal of Family Violence*, *18*(1), 43–57. https://doi.org/10.1023/A:1021453431252

Fantuzzo, J., De Paola, L., Lambert, L., Martino, T., Anderson, G., & Sutton, S. (1991). Effects of interparental violence on the psychological adjustment and competencies of young children. *Journal of Consulting and Clinical Psychology*, *59*, 258–265. https://doi.org/10.1037//0022-006x.59.2.258

Fergusson, D. M., Boden, J. M., & Horwood, J. (2006). Examining the intergenerational transmission of violence in a New Zealand cohort. *Child Abuse & Neglect, 30*, 89–108. doi:10.1016/j.chiabu.2005.10.006

Follingstad, D. (2007). Rethinking current approaches to psychological abuse: Conceptual and methodological issues. *Aggression and Violent Behavior, 12*(4), 439–458. https://doi.org/10.1016/j.avb.2006.07.004

Fox, R. (1994). *Parent Behavior Checklist*. Clinical Psychology Publishing.

Ganley, A. (2009). Domestic violence, parenting evaluations and parenting plans: Practice guide for parenting evaluators in family court proceedings. King County Coalition Against Domestic Violence, Family Law Work Group. https://endgv.org/wp-content/uploads/2016/03/PE-practice-Guide-final-08-13-09-compressed11.pdf

Garber, B. D. (2020). Sherlock Holmes and the case of resist/refuse dynamics: Confirmatory bias and abductive inference in child custody evaluations. *Family Court Review, 58*(2), 386–402. https://doi.org/10.1111/fcre.12478

Gerard, A. (1994). *Parent-Child Relationship Inventory*. Western Psychological Services.

Gould, J. (1999). Professional interdisciplinary collaboration and the development of psycholegal questions guiding court ordered child custody evaluations. *Juvenile and Family Court Journal, 50*(1), 43–52. https://doi.org/10.1111/j.1755-6988.1999.tb01277.x

Gould, J., Martindale, D., & Eidman, M. (2007). Assessing allegations of domestic violence. *Journal of Child Custody, 4*(1/2), 1–35. https://doi.org/10.1300/J190v04n01_01

Gould, J. W., & Martindale, D. A. (2013). Child custody evaluations: Current literature and practical applications. In I. Weiner (series editor) & R. K. Otto (volume editor), *Forensic psychology*, Vol. 11 of *The handbook of psychology* (2nd ed., pp. 101–138). Wiley.

Gould, J. W., & Stahl, P. M. (2000). The art and science of child custody evaluations: Integrating clinical and mental health models. *Family and Conciliation Courts Review, 38*(3), 392–414. https://doi.org/10.1111/j.174-1617.2000.tb00581.x

Greenberg, L. R., Fidler, B. J., & Saini, M. A. (2019). *Evidence-informed interventions for court-involved families*. Oxford University Press.

Grych, J., & Fincham, F. (1990). Marital conflict and children's adjustment: A cognitive-contexual framework. *Psychological Bulletin, 108*, 267–290. https://doi.org/10.1037/0033-2909.108.2.267

Gutierrez, K. (2008). Co-parenting counseling with high-conflict parents in the presence of domestic violence. In J. Hamel (Ed.), *Intimate partner and family abuse: A casebook of gender-inclusive therapy* (pp. 195–214). Springer.

Hamel, J. (2008). Beyond ideology: Alternative therapies for domestic violence. In J. Hamel (Ed.), *Intimate partner and family abuse: A casebook of gender-inclusive therapy* (pp. 3–25). Springer.

Hamel, J. (2011). In dubious battle: The politics of mandatory arrest and dominant aggressor laws. *Partner Abuse, 2*(2), 224–245. doi:10.1891/1946-6560.2.2.224

Hamel, J. (2014). *Gender-inclusive treatment of intimate partner abuse: Evidence-based approaches* (2nd ed.). Springer.

Hamel, J. (2016). In the best interests of children: What family law attorneys should know about domestic violence. *Journal of the American Academy of Matrimonial Lawyers, 28*, 201–228.

Hamel, J. (2019.) The evolution of evidence-based treatment for domestic violence perpetrators. In E. A. Bates & J. C. Taylor (Eds.), *Intimate partner violence: New perspectives in research and practice* (pp. 89–106). Routledge.

Hamel, J. (2020a). Perpetrator or victim? A review of the complexities of domestic violence cases. *Journal of Aggression, Conflict and Peace Research*, 12(2), 55–62. https://doi.org/10.1108/JACPR-12-2019-0464

Hamel, J. (2020b). Beyond gender: Finding common ground in evidence-based batterer intervention. In B. Russell (Ed.), *Intimate partner violence and the LGBT+ community: Understanding power dynamics* (pp. 195–226). Springer.

Hamel, J., Desmarais, S. L., Nicholls, T. L., Malley-Morrison, K., & Aaronson, J. (2009). Domestic violence and child custody: Are family court professionals' decisions based on erroneous beliefs? *Journal of Aggression, Conflict and Peace Research*, 1(2), 37–52. https://doi.org/10.1108/17596599200900011

Hamel, J., Jones, D., Dutton, D., & Graham-Kevan, N. (2015). The CAT: A gender-inclusive measure of abusive and controlling tactics questionnaire. *Violence and Victims*, 30(4), 547–580. https://doi.org/10.1891/0886-6708.VV-D-13-00027

Hamel, J., & Nicholls, T. (2007). *Family interventions in domestic violence: A handbook of gender-inclusive theory and treatment*. Springer.

Hardesty, J. L., Khaw, L., Chung, G. H., & Martin, J. M. (2008). Coparenting relationships after divorce: Variations by type of marital violence and father's role differentiation. *Family Relations*, 57(4), 479–491. https://doi.org/10.1111/j.1741-3729.2008.00516.x

Hardesty, J. L., Haselschwerdt, M. L., & Johnson, M. P. (2012). Domestic violence and child custody. In K. Kuehnle & L. Drozd (Eds.), *Parenting plan evaluations: Applied research for the family court* (p. 442–475). Oxford University Press.

Harman, J., Kruk, E., & Hines, D. (2018). Parental alienation behaviors an unacknowledged form of family violence. *Psychological Bulletin*, 144(12), 1275–1299. http://dx.doi.org/10.1037/bul0000175

Harman, J., & Lorandos, D. (2021). Allegations of family violence in court: How parental alienation affects judicial outcomes. *Psychology, Public Policy, and Law*, 27(2), 184–208. http://dx.doi.org/10.1037/law0000301

Harned, M. (2001). Abused women or abused men? An examination of the context and outcomes of dating violence. *Violence and Victims*, 16(3), 269–285. doi:10.1891/0886-6708.16.3.269

Hines, D. (2014). Extent and implications of the presentation of false facts by domestic violence agencies in the United States. *Partner Abuse*, 5(1), 69–82. https://doi.org/10.1891/1946-6560.5.1.69

Hines, D., & Douglas, E. (2015). Health problems of partner violence victims: Comparing help-seeking men to a population-based sample. *American Journal of Preventive Medicine*, 48(2), 136–144. doi:10.1016/j.amepre.2014.08.022

Hines, D., & Douglas, E. (2018). Influence of intimate terrorism, situational couple violence, and mutual violent control on male victims. *Psychology of Men & Masculinity*, 19(4), 612–623. doi:10.1037/men0000142

Hines, D., Douglas, E., & Berger, J. (2015). A self-report measure of legal and administrative aggression within intimate relationships. *Aggressive Behavior*, 41(4), 295–309. https://doi.org/10.1002/ab.21540

Hines, D. A., & Douglas, E. M. (2010). A closer look at men who sustain intimate terrorism by women. *Partner Abuse*, 1(3), 286–313. doi:10.1891/1946-6560.1.3.286

Holtzworth-Munroe, A., Beck, C. J. A., & Applegate, A. G. (2010). The mediator's assessment of safety issues and concerns (MASIC): A screening interview for intimate partner violence and abuse available in the public domain. *Family Court Review*, *48*(4), 646–662. https://doi.org/10.1111/j.1744-1617.2010.001339.x

Holtzworth-Munroe, A., & Stewart, G. L. (1994). Typologies of male batterers: Three subtypes and the differences among them. *Psychological Bulletin*, *116*, 476–497. doi:10.1037/0033-2909.116.3.476

Hynan, D. J. (2003). Parent child observations in custody evaluations. *Family Court Review*, *41*(2), 214–223. https://doi.org/10.1111/j.174-1617.2003.tb00885.x

Jacobsen, N., & Gottman, J. (1998). *When men batter women*. Simon & Schuster.

Jaffe, P., & Geffner, R. (1998). Child custody disputes and domestic violence: Critical issues for mental health, social service, and legal professionals. In G. Holden, R. Geffner, & E. Jouriles (Eds.), *Children exposed to marital violence: Theory, research and applied issues* (pp. 371–408). American Psychological Association.

Jaffe, P. G., Johnston, J. R., Crooks, C., & Bala, N. (2008). Toward a differentiated view of parenting plans. *Family Court Review*, *46*, 500–522. https://doi.org/10.1111/j.1744-1617.2008.00216.x

Jasinski, J., Blumenstein, L., & Morgan, R. (2014). Testing Johnson's typology: Is there gender symmetry in intimate terrorism? *Violence and Victims*, *29*(1), 73–88.

Johnson, M. P. (2005). Apples and oranges in child custody disputes: Intimate terrorism versus situational couple violence. *Journal of Child Custody*, *2*, 43–52. https://doi.org/10.1300/J190v02n04_03

Johnson, M. (2008). *A typology of domestic violence: Intimate terrorism, violence resistance, and situational couple violence*. Northeastern University Press.

Johnson, M. (2011). Gender and types of intimate partner violence: A response to antifeminist literature review. *Aggression and Violent Behavior*, *16*(4), 290–296. doi:10.1016/j.avb.2011.04.006

Johnston, J., & Campbell, L. (1993). A clinical typology of interpersonal violence in disputed-custody cases. *American Journal of Orthopsychiatry*, *63*(2), 190–199. doi:10.1037/h0079425

Johnston, J., Lee, S., Olesen, N., & Walters, M. (2005). Allegations and substantiations of abuse in custody disputing families. *Family Court Review*, *43*(2), 283–294. https://doi.org/10.1111/j.1744-1617.2005.00029.x

Johnston, J., & Sullivan, M. (2020). Parental alienation: In search of common ground for a more differentiated theory. *Family Court Review*, *58*(2), 270–292. https://doi.org/10.1111/fcre.12472

Johnston, J. R., Roseby, V., & Kuehnle, K. (2009). *In the name of the child: A developmental approach to understanding and helping children of conflicted and violent divorce* (2nd ed.). Springer.

Jouriles, E. N., McDonald, R., Smith-Slep, A. M., Heyman, R. E., & Garrido, E. (2008). Child abuse in the context of domestic violence: Prevalence, explanations, and practice implications. *Violence and Victims*, *23*(2), 221–235. doi:10.1891/0886-6708.23.2.221

Jouriles, E. N., Norwoodd, W. D., McDonald, R., & Peters, B. (2001). Domestic violence and child adjustment. In J. H. Grych & F. D. Fincham (Eds.), *Interpersonal conflict and child development: Theory, research, and applications* (pp. 315–336). Cambridge University Press.

Kelly, J. B., & Johnston, J. R. (2001). The alienated child: A reformulation of parental alienation syndrome. *Family Court Review*, 39(3), 249–266. https://doi.org/10.1111/j.174-1617.2001.tb00609.x

Kelly, J. B., & Johnston, M. P. (2008). Differentiation among types of intimate partner violence: Research update and implications for interventions. *Family Court Review*, 46(3), 476–499. https://doi.org/10.1111/j.1744-1617.2008.00215.x

Kerig, P., & Lindahl, K. M. (Eds.) (2001). *Family observational coding systems: Resources for systemic research*. Erlbaum.

Kernic, M. (2020). Interdisciplinary evaluation of child custody decision-making among intimate partner violence families. Office of Justice Programs. Document number 255926. Retrieved 5/1/2020 from: https://www.ojp.gov/library/publications/interdisciplinary-evaluation-child-custody-decision-making-among-intimate

Kernic, M., Monary-Ernsdorff, D., Koepsell, J., & Holt, V. (2005). Child custody determinations among couples with a history of intimate partner violence. *Violence Against Women*, 11(8), 991–1021. https://doi.org/10.1177/1077801205278042

Kimber, M., Adhama, Gillb, S., McTavisha, J., & MacMillana, H. L. (2018). The association between child exposure to intimate partner violence (IPV) and perpetration of IPV in adulthood—A systematic review *Child Abuse & Neglect*, 76, 273–286. doi:10.1016/j.chiabu.2017.11.007

Kitzmann, K. M., Gaylord, N. K., Holt, A. R., & Kenny, E. D. (2003). Child witnesses to domestic violence: A meta-analytic review. *Journal of Consulting and Clinical Psychology*, 71(2), 339–352. https://doi.org/10.1037/0022-006X.71.2.339

Langhinrichsen-Rohling, J., Misra, T. A., Selwyn, C., & Rohling, M. L. (2012). Rates of bi-directional versus unidirectional intimate partner violence across samples, sexual orientations, and race/ethnicities: A comprehensive review. *Partner Abuse*, 3(2), 199–230. doi:10.1891/1946-6560.3.2.199

Laroche, D. (2005). Aspects of the context and consequences of domestic violence: Situational couple violence and intimate terrorism in Canada in 1999. Institut de la statistique du Quebec. https://www.stat.gouv.qc.ca

Laumakis, M., Margolin, G., & John, R. S. (1998). The emotional, cognitive, and coping responses of preadolescent children to different dimensions of marital conflict. In G. Holden, R. Geffner, & E. Jouriles (Eds.), *Children exposed to marital violence* (pp. 257–288). American Psychological Association.

Lawrence, E., Oringo, A., & Brock, R. (2012). The impact of partner abuse on partners. *Partner Abuse*, 3(4), 406–428. doi:10.1891/1946-6560.3.4.406

Levendosky, A. A., Leahy, K. L., Bogat, G. A., Davidson, W. S., & von Eye, A. (2007). Domestic violence, maternal parenting, maternal mental health, and infant externalizing behavior. *Journal of Family Psychology*, 20(4), 544–552.

Lynch, M., & Ciccheti, D. (1998). An ecological-transactional analysis of children and contexts. *Developmental Psychopathology*, 10, 235–257. DOI:10.1017/S095457949800159X

MacDonnel, K. W. (2012). The combined and independent impact of witnessed interparental violence and child maltreatment. *Partner Abuse*, 3(3), 358–378. doi:10.1891/1946-6560.3.3.358

McDonald, R., Jouriles, E., Ramisetty-Mikler, S., Caetano, R., & Green, C. (2006). Estimating the number of American children living in partner-violent families. *Journal of Family Psychology*, 20(1), 137–142. doi:10.1037/0893-3200.20.1.137.

Margolin, G., & Gordis, E. (2003). Co-occurrence between marital aggression and parent's child abuse potential: The impact of cumulative stress. *Violence & Victims, 18*, 243–258. https://doi.org/10.1891/vivi.2003.18.3.243

Mauricio, A. M., Tein, J. Y., & Lopzez, F. G. (2007). Borderline and antisocial personality scores as mediators between attachment and intimate partner violence. *Violence and Victims, 22*(2), 139–157. doi:10.1891/088667007780477339

Medoff, D. (1999). MMPI-2 validity scales in child custody evaluations: Clinical versus statistical significance. *Behavioral Sciences & The Law, 17*(4), 409–411. https://doi.org/10.1002/(SICI)1099-0798(199910/12)17:4<409::AID-BSL357>3.0.CO;2-N

Miller, H. A. (2001). *M-FAST: Miller Forensic Assessment of Symptoms Test professional manual*. PAR.

Moore, T. E., & Pepler, D. J. (1998). Correlates of adjustment in children at risk. In G. W. Holden, R. Geffner, & E. N. Jouriles (Eds.), *APA science Vols. Children exposed to marital violence: Theory, research, and applied issues* (pp. 157–184). American Psychological Association. https://doi.org/10.1037/10257-005

Morrill, A., Dai, J., Dunn, S., Sung, I., & Smith, K. (2005). Child custody and visitation decisions when the father has perpetrated violence against the mother. *Violence Against Women, 11*(8), 1076–1107. doi:10.1177/1077801205278046

Muller, R., Nicholls, T., Desmarais, S., & Hamel, J. (2009). Do judicial responses to restraining order requests discriminate against male victims? *Journal of Family Violence, 24*, 625–637. doi:10.1007/s10896-009-9261-4

Munro, O. E., & Sellbom, M. (2020). Elucidating the relationship between borderline personality pisorder and intimate partner violence. *Personality and Mental Health, 14*(3), 284–303. https://doi.org/10.1002/pmh.1480

Murphy, C., & Eckhardt, C. (2005). *Treating the abusive partner: An individualized cognitive-behavioral approach*. Guilford Press.

Nicholls, T., Pritchard, M., Reeves, K., & Hilterman, E. (2013). Risk assessment in intimate partner violence: A review of contemporary approaches. *Partner Abuse, 4*(1), 76–168. doi:10.1891/1946-6560.4.1.76

Nielsen, L. (2017). Re-examining the research on parental conflict, coparenting, and custody arrangements. *Psychology, Public Policy, and Law, 23*(2), 211–231. https://doi.org/10.1037/law0000109

Pratt, D., & Chapman, T. (2007). Family violence groups. In J. Hamel & T. Nicholls (Eds.), *Family interventions in domestic violence: A handbook of gender-inclusive theory and treatment* (pp. 519–540). Springer.

Rosen, L., & O'Sullivan, C. (2005). Outcomes of custody and visitation petitions when fathers are restrained by protective orders: The case of the New York family courts. *Violence Against Women, 11*(8), 1054–1075. https://doi.org/10.1177/1077801205278045

Saccuzzo, D. P., & Johnson, N. E. (2004). Child custody's mediation's failure to protect: Why should the criminal justice system care? *National Institute of Justice Journal, 251*, 1–30.

Saini, M., Drozd, L., & Olesen, N. (2017). Adaptive and maladaptive gatekeeping behaviors and attitudes: Implications for child outcomes after separation and divorce. *Family Court Review, 55*(2), 260–272. https://doi.org/10.1111/fcre.12276

Salem, P., & Dunford-Jackson, B. (2008). Beyond politics and positions: A call for collaboration between family court and domestic violence professionals. *Family Court Review, 46*(3), 437–453. https://doi.org/10.1111/j.1744-1617.2008.00213.x

Salzinger, S., Feldman, R. S., Ng-Mak, D. S., Mojica, E., Stockhammer, T., & Rosario, M. (2002). Effects of partner violence and physical child Abuse on child behavior: A Study of abused and comparison children. *Journal of Family Violence, 17*(1), 23–52. https://doi.org/10.1023/A:1013656906303

Saunders, D., Tolman, R., & Faller, K. (2013). Factors associated with child custody evaluators' recommendations in cases of intimate partner violence. *Journal of Family Psychology, 27*(3), 473–483. doi:10.1037/a0032164

Saunders, D. G. (2015). Research based recommendations for child custody evaluation practices and policies in cases of intimate partner violence. *Journal of Child Custody, 12*(1), 71–92. https://doi.org/10.1080/15379418.2015.1037052

Simmons, C., Lehmann, P., Cobb, N., & Fowler, C. (2005). Personality profiles of women and men arrested for domestic violence: An analysis of similarities and differences. *Journal of Offender Rehabilitation, 41*(4), 63–81.

Simonelli, C., & Ingram, K. (1998). Psychological distress among men experiencing physical and emotional abuse in heterosexual dating relationships. *Journal of Interpersonal Violence, 13*(6), 667–681. https://doi.org/10.1177/088626098013006001

Simpson, D., Doss, B., Wheeler, J., & Christensen, A. (2007). Relationship violence among couples seeking therapy: Common couple violence or battering? *Journal of Marital and Family Therapy, 33*(2), 270–283. https://doi.org/10.1111/j.1752-0606.2007.00021.x

Slep, A., & O'Leary, S. G. (2005). Parent and partner violence in families with young children: rates, patterns, and connections. *Journal of Consulting and Clinical Psychology, 73*(3), 435–444. https://doi.org/10.1037/0022-006X.73.3.435

Smith, L. S. (2016). Family-based therapy for parent-child reunification. *Journal of Clinical Psychology: In Session, 72*(5), 498–512. https://doi.org/10.1002/jclp.22259

Sonkin, D., Hamel, J., Ferreira, R., Buttell, F., & Frietas, M. (2019). The relationship between attachment anxiety, attachment avoidance and psychological violence in a sample of male and female court-mandated batterers. *Violence and Victims, 34*(6), 910–929.

Stahl, P. M. (1994). *Conducting child custody evaluations: A comprehensive guide*. Sage.

Stahl, P. M. (2011). *Conducting child custody evaluations: From basic to complex issues*. Sage.

Stanley, J. L., Bartholomew, K., Taylor, T., Oram, D., & Landolt, M. (2006). Intimate violence in male same-sex relationships. *Journal of Family Violence, 21*(1), 31–41. https://doi.org/10.1007/s10896-005-9008-9

Stark, E. (2007). *Coercive control: The entrapment of women in personal life*. Oxford University Press.

Statistics Canada. (2001). Family violence in Canada: A statistical profile 2001. Canadian Centre for Justice Statistics. htt[://www.statcan.ca

Stewart, L., Flight, J., & Slavin-Stewart, C. (2013). Applying effective corrections principles (RNR) to partner abuse interventions. *Partner Abuse, 4*(4), 494–534. https://doi.org/10.1891/1946-6560.4.4.494

Straus, M. (1992, September). *Children as witnesses to marital violence: A risk factor for lifelong problems among a nationally representative sample of American men and women*. Report of the Twenty-Third Ross Roundtable on Critical Approaches to Common Pediatric Problems. M5796.

Straus, M., Hamby, S., Boney-McCoy, S., & Sugarman, D. (1996). The revised conflict tactics scales (CTS2): Development and preliminary psychometric data. *Journal of Family Issues, 17*(3), 283–316.https://doi.org/10.1177/019251396017003001

Sturge-Apple, M. L., Davies, P. T., & Cummings, E. M. (2006). Impact of hostility and withdrawal in interparental conflict on parental emotional unavailability and children's adjustment difficulties. *Child Development, 77,* 1623–1641. https://doi.org/10.1111/j.1467-8624.2006.00963.x

Sturge-Apple, M. L., Skibo, M. A., & Davies, P. T. (2012). Impact of parental conflict and emotional abuse on children and families. *Partner Abuse, 3*(3), 379–400. https://doi.org/10.1891/1946-6560.3.3.379

Sullivan, M. (2008). Coparenting and the parenting coordination process. *Journal of Child Custody, 5*(1), 4–24. https://doi.org/10.1080/15379410802070351

Sullivan, M., & Burns, A. (2020). Effective use of parenting coordination: Considerations for legal and mental health professionals. *Family Court Review, 58*(3), 730–746. https://doi.org/10.1111/fcre.12509

Texas Family Code. (2019). Retrieved 4/19/21 from: https://texas.public.law/statutes/tex._fam._code_section_107.104

Ulman, A., & Straus, M. (2003). Violence by children against mothers in relation to violence between parents and corporal punishment by parents. *Journal of Comparative Family Studies, 34,* 41–60. https://doi.org/10.3138/jcfs.34.1.41

Ver Steegh, N. (2005). Differentiating types of domestic violence: Implications for child custody. *Louisiana Law Review, 65,* 1379–1431.

Warshak, R. (2013). *Severe cases of parental alienation.* In D. Lorandos, W. Bernet, & S. R. Sauber (Eds.), *Parental alienation: The handbook for mental health and legal professionals* (pp. 125–162). Charles C. Thomas.

Warshak, R. (2020). Parental alienation: How to prevent, manage, and remedy it. In D. Lorandos & W. Bernet (Eds.), *Parental alienation: Science and law.* Charles C. Thomas.

Wolak, J., & Finkelhor, D. (1998). Children exposed to partner violence. In J. Jasinski & L. Williams (Eds.), *Partner violence: A comprehensive review of 20 years of research* (pp. 73–112). Sage.

10

The Same Coin

Intimate Partner Violence, Child Abuse, and Parental Alienation

JENNIFER HARMAN AND EDWARD KRUK ■

The Duluth model is the most commonly used intervention in the United States and Canada for men who are court-sanctioned for domestic assault treatment (Corvo et al., 2009), and this model uses as a tool the *Power and Control Wheel* (Domestic Abuse Intervention Project [DAIP], 2011). One set of behaviors on this wheel is the "use of children" as a strategy to make women stay in their relationships with abusive men. For example, male abusers have been found to engage in prolonged custody battles and use parenting visitation as a way to continue abusing mothers (Bancroft & Silverman, 2002; Saunders, 1994), and they threaten to abduct or harm children if mothers do not comply with their wishes (Bancroft & Silverman, 2002). Children are also described as being manipulated to serve as informants to their abusive fathers regarding their mothers' behaviors as a means of control (e.g., McMahon & Pence, 1995). The use of children is reported to be frequent by women assaulted by a male partner (e.g., 88% of 156 battered women). The majority of these women report that the father attempted to turn their children against them (Beeble et al., 2007).

Women are not the only victims of intimate partner violence (IPV), however. Men are often reluctant to identify as IPV victims, and measures used to study the problem have not historically been tailored to capture male experiences (Hines et al., 2015). Thus, determining the prevalence and impact of IPV on male victims has posed research challenges (Walker et al., 2020). Despite these challenges, an estimated 5.2% of men, compared to 5.5% of women, are reported to be victims of IPV (sexual violence, physical violence, stalking) within the last 12 months. Similar proportions (34%–36%) of men and women report lifetime psychological aggression by an intimate partner (Smith et al., 2018). Although violence victimization rates and perpetration between women and men are similar, and most

IPV involves reciprocal abuse, women suffer the more significant share of severe, life-threatening injuries.

Many male victims of IPV describe their current or former partners as having used their children to control and abuse them. For example, male victims report that their female partners tell the children lies about them, undermine their authority and call them names in front of the children, tell them they will take their children away and threaten that they will never see them again, use the children for their personal gain, do not let them see their children, and make false allegations of abuse after leaving the relationship (Machado et al., 2020; Walker et al., 2020). Male victims of severe IPV report that one of the main reasons they do not leave their abusive partners is a fear of never seeing their children again. Their partners threaten to file false claims of abuse toward them if they leave the relationship (Hines & Douglas, 2010).

PARENTAL ALIENATING BEHAVIORS AS A FORM OF INTIMATE PARTNER VIOLENCE

Although the use of children has been accepted as a strategy of parents who use controlling-coercive violence (formerly known as "intimate terrorists" or batterers) to control and exert power over their victims, there has been considerable professional and scholarly resistance to labeling these actions as parental alienating behaviors (PABs). PABs are defined as patterns of behaviors executed by one parental figure (the alienating parent) over time, with the intent to harm the other parental figure's relationship with their children and or the target of the behaviors themselves (the targeted or alienated parent; Harman et al., 2018). A growing number of scholars considers PABs to be a form of family violence that includes IPV, given that the alienating parent uses the children to harm the targeted parent; the children are harmed in the process because this is a form of child psychological abuse (Harman et al., 2018; Kruk, 2018).

Harman and Matthewson (2020) recently used the power and control wheel to map PABs that have been documented in the empirical literature since 1985. Alienating parents use a wide variety of behaviors to coercively control and threaten the alienated parent. The use of children is one way to accomplish these acts. For example, alienating parents manipulate children to spy on the alienated parent, reward them for rejecting the parent, and tell the child that the alienated parent abandoned them and never loved them (Baker & Darnall, 2006). In more serious cases, the alienating parent abducts the child, hiding them away for years from the alienated parent (Poustie et al., 2018). Legal and administrative aggression is a particularly effective strategy to obtain and maintain custody of children (Harman & Lorandos, 2020), especially by mothers, because of social beliefs that men are more abusive than women (Hines et al., 2015). This form of aggression occurs when a parent uses legal and administrative systems, such as the courts, law enforcement, and child protection services, in a manipulative and abusive way when the relationship between the parties ends. This form of IPV involves legal manipulations such as false allegations of abuse and frivolous lawsuits (Berger et al., 2016), threats to ruin the target's reputation at work and in the community, and threats to take the target's money and possessions (Hines et al., 2015).

Across the research literature on PABs, parents who have been alienated from their children often report leaving their relationships with the alienating parent because they were abusive (e.g., 57% of mothers, 43% of fathers; Godbout & Parent, 2012; Lee-Maturana et al., 2021), and because the abusive parent, regardless of gender, has tried to or has succeeded in turning their child(ren) against them after leaving (Harman et al., 2018). Children witnessing parental abuse is a serious form of child abuse. Children witnessing PABs also fall into this category; Kruk (2010) found that targeted parents often disengage from their children as a protective measure in alienation situations. Further, parents who have been found by a court-appointed professional or court of law to have alienated their child(ren) are more likely to have a finding of some other form of abuse (e.g., physical IPV, child physical abuse) than parents who are only accused (not found) to have alienated their children, regardless of the gender of the parent (Sharples et al., 2021).

The impact of IPV is not dissimilar to the impact of PABs on parents; we argue they are identical because PABs as a form of IPV run parallel to IPV perpetrators' behaviors across the IPV research literature. Male victims of IPV report that police, court, and mental health professionals did not believe their reports of abuse, and that family and friends were often shocked and horrified to learn of their experience. These individuals downplayed the seriousness of their abuse. These reactions imply that it was the victim's fault for their experience (Machado et al., 2020; Walker et al., 2020). Female victims of IPV are also often blamed for their victimization (Meyer, 2016). Similarly, alienated parents have often blamed for their child(ren)'s rejection of them, are not believed, are told that there is no such thing as parental alienation, or their experience is minimized (e.g., "Do not worry, your children will return to you when they are ready"; Harman et al., 2018).

Alienated parents experience the ambiguous loss of their children (Tavares et al., 2020) and feel powerless to control or prevent the deterioration of their relationship with their children due to the alienating parent's behaviors (Balmer et al., 2018; Sauber, 2006). Consequently, alienated parents report experiencing symptoms of trauma, anxiety, depression, and extreme stress; having diminished life satisfaction and beliefs that the world is not fair and just; and a large proportion of them become suicidal (Balmer et al., 2018; Harman, Leder-Elder, et al., 2019; Poustie et al., 2018, Tavares et al., 2020). Mothers who are alienated from their children also report struggles with their identification as a parent, which is a central role/identity for many women (Finzi-Dottan et al., 2012). Likewise, research has found that victims of IPV suffer similar outcomes (e.g., Berger et al., 2016). For example, a meta-analysis of 207 studies that reported outcomes associated with IPV victimization found a positive association with depression, anxiety, and posttraumatic stress disorder (PTSD) symptoms, regardless of the gender of the victim (Spencer et al., 2019). Mothers who are victims of IPV also experience crises in their maternal identity (Gueta et al., 2016), and fathers report a dissociation with their gender and fatherhood identities as a result of their female-perpetrated IPV victimization (Corbally, 2015).

Abusive behaviors and their consequences are not the only similarities that victims of IPV and PABs share. Perpetrators of these forms of abuse share many characteristics, such as having pathologies like personality disorders (Gordon et al., 2008; Spencer et al., 2019), an unresolved trauma from their past (Gilbar et al., 2020; Lorandos, 2013), and being motivated to obtain and maintain control over the targets of their behaviors (Harman & Matthewson, 2020; Ubillos-Landa et al., 2020). Both IPV and PABs are proactive, patterned, predictable, and not reciprocated unless as a reactionary/protective response (e.g., self-defense, out of frustration) and the power dynamics between perpetrator and victim are asymmetrical (Harman et al., 2018, 2019; Walker, 1983; Warshak, 2015).

In summary, PABs have long been described by male and female victims of IPV but have not been labeled as such. IPV and PABs have been argued to be two sides of the same coin (Joshi, 2020); we argue they are one and the same. Later in this chapter, we will discuss why we believe there has been strong political, professional, and academic resistance to acknowledging PABs as a form of family violence. Before we do, we will first describe the impact of PABs on children.

IMPACT OF PARENTAL ALIENATING BEHAVIORS ON CHILDREN

Parental alienation refers to a mental condition in a child who has aligned strongly with one parent (the alienating parent) and rejects a relationship with the other parent (the alienated parent) *without legitimate justification* (Lorandos et al., 2013). It is essential to clarify that parental alienation is different from estrangement, which refers to a child's rejection of a parent or resistance to having a relationship with them, for *legitimate* reasons, such as the child being abused or neglected by the parent, or if a parent manifests a severe deficiency in their parenting skills (Harman et al., 2018). In the writings of Gardner, who originally coined the term "parental alienation syndrome," he stated that parental alienation would not be diagnosed for a child who was a victim of bona fide abuse by the parent that they are rejecting (Gardner, 1985, 1987). More recently, Baker (2018) and Bernet (2020a) have reinforced that the absence of abuse or neglect on the part of the alienated parent is central to the definition of parental alienation, as such abuse would provide a legitimate justification for the rejection of a parent.

When a child rejects a parent and refuses to have a relationship with them, many people assume that the rejected parent must have done something harmful to the child to warrant this behavior. Indeed, it does seem counterintuitive to infer that a child would reject a healthy, loving parent with whom they previously had a good relationship. Nevertheless, professionals who work with moderately and severely maltreated children (including victims of child physical abuse) report that the majority of these children engage in attachment-*enhancing* behaviors rather than attachment-*destructive* behaviors (Baker et al., 2019). Likewise, children in foster care yearn for their birth parents, experience fear and anxiety about being separated from them, and minimize the maltreatment that their birth parents perpetrated against them (Baker et al., 2016). In other words, children whom a parent abuses often engage in behaviors to preserve and protect the relationship (Baker, 2015); they do not seek to destroy it. It is notable that alienated children align with and reflexively support their alienating parent who engages in abusive, alienating behaviors (Harman & Matthewson, 2020), just as children who have been abused in other ways align with their abusive parent (Baker, 2015), and they resist reporting their abuse out of feelings of loyalty, guilt, fear, and shame (Sierau et al., 2018). The alienated child's alignment points to who the abusive parent most likely is in the family system.

It is not natural for a child to reject a parent because children's attachment to parents (even if abusive) increases their chances of survival (e.g., Bowlby, 1969). If this behavior is not normal, then why do alienated children do it, particularly when the child's emotional and physical rejection of the alienated parent results in the loss of a capable, loving parent in their life? Although PABs are not the only cause of a child's rejection of a parent, there is strong empirical support for them being one of the primary drivers of this effect (see Harman & Matthewson, 2020, for a review). When an abusive parent makes the child believe they were abandoned by or not loved by their other parent, this leads the child to be afraid of them or to believe they were harmed by them. In this way, the abusive parent undermines the attachment the child has to their other parent.

Teaching hatred of the other parent is tantamount to instilling self-hatred in the child, an alarming feature and one of the more serious and common effects of parental alienation. This self-hatred makes alienated children feel worthless, flawed, unloved, unwanted, endangered, and only of value in meeting another person's needs (Baker, 2005, 2010). Alienated children are also denied the opportunity to mourn or grieve the loss of this parent, as they cannot even talk about the alienated parent without feeling that they are betraying the alienating parent (Warshak, 2015). Unresolved grief can cause persistent anxiety, aggression (Dilworth & Hildreth, 1998), and dysphoria (Bonanno & Kaltman, 2001), and children tend to express their unresolved grief behaviorally rather than emotionally (Demi & Gilbert, 1987).

Unfortunately, the alienated parent is often powerless to correct the child's misperceptions and feelings toward them. The child interprets any provided explanations or clarifications of past events by the alienated parent as an attack on the alienating parent with whom they have aligned (Harman et al., 2018). In response to such attempts, the child will provide reflexive support to defend the alienating parent's actions. This response is driven by fear of losing the child's attachment to the alienator/abuser (Garner, 1985), who is the only attachment the child feels they have left—the child protects their abuser.

Reflexive support is one of eight manifestations of parental alienation that have been empirically supported in the scientific literature (e.g., Sîrbu et al., 2020). These manifestations are not likely to be found in children who have been abused in other ways. Alienated children display most, but not always, all of the manifestations of parental alienation to some level or degree. The other signs include a child's campaign of denigration against the alienated parent such that they vehemently and matter-of-factly state that they want nothing to do with the alienated parent because they despise or hate them (Clawar & Rivlin, 2013; Gottlieb, 2012). Such statements are made with an apparent lack of guilt about the alienated parent's feelings, which is the third manifestation of parental alienation. The child who is alienated feels anger, hurt, and rejected by the alienated parent due to the influence of the alienating parent. So the child suppresses all positive feelings toward the alienated parent and does not express any outward concern for how their words or behaviors affect them (e.g., Gardner, 1985; Gith, 2013; Moné & Biringen, 2012).

Another distinguishing manifestation of parental alienation is lack of ambivalence (Bernet et al., 2020), such that the child views the alienated parent as "all bad" and the alienating parent as "all good." These children view their parents in polarized, black and white terms, while children who have been abused or neglected in other ways feel ambivalent toward their abuser—they are upset and frightened, blame themselves, and yearn for things to be better. Consequently, children who have been abused in other ways engage in behaviors in an attempt to make their relationship with their abuser better (Baker et al., 2019), and their resistance to contact an abusive parent is not persistent or frequent (Freeman, 2020).

Alienated children encounter strong cognitive dissonance (Festinger, 1957): How do they justify rejecting a normal, healthy relationship with a parent to whom they were previously attached? In order to resolve this dissonance, the child must change their attitudes and or behavior toward the parent. No matter how "perfect" or "normal" the alienated parent is, an alienated child looks for some reason to justify their rejection of them. Hence, another manifestation of parental alienation is weak or frivolous rationalizations for the child's complaints about the alienated parent. For example, children will say they do not want to ever visit with the alienated parent because their house is boring, they do not like how they cook, or some other frivolous reason to resist contact. When challenged, these children will "double-down" and offer increasingly dramatic reasons for their rejection, escalating quickly from saying "his/her house is boring" to "they are abusive." No parent is perfect, and so weaknesses that most children would overlook or forgive are often exploited by alienated children (and the alienating parent) to provide a justification for rejection of the alienated parent (Harman & Matthewson, 2020).

Alienated children will also spontaneously claim that no one has told them to say bad things about the alienated parent, a phenomenon called "independent thinker." This out-of-context statement points to an agenda that the child is trying to accomplish: to argue that their rejection of the alienated parent is their own idea and that their rejection has not been influenced by the alienating parent (Bone, 2017). Likewise, the child may share "borrowed scenarios," which is another manifestation of parental alienation. Examples of borrowed scenarios are the use of age-inappropriate language or phrasing that was borrowed from an adult (e.g., a 4-year-old saying dad needs anger management classes; Harman &

Biringen, 2016), and "remembering" things that happened in the past related to the alienated parent that the child had no direct knowledge of or ability to recall, such as stating they know their mom never changed their diapers when they were little, or that their father cheated on their mother before they were born. Such scenarios may develop through coaching by the alienating parent (Baker & Darnall, 2006) or by overhearing the alienating parent talk to others about the alienated parent (Harman & Biringen, 2016).

The last manifestation of parental alienation is the spread of animosity. The child's anger and hatred toward the alienated parent are spread to other people with whom an alienated parent is associated. Alienated children will often refuse to communicate with or visit their grandparents, extended family, family friends, or neighbors that they believe to be on the alienated parent's "side." They will even reject family pets owned by the alienated parent. From the child's perspective, if their alienated parent is so awful and bad, then anyone associated with that individual must also be horrible, or they are guilty of enabling the alienated parent's behaviors (e.g., false beliefs of abuse; Gith, 2013). Children who have been abused in other ways do not appear to engage in this behavior, as they are more likely to have ambivalence toward their abuser rather than strong hatred.

Parental alienation results in very negative short- and long-term biopsychosocial consequences for children, leading a growing number of scholars to argue that a child protection response is necessary for its severe forms (Harman et al., 2018; Kruk, 2018). In the most severe cases of parental alienation, the harmful effects on children are profound (Balmer et al., 2018; Moné & Biringen, 2012; Moné et al., 2011). Alienated children experience disrupted social-emotional development, develop a lack of trust in relationships, social anxiety, and social isolation (Baker, 2005, 2010; Baker & Ben-Ami, 2011; Friedlander & Walters, 2010; Godbout & Parent, 2012). Such children have poor relationships with both parents when they become adults (Moné & Biringen, 2012). As adults, they tend to enter adult romantic partnerships earlier than their peers, are more likely to divorce or dissolve their cohabiting unions, are more likely to have children outside a committed relationship, and more likely to become alienated from their own children (Ben-Ami & Baker, 2012). Low self-sufficiency, lack of autonomy, and lingering dependence on the alienating parent also occur, and alienated children experience difficulties controlling their impulses, struggle with mental health and addiction, and are likely to engage in self-harm (Otowa et al., 2014).

OTHER CAUSES OF PARENTAL ALIENATION

While PABs are one of the primary causes of the alienation of a child from another parent, there are other less studied but hypothesized causes and contributions to this problem. Child affected by parental relationship distress (CAPRD) is a DSM-V (American Psychiatric Association, 2013) diagnostic category (V61.29) used by clinicians when the focus of clinical attention is on a child who has been negatively affected by problems in the parental relationship (e.g., high levels of conflict or disparagement, p. 716). CAPRD can result from passively witnessing IPV in the parental relationship and being pulled actively into the conflict. As previously described, parents who engage in a pattern of abuse intended to dominate the partner (coercive-controlling parents) will often use their children against the other parent, which can result in the child aligning with the abusive parent and rejecting the alienated parent, which is the parental alienation form of CAPRD (Bernet, Wambolt, & Narrow, 2016). Another form of CAPRD is a loyalty conflict which involves the child becoming triangulated between the parents and feeling like they are "put in the middle." In this situation, the child feels both their parents are trying to influence them to pick their side, and the child tries to maintain a positive relationship with both of them (Bernet et al., 2016; Schrodt & Afifi, 2018). This type of conflict more closely resembles a different form of IPV than described so far: situational couple violence (Johnson, 2008). In families where there is a loyalty conflict, the parent's behaviors are often reactionary, not predictable, are reciprocal, and the parents generally have the same level of power in the family system. If these loyalty conflicts become too intense, some children may start to align with one parent in order to alleviate the stress of being caught in the middle, leading to parental alienation (Bernet et al., 2016).

Less researched as a contributing factor of parental alienation is the impact of systems and institutions on the family (Harman & Biringen, 2016). Norms, policies, and laws that influence responses to allegations of abuse and PABs can often exacerbate family conflicts. The use of legal and administrative aggression against alienated parents can be an effective strategy of abusive and alienating parents to obtain a custody advantage (Harman & Lorandos, 2020; Hines et al., 2015). The protection of children from abuse is imperative; however, family court responses to allegations are often slow and can provide an opportunity for a parent who has made false or unsubstantiated allegations of abuse to have an extended period of time with the child in their exclusive care. This exclusive time provides the alienating parent ample time to influence and turn the child against the other parent (Kruk, 2013).

Definitions of IPV in the law can also create problems for legal and mental health professionals working with families. For example, although coercive control and other forms of psychological abuse are forms of IPV, the inclusion of power and control behaviors in legal definitions of abuse can potentially lead to misuse by abusive parents (e.g., Follingstad, 2007). For example, if an abusive and alienating parent tells the police or court that the other parent is controlling, overbearing, or argumentative, such a definition would classify the accused person as abusive and lead to criminal prosecution based solely on the self-report of the accuser. Without professional training regarding the differentiation of types of abuse, better assessment tools and standards of evidence, and the willingness to punish parents who misuse legal and administrative systems, innocent parents will be pushed out of their children's lives when abusive and alienating parents and their attorneys misuse such vague legal definitions.

Legal and physical custody "battles" and court orders can also contribute to and exacerbate parental alienation. The adversarial legal process of determining child custody fosters a situation where the parents become polarized and recalcitrant, whereas they were previously reasonable and cooperative with each other (Kruk, 2013). In order to obtain sole or primary physical and legal custody or to prevent the other parent from gaining such an advantage, parents (often at the encouragement of their attorneys) depict each other as less loving and capable of making decisions or caring for the children than them and or as being abusive. Parental alienation flourishes in situations where one parent has exclusive care and control of children. Suppose a parent has sole legal decision-making across all spheres of the child's life (e.g., medical, educational, religious, recreational) when the other parent is just as capable. In that case, this authority promotes an imbalance of power in the family system that an abusive parent easily exploits. This consolidation of parental authority also conveys an implicit message to the child that one parent is "better" than the other. Legal systems that remove a loving and capable parent from a child's life via sole custody or primary residence orders, and give all decision-making authority to one parent, are not only contributing to parental alienation; we assert that they are *engaging* in PABs at the systemic level.

ASSESSMENT OF ALIENATED CHILDREN

Parental alienation may be differentiated from other parent–child contact and conflict problems through the use of an empirically validated and supported Five-Factor model (Bernet, 2020a, 2020c). For parental alienation to be the explanation for a child's resistance/refusal to have a relationship with a parent, there needs to be evidence for the following five factors:

(1) a clear frequent and persistent rejection of the alienated parent by the child manifested in the form of contact refusal;
(2) a prior positive relationship between the child and the now rejected parent;
(3) an absence of child abuse or neglect, or maltreatment by the rejected parent;
(4) the use of alienating behaviors by the favored parent; and
(5) the presence of most of the eight behavioral manifestations of parental alienation in the child: a campaign of denigration, frivolous rationalizations for their deprecation, lack of ambivalence, independent thinker phenomenon, reflexive support, absence of guilt, presence of borrowed scenarios, and spread of animosity.

If there is evidence for all five factors, then the severity or degree of parental alienation must be determined, as this helps to inform what type of treatment and intervention will be most effective (Warshak, 2020). At the mild stage of parental alienation, the child starts to manifest some of the symptoms described in factor five. They still harbor positive feelings toward the alienated parent and even miss them when they are not in their presence, but they will not openly express this in the presence of the alienating parent. Transitions between parents are typically difficult, and it may take a few hours or even a day for the child to get back to "normal." There is often some resistance to contact or visitation, but once in the care of the alienated parent, the child enjoys their time with them (Bernet, 2020a).

At the moderate stage of parental alienation, the child displays more of the symptoms described in Factor Five, and transitions between homes are more difficult. The child is more resistant to communication and contact with the alienated parent and more openly defiant and disrespectful toward them. They may enjoy doing activities with the alienated parent (e.g., going to an amusement park) but will not enjoy it because they are doing it together. They will not admit to missing the alienated parent, will more openly disparage them, and yet at times, there may be indications that they still love them and want their approval. At its severest stage, the child has manifested most, if not all, of the symptoms described in factor five. There is much more refusal of contact with the alienated parent, and the children actively engage in behaviors to push the alienated parent out of their lives. They will not admit to positive feelings toward the parent and will lash out and hurt them with no apparent feelings of guilt (Bernet, 2020a).

To differentiate alienated children from estranged children and those involved in a loyalty conflict between their parents, evidence supporting these factors is reviewed. If a child has been estranged from a parent, there may be *some* evidence for factor one, but the resistance of a relationship with the rejected parent is not consistent or persistent over time. There also would be evidence of child maltreatment by the rejected parent, an absence of alienating behaviors by the favored parent (factor four), and few manifestations of parental alienation in factor five. Such children will express ambivalence toward their estranged parent, not a polarization of attitudes where the preferred parent is idolized and the rejected parent is demonized. In contrast, when children are embroiled in loyalty conflicts, they try to maintain positive relationships with both parents while the parents attempt to force the child into an alignment with them (Bernet et al., 2016). In this dynamic, one would not see evidence for factors one, three, or five. There would be evidence for factor two, and the behaviors that the parents' behaviors would be noticeably reciprocal, reactive, not patterned. The power between the two parents would be fairly symmetrical.

There are some situations in which a parent has been estranged from their child, and the other parent capitalizes on this situation by engaging in PABs to make the child completely reject them. Such cases are referred to as "hybrids." Some professionals believe hybrid cases are the "norm" and that true parental alienation is not common (e.g., Drozd & Oleson, 2004). Yet, of nearly 1,000 U.S. appellate cases, only about 20% involved a case where parental alienation was found, and the alienated parent had a finding of abuse against them (Harman & Lorandos, 2020). Differentiating hybrid from parental alienation cases can be challenging when allegations of abuse have been investigated across multiple administrative and legal systems with different outcomes. In such cases, a close examination of how and when allegations are made, how they may or may not evolve when professionals/third parties become involved, and how the allegations are resolved is required. False allegations of abuse are commonly made in high-conflict custody battles (Ceci & Bruck, 1995; Trocmé & Bala, 2005), and findings of abuse can be concluded based on an "inarticulable hunch" (Redleaf, 2019), particularly when legal definitions of abuse are vague. Consequently, many professionals assume that most parental alienation cases are actually hybrids and fail to recognize how alienating and abusive parents misuse legal and administrative systems to make it appear the alienated parent is abusive when they are not, all in an effort to gain and maintain power.

Some individuals consider themselves "protective parents" because they believe their behaviors serve to protect their children from abusive parents, not alienate them (e.g., Rosen, 2017). When there is actual child maltreatment, then it is, of course, imperative to protect a child. However, there are many ways to protect a child without engaging in PABs. Gatekeeping behaviors (e.g., blocking phone contact; supervised visitation) that restrict access between a parent and child may be necessary when there is a substantiated finding of abuse. In such cases, the behaviors would not be considered PABs. Healthy parents would not take advantage of such a situation and make a child feel worse than they already do about their abusive parent. These parents recognize that the parent is still an important person to the child and that the child just needs protection from the parent until they stop their abusive behaviors.

In contrast, if a parent unilaterally engages in gatekeeping behaviors in the absence of a court order or administrative action, and they do so based solely on their beliefs or claims of abuse rather than a substantiated finding, then a red flag is raised as to whether the behavior is a PAB. Looking more closely at such a case, the behavior would constitute a PAB if the parent is also engaging in other strategies over time to turn the child against their other parent. PABs are never justified—it is possible to protect children from abuse while still preserving their love and attachment for their other parent (Harman et al., 2018).

It is outside the scope of the current chapter to describe best practices for the treatment of parental alienation, but we note that the treatment recommendations are very similar to how other forms of child abuse are treated (Kruk, 2018; Warshak, 2020). At milder stages, psychoeducation, legal case management and oversight, and therapeutic support for all family members can be effective, with careful attention being made to preserve the balance of power and authority of the parents in the child's life. As the severity of parental alienation worsens, more intensive interventions must be employed to protect the child from the PABs of the alienating parent, and corrective actions are needed to address the child's unwarranted rejection of a loving and healthy parent. Respecting the child's wishes when they have been manipulated to reject a parent and allowing them to "choose" or decide for themselves whether to have a relationship with the alienated parent has been considered by some scholars to be the sanctioning of child abuse. Corrections must be made to repair the child's relationship with the alienated parent. This reparation is not just about the parent–child relationship—it is about repairing the psychological split that has occurred in the child that, if not addressed, creates long-term, negative consequences for the child through adulthood (see Warshak, 2020, for a review).

THE GENDER PARADIGM AND PARENTAL ALIENATION

Paradigms are perceptual frameworks, or worldviews, that serve to filter and organize information that is consistent with assumptions and to ignore, dispel, and ward off evidence that is inconsistent with them. Dutton (1994) has described how feminist theory has influenced a gendered paradigm within IPV research, and this paradigm creates a biased perspective that IPV is a "culturally supported male enterprise, and that female violence is always defensive and reactive" (Dutton & Nicholls, 2005, p. 683). As with the parallels we highlighted earlier between the IPV and parental alienation research literature, this gender paradigm also dominates the field of parental alienation and is driven by two interrelated beliefs: that men are more abusive than women and that mothers' behaviors are acceptable when they serve to "protect" children from abusive fathers. Mothers' allegations of abuse are more likely to be believed by professionals than fathers' allegations (e.g., Hines et al., 2015; Tilbrook et al., 2010), and these effects are largely explained by deeply entrenched beliefs that men are more aggressive than women. In early writings about parental alienation, Gardner (1985) noted that alienating parents often made false allegations of abuse about the alienated parent, and the majority of alienating parents in his clinical and forensic practice at the time were mothers. Over time, Gardner noted many more cases in which fathers were the alienating parent. Recent research using population-based and representative samples indicates that mothers and fathers are equally likely to be victims of PABs (e.g., Harman, Leder-Elder et al., 2016, 2019).

Approximately 75% of U.S. appellate court cases involve a mother as an alienating parent (Lorandos, 2020), which could be used to support a lingering belief that mothers are more likely to be alienating parents than fathers. However, there could be many explanations for this gender difference at higher levels of the legal process. For example, appeals are exceptionally expensive, and fathers may have more financial resources to pursue this legal avenue than mothers to address the problem. There are also gender differences in the use of aggression, including PABs. Alienating mothers have been found to use twice as many indirect forms of PABs (e.g., badmouthing the father to others) than direct forms (creating conflict with the parent at parenting time exchanges), while fathers use similar levels of both forms (Harman, Lorandos, et al., 2019). As a result, gender biases may occur in the assessment process because the PABs of alienating mothers may be more difficult to identify. Consequently, alienated fathers may have to utilize more legal and administrative resources than mothers to document and "prove" that parental alienation is occurring.

Another explanation for this gender difference is that a mother's PABs may be interpreted as more "acceptable" and "justified" as a means to protect children from an "abusive" father. In one experimental study, survey respondents were presented with a list of PABs that they rated in terms of their "acceptability." One third of the sample read that the behaviors were done by a mother, a father, or a generic parent. As predicted, although the PABs were not generally rated as acceptable, they were considered more acceptable for a mother to do than a father or a generic parent. In other words, the participants likely inferred there being *some* reason for the PABs, and that it was, therefore, more acceptable for a mother to engage in PABs than a father (Harman, Biringen, et al., 2016). As a result, alienated fathers may have a more difficult time getting mental health and legal professionals to take their concerns about being alienated seriously, and the PABs of the mother may be perceived as justified, particularly when one of the strategies used by the mother is to make a false allegation of abuse against the father. When the father claims they are being alienated, professionals interpret this claim as just a countermeasure to abuse allegations (e.g., Meier et al., 2019). Therefore, the alienated father's concerns are ignored because of underlying gendered beliefs about human aggression and who is responsible for protecting children.

CONTROVERSIES

Research on the topic of parental alienation has been characterized as "controversial," an argument that we believe is fueled by the gender paradigm and associated ideological beliefs, a misuse, mischaracterization, and misunderstanding of scientific research (Bernet, 2020b), and a lack of access to peer-reviewed research due to "paywalls" that restrict access to published articles unless the consumer subscribes to the journal or pays a fee. In this section, we will describe examples of the ways these controversies have plagued research on parental alienation. While it is not our intent, we are aware that these examples may be interpreted by some individuals or groups as ad hominem attacks. Consequently, we will not cite specific individuals, events, or organizations. We are open to direct communication with individuals who would like more specific documentation of the details described.

Denial of Parental Alienation

There are a number of vocal opponents to the concept of parental alienation, many of whom are attorneys working with domestic violence advocacy agencies. The primary basis of their position is a belief that parental alienation is just a legal defense used by abusive fathers as a way to counter physical and sexual abuse allegations and continue abusing mothers and their children (Bruch, 2001; Meier et al., 2019). This position represents a gross mischaracterization of the original work of Gardner (1985). He noted in his clinical work that a small number of cases of parental alienation involved false claims of child and sexual abuse about the alienated parent. This statement was wrongly interpreted by some women's advocates and attorneys to mean that denial of sexual abuse by abusive fathers was a central feature of the phenomenon and is grounded in a belief that children never lie or that they cannot be influenced to lie about abuse (Rand, 2013). This position ignores the fact that if there is bona fide abuse, experts have continuously stated that parental alienation needs to be ruled out as a concern (Baker, 2019; Gardner, 1985, 1987).

State of Parental Alienation Research

There are also controversies regarding the current state of research on parental alienation and the factors that cause it. There have been a handful of published research studies in which the authors have concluded that PABs do not cause parental alienation, and therefore parental alienation is not a supported "theory" (Clemente & Padilla-Racero, 2015; Rowen & Emery, 2019). Scholars have noted numerous problems with these studies, such as inaccurate operationalizations of the studies' constructs, incorrect analysis of the data, errors in the representation of the published literature, and illogical premises of the methods selected to test the study's hypotheses (e.g., Bernet et al., 2015).

Other critics have argued that there are *no* high-quality studies of parental alienation that have been published to date, for example. Saini, et al. (2016) have argued that parental alienation remains a "hypothesis" needing further empirical testing, even though the literature review that served as the foundation of this opinion included only a small fragment of the existing research published through 2015. A recent review of 43 published papers indicates that in just the few years prior to 2018, there has been substantial growth and investment in expanding research on parental alienation and that the research is "progressing productively" (Marquez et al., 2020). To date, more than 1,000 papers have been published on parental alienation (Vanderbilt University Medical Center, 2017), and the numbers of research studies published each year on the topic are increasing dramatically. Harman et al. (2019) point out that research on parental alienation has moved beyond preliminary descriptive studies, which are necessary at the early stages of a field of inquiry to build a knowledge base, and that the field has entered a "blossoming" stage of greater theoretical extension and development.

Minimization of Parental Alienation

There are also a number of professionals who do not deny that parental alienation exists; however, they minimize the prevalence and severity of the problem. These professionals have taken the position that in the majority of cases, both parents are responsible for the child's rejection of a parent. In other words, while a parent may actively alienate a child, these individuals have taken the position that the child's rejection of the alienated parent is also due to the alienated parent's behaviors. It is illogical to assume that parents who leave relationships with a coercively controlling partner are somehow, miraculously, just as responsible for the postseparation conflict as the abusive and alienating parent. This belief flies in the face of considerable research documenting different forms of IPV (Johnson, 2008), and the fact that abused and alienated parents have little power before they leave their relationships with the abusing and alienating parent, and still have little power when they leave, particularly after their children have been turned against them. Of 594 people from a representative panel of U.S. adults who had children with someone with whom they no longer lived in a relationship, 47.9% stated that both parents reciprocally engaged in PABs, which would make both parents responsible and create a loyalty conflict for the child. The remaining parents (52.0%) admitted being the primary perpetrator or the unreciprocating parent (Harman et al., 2019). Those who claim both parents are largely responsible for the child's rejection conflate the experience of loyalty conflict parents with alienated parents.

Minimization also takes the form of not regarding parental alienation as a serious mental health issue for either the child or affected parents and not recognizing it as either a form of family violence or child abuse. While alienated children suffer many short- and long-term effects (e.g., Kruk, 2018; Verrocchio et al., 2016, 2017), some children who have completely rejected a parent appear on the surface to be excelling in school or some other activity (sports, music). The appearance that the child is "better off" without their parent is misleading, as such children tend to cope with the psychological splitting they have experienced by compartmentalizing and focusing on such activities as a distraction from their unresolved grief. In contrast, some children are so harmed by the PABs of their parent that they are fragile and suicidal, leading legal and mental health practitioners to be afraid to change the status quo. In both of these circumstances, the child still needs mental health intervention, as the psychological splitting that has occurred explains both outcomes and will cause more damage to the child over time if left unaddressed.

Accessibility of Research

Within the sciences, there has been a growing movement for more open and transparent research practices across the entire research process (Chambers, 2017). Part of this movement is the call for research findings and publications to be openly accessible to the public. As Chambers (2017) describes, most of the population does not have access to published research findings because they are behind a "paywall" controlled by academic journal publishers. If one does not have a license or subscription to the journal, then individual articles must be purchased directly from the publisher. These licenses and subscriptions are extraordinarily expensive, and even prestigious universities such as Harvard have to suspend their subscriptions due to budgetary constraints (Chambers, 2017).

Consequently, mental health and legal professionals, policymakers, and politicians cannot easily access scientific advances. How are such individuals expected to form informed opinions, or create empirically based policies and laws, if they are only able to access a small body of accessible literature? The Partner Abuse State of Knowledge project, which has been published across six issues of the journal *Partner Abuse*, provides access to the latest research on IPV to professionals (Hamel et al., 2012). It would be invaluable to develop such a project for all the scholarly literature on parental alienation that is beyond a bibliographic listing (e.g., Vanderbilt University Medical Center, 2017). We believe that the lack of accessibility to peer-reviewed research has contributed to many of the controversies described here.

Means of Suppression

The perpetuation of these "controversies" is fueled by behaviors of deniers and minimizers of parental alienation research and media practices. Some scholars have created what are called "woozles," which are faulty, partial, or misinterpreted research claims that are used to mislead professionals working with families (Nielsen, 2014). When research findings are misreported or overgeneralized without acknowledging methodological limitations, or scholars quote and then misquote the works of other scholars (often without reading the original source), the original work becomes misrepresented and taken as "fact." For example, Bernet (2020b) has described in great detail five false statements about parental alienation that have been published in the psychological, medical, and legal literature. This "woozling" has led to professionals and the public adopting false beliefs that parental alienation is not scientific, is "junk science," and that there is no empirical evidence to support its validity. This campaign of misinformation has contributed to a divide between many family violence advocates and "fathers' rights" groups who do not see the common ground between them: PABs are abusive behaviors of a parent, regardless of gender. IPV and PABs are the same phenomena.

Legislative changes to include parental alienation as a form of child abuse have also been stymied by domestic violence advocates and "protective parents" in the United States. For example, in 2019, an alienating father in the state of Colorado was ordered to transfer custody of his child to the alienated mother. Upon learning of this outcome, the father returned home and killed his son before committing suicide. After a child fatality review team investigated, it was recommended that parental alienation be added to the state statutes for child abuse (Colorado Department of Human Services, 2020). A task force was created; however, no one from the team responded to the first author's offer to help by providing published empirical research on the topic and testimony. It was later learned that a nationally organized group of women's advocates interfered with the task force and forcefully excluded advocates who were in support of parental alienation being added to the statute as recommended. These excluded advocates were told that discussing parental alienation would not be "productive" and would detract from their task to define domestic violence in the state statutes more clearly. To support their position, this group continuously referred to a research study that has failed to replicate and has notable methodological, conceptual, and statistical flaws; they have called parental alienation "junk science" based on the misinformation they had heard from deniers of parental alienation, and they out of hand refused to review any other empirical research on the topic that was provided to them. We believe these actions are willfully ignorant, dangerous, and will harm many families who are experiencing parental alienation.

Scientists who study parental alienation have also been denied platforms to present their work at professional conferences on the topic of domestic violence. For example, the first author was invited to present her research on parental alienation as a form of family violence at a conference for domestic violence service providers. Upon learning of this invitation, the organizer was notified by the conference sponsor that funding would be withdrawn unless the author was taken off the schedule. By not allowing diverse opinions and presenting scientific data at such conferences, such professions run the risk of becoming echo chambers of individuals with the same opinion and the needs of mothers and fathers who are abused by their ex-partners through their relationship with their children are ignored.

Another example of this behavior occurred when the authors of this chapter organized a conference intended to bring together diverse opinions on the topic of shared parenting and family violence. The intent was to bring people from "opposing" sides to the table in order to identify common ground and paths forward. We were disappointed in how some scholars reacted to this invitation. Some individuals did not respond to our invitation at all, and others stated they did not want to participate if certain individuals were speaking at the conference. One individual even accepted the invitation, later withdrew when the schedule was released, and threatened to sue the organizers if their name was not removed from the schedule within the week because they did not want to be associated with those scheduled to speak. By not stepping up and coming to the table, diverse voices and opinions are not factored into the discussion, and opportunities for change are lost.

Another form of suppression in this arena includes attempts by professional associations to control the narrative about what research developments "mean" when findings contradict their position. For example, the first author of this chapter coauthored a paper where she failed to replicate the findings of another research team. The results of this study challenged one professional association's stance that parental alienation cases are typically hybrids (where both parents are responsible), among other beliefs of many of their members. The authors of the two papers were invited to record presentations of their work (not present live in a Q & A format, as would typically occur in scientific venues), and then a panel of three selected individuals was to provide commentary on the studies to "interpret" what they mean for their members. The authors of the two papers declined to participate in this transparent attempt to control a narrative of their work, particularly after their offer to present their work directly to the members was declined.

Role of the Media

The media also plays a significant role in fueling the controversies that have plagued scholarly work on parental alienation. The media is motivated to publish sensational stories to gain and maintain readership, and reporters often lack the scientific expertise to be critical of published reports and research studies. For example, Meier and colleagues (2019) received uncritical media attention for some findings they described in a paper that was published in a non-peer-reviewed law journal and had many noticeable methodological, statistical, and conceptual flaws (Harman & Lorandos, 2020). The Meier team (2019) offered findings such as mothers who claimed their children were abused were more likely to lose custody of their children and that fathers who claimed they were alienated from their child were more likely to get custody, even if they were proven to be abusive. One headline example from this coverage was, "Survivors of domestic abuse told to keep quiet about it in court or risk jeopardizing child custody" (Carmen, 2020), and no other scholarly perspective was included in this media coverage. This biased and uncritical coverage of the paper propagates stereotypes about men being abusive and women being victims. Harman and Lorandos (2020) conducted a separate study utilizing open science research practices and failed to find any support for the conclusions made by Meier et al. (2019). When their findings were sent to all of the media reporters who initially covered Meier et al.'s (2019) report, along with an offer to be interviewed for another story about the findings, Harman and Lorandos received no reply.

Interestingly, when other media coverage of parental alienation has attempted to portray it as a legitimate and real phenomenon, reporters are met with strong editorial resistance and are encouraged to get a "balanced" perspective from people who deny and minimize the problem. A recent example of this double standard was a story about parental alienation that was published in *The Atlantic* (Hagerty, 2020). When equal "air time" is given to individuals whose opinions are based on a poor or minimal understanding of the scientific literature, and or who have opinions rooted in biased beliefs and "woozles" rather than allowing more air time to legitimate scientific experts on the topic, the public can fall for what has been called a false equivalence logical fallacy (Hansson, 2017). For example, despite the retraction of Andrew Wakefield's *Lancet* article on the measles, mumps, and rubella (MMR) vaccine due to insufficient and incorrect data, scientific misrepresentation, and ethical violations, the "balanced" media coverage of the MMR arguments that gave equal weight to Wakefield's unsubstantiated position and the scientifically supported position led to the public inaccurately believing that doctors and scientists are "divided" over the safety of the vaccine (Dobson, 2003). It is concerning that the media is fueling the stereotypes underlying the gender paradigm that plagues parental alienation research, and we believe it creates the perception that there is a large divide between the "DV and PA worlds" when they are one and the same.

SOLUTIONS

Certainly, there are people who claim that they are being alienated from a child when they are not, just as there are people who claim they are being abused when they are not (Harman & Lorandos, 2020). False allegations of both forms of abuse should be of concern to everyone because they undermine the believability of and protection for true victims of abuse. One solution that can address this issue is greater training and education about IPV and PABs. Some parents' claims about being alienated from a child may be due to a misunderstanding of what are considered PABs (Harman, Leder-Elder, et al., 2019). For example, suppose a parent has court-ordered supervised visits because there were multiple substantiated findings of abuse. In that case, this restricted contact does not mean the other parent is alienating them. If the other parent were engaging in PABs on top of this restriction, it would be considered a hybrid case. There are also many mental health and legal professionals who do not know how to differentiate alienated children from children who have been abused in other ways (Warshak, 2020). There have been considerable advances in empirically supported assessment tools for family violence (including parental alienation), so it is important for professionals to become better trained on how to evaluate all forms of family violence. Once there is greater awareness and understanding of these issues, then progressive deterrents (e.g., fines) can be created and implemented when false allegations of any form of family violence are found to be deliberate attempts to abuse the target of the allegation.

As described earlier, a growing number of scholars are arguing for parental alienation to be considered a form of child psychological abuse that requires a child protection response (Harman et al., 2018; Kruk, 2018, von Boch Galhau, 2018). Recognizing the scientific and scholarly advances in our understanding of this problem as one that affects both mothers and fathers and as one that causes severe consequences for the targets of PABs (both alienated parents and children) is an important step toward bridging the false divide between IPV and parental alienation research and practice. When victims of IPV and PABs encounter professional misunderstanding of these problems, their needs are not met, and their victimization continues. If parental alienation is recognized as another form of child abuse in legal statutes and administrative policies, then affected children can receive protection from the behaviors of an abusive parent. These responses include both family support and family preservation programs, where children remain with both parents and receive parenting support from family service workers (at milder stages of parental alienation), as well as child removal interventions on the part of child welfare authorities, where children are apprehended from alienating parents in order to allow them to reestablish a relationship with the targeted parent and protect them from abusive PABs (in more severe cases; Warshak, 2020).

In some parts of the world, parental alienation is recognized as a criminal offense, similar to child physical and sexual abuse, and this approach aligns with the empirical evidence on parental alienation to date (e.g., Poustie et al., 2018). Brazil, for example, was the first country to criminalize the offense. This criminalization provides authorities more options for intervention, such as being able to mandate the offender to obtain mental health services, which many civil and family courts are not authorized to do (Feitor, 2014). Legal scholars have been grappling with how parental alienation can similarly be treated as a criminal offense in other parts of the world (e.g., Finland). Barriers to the criminal prosecution of perpetrators of all forms of family violence and to the protection of victims of family violence, including parental alienation, need to be acknowledged, recognized, and removed.

A rebuttable presumption of shared parenting is another solution that may help prevent or mitigate parental alienation. Shared parenting is defined as children spending equal amounts of time in each parent's household and parents sharing responsibility for all aspects of decision-making concerning children. This presumption will be rebutted if there is evidence of family violence that has not been remedied. It would be contraindicated to place children in the custody of a parent who has been abusing them and could lead to further abuse of them. Remedial action to address spousal and child abuse is imperative, with the goal of the child maintaining a healthy and loving relationship with both parents and minimizing conflict between the parents. In cases where a partner exercises considerable coercive control, co-parenting is not typically a viable option because abusive parents will use these interactions to continue to control and abuse the other parent. In such cases, firm and clear court orders regarding parenting time and parallel parenting plans where both parents contribute separately to decisions regarding the child in different domains can be effective in maintaining a similar level of power between the parents and minimizing conflict. Interventions to address parental alienation are most effective when there are strong legal sanctions for noncompliance with shared parenting orders (Templer et al., 2017). Such plans require substantial legal and administrative oversight to ensure that children are protected from abuse and that their time with the abusive parent is safe (whether supervised or unsupervised).

In cases where there is potential for mild cases of parental alienation, then the shared parenting presumption would apply. This approach utilizes a "responsibility-to-needs" framework, which focuses on the child's needs, parental responsibilities to those needs, and the responsibilities of social institutions to support parents in the fulfillment of their parental responsibilities. We know that mothers and fathers who are satisfied with their parenting arrangements are less conflicted (Fabricius et al., 2016; Kruk, 2013), and reduced conflict is associated with children's well-being (Kruk, 2013; Nielsen, 2018). New legislation regarding a rebuttal presumption of shared parenting thus needs to consider concerns of both feminist and fathers' advocacy groups regarding the need for a better understanding of different forms of family violence, better strategies for interventions and treatment, an understanding of the impact that parental loss has on children (e.g., Vezzetti, 2016), the importance of parent–child attachment, and child access enforcement (Kruk, 2013).

Shared parenting as a legal presumption is strongly associated with both parents' active involvement in the day-to-day parenting of children (Kruk, 2013), and the child's time with the potentially alienated parent can provide contradictory experiences that make them less susceptible to a false narrative promoted by the alienating parent. Shared parenting can be a protective factor for children in high-conflict families and potentially preventive of first-time parental alienation and family violence. Parental conflict levels go up in court-determined sole custody and primary residence arrangements and go down in shared parenting agreements; the risk of parental alienation and other forms of family violence is much higher when parental relationships are threatened within an adversarial "winner-takes-all" context (Bauserman, 2012; Melli & Brown, 2008).

Other family support services are essential to the prevention and intervention of family violence in all its forms. Divorce education programs, therapeutic family mediation, postdivorce family therapy, support groups, and parental coordination and coaching services are vitally important adjuncts. Unfortunately, when professionals who provide these services do not have the training or expertise to understand parental alienation, PABs, and other forms of family violence, they can do more harm than good. Indeed, traditional forms of psychotherapy with providers who do not understand parental alienation are contraindicated for children and make matters worse (Clawar & Rivlin, 2013). New guidelines and best practices for assessment and treatment are needed based on the growing accumulation of research evidence on all forms of violence.

CONCLUSION

PABs are a common form of family violence in contested child custody cases. They should be recognized as such by practitioners, policymakers, legal practitioners, and judicial and legislative bodies. Should the issue of PABs as a form of IPV be framed as gender-specific as "violence against women" or as a gender-neutral conceptualization, such as "partner abuse"? Based on the empirical evidence, the exclusive focus on fathers as perpetrators and mothers as exclusively the victims of violence is unwarranted. The gender paradigm in family violence and parental alienation research is wanting in many respects, particularly because female-to-male violence has been overlooked in IPV research. Male-to-female PABs have until recently been underemphasized in parental alienation research.

The perceived "divide" between IPV and parental alienation scholars and advocates is a lamentable outcome of continued adherence to the gender paradigm on the part of policymakers and professionals in the legal and mental health fields. We detailed a fragment of the parallel lines of research in these areas in an effort to demonstrate that, in actuality, the two streams have a common primary concern: the use of abusive behaviors to harm another person through the use of children. There is considerable research on the negative impact of childhood exposure to IPV (Crooks et al., 2010) and loyalty binds (e.g., Schrodt & Afifi, 2018). We believe the IPV literature would benefit greatly by incorporating the accumulated evidence of the impact of parental alienation on children, which is documented to occur in families formerly and currently characterized by severe coercive controlling behaviors, regardless of the gender of the perpetrator, and to recognize parental alienation as a form IPV. Child outcome studies conclude that witnessing parental abuse and experiencing parental alienation are serious forms of child abuse, with devastating outcomes for children's security and well-being. By challenging misinformation and gender biases and understanding that we all want healthy and safe children and families, our hope is that this imaginary divide can be bridged, and we can finally join together to find better solutions for these forms of family violence.

REFERENCES

American Psychiatric Association. (2013). *Diagnostic and statistical manual of mental disorders* (5th ed.). American Psychiatric Association.

Baker, A. J. L. (2005). The long-term effects of parental alienation on adult children: A qualitative research study. *American Journal of Family Therapy, 33*, 289–302. https://doi.org/10.1080/01926180590962129

Baker, A. J. L. (2010). Adult recall of parental alienation in a community sample: Prevalence and associations with psychological maltreatment. *Journal of Divorce & Remarriage, 51*, 16–35. https://doi.org/10.1080/10502550903423206

Baker, A. J. L. (2015). *Bonded to the abuser: How victims make sense of childhood abuse.* Rowman & Littlefield.

Baker, A. J. L. (2018). Reliability and validity of the four-factor model of parental alienation. *Journal of Family Therapy, 42*, 100–118. https://doi.org/10.1111/1467-6427.12253

Baker, A. J. L., & Ben-Ami, N. (2011). To turn a child against a parent is to turn a child against himself: The direct and indirect effects of exposure to parental alienation strategies and self-esteem and well-being. *Journal of Divorce & Remarriage, 52*(7), 472–489. https://doi.org/10.1080/10502556.2011.609424

Baker, A. J. L., Creegan, A., Quinones, A., & Rozelle, L. (2016). Foster children's views of their parents: A review of the literature. *Children and Youth Services Review, 67*, 177–183. https://doi.org/10.1016/j.childyouth.2016.06.004

Baker, A. J. L., & Darnall, D. (2006). Behaviors and strategies employed in parental alienation: A survey of parental experiences. *Journal of Divorce & Remarriage, 45*, 97–124. https://doi.org/10.1300/J087v45n01_06

Baker, A. J. L., Miller, S., Bernet, W., & Adebayo, T. (2019). The assessment of the attitudes and behaviors about physically abused children: A survey of mental health professionals. *Journal of Child and Family Studies, 28*, 3401–3411. https://doi.org/10.1007/s10826-019-01522-5

Balmer, S., Matthewson, M., & Haines, J. (2018). Parental alienation: Targeted parent perspective. *Australian Journal of Psychology, 70*(1), 91–99. https://doi.org/10.1111/ajpy.12159.

Bancroft, L., & Silverman, J. (2002). *The batterer as parent: Addressing the impact of domestic violence on family dynamics.* Sage.

Bauserman, R. (2012). A meta-analysis of parental satisfaction, adjustment, and conflict in joint custody and sole custody following divorce. *Journal of Divorce & Remarriage, 53*, 464–488.

Beeble, M. L., Bybee, D., & Sullivan, C. M. (2007). Abusive men's use of children to control their partners and ex-partners. *European Psychologist, 12*, 54–61. https://doi.org/10.1027/1016-9040.12.1.54

Ben-Ami, N., & Baker, A. J. L. (2012). The long-term correlates of childhood exposure to parental alienation on adult self-sufficiency and well-being. *American Journal of Family Therapy, 40*(2), 169–183. https://doi.org/10.1080/01926187.2011.601206

Berger, J. L., Douglas, E. M., & Hines, D. A. (2016). The mental health of male victims and their children affected by legal and administrative partner aggression. *Aggressive Behavior, 42*, 346–361. https://doi.org/10.1002/ab.21630

Bernet, W. (2020a). Introduction to parental alienation. In D. Lorandos & William Bernet (Eds.), *Parental alienation—Science and law* (pp. 5–43). Charles C. Thomas.

Bernet, W. (2020b). Parental alienation and misinformation proliferation. *Family Court Review, 58*, 293–307. https://doi.org/10.1111/fcre.12473

Bernet, W. (2020c). The Five-Factor Model for the diagnosis of parental alienation. *Feedback—Journal of the Family Therapy Association of Ireland, 6*(Summer), 3–15.

Bernet, W., Gregory, N., Rohner, R. P., & Reay, K. M. (2020). Measuring the difference between parental alienation and estrangement: The PARQ-Gap. *Journal of Forensic Sciences, 65*, 1225–1234. https://doi.org/10.1111/1556-4029.14300

Bernet, W., Verrocchio, M. C., & Korosi, S. (2015). Yes, children are susceptible to manipulation: Commentary on article by Clemente and Padilla-Racero. *Child and Youth Services Review, 56*, 135–138. https://doi.org/10.1016/j.childyouth.2015.07.004

Bernet, W., Wambolt, M. Z., & Narrow, W. E. (2016). Child affected by parental relationship distress. *Journal of the American Academy of Child & Adolescent Psychiatry, 55*, 571–579.

Bonanno, G. A., & Kaltman, S. (2001). The varieties of grief experience. *Clinical Psychology Review, 21*, 705–734.

Bone, J. M. (2017, March 10). The eight symptoms of parental alienation: Independent thinker phenomenon. https://www.jmichaelbone.com/blog1/the-eight-symptoms-of-parental-alienation-independent-thinker-phenomenon

Bowlby, J. (1969). *Attachment*. Basic Books.

Bruch, C. S. (2001). Parental alienation syndrome and parental alienation: Getting it wrong in child custody cases. *Family Law Quarterly, 35*(3), 527–552. https://law.ucdavis.edu/faculty/bruch/files/fam353_06_Bruch_527_552.pdf

Carmen, T. (2020, September 27). Survivors of domestic abuse told to keep quiet about it in court or risk jeopardizing child custody. CBC News. https://www.cbc.ca/news/canada/survivors-of-domestic-abuse-punishedfor-talking-about-it-in-child-custody-cases-1.5738149

Ceci, S. J., & Bruck, M. (1995). *Jeopardy in the courtroom: A scientific analysis of children's testimony*. American Psychological Association. https://doi.org/10.1037/10180-000

Chambers, C. (2017). *The 7 deadly sins of psychology: A manifesto for reforming the culture of scientific practice*. Princeton University Press.

Clawar, S. S., & Rivlin, B. V. (2013). *Children held hostage: Identifying brainwashed children, presenting a case, and crafting solutions* (2nd ed.). American Bar Association.

Clemente, M., & Padilla-Racero, D. (2015). Are children susceptible to manipulation? The best interest of children and their testimony. *Children & Youth Services Review*, *51*, 101–107. https://doi.org/10.1016/j.childyouth.2015.02.003

Colorado Department of Human Services. (2020). Case-specific executive review report: Non-confidential. Public identification case ID: 19-074.

Corbally, M. (2015). Accounting for intimate partner violence: A biographical analysis of narrative strategies used by men experiencing IPV from their female partners. *Journal of Interpersonal Violence*, *30*, 3112–3132. https://doi.org/10.1177/0886260514554429

Corvo, K., Dutton, D., & Chen, W. (2009). Do Duluth model interventions with perpetrators of domestic violence violate mental health professional ethics? *Ethics & Behavior*, *19*(4), 323–340. https://doi.org/10.1080/10508420903035323

Crooks, C. V., Jaffe, P. G., & Bala, N. (2010). Factoring in the effects of children's exposure to domestic violence in determining appropriate postseparation parenting plans. In M. T. Hannah & B. Goldstein (Eds.), *Domestic violence, abuse, and child custody: Legal strategies and policies, 22-1-22-25*. Civic Research Institute.

Demi, A. S., & Gilbert, C. M. (1987). Relationship of parental grief to sibling grief. *Archives of Psychiatriatric Nursing*, *1*, 385–391.

Dilworth, J. L., & Hildreth, G. J. (1998). Long-term unresolved grief: Applying Bowlby's variants to adult survivors of early parental death. *Omega: Journal of Death & Dying*, *36*, 147–159.

Dobson, R. (2003). Media mislead the public over the MMR vaccine, study says. *British Medical Journal*, *326*, 1107. https://doi.org/10.1136/bmj.326.7399.1107-a

Domestic Abuse Intervention Program. (2011). Wheel gallery. Home of the Duluth Model. http://www.theduluthmodel.org/training/wheels.html

Drozd, L., & Oleson, N. W. (2004). Is it abuse, alienation, and/or estrangement? A decision tree. *Journal of Child Custody*, *1*, 65–106. https://doi.org/10.1300/J190v01n03_05

Dutton, D. G. (1994). Patriarchy and wife assault: The ecological fallacy. *Violence and Victims*, *9*, 125–140.

Dutton, D. G., & Nicholls, T. L. (2005). The gender paradigm in domestic violence research and theory: Part 1—the conflict of theory and data. *Aggression & Violent Behavior*, *10*, 680–714. https://doi.org/10.1016/j.avb.2005.02.001

Fabricious, W. V., Sokol, K. R., Diaz, P., & Braver, S. L. (2016). Parent-child relationships: The missing link between parenting time and children's mental and physical health. In L. Drozd, M. Saini, & N. Oleson (Eds.), *Parenting plan evaluations: Applied research for the family court* (2nd ed., pp. 74–84). Oxford University Press.

Feitor, S. (2014). Alienação parental: Novos desafios, velhos problemas: Estudo de Jurisprudência e legislação. *Julgar*, *24*, 187–202.

Festinger, L. (1957). *A theory of cognitive dissonance*. Stanford University Press.

Finzi-Dottan, R., Goldblatt, H., & Cohen-Mascia, O. (2012). The experience of motherhood for alienated mothers. *Child & Family Social Work*, *17*, 316–325. https://doi.org/10.1111/j.1365-2206.2011.00782.x

Follingstad, D. R. (2007). Rethinking current approaches to psychological abuse: Conceptual and methodological issues. *Aggression & Violent Behavior*, *12*, 439–458. https://doi.org/10.1016/j.avb.2006.07.004

Freeman, B. W. (2020). The psychological assessment of contact refusal. In D. Lorandos & William Bernet (Eds.), *Parental alienation—Science and law* (pp. 44–81). Charles C. Thomas.

Friedlander, S., & Walters, M. G. (2010). When a child rejects a parent: Tailoring the intervention to fit the problem. *Family Court Review, 48*(1), 98–111. https://doi.org/10.1111/j.1744-1617.2009.01291.x

Gardner, R. A. (1985). Recent trends in divorce and custody litigation. *Academy Forum, 29*(2), 3–7.

Gardner, R. A. (1987). *The parental alienation syndrome and the differentiation between fabricated and genuine child sex abuse.* Creative Therapeutics.

Gilbar, O., Taft, C., & Dekel, R. (2020). Male intimate partner violence: Examining the roles of childhood trauma, PTSD symptoms, and dominance. *Journal of Family Psychology, 34,* 1004–1013. http://dx.doi.org/10.1037/fam0000669

Gith, E. (2013). The attitude of the Shari'a courts to parental alienation syndrome: Understanding the dynamics of the syndrome in Arab society. *Journal of Divorce & Remarriage, 54,* 537–549. https://doi.org/10.1080/10502556.2013.828982

Godbout, E., & Parent, C. (2012). The life paths and lived experiences of adults who have experienced parental alienation: A retrospective study. *Journal of Divorce & Remarriage, 53,* 34–54.

Gordon, R. M., & Stoffey Bottinelli, R. W. (2008). MMPI-2 findings of primitive defenses in alienating patients. *American Journal of Family Therapy, 36,* 211–228. https://doi.org/10.1080/01926180701643313

Gottlieb, L. J. (2012). *The parental alienation syndrome: A family therapy and collaborative systems approach to amelioration.* Charles C. Thomas.

Gueta, K., Peled, E., & Sander-Almonznino, N. (2016). "I used to be an ordinary mom": The maternal identity of women abused by an intimate partner. *American Journal of Orthopsychiatry, 86,* 456–466. http://dx.doi.org/10.1037/ort0000128

Hagerty, B. B. (2020, December). Can children be persuaded to love a partner they hate? *The Atlantic.* https://www.theatlantic.com/magazine/archive/2020/12/when-a-child-is-a-weapon/616931/

Hamel, J., Langhinrichsen-Rohling, J., & Hines, D. A. (2012). The partner abuse state of knowledge articles and online database. *Partner Abuse, 3,* 131–139.

Hansonn, S. O. (2017, April 11). Science and pseudo-science. *Stanford Encyclopedia of Philosophy.* https:plato.stanford.edu/entries/pseudo-science/

Harman, J. J., Bernet, W., & Harman, J. (2019). Parental alienation: The blossoming of a field of study. *Current Directions in Psychological Science, 28,* 212–217. https://doi.org/10.1177/0963721419827271

Harman, J. J., & Biringen, Z. (2016). *Parents acting badly: How institutions and societies promote the alienation of children from their loving families.* Colorado Parental Alienation Project, LLC.

Harman, J. J., Biringen, Z., Ratajack, E. M., Outland, P. L., & Kraus, A. (2016). Parents behaving badly: Gender biases in the perception of parental alienation. *Journal of Family Psychology, 30,* 866–874. https://doi.org/10.1037/fam0000232

Harman, J. J., Kruk, E., & Hines, D. (2018). Parental alienating behaviors: An unacknowledged form of family violence. *Psychological Bulletin, 144,* 1275–1299. http://dx.doi.org/10.1037/bul0000175

Harman, J. J., Leder-Elder, S., & Biringen, Z. (2016). Prevalence of parental alienation drawn from a representative poll. *Children & Youth Services Review, 66,* 62–66. https://doi.org/10.1016/j.childyouth.2016.04.021

Harman, J. J., Leder-Elder, S., & Biringen, Z. (2019). Prevalence of adults who are the targets of parental alienating behaviors and their impact: Results from three national polls. *Child & Youth Services Review, 106,* 1–13. https://doi.org/10.1016/jy.childyouth.2019.104471

Harman, J. J., & Lorandos, D. (2020). Allegations of family violence in court: How parental alienation affects judicial outcomes. *Psychology, Public Policy, & Law.* https://doi.org/10.1037/law0000301

Harman, J. J., Lorandos, D., Biringen, Z., & Grubb, C. (2019). Gender differences in the use of parental alienating behaviors. *Journal of Family Violence, 35,* 459–469. https://doi.org/10.1007/s10896-019-00097-5

Harman, J. J., & Matthewson, M. (2020). Parental alienating behaviors. In D. Lorandos & William Bernet (Eds.), *Parental alienation—Science and law* (pp. 82–141). Charles C. Thomas.

Hines, D. A., & Douglas, E. M. (2010). A closer look at men who sustain intimate terrorism by women. *Partner Abuse, 1,* 286–313. https://doi.org/10.1891/1946-6560.1.3.286

Hines, D. A., Douglas, E. M., & Berger, J. L. (2015). A self-report measure of legal and administrative aggression within intimate relationships. *Aggressive Behavior, 41,* 295–309. http://dx.doi.org/10.1002/ab.21540

Johnson, M. P. (2008). *A typology of domestic violence: Intimate terrorism, violent resistance and situational couple violence.* Northeastern University Press.

Joshi, A. (2020). Parental alienation and domestic violence: Two sides of the same coin. Part two of two. *Michigan Family Law Journal, 50,* 11–17.

Kruk, E. (2010). Parental and social institutional responsibilities to children's needs in the divorce transition: Fathers' perspectives. *Journal of Men's Studies, 18*(2), 159–178.

Kruk, E. (2013). *The equal parent presumption.* McGill-Queen's University Press.

Kruk, E. (2018). Parental alienation as a form of emotional child abuse: Current state of knowledge and future directions for research. *Family Science Review, 22*(4), 141–164.

Lee-Maturana, S., Matthewson, M., & Dwan, C. (2021). Understanding targeted parents' experience of parental alienation: A qualitative description from their own perspective. *The American Journal of Family Therapy 49*(5), 499–516. doi:10.1080/01926187.2020.1837035

Lorandos, D. (2013). Parental alienation and North American law. In D. Lorandos, W. Bernet, & S. R. Sauber (Eds.), *Parental alienation: The handbook for mental health and legal professionals* (pp. 348–424). Charles C. Thomas.

Lorandos, D. (2020). Parental alienation in U.S. courts, 1985–2018. *Family Court Review, 58,* 322–339. https://doi.org/10.1111/fcre.12475

Lorandos, D., Bernet, W., & Sauber, S. R. (2013). Overview of parental alienation. In D. Lorandos et al. (Eds.), *Parental alienation: The handbook for mental health and legal professionals* (pp. 5–46). Charles C. Thomas.

Machado, A., Hines, D., & Douglas, E. M. (2020). Male victims of female-perpetrated partner violence: A qualitative analysis of men's experiences, the impact of violence, and perceptions of their worth. *Psychology of Men & Masculinities, 21,* 612–621. http://dx.doi.org/10.1037/men0000285

Marquez, T. M., Narciso, I., & Ferreira, L. C. (2020). Empirical research on parental alienation: A descriptive literature review. *Children & Youth Services Review, 119*, 105572. https://doi.org/10.1016/j.childyouth.2020.105572

McMahon, M., & Pence, E. (1995). Doing more harm than good: Some cautions on visitation centers. In E. Peled, P. Jaffe, & J. Edleson (Eds.), *Ending the cycle of violence: Community responses to children of battered women* (pp. 186–206). Sage.

Meier, J. S., Dickson, S., O'Sullivan, C., Rosen, L., & Hayes, J. (2019). Child custody outcomes in cases involving parental alienation and abuse allegations (GWU Law School Public Law Research Paper No. 2019-56). *SSRN*. https://ssrn.com/abstracte_3448062

Melli, M. S., & Brown, P. R. (2008). Exploring a new family form: The shared time family. *International Journal of Law, Policy and the Family, 22*, 231–269.

Meyer, S. (2016). Still blaming the victim of intimate partner violence? Women's narratives of victim desistance and redemption and seeking support. *Theoretical Criminology, 20*, 75–90. https://doi.org/10.1177/13624806155853999

Moné, J., & Biringen, Z. (2012). Assessing parental alienation: Empirical assessment of college students' recollections of parental alienation during their childhoods. *Journal of Divorce & Remarriage, 53*, 157–177. https://doi.org/10.1080/10502556.2012.663265

Moné, J., McPhee, D., Anderson, S. K., & Banning, J. H. (2011). Family members' narratives of divorce and interparental conflict: Implications for parental alienation. *Journal of Divorce & Remarriage, 52*, 642–667. https://doi.org/10.1080/10502556.2011.619940

Nielsen, L. (2014). Woozles: Their role in custody law reform, parenting plans, and family court. *Psychology, Public Policy, and Law, 20*(2), 164–180. https://doi.org/10.1037/law0000004

Nielsen, L. (2018). Joint versus sole physical custody: Children's outcomes independent of parent–child relationships, income, and conflict in 60 studies. *Journal of Divorce and Remarriage, 59*(4), 247–281.

Otowa, T., York, T. P., Gardner, C. O., Kendler, K. S., & Hettema, J. M. (2014). The impact of childhood parental loss on risk for mood, anxiety and substance use disorders in a population-based sample of male twins. *Psychiatry Research, 220*, 404–409. https://doi.org/10.1016/j.psychres.2014.07.053

Poustie, C., Matthewson, M., & Balmer, S. (2018). The forgotten parent: The targeted parent perspective of parental alienation. *Journal of Family Issues, 39*, 3298–3323.

Rand, D. (2013). The history of parental alienation from early days to modern times. In D. Lorandos, W. Bernet, & S. R. Sauber (Eds.), *Parental alienation: The handbook for mental and legal health professionals* (pp. 291–321). Charles C. Thomas.

Redleaf, D. (2019, January 27). After the hotline call. *The Atlantic*. https://www.theatlantic.com/ideas/archive/2019/01/problem-child-protectiveservices/580771/

Rosen, L. (2017). *Beyond the hostage child: Towards empowering protective parents*. Createspace.

Rowen, J., & Emery, R. E. (2019) Parental denigration reports across parent–child dyads: Divorced parents underreport denigration behaviors compared to children. *Journal of Child Custody, 16*, 197–208. https://doi.org/10.1080/15379418.2019.1610135

Saini, M., Johnston, J. R., Fidler, B. J., & Bala, N. (2016). Empirical studies of alienation. In L. M. Drozd, M. Saini, & N. Olesen (Eds.), *Parenting plan evaluations: Applied research for the family court* (2nd ed., pp. 374–430). Oxford University Press. http://dxdoi.org/10.1093/med:psych/9780199396580.003.0013

Sauber, S. R (2006). PAS as a family tragedy: Roles of family members, professionals, and the justice system. In R. A. Gardner, S. R. Sauber, & D. Lorandos (Eds.), *The international handbook of parental alienation syndrome: Conceptual, clinical and legal considerations* (pp. 12–32). Charles C. Thomas.

Saunders, D. (1994). Child custody decisions in families experiencing woman abuse. *Social Work, 39*, 51–59.

Schrodt, P., & Afifi, T. D. (2018). Untying the ties that bind: Dispositional and relational patterns of negative relational disclosures and family members' feelings of being caught. *Journal of Family Issues, 39*, 1962–1983. https://doi.org/10.1177/0192513X17739050

Sharples, A., Harman, J. J., & Lorandos, D. (2021). The relationship between parental alienation and other forms of abuse. Manuscript in preparation.

Sierau, S., White, L. O., Klein, A. M., Manly, J. T., von Klitzing, K., & Herzberg, P. Y. (2018). Assessing psychological and physical abuse from children's perspective: Factor structure and psychometric properties of the picture-based, modularized child-report version of the Parent-Child Conflict Tactics Scale–Revised (CTSPC-R). *PLOS One, 13*, 1–14. https://doi.org/10.1371/journal.pone.0205401

Sîrbu, A. G., Vintila, M., Tisu, L., Ştefănuţ, A. M., Tudorel, O. I., Măguran, B., & Toma, R. A. (2020). Parental alienation-development and validation of a behavioral anchor scale. *Sustainability, 13*, 1–18, https://doi.org/10.3390/su13010316

Smith, S. G., Zhang, X., Basile, K. C., Merrick, M. T., Wang, J., Kresnow, M., & Chen, J. (2018, November).The National Intimate Partner and Sexual Violence Survey (NISVS): 2015 data brief—Updated release. Centers for Disease Control and Prevention. https://www.cdc.gov/violenceprevention/pdf/2015data-brief508.pdf

Spencer, C., Mallory, A. B., Cafferky, B. M., Kimmes, J. G., Beck, A. R., & Stith, S. M. (2019). Mental health factors and intimate partner violence perpetration and victimization: A meta-analysis. *Psychology of Violence, 9*, 1–17. http://dx.doi.org/10.1037/vio0000156

Tavares, A., Crespo, C., & Ribeiro, M. T. (2020). Psychological adaptation and beliefs in targeted parents: A study in the context of parental alienation. *Journal of Child & Family Studies, 29*, 2281–2289. https://doi.org/10.1007/s10826-020-01742-0

Templer, K., Matthewson, M., Haines, J., & Cox, G. (2017). Recommendations for best practice in response to parental alienation: Findings from a systematic review. *Journal of Family Therapy, 39*(1), 103–122. https://doi.org/10.1111/1467-6427.12137

Tilbrook, E., Allan, A., & Dear, G. (2010). *Intimate partner abuse of men*. Men's Advisory Network.

Trocmé, N., & Bala, N. (2005). False allegations of abuse and neglect when parents separate. *Child Abuse & Neglect, 29*(12), 1333–1345. https://doi.org/10.1016/j.chiabu.2004.06.016

Ubillos-Landa, S., Puente-Martinez, A., González-Castro, J. L., & Nieto-González, S. (2020). You belong to me! Meta-analytic review of the use of male control and dominance against women in intimate partner violence. *Aggression & Violent Behavior, 52*, 101392. https://doi.org/10.1016/j.avb.2020.101392

Verrocchio, M. C., Baker, A. J. L., & Bernet, W. (2016). Associations between exposure to parental alienating behaviors, anxiety, and depression in an Italian sample of adults. *Journal of Forensic Sciences, 61*, 692–698. http://dx.doi.org/10.1111/1556-4029.13046

Verrocchio, M. C., Baker, A. J. L., & Marchetti, D. (2017). Adult report of childhood exposure to parental alienation at different developmental time periods. *Journal of Family Therapy, 40*, 602–618. http://dx.doi.org/10.1111/1467-6427.12192

Vezzetti, V. C. (2016). New approaches to divorce with children: A problem of public health. *Health Psychology Open.* July-Dec 2016), 1–13.http://dx.doi.org/10.1177/2055102916678105

von Boch-Galhau, W. (2018). Parental alienation (syndrome)—A serious form of psychological child abuse. *Mental Health and Family Medicine, 14*, 725–739. http://mhfmjournal.com/pdf/MHFM-117.pdf

Walker, A., Lyall, K., Silva, D., Craigie, G., Mayshak, R., Costa, B., Hyder, S., & Bently, A. (2020). Male victims of female-perpetrated intimate partner violence, help-seeking, and reporting behaviors: A qualitative study. *Psychology of Men & Masculinities, 21*, 213–223. http://dx.doi.org/10.1037/men0000222

Walker, L. E. (1983). Victimology and the psychological perspectives of battered women. *Victimology, 8*, 82–104.

Warshak, R. A. (2015). Ten parental alienation fallacies that compromise decisions in court and in therapy. *Professional Psychology: Research and Practice, 46*, 235–249. https://doi.org/10.1037/pro0000031

Warshak, R. A. (2020). When evaluators get it wrong: False positive IDs and parental alienation. *Psychology, Public Policy, and Law, 26*(1), 54–68. https://doi.org/10.1037/law0000216

PART IV

Evidence-Based Interventions

11

Holding Perpetrators Accountable

Evidence-Based Interview and Assessment Procedures

JOHN HAMEL AND LIAM ENNIS ■

Intimate partner violence (IPV), also known as domestic violence, is a criminal offense in most developed countries, including the United States. In many ways, however, intervention policies treat IPV differently than other violent crimes. This is partly because, after four decades of increasing attention to this problem in the media and among criminal justice personnel, mental health professionals, and other stakeholders in the field, IPV remains mostly a private phenomenon, occurring "behind closed doors" among individuals in close relationships; and because IPV arrest, prosecution, and treatment policies have been shaped more by political considerations than empirical research findings.

There are serious limitations to arrest and prosecution policies and the manner in which they are implemented, concerning the rights of defendants to due process and the consequences of a criminal conviction (e.g., for child custody, employment opportunities, social stigma), and with respect to their actual effectiveness, as documented elsewhere in this volume. Indeed, a comparison of national surveys indicates that the overall annual prevalence of IPV has not only not been reduced but may have actually risen—from the 6 million males and 6 million females found in the National Family Violence Surveys of the 1980s (Straus & Gelles, 1990), to the 7 million males and 7 million females found in the more recent National Intimate Partner and Sexual Violence Survey (Black et al., 2011). In order for the crime of IPV to be adjudicated fairly and effectively, current policies will need to undergo some much-needed reforms to challenge and examine some prevailing biases and assumptions about IPV in the light of empirical research—among them the belief that IPV is largely a gender problem; that it necessarily involves attempts to dominate and control one's partner and only worsens over time; that there is a clear distinction between perpetrators and victims; that individuals designated as "victims" should always be believed, whereas attempts by those designated as "perpetrators" to explain any IPV incident as mutual or in self-defense should be regarded as victim-blaming and lack of responsibility-taking; and that individuals who engage in any form of IPV around their children, no matter how infrequent or inconsequential, or who engage in any type of psychological aggression deemed by someone as "power and control" are not fit parents (Dutton & Corvo, 2006; Hamel, 2020a).

The final section of this volume suggests a number of evidence-based reforms for overcoming such assumptions and ushering in, it is hoped, a more enlightened era in arrest, prosecution, and treatment policies. Within this reformist paradigm, guilty parties are held responsible and victims protected from further abuse, but the complex, heterogeneous, gender-inclusive, and systemic nature of IPV is acknowledged (Dutton, 2006; Hamel, 2014, 2020). A key consideration is an actual risk posed by the alleged perpetrator. Police arrest guidelines, especially in mandatory arrest states, cast a wide net due to vague, politically driven dominant aggressor guidelines. Further, the questionable assumption that low-level acts of IPV must be criminally prosecuted lest they become serious or possibly life-threatening leaves officers unable to adequately determine whether a crime has been committed and by whom. Police make an arrest and leave it up to the suspect to prove their innocence, a daunting task given current pro-conviction attitudes and the gender paradigm, one made exponentially more difficult for those who cannot afford quality legal representation.

In this chapter, we explore ways to better gauge the actual risk posed by IPV perpetrators, first through evidence-based interview techniques and, second, with validated, reliable assessment instruments.

INTERVIEW PROTOCOLS

The following should be considered generic recommendations. However, the content is relevant not only to police officers and prosecutors tasked with determining whether or not a suspect should be arrested and charged with a crime but also to attorneys wanting to mount an effective defense and child custody evaluators and expert witnesses. For intervention providers wanting to tailor treatment to client needs, these suggestions should help navigate the challenges IPV poses to those seeking to overcome resistance and assign responsibility for and gauge the impact of multidetermined and multimotivated behaviors within complex systems. How they are implemented depends, of course, on the particular setting, context, and population.

Lessons from Deception Detection Research

Developed in the United States by John E. Reid and Associates in the 1970s (Inbau et al., 2013), the Behavior Analysis Interview (BAI) consists of nonthreatening questions, as well as 14 intended to provoke a behavior response. It is assumed that guilty suspects are more likely than truth-tellers to display or "leak" nervous or anxiety-reducing behavior (Vrij, 2015b). However, a meta-analysis of 120 studies on the BAI, from laboratory studies and analyses of actual police interrogations (DePaulo et al., 2003), reported on 158 possible cues to deception and found numerous commonly held assumptions to be incorrect. Liars, for example, do not avert their gaze or fidget nor self-groom or avoid leaning forward more than truth-tellers. Findings of correlations between deception and certain behaviors are typically weak and inconsistent. Some behaviors have been found to indicate the opposite of what would be predicted—for example, that liars less likely to cross their legs and shift posture than truth-tellers. In fact, in one study of police investigations, "the more the officers endorsed the BAI's view on cues to detection, the worse they became at distinguishing between truth and lies" (Vrij, 2015b, p. 229). Although some of the 206 studies reported in the Bond and De Paulo (2006) meta-analysis found police officers to be better than civilians at deception detection, most studies found no difference between assumed "experts" and the lay public. Aside from the BAI, all anxiety-based procedures have been deemed unreliable, including voice stress analysis (VSA) and attempts to detect deception with facial micro-expressions (Vrij & Granhag, 2012).

In addition to its unreliability in detecting liars from truth-tellers, the Reid interview is an accusatory type of procedure, in which the interrogator seeks to manipulate levels of anxiety in the suspect with isolation and lengthy interviews, a series of pointed questions, the presentation of false evidence, and minimizing the consequences of confessing (Kassin et al., 2015; Redlich & Meissner, 2009). It has been found to increase the likelihood of both true and false confessions from suspects, and as a result, overconfident police may prematurely terminate an investigation. Accusatory types of procedures have also failed to detect deception in fraud investigations (Walsh & Bull, 2010) and among terrorism suspects (High-Value Detainee Interrogation Group, 2016) reliably.

Evidence-Based Interviewing

Research has identified more predictable cues to deception with the use of "strategic questioning" that focuses on the cognitive rather than emotional differences between liars and truth-tellers (Granhag & Hartwig, 2015; Redlich & Meissner, 2009). Drawing upon empirical findings on memory, communication, and interpersonal dynamics, the Cognitive Interview has been found effective with suspects, victims, and witnesses in increasing the amount of information elicited without significant loss in accuracy. In this approach, the interrogator obtains cooperation by establishing rapport with the suspect and encouraging him or her to talk freely (High Value Detainee Interrogation Group, 2016). Unlike the Reid technique, an information-gathering approach increases the likelihood of true rather than false confessions (Meissner et al., 2012). Similar procedures include the Observing Rapport-Based Interview Techniques (ORBIT), tested with terrorism suspects:

Interviewer behaviors consistent with Motivational Interviewing (showing acceptance and empathy being adaptive to the suspect's narrative, evoking the suspect's beliefs and views, and encouraging a sense of autonomy on the part of the suspect) had the largest direct effect on information yield. Motivational Interviewing techniques appeared to both directly increase yield and indirectly increased yield by improving adaptive interviewing, as well as decreasing maladaptive interviewing. (High Value Detainee Interrogation Group, 2016, pp. 26–27)

MOTIVATIONAL INTERVIEWING

A way of relating to suspects or clients in counseling settings rather than a specific treatment model, motivational interviewing (MI) is a nonconfrontational, client-centered approach that can help to elicit information from otherwise reluctant and defensive individuals by demonstrating respect, helping them examine and resolve ambivalence, and furthering responsibility taking. Motivation to change comes from the client, not imposed from without, and the relationship between interviewer and interviewee is a partnership (Dia et al., 2009; Stinson & Clark, 2017). Outcome studies with court-mandated IPV perpetrators indicate that substituting an MI interview for the traditional cursory intake results in a stronger client–facilitator alliance, fewer program dropouts, increased responsibility taking, homework compliance, group cohesion, and adherence to group norms. It also predicts lower psychological and physical abuse, based on victim reports (see Hamel, 2020b, for a review.) The effectiveness of MI can be attributed, at least in part, to the importance it places on what has been called the "common factors" in counseling and psychotherapy, responsible for the majority of positive treatment effects, with strong effect sizes as measured by Cohen's "d" for the following: therapist–client alliance (0.57), empathy (0.63), goal consensus/collaboration (0.72), and positive regard/affirmation (0.56) (Wampold & Imel, 2015).

The importance of client-centered approaches such as MI has been confirmed with participants in batterer intervention programs, among which there is a consensus that clients are more engaged and motivated when facilitators are caring and committed; are nonjudgmental; maintain a safe working group environment; are honest, humble, and genuine; and are willing to challenge client behaviors, but in nonconfrontational and respectful ways (Hamel, 2020b).

Establishing Trust and Cooperation

Expect resistance when interviewing involuntary clients, which may reflect a mistrust of authority or fear of being judged (e.g., as inadequate or morally reprehensible), and not always evidence of denial or unwillingness to change. It is the interviewer's task to elicit more truthful responses and facilitate accountability without unnecessarily alienating or shaming the person sitting across from them.

Self-Awareness

Recent research has found that most people actually depend on implicit, impressionistic cues (Hartwig & Bond, 2011). People are judged as deceptive when they appear incompetent or ambivalent, when their statements seem implausible, scripted, and lacking in details, and when they appear as unfriendly and uncooperative, which may be better objective predictors of deception. However, "even if perceivers displayed a perfect reliance on the most valid constellation of cues, their performance would not improve much. Instead, the results show that inaccuracy in lie judgments is primarily due to the weakness of behavioral cues to deception" (Hartwig & Granhag, 2015, p. 145).

While such System 1 "gut instinct" thinking can lead to the truth or provide clues for further investigation, they cannot be relied upon in forensic settings (Gilovich et al., 2002). This way of making judgments is seductive but easily vulnerable to bias. Be mindful, then, of the possible impact of your background and experience—if, for example, you grew up with family members in law enforcement or criminal defense or have been the victim of relationship violence or other violent crimes. Also, be alert for common cognitive biases such as the availability and representativeness heuristics and confirmatory bias (Gilovich et al., 2002; Nicholls et al., 2013). In the media and among criminal justice personnel, mental health professionals, victim advocates, and other domestic violence stakeholders, the focus is typically on male perpetrators and serious, lethal violence, reflective of the *gender paradigm* discussed elsewhere in this volume. As argued by Corvo and Johnson (2003), perceiving IPV suspects, especially male suspects, as "batterers" is:

> based on a closed system of logic, which begins by identifying the most violent perpetrators of domestic violence, labels them as "batterers," and then retrospectively analyzes the escalation of their violence as being inevitable. This focus on the most violent offender then appears to demonstrate the inevitability of escalation in all cases and reinforces commonly held assumptions and beliefs, such as that all domestic violence has the same pattern, all offenders have the same personality characteristics, and all perpetrator behavior is premeditated and strategic in nature. (p. 261)

Creating and Maintaining the Right Environment

The interview should be conducted, whenever possible, in a comfortable, open setting. In line with MI guidelines, you should maintain eye contact, smile, and exhibit a respectful but businesslike demeanor, knowledgeable and confident, yet warm and open-minded, eager to hear the client's account of the events for which he or she was accused of committing. Be sure to quickly separate yourself from the police and other authority figures who the client may resent. Show that you understand why the client may feel the way he or she does without defending or condemning those authority figures. The following are among the research-based techniques for establishing and maintaining client engagement throughout the interview process:

- Allow for an initial period of "chit-chat," allowing the interviewee to acclimate to their surroundings and get comfortable. The chit-chat can be about the weather, traffic, or a major ongoing news event, so long as it establishes, even just briefly, your connection to the client as another human being and does not appear forced and inauthentic.
- Obtain basic demographic and personal information, and conduct a general psychosocial history before asking about alleged IPV incidents. This allows you to show your concern for the client and build rapport.
- Raise the client's self-esteem by offering simple compliments, such as thanking them for being on time or deferring to their judgment when possible (e.g., giving them a choice of chairs to sit in). When appropriate, find a way to acknowledge a recent success, or their expertise on a particular topic, based on previous information or something they have disclosed during the interview.
- Acknowledge any resistance and frame it as normal and understandable.
- Show empathy with limited, careful self-disclosure and chit-chat (e.g., agreeing about the traffic outside, bad weather, an important sporting event, the stress of raising children).
- Any self-disclosure should be natural and not forced or awkward, or it will backfire. You do not want to be perceived as trying to be someone's buddy or being manipulative.
- Provide incentives to cooperate, as done in MI work, by promising to help the client achieve his or her positive goals (e.g., be happier or more confident, avoid jail, be a better example for the children) if they make a sincere effort to benefit from the counseling. This taps into the norm of reciprocity, which helps maintain trust and a working alliance between the interviewer and the client.
- Occasionally summarize the information they are providing you as you go through the interview to demonstrate respect and stay aligned with the client.
- Look for disclosures indicating positive values and motives and encourage the client to elaborate on those.
- Avoid passing judgment on negative, harmful, or illegal behavior. If pressed to comment, have the client think through the consequences of these behaviors and whether they have been in their best interest.

Detecting Deception

Before asking about the alleged IPV incidents, make sure you have first reviewed all the information you have about the client and the alleged crime in question, including police reports and other documents. This information and what you can gather with the initial psychosocial history will help guide your questioning. Begin with open-ended questions and give clients time to remember as much as possible about the IPV events. Have them provide details by asking them to put themselves back into the time and place of the event (e.g., physical environment, time of day, temperature, what they were feeling, and any conversations they may have had at the time), take the victim's perspective, or recall the events in backward order. Truthful renditions of an event are more likely to contain such details, whereas deceivers tend to be vague and to provide few sensory details (Amado et al., 2015; Vrij, 2015a, 2015c). They have a difficult time making up conversations, and they rely on *cognitive operations* in which details are talked about rather than directly presented—for example, "I must have had my coat on, because it was cold that night," as opposed to "I was freezing, so I grabbed my coat from the utility closet."

As discussed previously, truth-tellers cannot be distinguished from liars by some nonverbal signs commonly thought to indicate deception, such as fidgeting, making grooming gestures, or looking away. Both may have reasons to be nervous. According to self-presentational theory, both liars and truth-tellers want to be believed and try to convey a truthful impression. Truth-tellers are usually more relaxed, but sometimes honest but insecure people will be reluctant to tell the truth if they thinks it might make them look bad or harm others and may appear more nervous than liars who feel comfortable with what they have done (DePaulo et al., 2003).

> The self-presentational perspective underscores the similarities between truths and lies. Telling the whole truth and nothing but the truth is rarely possible or desirable. All self-presentations are edited. The question is whether the editing crosses the line from the honest highlighting of aspects of identity that are most relevant in the ongoing situation to a dishonest attempt to mislead. This suggests that truthful and deceptive self-presentations may be construed more aptly as aligned on a continuum rather that sorted into clear and distinct categories. (p. 105)

Liars and truth-tellers employ different strategies to achieve their goal of being believed, which can be exploited by interrogators (Granhag & Hartwig, 2008). After all, "guilty suspects have a transgression to cover up, while innocent suspects do not" (Hartwig et al., 2010, p. 11). Both engage in impression management, but only liars attempt to manipulate the information they choose to provide. Individuals who are trying to make up a false narrative will appear cautious and deliberate, with lots of pauses but less blinking and less hand and finger movements than truth-tellers, and their narrative will be more structured. These telltale signs of deception can be elicited by having a client recount an event backward and having them make eye contact with you as they do so; this increases their cognitive load, leading them to think harder to "keep their story straight."

Inconsistency between statements is not always, contrary to common belief, a reliable sign of evasiveness or lying. In fact, truth-tellers are less concerned with consistency between statements and more focused on remembering and reporting the events (Hartwig & Granhag, 2015). In contrast, truth-tellers have been found to have a *belief in a just world* and *the illusion of transparency*, by which they assume that they will more likely be believed if they are as accurate as possible because people want justice and can tell when someone is being genuine. For example, they will freely correct a previous statement or provide incidental details that are not as relevant to the event in question because they are not trying to edit themselves out of fear of being "found out." Their narratives often meander and appear unstructured.

Strategic Use of Evidence

This cutting-edge approach to police investigation is compatible with established, ethical, information-gathering types of police interrogation procedures, such as PEACE (Clarke & Milne, 2011; Meissner et al., 2012; Oxburgh & Dando, 2011). It draws upon research findings that guilty suspects have knowledge that, if disclosed, would give them away, so they enter the interview with the intent of not revealing that information; whereas innocent suspects, who also want to be believed but have nothing to hide, are motivated to be more open (Bond et al., 2015; Granhag & Hartwig, 2008; Hartwig et al., 2014). Guilty suspects may provide many details, but only those that are unverifiable (High Value Detainee Interrogation Group, 2016). Strategic use of evidence (SEU) takes advantage of the different information-management strategies between liars and truth-tellers: "By posing questions about the information that liars are motivated to conceal without revealing that one possesses this information, a questioner may lead liars to contradict these facts in their attempts to distance themselves from incriminating information" (Bond et al., 2015, p. 46).

SUE takes into account findings that inconsistency is far more relevant when it is between a client's statement and empirical evidence to the contrary (statement-evidence inconsistency); or when a client keeps changing his or her account of an event in order to make it fit the evidence presented (within-statement inconsistency). The interviewer who has evidence unknown to the suspect will more readily produce within-statement inconsistencies by revealing the evidence from general to specific. For example, if the interviewer has pictures of a victim with obvious facial injuries, he or she will first ask about possible injuries inflicted on the victim and only later mention the pictures. If the suspect has overestimated the amount of information held by the interviewer, he or she will volunteer more information than they had wanted to. If the suspect has underestimated the amount of information, he or she will be faced with incriminating inconsistencies.

SUE is most effective when you have solid information about the events—for example, police report, pictures, and other forensic evidence, statements from witnesses or family members other than the victim, or evidence of deception as revealed in the PDS or other questionnaires (see next section). Rather than suggesting that the client is a liar, better to address discrepancies between what the client has said and the information at your disposal. "Your version of the events," you might say, "is different from so and so," or "According to this test, you are trying to present a positive self-image. On the one hand, that is perfectly normal and human, but it's important that I know what happened." As with the Conflict Tactics Scales (CTS), the idea is to get the client to commit to admitting some wrongdoing and then methodically nudging them to make more disclosures.

Considerations in Interviewing Intimate Partner Violence Suspects

Interviewees accused of IPV have many reasons for not lying or omitting important details (see Box 11.1.) Reliable information is facilitated when relationship conflict and violence are viewed from a systemic perspective. Even when there is

---

Box 11.1

CLIENT-BASED REASONS WHY INTIMATE PARTNER VIOLENCE IS UNDERDETECTED

1. *Perception of physical violence as trivial or tolerable:* The couple regards minor acts of violence, such as grabbing or slapping, as not important enough to bring up in therapy.
2. *Physical violence viewed as a way to resolve conflict:* Physical violence is considered quasi normal behavior, particularly with couples who have witnessed parental violence as children.
3. *Too narrow a focus:* Some clients fail to recognize that the violence is related to their other problems. Others dismiss the aggression as merely symptomatic of deeper, more fundamental issues.
4. *Public image:* Admitting to violence would be inconsistent with the positive self-image these clients present in their social lives.
5. *Shame:* The abuse is concealed in an attempt to avoid public condemnation and humiliation. Men, who are socialized to present a brave facade, are especially reluctant to be viewed as victims and tend to underreport assaults against them.
6. *Fear of further victimization:* Chronically and severely abused clients fear the perpetrator may learn of the disclosure and attack them again.
7. *Love and dependency concerns:* Many victims are reluctant to disclose information that may result in the arrest and incarceration of someone they love or depend on, or may otherwise contribute to the breakup of the relationship.

SOURCE: From Hamel (2014).

a clear guilty party or dominant aggressor, the complex interactions and motives inherent in IPV relationships are more easily delineated, allowing for more productive questioning, the avoidance of judgment required for interviewee cooperation, and a more reliable way to assess victim statements. Disclosure is thus facilitated without the appearance of pandering or collusion on the part of the interviewer. An important consideration is the language around IPV. Terms such as "batterer," "violence," or "abuse" are necessary for certain circumstances but unhelpful in obtaining honest and accurate information, and their use can prejudice the kinds of questions asked and how questions are answered. The terms "verbal abuse" and "psychological abuse" may carry fewer negative connotations but are often cited as examples of so-called power and control behaviors, with definitions that have expanded to include rude and disrespectful, but common, behaviors within normal intimate relationships, with unwanted implications for how "dominant aggressors" are defined (Follingstad, 2007). In the following section, suggestions are made on how to ask about IPV without the use of such loaded terminology.

The Conflict Tactics Scales

The interviewer may choose to ask first about the incident for which they were arrested or accused, then about previous IPV, or proceed the other way around. To obtain the most accurate possible rates of past IPV incidents, avoid protocols in which the client feels inherently blamed. Studies have found that using a tool such as the Conflict Tactics Scales (CTS), which frames IPV within the context of relationship conflict, elicits significantly higher incidence rates than those in which assaults are framed as dangerous and unethical or criminal acts (Straus, 1999). The list of CTS items asked about first focus on verbal aggression, progress to minor acts of physical aggression (e.g., scratching, pushing, grabbing), and eventually to the most serious types of injury-producing violence (e.g., beating up, using a knife or firearm). Together with scales administered on abuse both perpetrated and received, this graduated process tends to lessen defensiveness (Straus, 1979).

As some critics have pointed out, the CTS does not account for the context in which the various behaviors occur—for example, who initiates, who is acting in self-defense, as well as the emotional and physical impact on the parties. This information, however, is more likely to be obtained later, after a baseline of behaviors has been established, and trust and cooperation have been developed between interviewer and interviewee. During the interview process, you must first obtain the most honest account of what happened from the client's point of view before you proceed to challenge the client's interpretation of the events. Relationship violence is often bidirectional, but even if it is not in the case at hand, it is preferable that the client admits to the behaviors in question with the belief, furthered by you, that they are normal and understandable, then trying to get a client to confess to engaging in criminal and unethical behaviors, and to take 100% responsibility for doing so.

Memory Research

How much a client remembers, or chooses not to remember, varies both by their motive (tell the truth or deceive) and the vagaries of human memory. Recent events are typically more easily remembered, so claims to not be able to remember those from the distant past are not necessarily indications of deception. In general, women have a better recollection of relationship events than do men. Compared to men, women display more detailed and accurate narrative memories overall. For example, they can provide precise dates for both personal events and relationship events (Skowronski et al., 1991), and the differences are even greater when the memories involve emotional content, whether positive or negative (Hsu et al., 2018). IPV prevalence surveys have consistently demonstrated the differences across sex, with reports based on a past-year time-frame similar between male and female perpetrators and lifetime rates finding significantly higher assault rates by men. In addition to memory differences, this is also because men tend to downplay IPV, both perpetrated and received, especially lower-level assaults that happened in the more distant past (Archer, 2002), making it difficult to determine if an interviewee is consciously attempting to deceive or simply cannot remember.

Obtaining Event Details

After obtaining a baseline of IPV acts with the CTS or other measures of relationship abuse, it is important to ask follow-up questions about specific incidents, particularly the more serious ones, to determine more about the context and circumstances around those behaviors. Doing so allows the interviewee a chance to explain their behaviors and the interviewer opportunities for identifying inconsistencies and possibly obtaining additional disclosures of wrongdoing.

Start by asking a general question (e.g., "What happened?") and see how the client answers. Usually, they are vague or want to describe the events leading up to the incident as a way to minimize their behavior, knowing that they are being judged. Allow them to do this, but you will soon need to ask them about the events themselves in a way that they do not feel incriminated. Let them know that there are all sorts of IPV dynamics, not just the ubiquitous three-phase unilateral battering model originally proposed by Lenore Walker (build-up, blow-up, contrition), but mutual abuse cycles as well (Hamel, 2012). You should be aware of the more common ones, including *attachment style* or how intimate partners connect emotionally with one another (Roberts & Noller, 1998, p. 327). If it becomes clear during the interview process that he or she does fit a particular style, alluding to it may be a useful strategy in demonstrating an understanding of the client's situation and giving them further cover to disclose wrongdoing and taking responsibility. Such "cover" may not work with psychopaths who lie purely out of self-interest, but most IPV suspects minimize their violence out of guilt and embarrassment or fear of disapproval and are more amenable to such an approach.

As they describe the event, ask questions that avoid the implication of blame so that the client is allowed to respond as though he or she only reacted to events outside their control, which is often exactly how they feel even when they initiated the violence itself. For example, do not automatically interpret complaints about a partner as denial and a means to deflect attention from their own behavior. While this can be a motive, clients also need to feel they are being treated fairly and to know that their partner will be held to the same standard of conduct. Instead of asking, "What did you do?" asking instead "How did you respond (or react) to that situation?" can help you come off as less accusatory, especially if you make it clear that such responses are common. When alluding to the conflict surrounding the incident, use neutral phrases such as "Things can get out of hand in these situations," or "Sometimes people can be difficult," "Sometimes it feels like all our buttons are getting pushed," or even "It's so easy to just lose it." Note that you are not saying it is permissible to be abusive, only that it can happen. If these phrases do not work, and you are reasonably certain that the client did perpetrate a physical assault, say something like "Psychological aggression can lead to responses at times." This provides the client a face-saving way of admitting to behavior they would not otherwise admit to. When dealing with a highly defensive client, you may want to be more explicit. "My job," you might say, "isn't to decide who's at fault. That's what the judge does, but not me. I'm not figuring out who's to blame. I'm more concerned with where you are, where you might want to be, and what we can do to get you there" (Stinson & Clark, 2017, p. 60).

IPV perpetrators often believe they have a *good reason* for resorting to violence. Typically, however, their focus is on the partner's behavior, which leads to blaming and denial about their own actions. At times, it is best for the interviewer to have the client focus on neither and instead help him or her focus on the *positive intentions* behind the abuse. Should you suspect that a client underreported on the CTS, you might precede further inquiry by suggesting that there are times when even with the best of intentions, "situations can get physical," and pointing out some examples of "well-intended motives" common in stressful, high-conflict situations (see Table 11.1). Then you might say, "Tell me when this has happened."

Table 11.1 "Well-Intended" Motives for Anger

Motive	Example
Make a connection	Latishia hurls a coffee pot at Rodney in a desperate attempt to get his attention.
Express moral outrage	Steve slaps his drug-addicted girlfriend after she leaves their toddler unsupervised for hours.
Communicate something important	Lupe comes home at 3 a.m., drunk again, and Manuel grabs her by the neck when she tries to laugh it off.
Set limits/assert oneself	Tired of Craig's verbal abuse, Joanne cracks a vase over his head.
Resolve a problem	Tom keeps his wife up past midnight, yelling and carrying on about their money issues, insisting that "We're going to solve this *now!*"

SOURCE: From Hamel (2014).

Occasionally a client will surprise you by admitting that their motive was, in fact, to dominate, to exact revenge, out of jealousy, and so on, but if they don't, you have given them "cover" to make further disclosures. When assessing a client for treatment, and there is a need for more than disclosure about wrongdoing, other techniques can be used for further motivation.[1]

Assessment Instruments

You can verify client truthfulness and the level of risk they may pose to victims with established instruments that measure response bias and client attempts to deceive and to present themselves in a favorable light, what is known as impression management (IM). In the MMPI-2 and MMPI-2-RF, response bias is captured by the L, F, and K scales (Goldstein & Posthuma, 2015), reflecting the presence of positive, negative, and inconsistent impression management, respectively. They have been found to correlate with IM among litigants in disputed child custody cases (Caldwell, 2005; Schenk, 1996). When the administration of the MMPI-2 is not required or not practical, an excellent alternative is the Paulhus Deception Scales (PDS; Paulhus, 1999). The PDS is a standalone measure of IM, as well as a separate construct, "self-deceptive enhancement," reflecting minimization and lack of insight rather than a conscious effort to deceive. Both the IM and SDE scale have strong correlations with the MMMPI-2 L scale (Goldstein & Posthuma, 2015), and the instrument has been validated with both general and forensic populations. It is a reliable, easy-to-administer, and easy-to-score alternative with populations where the motivation to deceive is higher than average. Although the PDS has not yet been field-tested with court-mandated IPV offenders, research findings "are supportive of the use of the BIDR/PDS in forensic contexts" (Lanyon & Carle, 2007, p. 16).

One study (Helfritz et al., 2006) found high scores on the MMPI-2 impression management items for family court litigants suspected of IPV perpetration. Interestingly, litigants at low risk for assaulting a partner did not score significantly different from those with a documented history of IPV arrest, even though the latter reported more incidents on direct measures of IPV perpetration, leading the authors to suggest that guilt or innocence cannot be determined by IM scores alone. That attempted deception may be "a reflection of the high stakes involved" (p. 178). Given this study's small sample size (N = 52), results should be regarded

---

1. Eventually, the client must find an *internal* basis for change. However, some legitimately seek to advance their own interests. At odds with their partners, many feel legitimately hurt, abused, or taken advantage of and are not motivated to please them. At least in the short run, it is therefore important that they find in treatment something of value for themselves. The counselor helps the client understand how their behavior has undermined their own best interests. Even clients who are unwilling to admit they are wrong can nonetheless understand cause and effect—the negative consequences of their actions. The counselor uses information gathered during the interview process to point out how abusive behaviors appear to bring about temporary success (getting a spouse to stop nagging) but ultimately fail by causing more dissension and chaos (withdrawal, more fighting.)

with caution. However, they do suggest that offenders will admit to some level of IPV because they "may be unable to estimate normal levels of aggression for the purposes of impression management" (p. 178). As with any self-administered instrument, its results must be understood in the context of other findings. The MMPI-2 impression management scales, for example, are less elevated among more educated, higher SES individuals who may be savvy to the purpose of the items (Friedman et al., 2015).

When interviewing someone who presents as the victim and claims psychological distress and trauma, administer a trauma measure that contains deception scales, such as the Trauma Symptoms Inventory-2 (Briere, 2011). Among the most well-regarded standalone measures with high validity and reliability are the Miller Forensic Assessment of Symptoms Test (Miller, 2001) and the Structured Interview of Reported Symptoms (Rogers et al., 2010).

Further Considerations

There are, of course, limitations to even the soundest interviews. Holding perpetrators accountable for their violence requires additional information that the client chooses not to disclose, and even when a client is entirely forthright about their behaviors, gauging the risk posed to victims entails a more comprehensive investigation, as discussed in the following section. Given the complex and often mutual nature of IPV, statements from victims and family members may not always be as accurate as those from objective witnesses. IPV allegations are not always based on fact. Sometimes they are a form of legal and administrative aggression (see Harman & Kruk, Chapter 10, this volume), instrumentally employed to advance one's interests (e.g., win a child custody dispute), or, in other cases, used to punish someone or retaliate for some transgression, such as having been unfaithful, perhaps to be retracted at some point in the judicial process (Hamel, 2020a). That said, a client that presents well in an interview may present a serious danger when additional evidence is gathered.

INTIMATE PARTNER VIOLENCE RISK ASSESSMENT INSTRUMENTS

There has been steady growth in the practice of violence risk assessment since structured tools to aid this process appeared in the 1990s and early 2000s. Prior to the development and validation of structured guides to the assessment of risk, assessors relied entirely on subjective and unstructured risk assessment processes, which, we later came to appreciate, yielded risk predictions that were wrong more often than they were right (Monahan, 1981). Clinical intuition was gradually abandoned in favor of structured risk assessments that, through a variety of methods, identify relevant risk factors in advance and specify procedures for coding the relevance of those factors and formulating opinions regarding the probability of criminal outcomes. Meta-analyses have revealed that structured methods outperform clinical judgement of violence risk (e.g., Grove et al., 2000;

Hilton et al., 2006). Several well-established tools are now available for measuring the risk of IPV recidivism among offenders (Graham et al., 2019).

An essential aspect of a risk assessment instrument's validity is its predictive accuracy, measured primarily in terms of relative risk or discrimination, which considers the instrument's ability to discriminate between recidivists and nonrecidivists. That is, are offenders with higher risk ratings relatively more likely to reoffend than offenders with lower risk ratings (Helmus et al., 2020)? Predictive accuracy is typically assessed using the receiving operator characteristic (ROC) area under the curve (AUC), a statistic that indicates a tool's overall predictive effect size, accounting for sensitivity (true positives) and specificity (avoidance of false positives) for all possible cut-off scores (Helmus & Quinsey, 2020). The statistic ranges from 0 to 1, such that an AUC of .50 indicates no predictive effect and AUCs over .50 and up to 1 indicate increasingly large effects in the positive direction (i.e., greater correspondence between risk scores and the likelihood of recidivism). An AUC over .71 is considered a large effect (Rice & Harris, 2005). Scores on the tools reviewed next all yield moderate AUCs on average; that is, in the range of approximately .64 to .70 (Rice & Harris, 2005).

The validity of a risk assessment tool is limited by the extent to which two or more assessors, working independently, come to the same score on a scale or draw the same conclusion about risk. This interrater reliability is usually evaluated using a correlation coefficient (that ranges from −1.0 for a perfect negative association to +1.0 for perfect agreement) or alternative statistics for categorical information.

Spousal Assault Risk Assessment

The Spousal Assault Risk Assessment (SARA) was developed to acknowledge that IPV perpetrators are a heterogeneous group and to provide assessors with a structured framework to ensure that an adequately broad range of risk factors are consistently considered while simultaneously accommodating for case-specific factors (Kropp et al., 1999). The authors of the SARA define IPV (or spousal assault) "as any actual, attempted, or threatened physical harm perpetrated by a man or a woman against someone with whom he or she has, or has had, an intimate, sexual relationship" (Kropp et al., 1999, p. 1). The authors further clarify that the definition of spousal assault "is not limited by gender of the victim or perpetrator" (p. 1).

The SARA utilizes a structured professional judgment (SPJ) approach in which the assessor considers a range of predetermined risk factors and then formulates opinions regarding the risk for reoffence as well as treatment needs and management recommendations (Garrington & Boer, 2020; Guy et al., 2012). Risk factors were selected based on a review of the clinical and empirical literature, and a list of 20 items was identified, covering criminal history, spousal assault history, and most recent offense, and psychosocial adjustment (e.g., relationship, employment, substance abuse, mental health, and behavioral problems). The assessor uses multiple sources of information to rate each SARA item, such as interviews with the offender and any victims, standardized measures of intimate partner abuse and substance abuse, and a review of official records. Each item is scored between 0 and 2 (0 = absent; 1 = partially/possibly present; 2 = present) for a total possible score of 40; however, the SPJ risk assessment schemes such as SARA are not intended to generate a numerical score. Rather, the assessment concludes with a summary risk judgment of low, moderate, or high for the risk of violence against a partner or against another person.

Interrater reliability on the SARA total score has been reported to be good (correlations over .80) but more variable for the summary risk rating and poorer for the selection of critical items (e.g., Grann & Wedin, 2002; Kropp & Hart, 2000). Interitem agreement between raters has ranged from 40% to 94% (Jung & Buro, 2017). When the SARA was scored by researchers from the case files of 32 offenders referred for police threat assessment, the interrater correlation coefficient was .70, and agreement on individual SARA items ranged from 31% to 94%, with a poorer agreement for items related to mental health and psychosocial adjustment (Hilton et al., 2021).

The SARA has been validated internationally, including studies in Canada (Hilton et al., 2008; Kropp & Hart, 2000; Pham et al., 2021), the United States (Heckert & Gondolf, 2004; Williams & Houghton, 2004; Wong & Hisashima, 2008), Spain (Andrés-Pueyo et al., 2008), and Sweden (Belfrage et al., 2012; Grann & Wedin, 2002). To our knowledge, the validity of the SARA has been tested exclusively with males who have committed IPV against female partners. Predictive validity studies have used the SARA score more often than the categorical judgment, but both total scores and judgments predicted IPV recidivism with medium effect sizes in a review of published and unpublished studies with samples drawn from police, corrections, and court-mandated treatment settings (average AUCs = .63 to .67; Helmus & Bourgon, 2011). A more recent review by Graham and colleagues (2019) reported that AUCs for SARA scores and judgments range from .52 to .72.

Spousal Assault Risk Assessment Version 3

The Spousal Assault Risk Assessment Version 3 (SARA v3; Kropp & Hart, 2015) is the 24-item revision of the SARA. The SARA v3 items have some overlap with the SARA but are reconfigured into three domains: nature of IPV, perpetrator risk factors, and victim vulnerability factors. In addition, the assessor evaluates each item in terms of its past and recent (i.e., within 1 year of the assessment) influence on behavior and identifies scenarios in which future violence is more likely to occur. Risk assessors using the SARA v3 conclude their assessment with the formulation of ratings reflecting overall risk (i.e., case prioritization), as well as imminence and severity of future violence.

Research establishing interrater reliability for the SARA v3 is limited. Initial research using researcher-derived scores for the past, recent, and total combined items found good interrater reliability overall, with correlations of .83 and larger in a sample of IPV threat assessment cases (Hilton et al., 2021). Unpublished research using researcher-generated SARA v3 ratings for 30 IPV cases (Ryan, 2016) found interrater correlations ranging from .73 to .89 for SARA v3 total score, ratings of risk factor presence and relevance on the Perpetrator Risk factor domain, and presence of risk factors in the Nature of IPV domain. However, interrater reliability was poorer for summary risk ratings reflecting case prioritization (.40), serious physical harm (.68), and imminent violence (.41).

There are no published validations of the SARA v3's predictive accuracy to date. We are aware of one study, currently under peer review, that has investigated the SARA v3's predictive validity in a sample of high-risk men referred for police threat assessment (Pham et al., 2021). SARA v3 summed total scores did not predict IPV or any violent recidivism in this nonroutine sample; however, they did predict general recidivism with small effects. Additionally, unpublished doctoral research (Ryan, 2016) investigated correlations between the SARA v3 and other established IPV risk measures and found moderate to large positive associations between SARA v3 total scores and scores on the ODARA DVRAG and DA.

Brief Spousal Assault Form for the Evaluation of Risk

The Brief Spousal Assault Form for the Evaluation of Risk (B-SAFER) is a shorter version of the SARA for frontline police officers (Kropp & Hart, 2004). It has 10 items that concern IPV history, attitudes, other serious offending, substance abuse, and problems in relationships, employment, and mental health. As with the SARA, each item is rated, and then a summary judgment is made as to whether the risk of life-threatening or imminent violence is high, moderate, or low. Assessors rate each of the items for their relevance to IPV in the 4 weeks immediately preceding the assessment and in the past (>4 weeks preassessment).

Gerbrandij et al. (2018) found excellent interrater reliability (.96) for B-SAFER total scores. Hilton et al. (2021), however, found a moderate-sized correlation (.70) between raters of cases referred by police for threat assessment but substantially poorer for ratings of recent than past relevance (Hilton et al., 2021). Agreement for B-SAFER risk judgments has ranged from .63 to .88 in cases assessed by clinicians (Gerbrandij et al., 2018) and .58 to .72 among police officers (Svalin et al., 2017). The average agreement on individual items was .57 among 12 cases coded from probation reports and .54 among 32 cases coded from threat assessment reports (Hilton et al., 2019; Thijssen & de Ruiter, 2011); as with the SARA, reliability was poorer for items related to mental health. In both development samples and in later research, mental disorder was among the items most likely to be omitted or rated not present (Kropp & Hart, 2004; Loinaz, 2014). Researchers have suggested that it may be challenging for police officers to judge mental disorder (Kropp & Hart, 2004) or that police file information provide limited information related to perpetrators' mental health (Hilton et al., 2021).

Graham and colleagues (2019) report only one validation study of the B-SAFER with an AUC better than .70. B-SAFER total scores predicted criminal recidivism among 40 men imprisoned for a violent or other offense against an intimate partner (AUC = .76; Loinaz, 2014) but did not significantly predict IPV recidivism among 158 men court-ordered to treatment for IPV violence or stalking (AUC = .55; Gerbrandij et al., 2018). Similarly, B-SAFER total scores did not predict IPV or any violent recidivism in a sample of 247 intimate partner abusive men referred for police threat assessment; however, it did predict general recidivism with small effects (AUC = .60; Pham et al., 2021).

Similarly, mixed findings have been reported for B-SAFER summary ratings. In one study, both total scores and the summary rating predicted new IPV assaults among 249 men with a police record of IPV (AUC = .70 for scores, AUC = .69 for ratings; Storey et al., 2014). However, Belfrage and Strand (2012) reported that police officers' summary ratings were not significantly related to new assaults against an intimate partner among 216 men (test statistics were not reported). Svalin et al. (2018) tested summary ratings of likelihood and severity for their association with several outcomes in 301 assessments (including 11 cases with female offenders) and reported only one significant effect.

Ontario Domestic Assault Risk Assessment

The Ontario Domestic Assault Risk Assessment (ODARA; Hilton et al., 2004, 2010) uses an actuarial approach. ODARA items were selected using an empirical method to identify the strongest unique predictors in a follow-up study of IPV offenders. Individual offenders' risk can be interpreted as a percentile (where the individual would stand in a line of 100 offenders in order of increasing risk) or in terms of comparable observed recidivism rates for similarly ranked IPV perpetrators.

The ODARA was designed for frontline police officers using 13 items that would normally be obtained during a routine investigation of a domestic assault (the index assault; Hilton et al., 2004). Items concern the perpetrator's prior domestic and nondomestic criminal history and substance use, events and statements at the index assault, the relationship history, and the victim's circumstances. All items are scored 0 (not present) or 1 (present), and the total ranges from 0 to 13. There is also a prorating procedure for up to five items when the available information is ambiguous. An actuarial table of data shows the rate of offenders with similar scores and the rate of IPV recidivism observed in the original follow-up research and initial validation studies involving more than 1,400 men with a police record of IPV against a female domestic partner (Hilton et al., 2010).

Interrater reliability between researchers scoring the ODARA from offender case files has ranged from .80 to .95 (Hilton & Eke, 2016; Hilton et al., 2010; Rettenberger & Eher, 2013). Classroom and online training for law enforcement and other professionals has also produced reliable scoring (Hilton & Ham, 2015; Hilton et al., 2007). Researchers coding the ODARA from threat assessment files reported a correlation of .84 (Hilton et al., 2021). Agreement on individual ODARA items has ranged from 69% to 100% (Hilton et al., 2021; Jung & Buro, 2017).

A systematic review by Graham and colleagues (2019) determined that the ODARA is one of the two most tested IPV risk assessment tools, along with the Danger Assessment (DA; see later). The ODARA has been validated in studies with male offenders sampled from police reports (Gerth et al., 2015, 2017; Hilton et al., 2004; Hilton & Harris, 2009; Hilton et al., 2008; Jung & Buro, 2017; Olver & Jung, 2017; Pham et al., 2021) and correctional service files (Hilton et al., 2010; Rettenberger & Eher, 2013). AUCs have ranged from .61 to .86 (Graham et al., 2019), corresponding to medium to large effects. A 2017 study by Seewald et al. demonstrated that ODARA scores calculated by research assistants were significantly more accurate for predicting future violence for IPV perpetrators than the unaided clinical judgments of licensed psychiatrists (AUC = .78 vs. .44). In meta-analytic studies, a significantly higher predictive accuracy has been reported for the ODARA than other tools (Hanson et al., 2007; Messing & Thaller, 2013).

Preliminary research suggests that the ODARA is valid for use with female IPV perpetrators. Hilton and colleagues (2014) found that the ODARA predicted women's IPV recidivism with an AUC of .72 in a small sample of 30 women in custody for IPV offenses. However, women reoffended at a lower rate than indicated by the actuarial data used to interpret ODARA scores for male offenders. The authors suggested the ODARA could be used to inform decisions about prioritizing interventions for female offenders, although more research is necessary to permit the application of actuarial data for women. To date, there have been no investigations of the ODARA's predictive validity in the context of homosexual relationships.

A recent study investigated the predictive accuracy of several IPV risk assessment instruments, including ODARA and SARA, among a nonroutine sample of high-risk male offenders (Pham et al., 2021). ODARA and the SARA performed well, predicting all recidivistic outcomes, but with accuracy that was lower than typically found in past research with these tools (e.g., to predict IPV recidivism, $ODARA_{AUC}$ = .59 in the index study vs. .67 in past research; $SARA_{AUC}$ = .54 in the index study vs. .63 in past research; Messing & Thaller, 2013). These findings suggest that it may be more difficult to discriminate recidivists from nonrecidivists among relatively high-risk cases using tools developed for lower-risk, routine populations. However, to the extent that IPV recidivism is predictable in this higher-risk group, actuarial-developed tools such as the ODARA and scales that focus on past offending such as the SARA criminal history subscale appeared most useful.

Domestic Violence Risk Appraisal Guide

The Domestic Violence Risk Appraisal Guide (DVRAG) was derived from research aimed at identifying existing assessments that could improve on the ODARA's predictive accuracy. Hilton and colleagues examined the SARA, the Domestic Violence Screening Instrument (DVSI; see later), the DA, the Psychopathy Checklist-Revised (PCL-R; Hare, 2003), and an actuarial risk assessment tool for general violent recidivism, the Violence Risk Appraisal Guide (VRAG; Harris et al., 2015). They also explored the contributions of child abuse and other adverse childhood experiences, attitudes, and indicators of mental health conditions. The measure that most consistently improved the assessment of risk was the PCL-R (psychopathy) score.

The DVRAG is recommended for use in cases where greater discriminative accuracy among higher-risk cases is desired and where more in-depth case information is available (Hilton et al., 2008, 2010). The DVRAG is essentially an algorithm for scoring the 13 ODARA items, some now weighted rather than all being scored dichotomously as in the ODARA, plus the PCL-R (Hare, 2003), which contributes from –1 to +6 points to the DVRAG score. Total DVRAG scores range from –10 to +41, and total scores correspond with percentile ranks and observed recidivism rates for similarly ranked male offenders.

Interrater reliability for the total DVRAG score is reported to be excellent (ICC = .90; Hilton et al., 2008). In cross-validation among 346 men with both a police record of IPV and a correctional history, the AUC for IPV was .70 (Hilton et al., 2008), and among 94 previously incarcerated offenders, the AUC for IPV was .71 (Gray, 2012). Rettenberger and Eher (2013) found that both the DVRAG and the ODARA predicted future IPV (AUC = .71) as well as violence and general offending (AUC = .66–.71) in a sample of 66 Austrian men convicted of sexual offenses against their intimate partners. The DVRAG can be scored using PCL-R Facet 4 items in lieu of the PCL-R total score. This modification, known as the DVRAG-4, had an AUC of .73 for IPV recidivism in the Hilton et al. (2008) cross-validation sample of 346 men (Hilton & Quinsey, 2017).

Domestic Violence Screening Instrument

The Domestic Violence Screening Instrument (DVSI) was developed for use by probation officers and counselors postarrest to inform arraignment decisions (Williams, 2012). It was developed using a combination of literature review, statistical analysis of the characteristics that distinguished repeat IPV offenders in a large sample of probationers, and feedback from users (Williams & Houghton, 2004). DVSI items reflect domestic and nondomestic criminal history (e.g., conviction, assault, restraining orders, community supervision, weapon use, presence of children during a domestic incident) as well as treatment history for IPV or substance use, unemployment, and variables relating to the victim (separation, restraining order). Assessors score each item using response options that vary from 0–1 to 0–3, which are then summed for a total risk score. In the revised version (DVSI-R), one item concerning restraining orders was dropped, and summary risk judgments of low, moderate, or high risk for imminent violence to the index victim or to another person were added (Williams & Grant, 2006).

Interrater reliability for the DVSI has not been reported, but a standard of 80% correct is required in training (Stansfield & Williams, 2014). The DVSI scores and summary risk ratings have been validated in several large-sample studies with AUCs ranging from .62 to .73 (Graham et al., 2019). Validation studies include large samples of US men and women arrested for IPV and other forms of family violence (Stansfield & Williams, 2014; Williams, 2012; Williams & Grant, 2006; Wong & Hisashima, 2008). As with the ODARA, research using the DVSI-R indicates that women generally reoffend less frequently and less quickly than men (Stansfield & Williams, 2014). The DVSI-R is the only risk appraisal instrument that has been tested for assessing IPV in same-sex relationships. Gerstenberger et al. (2019) studied the risk, as indicated by DVSI-R scores, and recidivism of 332 IPV perpetrators in same-sex relationships. The DVSI-R predicted future IPV equally well for perpetrators in male homosexual relationships (AUC = .63) as for male (AUC = .61) and female perpetrators (AUC = .63) in heterosexual relationships. The DVSI-R did not predict future IPV for female perpetrators in same-sex relationships (AUC = .56). Results further indicated that rearrest for IPV was nearly as common among female perpetrators in same-sex relationships as it was among male perpetrators in heterosexual relationships. In contrast, female perpetrators in heterosexual relationships demonstrated the lowest rates of rearrest compared to the other three relationship subgroups.

Danger Assessment

The Danger Assessment (DA) is a structured risk tool created to aid female victims of IPV to appraise their risk of being lethally assaulted by their intimate partners (Campbell, 1986). The DA joins the ODARA, the two most tested IPV risk assessment tools (Graham et al., 2019). Investigations of the DA's predictive validity have focused on risk for harm to female victims at the hands of male perpetrators. The DA comprises two components. First, the victim reviews the previous year's assaults using a calendar, and then she responds to several risk-related questions. Several DA items relate to the perpetrator's abusive behavior toward the victim. Others concern his employment status, access to firearms, alcohol problem, alcohol and drug use, suicide threats, and IPV not leading to arrest, as well as the victim's circumstances (e.g., tried to leave the perpetrator, has a child who is not the perpetrator's). The victim's belief that the perpetrator could kill her is also assessed. The total weighted DA score is tied to risk categories ranging from "variable danger" to "extreme danger" based on studies of women who were assaulted or killed by their partners. Victim suicidality is also assessed but not included in the risk score.

The principal 20-item version of the DA uses the strongest risk factors from a multisite study of 220 femicide victims and 343 female victims of nonfatal IPV (Campbell et al., 2003). It distinguished between these groups with a large effect size (AUC = .92; Campbell et al., 2009), DA scores among femicide victims have been shown to be significantly higher than DA scores of women who were abused but not killed (Glass et al., 2008). Modified versions of the DA have been created to identify the risk of severe violence and have been found to be very sensitive, capturing most cases of severe violence. Scores on the 11-item Lethality Screen version of the DA, designed for use by first responders to dichotomously classify danger as "high" or "not high," was significantly associated with victim-reported severe IPV among 440 female victims over a 6-month follow-up (Messing et al., 2013). The DA has also demonstrated associations with nonlethal IPV outcomes, including future assaults and serious threats (Goodman et al., 2000; Weisz et al., 2000), intimate partner sexual assault (Pengpid & Peltzer, 2014), and abuse severity (Nava et al., 2014).

Currently, there are several well-established tools for assessing risk for future violence among IPV perpetrators. Overall, these tools have demonstrated moderate predictive accuracy, which is to say that there is reasonably good, albeit imperfect, correspondence between ratings on risk appraisal tools and the probability of various criminal outcomes, including IPV. The research literature that underlies the development and validation of these risk instruments is based primarily and overwhelmingly on males who have aggressed against an intimate female partner. Preliminary research suggests that the ODARA and the DVSI-R scores predict future IPV for female perpetrators and may be helpful for informing case prioritization, but it also indicates that women appear to reoffend at lower rates than men, and correspondingly, probability estimates based on male offender norms should not be utilized for female perpetrators. There are also preliminary findings suggesting that existing instruments are valid for use for assessing risk in same-sex relationships; however, this research is very much in its infancy. Further research investigating the extent to which established IPV risk factors and associated risk assessment schemes, derived and validated based on male heterosexual abusers, can be applied for use with IPV perpetrators in same-sex relationships.

CONCLUSIONS

To be effective, domestic violence arrest, prosecution, and intervention policies must be grounded in sound empirical research rather than political considerations. Beginning with the arrival of police at the scene of a possible domestic disturbance, incorrect assumptions about the causes, dynamics, and consequences of IPV can result in the prosecution of innocent suspects and treatment recommendations that fail to address the needs of the parties involved. In this chapter, evidence-based approaches have been suggested to assess the actual risk posed to victims, so perpetrators can be properly motivated and helped to desist from the abuse they have perpetrated upon their loved ones. Based on the seriousness of the risk posed to the victims and the needs and learning style of the offender, an appropriate treatment plan can be formulated. The reader is encouraged to review the other chapters in the last section of this volume, including procedures for delivering batterer intervention groups based on risk-needs-responsivity (RNR) principles, as explained in Chapter 12 by Roberts (this volume); as well as alternative modalities such as couples and family counseling (Bennet et al., Chapter 13, this volume) and restorative justice interventions (Barocas & Shimizu, Chapter 14, this volume).

REFERENCES

Amado, B, Arce, R., & Farina, F. (2015). Undeutch hypothesis and criteria based content analysis: A meta-analytic review. *The European Journal of Psychology Applied to Legal Context, 7*, 3–12. https://doi.org/10.1016/j.ejpal.2014.11.002

Andrés-Pueyo, A., López, S., & Álvarez, E. (2008). Assessment of the risk of intimate partner violence and the SARA. *Papeles del Psicólogo, 29*, 107–122. http://www.papelesdelpsicologo.es/English/1543.pdf

Archer, J. (2002). Sex differences in physically aggressive acts between heterosexual partners: A meta-analytic review. *Aggression and Violent Behavior, 7*, 313–351. https://doi.org/10.1016/S1359-1789(01)00061-1

Belfrage, H., Strand, S., Storey, J. E., Gibas, A. L., Kropp, P. R., & Hart, S. D. (2012). Assessment and management of risk for intimate partner violence by police officers using the Spousal Assault Risk Assessment Guide. *Law and Human Behavior, 36*, 60–67. https://doi.org/10.1037/h0093948

Black, M. C., Basile, K. C., Breiding, M. J., Smith, S. G., Walters, M. L., & Merrick, M. T. (2011). *National Intimate Partner and Sexual Violence Survey (NISVS): 2010 summary report*. National Center for Injury Prevention and Control, Centers for Disease Control and Prevention. http://www.cdc.gov/ViolencePrevention/pdf/NISVS_Executive_Summary-a.pd

Bond, C., & DePaulo, B. (2006). Accuracy of deception judgments. *Personality and Social Psychology Review, 10*(3), 214–234. https://doi.org/10.1207/s15327957pspr1003_2

Bond, C., Levine, T., & Hartwig, M. (2015). New findings in non-verbal lie detection. In P. Granhag, A. Vrij, & B. Verschuere (Eds.), *Detecting deception: Current challenges and cognitive approaches* (pp. 37–58). John Wiley & Sons.

Briere, J. (2011). *Trauma Symptom Inventory-2 Professional Manual*. PAR.

Caldwell, A. B. (2005). How can the MMPI-2 help child custody examiners? *Journal of Child Custody, 2*(1), 83–117. https://doi.org/10.1300/J190v02n01_06

Campbell, J. C. (1986). Nursing assessment for risk of homicide with battered women. *Advances in Nursing Science, 8*, 36–51. https://doi.org/10.1097/00012272-198607000-00006

Campbell, J. C., Webster, D. W., & Glass, N. (2009). The Danger Assessment: Validation of a lethality risk assessment instrument for intimate partner femicide. *Journal of Interpersonal Violence, 24*, 653–674. https://doi.org/10.1177/0886260508317180

Campbell, J. C., Webster, D., & Koziol-McLain, J. (2003). Risk factors for femicide in abusive relationships: Results from a multisite case control study. *American Journal of Public Health, 93*, 1089–1097. https://doi.org/10.2105/ajph.93.7.1089

Clarke, C., & Milne, R. (2011, April.) National evaluation of the PEACE investigative interviewing course. Police Research Award Scheme, Report No: PRAS/149. https://www.academia.edu/1926581/A_National_Evaluation_of_the_ PEACE_Investigative_Interviewing_Course

Corvo, K., & Johnson, P. (2003). Vilification of the "batterer": How blame shapes domestic violence policy and interventions. *Aggression and Violent Behavior, 8*, 259–281. https://doi.org/10.1016/S1359-1789(01)00060-X

DePaulo, B., Lindsay, J., Malone, B., Muhlenbruck, L., Charlton, K., & Cooper, H. (2003). Cues to deception. *Psychological Bulletin, 129*(1), 74–118. https://doi.org/10.1037/0033-2909.129.1.74

Dia, D., Simmons, C., Oliver, M., & Cooper, L. (2009). Motivational interviewing for perpetrators of intimate partner violence. In P. Lehmann & C. Simmons (Eds.), *Strengths-based batterer intervention: A new paradigm in ending family violence* (pp. 87–112). Springer.

Dutton, D. (2006). *Rethinking domestic violence*. UBC Press.

Dutton, D., & Corvo, K. (2006) Transforming a flawed policy: A call to revive psychology and science in domestic violence research and practice. *Aggression and Violent Behavior, 11*, 457–483. https://doi.org/10.1016/j.avb.2006.01.007

Follingstad, D. (2007). Rethinking current approaches to psychological abuse: Conceptual and methodological issues. *Aggression and Violent Behavior, 12*(4), 439–458. https://doi.org/10.1016/j.avb.2006.07.004

Friedman, A. F., Bolinskey, P. K., Levak, R. W., & Nichols, D. S. (2015). *Psychological assessment with the MMPI-2/MMPI-2-RF* (3rd ed.). Routledge.

Garrington, C., & Boer, D. P. (2020). Structured professional judgement in violence risk assessment. In J. S. Wormith, L. A. Craig, & T. E. Hogue (Eds.), *What works in violence risk management: Theory, research, and practice* (pp. 145–162). Wiley Blackwell.

Gerbrandij, J., Rosenfeld, B., Nijdam-Jones, A., & Galietta, M. (2018). Evaluating risk assessment instruments for intimate partner stalking and intimate partner violence. *Journal of Threat Assessment and Management, 5*(2), 103–118. https://doi.org/10.1037/tam0000101

Gerstenberger, C., Stansfield, R., & Williams, K. R. (2019). Intimate partner violence in same-sex relationships: An analysis of risk and rearrest. *Criminal Justice and Behavior, 46*, 1515–1527.

Gerth, J., Rossegger, A., Bauch, E., & Endrass, J. (2017). Assessing the discrimination and calibration of the Ontario Domestic Assault Risk Assessment in Switzerland. *Partner Abuse, 8*(2), 168–189. https://doi.org/10.1891/1946-6560.8.2.168

Gerth, J., Rosseger, A., Singh, J. P., & Endrass, J. (2015). Assessing the risk of intimate partner violence: Validating the DyRiAS in Switzerland. *Archives of Forensic Psychology, 1*(2), 1–15.

Gilovich, T., Griffin, D. W., & Kahneman, D. (2002). *Heuristics and biases: The psychology of intuitive judgement*. Cambridge University Press.

Glass, D. J., Laughon, K., Rutto, C., Bevacqua, J., & Campbell, J. C. (2008). Young adult intimate partner femicide: An exploratory study. *Homicide Studies, 12*, 177–187. https://doi.org/10.1177/1088767907313303

Goldstein, M., & Posthuma, A. (2015). Use of the Paulhus Deception Scales and MMPI-2 with custody litigants. *American Journal of Forensic Psychology, 33*(3), 19–34.

Goodman, L. A., Dutton, M. A., & Bennett, L. (2000). Predicting repeat abuse among arrested batterers: Use of the Danger Assessment Scale in the criminal justice system. *Journal of Interpersonal Violence, 15*, 63–74. https://doi:10.1177/088626000015001005

Graham, L. M., Sahay, K. M., Rizo, C. F., Messing, J. T., & Macy, R. J. (2019). The validity and reliability of available intimate partner homicide and reassault risk assessment tools: A systematic review. *Trauma, Violence, & Abuse, 22*, 18–40. https://doi.org/10.1177/1524838018821952

Granhag, P., & Hartwig, M. (2008). A new theoretical perspective on deception detection: On the psychology of instrumental mind-reading. *Psychology, Crime & Law, 14*(3), 189–200. https://doi.org/10.1080/10683160701645181

Granhag, P., & Hartwig, M. (2015). The strategic use of evidence technique: A conceptual overview. In P. Granhag, A. Vrij, & B. Verschuere (Eds.), *Detecting deception: Current challenges and cognitive approaches* (pp. 231–252). John Wiley & Sons.

Grann, M., & Wedin, I. (2002). Risk factors for recidivism among spousal assault and spousal homicide offenders. *Psychology, Crime and Law, 8*, 5–23. https://doi.org/10.1080/10683160208401806

Gray, A. L. (2012). *Assessing risk for intimate partner violence: A cross-validation of the ODARA and DVRAG within a sample of incarcerated offenders* [Unpublished Master's thesis, Carleton University].

Grove, W. M., Zald, D. H., Lebow, S., Snitz, B. E., & Nelson, C. (2000). Clinical versus mechanical prediction: A meta-analysis. *Psychological Assessment, 12*, 19–30. https://doi.org/10.1037/1040-3590.12.1.19

Guy, L., Packer, I., & Warnken, W. (2012). Assessing risk of violence suing structured professional judgment guidelines. *Journal of Forensic Psychology Practice, 12*, 270–283. https://doi-org.login.ezproxy.library.ualberta.ca/10.1080/15228932.2012.674471

Hamel, J. (2012). "But she's violent, too!": Holding domestic violence offenders accountable within a systemic approach to batterer intervention. *Journal of Aggression, Conflict and Peace Research, 4*(3), 124–135. https://doi.org/10.1108/17596591211244139

Hamel, J. (2014). *Gender-inclusive treatment of intimate partner abuse: Evidence-based approaches* (2nd ed.). Springer.

Hamel, J. (2020a). Perpetrator or victim? A review of the complexities of domestic violence cases. *Journal of Aggression, Conflict and Peace Research, 12*(2), 55–62. https://doi.org/10.1108/JACPR-12-2019-0464

Hamel, J. (2020b). Beyond gender: Finding common ground in evidence-based batterer intervention. In B. Russell (Ed.), *Intimate partner violence and the LGBT+ community: Understanding power dynamics* (pp. 195–226). Springer.

Hanson, R. K., Helmus, L., & Bourgon, G. (2007). *The validity of risk assessments for intimate partner violence: A meta-analysis.* Public Safety Canada, unpublished report Cat. No.: PS3-1/2007-7. Retrieved 1/10/2022 from: https://www.publicsafety.gc.ca/cnt/rsrcs/pblctns/ntmt-prtnr-vlnce/index-en.aspx

Hare, R. D. (2003). *The Psychopathy Checklist-Revised* (2nd ed.). Multi-Health Systems.

Harris, G. T., Rice, M. E., Quinsey, V. L., & Cormier, C. A. (2015). *Violent offenders: Appraising and managing risk* (3rd ed.). American Psychological Association.

Hartwig, M., & Bond, C. (2011). Why do lie-catchers fail? A lens model meta-analysis of human lie judgments. *Psychological Bulletin, 1327*(4), 643–659. https://doi.org/10.1037/a0023589

Hartwig, M., & Granhag, P. (2015). Exploring the nature and origin of beliefs about deception: Implicit and explicit knowledge among lay people and presumed experts. In

P. Granhag, A. Vrij, & B. Verschuere (Eds.), *Detecting deception: Current challenges and cognitive approaches* (pp. 125–154). John Wiley & Sons.

Hartwig, M., Granhag, P., & Luke, T. (2014, February). Strategic use of evidence during investigative interviews: The state of the science. In D. Raskin, C. Honts, & J. Kircher (Eds.), *Credibility assessment: Scientific research and applications* (pp. 1–36). Academic Press.

Hartwig, M., Granhag, P., Stromwall, L., & Doering, N. (2010). Impression and information management: On the strategic self-regulation of innocent and guilty suspects. *The Open Criminology Journal, 3*, 10–16. doi:10.2174/1874917801003010010]

Heckert, D. A., & Gondolf, E. W. (2004). Battered women's perceptions of risk versus risk factors and instruments in predicting repeat reassault. *Journal of Interpersonal Violence, 19*, 778–800. https://doi.org/10.1177/0886260504265619

Helfritz, L. E., Stanford, M. S., Conklin, S. M., Greve, K. W., Villemarette-Pittman, N. R., & Houston, R. J. (2006). Usefulness of self-report instruments in assessing men accused of domestic violence. *The Psychological Record, 56*, 171–180. https://doi.org/10.1007/BF03395542

Helmus, L., & Bourgon, G. (2011). Taking stock of 15 years of research on the Spousal Assault Risk Assessment Guide (SARA): A critical review. *International Journal of Forensic Mental Health, 10*, 64–75. doi:10.1080/14999013.2010.551709

Helmus, L., Hanson, R. K., Thornton, D., Babchishin, K. M., & Harris, A. J. R. (2012). Absolute recidivism rates predicted by Static-99R and Static-2002R sex offender risk assessment tools vary across samples: A meta-analysis. *Criminal Justice and Behavior, 39*, 1148–1171. https://doi: 10.1177/0093854812443648

Helmus, L. M., & Quinsey, V. L. (2020). Predicting violent reoffending with the VRAG-R: Overview, controversies, and future directions for actuarial risk scales. In J. S. Wormith, L. Craig, & T. Hogue (Eds.), *What works in violence risk management: Theory, research and practice* (pp. 119–144). Wiley.

High Value Detainee Interrogation Group (2016, Sept.). Interrogation: A review of the science. https://www.fbi.gov/file-repository/hig-report-interrogation-a-review-of-the-science-september-2016.pdf/view

Hilton, N. Z., & Eke, A. W. (2016). Non-specialization of criminal careers among intimate partner violence offenders. *Criminal Justice and Behavior, 43*, 1347–1363. https://doi.org/ 10.1177/0093854816637886

Hilton, N. Z., & Ham, E. (2015). Cost-effectiveness of electronic training in domestic violence risk assessment: ODARA 101. *Journal of Interpersonal Violence, 30*, 1065–1073. https://doi.org/10.1177/0886260514539762

Hilton, N. Z., & Harris, G. T. (2009). How non-recidivism affects predictive accuracy: Evidence from a cross-validation of the Ontario Domestic Assault Risk Assessment (ODARA). *Journal of Interpersonal Violence, 24*, 326–337. https://doi.org/10.1177/0886260508316478

Hilton, N. Z., Harris, G. T., Popham, S., & Lang, C. (2010). Risk assessment among male incarcerated domestic offenders. *Criminal Justice and Behavior, 37*, 815–832. https://doi.org/10.1177/ 0093854810368937

Hilton, N. Z., Harris, G. T., & Rice, M. E. (2006). Sixty-six years of research on the clinical versus actuarial prediction of violence. *The Counselling Psychologist, 34*, 400–409. https://doi:10.1177/0011000005285877

Hilton, N. Z., Harris, G. T., & Rice, M. E. (2010). *Risk assessment for domestically violent men: Tools for criminal justice, offender intervention, and victim services.* American Psychological Association.

Hilton, N. Z., Harris, G. T., Rice, M. E., Eke, A. W., & Lowe-Wetmore, T. (2007). Training frontline users in the Ontario Domestic Assault Risk Assessment (ODARA), a tool for police domestic investigations. *Canadian Journal of Police and Security Services, 5*, 92–96.

Hilton, N. Z., Harris, G. T., Rice, M. E., Houghton, R. E., & Eke, A. W. (2008). An in depth actuarial assessment for wife assault recidivism: The Domestic Violence Risk Appraisal Guide. *Law and Human Behavior, 32*(2), 150–163. https://doi.org/10.1007/s10979-007-9088-6

Hilton, N. Z., Harris, G. T., Rice, M. E., Lang, C., Cormier, C. A., & Lines, K. J. (2004). A brief actuarial assessment for the prediction of wife assault recidivism: The Ontario Domestic Assault Risk Assessment. *Psychological Assessment, 16*, 267–275. https://doi.org/10.1037/1040-3590.16.3.267

Hilton, N. Z., Pham, A. T., Jung, S., Nunes, K. L., & Ennis, L. (2021). Risk scores and reliability of the SARA, SARAV3, B-SAFER, and ODARA among intimate partner violence (IPV) cases referred for threat assessment. *Police Practice and Research, 22*, 157–172. https://doi.org/10.1080/15614263.2020.1798235

Hilton, N. Z., Popham, S., Lang, C., & Harris G. T. (2014). Preliminary validation of the ODARA for female intimate partner violence offenders. *Partner Abuse, 5*, 189–203. https://doi.org/10.1891/1946-6560.5.2.189

Hilton, N. Z., & Quinsey, V. L. (2017). Domestic Violence Risk Appraisal Guide can be scored with PCL-R Facet 4. *Crime Scene, 24*, 14–16. https://cpa.ca/docs/File/Sections/Criminal%20Justice%20Psychology/Crime%20Scene%20-%20Spring%202017%20-%20issue%2024.pdf

Hsu, C. K. Kleim, B., Nicholson, E. L., Zuj, D. V., Cushing, P. J., Gray, K. E., Clark, L., & Felmingham, K. L. (2018, December). Sex differences in intrusive memories following trauma. *Plos One, 13*(12). https://doi.org/10.1371/journal.pone.0208575

Inbau, F., Reid, J., Buckley, J., & Jayne, B. (2013). *Criminal investigations and confessions* (5th ed.). Jones & Bartlett Learning.

Jung, S., & Buro, K. (2017). Appraising risk for intimate partner violence in a police context. *Criminal Justice and Behavior, 44*, 240–260. https://doi.org/10.1177/0093854816667974

Kassin, S., Perillo, J., Appleby, S., & Kukucka, J. (2015). Confessions. In: B. L. Cutler & P. A. Zapf (Eds.), *APA handbook of forensic psychology, volume 2: criminal investigation, adjudication, and sentencing outcomes* (pp. 245–270). American Psychological Association.

Kropp, P. R., & Hart, S. D. (2000). The Spousal Assault Risk Assessment (SARA) Guide: Reliability and validity in adult male offenders. *Law and Human Behavior, 24*, 101–118. https://doi.org/10.1023/A:1005430904495

Kropp, P. R., & Hart, S D. (2004). *The development of the Brief Spousal Assault Form for the Evaluation of Risk (B-SAFER): A tool for criminal justice professionals.* Department of Justice Canada. https://www.justice.gc.ca/eng/rp-pr/fl-lf/famil/rr05_fv1-rr05_vf1/index.html

Kropp, P. R., & Hart, S. D. (2015). *SARA-V3: User manual for version 3 of the Spousal Assault Risk Assessment Guide.* Proactive Resolutions.

Kropp, P. R., Hart, S. D., Webster, C. D., & Eaves, D. (1999). *Spousal Assault Risk Assessment Guide*. Multi-Health Systems.

Lanyon, R.I., & Carle, A. C. (2007). Internal and external validity of scores on the Balanced Inventory of Desirable Responding and the Paulhus Deceptions Scales. *Educational and Psychological Measurement, 67*, 859–876. https://doi.org/10.1177/0013164406299104

Loinaz, I. (2014). Typologies, risk and recidivism in partner-violent men with the B-SAFER: A pilot study. *Psychology, Crime & Law, 20*, 183–198. https://doi.org/10.1080/1068316x.2013.770854

Meissner, C. A., Redlich, A. D., Bhattt, S., & Brandon, S. (2012). Interview and interrogation methods and their effects on true and false confessions. *Campbell Systematic Reviews, 8*(13), 1–53. https://doi.org/10.4073/csr.2012.13

Messing, J. T., & Thaller, J. (2013). The average predictive validity of intimate partner violence risk assessment instruments. *Journal of Interpersonal Violence, 28*, 1537–1558. https://doi.org/10.1177/0886260512468250

Miller, H. A. (2001). *Miller Forensic Assessment of Symptoms Test*. PAR.

Monahan, J. (1981). *The prediction of violent behavior: An assessment of clinical techniques*. Sage.

Nava, A., McFarlane, J., Gilroy, H., & Maddoux, J. (2014). Acculturation and associated effects on abused immigrant women's safety and mental functioning: Results of entry data for a 7-year prospective study. *Journal of Immigrant and Minority Health, 16*, 1077–1084. doi:10.1007/s10903-013-9816-6

Nicholls, T., Pritchard, M., Reeves, K., & Hilterman, E. (2013). Risk assessment in intimate partner violence: A review of contemporary approaches. *Partner Abuse, 4*(1), 76–168. doi:10.1891/1946-6560.4.1.76

Olver, M. E., & Jung, S. (2017). Incremental prediction of intimate partner violence: An examination of three risk measures. *Law and Human Behavior, 41*, 440–453. https://doi.org/10.1037/lhb0000251

Oxburgh, G., & Dando, C. (2011). Psychology and interviewing: What direction now in our quest for reliable information? *British Journal of Forensic Practice, 13*, 135–147. https://doi.org/10.1108/14636641111134378

Paulhus, D. L. (1999). *Paulhus Deception Scales user's manual*. Multi-Health Systems.

Pengpid, S., & Peltzer, K. (2014). Sexual assault and other types of intimate partner violence in women with protection orders in Vhembe District, South Africa. *Violence and Victims, 29*(5), 857–871. doi:10.1891/0886-6708.VV-D-13-00008

Pham, A. T., Hilton, N. Z., Ennis, L., Nunes, K. L., & Jung, S. (2021). Predicting recidivism in a high risk sample of intimate partner violent men referred for police threat assessment. Manuscript under review.

Redlich, A., & Meissner, C. (2009). Techniques and controversies in the interrogation of suspects: The artful practice versus the scientific study. In J. Skeem, K. Douglas, & S. Lilienfeld (Eds.), *Psychological science in the courtroom: Consensus and controversy* (pp. 124–148). Guilford Press.

Rettenberger, M., & Eher, R. (2013). Actuarial risk assessment in sexually motivated intimate-partner violence. *Law and Human Behavior, 37*, 75–86. https://doi.org/10.1037/b0000001

Rice, M. E., & Harris, G. T. (2005). Comparing effect sizes in follow-up studies: ROC area, Cohen's d, and r. *Law and Human Behavior, 29,* 615–620. https://doi.org/10.1007/s10979-005-6832-7

Roberts, N., & Noller, P. (1998). The association between adult attachment and couple violence: The role of communication patterns and relationship satisfaction. In J. Simpson & W. Rholes (Eds.), *Attachment theory and close relationships* (pp. 317–350). Guilford Press.

Rogers, R., Sewell, K. W., & Gillard, N. D. (2010). *Structured Interview of Reported Symptoms* (2nd ed.). PAR.

Ryan, T. J. (2016). *An examination of the interrater reliability and concurrent validity of the Spousal Assault Risk Assessment Guide—version 3 (SARA-V3)* [Unpublished master's thesis, Simon Fraser University].

Schenk, P. W. (1996). MMPI-2 norms for child custody litigants. *Georgia Psychologist, 50*(2), 51–54.

Seewald, K., Rossegger, A., Urbaniok, F., & Endrass, J. (2017). Assessing the risk of intimate partner violence: Expert evaluations versus the Ontario Domestic Assault Risk Assessment. *Journal of Forensic Psychology Research and Practice, 17,* 217–231. https://doi.org/10.1080/24732850.2017.1326268

Skowronski, J. J., Betz, A., Thompson, C. P., & Shannon, L. (1991). Social memory in everyday life: Recall of self-events and other-events. *Journal of Personality and Social Psychology, 60*(6), 831–843. https://doi.org/10.1037/0022-3514.60.6.831

Stansfield, R., & Williams, K. R. (2014). Predicting family violence recidivism using the DVSI-R: Integrating survival analysis and perpetrator characteristics. *Criminal Justice and Behavior, 41,* 163–180. https://doi.org/10.1177/0093854813500776

Stinson, J. D., & Clark, M. D. (2017). *Motivational interviewing with offenders: Engagement, rehabilitation, and reentry.* Guilford Press.

Storey, J. E., Kropp, P. R., Hart, S. D., Belfrage, H., & Strand, S. (2014). Assessment and management of risk for intimate partner violence by police officers using the Brief Spousal Assault Form for the Evaluation of Risk. *Criminal Justice and Behavior, 41*(2), 256–271. https://doi.org/10.1177/0093854813503960

Straus, M. (1979, February). Measuring intrafamily conflict and violence: The Conflict Tactics (CT) Scales. *Journal of Marriage and the Family, 41*(1), 75–85.

Straus, M. (1999). The controversy over domestic violence by women: A methodological, theoretical, and sociology of science analysis. In X. Arriaga & S. Oskamp (Eds.), *Violence in intimate relationships* (pp. 17–44). Sage.

Straus, M., & Gelles, R. (1990). *Physical violence in American families.* Transaction.

Svalin, K., Mellgren, C., Levander, M. T., & Levander, S. (2017). The inter-rater reliability of violence risk assessment tools used by police employees in Swedish police settings. *Nordisk politiforskning, 4,* 9–28. https://www.idunn.no/file/pdf/66960155/the_inter-rater_reliability_of_violence_risk_assessment_too.pdf

Svalin, K., Mellgren, C., Levander, M. T., & Levander, S. (2018). Police employees' violence risk assessments: The predictive validity of the B-SAFER and the significance of protective actions. *International Journal of Law and Psychiatry, 56,* 71–79. https://doi.org/10.1016/j.ijlp.2017.09.001

Thijssen, J., & de Ruiter, C. (2011). Identifying subtypes of spousal assaulters using the B-SAFER. *Journal of Interpersonal Violence, 26,* 1307–1321. https://doi.org/10.1177/0886260510369129

Vrij, A. (2015a). Verbal lie detection tools: Statement validity analysis, reality monitoring, and scientific content analysis. In P. Granhag, A. Vrij, & B. Verschuere (Eds.), *Detecting deception: Current challenges and cognitive approaches* (pp. 3–36). John Wiley & Sons.

Vrij. A. (2015b). Deception detection. In: P. A. Granhag, A. Vrij, & B. Verschuere (Eds.), *APA handbook of forensic psychology, volume 2: Criminal investigation, adjudication, and sentencing outcomes* (pp. 225–244). American Psychological Association.

Vrij, A. (2015c). A cognitive approach to lie detection. In P. Granhag, A. Vrij, & B. Verschuere (Eds.), *Detecting deception: Current challenges and cognitive approaches* (pp. 205–230). John Wiley & Sons.

Vrij, A., & Granhag, P. A. (2012). Eliciting cues to deception and truth: What matters are the questions asked. *Journal of Applied Research in Memory and Cognition, 1*(2), 110–117. https://doi.org/10.1016/j.jarmac.2012.02.004

Walsh, D., & Bull, R. (2010). Interviewing suspects of fraud: An in-depth analysis of interviewing skills. *The Journal of Psychiatry and Law, 38*, Spring/Summer, 99–133.

Wampold, B. E., & Imel, Z. E. (2015). *The great psychotherapy debate: The evidence for what makes psychotherapy work* (2nd ed.) Routledge.

Weisz, A. N., Tolman, R. M., & Saunders, D. G. (2000). Assessing the risk of severe domestic violence: The importance of survivors' predictions. *Journal of Interpersonal Violence, 15*, 75–90. doi:10.1177/088626000015001006

Williams, K. R. (2012). Family violence risk assessment: A predictive cross-validation study of the Domestic Violence Screening Instrument-Revised (DVSI-R). *Law and Human Behavior, 36*, 120–129. https://doi.org/10.1037/h0093977

Williams, K. R., & Grant, S. R. (2006). Empirically examining the risk of intimate partner violence: The Revised Domestic Violence Screening Instrument (DVSI-R). *Public Health Reports, 121*, 400–408. https://doi.org/10.1177/003335490612100408

Williams, K. R., & Houghton, A. B. (2004). Assessing the risk of domestic violence reoffending: A validation study. *Law and Human Behavior, 28*, 437–455. https://doi.org/10.1023/b:lahu.0000039334.59297.f0

Wong, T., & Hisashima, J. (2008). *State of Hawaii, 2003–2007: Domestic violence exploratory study on the DVSI and SARA. Report No. 1.* Hawaii State Department of Health.

Risk-Needs-Responsivity-Informed Approaches to Batterer Intervention Treatment

AMIE ROBERTS ∎

Before we outline an alternative to batterer intervention treatment, let us clarify what it is not because it is common for courts in some jurisdictions to order anger management, mental health, or couples counseling as alternative treatments for court-mandated offenders intimate partner violence (IPV). While psychotherapy and anger management are essential components of offender treatment, depending on how they are incorporated, these treatment modalities are not well-suited for IPV treatment. In some cases, they can be inappropriate and even dangerous. They are not viable alternatives for most offenders, as most states mandate psychoeducational group formats specific to domestic violence treatment as the only recognized treatment modality.

"TRADITIONAL" BATTERER INTERVENTION TREATMENT AND THE ALTERNATIVES

The provision of domestic violence treatment requires specialized education, which is often not addressed within the training curriculums offered in most professional mental health counseling programs. Collusion with the offender and victim blaming are common with counselors who lack training in domestic violence offenders in individual mental health counseling. This only increases the risk to the victim and their children. Consider that an offender can maintain a calm and healthy demeanor during a couples counseling session. The counselor will assume that it is a safe space for the offender's partner to open up and express grievances. All seems fine on the surface. However, if a domestic violence offender has not made healthy cognitive and behavioral changes resulting from proper treatment, they may lash out at their partner after the session. Obviously, this also increases the risk to the victim.

A well-trained domestic violence professional should determine specific treatment options appropriate for each individual who has engaged in IPV, just as a specially trained substance abuse professional would make treatment recommendations for someone arrested for driving under the influence of drugs or alcohol. Batterer intervention typically includes an anger management component. However, anger management does not include batterer intervention treatment, which is designed to address more chronic, severe forms of physical violence and issues of power and control. When IPV has occurred, a typical anger management class may not be a suitable response. An offender may present with both an anger management problem and an IPV problem, in which case treatment, in the form of a batterer intervention program, can address both aspects and is fitting.

Domestic violence intervention treatment has been around since the late 1970s but really began to expand nationally in the 1980s and 1990s because of mandatory arrest laws for offenders. While there are no national standards in place, most states in the United States have standards in place for batterer intervention programs, although some are not mandated but rather serve as guidelines. Often, there is little to no funding for batterer intervention programs. Levels of qualification, education, and training of staff/facilitators tasked with treatment delivery differ substantially across programs and states. In the absence of a national standard (Stover & Lent, 2014), each state or county, and sometimes each individual treatment program, has developed its own versions of a treatment model. In places where there are limited local standards or the standards are merely guidelines, it is not unusual to find treatment programs that are staffed with facilitators who lack domestic violence training, collude with participants, or utilize punitive and shame-based approaches. Most batterer intervention programs are psychoeducational, although there are some which can be characterized as purely educational or therapeutic as well. It is for this reason that it is hard to define a "traditional" approach. In some states, batterer intervention programs are also referred to as IPV treatment programs to differentiate between a broader definition of domestic violence perpetrated against any member of the family and IPV perpetrated against an intimate partner.

Many researchers divide IPV treatment programs into two groups: those that use a cognitive-behavioral approach, focused on changing the thoughts that lead to abuse and providing the prosocial skills with which to improve the offender's emotion management and relationship skills, and those that use the Duluth model (Babcock, 2004), focused on changing the abuser's belief that they should exercise power and control over their partner. Nevertheless, most IPV treatment programs combine the two approaches (Cannon et al., 2016). Consider a program that utilizes the Power and Control Wheel (Pence & McMahon, 2008) in a particular session. Does that alone categorize the program as a "Duluth" model? What if that same program also incorporates mindfulness or dialectical behavior therapy (DBT) skills (Linehan, 2014)? How then would the program be categorized? Although many programs are heavily weighted with a cognitive-behavioral approach, they are not always overt about it, and they may not have a standardized curriculum, so that leaves doubt and subjective interpretation about their methods. How researchers divide and define programs is a question worth asking so that IPV treatment programs can get a more accurate picture of outcomes and shape their programs for success.

Regardless of how a batterer intervention program is shaped, it can only be as good as the system in which it operates. "Program effectiveness," according to Gondolf (2003), depends on the intervention system of which the program is a part (Gondolf, 2003). A batterer intervention program is responsible for continually evolving to use the most effective methods and standards possible. However, that effort is inadequate without ample court response for violations, more intensive programming for high-risk participants, and consistent risk monitoring (Gondolf, 2003). From law enforcement, the court, and probation to treatment, the entire system must function in a united fashion to yield the best results.

It is equally important to acknowledge the value of fundamental standards. In an evaluation among four geographically distributed cities to measure the effectiveness of treatment, Gondolf concluded that different treatment approaches could have similar successful outcomes when they share a common standard (Gondolf, 1999). Meaning, IPV treatment programs can have diverse and individualized approaches as long as they adhere to a common core standard. Consequently, what alternative approach to IPV treatment could successfully conform to fundamental standards, and what should those standards be? A broad sample of research into batterer treatment programs yields mixed results, mainly due to how programs are defined and measured, as mentioned earlier (Babcock et al., 2016). However, one common theme that does consistently emerge is the need to step away from a one-size-fits-all approach and move toward a more individualized, cognitive-behavioral approach. It is imperative to note that aside from an effective model and standards, other important factors are just as critical, such as group cohesion and the therapeutic relationship between the facilitator and the participants. A 2003 study found that the strongest predictors of outcome were group cohesion and the client–therapist alliance (Taft et al., 2003).

In this chapter, we will examine one example of an alternative approach to IPV treatment, which consists of the following components:

- education and training requirements for IPV treatment facilitators;
- a risk-needs-responsivity assessment, and treatment framework;
- a differentiated treatment model;
- a cognitive-behavioral treatment approach with a standardized core curriculum;
- core competencies and completion criteria for successful completion of treatment; and
- quality management.

This approach is from the State of Washington, which amended its IPV standards in response to a broad concern about the efficacy of IPV treatment. As a result, Washington State convened an IPV treatment advisory committee, contracted with national IPV experts, and gathered feedback from a large selection of stakeholders, including victim advocates and survivors. The resulting changes in IPV treatment standards were immense. The previous standards were revoked completely, and a new chapter of IPV treatment standards was adopted in the State of Washington on June 29, 2018. A fuller representation of these changes can be found at https://app.leg.wa.gov/wac/default.aspx?cite=388-60B.

Colorado incorporated a similar differentiated treatment approach in 2010 (McRee Lauch et al., 2017). The main differences between the Colorado and Washington models are the risk assessment tools and Colorado's mandated use of a multidisciplinary team to determine treatment progress and completion.

EDUCATION AND TRAINING REQUIREMENTS FOR INTIMATE PARTNER VIOLENCE TREATMENT FACILITATORS

There are three levels of direct treatment staff in certified IPV treatment programs in the State of Washington. The first level (trainee) requires a bachelor's degree, a counseling credential issued by the state, 30 hours of training in domestic violence victim advocacy, and 30 hours of training in providing IPV treatment. The second level (staff) requires the previous level's education, credential, and training, along with at least 50 hours of experience providing supervised, direct treatment at an IPV treatment program and 50 hours of experience working with domestic violence victims. The third level is that of "supervisor." The Washington State model requires that each state-certified IPV treatment program have at least one supervisor with the following qualifications:

- a master's degree from an accredited university in counseling, psychology, social work, or similar social services field;
- a counseling credential issued by the state;
- a minimum of 2 years of experience providing direct services at an IPV treatment program;
- at least 250 hours of direct treatment contact with participants at an IPV treatment program; and
- at least 100 hours of experience working with victims of domestic violence.

Supervisors are required to oversee the IPV treatment program by periodically observing assessments and treatments of all staff who provide direct client services in the IPV treatment program. Supervisors also review a sample of each direct treatment staff's assessments and client records for compliance with state standards and the program's own policies and procedures. Additionally, supervisors are required to report any critical incidents to the certifying department at the state, such as death, serious injury, or a violation of staff or client's rights at the program.

A well-educated, trained, and experienced workforce plays a crucial part in providing effective assessments and evidence-based treatment. The State of Washington requires all direct IPV treatment staff to attain a minimum of 20 hours of continuing education annually, about half of which is victim focused. The other half is treatment focused. Suicide prevention education is also required. Furthermore, the state performs on-site reviews of all certified IPV treatment programs to determine compliance with state standards and require corrective actions when needed.

A RISK, NEEDS, RESPONSIVITY ASSESSMENT AND TREATMENT FRAMEWORK

The risk, needs, responsivity (RNR) model is an evidence-based approach for working with participants in the criminal justice system. RNR (Andrews et al., 2006) has three principles:

Risk principle. We are looking specifically at the offender's risk to reoffend in IPV.

Needs principle. Criminogenic needs are assessed as part of the RNR model, but the State of Washington's approach also evaluates static and dynamic risk factors (other than criminogenic) and their associated treatment needs.

Responsivity principle: The State of Washington's approach individualizes treatment within a cognitive-behavioral model and considers the offender's learning style, motivations for healthy relationships, and personal strengths.

"RNR is derived from decades of research demonstrating that the best outcomes are achieved in the criminal justice system when (1) the intensity of criminal justice supervision is matched to participants' risk for criminal recidivism or likelihood of failure in rehabilitation (criminogenic risk) and (2) interventions focus on the specific disorders or conditions that are responsible for participants' crimes (criminogenic needs)" (Andrews et al., 2006, p. 1).

The RNR model has been incorporated into outpatient IPV treatment programs with documented success. According to one study conducted by Gabora, results for incarcerated male offenders in an IPV treatment program using RNR principles showed reduced attitudes that supported violence against women and higher prosocial skills overall. In the same study, feedback from parole officers reported positive changes in behavior and attitude associated with treatment. A follow-up with the offenders after release indicated that program completion significantly reduced spousal violence in addition to general violent recidivism. These results are encouraging and demonstrate that domestic violence programs respecting the RNR principles may effectively reduce IPV (Andrews et al., 2011; Stewart et al., 2015).

How does an outpatient program incorporate RNR into the assessment and treatment process? The Washington State model demonstrates one possibility by incorporating it into a robust behavioral assessment (https://app.leg.wa.gov/wac/default.aspx?cite=388-60B-0400). How RNR is integrated into the treatment process is explained later in this chapter. The Washington State model asserts the purpose of the assessment is to determine (1) the level of risk, needs, and responsivity for the participant; (2) the level of treatment the program will require for the participant; and (3) behaviorally focused, individualized treatment goals or objectives for an initial treatment plan.

BEHAVIORAL ASSESSMENT STANDARDS

The State of Washington requires the IPV behavioral assessment to include general information such as referral, demographic, and cultural information. The cultural information includes gender identity, preferred pronouns, sexual orientation, religious or spiritual beliefs, race, ethnicity, groups with which the participant identifies, and any possible cultural context for the participant's views about using violence in family relationships. A summary of historical information is gathered about the participant's domestic violence or sexual assault victimization and trauma history, which includes any complex trauma. Information on legal interventions is documented, including current or past protective orders, restraining orders, or any other court orders such as a parenting plan. A summary of police or incident reports for current and past incidents involving coercive or abusive behaviors is also included when applicable.

The assessment characterizes the types of abuse the participant has engaged in and whether abuse has affected any children. This is achieved by documenting the participant's specific abusive behaviors, whether there were children present during any incidents or in the immediate aftermath of an incident, and the children's exposure to the abuse, the victim's injuries, or property damage. The assessor gathers information to determine how children have been affected in any way by the participant's domestic violence and if a parenting class specific to perpetrators of domestic violence will be required by the program. Third-party and collateral sources are necessary to assess the participant's risks and needs are required components of the assessment. Those sources include, but are not limited to, information from probation or parole officers, the victim, previous partners, or a current partner if they choose to provide information, victim advocates, 911 tapes, guardians ad litem, Court Appointed Special Advocates (CASAs), or parenting evaluators, and child protective service workers.

The assessment compiles additional information into seven main domains, which constitute the core of the assessment document and include the following:

1. current and past high-risk factors as defined by the standards;
2. screening for traumatic brain injury, with documentation of making appropriate referrals for further assessment or treatment when needed;
3. a screening for indicators associated with the participant's mental health, with documentation of making appropriate referrals for further assessment or treatment when needed;
4. an assessment of the participant's belief system as it relates to hierarchical relationships, spiritual, cultural, or religious beliefs about gender and family roles that condone partner violence;
5. screening for substance use, with documentation of making appropriate referrals for further assessment or treatment by a substance use disorder professional when needed;
6. an assessment of the participant's environmental factors which must include a criminal history from the participant's self-report, a background check that covers each state they have lived in over the last 10 years, and collateral sources. The environmental factors include criminogenic needs as defined later in this chapter; and
7. documentation of the results from an evidence-based, standardized test that provides empirical and objective data regarding risk, lethality, or needs for domestic violence perpetrators. Documentation of a separate evidence-based test and the participant's level of psychopathy must be completed when needed based on the assessment interview, background check, or input from a third party or collateral sources.

In addition to the seven domains of the assessment, the assessor also estimates the participant's readiness to change, the current level of accountability, motivations for healthy relationships, and their perceived strengths. The assessor then notes the absence or presence of acute or critical factors, which indicate the participant is at a higher risk for lethality or recidivism:

- previous incidents of physical assaults causing injury, sexual assaults, strangulation, or previously reported incidents toward more than one partner;
- stalking behaviors;
- physical, sexual, or assaultive violence against children, pets, or an elderly person;
- attempts or threats of homicide or suicide in the last 12 months;
- repeated violations of probation, no contact orders, protective orders, or similar orders; or
- a demonstration of medium to high levels of traits and characteristics associated with psychopathy.

Participants may be determined to have a high level of risk, need, or lethality, even if they do not meet any of the critical or acute factors listed earlier.

Finally, the assessment summary includes findings from the behavioral assessment and interview with the participant, collateral information, and input from third-party sources, which are public record or have been released to be shared in the assessment by the source of information. The summary contains a recommendation and rationale for no treatment or placement into one of four levels of treatment. The assessment is contained in a single document. However, it is an ongoing process of gathering information throughout treatment from the participant and third-party contacts, with particular attention to dynamic risk factors. The assessment process collects information that assists the program in developing an individualized treatment plan, which includes the program's general and specific responsivity as defined by the RNR model (Andrews & Bonta, 2010).

Programs can produce significant reductions in recidivism when program facilitators adhere to the RNR model. The risk principle has two components. The first part emphasizes the importance of predicting criminal behavior, which is why the State of Washington requires evidence-based testing for risk or lethality. The second component focuses on the need to appropriately match the level of IPV treatment to the offender's risk level. As the risk level increases, the amount of treatment needed to reduce recidivism also rises (Andrews & Dowden, 2005). General responsivity in the Washington State model includes a trauma-informed cognitive-behavioral approach. Specific responsivity considers strengths, learning style, personality, motivation, and biosocial (e.g., gender, race) characteristics of the individual.

A DIFFERENTIATED TREATMENT MODEL

Once the assessment determines risks, needs, and lethality, the participant is recommended to either no treatment or to one of four levels of treatment (see Table 12.1). The interview with the participant, evidence-based testing, criminal history, and input from a third party and collateral sources determine the level of

Table 12.1 Differentiated Levels for Intimate Partner Violence Treatment in the State of Washington

Treatment Level	Brief Description	Minimum Treatment Length
No treatment	Possible referral to victim services or not amenable to treatment	NA
Level 1	Low risk and need	6 months
Level 2	Medium risk or need	9 months
Level 3	High risk or need	12 months
Level 4	Medium to high levels of traits and characteristics associated with psychopathy as evidenced by testing, criminal history, or collateral contacts	18 months

risk, needs, and lethality in the assessment. In order to qualify for level-one treatment, participants must have engaged in abusive and controlling behaviors with an intimate partner but have no previous domestic violence charges, regardless of an arrest or legal outcomes. Suppose the assessor cannot obtain information from any collateral or third-party sources. In that case, the assessor does not have sufficient information to categorize the participant as "low risk" and cannot place them in level-one treatment.

One prominent factor that separates level three from level two is the presence of criminogenic needs or traits associated with an antisocial personality. Participants with several criminogenic needs or antisocial traits will require more time in treatment, and they will be recommended for level-three treatment (see Table 12.2).

> Criminogenic needs are dynamic risk factors that are directly linked to criminal behavior. Criminogenic needs can come and go unlike static risk factors that can only change in one direction (increase risk) and are immutable to treatment intervention. Offenders have many needs deserving of treatment but not all of these needs are associated with their criminal behavior. These criminogenic needs are subsumed under the major predictors of criminal behavior referred to as "central eight" risk/needs factors. (Andrews et al., 2006, p.1)

Level-four treatment is reserved for participants with medium to high levels of traits and characteristics associated with psychopathy and focuses almost entirely on criminogenic needs and intrinsic motivations for change.

A COGNITIVE-BEHAVIORAL TREATMENT APPROACH AND STANDARDIZED CORE CURRICULUM

Using a trauma-informed, cognitive-behavioral treatment approach is a requirement of the Washington State model (https://app.leg.wa.gov/wac/default.aspx?cite=388-60B-0320), but that does not exclude an augmentation to the approach with DBT, Internal Family Systems (IFS), mindfulness, or other evidence-based approaches. The University of Washington (Harborview) developed the "Cognitive Behavioral Treatment Guide for Intimate Partner Violence" (Berliner et al., 2020), and it meets the requirements of the Washington State rules for treatment in levels one, two, and three. The guide is for the facilitator, and it includes mindfulness activities, information about the session topic, and links to homework documents. The guide consists of 29 sessions, including those orienting the participant to the curriculum and providing definitions; and those providing information in overcoming unhelpful thinking, coping with emotional dysregulation, managing anger and other challenging emotions, developing empathy for victims, and improving one's communication, conflict resolution, and parenting skills (Berliner et al., 2020). The guide is available, free of charge, and

Table 12.2 CRIMINOGENIC NEEDS, INDICATORS, AND GOALS

The Seven Major Risk/Need Factors along with Some Minor Risk/Need Factors Major Risk/Need Factor	Indicators	Intervention Goals
Antisocial personality pattern	Impulsive, adventurous, pleasure seeking, restlessly aggressive, and irritable	Build self-management skills, teach anger management
Procriminal attitudes	Rationalizations for crime, negative attitudes toward the law	Counter rationalizations with prosocial attitudes; build up a prosocial identity
Social supports for crime	Criminal friends, isolation from prosocial others	Replace procriminal friends and associates with prosocial friends and associates
Substance abuse	Abuse of alcohol and/or drugs	Reduce substance abuse, enhance alternatives to substance use
Family/marital relationships	Inappropriate parental monitoring and disciplining, poor family relationships	Teaching parenting skills, enhance warmth and caring
School/work	Poor performance, low levels of satisfactions	Enhance work/study skills, nurture interpersonal relationships within the context of work and school
Prosocial recreational activities	Lack of involvement in prosocial recreational/leisure activities	Encourage participation in prosocial recreational activities, teach prosocial hobbies and sports

SOURCE: Andrews & Dowden, 2005; Lowenkamp & Latessa, 2004; Lowenkamp, 2006; Taxman & Marlowe, 2006.

can be viewed or downloaded from the State of Washington's website: https://www.dshs.wa.gov/esa/community-services-offices/domestic-violence-intervention-treatment.

IPV treatment groups in the State of Washington are typically open, and as a result, there is no specific order to the treatment guide. Facilitators are encouraged to use the guide as a "core" curriculum and add to it in order to meet the individual needs of the participants in the group. Having a standardized core curriculum helps deliver a more consistent treatment, and flexibility for augmentation

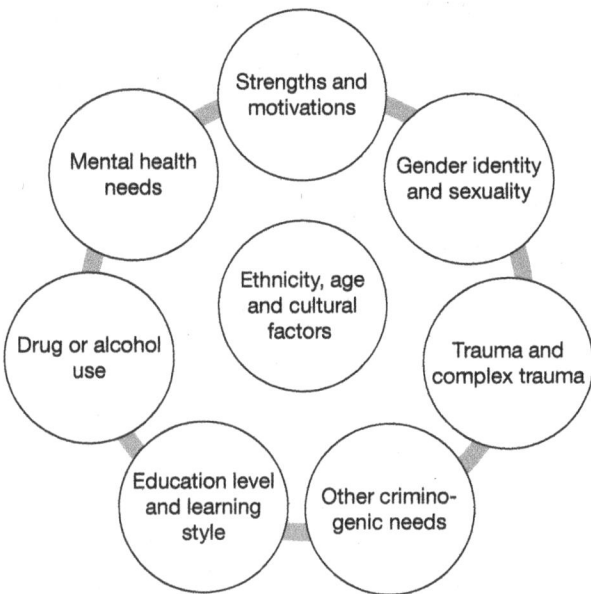

Figure 12.1 Individualized Intimate Partner Violence Treatment in the State of Washington (created by Amie Roberts, LMHC, State of Washington)

allows the program to address the participant's individual needs. Figure 12.1 demonstrates the almost infinite combination of individual needs of participants in IPV treatment. Although the core curriculum is a consistent deliverable for all group members, numerous other factors may be present in each category surrounding the core standards. When enough group members share a common factor outside the core curriculum, it is simple for the group facilitator to incorporate it into group treatment. When just one or two group members have additional needs that are not met in the core curriculum, facilitators can use individual sessions to meet the participant's needs. The State of Washington's model allows for a group, individual, or a combination of group and individual sessions for high-risk/need participants.

CORE COMPETENCIES AND COMPLETION CRITERIA

Dynamic risk factors must improve during IPV treatment. Examples of stable and acute dynamic risk factors could include substance abuse, unemployment, emotional regulation difficulties, few prosocial friends, arguing with coworkers, intense negative emotional state when arguing with their intimate partner, and using physical and verbal abuse to get their way, to "win," or as a means to end arguments. Documentation of the following core competencies and completion criteria are required to successfully complete levels one, two, and three IPV treatment in the Washington State model:

- documentation of the participant's cognitive and behavioral changes;
- documentation that the participant has met all of the treatment program's requirements for completion;
- evidence that the participant has remained in compliance with any co-occurring treatments required in their treatment plan;
- the knowledge that there have been no reports of physical violence in the last 6 months;
- documentation that the participant has met the minimum treatment period requirements for their level of treatment;
- proof that the participant complies with all related court orders;
- documentation of the participant's accountability and adherence to their accountability plan; and
- documentation of the participant's knowledge of their primary personal motivations for using abusive or controlling behaviors and alternative ways to meet their needs in a nonabusive manner.

Level-four participants have a unique treatment approach and completion criteria outlined in the Washington State standards (https://app.leg.wa.gov/wac/default.aspx?cite=388-60B-0430). The Washington State model also has standards for quality management to improve each IPV treatment program (https://app.leg.wa.gov/wac/default.aspx?cite=388-60B-0125) continually.

As part of the quality management plan, participants are asked to complete outcome data forms at the end of treatment, which measure demographics, their understanding of the cognitive-behavioral paradigm, healthy relationship skills, and their use of abusive behaviors before, during, and after treatment. The outcome data form is voluntary and confidential. Completed forms are sent to the State of Washington to compile the data and provide program feedback. Over 600 data outcome forms were submitted to the State of Washington in the first 2 years of implementing the new standards. The data help compile quantitative and qualitative information to facilitate continuous improvement in IPV treatment programs. For more information about this alternative IPV treatment approach or the core curriculum, you can contact:

State of Washington
Department of Social and Health Services
Domestic Violence Perpetrator Treatment Program Manager
https://www.dshs.wa.gov/esa/community-services-offices/contact-information

REFERENCES

Andrews, D., & Bonta, J. (2010). *The psychology of criminal conduct* (5th ed.). Anderson.

Andrews, D. A., Bonta, J., & Wormith, J. (2011). The risk-need-responsivity RNR model. *Criminal Justice and Behavior, 38,* 735–755. https://psycnet.apa.org/doi/10.1177/0093854811406356

Andrews, D. A., Bonta, J., & Wormith, J. S. (2006). The recent past and near future of risk and/or need assessment. *Crime & Delinquency, 52*(1), 7–27. https://doi.org/10.1177/0011128705281756

Andrews, D. A., & Dowden, C. (2005). Managing correctional treatment for reduced recidivism: A meta-analytic review of program integrity. *Legal and Criminological Psychology, 10,* 173–187. https://doi.org/10.1348/135532505X36723

Andrews, D. A., Zinger, I., Hoge, R. D., Bonta, J., Gendreau, P., & Cullen, F. T. (1990). Does correctional treatment work? A clinically relevant and psychologically informed meta-analysis. *Criminology, 28*(3), 369–404. https://doi.org/10.1111/j.1745-9125.1990.tb01330.x

Babcock, J., Cannon, C., Lauve-Moon, K., Ferreira, R., Cantos, A., Hamel, J., Kelly, D., Leisring, P.A., Murphy, C., O'Leary, K.D., Bannon, S., Salis, K. L., & Solono, I. (2016). Domestic violence perpetrator programs: A proposal for evidence- based standards in the United States. *Partner Abuse, 7*(4), 1–107. https://doi.org/10.1016/j.cpr.2002.07.001

Babcock, J., Green, C., & Robie, C. (2004). Does batterers' treatment work? A meta-analytic review of domestic violence treatment. *Clinical Psychology Review, 23*(8), 1023–1053. doi:10.1891/1946-6560.7.4.355

Berliner, L., Merchant, L., Roberts, A., & Martin, D. (2020). CBT guide for intimate partner violence. https://www.dshs.wa.gov/esa/community-services-offices/domestic-violence-intervention-treatment.

Bonta, J., & Andrews, D. A. (2007). *Risk need responsivity model for offender assessment and rehabilitation.* Her Majesty the Queen in Right of Canada.

Cannon, C., Hamel, J., Buttell, F. P., & Ferreira, R. J. (2016). A survey of domestic violence perpetrator programs in the U.S. and Canada: Findings and implications for policy intervention. *Partner Abuse, 7*(3), 226–276. doi:10.1891/1946-6560.7.3.226

Gendreau, P., Smith, P., & French, S. A. (2006). The theory of effective correctional intervention: Empirical status and future directions. In F. T. Cullen, J. P. Wright, & K. R. Blevins (Eds.), *Taking stock: The status of criminological theory (vol. 15). Advances in criminological theory* (pp. 419–446). Transaction.

Gondolf, E. W. (1999). A comparison of four batterer intervention systems: Do court referral, program length, and services matter? *Journal of Interpersonal Violence, 14*(1), 41–61. https://doi.org/10.1177/088626099014001003

Gondolf, E. W. (2003). Evaluating batterer counseling programs: A difficult task showing some effects and implications. https://www.iup.edu/marti/publications/edward-gondolf/

McRee Lauch, K., Hart, K. J., & Bresler, S. (2017). Predictors of treatment completion and recidivism among intimate partner violence offenders. *Journal of Aggression, Maltreatment & Trauma, 26*(5), 543–557. doi:10.1080/10926771.2017.1299824

Linehan, M. M. (2014). *DBT training manual.* The Guilford Press.

Lipsey, M. W., & Cullen, F. T. (2007). The effectiveness of correctional rehabilitation: A review of systematic reviews. *Annual Review of Law & Social Science, 3,* 279–320. https://doi.org/10.1146/annurev.lawsocsci.3.081806.112833

Lowenkamp, C. T., & Latessa, E. J. (2004). Understanding the risk principle: How and why correctional interventions can harm low-risk offenders. *Topics in Community Corrections*, 3–8. https://dvrisc.org/wp-content/uploads/2021/09/Understanding-the-Risk-Principle.pdf

Lowenkamp, C. T., Latessa, E. J., & Holsinger, A. M. (2006). The risk principle in action: What have we learned from 13,676 offenders and 97 correctional programs? *Crime & Delinquency*, 52(1), 77–93. https://doi.org/10.1177/0011128705281747

Pence, E., & McMahon, M. (2008). Power and control wheel. In C. M. Renzetti & J. L. Edleson (Eds.), *Encyclopedia of interpersonal violence* (Vol. 1, pp. 525–526). Sage. https://www.doi.org/10.4135/9781412963923.n351

Smith, P., Gendreau, P., & Swartz, K. (2009). Validating the principles of effective intervention: A systematic review of the contributions of meta-analysis in the field of corrections. *Victims & Offenders*, 4(2), 148–169. https://doi.org/10.1080/15564880802612581

Stewart, L. A., Gabora, N., Kropp, P. R. & Lee, Z. (2015). Erratum to: Effectiveness of risk-needs-responsivity-based family violence programs with male offenders. *Journal of Family Violence*, 30, 673. https://doi.org/10.1007/s10896-015-9707-9

Stover, C. S., & Lent, K. (2014). Training and certification for domestic violence service providers: The need for a national standard curriculum and training approach. *Psychology of Violence*, 4(2), 117–127. doi:10.1037/a0036022.

Taft, C. T., Murphy, C. M., King, D. W., Musser, P. H., & DeDeyn, J. M. (2003). Process and treatment adherence factors in group cognitive-behavioral therapy for partner violent men. *Journal of Consulting and Clinical Psychology*, 71(4), 812–820. https://doi.org/10.1037/0022-006X.71.4.812

Taxman, F. S., & Marlowe, D. B. (Eds.) (2006). Risk, needs, responsivity: In action or inaction? (Special issue). *Crime & Delinquency*, 52(1), 3–6. doi:10.1177/0011128705281757

Couples and Family Interventions for Intimate Partner Violence

VICTORIA E. BENNETT, JANELLA CHU, DEANNA POLLARD, AND JULIA BABCOCK ■

Intimate partner violence (IPV) is a pervasive public health problem that has significant consequences for couples, their children, and their entire family unit. The Centers for Disease Control (CDC) defines IPV as physical, sexual, and psychological abuse committed against current or former romantic partners (Breiding et al., 2015). Twelve-month prevalence rates reported by the National Intimate Partner and Sexual Violence Survey (NISVS) indicate that 4.3 million women (3.6%) and 5.1 million men (4.5%) have experienced minor physical assault (e.g., slapping/hitting, kicking). The data also report that 3.2 million women (2.7%) and 2.2 million men (2%) have experienced severe physical abuse (e.g., choking, punching, burning) (Breiding et al., 2014). Twelve-month victimization rates indicate that 686,000 women (0.6%) experienced rape by an intimate partner, and 2.7 million women (2.3%) experienced other forms of sexual abuse (e.g., unwanted sexual contact, sexual coercion). Due to low reporting among men, the NISVS was unable to provide 12-month prevalence rates for rape committed by an intimate partner. However, the data showed that 2.8 million men (2.5%) reported experiencing other forms of sexual aggression (Breiding et al., 2014).

Psychological aggression is one of the most prevalent forms of IPV and is the most poorly defined. Depending on the source, psychologically abusive behaviors range from common relationship behaviors, such as yelling and swearing, to more severe forms of emotional abuse such as coercive control, manipulative behaviors, and isolation (Follingstad & Rogers, 2013). Twelve-month prevalence rates indicate that 18.1% of men and 13.9% of women have been psychologically victimized. Cyber abuse is a form of psychological aggression that has gained significant attention in recent years. Cyber abuse is defined as using technology, including the Internet, social media, and text messages to threaten, track, embarrass, or ridicule a romantic partner (Watkins et al., 2018). A recent study found that 81% of men referred to a batterer intervention program (BIP) engaged in at least one act of cyber abuse in the 12 months prior to starting treatment (Brem et al., 2019).

IPV results in a number of physical and behavioral health problems, including chronic pain, IPV-related injuries, gastrointestinal distress, difficulty sleeping, anxiety, posttraumatic stress disorder (PTSD), depression, substance abuse, and suicide (Bennett et al., 2020; Karakurt et al., 2014; Simpson et al., 2019, Warshaw et al., 2009). Subsequently, IPV results in an economic burden totaling $3.6 trillion over the course of survivors' lives, and it includes an estimated $2 trillion in health care costs, $1 trillion in lost wages, $73 billion for the criminal justice system, and $62 billion for other expenses. Broken down, IPV costs the United States $100,000 for every woman and $23,000 for every man who has been victimized (Peterson et al., 2018).

RISK FACTORS

There are several risk factors for IPV, including conflict, relationship dissatisfaction, ineffective communication skills, personality disorder characteristics, poor anger regulation, and hostility (Babcock et al., 2004; Birkley & Eckhardt, 2015; Costa & Babcock, 2008; Elmquist et al., 2014). Stith and colleagues (2008) found that higher rates of marital conflict and relationship dissatisfaction were positively associated with greater levels of physical abuse. They also found that men who perpetrated abuse tended to report that they were more dissatisfied with their relationships than women who perpetrated abuse. Vives-Cases and colleagues (2009) found a similar relationship between marital conflict and wife abuse, supporting the theory that relatively high levels of conflict coupled with relationship dissatisfaction increases the likelihood of IPV.

Maladaptive communication skills are a related, yet distinct, risk factor for IPV (Babcock et al., 1993). Research has found that couples with poor communication are more likely to report IPV compared to couples with good communication (Messinger et al., 2012; Ronan et al., 2004). Several research studies have indicated that specific negative communication behaviors are linked with IPV perpetration. Recently, Sommer et al. (2019) found that contempt and anger were associated with couples' own physical abuse perpetration. In contrast, they found that contempt was associated with partners' physical assault perpetration. Other studies have found that the demand-withdrawal interaction pattern, contempt, and belligerence are positively associated with IPV (Berns et al., 1999; Coan et al., 1997; Gordis et al., 2005). These results provide insight into the specific communication behaviors that predict IPV, thus allowing for more targeted interventions than general communication skills training.

Personality disorder characteristics are some of the most widely studied risk factors for IPV, with a wealth of research examining borderline and antisocial personality disorder (Brem et al., 2018; Shaffer et al., 2021). A meta-analysis examining the relations among depression, anxiety, PTSD, borderline personality disorder, and antisocial personality disorder with the perpetration of physical IPV found that borderline and antisocial personality disorder demonstrated stronger correlations with IPV perpetration than IPV victimization (Spencer et al., 2019). Narcissistic personality disorder has also been found to increase the risk of IPV. Larson and colleagues (2015) found that individuals who reported more symptoms of narcissistic personality disorder and reported lower self-control were more likely than other individuals to engage in IPV. Taken together, these results suggest that Cluster B personality disorders (erratic, dramatic, and overly emotional types) are strongly related to IPV perpetration.

Anger and hostility are often-cited risk factors for IPV perpetration (Costa & Babcock, 2008; Wolf & Foshee, 2003). Perpetrators of IPV tend to exhibit more hostility than nonperpetrators and subsequently endorse greater levels of state and trait anger (Norlander & Eckhardt, 2005). A recent meta-analysis of 61 studies (Birkley & Eckhardt, 2015) found that anger, hostility, and negative affect suppression were significant predictors of IPV perpetration. However, this effect was stronger for moderate to severe violence perpetration. Studies have also found that low anger control and high anger expressivity are associated with greater rates of IPV recidivism, including the issuing and violation of protective orders (Farzan-Kashani & Murphy, 2017). Taken together, it is possible that poor anger and hostility regulation are underlying mechanisms between limited conflict resolution skills and IPV perpetration.

TYPOLOGIES OF PERPETRATORS

As researchers began to recognize the multitude of risk factors for IPV perpetration and move away from the traditional models of IPV, the field began proposing we conceptualize IPV using typologies. The most widely cited perpetrator typologies are Holtzworth-Munroe and Stuart's (1994): "family only," "dysphoric/borderline," and "generally violent/antisocial." These typologies differed primarily on IPV severity, general violence, and psychopathology.

The "family only" are thought to only engage in relatively minor physical and psychological abuse, only engage in IPV, and exhibit few symptoms of psychopathology or personality disorder traits. In contrast, the "dysphoric/borderline" are thought to engage in moderate to severe levels of abuse, engage in IPV and general violence, and display symptoms of emotional volatility and borderline personality disorder. The "generally violent/antisocial" perpetrate severe IPV, engage in general violence, and display symptoms of antisocial personality disorder or psychopathy (Holtzworth-Munroe & Stuart, 1994).

Following Johnson's (2008) typology publication that classifies couples based on levels of coercive control and severity, the typologies have been simplified to characterological violence and situational couple violence (Babcock et al., 2007; Kelly & Johnson, 2008). Characterological violence is like the Generally Violent/Antisocial typology, with primarily asymmetrical severe IPV that stems from motivations to dominate and control one's partner. Characterologically violent perpetrators will likely minimize the IPV and demonstrate little remorse (Babcock et al., 2017). Situational violence, in contrast, is mutual, and often occurs due to frustrating disagreements, though both partners likely display remorse during repair attempts (Armenti & Babcock, 2016). Johnson and Leone (2005) found that 65% of couples experiencing violence could be classified as experiencing situational violence.

COUPLES THERAPY FOR INTIMATE PARTNER VIOLENCE

Although there is a wealth of research demonstrating which variables increase the risk for IPV, meta-analytic research indicates that the predominant BIP, the Duluth model, does little to stop IPV (Arias et al., 2013; Babcock et al., 2004). Developed through interviews with women seeking shelter services in the 1970s, the Duluth model theorizes that IPV occurs because of men's need to exert power and control over women caused by internalized sexist and patriarchal beliefs (Babcock et al., 2007; Pence & Paymar, 1993). Along this vein, the Duluth model promotes the belief that IPV is asymmetrical, with men as the perpetrators and women as the victims. If women engage in violence, it is in self-defense (Babcock et al., 2007). However, in the United States, legal definitions of domestic violence are much broader than the male characterological abuse delineated by the Duluth model. The Duluth model is not applicable for situational IPV, gay and lesbian couples, or female-perpetrated violence. Thus, IPV appears to be a much more nuanced phenomenon than originally believed. This may explain why the Duluth model's one-size-fits-all approach is not highly effective in stopping IPV recidivism.

Couples therapy may be an effective modality for treating IPV, as ineffective and unhealthy communication are more prevalent among couples experiencing IPV and are often cited reasons for using aggression to resolve conflict (Elmquist et al., 2014; Langhinrichsen-Rohling et al., 2012). Communication skills training may be one helpful intervention for couples that experience situational violence and want to stay together (Bennett et al., 2020; Kreig Mayer, 2017). However, the notion of addressing IPV within the dyad is quite controversial because couples therapy typically assumes that both partners equally contribute to problems within the relationship (Babcock et al., 2017). Theoretically, couples therapy for IPV could compromise women's safety by reinforcing men's belief that women are to blame for being abused and result in them seeking retribution for topics discussed in therapy (Babcock et al., 2017; Stith et al., 2012). However, some argue that traditional approaches may compromise the safety of couples who choose to stay together or are co-parenting because gender-specific services often do not address their specific needs (Krieg Mayer, 2017). Several researchers and clinicians maintain that couples therapy can be done safely with couples experiencing situational violence when they are carefully screened at the beginning of and throughout treatment for any safety concerns (Krieg Mayer, 2017; Stith et al., 2012).

Intervention Programs

Given the controversy surrounding interventions for couples, it comes as no surprise that there are very few studies that have empirically tested couples therapy for IPV. However, a recent meta-analysis of six studies testing the effectiveness of couples therapy for IPV found that when compared to an active treatment or a no-treatment control, couples therapy reduces IPV recidivism by a significant amount ($d = -.84$) (Karakurt et al., 2016). This is a large effect. Cohen's d is an effect size, which allows researchers to capture how well an intervention works for the outcome of interest when compared to another treatment or a no-treatment control group. In this case, Cohen's d gives an estimate of how well specific therapies work at stopping and reducing IPV recidivism. A Cohen's d effect size is said to be small at .2, medium at .5, and large at .8 (Coe, 2002). When compared to the standard Duluth intervention, couples therapy appears to be slightly more effective at stopping IPV recidivism (Karakurt et al., 2016).

The two earliest published studies that tested the effect of couples therapy for IPV utilized quasi-experimental designs to compare multicouple group interventions with gender-specific Duluth-based groups (Brannen & Rubin, 1996; O'Leary et al., 1999). Multicouple group interventions teach skills to address relationship patterns that maintain conflict and potentially lead to violence, whereas the Duluth model challenges men's beliefs about dominating and controlling women (Babcock et al., 2007; Stith et al., 2012). Brannen and Rubin (1996) found no difference in 6-month recidivism rates between the multicouple group intervention and the gender-specific Duluth-based intervention ($d = -.09$; see Table 13.1). However, when combining the 6-month recidivism data ($n = 26$) from both interventions, 92% reported no new incidents of violence. This suggests that both interventions were equally effective at stopping IPV. When examining recidivism rates among men with alcohol problems, the multicouple group was superior to the gender-specific Duluth-based intervention ($d = -3.64$) (Brannen & Rubin, 1996), further supporting that Duluth's one-size-fits-all approach is too narrow.

Using a community sample of 75 couples, O'Leary et al. (1999) tested a similar quasi-experimental design in which they compared the recidivism rates of a multicouple group and a men's only Duluth-based group. They found no difference in 1-year recidivism rates between the two therapy conditions for moderate ($d = -.14$) and severe ($d = -.12$) physical assault (O'Leary et al., 1999). When recidivism was combined across interventions, moderate physical assault decreased by 55% and severe physical assault decreased by 51%, also suggesting that both

Table 13.1 Evidenced-Based Couples Interventions for IPV

Study	Sample Type	Intervention	Participants	Recidivism Measure and Length of Follow-up	% Recidivated	Effect Size
Brannen & Rubin (1996)	Court-Mandated	Multi-couple group vs. Gender-specific Duluth-based Group	26 couples	Binary (yes/no) partner-report at 6-month follow-up	Total sample: 92% violence cessation	$d = -0.09$
O'Leary et al. (1999)	Community Sample	Multi-couple group vs. Men's Only Duluth-based Group	75 couples	Partner-report CTS2[a] at 1 year follow-up	Total sample: 26% ceased physical violence; 55% reduction in moderate physical assault; 51% reduction in severe physical assault	Moderate physical assault: $d = -0.14$ Severe physical assault: $d = -0.16$
Stith et al. (2004)	Court-Mandated	Domestic Violence Focused Couples Therapy (DVFCT): Multi-couple vs. Dyadic couple vs. Control	39 couples	Partner-report CTS2 at 2 year follow-up	Dyadic couples therapy: 0% recidivism Multi-couple group: 13% recidivism Control group: 50% recidivism	Dyadic Couples Therapy vs. Control: $d = 0.84$ Multi-Couple vs. Control: $d = 0.72$

Study	Sample	Intervention	N	Measure	Results	Effect Size
Wray et al. (2013)	Court-Mandated	Gottman Method/ CBT-based intervention	92 couples	Partner-report CTS2 and police report at 12-month follow-up	Both partners completed: 4% recidivism Men-only completed: 8.3% Women-only completed: 10% Neither partner completed: 50%	Both vs. neither: $d = 1.75$ Both vs. Men-only: $d = 0.43$ Both vs. Women-only: $d = 0.54$
Cleary Bradley et al. (2014); Personal communication (2021)	Community Sample	Creating Healthy Relationships Program (CHRP) vs. Control group	115 couples	Partner-report CTS2 at 12-month follow-up	CHRP: 50% recidivism Control: 66.7% recidivism	$d = 0.38$
Mills et al. (2019)	Court-Mandated	Circle of Peace Restorative Justice vs. Duluth	222 men	Police report at 2-year follow up	Reduction in recidivism: 53%	$d = 0.67$

[a]CTS2, Conflict Tactics Scale Revised.

interventions were equally effective at reducing physical IPV. However, only 26% of men engaged in no physical violence during the 1 year following treatment. This is in stark contrast to Brannen and Rubin's (1996) findings, in which 92% of their sample stopped IPV perpetration. However, O'Leary and colleagues (1999) had a longer follow-up period (1 year vs. 6 months), a community sample, and a lower completion rate (49% vs. 86%). Findings from meta-analytic studies suggest that court-mandated samples tend to have higher completion rates, and treatment completers tend to have lower recidivism rates than treatment dropouts (Babcock et al., 2004). Further, men from court-mandated samples are more likely to have protective orders issued against them prohibiting contact with the victim (O'Leary et al., 1999).

Domestic Violence Focused Couples Therapy

Domestic violence focused couples therapy (DVFCT) is an 18-week treatment program that was designed specifically for couples experiencing situational violence who want to stay together (Stith et al., 2004, 2011). Given the importance of safety, couples are carefully screened before starting the program and before and after each session. DVFCT is offered in two formats: a multicouple group or dyadic couples therapy. Based on solution-focused therapy, DVFCT aims to stop physical, sexual, and psychological abuse through two primary objectives: (1) teaching conflict-resolution skills and (2) building on the strengths of the relationship. By learning effective communication strategies, such as time-outs, couples learn to discuss areas of disagreement without becoming violent and, if necessary, the emotion regulation skills to deescalate conflict. Similarly, by focusing on the relationship strengths rather than deficits, couples are more motivated to change their behavior (Stith et al., 2011). In a quasi-experimental design, Stith and colleagues (2004) tested the efficacy of DVFCT in a sample of 39 court-mandated couples, with 16 in the multicouple group, 14 receiving dyadic couples, and 9 couples who completed questionnaire data but did not attend any treatment sessions making up the no-treatment control group. At 2-year follow-up (59% response), couples receiving dyadic couples therapy reported 0% of men recidivated, followed by men in the multicouple group (13%), and men in the control group (50%). Using the intent-to-treat sample, the authors estimated large effects for the dyadic couple intervention ($d = .84$) and the multicouple group intervention ($d = .72$) when compared to the no-treatment control group. These are far larger than the average effect size of traditional Duluth-type men's groups ($d = .16$; Babcock, 2021; Babcock et al., 2004).

DVFCT has been culturally adapted to meet the needs of couples living in Colombia, Iran, and Finland; however, case study data exist only for the programs in Colombia and Iran (Stith et al., 2020). In Colombian society, there is a significant stigma against mental health/therapy. Although there are some legal protections against violence toward women and the family, the majority of men and women in Colombia hold permissive attitudes toward IPV. Based on this information, the original DVFCT curriculum was modified and shortened to eight sessions to meet the needs of couples in Colombia. DVFCT was delivered in the multicouple group format, focusing on couples' conflict resolution, communication, mindfulness, and anger regulation skills. Of the three couples that completed the Colombian DVFCT adaptation, none reported physical abuse at the end of treatment. Further, all three couples reported decreased psychological abuse and improved relationship functioning.

Iranian culture places significant value on the family unit and teaches couples that marriages are to be preserved at all costs. There is also stigma associated with publicly discussing one's marriage; thus, the Iranian DVFCT adaptation was only provided in a dyadic couple format with a female therapist. Two sessions were added to the first phase of treatment to allow for couples to gain a foundation in basic communication, and another two sessions were added to the second phase to increase couples comfort with discussing their sexual relationship, increasing the total number of weekly sessions to 22. The first phase of treatment focused on teaching communication skills, and the second phase was tailored to address each couple's specific issues; however, the theme of positivism was an area of focus for all couples. Of the four couples that completed treatment, all reported decreased physical abuse and improved relationship satisfaction and communication. Though the findings from these adaptations are preliminary, they provide some indication that evidence-based interventions can be helpful for couples in other countries when culturally adapted.

Gottman Method/Creating Healthy Relationships Program

Multiple studies have examined the efficacy of the Gottman Method for couples experiencing IPV. Wray et al. (2013) provided a Gottman Method/cognitive-behavioral therapy–based intervention to 92 couples court-mandated to treatment for mutual IPV. This 12-session intervention focused on increasing positive relationship behaviors and decreasing the negative, including IPV, by teaching couples emotional awareness, relationship skills, and parenting skills. Because of safety concerns, the interventions were taught in gender-specific groups. However, in contrast to the curriculums taught in previous studies (e.g., Brannen & Rubin, 1996; O'Leary et al., 1999), both partners received the same intervention. Results indicated that at 12-month follow-up, recidivism rates were lowest for couples when both partners completed treatment (4%) and highest for couples when both partners dropped out of treatment (50%).

The Creating Healthy Relationships Program (CHRP) is a multicouple group intervention based on Gottman-Method couples therapy designed specifically for couples experiencing situational couple violence (Cleary Bradley et al., 2011). The CHRP is a 22-week psychoeducational multicouple intervention that is based on Gottman's (1999) sound relationship house theory. CHRP seeks to reduce violence by strengthening the relationship and teaching effective communication and conflict resolution skills. Voluntary community couples reporting low-level situational violence were randomly assigned to complete CHRP or a control condition. At 12-month follow-up, couples that completed at least 11 out of the 22 CHRP sessions had significantly decreased psychological abuse. While couples CHRP group tended to report lower IPV at follow-up, there was no significant difference in self-reported physical IPV between the treatment and control groups. However, a significant difference was found between both groups when using partner reported physical IPV ($d = .38$) (personal communication, 2021).

The next step would be to apply CHRP to a court-mandated sample of situationally violent couples. Babcock and colleagues (2017) attempted to compare CHRP with Duluth in a court-mandated sample in Oregon. Couples were carefully screened using the Situational Violence Screening Tool (SVST) before being eligible for CHRP (Friend et al., 2011). Six couples completed the group intervention and expressed high satisfaction with the group. Plans were made to adopt the intervention to a Spanish-speaking group. However, an oversight committee was concerned about the safety of couples therapy for IPV and shut down the study. Accused "either directly or by insinuation, of being unethical, antifeminist, and callous to women's safety" Babcock et al. (2017, p. 113) concluded that multicouple group interventions were not feasible in that current political climate (Babcock et al., 2018).

Restorative Justice Programs

One of the most promising new interventions for IPV is a restorative justice program that includes the victim in the intervention process (see Barocas & Shimizu, Chapter 14, this volume). Although it is not couples therapy, victims and others affected by IPV (e.g., friends, clergy, other family members) are engaged in speaking about the impact and aftermath that the violence has had on them (Mills, 2006). Restorative justice interventions are similarly controversial as couples' interventions due to the inclusion of victims. Rather than putting them at risk, restorative justice interventions' inclusion of IPV victims gives them a voice. A randomized clinical trial of IPV offenders ($N = 222$) attending the Circles of Peace restorative justice intervention compared to a Duluth-model group intervention revealed a medium effect size of ($d = .67$) for stopping IPV recidivism (Mills et al., 2019). This is the largest of all the true experiments of IPV interventions conducted to date, especially impressive considering that the effect size reflects the difference between two active treatments (Babcock, 2021).

FAMILY INTERVENTIONS FOR WITNESSING INTIMATE PARTNER VIOLENCE

In the United States alone, approximately 10%–20% of children witness at least one incident of IPV in their lifetimes (Carlson, 2000; Finkelhor et al., 2015; Wolak & Finkelhor, 1998). This prevalence is problematic given that cross-sectional and longitudinal research has identified several negative psychological consequences for witnessing IPV between one's parents during childhood (Bennett et al., 2020). Exposure to physical and psychological IPV in infancy and early childhood predicts later internalizing and externalizing behavioral problems in children ages 10 to 11 years, with repeated psychological IPV exposure predicting greater behavioral problems (Westrupp et al., 2018). In adolescents, Izaguirre and Calvete (2018) found that witnessing psychological IPV predicted later increases in internalizing and externalizing behaviors, such as anxiety and depressive symptoms, aggression, and trouble-making behaviors. Studies have also found that, compared to children who did not witness interparental violence, children exposed to IPV performed poorer on IQ tests and demonstrated lower verbal ability and decreased explicit memory (Graham-Bermann et al., 2010; Jouriles et al., 2008; Koenen et al., 2003). These findings suggest that childhood IPV exposure can adversely impact children's cognitive development. Furthermore, IPV exposure is associated with later development of psychopathology, including posttraumatic stress (DeJonghe et al., 2005; Showalter et al., 2020) and borderline personality disorder (Sharp et al., 2020).

In addition to the adverse effects on children's development, there is also an intergenerational cycle of violence transmitted to children who witness caregivers' IPV (Stith et al., 2000). Research finds an association between witnessing IPV in childhood and IPV perpetration in adulthood, with some suggesting that psychopathology, perhaps developed because of witnessing interparental violence, mediates that relation (Ehrensaft et al., 2003; Latzman et al., 2015; Vu et al., 2016). For example, depressive symptoms (Madruga et al., 2017) and externalizing behaviors (Low et al., 2019) have been shown to mediate the association between childhood IPV exposure and later perpetration in adulthood. These findings suggest that witnessing interparental violence may increase children's susceptibility to developmental pathways associated with antisocial behaviors, including IPV perpetration (Ehrensaft et al., 2003).

Types of Interventions

INTERVENTIONS FOR TREATING CHILDHOOD EXPOSURE TO INTIMATE PARTNER VIOLENCE

In response to the research demonstrating the adverse effects of IPV exposure on children, several interventions have been developed to attenuate the impact of IPV exposure on children's psychosocial and behavioral outcomes. Treatments for IPV exposure come in several forms, including individual and sibling play therapy (Kot et al., 1998; Tyndall-Lind et al., 2001), group therapy (McWhirter, 2008; Pepler et al., 2000; Sudermann et al., 2000; Wagar & Rodway, 1995), trauma-based cognitive-behavioral therapies (Cohen et al., 2011), and therapies that include or primarily target the abused parent or caregiver (Graham-Bermann et al., 2007; Jouriles et al., 2009). Such programs improve children's functioning by reducing feelings of blame, reducing trauma-based symptoms, addressing myths and attitudes toward violence, and improving children's coping, communication, conflict resolution, and problem-solving skills (Rizo et al., 2011).

Additionally, there is evidence suggesting that interventions for IPV-exposed children may also reduce negative conduct-related behaviors. One such intervention is a community-based family violence therapy that targets children's behavioral problems via separate services for children and their mothers. The child intervention focuses on educating children about family violence; correcting maladaptive attitudes and beliefs developed about families and family violence; and improving children's emotional and social adjustment. During the mothers' intervention, they are given tools to bolster their parenting and disciplinary skills and their own social and emotional adjustment. When Graham-Bermann and colleagues (2007) evaluated the effectiveness of this intervention program, they found that most children who participated scored below the clinical range for externalizing and internalizing behaviors post treatment. Notably, children whose mothers participated in the parent component of this treatment saw the most improvements in externalizing ($d = 1.13$) and internalizing ($d = .85$) behaviors when compared to children who participated in the child intervention alone (see Table 13.2). Indeed, consistent with research suggesting that parenting practices mediated the association between IPV exposure and externalizing behaviors (Levendosky & Graham-Bermann, 2000), IPV-exposed children appear to benefit from interventions that target caregivers' behaviors and psychological functioning (Jouriles et al., 2009; Sharp et al., 2021; Timmer et al., 2010).

Project SUPPORT is another intervention that mitigates the effects of IPV exposure on children by teaching mothers effective parenting skills and providing them with in-home emotional and instrumental support during the transition out of living in a women's shelter (Hamel, 2014; McDonald et al., 2006). In a study of 66 families transitioning out of a domestic violence shelter, Jouriles et al. (2009) found that children of mothers who participated in Project SUPPORT exhibited significantly fewer behavioral problems ($d = .66$) than did children whose mothers were in a control condition. Furthermore, changes in these children's problems were mediated by mothers' improved behavioral and psychological outcomes (Jouriles et al., 2009).

In a recent meta-analysis of 21 studies, Romano et al. (2021) found interventions for treating IPV-exposed children yielded a moderate effect size ($d = .49$) in reducing overall adverse outcomes at posttreatment. Additionally, nonmanualized

($d = .61$) and non-trauma-specific interventions ($d = .66$) produced better outcomes than manualized and trauma-based interventions (Romano et al., 2021). Perhaps trauma-based interventions are too focused, and treatments for children exposed to IPV should be broad enough to address the vast array of adverse outcomes associated with IPV exposure (e.g., externalizing/internalizing behaviors, social problems; Romano et al., 2021). Furthermore, play therapy ($d = .86$) yielded the largest effect size among all the therapy modalities examined in reducing problem behavior among children exposed to IPV.

INTIMATE PARTNER VIOLENCE PREVENTION PROGRAMS

Since young adults are at heightened risk for perpetrating violence in their intimate relationships (Kim et al., 2008; O'Leary, 1999), the teenage years are an ideal developmental period for interrupting the intergenerational transmission of violence (Bennett et al., 2020; Hagan et al., 2020). Several prevention programs have been developed to reduce teens' likelihood of engaging in dating violence (Doucette et al., 2021). Although not all of these programs were designed to target IPV-exposed teens specifically, they all share the goal of preventing teen dating violence (TDV) and later IPV in adult relationships.

Two teen-based interventions for preventing the intergenerational transmission of violence are Safe Dates (Foshee et al., 1998, 2005) and Fourth R (Wolfe et al., 2009). These programs are both delivered to teens (eighth- to ninth-grade students) in a school setting and include a parent component in the form of psychoeducational newsletters. Both programs share similar objectives in promoting healthy relationships and reducing TDV and incorporate skills components that allow teens to practice the skills covered in these programs. When compared with teens who only received community-based support, involvement in Safe Dates plus community-based support was associated with greater reductions in TDV perpetration ($d = -.06$) and victimization ($d = -.06$), improvements in attitudes about TDV, attitudes about gender, and 29% greater awareness of TDV-related community services (Foshee et al., 1998, 2000, 2005). Similarly, compared to teens whose schools did not implement Fourth R, teens that participated in the Fourth R prevention program perpetrated less physical TDV ($d = .49$) at 2.5-year follow-up (Crooks et al., 2008; Wolfe et al., 2009, 2012).

Other programs and initiatives found to reduce TDV perpetration and victimization are family based and community based, such as Project STRONG (Rizzo et al., 2021), Moms and Teens for Safe Dates (MTSD; Foshee et al., 2015), and Dating Matters: Strategies to Promote Healthy Teen Relationships (Tharp, 2012; Tharp et al., 2011). Project STRONG is a Web-based intervention developed for middle-school-aged boys and their caregivers to reduce adolescent boys' risk of perpetrating TDV. Project STRONG consists of six modules that span over four sessions that can be completed at home. The first module is shorter and completed only by parents to increase their engagement in the program, whereas the other five are completed by a parent and adolescent together and are 30 minutes in length. Like previously mentioned interventions, Project STRONG aims to promote healthy relationships and improve communication and emotion regulation.

Table 13.2 EVIDENCED-BASED INTERVENTIONS FOR CHILD WITNESSES AND THE PREVENTION OF IPV

Study	Sample type	Intervention	Participants	Outcome Measure and Length of Follow-up	Risk Reduction	Effect Size
Graham-Bermann et al. (2007)	Community	Community-based Family Violence Therapy	181 children and their mothers	Mother-report CBCL[a] scores at 8-month follow-up	Clinical Externalizing behaviors: Child-only = 35% fewer children; Child + Mother = 79% fewer children Clinical Internalizing behaviors: Child-only = 50% fewer children; Child + Mother = 77% fewer children	Child + Mother vs. Child Alone Externalizing behaviors: $d = 1.13$ Child + Mother vs. Child Alone Internalizing behaviors: $d = .85$
Jouriles et al. (2009)	Shelter	Project SUPPORT vs. Control	66 children diagnosed with CD or ODD and their mothers	Mother-report CBCL scores at 20-month follow up	Project SUPPORT: 69.3% fewer children with clinical CBCL scores Control: 32.4% fewer children with clinical CBCL scores	$d = 0.63$
Foshee et al. (2005)	Eighth and Ninth Grade Students	Safe Dates plus Community-based support vs. Only Community-based support	1332 teens at 14 schools	Self-report SDDAS[b] at 4 year follow up (2005)	Information not provided	TDV Perpetration: $d = -0.06$ TDV Victimization: $d = -0.06$
Wolfe et al. (2009)	Eighth and Ninth Grade Students	Fourth R vs. Control	1722 teens at 20 schools	Self-report CARDI[c] scores at 2.5 year follow up	Fourth R: 7.4% reported TDV Control: 9.8% reported TDV	$d = 0.49$

Rizzo et al. (2020)	Middle School Boys	Project STRONG vs. Waitlist Control	119 teen boys and their parents	Self-report CARDI scores at 9-month follow up	Project STRONG: 64.5% more likely to report TDV Control: 156% more likely to report TDV	$d = -0.37$
Foshee et al. (2015)	High-Risk Teens	Moms and Teens for Safe Dates (MTSD)	409 teens and their mothers	Teen self-report SDDAS and TATR[d] reports at 6-month post-intervention completion	Not enough information to calculate	Psychological victimization: $d = 0.17$ Physical victimization: $d = 0.14$ Physical perpetration: $d = 0.24$ Cyber perpetration: $d = 0.15$
Niolon et al. (2019)	High-Risk Middle School Students	Dating Matters: Strategies to Promote Healthy Teen Relationships vs. Safe Dates	2349 teens at 46 middle schools	Self-report CARDI scores at 4 months follow up	TDV-Perpetration: reduced by 8.43% TDV-Victimization: reduced by 9.78%	TDV-Perpetration: $d = -0.01$ TDV-Victimization: $d = -0.01$

[a]CBCL, Child Behavior Checklist; [b]SDDAS, Safe Dates Dating Abuse Scales; [c]CARDI, Conflict in Adolescent Dating Relationships Inventory; [d]TATR, Tech Abuse in Teen Relationships.

Rizzo et al. (2021) found that teen boys in the wait-list condition were more likely to experience TDV at 9-month follow-up than teen boys who participated in Project STRONG with their families ($d = -.37$). Parents who participated in Project STRONG also endorsed fewer accepting attitudes toward TDV at 3-month ($d = .19$) and 9-month ($d = .20$) follow-up than parents in the wait-list condition (Rizzo et al., 2021).

In contrast to previously mentioned primary prevention programs, MTSD and Dating Matters specifically target teens that are perceived to be at higher risk for TDV perpetration or victimization (Doucette et al., 2021). MTSD is a family-based secondary prevention program directly created for caregivers and teens exposed to IPV (Doucette et al., 2021; Foshee et al., 2015). This program includes six pamphlet-based modules to be self-administered by the participating families at home. The primary objectives of this intervention are to reduce the risk of TDV, increase caregivers' engagement in TDV prevention, and improve family cohesion. Compared to teens who did not participate in MTSD, teens whose families participated in MTSD exhibited reductions in psychological ($d = .17$) and physical ($d = .14$) TDV victimization and psychological ($d = .24$) and cyber abuse perpetration ($d = .15$) at 6-month follow-up (Foshee et al., 2015). Notably, teens exposed to the highest rates of IPV were the only ones to exhibit these reductions (Foshee et al., 2015). Involvement in MTSD also increased mothers' comfort communicating with their teens, perceptions of relationship violence severity, self-efficacy in preventing TDV, and teen monitoring (Foshee et al., 2015).

Finally, the Dating Matters: Strategies to Promote Healthy Teen Relationships initiative is a comprehensive IPV secondary prevention program created by the CDC for high-risk middle-school students (Tharp et al., 2011). This intervention aims to promote healthy relationship behaviors for at-risk teens at the individual, family, neighborhood, and community levels (Niolon et al., 2019; Tharp, 2012; Tharp et al., 2011). Dating Matters includes developmentally appropriate school based TDV prevention, parent training, teacher and staff training, youth communications, and policies and data tracking programs (Niolon et al., 2019). The teen and parent training programs incorporate pre-existing interventions, including Safe Dates for eighth graders (Niolon et al., 2019). In a randomized controlled trial (RCT) comparing teens that participated in Dating Matters with those who only participated in Safe Dates, high-risk teens that participated in Dating Matters used 5.52% fewer negative conflict resolution tactics and experienced 8.43% less TDV perpetration and 9.72% less TDV victimization (Niolon et al., 2019). These findings suggest that multicomponent prevention initiatives may be more effective at promoting healthy relationship behaviors than initiatives that only target teens or teens and their caregivers.

SUMMARY AND FUTURE DIRECTIONS

Given the far-reaching consequences of IPV and the limited efficacy of the standard Duluth model men's group, different treatment options are warranted.

Couple interventions appear to be a safe and effective alternative treatment option for couples experiencing low-level situational couple violence (Karakurt et al., 2016). As communication skills training was a core component of all couple interventions reviewed, couples therapy would likely be the preferred IPV treatment option for couples that want to stay together and exhibit unhealthy communication patterns and poor conflict resolution skills (Krieg Mayer, 2017). However, many of the couple interventions were as equally effective as the standard interventions, suggesting that there may be other interventions that would be important to add to couple treatment packages. Indeed, except for O'Leary et al. (1999), none of the studies examined the efficacy of the couple interventions for common IPV comorbidities and risk factors such as personality disorders, poor anger regulation skills, PTSD, and substance use disorders. With these continued gaps, it is necessary to obtain funding for IPV intervention research to determine which interventions are most effective and appropriate for common IPV presentations. Further, many of the studies utilized a quasi-experimental design and had small samples sizes; thus, it would be important to replicate them with much larger samples in a randomized controlled trial or a matched control quasi-experimental design.

The child witness literature has also consistently demonstrated the link between childhood and adolescent IPV exposure and IPV in adulthood. Although not conclusive, there is significant, convincing evidence that psychopathology, perhaps developed as a result of IPV exposure during key periods of development and subsequent maternal parenting and emotion dysregulation issues, is an underlying mechanism of change. Thus, the best way to intervene and stop IPV may be through early prevention efforts. Indeed, the existing interventions geared toward IPV-exposed children and those at high risk for teen dating violence exhibit medium to large effects. The next steps may be to promote early identification of IPV-exposed children and teens at greater risk for TDV to intervene and stop the intergenerational cycle of violence.

REFERENCES

Arias, E., Arce, R., & Vilariño, M. (2013). Batterer intervention programmes: A meta-analytic review of effectiveness. *Psychosocial Intervention*, *22*(2), 153–160. https://doi.org/10.5093/in2013a18

Armenti, N. A., & Babcock, J. C. (2016). Conjoint treatment for intimate partner violence: A systematic review and implications. *Couple and Family Psychology: Research and Practice*, *5*(2), 109.

Babcock, J. C. (2021, April). *What to do to improve batterers' interventions*. Invited address to Oregon State Bar, Criminal Law Division. Portland, OR.

Babcock, J. C., Armenti, N. A., Bennett, V. E., & Snead, A. L. (2018, July). *The trials and tribulations of testing couples therapies for intimate partner violence*. Talk delivered at the Association of Domestic Violence Intervention Programs Conference. Portsmouth, NH.

Babcock, J. C., Armenti, N. A., & Warford, P. (2017). The trials and tribulations of testing couples-based interventions for intimate partner violence. *Partner Abuse, 8*(1), 110–124. https://doi.org/10.1891/1946-6560.8.1.110

Babcock, J. C., Canady, B. E., Graham, K., & Schart, L. (2007). The evolution of battering interventions: From the dark ages into the scientific ages. In J. Hamel & T. L. Nicholls (Eds.), *Family interventions in domestic violence: A handbook of gender-inclusive theory and treatment* (pp. 215–244). Springer.

Babcock, J. C., Costa, D. M., Green, C. E., & Eckhardt, C. I. (2004). What situations induce intimate partner violence? A reliability and validity study of the proximal antecedents to violent episodes (PAVE) scale. *Journal of Family Psychology, 18*(3), 433–442. https://doi.org/10.1037/0893-3200.18.3.433

Babcock, J. C., Green, C. E., & Robie, C. (2004). Does batterers' treatment work? A meta-analytic review of domestic violence treatment. *Clinical Psychology Review, 23*(8), 1023–1053. https://doi.org/10.1016/j.cpr.2002.07.001

Babcock, J. C., Waltz, J., Jacobson, N. S., & Gottman, J. M. (1993). Power and violence: The relation between communication patterns, power discrepancies, and domestic violence. *Journal of Consulting and Clinical Psychology, 61*(1), 40–50. https://doi.org/10.1037/0022-006X.61.1.40

Bennett, V. E., Godfrey, D. A., Snead, A. L., Kehoe, C., Bastardas-Albero, A., & Babcock, J. C. (2020). Couples and family interventions for intimate partner aggression: A comprehensive review. *Partner Abuse*. https://doi.org/10.1891/PA-2020-0011

Berns, S., Jacobson, N., & Gottman, J. (1999). Demand-withdraw interaction in couples with a violent husband. *Journal of Consulting and Clinical Psychology, 67*(5), 666–674. https://doi.org/10.1037/0022-006X.67.5.666

Birkley, E. L., & Eckhardt, C. I. (2015). Anger, hostility, internalizing negative emotions, and intimate partner violence perpetration: A meta-analytic review. *Clinical Psychology Review, 37,* 40–56.

Brannen, S. J., & Rubin, A. (1996). Comparing the effectiveness of gender-specific and couples groups in a court-mandated spouse abuse treatment program. *Research on Social Work Practice, 6*(4), 405–424. https://doi.org/10.1177/104973159600600401

Breiding, M. J., Basile, K. C., Smith, S. G., Black, M. C., & Mahendra, R. R. (2015). *Intimate partner violence surveillance: Uniform definitions and recommended data elements, version 2.0.* National Center for Injury Prevention and Control, Centers for Disease Control and Prevention.

Breiding, M. J., Chen, J., & Black, M. C. (2014). *Intimate partner violence in the United States—2010.* National Center for Injury Prevention and Control, Centers for Disease Control and Prevention.

Brem, M. J., Florimbio, A. R., Elmquist, J., Shorey, R. C., & Stuart, G. L. (2018). Antisocial traits, distress tolerance, and alcohol problems as predictors of intimate partner violence in men arrested for domestic violence. *Psychology of Violence, 8*(1), 132–139. https://doi.org/10.1037/vio0000088

Brem, M. J., Florimbio, A. R., Grigorian, H., Wolford-Clevenger, C., Elmquist, J., Shorey, R. C., & Stuart, G. L. (2019). Cyber abuse among men arrested for domestic violence: Cyber monitoring moderates the relationship between alcohol problems and intimate partner violence. *Psychology of Violence, 9*(4), 410–418. https://doi.org/10.1037/vio0000130

Carlson, B. E. (2000). Children exposed to intimate partner violence: Research findings and implications for intervention. *Trauma, Violence, & Abuse, 1*(4), 321–342. https://doi.org/10.1177/1524838000001004002

Cleary Bradley, R. P., Friend, D. J., & Gottman, J. M. (2011). Supporting healthy relationships in low-income, violent couples: Reducing conflict and strengthening relationship skills and satisfaction. *Journal of Couple & Relationship Therapy, 10*, 97–116. https://doi.org/10.1080/15332691.2011.562808

Coan, J., Gottman, J. M., Babcock, J., & Jacobson, N. (1997). Battering and the male rejection of influence from women. *Aggressive Behavior, 23*(5), 375–388. https://doi.org/10.1002/(SICI)1098-2337(1997)23:5<375::AID-AB6>3.0.CO;2-H

Coe, R. (2002, September). It's the effect size, stupid. Paper presented at the Annual Conference of the British Educational Research Association. University of Exeter, England.

Cohen, J. A., Mannarino, A. P., & Iyengar, S. (2011). Community treatment of posttraumatic stress disorder for children exposed to intimate partner violence: A randomized controlled trial. *Archives of Pediatrics & Adolescent Medicine, 165*(1), 16–21. https://doi.org/10.1001/archpediatrics.2010.247

Costa, D. M., & Babcock, J. C. (2008). Articulated thoughts of intimate partner abusive men during anger arousal: Correlates with personality disorder features. *Journal of Family Violence, 23*(6), 395–402. https://doi.org/10.1007/s10896-008-9163-x

Crooks, C. V., Wolfe, D. A., Hughes, R., Jaffe, P. G., & Chiodo, D. (2008). Development, evaluation and national implementation of a school-based program to reduce violence and related risk behaviours: Lessons from the fourth R. *IPC Review, 2*(2), 109–135.

DeJonghe, E. S., Bogat, G. A., Levendosky, A. A., Von Eye, A., & Davidson, W. S. (2005). Infant exposure to domestic violence predicts heightened sensitivity to adult verbal conflict. *Infant Mental Health Journal: Official Publication of The World Association for Infant Mental Health, 26*(3), 268–281. https://doi.org/10.1002/imhj.20048

Doucette, H., Collibee, C., & Rizzo, C. J. (2021). A review of parent-and family-based prevention efforts for adolescent dating violence. *Aggression and Violent Behavior,* 101548. https://doi.org/10.1016/j.avb.2021.101548

Ehrensaft, M. K., Cohen, P., Brown, J., Smailes, E., Chen, H., & Johnson, J. G. (2003). Intergenerational transmission of partner violence: A 20-year prospective study. *Journal of Consulting and Clinical Psychology, 71*(4), 741–753. https://doi.org/10.1037/0022-006X.71.4.741

Elmquist, J., Hamel, J., Shorey, R. C., Labrecque, L., Ninnemann, A., & Stuart, G. L. (2014). Motivations for intimate partner violence in men and women arrested for domestic violence and court referred to batterer intervention programs. *Partner Abuse, 5*(4), 359–374. https://doi.org/10.1891/1946-6560.5.4.359

Farzan-Kashani, J., & Murphy, C. M. (2017). Anger problems predict long-term criminal recidivism in partner violent men. *Journal of Interpersonal Violence, 32*(23), 3541–3555. https://doi.org/10.1177/0886260515600164

Finkelhor, D., Turner, H. A., Shattuck, A., & Hamby, S. L. (2015). Prevalence of childhood exposure to violence, crime, and abuse: Results from the national survey of children's exposure to violence. *JAMA Pediatrics, 169*(8), 746–754. https://doi.org/10.1001/jamapediatrics.2015.0676

Follingstad, D. R., & Rogers, M. J. (2013). Validity concerns in the measurement of women's and men's reports of intimate partner violence. *Sex Roles*, *69*(3–4), 149–167. https://doi.org/10.1007/s11199-013-0264-5

Foshee, V. A., Bauman, K. E., Arriaga, X. B., Helms, R. W., Koch, G. G., & Linder, G. F. (1998). An evaluation of Safe Dates, an adolescent dating violence prevention program. *American Journal of Public Health*, *88*(1), 45–50. https://doi.org/10.2105/AJPH.88.1.45

Foshee, V. A., Bauman, K. E., Ennett, S. T., Suchindran, C., Benefield, T., & Linder, G. F. (2005). Assessing the effects of the dating violence prevention program "Safe Dates" using random coefficient regression modeling. *Prevention Science*, *6*(3), 245–258. https://doi.org/10.1007/s11121-005-0007-0

Foshee, V. A., Bauman, K. E., Greene, W. F., Koch, G. G., Linder, G. F., & MacDougall, J. E. (2000). The Safe Dates program: 1-year follow-up results. *American Journal of Public Health*, *90*(10), 1619–1622. https://doi.org/10.2105/ajph.90.10.1619

Foshee, V. A., Benefield, T., Dixon, K. S., Chang, L. Y., Senkomago, V., Ennett, S. T., . . . Bowling, J. M. (2015). The effects of moms and teens for safe dates: A dating abuse prevention program for adolescents exposed to domestic violence. *Journal of Youth and Adolescence*, *44*(5), 995–1010. https://doi.org/10.1007/s10964-015-0272-6

Friend, D. J., Cleary Bradley, R. P., Thatcher, R., & Gottman, J. M. (2011). Typologies of intimate partner violence: Evaluation of a screening instrument for differentiation. *Journal of Family Violence*, *26*, 551–563. https://doi.org/10.1007/s10896-011-9392-2

Gordis, E. B., Margolin, G., & Vickerman, K. (2005). Communication and frightening behavior among couples with past and recent histories of physical marital aggression. *American Journal of Community Psychology*, *36*(1–2), 177–191. https://doi.org/10.1007/s10464-005-6241-6

Gottman, J. (1999). *The marriage clinic: A scientifically-based marital therapy*. W.W. Norton.

Graham-Bermann, S. A., Howell, K. H., Miller, L. E., Kwek, J., & Lilly, M. M. (2010). Traumatic events and maternal education as predictors of verbal ability for preschool children exposed to intimate partner violence (IPV). *Journal of Family Violence*, *25*(4), 383–392. https://doi.org/10.1007/s10896-009-9299-3

Graham-Bermann, S. A., Lynch, S., Banyard, V., DeVoe, E. R., & Halabu, H. (2007). Community-based intervention for children exposed to intimate partner violence: An efficacy trial. *Journal of Consulting and Clinical Psychology*, *75*(2), 199–209. https://doi.org/10.1037/0022-006X.75.2.199

Hagan, M. J., Waters, S. F., Holley, S., Moctezuma, L., & Gentry, M. (2020). The interactive effect of family conflict history and physiological reactivity on different forms of aggression in young women. *Biological Psychology*, *153*. https://doi.org/10.1016/j.biopsycho.2020.107888

Hamel, J. (2014). Working with families. In J. Hamel (Eds.), *Gender-inclusive treatment of intimate partner abuse: Evidence-based approaches* (2nd ed., pp. 167–184). Springer.

Holtzworth-Munroe, A., & Stuart, G. L. (1994). Typologies of male batterers: Three subtypes and the differences among them. *Psychological Bulletin*, *116*(3), 476–497. https://do.org/10.1037/0033-2909.116.3.476

Izaguirre, A., & Calvete, E. (2018). Exposure to family violence and internalizing and externalizing problems among Spanish adolescents. *Violence and Victims*, *33*(2), 368–382. https://doi.org/10.1891/0886-6708.VV-D-17-00016

Johnson, M. P., & Leone, J. M. (2005). The differential effects of intimate terrorism and situational couple violence: Findings from the National Violence Against Women Survey. *Journal of Family Issues, 26*(3), 322–349. https://doi.org/10.1177/0192513X04270345

Johnson, M. P. (2008). *A typology of domestic violence: Intimate terrorism, violent resistance, and situational couple violence*. Boston: Northeastern University Press.

Jouriles, E. N., Brown, A. S., McDonald, R., Rosenfield, D., Leahy, M. M., & Silver, C. (2008). Intimate partner violence and preschoolers' explicit memory functioning. *Journal of Family Psychology, 22*(3), 420–428. https://doi.org/10.1037/0893-3200.22.3.420

Jouriles, E. N., McDonald, R., Rosenfield, D., Stephens, N., Corbitt-Shindler, D., & Miller, P. C. (2009). Reducing conduct problems among children exposed to intimate partner violence: A randomized clinical trial examining effects of Project Support. *Journal of Consulting and Clinical Psychology, 77*(4), 705–717. https://doi.org/10.1037/a0015994

Karakurt, G., Smith, D., & Whiting, J. (2014). Impact of intimate partner violence on women's mental health. *Journal of Family Violence, 29*(7), 693–702. https://doi.org/10.1007/s10896-014-9633-2

Karakurt, G., Whiting, K., Van Esch, C., Bolen, S. D., & Calabrese, J. R. (2016). Couples therapy for intimate partner violence: A systematic review and meta-analysis. *Journal of Marital and Family Therapy, 42*(4), 567–583. https://doi.org/10.1111/jmft.12178

Kelly, J. B., & Johnson, M. P. (2008). Differentiation among types of intimate partner violence: Research update and implications for interventions. *Family Court Review, 46*(3), 476–499.

Kim, H. K., Laurent, H. K., Capaldi, D. M., & Feingold, A. (2008). Men's aggression toward women: A 10-year panel study. *Journal of Marriage and Family, 70*(5), 1169–1187. https://doi.org/10.1111/j.1741-3737.2008.00558.x

Koenen, K. C., Moffitt, T. E., Caspi, A., Taylor, A., & Purcell, S. (2003). Domestic violence is associated with environmental suppression of IQ in young children. *Development and Psychopathology, 15*(2), 297–311. https://doi.org/10.1017/S0954579403000166

Kot, S., Landreth, G., & Giordano, M. (1998). Intensive child-centered play therapy with child witnesses of domestic violence. *International Journal of Play Therapy, 7*, 17–36. http://doi.org/10.1037/h0089421

Krieg Mayer, A. G. (2017). Intervening with couples experiencing domestic violence: Development of a systemic framework. *Australian and New Zealand Journal of Family Therapy, 38*(2), 244–255. https://doi.org/10.1002/anzf.1217

Langhinrichsen-Rohling, J., McCullars, A., & Misra, T. A. (2012). Motivations for men and women's intimate partner violence perpetration: A comprehensive review. *Partner Abuse, 3*(4), 429–468. https://doi.org/10.1891/1946-6560.3.4.429

Larson, M., Vaughn, M. G., Salas-Wright, C. P., & Delisi, M. (2015). Narcissism, low self-control, and violence among a nationally representative sample. *Criminal Justice and Behavior, 42*(6), 644–661. https://doi.org/10.1177/0093854814553097

Latzman, N. E., Vivolo-Kantor, A. M., Holditch Niolon, P., & Ghazarian, S. R. (2015). Predicting adolescent dating violence perpetration: Role of exposure to intimate partner violence and parenting practices. *American Journal of Preventive Medicine, 49*(3), 476–482. https://doi.org/10.1016/j.amepre.2015.06.006

Low, S., Tiberio, S. S., Shortt, J. W., Mulford, C., Eddy, J. M., & Capaldi, D. M. (2019). Intergenerational transmission of violence: The mediating role of adolescent psychopathology symptoms. *Development and Psychopathology, 31*(1), 233–245. https://doi.org/10.1017/S0954579417001833

Madruga, C. S., Viana, M. C., Abdalla, R. R., Caetano, R., & Laranjeira, R. (2017). Pathways from witnessing parental violence during childhood to involvement in intimate partner violence in adult life: The roles of depression and substance use. *Drug and Alcohol Review, 36*(1), 107–114. https://doi.org/10.1111/dar.12514

McDonald, R., Jouriles, E. N., & Skopp, N. A. (2006). Reducing conduct problems among children brought to women's shelters: Intervention effects 24 months following termination of services. *Journal of Family Psychology, 20*(1), 127–136. https://doi.org/10.1037/0893-3200.20.1.127

McWhirter, P. T. (2008). An empirical evaluation of a collaborative child and family violence prevention and intervention program. In G. R. Walz, J. C. Bleuer, R. K. Yep, G. R. Walz, J. C. Bleuer, & R. K. Yep (Eds.), *Compelling counseling interventions: Celebrating VISTAS' fifth anniversary* (pp. 221–227). American Counseling Association.

Messinger, A. M., Rickert, V. I., Fry, D. A., Lessel, H., & Davidson, L. L. (2012). Revisiting the role of communication in adolescent intimate partner violence. *Journal of Interpersonal Violence, 27*(14), 2920–2935. https://doi.org/10.1177/0886260512438276

Mills, L. G. (2006). *Insult to injury: Rethinking our responses to intimate abuse.* Princeton University Press.

Mills, L. G., Barocas, B., Butters, R. P., & Ariel, B. (2019). A randomized controlled trial of restorative justice-informed treatment for domestic violence crimes. *Nature Human Behaviour, 3*(12), 1284–1294. https://doi.org/10.1038/s41562-019-0724-1

Niolon, P. H., Vivolo-Kantor, A. M., Tracy, A. J., Latzman, N. E., Little, T. D., DeGue, S., ... Tharp, A. T. (2019). An RCT of dating matters: Effects on teen dating violence and relationship behaviors. *American Journal of Preventive Medicine, 57*(1), 13–23. https://doi.org/10.1016/j.amepre.2019.02.022

Norlander, B., & Eckhardt, C. (2005). Anger, hostility, and male perpetrators of intimate partner violence: A meta-analytic review. *Clinical Psychology Review, 25*(2), 119–152.

O'Leary, K. D. (1999). Developmental and affective issues in assessing and treating partner aggression. *Clinical Psychology: Science and Practice, 6*(4), 400–414. https://doi.org/10.1093/clipsy.6.4.400

O'Leary, K. D., Heyman, R. E., & Neidig, P. H. (1999). Treatment of wife abuse: A comparison of gender-specific and conjoint approaches. *Behavior Therapy, 30*(3), 475–505. https://doi.org/10.1016/S0005-7893(99)80021-5

Pence, E., & Paymar, M. (1993). *Education groups for men who batter: The Duluth model.* Springer.

Pepler, D. J., Catallo, R., & Moore, T. E. (2000). Consider the children: Research informing interventions for children exposed to domestic violence. *Journal of Aggression, Maltreatment & Trauma, 3*(1), 37–57. https://doi.org/10.1300/J146v03n01_04

Peterson, C., Kearns, M. C., McIntosh, W. L., Estefan, L. F., Nicolaidis, C., McCollister, K. E., Gordon, A., & Florence, C. (2018). Lifetime economic burden of intimate partner violence among U.S. adults. *American Journal of Preventive Medicine, 55*(4), 433–444. https://doi.org/10.1016/j.amepre.2018.04.049

Rizo, C. F., Macy, R. J., Ermentrout, D. M., & Johns, N. B. (2011). A review of family interventions for intimate partner violence with a child focus or child component. *Aggression and Violent Behavior*, 16(2), 144–166. https://doi.org/10.1016/j.avb.2011.02.004

Rizzo, C. J., Houck, C., Barker, D., Collibee, C., Hood, E., & Bala, K. (2021). Project STRONG: An online, parent–son intervention for the prevention of dating violence among early adolescent boys. *Prevention Science*, 22(2), 193–204. https://doi.org/10.1007/s11121-020-01168-6

Romano, E., Weegar, K., Gallitto, E., Zak, S., & Saini, M. (2021). Meta-analysis on interventions for children exposed to intimate partner violence. *Trauma, Violence & Abuse*, 22(4), 728–738. https://doi.org/10.1177/1524838019881737

Ronan, G. F., Dreer, L. E., Dollard, K. M., & Ronan, D. W. (2004). Violent couples: Coping and communication skills. *Journal of Family Violence*, 19(2), 131–137. https://doi.org/10.1023/B:JOFV.0000019843.26331.cf

Shaffer, C. S., Gatner, D. T., McCuish, E., Douglas, K. S., & Viljoen, J. L. (2021). The role of psychopathic features and developmental risk factors in trajectories of physical intimate partner violence. *Psychology of Violence*. https://doi.org/10.1037/vio0000313

Sharp, C., Kulesz, P., Marais, L., Shohet, C., Rani, K., Lenka, M., Cloete, J., Vanwoerden, S., Givon, D., & Boivin, M. (2021). Mediational intervention for sensitizing caregivers to improve mental health outcomes in orphaned and vulnerable children. *Journal of Clinical Child and Adolescent Psychology*, 1–16. https://doi.org/10.1080/15374416.2021.1881903

Sharp, C., Vanwoerden, S., Jouriles, E. N., Godfrey, D. A., Babcock, J., McLaren, V., & Temple, J. R. (2020). Exposure to interparental intimate partner violence and the development of borderline features in adolescents. *Child Abuse & Neglect*, 103, 104448. https://doi.org/10.1016/j.chiabu.2020.104448

Showalter, K., Yoon, S., Maguire-Jack, K., Wolf, K. G., & Letson, M. (2020). Are dual and single exposures differently associated with clinical levels of trauma symptoms? Examining physical abuse and witnessing intimate partner violence among young children. *Child & Family Social Work*, 25(2), 439–447. https://doi.org/10.1111/cfs.12700

Simpson Rowe, L., & Jouriles, E. N. (2019). Intimate partner violence and the family. In B. H. Fiese, M. Celano, K. Deater-Deckard, E. N. Jouriles, & M. A. Whisman (Eds.), *APA handbook of contemporary family psychology: Applications and broad impact of family psychology* (Vol. 2, pp. 399–416). American Psychological Association. https://doi.org/10.1037/0000100-025

Snead, A. L., & Babcock, J. C. (2019). Differential predictors of intimate partner sexual coercion versus physical assault perpetration. *Journal of Sexual Aggression*, 25(2), 146–160. https://doi.org/10.1080/13552600.2019.1581282

Sommer, J., Iyican, S., & Babcock, J. (2019). The relation between contempt, anger, and intimate partner violence: A dyadic approach. *Journal of Interpersonal Violence*, 34(15), 3059–3079. https://doi.org/10.1177/0886260516665107

Spencer, C., Mallory, A. B., Cafferky, B. M., Kimmes, J. G., Beck, A. R., & Stith, S. M. (2019). Mental health factors and intimate partner violence perpetration and victimization: A meta-analysis. *Psychology of Violence*, 9(1), 1–17. https://doi.org/10.1037/vio0000156

Stith, S. M., Green, N. M., Smith, D. B., & Ward, D. B. (2008). Marital satisfaction and marital discord as risk markers for intimate partner violence: A meta-analytic review. *Journal of Family Violence*, 23(3), 149–160. https://doi.org/10.1007/s10896-007-9137-4

Stith, S. M., McCollum, E. E., Amanor-Boadu, Y., & Smith, D. (2012). Systemic perspectives on intimate partner violence treatment. *Journal of Marital & Family Therapy*, 38(1), 220–240. https://doi.org/10.1111/j.1752-0606.2011.00245.x

Stith, S. M., McCollum, E. E., & Rosen, K. H. (2011). *Couples therapy for domestic violence: Finding safe solutions*. American Psychological Association.

Stith, S. M., Rosen, K. H., Middleton, K. A., Busch, A. L., Lundeberg, K., & Carlton, R. P. (2000). The intergenerational transmission of spouse abuse: A meta-analysis. *Journal of Marriage and Family*, 62(3), 640–654.

Stith, S. M., Spencer, C. M., Ripoll-Núñez, K. J., Jaramillo-Sierra, A. L., Khodadadi-Andariyeh, F., Nikparvar, F., . . . Metelinen, J. (2020). International adaptation of a treatment program for situational couple violence. *Journal of Marital and Family Therapy*, 46(2), 272–288. https://doi.org/10.1111/jmft.12397

Sudermann, M., Marshall, L., & Loosely, S. (2000). Evaluation of the London (Ontario) community group treatment programme for children who have witnessed woman abuse. *Journal of Aggression, Maltreatment & Trauma*, 3(1), 127–146. https://doi.org/10.1300/J146v03n01_09

Tharp, A. T. (2012). Dating matters™: The next generation of teen dating violence prevention. *Prevention Science*, 13(4), 398–401. https://doi.org/10.1007/s11121-012-0307-0

Tharp, A. T., Burton, T., Freire, K., Hall, D. M., Harrier, S., Latzman, N. E., . . . Vagi, K. J. (2011). Dating Matters™: Strategies to promote healthy teen relationships. *Journal of Women's Health*, 20(12), 1761–1765. https://doi.org/10.1089/jwh.2011.3177

Timmer, S. G., Ware, L. M., Urquiza, A. J., & Zebell, N. M. (2010). The effectiveness of parent-child interaction therapy for victims of interparental violence. *Violence and Victims*, 25(4), 486–503. https://doi.org/10.1891/0886-6708.25.4.486

Tyndall-Lind, A., Landreth, G. L., & Giordano, M. A. (2001). Intensive group play therapy with child witnesses of domestic violence. *International Journal of Play Therapy*, 10(1), 53–83. https://doi.org/10.1037/h0089443

Vives-Cases, C., Gil-González, D., & Carrasco-Portiño, M. (2009). Verbal marital conflict and male domination in the family as risk factors of intimate partner violence. *Trauma, Violence, & Abuse*, 10(2), 171–180. https://doi.org/10.1177/1524838008331193

Vu, N. L., Jouriles, E. N., McDonald, R., & Rosenfield, D. (2016). Children's exposure to intimate partner violence: A meta-analysis of longitudinal associations with child adjustment problems. *Clinical Psychology Review*, 46, 25–33. https://doi.org/10.1016/j.cpr.2016.04.003

Warshaw, C., Brashler, P., & Gil, J. (2009). Mental health consequences of intimate partner violence. In C. Mitchell & D. Anglin (Eds.), *Intimate partner violence: A health-based perspective* (pp. 147–171). Oxford University Press.

Watkins, L. E., Maldonado, R. C., & DiLillo, D. (2018). The cyber aggression in relationships scale: A new multidimensional measure of technology-based intimate partner aggression. *Assessment*, 25(5), 608–626. https://doi.org/10.1177/1073191116665696

Wagar, J., & Rodway, M. (1995). An evaluation of a group treatment approach for children who have witnessed wife abuse. *Journal of Family Violence, 10*(3), 295–305.

Westrupp, E. M., Brown, S., Woolhouse, H., Gartland, D., & Nicholson, J. M. (2018). Repeated early-life exposure to inter-parental conflict increases the risk of preadolescent mental health problems. *European Journal of Pediatrics, 177*(3), 419–427. https://doi.org/10.1007/s00431-017-3071-0

Wolak, J., & Finkelhor, D. (1998). *Children exposed to partner violence.* In J. L. Jasinski & L. M. Williams (Eds.), *Partner violence: A comprehensive review of 20 years of research* (p. 73–112). Sage.

Wolf, K. A., & Foshee, V. A. (2003). Family violence, anger expression styles, and adolescent dating violence. *Journal of Family Violence, 18*(6), 309–316. https://doi.org/10.1023/A:1026237914406

Wolfe, D. A., Crooks, C. V., Chiodo, D., Hughes, R., & Ellis, W. (2012). Observations of adolescent peer resistance skills following a classroom-based healthy relationship program: A post-intervention comparison. *Prevention Science, 13*(2), 196–205. https://doi.org/10.1007/s11121-011-0256-z

Wolfe, D. A., Crooks, C., Jaffe, P., Chiodo, D., Hughes, R., Ellis, W., & Donner, A. (2009). A school-based program to prevent adolescent dating violence: A cluster randomized trial. *Archives of Pediatrics & Adolescent Medicine, 163*(8), 692–699. https://doi.org/10.1001/archpediatrics.2009.69

Wray, A. M., Hoyt, T., & Gerstle, M. (2013). Preliminary examination of a mutual intimate partner violence intervention among treatment-mandated couples. *Journal of Family Psychology, 27*(4), 664–670. https://doi.org/10.1037/a0032912

14

Restorative Justice Alternatives

BRIANA BAROCAS AND REI SHIMIZU ■

Domestic violence (DV) is a global public health phenomenon negatively affecting individuals, families, and communities. In the United States, every state now criminalizes DV. Legal definitions of DV apply to both male and female offenders and tend to be broad: It can include intimate partner violence (IPV), family violence (e.g., adult child and parent), and in some states, conflicts between roommates with no romantic relationship. These are important distinctions given the legal context in which these various forms of violence are considered DV. However, the terms DV and IPV are often used interchangeably in the field and literature about IPV. Yet IPV is considered only one form of DV in many states, where DV includes various forms of violence that are otherwise known as family violence or, in some states, roommate violence. The focus of this chapter is IPV, specifically defined as aggressive or abusive behavior that occurs in romantic relationships, including physical, sexual, and emotional violence, as well as stalking. IPV can also vary in severity and frequency, ranging from one instance of violence to chronic episodes over time (Centers for Disease Control and Prevention, 2020). IPV is a violation of human rights with detrimental emotional and physical effects that can be both short and long term. The relationship between IPV and the increased risk of psychiatric symptoms, such as anxiety, depression, posttraumatic stress disorder, and social isolation, and an increase in adverse physical symptoms such as chronic pain is well established (World Health Organization, 2021). Considering these significant adverse outcomes associated with IPV, the criminal legal system recognizes IPV as a DV crime.

Despite there being legal consequences for its perpetration, IPV, unfortunately, continues to be a common public health issue worldwide (World Health Organization, 2021). In the United States, 52% of violent crimes that are reported to the police were domestic in nature, of which 58% were specifically IPV crimes (US Department of Justice, 2020a). Furthermore, approximately 36% of women and 34% of men report having experienced some form of IPV in their lifetime (Centers for Disease Control and Prevention, 2018). It is estimated that the lifetime prevalence rate for psychological aggression is 47% for both men and women (Centers for Disease Control, 2018). Overall, these prevalence rates are expected to be higher, considering unreported incidents due to the stigma and barriers that individuals face when seeking help for IPV or reporting it to legal authorities (Overstreet & Quinn, 2013). Additionally, there are disparities in IPV prevalence rates and help-seeking behavior by age (Johnson et al., 2015), ableism (Breiding & Armour, 2015), race/ethnicity, and sexual identity (Carvalho et al., 2011; Lipsky et al., 2006; Satyen et al., 2019). In the United States, Black, Indigenous, and People of Color (BIPOC) overall have higher victimization rates of sexual violence and stalking (Centers for Disease Control and Prevention, 2014). For example, the National Intimate Partner and Sexual Violence Survey results indicate that more than 80% of American Indian and Alaska Native women and men (84% of women and 82% of men) have experienced IPV in their lifetime (Rosay, 2016).

Committing DV and or IPV has legal consequences. Traditional responses to DV crimes include mandatory arrest, incarceration, probation, and intervention programs for DV offenders, focusing on retributive justice. Serious questions have been raised about a retributive/punitive justice approach and the efficacy of these traditional, often one-size-fits-all responses, leading to new and innovative approaches to IPV such as those based on the risk-needs-responsivity model (see Roberts, Chapter 12, this volume) and those utilizing couples and family counseling (see Bennet et al., Chapter 13, this volume). This chapter presents an overview of restorative justice (RJ) theory and practice and its applications to addressing DV crimes, and more specifically, IPV. It highlights research on the use of RJ for IPV, as well as challenges and future considerations.

RESTORATIVE JUSTICE

History of Restorative Justice

RJ has been used worldwide to address a variety of crimes and issues that call for healing. In the United States, RJ first took hold in the 1970s in response to the growing dissatisfaction with the criminal legal system. During this time, incarceration rates were increasing due to policy changes that required harsher legal punishment for any crimes committed (Travis et al., 2014). The US criminal legal system has historically taken a retributive or punitive approach where the primary function of the criminal legal system is to determine who is responsible for a crime and the appropriate punishment that should be given (Leonard, 2010). Under the punitive framework, the offender is held accountable for their criminal sentence and enduring the punishment (such as incarceration, legal restrictions, and or mandatory community service/treatment) (Duff, 2003). Therefore, overall, the punishment within a punitive framework serves two purposes: one, to serve justice by adjudicating a punishment appropriate to the legal infraction and, second, to deter the offender and others from breaking the law.

The RJ approach differs from the punitive legal framework because its primary aim is to repair the harm that was caused by the crime; therefore, it addresses three major areas that are not fully addressed by the retributive or punitive approach. First, RJ is grounded in the belief that taking responsibility and restitution occur due to making positive intrapersonal and interpersonal changes. In contrast, the punitive approach emphasizes the importance of obedience and compliance (Zehr & Mika, 1998). Furthermore, these personal changes that result from the restorative process are expected to have lasting positive effects on the well-being of the offender[1] (the person who has caused harm), the victim[2] (the person who has been harmed), and the community. Justice in RJ is, therefore, rehabilitative as the notion of justice is relational, integrative, and collaborative, rather than isolating individuals from the community or coercing them into punitive mechanisms.

Second, RJ incorporates the victims and their needs. This notable component of RJ as it emerged in the 1970s derived partly from the growing victims' rights movements, which had questioned the absence of victim perspectives in the criminal legal system and its inability to meet victim needs (Richards, 2009). In a punitive justice system, the victims' needs are not directly addressed by the offender. The legal framework does not formally include victims in the judicial process of determining whether a legal violation occurred and what the appropriate response would be. However, within RJ, victims are allowed to participate. At the heart of RJ is a transformative process of personal change. This personal transformation is relational and facilitated by engaging in conversations with others, including the victims, if they choose to participate. Even if the victims do not participate, other participants such as facilitators, victim advocates, community volunteers, supportive family, and friends offer support and feedback so the offender can make tangible and rehabilitative behavioral changes to rectify the harm caused and to prevent future harm. This relational component in RJ addresses the significant gap in the punitive approach, as enduring a punishment does not necessarily lead to meaningful reflection about wrongdoings, nor does it mean that the offenders will be equipped with the behavioral and emotional tools necessary to avoid reoffending.

Victim safety is paramount. It is important to emphasize that victims' participation in these conversations is voluntary. There are nondirect ways for victims to participate (e.g., through letters), especially when direct contact would jeopardize

---

1. In keeping true to RJ principles, RJ practitioners avoid utilizing prescriptive, value-laden language that may stigmatize individuals. "Offenders" are usually referred to as the person who caused harm and the "victim" as the person who was harmed. However, in the context of the terminology used in this book and within the criminal legal system, "offender" and "victim" are used in this chapter.

2. We understand that the term "survivor(s)" is utilized in reference to those who have been harmed by IPV. We also align with this empowerment perspective. However, as we are discussing IPV in reference to an instance of a domestic violence crime, we use the term "victim(s)" throughout, which is the conventional term in the criminal justice literature.

safety. Additionally, victim advocates, who are trained to assist victims of DV crimes, may represent victims' voices and perspectives in the conversations. Most importantly, RJ provides victims a choice: If a victim desires to participate, they can, which is an option that is not available in the traditional punitive system.

Lastly, RJ utilizes the power of the community. While the punitive approach relies primarily on the criminal legal system and the legal professionals to achieve justice (Leonard, 2010), RJ depends on social and inclusive opportunities "to demonstrate mutual accountability—the collective responsibility of citizens to care about and take care of one another" (Pranis as cited in Wachtel & McCold, 2001, p. 114). At the core of RJ is the belief that offenders, victims, and the community are all stakeholders that are invested in the well-being of all. Therefore, inclusivity is an important component of RJ, to be free of gender binaries, sexual identities, racial biases, or other preconceived notions/paradigms that may inhibit one's ability to understand the other for who they are. Therefore, the restorative process is a personal and transformative experience for all involved, not limited to offenders and victims.

Consequently, the community is responsible for providing, as much as possible, a supportive environment so that the offenders can fulfill their responsibility to repair the harm they caused. The community also has a primary responsibility to empower the victims and secure and maintain their safety, to effectively engage in recovery from the harm (Zehr & Mika, 1998). A unique contribution of the RJ framework is the underlying belief that the community is overall responsible for maintaining social conditions that promote peaceful communities and restorative conflict resolution.

Restorative Justice Definition and Restorative Justice in Practice

The United Nations defines the restorative process as "any process in which the victim, the offender, and/or any other individuals or community members affected by a crime actively participate together in the resolution of matters arising from crime, often with the help of a fair and impartial third party" (United Nations, 2006, p. 7). Accordingly, RJ practices are utilized in many areas that need conflict resolution (Van Wormer, 2006).

RJ can be practiced in various ways, and three main methods have emerged: mediation/dialogue, conferencing, and circles. All three methods have a shared goal of identifying the harm that was caused, its impact, and how to address the harm. All methods also involve a neutral third party trained in restorative processes, who acts as a facilitator or coordinator, and all the stakeholders participate on a voluntary basis. Each participant is given information regarding the meetings and the RJ process, to be well-informed and prepared beforehand. The restorative process is also guided by a set of shared values and rules that usually include statements about the aim of the RJ process and the code of conduct that help create an egalitarian, respectful space (e.g., engaging in equitable dialogue and decision-making, respect, active listening, and authenticity). In some RJ processes, participants spend time in their first session to collectively add to and affirm these rules to become shared values. Initial assessments are conducted on a case-by-case basis to determine whether meeting face to face is appropriate to avoid traumatization, retraumatization, or other adverse outcomes. Hence, all meetings have an assignment phase for evaluative purposes. If face-to-face contact would jeopardize participant safety, nondirect methods of participation can be arranged, such as "shuttling" (using letters) or inviting a representative third party (Sasson, 2016).

Victim-offender mediation or dialogue is the oldest form of RJ (Umbreit, 1994). It is the most common form utilized in the United States, usually for criminal cases and juvenile justice (Beck & Wood, 2010). The participants in mediation are typically the mediator, victim, offender, and support persons (close family and friends). The mediator holds informational meetings with the offender and victim to prepare them for the mediation, create rapport between the mediator and the participants, and start building a respectful and trusting environment. Once all participants are ready to meet, mediation is scheduled. In the mediation, each person is given the opportunity to speak about the issue at hand, and both parties, with the mediator, are involved in diplomatically creating the restitution process. Once an agreed-upon process is created, there is a follow-up process of checking in to monitor progress and adherence, resulting in another face-to-face meeting to make further adjustments (Beck & Wood, 2010).

Family-group conferencing (FGC) is another method utilized primarily for juvenile justice and child custody cases. FGC utilizes a similar process as mediation but is unique because it often involves the immediate family members and the extended family, social service providers, and community members. FGC focuses on the culture, strength, and resilience of the particular family unit. In cases where it is deemed appropriate, stakeholders can meet privately to discuss and form the retributive process. The family unit then presents its final family agreement to the coordinator for consensus or further discussion (Olson, 2009; Pennell & Burford, 2000).

Circles are another method of RJ in practice. It borrows from peacemaking practices in Indigenous communities such as the First Nations communities in Canada and Native American communities in the United States (e.g., the Navajo peacemaking ritual) to resolve conflict or crime. The Circle begins with the circle keeper or facilitator who reviews the group guidelines and rules. The Circle participants then engage in an opening ceremony, which can be reciting a quote, a prayer, or any meaningful ritual that the circle keeper facilitates. The circle keeper will then pose questions and discussion topics to the group. The stakeholders, in response, take turns talking in a circle using the talking piece. A talking piece may be any object that can be physically passed around in a circle, allowing each person the opportunity to participate in turn. Participants can talk only when they hold the talking piece, and others must engage in active listening. Individuals may skip their turn if they do not wish to speak. Circle participants usually involve a circle keeper/facilitator, the victim and offender, support persons, community advocates (e.g., victim advocates in DV or IPV cases), and community volunteers. Circles also do not require an agreement or finalized plan between the victim and offender to end the session, as is the case with mediation or FGC. However, all Circles conclude with a closing ceremony, which can summarize the discussion and offer concluding remarks, a closing quote or prayer, or a meaningful ritual that the circle keeper facilitates. Circles can also take on many forms for different purposes and are named accordingly (e.g., Healing Circles, Sentencing Circles) (Beck & Wood, 2010; Mills, 2008; Pranis et al., 2003).

RESTORATIVE JUSTICE TO ADDRESS INTIMATE PARTNER VIOLENCE CRIMES

Restorative Justice as an Alternative Framework for Domestic Violence and Intimate Partner Violence

The first known application of RJ in the mainstream criminal legal system[3] was a victim-offender mediation program for a case of vandalism (Liebmann, 2007). In 1974 in Kitchener, Ontario, two teenagers who had vandalized some homes were escorted by their probation officer to meet with 22 of their victims face to face, apologize, and converse about the harm they caused (Zehr, 1990). The success of this approach then expanded into various victim-offender mediation programs in Canada and the United States (Liebmann, 2007). RJ has now been successfully applied to address several areas within criminal justice, including sexual assault (Bletzer & Koss, 2012) and other serious crimes (Rugge & Cormier, 2013). However, the application of RJ to address IPV has faced various challenges and continues to be debated among scholars, practitioners, and policymakers. First, concerns about the compatibility of RJ and IPV have been raised by feminist activists and scholars, some of whom consider the application of RJ to IPV a step backward. Following years of advocacy and lobbying, they worry that moving IPV out of courthouses and the criminal legal system undermines the issue's significance. These feminists have raised concerns about the danger of physical and/or psychological harm to victims (Augusta-Scott et al., 2018; Van Wormer, 2009), the decriminalization of IPV, the failure to convey antiviolence norms to the public, and the focus on the person who caused harm and their rehabilitation while not addressing the needs of victims who were harmed (Hooper & Busch, 1996; Lewis et al., 2001; Stubbs, 2002). Nevertheless, despite originating from different concerns about crime, it has been noted that opponents and proponents of RJ have in common several similar critiques of the criminal legal system. Both

---

3. We are deliberate about using the term "mainstream" and refer to RJ specifically in this context because Indigenous/native communities have embraced RJ principles and practices long before RJ emerged in conversations in non-Indigenous communities.

contend that existing solutions provided by the law fail victims and offenders, and both movements advocate for a justice system that is victim-centric.

Second, policy-level challenges can create difficulties in implementing RJ to address IPV. Despite interest in face-to-face meetings expressed by some couples, the use of RJ for IPV has been prohibited in some jurisdictions in the United States (as well as Britain and Australia) due to safety concerns. For example, in the United States, if RJ is used as an intervention following the conviction of a DV crime, mandated offender treatment programs must adhere to state standards and guidelines that may not allow for conjoint treatment where an offender and a victim are brought together in the treatment process (Barocas et al., 2016). In states where conjoint treatment is forbidden, victim participation is impossible, even if the victim wants to participate. Thus, the application of RJ to IPV crimes can be limited if no coinciding policy changes allow for it. As Pennell et al. (2021) note, "Growing restorative approaches in the United States requires lifting prohibitions in law and policy that prevent face-to-face meetings of those harmed and those causing harm and instituting legislation, policy, and funding that enable program initiation, implementation, and evaluation" (p. 1625).

Despite these challenges, examples can be found of RJ programs/interventions utilized to address IPV crimes and have been empirically tested. These interventions are designed ultimately to address root causes and cycles of violence that often occur from one generation to the next. The following section will introduce how RJ has been implemented to address IPV and what has emerged from existing research.

Restorative Justice to Address Domestic Violence and Intimate Partner Violence Crimes

RJ has been used to address DV worldwide (Wolthuis & Lünnemann, 2016), and there is a growing interest in its application to IPV cases. An RJ approach is seen as potentially valuable in situations where victims and offenders remain connected through various circumstances, including continued romantic relationships, shared community and peers, co-parenting, and finances (Ptacek, 2009). Additionally, RJ's approaches tend to be inclusive and not limited to a prescriptive syllabus based on binary gender norms that often inform traditional batterer intervention programs (BIPs) (Cannon et al., 2015). The implementation of RJ to address DV and, more specifically, IPV crimes is affected by various factors, including the severity of the crime, the different RJ methods available, and the timing in which programs are implemented.

Severity (Felony/Misdemeanor)

Applications of RJ to IPV need to be viewed in the context of DV as a crime and the severity of that crime. Criminal codes related to DV and IPV vary by state, district, and territory (US Department of Justice, n.d.). Only two states have criminalized coercive control or the sustained oppression that most victims experience as a DV crime (Americas Conference to End Coercive Control, 2020). Additionally, there are encompassing federal laws under the Violence Against Women's Act (VAWA), passed by Congress in 1994, which recognizes DV as a federal crime that can be tried in federal court, providing legal avenues to address DV and IPV where state laws may falter (US Department of Justice, 2020b).

Overall, both state and federal laws classify crimes as felonies or misdemeanors. A felony is more serious than a misdemeanor, referring to crimes that can result in imprisonment for more than a year, including the death penalty. Misdemeanors refer to less severe crimes that can result in imprisonment for a year or less. Commonly, the outcome of a misdemeanor crime is negotiated as part of a guilty plea bargain, resulting in community service, mandatory participation in intervention programs, probation, and or fines (Legal Information Institute, n.d.). In the context of DV, and more specifically IPV crimes, whether an assault is judged a felony or a misdemeanor depends on multiple contextual factors such as the severity of physical harm that was caused by assault, intent to harm, previous DV or IPV convictions, previous threats to harm, and the use of a weapon (Fagan, 1996). Whether a specific charge (e.g., aggravated assault, battery, strangulation) is filed as a felony or a misdemeanor is determined by each state, district, and territory (Battered Women's Justice Project, 2015).

RJ programs for IPV are available for offenders who have been charged with either felony or misdemeanor DV crimes, or both. For example, the AHIMSA Collective provides an RJ circle program that specifically addresses intimate violence called Realize for inmates incarcerated in California prisons. The circle program focuses on addressing experiences with violence within intimate relationships, including family violence, sexual abuse, and other forms of DV. The program also explores specific topics pertinent to intimate violence, such as trauma, gender norms/structure, accountability, and the impact that the violence has on victims. They are unique because their circles are facilitated by peer educators or "incarcerated leaders" and individuals who are not incarcerated (The AHIMSA Collective, 2020).

The AHIMSA Collective also provides a circle program for inmates with a deeper focus on victim narratives and experiences, called Empathize. Participants in Empathize write an apology letter to the victim within the 1-year program, filed with the Office of Victim Services. Although "Empathize" is not specific to intimate violence (The AHIMSA Collective, 2020), programs such as Realize and Empathize are available for offenders who may be incarcerated for more serious DV crimes. RJ programs that address IPV are particularly impactful for inmates with long-term sentences to be able to reconcile or express remorse for the harm they caused (Fraley, 2001). Inmates with longer sentences tend to be more removed or disconnected with the harm they caused, the victims, their support systems, and the larger community (Fraley, 2001). RJ programs with community involvement and multiple stakeholders who represent victim narratives, therefore, may provide a critical opportunity for long-term inmates to express remorse and begin to repair and take accountability for the harm they caused (Hurley, 2009).

Most misdemeanor DV crimes are addressed through mandated BIPs, as misdemeanors often conclude with a plea bargain. In a plea bargain, the offender usually pleads guilty to the crime, and in return, receives an alternative mandate instead of incarceration, such as mandated treatment, probation, community service, or a fine. In the context of DV and IPV, the alternative mandate is usually participation in a BIP. Therefore, many offenders who participate in RJ programs for IPV in the community are charged with misdemeanor DV crimes.

DIFFERENT METHODS OF RESTORATIVE JUSTICE

The implementation of RJ programs to address IPV is also influenced by the different RJ processes available. In 2019, the Center for Court Innovation published a report on IPV-related RJ programs across the country (Cissner et al., 2019). The report highlights how RJ is being applied to IPV in the United States based on a survey of 34 programs, including five in-depth case studies. The survey responses included programs that used various restorative methods. The most common was peacemaking circles, followed by support circles for persons harmed, family group conferences, and some programs employing more than one method. The case studies focused on the various methods employed in RJ and the processes involved, including conferencing (e.g., EPIC "Ohana in Hawaii), family group decision-making (e.g., Family Service Rochester in Minnesota), and circles (e.g., Men as Peacemakers in Duluth, Minnesota). Some programs engage with the person who has been harmed, some with the person who has caused harm, and some with both, either together or separately. Programs receive referrals in various ways, including from child welfare (when there is a co-occurrence with DV), from the court in cases of IPV, and the community. In a qualitative comparative analysis study of the programs that utilized peacemaking circles and family group conferencing, Pennell et al. (2021) found that programs grounded in the peacemaking circles method pursued options other than traditional BIPs or legal action. They looked to approaches grounded in Indigenous restorative practice and were open to receiving legal referrals. In contrast, programs based on the family group conferencing method sought to further practices that centered on the family, and safely maintaining the family unit through culturally appropriate family-oriented programs, with referrals from child welfare. As the examples show, existing programs in the United States draw on the variety of methods employed in RJ. These methods are then applied at various points in time in the context of the criminal legal system.

TIMING (PRETRIAL, PRESENTENCING AND SENTENCING, POSTSENTENCE)
Pretrial Restorative Justice

The timing of RJ program implementation can vary as programs can be implemented as a diversionary measure, at presentence or sentencing, and as an alternative to incarceration postconviction/postsentence. In general, diversionary programs offer offenders an alternative to traditional criminal proceedings. The specificities of diversionary programs differ by jurisdiction as some are implemented at pretrial, while others are implemented at presentencing, or to defer sentencing. Some diversionary programs require an admission of guilt, while others do not. Sadusky (2003) provides an encompassing definition of diversionary programs for DV crimes as one that "suspends criminal justice case processing of a domestic violence related charge with one or more of the following: no charges files, charges dismissed, or charges expunged" (p. 2).

There was a notable rise in diversionary programs for DV crimes in the 1980s as they were implemented to divert first-time offenders with low-level misdemeanor DV crimes from the traditional criminal legal system. The idea behind diversionary programs was to offer an opportunity for offenders to get the rehabilitative services they need to rectify the issue that led to the DV crime (e.g., counseling programs for anger management, substance use, etc.) instead of being incarcerated. Allowing diversionary options also alleviated the administrative and financial burden of the criminal legal system that was being overloaded because of the harsh retributive policies in the 1970s (Sadusky, 2003). However, advocates for victims of DV and IPV were quick to point out flaws in diversionary programs for DV crimes. One of their main arguments was the inability in first-time arrest cases to accurately predict whether the incident that led to the arrest was, in fact, the first instance of violence in the relationship. Furthermore, as diversionary programs were intended for low-level crimes, it was argued that treating DV as a misdemeanor would diminish the gravity of DV crimes in general. Additionally, advocates argued that diversionary programs failed to hold DV offenders accountable, as the outcome of a diversionary program usually resulted in an official verdict of not guilty (Sadusky, 2003).

The most recent report by the National Conference for State Legislatures (2017) cites only 10 states in the United States that offer DV diversionary programs, with eligibility criteria specific to each jurisdiction. It is not surprising that RJ diversionary programs are even more of a rarity in the United States. Most RJ diversionary programs in the United States have specifically intended for substance use and mental illness–related offenses as well as for first-time juvenile offenders (US Department of Justice, 1998, 2001). In Vermont and other states with RJ diversionary programs for non-DV misdemeanor crimes, DV and IPV cases are deliberatively excluded, due to objections from advocates (e.g., that approaches in RJ, in treating offenders, victims, and the community as equals, wrongfully dismiss the inherent power dynamics that are pertinent to DV and IPV; The Vermont Network Against Domestic and Sexual Violence, 2019). Similarly, one of the most well-known diversionary RJ programs, RESTORE, also excluded cases with a history of DV or ongoing violence in the intimate relationship. A diversionary RJ program specifically for sex crimes, RESTORE was implemented in Pima County, Arizona, from 2003 to 2004 (Koss, 2010, 2014). It was developed using robust community-based approaches in program development, in close consultation with stakeholders in the field of DV and IPV, including victims and offenders. While there are no publicly available records that explain why DV and IPV cases were excluded, a community-based decision was made not to include DV and IPV in the diversionary program (Koss, 2010, 2014).

There are two separate but related debates around the acceptability and implementation of RJ diversion programs: whether diversionary programs are appropriate for DV and IPV cases compared to the current judicial system, and the other is whether RJ overall is appropriate for DV and IPV cases, especially in the context of diversionary programs. Deciding whether RJ is appropriate for DV and IPV cases is a problem when diversionary programs themselves are uncommon. Therefore, it is likely that the lack of diversionary RJ programs for IPV in the United States, Canada, and New Zealand is at least partly due to the overall lack of enthusiasm toward utilizing diversionary programs to address DV crimes.

Restorative Justice at Presentencing or Sentencing

A more common way RJ is integrated into the criminal legal system is at presentencing or sentencing. An RJ program or mechanism implemented before sentencing or in the sentencing procedure allows the community and the victim to influence the outcome of the sentence. In other words, they are included in deciding what a just punishment should be for the harm that was caused.[4]

In the United States, RJ programs can also be integrated into the criminal legal system at presentencing and sentencing, using delivery methods such as sentencing circles and mediation. Sentencing circles are offered in the circle format described previously, but unique from healing circles as they not only involve community members, victims, and offenders, as well as support persons such as friends and family members, but can also involve court personnel such as judges, police, legal counsel, and other community members (e.g., witnesses to the crime). It is important to note that while public discourse about the use of RJ to address crimes and their effects has increased in recent years, RJ has been utilized in Indigenous communities for centuries (Chartrand & Horn, 2016). While the Western retributive criminal legal system continues to dominate as the mainstream form of justice, it can integrate or overlap with Indigenous restorative practices through tribal courts and laws.[5]

In the United States, there are currently 32 states with tribal courts; Alaska is one of them. In Alaska, the tribal courts and the state have overlapping jurisdiction over DV crimes. The court that initiates the case generally has jurisdiction over the DV crime with opportunities to transfer, so cases that the state court initiated may proceed as is or be transferred to tribal courts and vice versa (Alaska

---

4. In the United States, the right for victims to be heard and involved in the judicial process is defined in federal law. Therefore, there are mechanisms such as the victim impact statement that can be utilized for victim voices to be considered in the judicial process. Some consider this to be a move toward RJ, but for the sake of this chapter, we focus on introducing RJ-specific programs/interventions.

5. Describing the intricacies of jurisdiction which is informed by the intersections among the constitution, treaties, specific federal laws, and state-level agreements between states and tribes is beyond the scope of this chapter. Attempting to do so will merely oversimplify the topic. However, we acknowledge that there is a discussion to be had about tribal sovereignty, recognizing Indigenous nations as a separate self-determining government body.

Legal Services, 2012). When a DV crime is adjudicated in the tribal courts, the tribes have the freedom to proceed with the case using non-Western restorative and community-engaged adjudication and enforcement practices of their choice. Furthermore, the sentence and or orders of protection the tribal courts issue are also enforced by the state (Alaska Legal Services, 2012; Forston & Carbaugh, 2014).

Moreover, Alaska is unique as offenders, victims, and their communities may have access to RJ legal proceedings even if their case is not adjudicated in tribal courts through the RJ referral process (Alaska Court System, n.d.b). When a case is referred to the RJ process either by the tribe/organization or the state court, the state court retains jurisdiction over the criminal cases, but sentencing recommendations are made based on a restorative process. Some restorative processes will occur through tribal RJ sentencing circles or other community-based RJ programs. A state judge then adjudicates the final sentencing considering the recommendations (Alaska Court System, n.d.b; Forston & Carbaugh, 2014). Alaska also provides mediation programs at presentencing so that individuals can resolve issues without opening a legal case. DV and IPV issues are eligible for mediation upon consultation with the mediator. If a DV dispute resolution proceeds to mediation, the victim can bring a support person or an advocate. Victim participation is completely voluntary, and mediation of a DV case must be facilitated by a specific mediator who has been trained in DV and IPV dynamics and issues (Alaska Court System, n.d.a).

Outside of Alaska and the tribal context, sentencing is also utilized in Washington County, Minnesota, for IPV cases, most notably through the Washington County Community Circles (WCCC) program. Like the RJ referral program in Alaska, the WCCC works in conjunction with the justice system to offer recommendations for sentencing through sentencing circles (Washington County Community Circles, 2021). They also offer posttrial presentence circle programs for offenders who enter a plea on the condition that the offender completes a Circles program, where the charges are dismissed upon successful completion (Cissner et al., 2019).

As the examples illustrate, integrating RJ programs or strategies at presentencing and sentencing within the Western criminal legal system is possible for DV and IPV cases. According to a study in Canada that examined attitudes toward sentencing circles for IPV cases among Canadian judges, 74% were favorable to utilizing sentencing circles for IPV cases. Notably, these judges discussed the ability of sentencing circles to increase community awareness and community involvement, and to hold offenders responsible in meaningful ways (Belknap & McDonald, 2010). Therefore, while the use of RJ at presentencing and sentencing is far from mainstream, there are positive examples and attitudes toward integrating RJ presentencing and sentencing practices into the criminal legal system.

Postconviction/Postsentence Restorative Justice

RJ programs to address DV and IPV crimes are most often implemented at postconviction or postsentencing, where the sentence can be fulfilled, in whole or in part, through completion of an RJ program. An example of a postconviction program is the Circles of Peace (CP) model developed by New York University's

Center on Violence and Recovery. The model is the first of its kind in the United States to use RJ as an alternative treatment approach to standard BIPs for those sentenced to treatment for a misdemeanor DV crime. It was developed in response to growing interest in alternative approaches that included victim participation (Mills, 2008; Mills et al., 2013, 2019). CP uses the peacemaking circle method and RJ practices to bring together individuals who have been abusive with willing partners/family members (victims can choose to participate), support persons, trained professional facilitators, and community volunteers to address the DV that has occurred.

The goal of CP is to create meaningful and lasting change. This is done by monitoring participant safety carefully, encouraging dialogue about the violent incident(s), exploring gender dynamics, and uncovering the family histories of violence. The CP model is flexible, culturally sensitive, and works with the criminal legal system to bring about healing and transformation in individuals, families, and communities. The model moves beyond the IPV gender paradigm and can address the various types of DV cases that encounter the criminal legal system, including IPV cases involving men abusing women, female offenders, and same-sex and transgender intimate partners. The model has been adapted to the local context and state standards for DV offender treatment and implemented in Nogales, Arizona (in 2004); Salt Lake City, Utah (in 2012); and Windsor County, Vermont (in 2019).

RJ can be implemented in various ways, as a diversionary program, as an alternative or complementary process at presentencing and sentencing, or as a court-mandated RJ program for DV offenders. Because the use of RJ for DV and IPV cases is clearly an emerging approach in criminal justice, it is crucial to have a robust evidence base for RJ outreach and program implementation. Fortunately, an increasing number of studies have been conducted in recent years. The following section synthesizes the current state of research examining the efficacy of RJ DV offender programs and various areas in need of further investigation.

The Evidence Base for Restorative Justice Interventions

The use of RJ to address DV, and more specifically, IPV crimes is promising, and, although still limited, there is a growing body of research that supports this. In what follows the empirical evidence is highlighted, and existing gaps in the research literature are noted.

Existing research ranges from a national study that describes but does not evaluate restorative programs across the country (Cissner et al., 2019); to studies that focus on understanding justice preferences, how they are aligned with RJ goals, and how IPV survivors are defined (Decker et al., 2020); to randomized controlled trials of RJ interventions for those sentenced to treatment for DV crimes (Mills et al., 2013, 2019). Recently a comprehensive review on RJ interventions for IPV was conducted utilizing a systematic, wide-net search of empirical studies and theoretical/conceptual discussions about RJ interventions for IPV (Barocas et al.,

2020). Two of its major aims were to summarize the empirical studies and theoretical discussions regarding RJ interventions for IPV and identify the research gaps that remain to be addressed (Barocas et al., 2020).

Based on the results of the empirical studies that tested intervention effectiveness (Barocas et al., 2020), RJ was found to be a viable option for IPV. The interventions either had positive outcomes on victim satisfaction, better outcomes regarding recidivism compared to the traditional BIP models, or showed no differences compared to traditional BIP models. For example, in a randomized controlled trial comparing a standard BIP and the CP model at postconviction for offenders mandated to treatment for misdemeanor DV crimes (including IPV) in Nogales, Arizona, Mills et al. (2013) found that participants randomly assigned to CP experienced less recidivism at all follow-up comparisons over 24 months. However, statistically significant differences were found only for the 12-month follow-up comparisons for non-DV rearrests, and no statistically significant differences were found for the DV rearrests. This equivocal finding for DV rearrests, with comparable outcomes between groups, supports CP as a feasible alternative to traditional BIPs. Although CP may be more effective in reducing non-DV than DV arrests, results would seem to refute the claim that it is dangerous to use RJ for DV, including IPV (since it brings together an offender and voluntary victim). In a subsequent study in Salt Lake City, Utah, Mills et al. (2019) compared a standard BIP to a hybrid intervention, a BIP that includes a component informed by RJ and CP (BIP+CP). They found statistically significant differences between the two models over 2 years. Specifically, BIP+CP resulted in statistically significant reductions, for all offenses, including DV, in new arrests (53%) and severity of the crime (52%) (Mills et al., 2019).

In another randomized controlled study, victims reported higher satisfaction when their offenders were sent to a mediation process after prosecution than victims whose offenders only experienced prosecution (Davis, 2009). Statistically significant differences were not found in recidivism between offenders who experienced prosecution and mediation and those who experienced only prosecution, indicating that the mediation process after prosecution performed just as well as prosecution only. One could, therefore, argue that including the mediation process may improve the prosecution-only system because while recidivism does not differ, the mediation process improved victim satisfaction, a critical component largely missing in the criminal legal system addressing IPV.

The review also found that RJ may be particularly useful for the many IPV victims who choose to continue a relationship with their offender (Barocas et al., 2020). For example, one study found that 71% of the offender-victim dyads in the sample continued their romantic relationship after the IPV offense (Hargovan, 2010). Many of the studies cited in the review emphasized that RJ does not necessarily seek to reconcile romantic partners unless they mutually agree to do so. The typical outcome of the RJ process, particularly in the context of IPV, is for closure to be provided so that the victims, offenders, and others that were impacted can move on. Through the restorative process, victims and offenders may create an amicable relationship and improve communication skills, especially if they are co-parenting or facing other situations where they must interact due to circumstance, for example, financial partnerships, participation in shared community events, and cultural obligations.

Often missing in the discourse regarding BIPs is the genuine desire of offenders to directly express remorse and guilt to those they harmed (or to surrogates such as community volunteers, advocates, and support people who may be representative of those they have harmed). Not all offenders are chronic recidivists with a lengthy criminal history of DV or IPV charges or violent offenses. Some cases are purely situational, limited to one instance that occurred because of accumulated stressors. We do not minimize any type of abuse, but situational violence involves significantly different dynamics from more serious ongoing violence that persist throughout the relationship (Johnson, 2010). Depending on the circumstances, some offenders may seek to make amends and would do so if given a choice. These opportunities for offender rehabilitation and accountability are an active component of RJ lacking from the punitive criminal legal system focused on punishment. Considering these benefits, RJ programs, whether they are offered as diversionary, sentencing, or postconviction/postsentencing programs, can provide opportunities to the victims and offenders to recover from harm.

Gaps in the Evidence Base

Although there has been some promising research on using RJ to address IPV, gaps in the research literature remain. These gaps include increasing public awareness of RJ, clarifying the meaning of community in this approach, understanding optimal timing of program implementation, and understanding what populations RJ programs are best suited for (Barocas et al., 2020).

RESTORATIVE JUSTICE PUBLIC AWARENESS

The comprehensive review of RJ interventions for IPV crimes found that many stakeholders lacked knowledge about RJ and its different modalities (Barocas et al., 2020). Lack of awareness and knowledge poses challenges to RJ advocacy and program implementation. Therefore, proposing a RJ framework or program must begin with an in-depth explanation of what it is and a frank acknowledgment of current debates around the subject matter, before proposing benefits and other details specific to program implementation. As a result, getting buy-in for RJ programs, particularly for IPV, can be time-consuming in comparison to programs that utilize well-known modalities like cognitive-behavioral therapy. Additionally, even if the program is implemented, victims and offenders who do not know about RJ cannot ask for it.

Importantly, the review also found that those in favor of RJ for DV and IPV crimes were those with firsthand experience of RJ (Barocas et al., 2020). RJ as a framework, its approach, and the specific modalities are complex, multilayered, and multifaceted, and its benefits can be difficult to convey. Consequently, RJ training programs are mostly experiential. Current and future advocates of RJ

COMMUNITY IN RESTORATIVE JUSTICE

The review found that the concept of community in RJ may need clarifying (Barocas et al., 2020). Shifting the responsibility of crime to the community is a unique feature of RJ that distinguishes it from the traditional criminal legal approach. However, the review identified multiple studies that questioned what community means in RJ and whether negative/harmful dynamics are addressed or mitigated, whether interpersonal or systemic (Barocas et al., 2020), such as oppression, bias, and prejudice. These issues were salient in the discussion where the RJ programs were enmeshed with agencies within the criminal legal systems such as courts, police, and opposing legal counsel. Certain participants may be subject to unequal power dynamics and may distrust these authoritative institutions. Others also questioned whether RJ addressed dynamics within small and insular communities where confidentiality and impartiality may be at risk or communities where cultural norms may contradict victims' desires, such as beliefs and values opposed to separation and divorce. They can also be misaligned with participating victims and offenders if the community is not inclusive or representative of various demographics within that geographical location.

These concerns are valid and need further investigation. However, the review also found that many of the participants and stakeholders reported that the integration of community was a beneficial and distinct characteristic of RJ interventions that address IPV crimes (Barocas et al., 2020). RJ processes, like circles that occur over multiple sessions, often result in a rapport between the participants, where the circle itself becomes a supportive community that provides opportunities to connect with others. Considering these beneficial aspects of community, it is essential for future research on RJ to identify what community means for restorative processes in the context of DV and IPV and how victims and offenders relate to it.

Optimal Timing

More research is also needed to understand the optimal timing of RJ program implementation. Some have argued that utilizing RJ to address DV and IPV may minimize the gravity and criminal nature of partner abuse, referring to RJ as a form of "soft justice" (Barocas et al., 2020). While such arguments may be applicable to diversionary cases, participation in sentencing and postsentencing models nevertheless does not preclude offenders from being convicted of a crime (in the traditional legal sense). One of the significant benefits of RJ, at least for nondiversionary models such as sentencing and postsentencing programs, is that it provides a specific space for victims to be included in the sentencing/judicial process. There is a need for research using randomized controlled trials with multiple intervention arms to examine any differences in outcomes (e.g., recidivism, process, victim and offender experiences, and satisfaction) by the timing of RJ programs implementation, with the traditional BIP approach as the control group.

BEST FIT—RESTORATIVE JUSTICE FOR WHOM?

Another highly debated question among RJ advocates is which DV and IPV cases RJ programs are best suited for and for whom are they intended. Violence in romantic relationships comes in many forms, within various contexts, and involves varying needs. Outcome studies have found that the one-size-fits-all approach in traditional BIPs is flawed because it does not adequately cater to the heterogeneity of cases (Cantos & O'Leary, 2014). According to the comprehensive review by Barocas et al. (2020), about half of the published studies concluded that RJ interventions were suitable for some but not for all. Such findings indicate the need for future research to examine what differentiates offenders' and victims' RJ experiences when addressing IPV crimes and the mechanisms (specific components of the intervention) that affect intervention effectiveness (Barocas et al., 2020). Identifying the "best fit" is necessary in order to cater to the varying needs of IPV offenders and victims, to reduce and repair harm, and to reduce recidivism and violence overall.

After examining a total of 19 theoretical and empirical publications, the comprehensive review found that RJ, in the context of IPV, as a field, is in its early stages and is in the process of establishing what intervention success means (Barocas et al., 2020). Some studies utilized participant satisfaction as a measure of program success (a subjective outcome), while others operationalized program success as reduced recidivism, reduced severity of crimes, and reports of behavioral change postintervention (objective outcomes). The ways in which program success is measured are varied and align with the process-oriented nature of RJ but make it challenging to synthesize the findings and make a collective statement about program effectiveness.

CONCLUSION

RJ can be an alternative or a complement to criminal legal system responses to IPV. The use of RJ to address IPV is increasingly acknowledged, and interest in its application to IPV is growing. The New York City Mayor's Office to End Domestic and Gender-Based Violence recently published a blueprint outlining ways to develop restorative and community-based approaches to IPV (Sasson & Allen, 2020). Additionally, New York University's Center on Violence and Recovery has an over 15-year history of collaborating with local judges and other justice court personnel, community-based treatment providers (including social service agencies and a justice center), victim advocates, and community members in implementing and studying the CP model in the criminal legal systems in Nogales, Arizona; Salt Lake City, Utah; and more recently, Windsor County, Vermont. Interest in the model by other communities continues to grow based on the Arizona and Utah studies that show promising findings (Mills et al., 2013, 2019).

There are also growing opportunities for RJ implementation as the criminal legal system, particularly in response to IPV, shifts toward an evidence-informed rehabilitative model. For example, Colorado, Utah, and Washington have all implemented various versions of a differentiated intervention approach for DV offenders, rooted in the risk-needs- responsivity (RNR) framework. This framework aligns well with RJ principles as RNR recognizes the importance of rehabilitation, the community, and the shortcomings of a traditional one-size-fits-all approach (Bonta & Andrews, 2007). In RNR-based programs, offenders are categorized into low risk, medium risk, or high risk, to determine the corresponding level of treatment (low-level, medium-level, high-level treatment), with differing program/treatment goals, length, and intensity of treatment at each level. This shift of the criminal legal system toward RNR, however tentative it may be, represents an attempt to address the heart of the issue by catering to the unique needs of each offender, with implications for RJ to the extent that such approaches align with RJ principles. Hopefully, the implementation of RNR will create more opportunities for RJ programs in general (Latimer et al., 2005) and for RJ programs that specifically address DV and IPV crimes.

Implementing RJ approaches to addressing IPV requires multiple stakeholders, including policymakers, judges, probation officers, victim advocates, treatment providers, and clinicians, among others, from multiple systems (government, criminal justice, child welfare, service delivery, etc.). Research is central in establishing the evidence base for using RJ to address IPV and persuading stakeholders that RJ is a compelling alternative in addressing violence and repairing harm, particularly in cases like IPV, where the standard approaches do little to improve the lives of those affected. Coupled with the need for more research is the need for policies that allow for RJ in cases of IPV. Intervention programs for DV crimes need to adhere to state standards and guidelines, and this influences how RJ models are implemented (Barocas et al., 2016). Some states allow for RJ options to be offered instead of BIP treatment (e.g., Arizona); other states require that conjoint programs (including RJ) be offered after a period of BIP treatment (e.g., Utah). There is now evidence to suggest that combining traditional approaches like BIP with other treatment components can improve overall effectiveness (see, for example, Lila et al., 2018; Romero-Martinez et al., 2018). Thus, the application of RJ to DV, and in particular, IPV, continues to evolve with emerging hybrid-based intervention programs that include features from traditional interventions, like BIP, and elements of RJ, like CP, and there is research evidence to support this evolution (Mills et al., 2019).

The COVID-19 pandemic presents new challenges and considerations for the application of RJ to IPV. The use of technology (e.g., video platforms) during the pandemic raises issues on how technology should be incorporated into responses to IPV, including RJ. Other considerations for the application of RJ to IPV include the timing of a RJ approach (e.g., presentencing, sentencing, postconviction/postsentencing), the type of RJ model employed (e.g., conferencing, family group decision-making, circles, etc.), policy and other issues related to the ability to bring together offenders and victims (e.g., state standards for DV intervention programs) as well as other legal considerations, RJ training and facilitator background (e.g., licensed social service provider), funding issues and the costs associated with RJ, and attitudinal issues. Thus, there is a need for more research to explore these new challenges and other considerations and the outcomes of RJ for DV and, more specifically, IPV. Today, a range of approaches are crucial to meet the needs of victims, offenders, families, and communities in addressing IPV and should include options such as RJ that seek to address the harm and promote restoration and healing while also moving beyond the gender paradigm.

REFERENCES

The AHIMSA Collective. (2020). What we do. https://www.ahimsacollective.net/what-we-do

Alaska Court System. (n.d.a). Mediation—Frequently asked questions. https://www.courts.alaska.gov/mediation/index.htm

Alaska Court System. (n.d.b). Restorative justice programs. https://courts.alaska.gov/trialcourts/rjp.htm

Alaska Legal Services. (2012). Tribal jurisdiction in Alaska. http://www.akleg.gov/basis/get_documents.asp?session=29&docid=1426

Americas Conference to End Coercive Control. (2020, November 13). Hawaii and California lead the way signing the first coercive control bills in the Americas. https://www.theacecc.com/post/hawaii-and-california-lead-the-way-signing-the-first-coercive-control-bills-in-the-americas

Augusta-Scott, T., Harrison, P., & Singer, V. (2018). Creating safety, respect, and equality for women. In T. Augusta-Scott, K. Scotty, & L. M. Tutty (Eds.), *Innovations in interventions to address intimate partner violence* (pp. 156–173). Routledge/Taylor & Francis Group.

Barocas, B., Avieli, H., & Shimizu, R. (2020). Restorative justice approaches to intimate partner violence: A review of interventions. *Partner Abuse, 11*(3), 318–349. https://doi.org/10.1891/PA-2020-0010

Barocas, B., Emery, D., & Mills, L. G. (2016). Changing the domestic violence narrative: Aligning definitions and standards. *Journal of Family Violence, 31*(8), 941–947. https://doi.org/10.1007/s10896-016-9885-0

Battered Women's Justice Project. (2015). State statutes: Misdemeanor crimes of domestic violence. https://www.bwjp.org/assets/documents/pdfs/ncpoffc-state-statutes-misdemeanor-crimes-of-domesti.pdf

Beck, E., & Wood, A. (2010). Restorative justice practice. In E. Beck, N. P. Kropf, & P. B. Leonard (Eds.), *Social work and restorative justice: Skills for dialogue, peacemaking, and reconciliation* (pp. 64–89). Oxford University Press. https://doi.org/10.1093/acprof:oso/9780195394641.001.0001

Belknap, J., & McDonald, C. (2010). Judges' attitudes about and experiences with sentencing circles in intimate-partner abuse cases. *Canadian Journal of Criminology & Criminal Justice, 52*(4), 369–395. https://doi.org/10.3138/cjccj.52.4.369

Bletzer, K. V., & Koss, M. P. (2012). From parallel to intersecting narratives in cases of sexual assault. *Qualitative Health Research, 22*(3), 291–303. https://doi.org/10.1177/1049732311430948

Bonta, J., & Andrews, D. A. (2007). Risk-need-responsivity model for offender assessment and rehabilitation. *Rehabilitation*, 6(1), 1–22.

Breiding, M. J., & Armour, B. S. (2015). The association between disability and intimate partner violence in the United States. *Annals of Epidemiology*, 25(6), 455–457. https://doi.org/10.1016/j.annepidem.2015.03.017

Cannon, C., Lauve-Moon, K., & Buttell, F. (2015). Re-theorizing intimate partner violence through post-structural feminism, queer theory, and the sociology of gender. *Social Sciences*, 4(3), 668–687. https://doi.org/10.3390/socsci4030668

Cantos, A. L., & O'Leary, K. D. (2014). One size does not fit all in treatment of intimate partner violence. *Partner Abuse*, 5(2), 204–236. https://doi.org/10.1891/1946-6560.5.2.204

Carvalho, A. F., Lewis, R. J., Derlega, V. J., Winstead, B. A., & Viggiano, C. (2011). Internalized sexual minority stressors and same-sex intimate partner violence. *Journal of Family Violence*, 26(7), 501–509. https://doi.org/10.1007/s10896-011-9384-2

Centers for Disease Control and Prevention. (2014). Prevalence and characteristics of sexual violence, stalking, and intimate partner violence victimization—National Intimate Partner and Sexual Violence Survey, United States, 2011. https://www.cdc.gov/mmwr/pdf/ss/ss6308.pdf

Centers for Disease Control and Prevention. (2018). The National Intimate Partner and Sexual Violence Survey: 2015 data brief—Updated release. https://www.cdc.gov/violenceprevention/pdf/2015data-brief508.pdf

Centers for Disease Control and Prevention. (2020, October 10). Intimate partner violence. https://www.cdc.gov/violenceprevention/intimatepartnerviolence/index.html

Chartrand, L., & Horn, K. (2016). A report on the relationships between restorative justice and indigenous legal traditions in Canada. https://www.justice.gc.ca/eng/rp-pr/jr/rjilt-jrtja/rjilt-jrtja.pdf

Cissner, A., Sasson, E., Thomforde Hauser, R., Packer, H., Pennell, J., Smith, E. L., ... Burford, G. (2019). A national portrait of restorative approaches to intimate partner violence: Pathways to safety, accountability, healing, and well-being. Center for Court Innovation. https://www.courtinnovation.org/sites/default/files/media/document/2019/Report_IPV_12032019.pdf

Davis, R. C. (2009). The Brooklyn mediation field test. *Journal of Experimental Criminology*, 5(1), 25–39. https://doi.org/10.1007/s11292-008-9067-z

Duff, A. (2003). Restoration and retribution. In A. von Hirsch, J. Roberts, A. E. Bottoms, K. Roach, & M. Schiff (Eds.), *Restorative justice and criminal justice: Competing or reconcilable paradigms?* (pp. 43–59). Hart.

Fagan, J. (1996). The criminalization of domestic violence: Promises and limits. https://www.ojp.gov/pdffiles/crimdom.pdf

Fortson, R., & Carbaugh, J. A. (2014). Survey of tribal court effectiveness studies. *Alaska Justice Forum*, 31(3–4), 15–20. http://hdl.handle.net/11122/6575

Fraley, S. (2001). The meaning of reconciliation for prisoners serving long sentences. *Contemporary Justice Review*, 4(1), 59–74.

Hargovan, H. (2010). Doing justice differently: Is restorative justice appropriate for domestic violence? *Acta Criminologica*, 2, 25–41. https://hdl.handle.net/10520/EJC28601

Holder, R. L. (2016). Untangling the meanings of justice: A longitudinal mixed methods study. *Journal of Mixed Methods Research, 12*(2), 204–220. https://doi.org/10.1177/1558689816653308

Hooper, S., & Busch, R. (1996). Domestic violence and the restorative justice initiatives: The risks of a new panacea. *Waikato Law Review, 4*, 101.

Hurley, M. H. (2009). Restorative practices in institutional settings and at release: Victim wrap around programs. *Federal Probation, 73*(1), 16–22.

Johnson, M. P. (2010). *A typology of domestic violence: Intimate terrorism, violent resistance, and situational couple violence*. Northeastern University Press

Johnson, W. L., Giordano, P. C., Manning, W. D., & Longmore, M. A. (2015). The age-IPV curve: Changes in the perpetration of intimate partner violence during adolescence and young adulthood. *Journal of Youth and Adolescence, 44*(3), 708–726. https://doi.org/10.1007/s10964-014-0158-z

Koss, M. P. (2010). Restorative justice for acquaintance rape and misdemeanor sex crimes. In J. Ptacek (Ed.), *Restorative justice and violence against women* (pp. 218–238). Oxford University Press.

Koss, M. P. (2014). The RESTORE program of restorative justice for sex crimes: Vision, process, and outcomes. *Journal of Interpersonal Violence, 29*(9), 1623–1660. https://doi.org/10.1177/0886260513511537

Latimer, J., Dowden, C., & Muise, D. (2005). The effectiveness of restorative justice practices: A meta-analysis. *The Prison Journal, 85*(2), 127–144. https://doi.org/10.1177/0032885505276969

Legal Information Institute. (n.d.). Misdemeanor. https://www.law.cornell.edu/wex/misdemeanor

Leonard, P. B. (2010). An introduction to restorative justice. In E. Beck, N. P. Kropf, & P. B. Leonard (Eds.), *Social work and restorative justice: Skills for dialogue, peacemaking, and reconciliation* (pp. 31–63). Oxford University Press. https://doi.org/10.1093/acprof:oso/9780195394641.001.0001

Lewis, R., Dobash, R. E., Dobash, R. P., & Cavanagh, K. (2001). Law's progressive potential: The value of engagement with the law for domestic violence. *Social & Legal Studies, 10*(1), 105–130. https://doi.org/10.1177/a017834

Liebmann, M. (2007). *Restorative justice: How it works*. Jessica Kingsley.

Lila, M., Gracia, E., & Catalá-Miñana, A. (2018). Individualized motivational plans in batterer intervention programs: A randomized clinical trial. *Journal of Consulting and Clinical Psychology, 86*(4), 309–320. https://doi.org/10.1037/ccp0000291

Lipsky, S., Caetano, R., Field, C. A. & Larkin, G. L. (2006). The role of intimate partner violence, race, and ethnicity in help-seeking behaviors. *Ethnicity and Health, 11*(1), 81–100. https://doi.org/10.1080/13557850500391410

Mills, L. (2008). *Violent partners: A breakthrough plan for ending the cycle of abuse*. Basic Books.

Mills, L. G., Barocas, B., & Ariel, B. (2013). The next generation of court-mandated domestic violence treatment: A comparison study of batterer intervention and restorative justice programs. *Journal of Experimental Criminology, 9*(1), 65–90. https://doi.org/10.1007/s11292-012-9164-x

Mills, L. G., Barocas, B., Butters, R. P., & Ariel, B. (2019). A randomized controlled trial of restorative justice-informed treatment for domestic violence crimes. *Nature Human Behaviour, 3*(12), 1284–1294. https://doi.org/10.1038/s41562-019-0724-1

National Conference of State Legislatures. (2017). Pretrial diversion. https://www.ncsl.org/research/civil-and-criminal-justice/pretrial-diversion.aspx

Olson, K. B. (2009). Family group conferencing and child protection mediation: Essential tools for prioritizing family engagement in child welfare cases. *Family Court Review*, *47*(1), 53–68. https://doi.org/10.1111/j.1744-1617.2009.00239.x

Overstreet, N. M., & Quinn, D. M. (2013). The intimate partner violence stigmatization model and barriers to help seeking. *Basic and Applied Social Psychology*, *35*(1), 109–122. https://doi.org/10.1080/01973533.2012.746599

Pennell, J., & Burford, G. (2000). Family group decision making: Protecting children and women. *Child Welfare*, *79*(2), 131–158.

Pennell, J., Burford, G., Sasson, E., Packer, H., & Smith, E. L. (2021). Family and community approaches to intimate partner violence: Restorative programs in the United States. *Violence Against Women*, *27*(10), 1608–1629. https://doi.org/10.1177/1077801220945030

Ptacek, J. (2009). *Restorative justice and violence against women*. Oxford University Press.

Richards, K. (2009). Taking victims seriously? The role of victims' rights movements in the emergence of restorative justice. *Current Issues in Criminal Justice*, *21*(2), 302–320. https://doi.org/10.1080/10345329.2009.12035847

Romero-Martínez, A., Lila, M., Garcia, E., & Moya-Albiol, L. (2018). Improving empathy with motivational strategies in batterer intervention programmes: Results of a randomized controlled trial. *British Journal of Clinical Psychology*, *58*(2), 125–139. https://doi.org/10.1111/bjc.12204

Rosay, A. B. (2016) Violence against American Indian and Alaska native women and men. *National Institute of Justice Journal*, *277*, 38–45. http://hdl.handle.net/11122/7030

Rugge, T., & Cormier, R. (2013). Restorative justice in cases of serious crime: An evaluation. In E. Elliott & R. M. Gordon (Eds.), *New directions in restorative justice* (pp. 290–301). Wilan.

Sadusky, J. (2003). Prosecution diversion in domestic violence: Issues and context. https://www.bwjp.org/assets/documents/pdfs/prosecution_diversion_domestic_violence_cases.pdf

Sasson, E. (2016). Can restorative practices address intimate partner violence? Summary of a roundtable discussion. Center for Court Innovation. https://www.courtinnovation.org/sites/default/files/documents/Intimate_Partner_Restorative_Roundtable.pdf

Sasson, E., & Allen, C. (2020). Using restorative approaches to address intimate partner violence. Center for Court Innovation. https://www.courtinnovation.org/publications/restorative-approaches-address-intimate-partner-violence

Satyen, L., Rogic, A. C., & Supol, M. (2019). Intimate partner violence and help-seeking behaviour: A systematic review of cross-cultural differences. *Journal of Immigrant and Minority Health*, *21*(4), 879–892. https://doi.org/10.1007/s10903-018-0803-9

Stubbs, J. (2002). Domestic violence and women's safety: Feminist challenges to restorative justice. In H. Strang & J. Braithwaite (Eds.), *Restorative justice and family violence* (pp. 42–61). Cambridge University Press.

Travis, J., Western, B., & Redburn, S. (2014). *The growth of incarceration in the United States*. The National Academies Press.

Umbreit, M. (1994). *Victim meets offender: The impact of restorative justice in mediation*. Criminal Justice Press.

United Nations. (2006). Handbook on restorative justice programmes. https://www.unodc.org/pdf/criminal_justice/Handbook_on_Restorative_Justice_Programmes.pdf

US Department of Justice. (n.d.). Domestic violence. https://www.justice.gov/ovw/domestic-violence

US Department of Justice. (1998). National Institute of Justice Restorative Justice Symposia Summary. https://www.ojp.gov/pdffiles1/nij/248890.pdf

US Department of Justice. (2001). A comparison of four restorative conferencing models. https://www.ojp.gov/pdffiles1/ojjdp/184738.pdf

US Department of Justice. (2020a). Criminal victimization, 2019. https://www.bjs.gov/content/pub/pdf/cv19.pdf

US Department of Justice. (2020b). The Violence Against Women Act—An ongoing fixture in the nation's response to domestic violence, dating violence, sexual assault, and stalking. https://www.justice.gov/archives/ovw/blog/violence-against-women-act-ongoing-fixture-nation-s-response-domestic-violence-dating

Van Wormer, K. (2006). The case for restorative justice: A crucial adjunct to the social work curriculum. *Journal of Teaching in Social Work*, 26(3–4), 57–69. https://doi.org/10.1300/J067v26n03_04

Van Wormer, K. (2009). Restorative justice as social justice for victims of gendered violence: A standpoint feminist perspective. *Social Work*, 54(2), 107–116. https://doi.org/10.1093/sw/54.2.107

The Vermont Network Against Domestic and Sexual Violence. (2019). Final report to the general assembly of the restorative justice study committee. https://legislature.vermont.gov/Documents/2020/WorkGroups/Justice%20Oversight/Incarceration%20Issues/W~Sarah%20Robinson~Final%20Report%20of%20the%20Restorative%20Justice%20Study%20Committee~9-6-2019.pdf

Wachtel, T., & McCold, P. (2001). Restorative justice in everyday life. In H. Strang & J. Braithwaite (Eds.), *Restorative justice and civil society* (pp. 114–129). Cambridge University Press.

Wolthuis, A., & Lünnemann, K. (2016). Restorative justice and domestic violence: A guide for practitioners. https://www.unodc.org/e4j/data/_university_uni_/restorative_justice_and_domestic_violence_a_guide_for_practitioners.html?lng=en

Washington County Community Circles. (2021). Types of circles. https://www.peacemakingcircles.org/types-of-circles

World Health Organization. (2021). Violence and injury prevention. https://www.who.int/violence_injury_prevention/violence/sexual/en/

Zehr, H. (1990). A restorative lens. In H. Zehr (Ed.), *Changing lenses: A new focus for crime and justice* (pp. 177–214). Herald Press.

Zehr, H., & Mika, H. (1998). Fundamental concepts of restorative justice. In D. Roche (Ed.), *Restorative justice* (pp. 73–81). Routledge.

AFTERWORD: RECOMMENDATIONS AND RESOURCES

JOHN HAMEL, BRENDA RUSSELL,
DON DUTTON, AND JENNIFER COX ■

The promise of social progress that includes a criminal justice system based on rational ethical principles, products of the Enlightenment period in France and England, and reflected in the US Declaration of Independence and the Constitution, has yet to be fully met. Despite the gradual expansion of rights for individuals who have been traditionally oppressed and marginalized due to their social class, ethnicity, sex, gender identification, or sexual orientation, progress has been slow, uneven, and often obstructed by setbacks. Consider, for example, that individuals with scant financial resources, among them African Americans and other ethnic minority groups, have reduced access to competent legal representation, or that sexual harassment of women has only recently been given the attention it deserves. As well, despite federal laws providing same-sex couples the right to marry, it is still legal in many states for employers to deny employment to individuals based on their sexual orientation. One glaring exception is the change in child custody laws that once favored fathers but now discriminates against them, often to the detriment of children. The evolution of domestic violence arrest and intervention policies can best be understood as a subset of these general trends.

Before the 1980s, the law enforcement response to violence between married, cohabitating, or dating couples was weak and inadequate. Domestic violence was regarded mostly as a private matter. Police were reluctant to arrest offenders, presuming they were innocent or required at most some admonishment and a request to go for a walk and "cool off." In this period, it was the rights of victims that were compromised, and as now, it was women who endured the most severe assaults and were most at risk of being killed. The Battered Women's Movement brought much-needed attention to this problem, leading to widespread judicial reforms throughout the United States that would better protect victims and hold offenders accountable.

However, with the advent of mandatory arrest, no-drop prosecution, and confusing, ideologically driven dominant aggressor laws, the overly zealous protection of victims increasingly began to compromise the rights of the accused, mostly men but often women, and ironically weakening the effectiveness of the very policies designed to protect victims. This occurred, as discussed in the introductory chapter of this volume, despite early research by Straus and others documenting the high rates of female-perpetrated and bidirectional domestic violence. Happily, research challenging the gender paradigm would continue, occasionally finding its way into some of the peer-reviewed journals. Among the first wave of publications that traditional stakeholders could not ignore were investigations into the phenomena of same-sex domestic violence, compelling arguments by feminist therapists for the viability of couples counseling, the demand for family-oriented interventions by clinicians working with Latino families, and a growing typology literature finding domestic violence to not be the unitary phenomenon previously assumed (Hamel, 2007, 2019).

Along the way, results of several large-scale national surveys, comprehensive literature reviews, and meta-analyses vindicated and expanded upon the early research by Straus and colleagues on rates of physical abuse, revealing indisputable evidence of gender symmetry in rates of psychological abuse, risk factors, motivation, and the long-term repercussions of witnessed violence on children. These results are now accepted, with minor exceptions, as settled social science by the mainstream research community. They are cited by reform-minded legal reformers and treatment providers (see later discussion) and, occasionally, by traditional victim organizations who now cite results from the National Intimate Partner and Sexual Violence Survey (NISVS) rather than referring to misleading and outdated crime statistics. Evidence of progress toward the recognition of intimate partner violence (IPV) as a human problem is evident as the Violence Against Women Act (VAWA) was finally amended in 2013 to allow for the funding of services for male and LGBTQ+ victims, establishing "a nondiscrimination provision to ensure that victims are not denied services and are not subjected to discrimination based on actual or perceived race, color, religion, national origin, sex, gender identity, sexual orientation, or disability" (Sacco, 2019, p. 18). Progress is also evident in the states of Colorado and Washington, where one-size-fits-all perpetrator treatment programs have been replaced with a group model based on risk-needs-responsivity (RNR) principles.

Real progress, however, has only begun, and there is sure to be resistance in some quarters for even the most modest calls for reform. Still, the research presented in this volume demands that current policies be recalibrated so that victim safety and offender accountability can be balanced with the rights of criminal defendants, with safeguards against overpolicing and legal system abuse (e.g., by parents involved in child custody cases). We believe that this can be done only in a collective effort among all domestic violence stakeholders, and only with a firm commitment to the research evidence. Following are our recommendations for judicial reform of arrest and prosecution policies, followed by a list of

ARREST AND PROSECUTION

Presumption of Innocence

Individuals who call the police to report an incident of domestic violence cannot be assumed always to be the actual victim, given the various motives, especially among disputed child custody litigants, to fabricate, exaggerate, or otherwise distort the events in question. Unless they have been adjudicated as victims, they remain *complainants* and should be legally regarded as such, including within the family court system unless compelling evidence to the contrary is evident. The states of California, New York, New Jersey, and Connecticut have enacted statutes making it illegal to make false 911 reports of harassment based on race, sex, or sexual orientation. The remaining states should pass similar legislation.

Arrest versus No Arrest

- *No Physical Aggression.* Complaints that do not involve actual physical aggression are made not only by those who seek to profit from false or exaggerated allegations, but sometimes from high-conflict couples who naively expect the police to act as mediators in their disputes or by neighbors concerned about a loud argument. In general, no arrest ought to be made in abuse incidents that are nonphysical and involve no previous domestic violence calls or outstanding warrants. In such cases, police should proceed according to procedures of *deflection*, currently employed in over 250 jurisdictions nationwide. As described in the article by Charlier (2017) of the John Jay College of Criminal Justice, this entails the provision of domestic violence resources, including contact information on local shelters, mental health treatment, and helplines for both victims and perpetrators. The most widely known hotline for victims is the National Domestic Violence Hotline (see http://www.thehotline.org). For perpetrators, actual or potential, a listing of hotlines, including the 10 to 10 Helpline, can be found in Tadepalli (2021). Police officers on the scene should advise the parties to avail themselves of these resources, according to their needs.
- *Minor Injury, First Offense.* First-time domestic violence offenses that involve allegations of physical violence, but where there are no visible physical injuries, or minor injuries, should be processed according to the deflection procedure described earlier unless there is evidence of fear among either party and the officer reasonably suspects that there is a possibility of further aggression, as evidenced, for example, by continued

displays of anger, impairment due to alcohol or drug use, or emotional or mental instability. In such cases, the officer should proceed with the steps outlined later.

- *Low Injury, Previous Arrest.* In cases that do not involve the infliction of serious physical injury, but where one person has previously been arrested but not convicted of a domestic violence charge, depending on the state/jurisdiction, the responding police officer should issue a civil citation or otherwise refer the parties for further assessment (Young et al., 2007), after which it can be determined in a thorough assessment whether he or she would be a suitable candidate for *diversion*, in which prosecution is deferred and the guilty plea withdrawn upon successful completion of a treatment program. The officer on the scene should also strongly encourage a voluntary period of separation and provide the parties instructions and assistance on how to obtain a restraining order, find temporary shelter, and enlist the aid of a victim advocate.

  Unless there is compelling physical evidence for unilateral violence by one party, police should cite both persons, and the type of diversion program offered, if any, to one or both parties, should be determined through the formal assessment process. This alternative to immediate arrest avoids the unnecessary detention of individuals who pose no immediate risk to their partner, allowing them to continue working, reduces jail populations, saves governmental resources for use in the prosecution of more serious offenders, and provides victims with additional resources. Unless it undermines victim interests, diversion is a useful approach to reducing rates of domestic violence (Winick, 2001). The various types of diversion programs, currently offered in jurisdictions across the country, are summarized in Camilletti (2010).

  Assessment for treatment diversion should be conducted by experienced mental health professionals with forensic experience and expertise in the area of family violence, including knowledge of best practices in the treatment of perpetrators, victims, and their families. They should be aware of the advantages and limitations of all treatment modalities—group, individual, couple, family, and restorative justice—as discussed in this volume and elsewhere. Examples of how such assessments can be conducted, either presentencing or postsentencing, can be found in the current Colorado State standards for batterer intervention (Colorado Domestic Violence Offender Management Board, 2021).

- *Moderate to Severe Injury or Previous Conviction.* Arrest should be made according to traditional procedures in cases where there is moderate to serious physical injury to a victim, or minor injury with a previous domestic violence conviction. However, dual arrests should not be discouraged. Without evidence that one party responded strictly in self-defense, a mutual arrest should be made where both parties have engaged in physical assaults, and both persons should be considered for prosecution. Whether or not one party may have been the predominant aggressor in the relationship should not be determined by the arresting officer. This should instead be decided by the prosecuting team, using only validated, research-based instruments, who would then have the option of drawing upon such information in their sentencing and treatment recommendations.

Police Training

As discussed in the chapter by Hamel and Ennis (Chapter 11, this volume), police officers are notoriously deficient in accurately assessing a suspect's guilt or innocence generally; and as documented by Hamel and Russell (2013), training programs for law enforcement officers generally contain information on domestic violence that is outdated, inaccurate, or outright biased. This can be addressed by adding appropriate language to the Violence Against Women Act, such as what has previously been proposed (Congress.Gov, 2013): "Requirement for scientifically valid programs. — All grant funds made available by this Act shall be used to provide scientifically valid educational programming, training, and public awareness communications regarding domestic violence, dating violence, sexual assault, and stalking that is produced by accredited entities, as appropriate."

Prosecution Policies

Current "no-drop" prosecution policies, while perhaps well-intended, have been roundly criticized by a broad spectrum of domestic violence stakeholders, including victim advocates, because they reduce the rate of successful prosecution, with the effect of both compromising the due process rights of the accused and making victims less safe from potentially dangerous offenders (e.g., Mills, 2003). According to the National District Attorneys Association (NDAA):

> In some communities, prosecutors have attempted to implement a no-drop policy, advocating for the filing of all cases and refusing to dismiss any cases once charges are filed. The NDAA does not support this approach. Neither the American Bar Association standards nor the filing standards for the NDAA support the prosecution of cases when the evidence does not support a reasonable likelihood of conviction. (National District Attorneys Association, 2020, p. 13)

Both deflection and diversion, discussed previously, are reasonable alternatives in cases where victim safety is an issue, but there is either insufficient evidence or victim resistance to prosecution.

INTERVENTION

States are encouraged to revise their standards for the treatment of individuals convicted of domestic violence based on empirical evidence. A comprehensive review of the prevalence, causes, dynamics, and consequences of domestic violence, their implications for effective treatment, and recommendations for intervention standards based on this evidence can be found in Babcock et al. (2016). As this review indicates, and as described at length in the chapters included in Part IV of this volume, interventions for perpetrators, whether in the context of a deferred prosecution agreement or postconviction, should explicitly reject a rigid "one-size-fits-all" approach and instead feature the following:

- The type and duration of the intervention should be based on the needs of the perpetrator, based on a thorough assessment conducted by mental health professionals who have expertise in the area of family violence, including the research on best practices as mentioned earlier.
- Interventions should generally follow the risk-need-responsivity (RNR) principles that for many years have guided treatment for general correctional populations and conform to current typology research. This research reveals a wide range of offender types, ranging from those whose violence is rare, poses minimal risks to the partner, and occurs within the context of normal interpersonal conflict, to more dangerous, repeat offenders with serious mental health and personality disorders.
- It should be acknowledged that the psychoeducational group format, currently the primary treatment modality for perpetrator treatment, has its limitations as well as its advantages, and should be required only for clients who in fact might benefit. As well, there are large differences among the primary models (e.g., Duluth, cognitive-behavioral therapy, trauma-informed) and no single model is appropriate for everyone, even when conducted according to best practice standards—for example, compelling an egalitarian man to attend a Duluth-type program. Other modalities, such as individual, couples, family, or restorative justice, should be considered based on the particular needs of the client and the likelihood of treatment success.
- Treatment providers should first become officially certified after completing an appropriate training program. Such a program ought to include information on all aspects of domestic violence prevalence, dynamics, consequences, assessment, and treatment, including the role of victim service programs, and accurately reflect the extant body of empirical research (see Resources section).
- Additionally, intervention programs should only be conducted by licensed mental health professionals with substantial training in the particular modality they are working in, whether group or otherwise. An exception may be made for those who conduct strictly educational

groups, who would be permitted to work under the supervision of a licensed mental health professional with a minimum of a master's degree.

REFORM INITIATIVES

A number of promising reform initiatives have been launched around the country, even if not all focused specifically on domestic violence, and not necessarily including the precise recommendations outlined earlier. Following the police killings of George Floyd and other African Americans, as well as the less publicized killings of other suspects under dubious circumstances, a number of initiatives have been launched to reform current policies on arrest, prosecution, and intervention for the alleged perpetration of various violent crimes. Recently, nearly every established state coalition against domestic violence assault in the United States (46) has endorsed the Moment of Truth declaration by the Wisconsin Coalition Against Sexual Assault, which dresses the many shortcomings of current domestic violence policies as they impact upon the African American community. "We have," the document declares, "promoted false solutions of reforming systems that are designed to control people, rather than real community-based solutions that support healing and liberation" (see https://www.endabusewi.org/moment-of-truth/). In a similar vein, the MacArthur Foundation is working to reduce jail incarceration by promoting diversion programs, second-look hearings, bail reform, drug treatment, re-entry programs, and mental health services. The goal of their Safety and Justice Challenge is "to support policies and practices that will safely reduce jail populations by 50% ... by 2025 and eliminate racial inequities" (see https://safetyandjusticechallenge.org/).

While these specific initiatives focus on racial and ethnic minority populations, they are relevant to all marginalized low socioeconomic status (SES) populations, and ought to appeal to a broad range of stakeholders. Enacted into law in February 2021, the Illinois Pretrial Fairness Act, crafted by the Network Advocating Against Domestic Violence, acknowledges that "it is long past time that the criminal justice system learns how to accurately, fairly, and in a non-racist or classist manner, attend to the real threats that people charged with a crime do or do not pose" (see https://citizennewspapergroup.com/news/2021/feb/05/advocates-domestic-violence-survivors-join-illinoi/). The National Association of Social Workers (NASW) issued a social justice brief online, *Reimagining Policing: Strategies for Community Reinvestment*, in which they reaffirm the role of social workers as agents of change who can advocate for "the implementation of police reform models that can have a mitigating impact on reducing police encounters." In this report, we are reminded that although police are not licensed mental health professionals, they nevertheless remain the "de facto response to situations that call for social work intervention. Issues of drug use, homelessness, mental illness, and domestic violence disputes all too frequently lead to police responses. Tragically, we have seen over and over how these calls lead to harmful escalation instead of peaceful resolution" (see https://www.socialworkers.org/LinkClick.aspx?fileticket=WTrDbQ6CHxI%3D&portalid=0).

A new law was recently passed in the state of California that promises to provide funding for expanded community-based alternatives to policing, including funds for organizations that are capable of addressing domestic violence incidents outside the usual arrest and prosecution procedures of the criminal justice system. The first section of this Community Response Initiative to Strengthen Emergency Systems Act states:

> The complexities of emergency issues surrounding crises in mental health, intimate partner violence, community violence, substance abuse, and natural disasters can, at times, be addressed more safely, with greater impact, and more cost-effectively and efficiently with community organizations, which often have deeper knowledge and understanding of the issues, trusted relationships with the people and communities involved, and specific knowledge and relationships surrounding the emergency. (California Legislative Information, 2020)

Elsewhere, the Right on Crime organization, whose name suggests its political leanings, has published a number of reports calling for diversion programs and similar criminal justice reforms. "Incarceration," they reiterate, "is a significant and necessary factor in public safety." Other factors, however, are necessary. In fact, a "strategy of vigorous, data-driven law enforcement that results in more crimes being deterred and solved—coupled with effective probation strategies that emphasize restitution, work, and treatment—is essential for protecting communities" (see https://rightoncrime.com/the-conservative-case-for-reform/). More recently, reform recommendations have been advanced before Congress during testimony in October 2021 on reauthorization of the Violence Against Women Act, supported by many lawmakers, including calls for restorative justice programs by Vermont senator and former prosecutor Patrick Leahy (see http://endtodv.org/pr/cedv-commends-sen-patrick-leahy-for-leading-drive-to-include-restorative-justice-in-vawa-bill/).

RESOURCES

The influence of the National Coalition Against Domestic Violence (NCADV; see https://www.ncadv.org/) and its state affiliates on domestic violence arrest, prosecution, and intervention policy cannot be underestimated. While its fealty to the prevailing gender paradigm is evident throughout their pages, and the research data presented are often suspect (e.g., Hines, 2014), the websites on both the national and state levels remain important sources of information on available resources and current trends in arrest, prosecution, and intervention policy. Still, readers are strongly encouraged to familiarize themselves with alternative sources of information, as outlined here:

- The most comprehensive and accurate sources of information on domestic violence prevalence, dynamics, risk factors, assessment, and treatment are the results from the National Intimate Partner and Sexual Violence Survey (NISVS) and the Partner Abuse State of Knowledge Project (PASK), which can be found at www.domesticviolenceresearch.org. For those who desire an even broader understanding of domestic violence, the website also provides contact information for some of the most respected scholars worldwide, who are publishing the most cutting-edge research in the field.
- Stop Abuse for Everyone (https://www.stopabuseforeveryone.org/) offers supportive victim services and referrals, to "anyone regardless of age, race, gender, or sexual orientation." They have a speaker's bureau of renowned experts available to provide training and information on a variety of topics related to domestic violence, as well as a comprehensive national directory of resources for undeserved victims. The National Coalition of Anti-Violence Programs (NCAVP), now in its fortieth year, provides support and resources specifically for LGBTQ+ victims of violence, including violence in intimate relationships (see https://avp.org/ncavp/), as does the Gay Men's Domestic Violence Project (see http://gmdvp.org/gmdvp/).
- How family courts can better resolve disputed child custody cases involving accusations of domestic abuse is a primary concern of the International Council on Shared Parenting (https://icsp.erisunleashed.com/).
- The website of the Association of Domestic Violence Intervention Providers (ADVIP), an international organization whose motto is "Holding Perpetrators Accountable, Keeping Victims Safe," at www.domesticviolenceintervention.net, showcases a wealth of peer-reviewed research, podcasts, and videos on best practices in perpetrator intervention. For more information on ongoing efforts to reform the criminal justice system, the interested reader is referred to the Coalition to End Domestic Violence at https://endtodv.org/.

CONCLUSION

Domestic violence laws, as currently written, have been unduly influenced by ideologues for both the gender paradigm and overzealous policing practices on all sides of the political spectrum. These laws are badly written, loosely grounded in the body of empirical evidence, or unevenly applied and, ultimately, unfair legally and therapeutically inadequate. In universal human rights terms, the gender paradigm has fostered injustice for men and sexual minority groups just as still-present inequities in the criminal justice system have had deleterious consequences for low-SES and ethnic minority populations. A group can enjoy a higher overall degree of privilege compared to other groups and yet suffer discrimination, as documented in this book with respect to men accused of a domestic violence offense; and at the same time, certain marginalized subpopulations may find themselves at a disadvantage within a larger marginalized subgroup, as was the case for women of color throughout the first decades of the Battered Women's Movement, whose principles and tactics were decided mostly by bourgeois Whites. It is expressly prohibited by the Equal Protection Clause of the Fourteenth Amendment to the US Constitution for any state to deny individuals their basic rights, and proscribes that an individual be treated as any other person in similar circumstances. Civil libertarians understand this, and it is high time for all domestic violence stakeholders to unequivocally embrace this fundamental legal principle. It is the right and proper thing to do and essential to our collective efforts to competently reduce the intergenerational transmission of domestic violence.

REFERENCES

Babcock, J., Cannon, C., Lauve-Moon, K., Ferreira, R., Cantos, A., Hamel, J., Kelly, D., Leisring, P.A., Murphy, C., O'Leary, K.D., Bannon, S., Salis, K. L., & Solono, I. (2016). Domestic violence perpetrator programs: A proposal for evidence-based standards in the United States. *Partner Abuse, 7*(4), 1–107.

California Legislative Information. (2020). AB-2054 Emergency services: Community response grant program. https://leginfo.legislature.ca.gov/faces/billCompareClient.xhtml?bill_id=201920200AB2054&showamends=false

Camilletti, C. (2010). Pretrial diversion programs research summary. Bureau of Justice Assistance, U.S. Department of Justice. https://bja.ojp.gov/sites/g/files/xyckuh186/files/media/document/PretrialDiversionResearchSummary.pdf

Charlier, J. (2017, March). The "deflection" surge: Key to reducing re-arrests. The Crime Report. Center on Media, Crime and Justice at the John Jay College of Criminal Justice. https://thecrimereport.org/2017/03/21/the-deflection-surge-key-to-reducing-re-arrests/

Colorado Domestic Violence Offender Management Board. (2021). Standards and guidelines for the assessment, evaluation, treatment, and behavioral monitoring of domestic violence offenders. https://cdpsdocs.state.co.us/dcj/DCJ%20External%20Website/DVOMB/DVOMB%20Standards%20(2.23.2021).pdf

Congress.Gov (2013, February). Vol. 159, No. 19, Daily Edition. https://www.congress.gov/congressional-record/2013/02/07/senate-section/article/S528-2

Hamel, J. (2007). Gender inclusive family interventions in domestic violence: An overview. In J. Hamel & T. Nicholls (Eds.), *Family interventions in domestic violence: A handbook of gender-inclusive theory and treatment* (pp. 247–274). Springer.

Hamel, J. (2019). The evolution of evidence-based treatment for domestic violence perpetrators. In E. A. Bates & J. C. Taylor (Eds.), *Intimate partner violence: New perspectives in research and practice* (pp. 89–106). Routledge.

Hamel, J., & Russell, B. (2013). The Partner Abuse State of Knowledge Project: Implications for law enforcement responses to domestic violence. In B. Russell (Ed.), *Perceptions of female offenders: How stereotypes and social norms affect criminal justice responses* (pp. 151–180). Springer.

Hines, D. (2014). Extent and implications of the presentation of false facts by domestic violence agencies in the United States. *Partner Abuse, 5*(1), 69–82.

Mills, L. (2003). *Insult to injury: Rethinking our responses to intimate abuse.* Princeton University Press.

National District Attorneys Association. (2020). The national domestic violence prosecution best practices guide. https://ndaa.org/wp-content/uploads/NDAA-DV-White-Paper-FINAL-revised-June-23-2020-1.pdf

Sacco, L. N. (2019). The Violence Against Women Act (VAWA): Historical overview, funding, and reauthorization. Congressional Research Services. https://www.everycrsreport.com/files/20190423_R45410_672f9e33bc12ac7ff52d47a8e6bd974d96e92f02.pdf

Tadepalli, S. (2021, October 29). These organizations want to help survivors of domestic violence—without calling the police. *The Lily.* https://www.thelily.com/these-organizations-want-to-help-survivors-of-domestic-violence-without-calling-the-police/?

Winick, B. (2001). Applying the law therapeutically in domestic violence cases. *UMKC Law Review, 69*(1), 33–92.

Young, C., Cook, P., Smith, S., Turteltaub, J., & Hazelwood, L. R. (2007). Domestic violence: New visions, new solutions. In J. Hamel & T. Nicholls (Eds.), *Family interventions in domestic violence: A handbook of gender-inclusive theory and treatment* (pp. 601–620). Springer.

INDEX

For the benefit of digital users, indexed terms that span two pages (e.g., 52–53) may, on occasion, appear on only one of those pages.

Tables and figures are indicated by *t* and *f* following the page number

10 to 10 Helpline, 401

ABA. *See* American Bar Association
abandonment homicide, 145
Abramsky, T., 31
abusive victims, 220
adverse childhood experiences (ACEs), 31–33, 211
ADVIP. *See* Association of Domestic Violence Intervention Providers
AFCC. *See* Association of Family and Conciliation Courts
age of denial, 22
AHIMSA Collective, 383
American Bar Association (ABA)
  focus on rights of female victims, 4–5
  prosecution policies, 403
  rewriting judicial instructions, 186
American Psychological Association (APA), 244, 246, 248
Anderson, E. A., 101
anger management programs
  as alternative to prosecution, 123, 337
  versus batterer intervention programs, 12–13, 338
  child abuse and, 221
  in child custody litigation, 257, 260–61, 262*t*, 265
  criminogenic needs, indicators, and intervention goals, 346*t*
  motivation for participation, 265
antisocial personality disorder (APD), 236, 345, 346*t*, 352–53
anxiety over abandonment, 236
APA. *See* American Psychological Association
Appel, A. E., 40
Archer, J., 24–25, 130–31
Arias, I., 24
arrest and prosecution policies. *See also* prosecutorial discretion
  effect of gender paradigm on, 4–5
  evidence-based prosecution, 95
  limited effectiveness of, 12–13
  mandatory arrest, proarrest, and discretionary arrest, 61–64
  need for empirically-based, 8–9
  no-drop policies, 11, 94–95, 403
  recommendations and resources
    arrest versus no arrest, 401–3
    police training, 403
    presumption of innocence, 401
    prosecution policies, 403
  as undermining to defendant rights, 9–12
  vertical prosecution, 95

Asch, S. E., 184
assessment. *See also* risk assessment for IPV
  of alienated children, 284–87
  behavioral assessment standards in BIPs, 342–44
  Danger Assessment (DA) Scale, 145–46
  evidence-based, 242
  Five-Factor Model for parental alienation, 284–87
  Four-Factor Model for parental alienation, 256
  instruments for, 319–20
  Mediator's Assessment of Safety Issues and Concerns (MASIC), 248, 250
  Miller Forensic Assessment of Symptoms Test (M-FAST), 249
  Partial Parenting Plan Assessment, 221–22
  perpetrator assessment procedures
    considerations in interviewing suspects, 315–20
    creating and maintaining correct environment, 311–12
    deception detection research, 308–9
    detecting deception, 312–14
    establishing trust and cooperation, 310–11
    evidence-based interviewing, 309–10
    motives for anger, 318*t*
    overcoming assumptions concerning IPV, 307–8
    overview of, 328–29
    risk assessment, 320–28
    strategic use of evidence, 314–15
    why IPV is underdetected, 315*t*
  Personality Assessment Inventory (PAI), 248–49
Association of Domestic Violence Intervention Providers (ADVIP), 407
Association of Family and Conciliation Courts (AFCC), 234, 236, 244–46, 248, 254
attachment-enhancing behaviors, 279–80
attachment theory, 144–45, 317
Austin, W., 237–38, 242–43
automodulation of rage, 145

Babcock, J., 404
background checks, 226
BAI. *See* Behavior Analysis Interview
Baker, A. J. L., 279
Baker, Amy, 256
Balanced Inventory of Desirable Responding (BIDR), 319
Bandyopadhyay, S., 101
Barner, J. R., 28–29
Basow, S. A., 92
Bates, E. A., 25, 27, 28, 29, 30, 43, 170–71
battered woman/battered person syndrome
  definition of term, 137
  expert testimony and, 130, 188–91
  intimate partner homicide and, 146–49
  jury decision-making and, 177
  not admitted as evidence, 189
  questions prosecutors should consider, 100
  versus retribution in mutual abuse, 141
  stereotypes associated with, 177
  weak evidence for existence of, 147–48
Battered Women's Movement
  advocation for police response to IPV, 60–61
  long-lasting value achieved by, 8–9
  recognition of contributors of domestic violence, 60
batterer intervention programs (BIPs)
  emphasis of gender role factors in, 12–13
  interventions in child custody litigation, 262*t*
  male versus female requirements for, 234
  risk-needs-responsivity-informed approaches
    assessment and treatment framework, 341–42
    behavioral assessment standards, 342–44
    cognitive-behavioral treatment approach, 345–47
    core competencies and completion criteria, 347–48
    criminogenic needs, indicators, and intervention goals, 346*t*

Index

differentiated treatment model, 344t, 344–45
education and training requirements, 340–41
individualized IPV treatment in state of Washington, 347f
recognized treatment modalities, 337
traditional versus alternative treatments, 337–40
variations in, 260–61
battering
  definition of term, 236
  forms of, 237
Beckmann, L., 42
Behavior Analysis Interview (BAI), 308–9
benevolent sexist ideologies, 8
Berk, R., 61–62
Bernet, W., 279, 291
best interest of the child (BIC), 214–17, 231–33
Bet Tzedek, 212
bias, overcoming in courtrooms
  ability to leave relationship, 169–71
  confrontational versus nonconfrontational situations, 168
  controlling and coercive behaviors, 172–73
  decision-making in juries, 181–85
  definition of IPH, 166
  expert testimony, 188–91
  gender symmetry in IPV, 171–72
  heterosexual males and LGBTQ+ victimization, 178–80
  imminent danger requirement, 167–68
  judicial instructions, 185–87
  motivations for IPV and IPH, 174
  nontypical victims and perpetrators, 177–78
  overview of, 191–92
  race, ethnicity, and socioeconomic differences, 180–81
  role of defendant gender, 178
  role of juror gender, 187–88
  self-defense argument, 166–67
  stereotypes and scripts, 174–77
  stereotypes surrounding IPV, 165–66
  use of deadly force, 169
Bibas, S., 87

bidirectional violence, 27–29, 91, 134–35
Biehal, N., 42–43
BIPs. *See* batterer intervention programs
Bishop, D. M., 101
Black, M., 28–29
Block, C. R., 142
Bond, C., 308–9
borderline personality disorder (BPD), 144–45, 236, 352–53
Bornstein, B. H., 186
Bow, J., 242
Bowlby, J., 144
Boxer, P., 242
BPS. *See* battered woman/battered person syndrome
Brannen, S. J., 355–58
Brief Spousal Assault Form for the Evaluation of Risk (B-SAFER), 323–24
Bruns, D., 73
B-SAFER. *See* Brief Spousal Assault Form for the Evaluation of Risk
Bushway, S. D., 86–87
BWS. *See* battered woman/battered person syndrome

California Association of Family and Conciliation Courts, 259
California Family Code
  Code 3020, 216
  Code 3044, 210, 212–13, 216, 231–32
  Code 6032, 232
  Code 6345, 213
California Law Enforcement Telecommunications System (CLETS), 226
California POST manual (California Commission on Peace Officer Standards and Training), 68
Calvete, E., 361
Campbell, A., 25–26
Campbell, J., 145–46
Campbell, L., 243
Capaldi, D. M., 31, 32, 33
CAPRD. *See* child affected by parental relationship distress
Carney, M. M., 28–29
Carolla, M., 261–64

CCV. *See* controlling-coercive violence
Center for Court Innovation, 384
Chambers, C., 290
characterological violence, 353–54
child affected by parental relationship distress (CAPRD), 282–83
child custody
  gender-inclusive recommendations
    best interest of the child standards, 231–33
    case studies, 229–30
    challenges of evaluating claims, 230–31
    complexities of family abuse, 239–41
    custody protocols, 243–56
    custody recommendations, 256–65, 262t
    evaluation procedures, 242–43
    gender paradigm and, 231
    lack of accurate knowledge about IPV, 233–35
    psychological abuse and coercive control, 238–39
    recognition of need for change, 231
    typologies, 235–38
  litigation guidelines
    best interest of the child, 214–17
    challenges of litigation, 222–25
    child custody evaluators and other experts, 219–20
    constitutional rights involved, 213–14
    costs of litigation, 212
    custody and parental rights, 212–13
    effects of domestic violence, 211–12
    intersection of domestic violence and child custody, 210–11
    key questions, 217–19
    range of domestic violence and abuse, 208–10
    restraining orders, 220
    role of co-issues, 221–22
    suggestions to improve current system, 225–27
child custody evaluations (CCEs), 219–20, 233–35, 242–43
child maltreatment (CM), links to other types of family violence, 38–40. *See also* parental alienation
children
  impact of IPV on, 35–38
  interventions for witnessing IPV, 361
Children's Exposure to Domestic Violence (CEDV), 249
child-to-parent violence (CPV), links to other types of family violence, 38–40
Christakos, A., 142
chronic batterers, 143
Circles of Peace (CP), 360, 380–81, 387–88
classification schemes. *See* typologies
Clawar, S., 256
CLETS. *See* California Law Enforcement Telecommunications System
Cluster B personality disorders, 352–53
coabuse, 91
coercive control, 171, 208, 238–39, 353–54
cognitive-behavioral approach, 338–39, 345–47, 347f
"Cognitive Behavioral Treatment Guide for Intimate Partner Violence" (Univ. of Washington), 345–46
Cognitive Interview, 309
common battering, 237
common couple violence, 27, 67
communication skills, 352, 354–55
Community Response Initiative to Strengthen Emergency Systems Act, 406
Concealment of Mate, 138
Conflict Tactics Scales (CTS), 23–26, 248, 314–15, 316
confrontational situations, 168
conjoint counseling, 261–65, 262t
constitutional rights, 10, 213–14
Controlling and Abusive Tactics Questionnaire (CAT-2-C), 248
controlling-coercive violence (CCV), 131, 172–73, 236, 237–38, 277
Cooper, J., 261–64
Corvo, K., 311
couples and family interventions
  childhood exposure to IPV, 361–63
  couples therapy for IPV, 354–55
  Creating Healthy Relationships Program (CHRP), 359–60

Index

domestic violence focused couples therapy (DVFCT), 358–59
family counseling, 261–65, 262t
future directions, 366–67
Gottman Method, 359
impact of IPV on families, 35–38
intervention programs, 355–58
interventions for witnessing IPV, 361
IPV prevention programs, 363–66
prevalence and incidence of IPV, 351–52
restorative justice programs, 360
risk factors for IPV, 352–53
typologies of perpetrators, 353–54
court-involved therapists (CITs), 259
Cox, J., 98
CPV. See child-to-parent violence
Crawford, M., 135–36
Creating Healthy Relationships Program (CHRP), 359–60
criminogenic needs
  definition of term, 345
  needs, indicators, and intervention goals, 346t
Cripps, J., 191
Cross, C.P., 25–26
CTS. See Conflict Tactics Scales
cultural awareness, 227
Cunradi, C. B., 31
custody protocols. See also child custody
  beginning assessment, 244–46
  information gathering
    ascertaining specific details, 247
    collateral information, 253–55
    corroborating evidence, 248
    family interviews, 246–47
    interviews, 250–52
    legal and administrative aggression, 247–48
    minimizing bias in, 247
    parent-child observations, 252–53
    synthesizing data, 255–56
    testing instruments, 248–49
  preparing to conduct evaluations, 243–44
Cycle of Violence, 6–7

DA. See Danger Assessment
Daly, M., 135, 145

Danger Assessment (DA), 145–46, 325, 327–28
Dating Matters: Strategies to Promote Healthy Teen Relationships, 366
dating violence, 363
Daubert testimony standards, 147–48
Davis, D., 71
Davis, R. C., 94–95
deadly force, 168–69
deception, detecting, 308–9, 312–14
defendant rights, undermined by current policies, 9–12
defense strategies
  collateral consequences of IPV charges, 112
  example cases and legal strategies, 115–17
  expert witnesses, 119
  guiding clients through the process, 114–15
  initial case evaluation and interview, 110–12
  managing trial dynamics, 125–27
  mandatory arrest and dominant aggressor laws, 120–25
  power dynamics of relationships, 110–14
  role of sex and gender, 118–19
deflection procedures, 401
DeKeseredy, W. S., 22, 30
DePaulo, B., 308–9
deportation, 112
Desmarais, S. L., 24–25, 130–31
differentiated treatment model, 344t, 344–45
Dillehay, R. C., 183–84
Direct Mate Guarding, 138–39
discretionary arrest laws, 61–64
disturbing the peace of the other party, 208–10, 232–33, 238–39
diversion programs, 402
Dixon, L., 35
Domestic Abuse Intervention Project (DAIP), 276
domestic violence. See intimate partner violence
domestic violence fatality review teams (DVFRTs), 146

domestic violence focused couples therapy (DVFCT), 358–59
Domestic Violence in Child Custody (DVCC), 248
Domestic Violence Prevention Act, 213
Domestic Violence Prevention Temporary Restraining Order. *See* temporary restraining orders
domestic violence restraining order (DVRO), 210–11. *See also* temporary restraining orders
Domestic Violence Risk Appraisal Guide (DVRAG), 325–26
Domestic Violence Screening Instrument (DVSI), 325–27
dominant aggressor laws. *See* predominant aggressor guidelines
Douglas, E. M., 29, 175
Drozd, L., 237–38, 242–43
dual-process models, 182–83
Duluth model, 22, 261, 276, 338–39, 354–58, 366–67
Duluth Power and Control Wheel, 6–7, 22, 276
Durfee, A., 64
Dutton, D. G., 22, 23, 136, 143, 145, 287
Dutton, Donald, 4
DVCC. *See* Domestic Violence in Child Custody
DVFCT. *See* domestic violence focused couples therapy
DVFRTs. *See* domestic violence fatality review teams
DVRAG. *See* Domestic Violence Risk Appraisal Guide
DVRO. *See* domestic violence restraining order
DVSI. *See* Domestic Violence Screening Instrument
dysphoric-borderline type, 131, 353–54

Eckhardt, C. I., 261–64
Eckstein, J. J., 170–71
Edmundson, M., 29
elder abuse, 38–40
Elements of Child Custody Evaluation, 246–47

emotional terrorism, 237
Empathize program, 383
equal air time, 293
Eriksen, S., 133
estrangement, 145, 279
evidence-based practice
  assessment protocols, 242
  batterer intervention treatment
    assessment and treatment framework, 341–42
    behavioral assessment standards, 342–44
    cognitive-behavioral treatment approach, 345–47
    core competencies and completion criteria, 347–48
    criminogenic needs, indicators, and intervention goals, 346*t*
    differentiated treatment model, 344*t*, 344–45
    education and training requirements, 340–41
    individualized IPV treatment in state of Washington, 347*f*
    recognized treatment modalities, 337
    traditional versus alternative treatments, 337–40
  couples and family interventions
    childhood exposure to IPV, 361–63
    couples therapy for IPV, 354–55
    Creating Healthy Relationships Program (CHRP), 359–60
    domestic violence focused couples therapy (DVFCT), 358–59
    future directions, 366–67
    Gottman Method, 359
    intervention programs, 355–58
    interventions for witnessing IPV, 361
    IPV prevention programs, 363–66
    prevalence and incidence of IPV, 351–52
    restorative justice programs, 360
    risk factors for IPV, 352–53
    typologies of perpetrators, 353–54
  evidence-based prosecution, 95
  overview of section, 15–16
  perpetrator interview and assessment

Index

considerations in interviewing
  suspects, 315–20
creating and maintaining correct
  environment, 311–12
deception detection research, 308–9
detecting deception, 312–14
establishing trust and
  cooperation, 310–11
evidence-based interviewing, 309–10
motives for anger, 318t
overcoming assumptions concerning
  IPV, 307–8
overview of, 328–29
risk assessment, 320–28
strategic use of evidence, 314–15
why IPV is underdetected, 315t
restorative justice
  to address IPV crimes, 382–88
  as alternative framework for
    IPV, 381–82
  definition of, 379
  evidence base for, 388–90
  gaps in evidence base, 390–91
  history of, 377–79
  optimal timing for, 391–92
  overview of, 392–94
  in practice, 379–81
  prevalence and incidence of
    IPV, 376–77
expert testimony, 119, 188–91, 219–20

failure to protect charges, 9–10
false accusations
  of parental alienation, 285–86, 288–89
  sanctions imposed for, 226–27
  to secure custody, 243
false equivalence logical fallacy, 293
family-group conferencing (FGC), 380
family interventions. *See* couples and
  family interventions
family law. *See also* arrest and prosecution
  policies; litigation
  child custody litigation
    best interest of the child, 214–17
    challenges of litigation, 222–25
    child custody evaluators and other
      experts, 219–20

constitutional rights involved, 213–14
costs of litigation, 212
custody and parental rights, 212–13
effects of domestic violence, 211–12
impact of domestic violence given
  other problems, 221–22
intersection of domestic violence and
  child custody, 210–11
key questions, 217–19
range of domestic violence and
  abuse, 208–10
restraining orders, 220
suggestion to improve current family
  law system, 225–27
gender-inclusive recommendations for
  child custody
  best interest of the child
    standards, 231–33
  case studies, 229–30
  challenges of evaluating
    claims, 230–31
  complexities of family abuse, 239–41
  custody protocols, 243–56
  custody recommendations, 256–65, 262t
  evaluation procedures, 242–43
  gender paradigm and, 231
  lack of accurate knowledge about
    IPV, 233–35
  psychological abuse and coercive
    control, 238–39
  recognition of need for change, 231
  typologies, 235–38
IPV, child abuse, and parental alienation
  assessment of alienated
    children, 284–87
  controversies over parental
    alienation, 288–93
  Duluth model and, 276
  gender paradigm and parental
    alienation, 287–88
  impact of parental alienation on
    children, 279–82
  male victims of IPV, 276–77
  other causes of parental
    alienation, 282–84
  overview of, 296–97

family law (*cont.*)
    parental alienating behaviors as IPV, 277–79
    potential solutions to, 294–96
    use of children strategy, 277
  overview of section, 15
Family Problem Solving Guide (FAMPROS), 253
family violence
  links to IPV, 38–40
  types of, 38–39
Family Violence Act (1986), 60–61
Farris, E. M., 68
Feder, L., 72, 96, 97, 166
Felson, R., 141
feminist movement
  feminist perspective, 4
  focus of, 22
  motivations of IPV, 30–31
Finkelhor, D., 40
Finneran, C., 176
Five-Factor Model for assessment of parental alienation, 284–87
Follingstad, D. R., 29, 147
Ford, C. L., 69
Four-Factor Model for assessment of parental alienation, 256
Fourth R program, 363
Franklin, C. A., 66
Frazier, C. R., 101
Frederick, B., 86
Freiburger, T. L., 97

Garber, B. D., 245
Gardner, R. A., 279, 287, 288–89
Gartner, R., 135–36
gatekeeping behaviors, 286
Gay Men's Domestic Violence Project, 407
gender-inclusive framework
  battered person syndrome, 147–48
  complex reality of IPV, 98–99
  custody and intervention recommendations
    best interest of the child standards, 231–33
    case studies, 229–30
    challenges of evaluating claims, 230–31
    complexities of family abuse, 239–41
    custody protocols, 243–56
    custody recommendations, 256–65, 262t
    evaluation procedures, 242–43
    gender paradigm and, 231
    lack of accurate knowledge about IPV, 233–35
    psychological abuse and coercive control, 238–39
    recognition of need for change, 231
    typologies, 235–38
  effect on research results, 24–25
  gendered language in law enforcement training manuals, 68–69
  recommendations for prosecutors, 99–100
gender-inverted IPV
  perceptions of, 88–91
  prosecuting, 96–97, 101
gender paradigm. *See also* stereotypes
  bias confirmed by studies, 12
  consequences of, 7–8
  couple conflict and self-defense, 139–41
  decreased ability of males to achieve justice, 8
  definition of term, 4
  effect on policy creation, 4–5
  false distinction of motives resulting from, 5
  female-perpetrated IPH and intimate terrorism, 138–39
  female-perpetrated IPH and violent resistance, 137–38
  Johnson's typology of IPV, 26–27
  lack of concern for male's constitutional rights, 10
  lack of support for, 27
  law enforcement and, 57–59, 63–64
  male-perpetrated IPH and intimate terrorism, 136–37
  male-perpetrated IPH and violent resistance, 139
  moving beyond, 16
  parental alienating behaviors and, 287–88
  perception of IPV suspects and, 311
  recommendations and resources, 407–8

research evidence discrediting, 5–7, 25
stereotypes and scripts, 174–81
suggestions of fewer female
    perpetrators, 24
gender symmetry
    debate over figures supporting,
        23–24
    in IPV, 7, 132–34, 171–72
    statistical anomalies to, 25–26
    studies supporting, 237
generally violent antisocial type,
    131, 353–54
generally violent women, 131
General Social Survey data (1999), 25
Gerbrandij, J., 323
Goldman, Ronald, 208
Gondolf, E. W., 339
Goodmark, L., 67–68
Gottman Method, 359
Graham, L. M., 324, 325
Graham-Bermann, S. A., 362
Graham-Kevan, N., 25, 35
Greenberg, L. R., 261–64
Greene, E., 186
group decision-making, 183–85
Guadalupe-Diaz, X. L., 93
Guidelines for Examining Intimate Partner Violence (AFCC), 236, 244

Hamberger, L. K., 26–27
Hamby, S., 40, 89
Hamel, John, 63, 68–69, 99–100, 134–35,
    235, 261–64, 403
Hammett, J. F., 29
Hardesty, J. L., 237
Harman, J. J., 277–78, 293
Harvard Family Pathways Study, 145
Hastie, R., 183–84
Henning, K., 58, 72, 96, 97, 98, 166
Heuer, L., 186
Hilton, N. Z., 323
Hines, D., 4, 29, 175
Hirschel, D., 59
Holden, G. W., 40
Holleran, D., 96
Holman, M. R., 68
Holtzworth-Munroe, A., 143, 250, 353
Holtzworth-Munroe typology, 131, 353

hostile sexism, 8
hybrid cases of parental alienation,
    285–86, 292
Hynan, D. J., 253

Ibabe, I., 32
identity abuse, 171
Illinois Pretrial Fairness Act, 405–6
immigration-related law, 112, 171
imminent danger requirement
    confrontational versus
        nonconfrontational situations, 168
    understanding and overcoming bias in
        courtrooms, 167–68
impression management (IM), 319
intergenerational cycle of family violence
    due to witnessing IPV, 361
    increased risk of continuing, 32–33, 43
    increased risk to perpetrate domestic
        violence, 211
    IPV prevention programs, 363
International Association of Chiefs of
        Police (IACP)
    guidance on evidence collection, 67–68
    IACP National Law Enforcement Policy
        Center, 70–71
    policies for officer-involved domestic
        violence, 69–71
    predominant aggressor guidelines,
        10–11, 62–64
International Council on Shared
    Parenting, 407
interventions
    for batterers
        assessment and treatment
            framework, 341–42
        behavioral assessment
            standards, 342–44
        cognitive-behavioral treatment
            approach, 345–47
        core competencies and completion
            criteria, 347–48
        criminogenic needs, indicators, and
            intervention goals, 346t
        differentiated treatment model,
            344t, 344–45
        education and training
            requirements, 340–41

interventions (cont.)
- individualized IPV treatment in state of Washington, 347f
- recognized treatment modalities, 337
- traditional versus alternative treatments, 337–40

child custody
- best interest of the child standards, 231–33
- case studies, 229–30
- challenges of evaluating claims, 230–31
- complexities of family abuse, 239–41
- custody protocols, 243–56
- custody recommendations, 256–65, 262t
- evaluation procedures, 242–43
- gender paradigm and, 231
- lack of accurate knowledge about IPV, 233–35
- psychological abuse and coercive control, 238–39
- recognition of need for change, 231
- typologies, 235–38

for couples and families
- childhood exposure to IPV, 361–63
- couples therapy for IPV, 354–55
- Creating Healthy Relationships Program (CHRP), 359–60
- domestic violence focused couples therapy (DVFCT), 358–59
- future directions, 366–67
- Gottman Method, 359
- intervention programs, 355–58
- interventions for witnessing IPV, 361
- IPV prevention programs, 363–66
- prevalence and incidence of IPV, 351–52
- restorative justice programs, 360
- risk factors for IPV, 352–53
- typologies of perpetrators, 353–54

limited effectiveness of current policies, 12–13
recommendations and resources, 404–5

interviews
- during custody disputes, 250–52
- family interviews, 246–47
- initial case evaluation and interview, 110–12

perpetrator interview procedures
- considerations in interviewing suspects, 315–20
- creating and maintaining correct environment, 311–12
- deception detection research, 308–9
- detecting deception, 312–14
- establishing trust and cooperation, 310–11
- evidence-based interviewing, 309–10
- motives for anger, 318t
- overcoming assumptions concerning IPV, 307–8
- overview of, 328–29
- risk assessment, 320–28
- strategic use of evidence, 314–15
- why IPV is underdetected, 315t

questions relevant to adjudication, 162–64

intimate partner homicide (IPH)
- battered women's syndrome and, 146–49
- benefits of disaggregating IPH, 129
- bidirectional IPV, 134–35
- couple conflict and self-defense, 139–41
- gender symmetry in IPV, 132–34
- historical perspective, 130
- overview of, 149–50
- predictors of, 142–45
- prevalence rates of, 135–36
- as preventable, 130
- questions relevant to adjudication, 162–64
- risk assessment, 145–46
- types of IPH, 136–39
- types of IPV, 130–32

intimate partner violence (IPV). *See also* evidence-based practice; family law; litigation
gender paradigm and
- consequences of, 7–8
- effect on policy creation, 4–5
- false distinction of motives resulting from, 5
- moving beyond, 16
- research evidence discrediting, 5–7

Index

incidence and types of, 351–52, 376–77
law enforcement response to
  arrest policies, 61–64
  foundation and evolution of, 59–61
  gender paradigm and, 57–59
  officer discretion, 71–72
  officer-involved domestic
    violence, 69–71
  officer training concerning
    IPV, 66–69
  officer understanding of IPV, 72–73
  social stereotypes and, 64–66
overview of section, 13–14
prevalence, causes, and dynamics of
  bidirectional violence, 27–29
  definition of term, 4
  forms of, 28–29, 171–74
  historical context, 22
  impact on partners, 33–35
  impacts on family, 35–38
  Johnson's typology, 26–27
  links with other types of family
    violence, 38–40
  motivations, 30–31, 174
  overview of, 43–44
  prevalence based on data
    sources, 23–26
  risk factors and antecedents, 31–33
intimate terrorism
  definition of term, 131
  female-perpetrated IPH and, 138–39
  in Johnson's typology, 27, 236
  male-perpetrated IPH and, 136–37
  parental alienating behaviors and, 277
  police training concerning, 67
IPV. See intimate partner violence
Iyengar, R., 94
Izaguirre, A., 361

Jackson, A., 89
Jasinski, J., 93
Jensen, V., 133
Johnson, Michael, 236
Johnson, M. P., 26–27, 28, 29, 88, 353–54
Johnson, P., 311
Johnson's typology, 26–27, 28, 29, 88, 236–38, 353–54

Johnston, J., 243, 264
judicial instructions, 185–87
junk science, 291
jury decision-making
  battered women's syndrome (BWS)
    and, 177
  dual-process models, 182–83
  expert testimony, 188–91
  group decision-making, 183–85
  judicial instructions, 185–87
  overview of, 191–92
  race and ethnicity and, 180–81
  role of juror gender, 187–88
  story models, 181–82

Kalvin, H., 183–84
Kerker, B. D., 40–41
Kerry, G., 143
Kimmel, M. S., 25–26
Kitzmann, K. M., 37–38, 240–41
Kivisto, A., 143
Krauss, D. A., 183–84
Kurdyla, V., 93

Landes, W. M., 86–87
Langhinrichsen-Rohling, J., 28, 30–31
Lantz, B., 98–99, 102
Larsen, S. E., 26–27
Lautenberg Amendment (1996), 70
Lavelle v. Regina (1990), 190
law enforcement response to IPV
  arrest policies, 61–64
  foundation and evolution of, 59–61
  gender paradigm and, 57–59
  officer discretion, 71–72
  officer-involved domestic violence, 69–71
  officer training, 66–69
  officer understanding of IPV, 72–73
  social stereotypes and, 64–66
learned helplessness, 137
leaving abusive relationships
  employment and child welfare
    issues, 224
  fear of death, 223
  more frequent violence due to, 169–70
  number of attempts before
    success, 223–24

leaving abusive relationships (*cont.*)
  obstacles to, 170–71
  restraining orders and, 224
  sexual minority and immigrant populations, 171
  spillover effect, 239
  stressors brought on by, 170
legal aid, 212
Legal Aid Foundation, 212
legal and administrative aggression
  against alienated parents, 283
  as coercive control, 238, 239
  counseling and, 265
  definition of term, 247–48
  examples of, 247–48
  false allegations as form of, 122
  IPV allegations as, 320
  recommendations following use of, 257
  as strategy to obtain custody, 277–78
  subheads, 11
Leone, J. M., 353–54
Lieberman, J. D., 183–84
Liederbach, J., 70
litigation. *See also* family law
  cost of in child custody cases, 212
  intimate partner homicide
    battered women's syndrome and, 146–49
    benefits of disaggregating IPH, 129
    bidirectional IPV, 134–35
    couple conflict and self-defense, 139–41
    gender symmetry in IPV, 132–34
    historical perspective, 130
    overview of, 149–50
    predictors of, 142–45
    prevalence rates of, 135–36
    as preventable, 130
    questions relevant to adjudication, 162–64
    risk assessment, 145–46
    types of IPH, 136–39
    types of IPV, 130–32
  jury decision-making
    ability to leave relationship, 169–71
    confrontational versus nonconfrontational situations, 168
    controlling and coercive behaviors, 172–73
    decision-making in juries, 181–85
    definition of IPH, 166
    expert testimony, 188–91
    gender symmetry in IPV, 171–72
    heterosexual males and LGBTQ+ victimization, 178–80
    imminent danger requirement, 167–68
    judicial instructions, 185–87
    motivations for IPV and IPH, 174
    nontypical victims and perpetrators, 177–78
    overview of, 191–92
    race, ethnicity, and socioeconomic differences, 180–81
    role of defendant gender, 178
    role of juror gender, 187–88
    self-defense argument, 166–67
    stereotypes and scripts, 174–77
    stereotypes surrounding IPV, 165–66
    use of deadly force, 169
  legal defenses in IPV cases
    collateral consequences of IPV charges, 112
    example cases and legal strategies, 115–17
    expert witnesses, 119
    guiding clients through the process, 114–15
    initial case evaluation and interview, 110–12
    managing trial dynamics, 125–27
    mandatory arrest and dominant aggressor laws, 120–25
    power dynamics of relationships, 110–14
    role of sex and gender, 118–19
  overview of section, 4–15
  prosecutorial discretion
    differences based on prosecutor gender, 93
    directions for research, 100–1
    historical context, 85–86
    overview of, 101–2
    perceptions of gender-inverted IPV, 88–91
    perceptions of same-sex IPV, 91–92

perceptions of trans and gender-diverse IPV, 92–93
practice implications, 98–100
prosecuting gender-inverted IPV, 96–97
prosecuting same-sex, trans, and gender diverse IPV, 97–98
prosecution of IPV, 94–96
prosecutorial decision-making, 86–87
theories of IPV, 87–88
Loftus, E. F., 186
Lorandos, D., 293
Lysova, A., 170–71

MacArthur Foundation, 405
MacDonell, K. W., 37
MacDonnel, K. W., 240
Mackay, J., 32, 33
MacNeil, E., 96–97
Maeder, E. M., 180
maladaptive communication skills, 352
mandatory arrest laws
  historical context, 61–64
  legal defenses and, 120–25
  limited effectiveness of, 12–13
  questionable efficacy of, 94
  as undermining to defendant rights, 9–12
Mann, C. R., 140
mate guarding, 137, 138–39
mate retention, 137
Mate Retention Inventory (MRI), 138
Matthewson, M., 277–78
Maxwell, C., 94
McCannon, B. C., 101
McCormack, P. D., 59
McKimmie, B. M., 186
media coverage, 293
Mediator's Assessment of Safety Issues and Concerns, 248
Mediators Assessment of Safety Issues and Concerns (MASIC), 250
Meier, J. S., 293
Melillo, L. S., 177
memory research, 317
Men as Peacemaker, 384
mental health professionals (MHPs), 244–45

mentally ill group, 143
Messing, J. T., 96
Messner, S., 141
Miller Forensic Assessment of Symptoms Test (M-FAST), 249
Millon Clinical Multiaxial Inventory (MCMI-III), 248–49
Mills, L. G., 94–95, 389
Minnesota Multiphasic Personality Inventory (MMPI), 143, 248–49, 319–20
Model Code on domestic and family violence, 235, 239–40
Model Standards (AFCC, 2006), 244–46, 248, 254
Modern Sexism Scale, 233–34
Moment of Truth declaration, 405
Moms and Teens for Safe Dates (MTSD), 363–66
Monopolization of Time, 138
motivational interviewing (MI), 309–10
MRI. *See* Mate Retention Inventory
mutual violent control, 28, 131, 236
Myhill, A., 71–72

narcissistic personality disorder, 352–53
NASW. *See* National Association of Social Workers
National Association of Social Workers (NASW), 405–6
National Coalition Against Domestic Violence (NCADV), 4, 211–12, 234, 406
National Coalition of Anti-Violence Programs (NCAVP), 59, 407
National Conference for State Legislatures (NCSL), 66–67, 385
National Crime Victimization Survey, 26, 58–59
National District Attorneys Association (NDAA), 11, 99, 403
National Domestic Violence Hotline, 401
National Family Violence surveys, 133–34
National Incident-Based Reporting Systems (NIBRS), 59, 98
National Institute of Justice's Spouse Assault Replication Program, 94

National Intimate Partner and Sexual
	Violence Survey (NISVS), 58–59,
	89, 130–31, 134–35, 400, 407
National Longitudinal Study of Adolescent
	Health, 29
National Violence Against Women
	Survey, 27
National Violent Death Reporting
	System, 142–43
NCADV. *See* National Coalition Against
	Domestic Violence
needs principle, 341
Nemeth, C. J., 184
Network Advocating Against Domestic
	Violence, 405–6
Nicholls, T., 261–64
no-drop prosecution policies, 11, 94–
	95, 403
nonconfrontational situations, 168
NVAVP. *See* National Coalition of Anti-
	Violence Programs

Obergefell v. Hodges (2015), 96
Observing Rapport-Based Interview
	Techniques (ORBIT), 309
ODARA. *See* Ontario Domestic Assault
	Risk Assessment
officer-involved domestic violence
	(OIDV), 69–71
officer training, 66–69
Ogloff, J. R., 184–85
O'Leary, K. D., 355–58, 366–67
O'Neal, Eryn, 96, 100
Ontario Domestic Assault Risk Assessment
	(ODARA), 259–60, 324–25
order of protection. *See* protection order

Papamichail, A., 43
parental alienating behaviors (PABs). *See
	also* parental alienation
  as abusive behavior, 291
  alternatives to, 286–87
  consequences of, 294
  definition of term, 277
  engaging in a systematic level, 283–84
  as a form of IPV, 277–79
  gender paradigm and, 287–88
  hybrid cases and, 285–86

  impact on children, 279–82
  lack of professional training
	concerning, 296
  minimization of, 289–90
  overview of, 296–97
  parental alienation and, 289
  policies exacerbating family
	conflicts, 283
  training and education about, 294
parental alienation (PA). *See also* parental
	alienating behaviors
  assessment of alienated children, 284–87
  in child custody litigation, 256
  controversies over parental
	alienation, 288–93
  definition of term, 279
  denial of, 288–89
  gender paradigm and, 287–88
  levels of, 218–19
  minimization of, 289–93
  other causes of parental
	alienation, 282–84
  results of, 282
  state of research on, 289
parental rights, 212–13
Parent Behavior Checklist (PBC), 248–49
Parent-Child Relationship Inventory
	(PCRI), 248–49
Parenting Stress Index, 248–49
Partial Parenting Plan Assessment, 221–22
Partner Abuse State of Knowledge (PASK)
  bidirectional violence, 28
  expressive and coercive violence, 28–29
  prevalence of victimization, 24–25
  research accessed through, 134–
	35, 290–91
  resources offered by, 407
PASK. *See* Partner Abuse State of
	Knowledge
Paterson, R., 41
patriarchal terrorism, 27
Paulhus Deception Scales (PDS), 319
PBC. *See* Parent Behavior Checklist
PCL-R. *See* Psychopathy Checklist-Revised
PCRI. *See* Parent-Child Relationship
	Inventory
Peitzmeier, S. M., 92
Pennell, J., 382, 384

Penrod, S., 186
People of New York v. Arlene Mohammed (1987), 179
People v. Bush (1978), 169
Personality Assessment Inventory (PAI), 248–49
Petersen, N., 96
physical terrorism, 237
Pico-Alfonso, M. A., 34–35
Pizzey, Erin, 22
PO. *See* protection order
Poorman, P. B., 93
post-traumatic stress disorder (PTSD), 149, 189–90, 209–10, 278–79
Power and Control Wheel, 276, 338–39
predominant aggressor guidelines, 10–11, 62–64, 120–25
presumption of innocence, 401
proarrest statutes
  historical context, 61–64
  limited effectiveness of, 12–13
  as undermining to defendant rights, 9–12
professional licenses, 112
Project STRONG, 363–66
Project SUPPORT, 362
proprietariness theory, 136–37
prosecutorial discretion
  differences based on prosecutor gender, 93
  directions for research, 100–1
  historical context, 85–86
  overview of, 101–2
  perceptions of gender-inverted IPV, 88–91
  perceptions of same-sex IPV, 91–92
  perceptions of trans and gender-diverse IPV, 92–93
  practice implications, 98–100
  prosecuting gender-inverted IPV, 96–97
  prosecuting same-sex, trans, and gender diverse IPV, 97–98
  prosecution of IPV, 94–96
  prosecutorial decision-making, 86–87
  theories of IPV, 87–88
protection order (PO), 170. *See also* temporary restraining orders
psychiatric/pathological motives, 142–43

psychic freezing, 147
psychological abuse and violence
  gender-inclusive recommendations for child custody, 238–39
  impact on partners, 34–35
  incidence and types of, 351–52
  prevalence of, 28–29
Psychopathy Checklist-Revised (PCL-R), 325–26

readiness to change, 343
rebuttable presumption, 210–11
recommendations and resources
  arrest and prosecution
    arrest versus no arrest, 401–3
    police training, 403
    presumption of innocence, 401
    prosecution policies, 403
  gender paradigm, 407–8
  historical social and legal trends, 399–401
  interventions, 404–5
  reform initiatives, 405–6
  resources, 406–7
Redlich, A. D., 87
reform initiatives, 405–6
Reid, John E., 308–9
Reifman, A., 186
Reimagining Policing: Strategies for Community Reinvestment (NASW), 405–6
released on own recognizance (ROR), 72
Renauer, B., 58, 98
research evidence
  accessed through PASK, 134–35, 290–91
  beginnings of research movement, 22
  child custody case studies, 229–30
  deception detection research, 308–9
  discrediting gender paradigm, 5–7, 25
  gender-inclusive framework, 24–25
  memory research, 317
  on parental alienation, 289
  studies supporting gender symmetry, 237
  supporting gender paradigm, 12
responsibility-to-needs framework, 295. *See also* risk-needs-responsivity-informed approaches

responsivity principle, 259–60, 341
restorative justice (RJ)
    to address IPV crimes, 382–88
    as alternative framework for IPV, 381–82
    Circles of Peace, 360
    definition of, 379
    evidence base for, 388–90
    gaps in evidence base, 390–91
    history of, 377–79
    optimal timing for, 391–92
    overview of, 392–94
    in practice, 379–81
    prevalence and incidence of IPV, 376–77
RESTORE program, 385
Restraining Order Center (ROC), 212
restraining orders, 170, 209–10, 213, 220
Ricketts v. Columbia (1993), 61
Right on Crime organization, 406
risk assessment for IPV
    benefits of structured methods, 320–21
    Brief Spousal Assault Form for the Evaluation of Risk, 323–24
    Danger Assessment, 327–28
    Domestic Violence Risk Appraisal Guide, 325–26
    Domestic Violence Screening Instrument, 326–27
    Ontario Domestic Assault Risk Assessment, 324–25
    overview of, 328
    predictive accuracy of, 321
    Spousal Assault Risk Assessment, 321–22
    Spousal Assault Risk Assessment Version 3, 322–23
risk factors for IPH
    attachment theory, 144–45
    classification schemes, 143
    lifestyle and relationship factors, 142
    mental health issues, 142–43
    personality, 142
    risk assessment, 145–46
    spousal homicide, 143
risk factors for IPV
    adverse childhood experiences, 31–33
    anger and hostility, 353
    demographic factors, 31
    general offending and links with other crime, 33
    maladaptive communication skills, 352, 354–55
    overview of, 352
    personality disorder characteristics, 352–53
risk-needs-responsivity-informed approaches
    to batterer intervention
    assessment and treatment framework, 341–42
    behavioral assessment standards, 342–44
    cognitive-behavioral treatment approach, 345–47
    core competencies and completion criteria, 347–48
    criminogenic needs, indicators, and intervention goals, 346t
    differentiated treatment model, 344t, 344–45
    education and training requirements, 340–41
    individualized IPV treatment in state of Washington, 347f
    recognized treatment modalities, 337
    traditional versus alternative treatments, 337–40
    risk-needs-responsivity model, 259–60, 262t
    risk-needs-responsivity principles, 341–42, 400, 404
risk principle, 341
Rivlin, B., 256
RNR model. *See* risk-needs-responsivity-informed approaches
Rogers, M. J., 29
Romain, D. M., 97
Romano, E., 362–63
Rorschach test, 248–49
Rose, V. G., 184–85
Rubin, A., 355–58
Russell, Brenda, 11–12, 58, 68–70, 177, 403

Index

Sadusky, J., 384–85
Safe Dates program, 363
Safety and Justice Challenge, 405
Saini, M., 289
Sandys, M., 183–84
SARA. *See* Spousal Assault Risk Assessment
SARA 3. *See* Spousal Assault Risk Assessment Version 3
Sarat, A., 186
Saunders, D. G., 68, 233–34
Saxton, M., 44
schemas, 175
Schore, A. N., 145
Schuller, R. A., 189–90, 191
SCV. *See* situational couple violence
Sebire, J., 140, 142–43
Seewald, K., 325
self-awareness, 311
self-deceptive enhancement, 319
self-defense. *See also* jury decision-making
  and couple conflict, 139–41
  successful argument of in litigation, 188–89
  understanding and overcoming bias in courtrooms, 166–67
self-help centers, 212
separating from abuser, 169–71. *See also* leaving abusive relationships
sequential perpetrator model, 40–41
SEU. *See* strategic use of evidence
seven domains of assessment, 342–43
Severance, L. J., 186
sexual minorities
  coercive controls, 171, 173
  decreased ability to achieve justice, 8
  gender, sex, and prosecution of IPV
    nuances of experiences with criminal justice system, 89
    perceptions of same-sex IPV, 91–92
    perceptions of trans and gender-diverse IPV, 92–93
    prosecuting same-sex, trans, and gender diverse IPV, 97–98
    impact of IPV on men who have sex with men, 34
  lack of concern for constitutional rights, 10
  law enforcement response to IPV
    differential treatment of sexual minorities, 59, 71–72
    effect of homophobia, 72–73
    identification of primary aggressor, 64
    IPV rates among sexual minorities, 58–59
    officer training, 67–69
    social stereotypes and, 64–66
  mutual restraining orders, 170
  predominant aggressor guidelines and, 10–11
  stereotypes and IPV, 175–80
sexual selection theory, 136–37
shadow model (of a trial), 86–87
Shechter, S., 172
Sherman, L., 61–62
Shernock, S., 11–12, 58
sibling violence, 38–40
silver bullet strategy, 210
Simpson, Nicole, 208
situational couple violence (SCV), 27, 67, 73, 131, 236, 237–38, 353–54
social agency theory, 148
social framework evidence, 148
social stereotypes, law enforcement response and, 64–66
socioeconomic differences, 180–81
spillover effect, 239
SPJ. *See* structured professional judgment
Spohn, Cassia, 100, 101
Spousal Assault Risk Assessment (SARA), 259–60, 321–22
Spousal Assault Risk Assessment Version 3 (SARA v3), 322–23
Stahl, P. M., 250
Stanziani, M., 91, 187
Stark, E., 72–73, 172
State v. Anaya (1983), 177, 190
Stemen, D., 86
Stephenson, R., 176
stereotypes. *See also* gender paradigm
  battered person syndrome, 177
  gender, 178

stereotypes (*cont.*)
   heterosexual males and LGBTQ+ victimization, 178–80
   nature of IPV, 175–77
   nontypical victims and perpetrators, 177–78
   race, ethnicity, and socioeconomic differences, 180–81
   role of schemas, 174–75
   surrounding IPV, 165–66
Stewart, L., 259–60
St. George, S., 101
Stinson, P. M., 70
Stith, S. M., 32
Stop Abuse for Everyone, 407
story models, 181–82
strategic questioning, 309
strategic use of evidence (SEU), 314–15
Straus, M. A., 23–24, 26, 133–34, 400
structured professional judgment (SPJ), 321–22
Stuart, G., 143, 353
Stuntz, W. J., 87
Submission and Debasement, 138–39
substance abuse, 221
Summers, A., 87
System for Coding Interactions and Family Functioning (SCIFF), 253
Szinovacz, M. E., 24

Tadepalli, S., 401
Taft, C. T., 34–35
Tannenbaum, R., 69–70
TDV. *See* teen dating violence
teen dating violence (TDV), 363
temporary restraining orders (TROs), 170, 209–10, 213, 220
Tesch, B. P., 69
testing instruments, 248–49
Thematic Apperception Test (TAT), 248–49
therapeutic supervised visitation, 261–64
Thompson, J., 92
Thurman, Charles, 60–61
Thurman, Tracey, 60–61
Thurman v. Torrington (1984), 60–61

trans and gender-diverse persons. *See* sexual minorities
TROs. *See* temporary restraining orders
true victims, 219–20
typologies
   Dixon's, 143
   gender-inclusive framework and, 235–38
   Holtzworth-Munroe, 131, 143, 353
   of IPV perpetrators, 353–54
   Johnson's, 26–27, 28, 29, 88, 236–38, 353–54
   Kivisto, 143

Ulloa, E. C., 29
undercontrolled/dysregulated category, 143
universal human rights, 407–8
use of children strategy, 276–77

VAWA. *See* Violence Against Women Act
Velopulos, C., 141
vertical prosecution, 95
Vetere, A., 261–64
victim-offender mediation, 380, 381–82
Vidmar, N., 183
Vigilance, 138
Violence Against Women Act (VAWA), 61, 87–88, 208, 382–83, 403, 406
Violence Risk Appraisal Guide (VRAG), 325–26
violent resistance, 132, 137–38, 139, 236
visitation, 257–59, 262*t*
voice stress analysis (VSA), 308–9
VRAG. *See* Violence Risk Appraisal Guide
VSA. *See* voice stress analysis

Walker, Lenore, 6–7, 30, 137, 146–48, 188–89
Warshak, R., 264
Wasarhaley, N. E., 91
Washington County Community Circles (WCCC) program, 387
Washington State model, 345–46, 347*f*
WCCC. *See* Washington County Community Circles
Wetendorf, D., 71

WHO Multi-country Study on Women's Health and Domestic Violence, 31
Williams Institute Report, 69
Willis, C. E., 180
Wilson, M., 135, 145
Wisconsin Coalition Against Sexual Assault, 405
"women are wonderful" effect, 8
women's shelters, 22
woozles, 291, 293

Yakubovich, A. R., 31
Yglesias, J., 93
Young, C., 73

Zeisel, H., 183–84